A Nation in Bondage: Slavery and United States History

A Primary Source Reader

Dean T. Ferguson

Published by Linus Learning

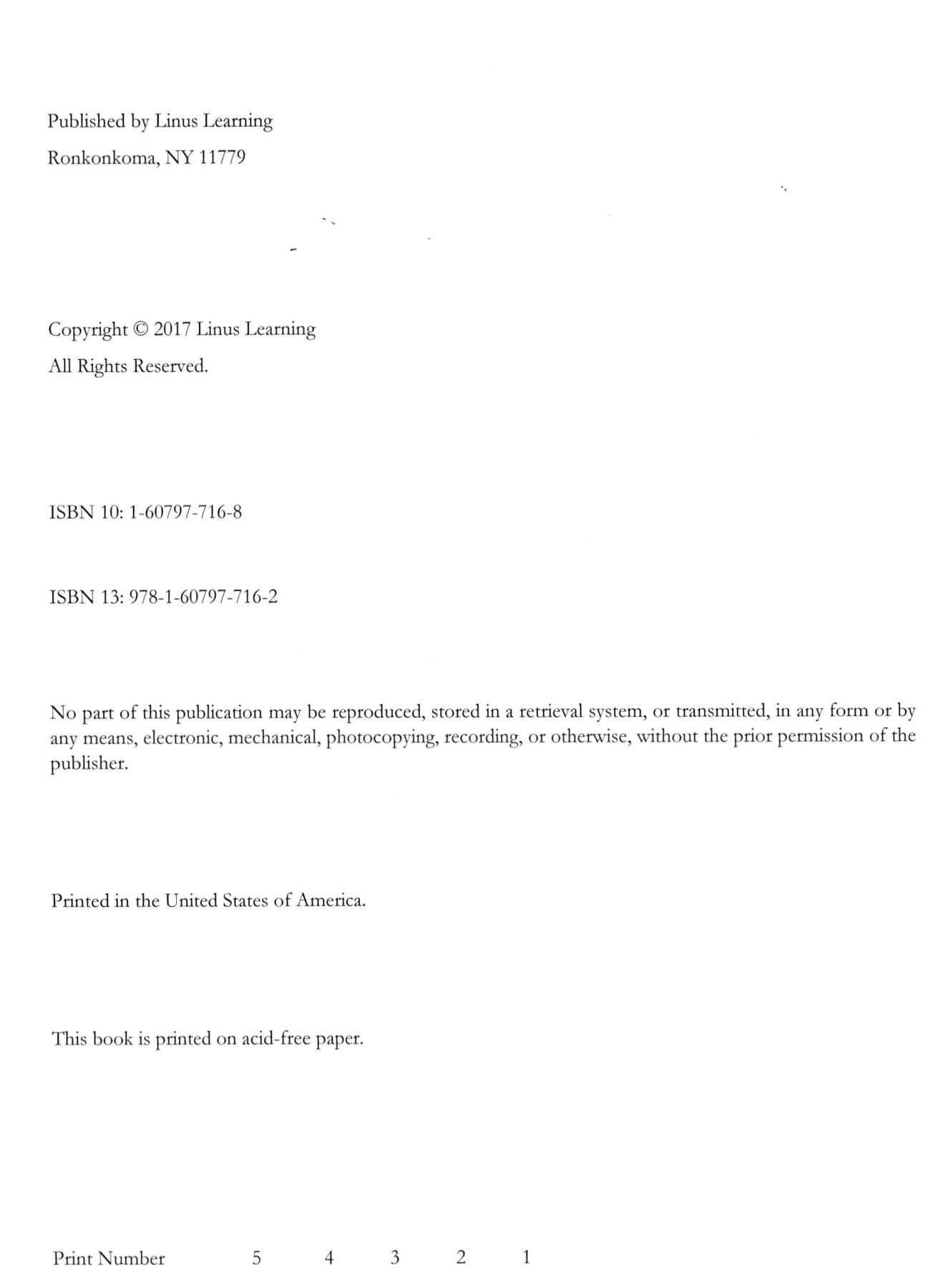

Ronkonkoma, NY 11779

Copyright © 2017 Linus Learning

All Rights Reserved.

ISBN 10: 1-60797-716-8

ISBN 13: 978-1-60797-716-2

No part of this publication may be reproduced, stored in a retrieval system, or transmitted, in any form or by any means, electronic, mechanical, photocopying, recording, or otherwise, without the prior permission of the publisher.

Printed in the United States of America.

This book is printed on acid-free paper.

Print Number   5   4   3   2   1

Table of Contents

Introduction: Slavery as the Centerpiece of a Course in United States History before 1877 V

Chapter 1:

The Atlantic Slave System—Africans as a Commodity in the "New World" 1

Chapter 2

Regional Variations in the American South: Virginia and the Carolinas 23

Chapter 3

Slavery Above the Mason-Dixon Line 47

Chapter 4

Afro-European Culture in the Americas: Africans and Colonial Society 67

Chapter 5

"Be not then, ye Negroes, tempted": Slavery and the American Revolution 89

Chapter 6

"A Covenant with Death and An Agreement with Hell": Slavery at the Constitutional Convention 113

Chapter 7

Black Founders, American Democracy, and White Supremacy 141

Chapter 8

Cotton, Capital, and Industry—Slaves and the Making of the American Economy 165

Chapter 9
Gender and Family On and Off the Plantation 197

Chapter 10
"Was Not Christ Crucified": Rebellion, Redemption, and Repression 223

Chapter 11
Antebellum Culture Wars 257

Chapter 12
"Oh, Liberty! What Crimes Have been Committed in Thy Name:"
Manifest Destiny and the Politics of Slavery 295

Chapter 13
"Cannot we Prove Ourselves Men!": Civil War and Emancipation 323

Epilogue
Reconstruction 353

Introduction

SLAVERY AS THE CENTERPIECE OF A COURSE IN UNITED STATE HISTORY BEFORE 1877

The titles of American history textbooks used in college classrooms tell their own story. The title of the text your professor has adopted may also provide some hint to his or her priorities in the classroom. One text employed often is Eric Foner's *Give Me Liberty: An American History*. Foner, an eminent scholar of the history of slavery, not surprisingly situates the pursuit of liberty and the many barriers that have been placed in the way of that pursuit at the heart of his story. James West Davidson's *A Nation of Nations*, a text I have often used, highlights the nation's diversity and the multiplicity of cultural and ethnic influences that came together to fashion our national identity. Alan Brinkley's *The Unfinished Nation* details the processes, still unfolding, of the development of the United States. James Henretta titled one of the many textbooks he has authored, *Evolution and Revolution*. Henretta in his text, juxtaposes incremental but no less important changes to American economic, cultural, demographic, and political life with the country's frequent moments of explosive and sometimes violent social and political transformations.

Document collections, or primary source readers like this one, often reveal similar agendas in their titles. Randy Roberts and Elliott Gorn, who edited *Constructing the American Past*, direct students to particular problems that the American nation has faced over the course of its history and provide readers with a collection of primary sources representing contrasting perspectives on these issues. John Murrin and Pekka Hämälleinen entitled their reader, *Liberty, Equality, and Power*, a nod to both the ideals of liberty and equality reverenced in the Declaration of Independence. But Murrin and Hämälleinen also confront the power struggles between dominant and subordinate groups over the meaning and extent of liberty and equality. In both cases, however, the authors of these teaching tools offer a panoramic view of the American past and engage students with a wide range of issues.

This reader, in contrast to the examples above, explicitly centers on the role played by the institution of slavery in American history and directs readers to documents that highlight the ways in which the "peculiar institution" and the presence of slaves in the Americas shaped both the development of the nation that would become the United States and featured in the critical junctures of the nation's history. This decision to focus on slavery is not an arbitrary one. It reflects the conviction that no other feature of the American past has done so much to shape the historical development of the United States. And no other feature of the American past better explains contemporary persistent social, economic, and political controversies.

SEEING SLAVERY AND THE SLAVE IN THE AMERICAN PAST

Perhaps the most immediate and obvious evidence of the place of slavery in United States history are the bodies and persons of African Americans, descendants of the slaves brought to the British colonies in North America and later to the United States between 1776 and 1808. The slaves imported into this region made up only a small percentage, perhaps less than five percent, of those exported to the Americas from Africa. But, across the Americas, Africans represented by a wide measure the vast majority of the population of immigrants arriving from the Old World. Of the 6.5 million immigrants settling in the Western Hemisphere between 1492 and 1776, only 1 million were Europeans. The "peopling of the Americas," as Daniel Boorstein rather myopically wrote--forgetting the Native Americans already resident in the "New World"--rested on the transport across the Atlantic of over 5.5 million Africans. The number of slaves exported to the British colonies in North America, perhaps half a million, was dwarfed by the numbers transported to Brazil and the Caribbean. However, natural growth and small numbers of illegally imported slaves after 1808 resulted in an enslaved population, according to the 1860 census, of over 3.9 million slaves in the antebellum United States. While this number represented only 13% of the American population—a proportion roughly comparable to the proportion of African Americans in the 2010 census—in Southern states slaves made up a much higher proportion, as much as fifty-seven percent in South Carolina and fifty-five percent in Mississippi.

The presence of African Americans in the cities and rural counties of the United States visibly speak to the enslavement of Africans. Less immediately obvious is the role slavery played in the economic foundation of American, and European, prosperity. Whether or not slavery created the capital that financed the Industrial Revolution, a hotly-debated historical issue, slavery was indispensable to European settlement and the development of the "New World." It is doubtful that widespread European settlement of the Americas would have taken place without the labor of slaves, or the profits generated by the commodities that slaves produced. Slave labor produced the principle consumer items—sugar, tobacco, coffee, rum, cotton—that satisfied the changing tastes of European and American households. And whole constellations of products from tea sets to pipes to ready-to-wear clothing made possible that consumption. For pre-Civil War America, the case for the significance of slave labor to the economy of the United States cannot be clearer. It has been argued that the United States sustained its revolution against Great Britain with profits earned from tobacco, a crop largely dependent on slave labor. And, when tobacco ceased to represent the forward edge of the American economy, cotton became king. As early as 1840, the American South grew sixty percent of the world's cotton; this one crop provided over half of all U.S. export earnings. Moreover, while Southern plantations generated profits directly from the labor of enslaved Africans, Northern meat packers, insurance companies, banks, shippers, clothiers, and textile mills provided services to the slave South, sustaining and profiting indirectly from slavery.

The lasting impact of slavery and the slave trade on the American economy is sometimes less than immediately obvious. It is perhaps much too easy to argue that the economic legacy of slavery is behind us. A cursory look at a number of American corporations (and other institutions) that benefited from slavery, however, makes it clear that association with slavery sullies many of the nation's most iconic brands. For example, Aetna Insurance, in the 1850s and 1860s sold policies on slaves to plantation owners eager to insure their valuable property. Aetna is not alone. Among the first thousand policies found in the archives of New York Life, one of the nation's largest life insurance companies, are 339 policies written on the lives of slaves. Of course, on the death of a slave insured by New York Life, or any other insurance company, the slave's spouse and children would receive no benefits. Instead, the benefit would accrue to the slave's owner and his heirs. Insurers were not the only contemporary financial institutions to profit from slavery. The gigantic banking firms, J.P. Morgan Chase, Barclay's Bank, and Wells Fargo, either directly or through former subsidiaries, profited from credit given to plantation owners, often with slaves standing as collateral underwriting the loans. Citizens Bank and Canal Bank, former subsidiaries of J.P. Morgan Chase, held as collateral nearly 13,000 slaves in 1860, a value of perhaps $13 million at the time. Insurance and banking were not the only industries that profited from slavery. Railroads were built with slave labor. Clothiers—Brooks Brothers most famously—profited from supplying slave owners with cheap clothing. Indeed, while slavery featured most prominently in the Southern economy, the entire economy—and many corporations that still do business in the United States—benefited from slavery.

But modern corporations are not alone among contemporary institutions in being implicated in the history of slavery. America's colleges and universities owe a great debt to the labor of slaves who manicured their grounds and cared for students, much as poorly paid workers often do today. But, the indebtedness of many of America's most renowned colleges and universities extends far beyond the labor of slaves. Georgetown University has recently acknowledged its obligation to the descendants of 272 slaves sold by the institution to enable the university to keep open its doors. And, Brown University has forthrightly apologized for the role of its namesake, James Brown, and his numerous family's prominent role in the African trade that saw countless Africans transported into slavery during the eighteenth century aboard Brown family ships. It is no exaggeration to suggest that Brown University, not unlike many other Ivy League and elite East Coast universities, owed its existence to an endowment secured by the blood and sweat of African slaves.

It is patently clear that America was shaped demographically and economically by the presence of slaves in the United States. Additionally, the presence of Africans on farms, plantations, and in urban households played a significant role in the shaping of what can only fairly be described as an Afro-European culture in the Americas. Borrowing from African cultures is often most immediately seen in language. The list of African loan words for food items (banana, cola, okra, gumbo, yam, goober, to name only a few examples) illustrates the place of African food in American cuisine. Goober, a term for peanut, is suggestive of how often language has wider cultural implications; a goober is someone who lacks basic common sense, a connotation derived from African usage of the term. Some words that have iconic association with the American West and with cattle culture, cowboy and buckaroo, for example, bear the markings of the slave-based economy. The first men in English America who were called cowboys were African cattle herders, men who were denied the status of men. Buckaroo is a term occasionally interchanged with cowboy. It derives from the term *buckra*, a derogatory term for white overseers and masters who often lorded it over their slaves from their position high atop their horses. On our very language, slavery has left a significant mark, often in ways that are not easily recognized.

The presence of Africans in large numbers has also shaped other aspects of the wider American culture. The prominence in the United States of religious groups that emphasized ecstatic forms of religious worship (laying on of hands in spiritual healing, falling into trancelike states or speaking in tongues, and building spiritual enthusiasm through music) resulted from the cultural fusion of African spirituality and the devotional methods of European worshipers. Food ways were also impacted by the presence of African slaves in their masters' kitchens. Deep frying meats, particularly chicken, and rubbing spices on pork and beef, before slow-cooking the meat in a bed of coals, were practices without parallels in European cuisine. Barbecue, though the name derives from a Caribbean Indian term, is an African contribution to the American diet. Childrearing also bears the impress of the slave men and women who were often charged with caring for the children of their white masters and mistresses. When Southern children today hear their parents admonish them with the warning "don't you dare sass me," they are repeating a phrase with likely African origins. Americans indeed grow up, often unawares, in an Afro-European culture. The aim of this reader is to engage at least some of the ways that this development emerged during the first centuries of the history of what would become the United States of America.

STRUCTURE OF THE READER

To argue that the African contribution to American economic fortunes, cultural traditions, and demographic makeup was significant, and thus warrants greater attention in American History textbooks is not a novel proposition. And a great deal has been done to remedy this imbalance. This reader is not principally designed to tell the story of African American contributions to American culture and history. Instead, this reader is designed to revisit each of the key moments in the historical development of the United States, from its origins to the aftermath of the American Civil War, in much the same way that traditional primary source readers follow the standard narrative of the nation's history. The structure of the book will therefore follow standard narrative lines of American history before 1877: settlement and colonization, eighteenth-century maturation of colonial society, the American Revolution and early republican period, the "Market Revolution" and Jacksonian expansion of democracy, Manifest Destiny and western expansion, the lead-up to the Civil War, the Civil War itself, and the failing of Reconstruction. The chapter divisions of this primary source reader will then look very much like those found in other similar readers.

However, in every case, the impact of slavery and the voices of slaves and free blacks will be the focal point of each chapter. This reader will then begin with an exploration of the development of an Atlantic economy dependent upon African laborers to produce a host of commodities consumed in the cities of Europe and North America. In the process, Africans themselves would become a commodity transported and traded across the Atlantic world. Chapters Two and Three will examine the settlement of the American colonies. The place of Africans in this development will be central, rather than peripheral, to the explorers and conquerors who spread European dominance across the Americas, or to the farmers and planters that transformed the landscape of colonial America. Rather than privileging the place of Puritan settlers in Massachusetts, or of the Jamestown founders, this reader will provide primary sources that explore the place of African slaves in clearing the land, laboring on farms, plantations, and the docks or in households from Massachusetts to Barbados. The construction of an Afro-European culture in the Americas during the colonial period and after will be taken up in Chapter Four, using a variety of primary sources to illustrate African influences on religion, work lives, spatial understandings, and language in colonial America.

After this survey of the colonial period, students will be asked to engage the grievances that would result in the rupture between Great Britain and the colonies as well as the social and political challenges that faced the founders of the new American republic. In Chapter Five we will turn our attention to the factors leading to the American Revolution and to the founding of the republic. It will come to no one's surprise to hear that many of the leading figures in the American Revolutionary period were either slave holders themselves (George Washington, Thomas Jefferson, Benjamin Franklin, Patrick Henry and Alexander Hamilton were slave owners) or profited from the "carrying trade" that transported slaves or the commodities they produced. Protection of the right to own slaves and fears of Great Britain's declining enthusiasm for the slave trade, however, have not featured often in the story of the coming of the American Revolution. This reader will introduce students to evidence that places slavery at the center of the factors leading to the revolution. Chapter Six takes up the place of slavery in the debates of the Constitutional Convention. William Lloyd Garrison called the Constitution a "Covenant with Death and an Agreement with Hell." Without forgetting that the Constitution has been amended to remedy its defense of slavery and to expand the liberties that were its stated purpose, in this chapter we will take Garrison's critique seriously, exploring the discussions and power struggles at the convention over the "peculiar institution." Chapter Seven will then examine the ways in which slavery was implicated in the political struggles of the early republic and national period. In particular in this chapter we will focus on the "Black Founders" who called the nation to live up to the ideals of the Declaration of Independence and on the ways that white men of property and power gradually extended the suffrage thereby constructing a political system that was self-described as democratic, but which can only be characterized as white supremacist.

The next two chapters explore the place of slavery in the making of the antebellum American economy and culture. Critics of capitalism have often observed that the profits earned from the sale and labor of slaves provided the early impetus to the development of capitalism in both Great Britain and the United States. The degree to which this was the case will be evaluated in Chapter Eight by looking at ways in which slavery was implicated in the inter-related "Market Revolution" and "Industrial Revolution" that combined to both integrate the American economy and transform it from an agrarian and commercial economy into an economy that combined a plantation economy producing cash crops for a global market with a Midwestern economy that produced both staple crops and raw materials needed by a growing urban manufacturing sector in the American Northeast. Chapter Nine will then explore the many ways in which gender and family relations in the antebellum period were constructed both on the plantation and in opposition to the institution of slavery. In this chapter students will encounter sources that illustrate the degree to which both African American and white ideas of masculinity and feminity both were both shaped by ideals of domesticity and confronted those same ideals as lived experience. These two chapters will also encourage readers to reflect on the ways in which slavery has shaped the American economy to the present and the continuing regional and cultural developments that, in no small part, help explain political and cultural cleavages that still divide the nation.

Often students ask me, "Why didn't slaves rebel against the injustices of plantation slavery?" Students are not alone in posing this question. Historians have likewise pondered what was characterized as the relative docility of American slaves in the face of the violence and inhumanity of slavery. The claim that African-American slaves rarely rose up in violent reaction was often touted as evidence of a failing virility; African-American men, unlike Spartacus of old, never mustered the courage to strike even a suicidal blow against their oppressors. Claims that slaves did not resist were perversely employed to justify the very system that tyrannized the slaves. As a result, when historians began to document the many ways in which slaves resisted and rose up in righteous revolt, both the benevolence of the plantation system and the docility of the slaves was called into question. Chapter Ten of this reader will then look closely at a number of slave rebellions, as slave insurrection was not an uncommon occurrence. And, despite the suicidal failure of all of the rebellions that took place in the United States, the fear of slave risings—a fear that curdled the blood of masters and mistresses across the South—resulted in a variety of policing and legal practices that have shaped the relationship between African Americans and the law to the present day.

The ensuing chapters in this reader will then seek to explain factors that ultimately resulted in the cataclysm of internecine violence that was the American Civil War. Chapter Eleven will introduce students to both the arguments put forth against slavery by ardent abolitionists and the predictable defense of slavery by those who depended upon African-American labor and obedience for their economic survival. It is often easier for American students to understand the perspective of abolitionists and to presume the inevitable demise of slavery than it is to hear arguments made by pro-slavery apologists. But, the confrontation between southern pro-slavery advocates and abolitionists was not merely an intellectual and cultural confrontation. It also had very real political dimensions that were most evident when American expansionism threatened to unsettle the balance of power between slaveholding and non-slaveholding states. Chapter Twelve addresses the relationship between territorial expansion, Manifest Destiny, the imperatives of the cotton economy and growing sectional political rivalries. Recognition that western expansion exacerbated sectional rivalries and highlighted is not new. This chapter will trace the familiar story of the debates over the Missouri compromise, the Texas "Revolution," and the Mexican American War, but with a heightened emphasis on the place of slavery in each.

In the final section of this reader students will be asked to examine the Civil War and its aftermath. The first chapter in this section will examine the Civil War itself. There are still those who argue that the Civil War primarily confronted northern interests that favored an interventionist national government against southerners intent on defending states rights. And, the predominant portrayals of the Civil War rarely emphasize the active participation of people of color in both defining and fighting for their freedom. Chapter Thirteen will seek to answer how the Civil War was transformed from a limited conflict designed to conclusively determine the political character of the union established "four score and seven years" prior into a crusade to end slavery consecrated by the blood of hundreds of thousands of men on both sides of the conflict. Additionally, however, the role of some 200,000 African-American men and women who fought to gain their freedom will be highlighted and their voices heard. The promise of a more perfect union, however, after an auspicious start, ultimately was not fulfilled. The final chapter of the reader, in the form of an epilogue, examines how Reconstruction ultimately failed to live up to the expectations of freedmen. Nor did Northern cities and small towns prove to be more welcoming to African-American citizens. This brief examination of Reconstruction will wrestle with the inability of the American republic to live up to the "better angels of our nature," and the ways in which African Americans, despite the fading promise of justice and liberty, sought to define and assert their freedom, often in the face of bitter resistance, legal retrenchment, and their abandonment by their erstwhile allies in the North.

A DOCUMENT READER FOR A "POST-RACIAL" AGE

Barack Obama in 2008 was elected to the presidency of the United States. His inauguration, which took place in the bitter cold of a Washington, D.C. January, was attended by perhaps the largest audience ever present at an event in the nation's capital. It is estimated that over 1.8 million Americans, including my son, braved the sub-zero temperatures to witness what could only have been characterized as unthinkable less than fifty years prior. African-American students meeting in a sociology classroom across the hall from where I was proctoring an exam shouted exuberantly when the president took the oath of office. One young man exclaimed, "We have the quarterback. We have the President. We have everything." The promise of American liberty had apparently been finally realized. Pundits proclaimed that the inauguration of an African-American man as President of the United States heralded a post-racial age. Sadly, this has not been the case.

Hardly eight years later, the promise of that auspicious moment seemed once again a shattered dream. The Black Lives Matter (BLM) movement has arisen in response to a spate of police shootings of unarmed black men. President Barack Obama has faced an unprecedented level of intransigence on the part of his legislative opposition, and every achievement or policy success has been accomplished only at great political cost. Additionally, Obama has encountered challenges to his legitimacy that few presidents have faced, including ongoing efforts to characterize him as a foreign national (despite his birth in Hawaii) and as a Muslim educated in a madrasa. For many, his legitimacy has been in question, even without these unprecedented assaults, simply because he is a black man. On the day of his inauguration, rather than celebrating the nation's belated acknowledgment of the full citizenship of its African-American population, the leadership of the Republican Party pledged to ensure Obama would have a single term in office. And, after eight years of the Obama administration, it can hardly be said that the ghosts of racial antipathy and discrimination had been overcome and the legacy of slavery had been effaced. The ways in which racial antipathy has intruded into the political discourse of the 2016 presidential election make it clear that, as much as at any time in the recent past, the history of slavery and its role in the development of the United States' peculiar relationship with racial animus must be re-engaged.

This Document reader then is an attempt to come to grips with the lasting impact of slavery and to acknowledge the many ways in which African Americans have contributed to the shaping of this nation. With all humility and with a healthy dose of caution, the goal of this reader is to illustrate the many ways in which black lives have mattered to the history of the United States from its very beginnings and the degree to which black lives have impacted the narrative of the American past at every pivotal moment in the history of the nation. Moreover, the intention of this reader is to make it clear that until black lives matter both historically and in contemporary society, all Americans' lives are diminished.

The Atlantic Slave System—Africans as a Commodity in the "New World"

In 1618, Richard Jobson, an Englishman trading in West Africa for gold and ivory was offered slaves by an Arab merchant. As Jobson described the offer, "hee shewed unto mee, certaine young blacke women, who were standing by themselves, and had white strings cross their bodies, which hee told me were slaves, brought for me to buy." Jobson refused to purchase the slaves explaining to the merchant, "We were a people, who did not deale in any such commodities, neither did wee buy or sell one another, or any that had our owne shapes." The tradesman was surprised at Jobson's disinterest and noted that there were other "white men, who earnestly desired them…" Within the century, however, the English had joined Portuguese, Spanish, Dutch, and French traders in this trade in Africans. Africans had become one of the most widely traded commodities in the global marketplace. How this became a horrible reality for Africans across the continent and how these Africans contributed to the settlement and development of the Americas is the subject of this chapter. Africans were not merely commodities, of course; they were also labor. Most significantly they provided the agricultural labor force that produced what Pierre Pomet called a drug, sugar. Today, Americans are once again remarking on the addictive qualities of sugar. The obesity epidemic frequently touted in American tabloids and television shows, may in part be attributed to our addition to this drug. Though slaves, both African and Indian, were employed in a wide variety of agricultural and mining activities in the sixteenth and seventeenth centuries, it was on the sugar islands of the Caribbean and in Brazil that the profitable nexus between sugar and slavery was formed.

While Richard Jobson may have expressed an unwillingness to enter into a trade for the young women the Arab merchant had to sell, by 1618, the practice of enslaving human beings had an ancient history, and the African slave trade had also been under way for some time. At the time that Jobson was writing, as Seymour Drescher has observed, "freedom, not slavery, was the peculiar institution." Ancient Greeks had slaves. The Roman Empire at its height had depended on two to three million enslaved persons. Incas and Aztecs relied on slave labor. The term slave itself had ancient origins; it reflected the Roman, and later Arab practice of using "Slavs" from central Europe as captive laborers. Most African kingdoms also practiced slavery. African slaves were acquired either as prisoners of war, debtors, or occasionally for small criminal offenses.

The Atlantic slave trade, which began in the late 15th century and continued for the next 400 years, nonetheless represented a departure from ancient and medieval slavery and from the way slavery operated in Africa. African slaves were not generally "chattel," as they couldn't be bought and sold in the same way as European property. This was not the case where African economies were connected to the Islamic world as African slaves had for some time been traded to merchants along the trans-Saharan trade routes and in the markets of the Swahili coast of East

Africa. The introduction of European demand for African slaves, however, would redirect the trade and increase enormously the number of Africans sought for sale in the new marketplace. While African slaves had been traded for centuries along trans-Saharan trade routes to the Mediterranean and Islamic worlds, the ferocity of the Atlantic slave trade, and the sheer scale of the trade and profits that were accrued from trans-Atlantic commerce were a striking departure. The trans-Atlantic slave trade was the largest forced migration in history. More Africans by 1807, perhaps 12 million, left the "Old World" aboard ships for transport to the "New World," than did Europeans during the same period. By 1807, when Great Britain effectively ended the trans-Atlantic export of enslaved Africans, only 2.5 million whites had emigrated to the Western Hemisphere.

The Portuguese, who first began to trade for African slaves in the late 15th century thus entered into a trade in human beings that had a long history. But, they were not militarily or politically able to impose their demand for African laborers on African kingdoms. Instead, they relied on African rulers and traders to supply them with slaves purchased with trade items that African rulers, traders, and consumers desired. In fact, very few Europeans directly participated in acquiring slaves in the interior of Africa. While each European nation authorized its own slavers to go to Africa and trade for slaves with African traders, they did not with few exceptions enter into Africa to acquire slaves directly. In fact, when Europeans attempted to do so, they were often subjected to severe reprisals from the rulers who controlled coastal kingdoms.

It must also be said that in no way did Portuguese explorers and merchants encounter peoples that they understood to be "inferior" or "backward." Notions of the racial, cultural or intellectual inferiority of Africans emerged and were perpetuated only after the slave trade had transported millions of Africans to the western hemisphere. It was a myth that served to justify European cruelties in the slave trade. Instead, Europeans initially justified their purchase, transport and enslavement of Africans using arguments about slavery that derived from Greek and Roman philosophers, or from views about the proper treatment by Christians of non-believers. In fact, the "culture gap" between Europe and Africa was in no way a large one. In various parts of Africa, large empires had been forged. In other parts of Africa there were more fragmented but nonetheless well-developed kingdoms. Elsewhere long-established city-states had a history of interaction and cultural sharing with the sophisticated and technologically advanced Islamic world. Thus, Africans were not disconnected from the major currents of world economic and cultural interaction when Europeans began to trade for Africans to labor in the plantations of the "New World."

If Africans were not imagined as culturally inferior or weak and therefore available for exploitation, why did Africa become the labor source for Europeans interested in profiting from their new position of power in the Americas? Most immediately, the trade in and commodification of African men and women resulted directly from the opening of a new circuit of trans-regional trade linking European markets (the consumers of commodities produced in the Americas) with newly available agricultural land in the Americas. The profits to be had by utilizing enslaved persons, people who were excluded by definition as consumers, to produce the commodities for sale in Europe was apparent immediately.

The trade in Africans, it should also be remembered, did not imply a conscious choice to forego enslaving or coercing Amerindians to labor in mines, sugar plantations, or other European enterprises. In fact, over the entire history of the African slave trade, and even after its abolition, Amerindians were also enslaved. Initially, Carib Indians were captured for transport to the slave markets of Europe. Columbus, in his second voyage to America, wrote to Ferdinand and Isabella about the commercial possibilities of Amerindian slavery, urging that consideration be given to capturing Carib Indians, "for I believe we could take many of the males every year and an infinite number of women." Columbus went on to point out that "one of them would be worth more than three black slaves from Guinea [on the West African coast] in strength and ingenuity...." In February 1595, the Admiral of the Ocean Sea, a title Columbus proudly held, shipped 550 Indians from Hispaniola to slave markets in southern Spain. And, of course, many Amerindians were enslaved in the mines of Peru and Bolivia, and put to work in agriculture across New Spain. The English, when they arrived in North America would also, when it was possible, capture Native-Americans, buy and sell them, and coerce their labor.

The demand for African labor, however, was predicated on the population crisis that struck the Americas in the sixteenth century. When Columbus arrived in the Americas, the region may have had a population of perhaps 140 million inhabitants. But with the introduction of European diseases, oppressive labor systems, and the dislocation occasioned by endemic warfare in community after community populations precipitously declined. Central Mexico's population fell by almost 95% in the first century after conquest—from more than 25,000,000 people to barely 1,300,000. In northern Mexico, the population declined from 2.5 million residents to perhaps as few as 320,000. The area of the Isthmus of Panama saw a reduction in population from 1 million to less than 10,000. In Peru and Chile, the region of the Inca Empire, estimations are that between 9 million and 14 million inhabitants could be found living scattered from the coastal plains to the Andean highlands before the Europeans arrived. Smallpox preceded the Europeans, and then the scourge of civil war, European invasion, and enslavement of the local populace reduced the population in the region to as few as 500,000 residents. As a result of the decline in Amerindian populations, when Europeans sought to profit from newly acquired lands in the Americas, it took little imagination to turn instead to sources of labor in Africa.

Land in the Americas and labor in Africa, however were only profitably exploited if there were markets elsewhere. The key factor driving European demand for African slaves was the emergence in the 16th century and 17th century of a number of important markets for cash crops, most importantly sugar, and later cotton, but also tobacco, indigo, coffee, rice, and other monocultures. The central problem faced by plantation owners was how to acquire the labor needed to maximize their investments. Europeans could not be easily coerced into these relations—although plantation owners had few scruples about mistreating and exploiting European indentured servants and laborers. There were legal and cultural protections that Europeans could claim that Africans and Amerindians were denied outright or struggled to attain. But, this was not the primary reason that European labor was not relied on in the plantation economies that emerged in the Americas. European planters and merchants depended upon "free" laborers to purchase the refined sugar, rum, molasses, cotton textiles, tobacco, and other products that slaves produced. Capitalism has a central contradiction, namely that manufacturers and investors must have a market for their products. Slaves (and low-wage laborers today) do not make a good market for products they cannot afford. In a sense then, the "free labor" system of Europe which gradually developed during the course of the early modern period made up of wage earners who became consumers, in fundamental ways depended upon the expansion of "un-free labor" in the Americas, regardless of the color of skin of the laborer.

The connection can be more explicitly made. The slaves in the West Indies, for example, produced sugar, taken either as rum or refined and semi-refined sugar consumed in cups of tea or coffee. Tea, coffee, and later sodas are merely "delivery systems for sugar," much as cigarettes are delivery systems for nicotine. Sugar, which had been a luxury few Europeans could afford before the sixteenth century, rapidly became an important source of calories for European workers (an energy boost of 250 calories per day in a diet that often hovered at just above 2400 calories daily). Tobacco served a similar purpose. The earliest consumption of tobacco by Europeans was as a novelty item and social lubricant; tobacco was often taken in social settings not unlike cafés. Very quickly, however, this powerful narcotic, which eased hunger pangs, would serve to distract European workers in dismal, repetitive, and low-paid labor in industrial factories. Later, cotton plantations would provide English textile mills with the raw materials necessary to compete with Indian textiles, which were of cheaper and higher quality until late in the 18th century. Cotton would also enrich plantation owners in the United States, who would become, like the West Indian sugar barons before them, among the wealthiest people in the world.

As you will see in the primary sources that follow, the rise of the Atlantic slave trade and the commodification of African bodies and labor was not an obvious choice. The earliest Europeans to reach the Americas were quite content to enslave Amerindians, though the Spanish did express misgivings at the practice and endeavored to curtail it. But the profits that could be had by the production of tobacco, sugar, and other commodities for the European market would soon motivate Portuguese, Dutch, French, and English slave traders to bargain with African merchants and rulers for the labor force that was so in need in the Americas. To fill that need, Africans were then captured and transported, under horrible conditions, to plantations in the Caribbean and on the American continents. They were then employed on sugar plantations that could only be described as slave labor camps where brutal living and working conditions took a surprising toll in life and limb.

PRIMARY SOURCES

Document 1   "How we Captured Many Indians and Returned to Spain with Some of them" from Michele de Cueno's Letter on Columbus's 2nd Voyage[1]

One of those days while we were lying at anchor we saw coming from a cape a canoe, that is to say a boat, which is how they call it in their language, going along with oars so that it looked like a well-manned *bergantino,* on which there were three or four Carib men with two Carib women and two Indian slaves…. when we saw that canoe coming, [we] quickly jumped into the boat and gave chase to that canoe. While we were approaching her the Caribs began shooting at us with their bows in such a manner that, had it not been for the shields, half of us would have been wounded. But I must tell you that to one of the seamen who had a shield in his hand came an arrow, which went through the shield and penetrated his chest three inches, so that he died in a few days. We captured that canoe with all the men, and one Carib was wounded by a spear in such a way that we thought he was dead, and cast him for dead into the sea, but instantly saw

---

[1] "How we Captured Many Indians and Returned to Spain with Some of them" from Michele de Cueno's Letter on Columbus's 2nd Voyage, pp. 226-227. http://www2.fiu.edu/~cookn/cuneo2.pdf

him swim. In so doing we caught him and with the grapple hauled him over the bulwarks of the ship where we cut his head with an axe. The other Caribs, together with those slaves, we later sent to Spain. While I was in the boat I captured a very beautiful Carib woman whom the said Lord Admiral [Christopher Columbus] gave to me, and with whom, having taken her into my cabin, she being naked according to their custom, I conceived a desire to take pleasure. I wanted to put my desire into execution but she did not want it and treated me with her finger nails in such a manner that I wished I had never begun. But seeing that, (to tell you the end of it all), I took a rope and thrashed her well, for which she raised such unheard of screams that you would not have believed your ears. Finally we came to an agreement in such manner that I can tell you that she seemed to have been brought up in a school of harlots. To that cape of the island the Admiral gave the name Cape of the Arrow because of the one who had died of the arrow.

When our caravels in which I wished to go home had to leave for Spain, we gathered together in our settlement 1600 people male and female of those Indians, of whom, among the best males and females, we embarked on our caravels on 17 February 1495, 550 souls. Of the rest who were left the announcement went around that whoever wanted them could take as many as he pleased; and this was done. And when everybody had been supplied there were some 400 of them left to whom permission was granted to go wherever they wanted. Among them were many women, who had infants at the breast. They, in order the better to escape us, since they were afraid we would turn to catch them again, left their infants anywhere on the ground and started to flee like desperate people; and some fled so far that they were removed from our settlement of Isabela 7 or 8 days beyond the mountains and across huge rivers; wherefore from now on scarcely any will be had. Among these people who were taken was one of their kings with two chiefs, who it was decided should be killed with arrows on the following day, so they were tied up; but in the night they knew so well how to gnaw one another's ropes with their teeth, that they were freed from their bonds and escaped.

…when we reached the waters around Spain about 200 of those Indians died, I believe because of the unaccustomed air, colder than theirs. We cast them into the sea. The first land we saw was Cape Spartel and very soon after we reached Cadiz, in which place we disembarked all the slaves, half of whom were sick. For your information they are not working people and they very much fear cold, nor have they long life.

Document 2 *True Relation of the Hardships suffered by Governor Hernando De Soto and Certain Portuguese Gentlemen during the Discovery of Florida, 1539-1543.*[2]

The next day the Governor asked for *tamemes* and one hundred Indian women, and the cacique gave them four hundred *tamemes* and said that he would give them the rest of the *tamemes* and the women in Mabila, the province of a principal vassal of his, and the Governor was content that the rest of his unjust demand would be satisfied in Mabila. And he commanded that he be given a horse and some buckskins and a cloak of scarlet cloth to keep him content. But as the cacique had already given him four hundred *tamemes*, or more accurately slaves, and was to give him one hundred women in Mabila….

---

2 Excerpts from the Soto Chronicles, De Soto to North America in 1539-1543, Volume 1, edited by Lawrence A. Clayton, Vernon James Knight, and Edward C. Moore, (Tuscaloosa, AL: The University of Alabama Press, 1993), 70, 291.

... From there the governor sent two captains, each one in a different direction, in search of the Indians. They captured a hundred head, among Indian men and women. Of the latter, there, as well as in any other part where forays were made, the captain selected one or two for the governor and the others were divided among themselves and those who went with them. These Indians they took along in chains with collars about their necks and they were used for carrying the baggage and grinding the maize and for other services which so fastened in this manner they could perform. Sometimes it happened that when they went with them for firewood or maize they would kill the Christian who was leading them and would escape with the chain. Others at night would file the chain off with a bit of stone which they have in place of iron tools, and with which they cut it. Those who were caught at it paid for themselves and for those others, so that on another day they might not dare do likewise. As soon as the women and young children were a hundred leagues from their land, having become unmindful, they were taken along unbound, and served in that way, and in a very short time learned the language of the Christians.

Document 3   Sugar and Rum Imports for Home Consumption: England And Wales, 1663-1799[3]

Years	Sugar: lbs per capita (annual average)	Rum: gallons per capita (annual average)
1663, 1669	2.13	n.a.
1690, 1698-99	4.01	n.a
1700-1709	5.81	<0.01
1710-1719	8.23	<0.01
1720-1729	12.02	0.02
1730-1739	14.90	0.06
1740-1749	12.73	0.08
1750-1759	16.94	0.14
1760-1769	20.20	0.15
1770-1779	23.02	0.22
1780-1789	21.14	0.17
1790-1799	24.16	0.24
*for comparison: U.S. 2015	101.39	

---

3   Carol Shammas, "Changes in English and Anglo-American Consumption from 1550 to 1800," in Consumption and the World of Goods, John Brewer and Roy Porter, eds. (London: Routledge, 1993), p. 182.

Document 4 Population of the English Colonies in America, 1650-1770 (in thousands)[4]

Region	1650	1700	1750	1770
West Indies	59,000	148,000	330,000	479,000
Lower South		16,400	142,200	344,800
Upper South	12,700	98,100	377,800	649,600
Plantation Colonies	71,700	262,500	850,000	1,473,400
Continental Colonies	55,000	265,000	1,206,000	2,283,000
TOTAL	114,000	412,000	1,536,000	2,762,000

Document 5 "The Sugar Works," in Pierre Pomet, *A Complete History of Drugs*, 1748.[5]

---

4   Russell R. Menard, "Plantation Empire: How Sugar and Tobacco Planters built their Industries and Raised an Empire," Agricultural History 81:3 (Summer 2007), p. 314.

5   "The Sugar Works," in Pierre Pomet, A Complete History of Drugs (London: J.J. Bonwicke, 1748), p. 57.

Document 6 Richard Ligon, *A True and Exact History of the Island of Barbadoes,* 1673.[6]

And so upon discourse with some of the most knowing men of the Island, we found that it was far better, for a man that had money, goods, or Credit, to purchase a Plantation there ready furnish'd, and stockt with Servants, Slaves, Horses, Cattle, Assinigoes, Camels &c., with a Sugar work and an Ingenio: than to begin upon a place, where land is to be had for nothing, but a trivial Rent, and to indure all hardships, and a tedious expectation, of what profit or pleasure may arise in many years patience: and that, not to be expected, without large and frequent supplies from *England*; and yet fare, and labour hard. This knowledge, was a spur to set on Colonel Modiford, who had both goods and credit, to make enquiry for such a purchase, which in very few days he lighted on; making a visit to the Governour Mr. *Phillip Bell,* met there with Major *William Hilliard,* an eminent Planter of the Island, and a Councellor, who had been long there, and was now desirous to suck in some of the sweet air of *England*: And glad to find a man likely to perform with him, took him home to his house, and began to treat with him, for half the Plantation upon which he lived; which had in it 500 Acres of Land, with a fair dwelling house, filling room, Cisterns, and Still-house; with a Carding house, of 100 foot long, and 40 foot broad; with stables, Smiths forge, and rooms to lay provisions, of Corn and Bonavist; Houses for *Negroes* and *Indian* slaves, with 96 *Negroes* and three *Indian* women, with their Children; 28 Christians, 45 Cattle for work, 8 Milch Cows, a dozen Horses and Mares, 16 Assinigoes.

After a Months treaty, the bargain was concluded, and Colonel *Modiford* was to pay for the Moiety of this Plantation, 7000£ to be payed, 1000£ in hand, the rest 2000£ a time, at six and six months, and Colonel *Modiford* to receive the profit of half the Plantation as it rose, keeping the account together, both of the expence and profit.

In this Plantation of 500 acres of land, there was imployed for sugar somewhat more than 200 acres; above 80 acres for pasture, 120 for wood, 30 for Tobacco, 5 for Ginger, as many for Cotton wool, and 70 acres for provisions: *viz.* Corn, Potatoes, Plantaines, Cassava, and Bonavist; some few acres of which for fruit; *viz.* Pines, Plantaines, Milions, Bananas, Guavas, Water Milions, Oranges, Limon Limes, &c. most of these onely for the table.

Upon this Plantation I lived with these two partners a while, But with Colonel *Modiford* three years; for the other went for *England,* and left Colonel *Modiford* to manage the imployment alone; and I to give what assistance I could for the benefit of both….

---

6   Richard Ligon, A True and Exact History of the Island of Barbadoes (London: Peter Parker, bookseller, 1673), p. 22. https://archive.org/details/mobot31753000818390

THE ATLANTIC SLAVE SYSTEM—AFRICANS AS A COMMODITY IN THE "NEW WORLD" 9

Document 7   *Crops grown in Africa purchased by slave ships.*[7]

African Origin	New World Origin	Asian Origin
Malegueta pepper	Peanut	Coconuts
African rice	Manioc	Bananas
Sorghum	Tobacco	Plantains
Yams	Maize	Asian rice
Pearl millet		
Tamarind		
Oil palm		
Sesame		

Document 8   John Barbot, *Description of the Coasts of North and South-Guinea*, 1732.[8]

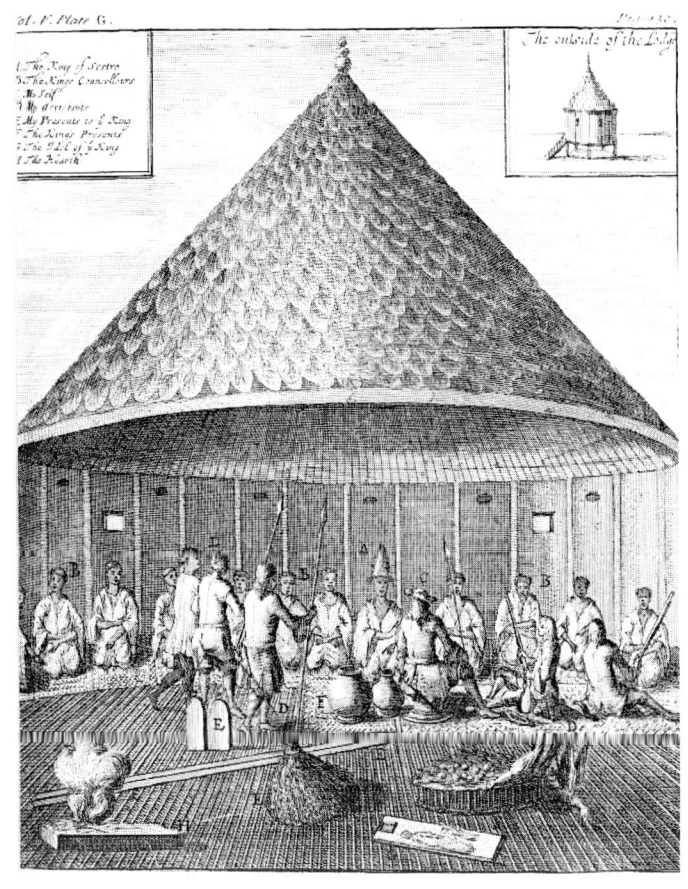

---

7   Adapted from Judith A. Carney, "African Rice in the Columbian Exchange," *Journal of African History* 42:3 (2001), p. 382.

8   John Barbot, Description of the Coasts of North and South-Guinea, ... (London: Churchill, 1732) p. 130.

Document 9 Ottobah Cugoano, *Thoughts and Sentiments on the Evil And Wicked Traffic of the Slavery and Commerce of the Human Species*, 1787.[9]

I was born in the city of Agimaque, on the coast of Fantyn; my father was a companion to the chief in that part of the country of Fantee, and when the old king died I was left in his house with his family; soon after I was sent for by his nephew, Ambro Accasa, who succeeded the old king in the chiefdom of that part of Fantee known by the name of Agimaque and Assinee. I lived with his children, enjoying peace and tranquillity, about twenty moons, which, according to their way of reckoning time, is two years. I was sent for to visit an uncle, who lived at a considerable distance from Agimaque. The first day after we set out we arrived at Assinee, and the third day at my uncle's habitation, where I lived about three months, and was then thinking of returning to my father and young companion at Agimaque; but by this time I had got well acquainted with some of the children of my uncle's hundreds of relations, and we were some days too venturesome in going into the woods to gather fruit and catch birds, and such amusements as pleased us. One day I refused to go with the rest, being rather apprehensive that something might happen to us; till one of my play-fellows said to me, because you belong to the great men, you are afraid to venture your carcase, or else of the *bounsam*, which is the devil. This enraged me so much, that I set a resolution to join the rest, and we went into the woods as usual; but we had not been above two hours before our troubles began, when several great ruffians came upon us suddenly, and said we must go and answer for it ourselves before him.

Some of us attempted in vain to run away, but pistols and cutlasses were soon introduced, threatening, that if we offered to stir we should all lie dead on the spot. One of them pretended to be more friendly than the rest, and said, that he would speak to their lord to get us clear, and desired that we should follow him; we were then immediately divided into different parties, and drove after him. We were soon led out of the way which we knew, and towards the evening, as we came in sight of a town, they told us that this great man of theirs lived there, but pretended it was too late to go and see him that night. Next morning there came three other men, whose language differed from ours, and spoke to some of those who watched us all the night, but he that pretended to be our friend with the great man, and some others, were gone away. We asked our keepers what these men had been saying to them, and they answered, that they had been asking them, and us together, to go and feast with them that day, and that we must put off seeing the great man till after; little thinking that our doom was so nigh, or that these villains meant to feast on us as their prey. We went with them again about half a day's journey, and came to a great multitude of people, having different music playing; and all the day after we got there, we were very merry with the music, dancing and singing. Towards the evening, we were again persuaded that we could not get back to where the great man lived till next day; and when bedtime came, we were separated into different houses with different people. When the next morning came, I asked for the men that brought me there, and for the rest of my companions; and I was told that they were gone to the sea side to bring home some rum, guns, and powder, and that some of my companions were gone with them, and that some were gone to the fields to do something or other. This gave me strong suspicion that there was some treachery in the cause, and I began to think

---

[9] Ottobah Cugoano, Thoughts and Sentiments on the Evil And Wicked Traffic of the Slavery and Commerce of the Human Species, (London, 1787).

that my hopes of returning home again were all over. I soon became very unesy, not knowing what to do, and refused to eat or drink for whole days together, till the man of the house told me that he would do all in his power to get me back to my uncle; then I ate a little fruit with him, and had some thoughts that I should be sought after, as I would then be missing at home about five or six days. I enquired every day if the men had come back, and for the rest of my companions, but could get no answer of any satisfaction. I was kept about six days at this man's house, and in the evening there was another man came and talked with him a good while, and I heard the one say to the other he must go, and the other said the sooner the better; that man came out and told me that he knew my relations in Agimaque, and that we must set out tomorrow morning, and he would convey me there. Accordingly we set out next day, and travelled till dark, when we came to a place where we had some supper and slept. He carried a large bag with some gold dust, which he said he had to buy some goods at the sea side to take with him to Agimaque. Next day we travelled on, and in the evening came to a town, where I saw several white people, which made me afraid that they would eat me, according to our notion as children in the inland parts of the country. This made me rest very uneasy all the night, and next morning I had some victuals brought, desiring me to eat and make haste, as my guide and kidnapper told me that he had to go to the castle with some company that we are going there, as he had told me before, to get some goods. After I was ordered out, the horrors I soon saw and felt, cannot be well described; I saw many of my miserable countrymen chained two and two, some hand-cuffed, and some with their hands tied behind. We were conducted along by a guard, and when we arrived at the castle, I asked my guide what I was brought there for, he told me to learn the ways of the *browfow*, that is the white faced people. I saw him take a gun, a piece of cloth, and some lead for me, and then he told me that he must now leave me there, and went off. This made me cry bitterly, but I was soon conducted to a prison, for three days, where I heard the groans and cries of many, and saw some of my fellow captives. But when a vessel arrived to conduct us away to the ship, it was a most horrible scene; there was nothing to be heard but rattling of chains, smacking of whips, and the groans and cries of our fellow-men. Some would not stir from the ground, when they were lashed and beat in the most horrible manner. I have forgot the name of this infernal fort; but we were taken in the ship that came for us, to another that was ready to sail from Cape Coast. When we were put into the ship, we saw several black merchants coming on board, but we were all drove into our holes, and not suffered to speak to any of them. In this situation we continued several days in sight of our native land; but I could find no good person to give any information of my situation to Accasa at Agimaque. And when we found ourselves at last taken away, death was more preferable than life, and a plan was concerted amongst us, that we might burn and blow up the ship, and to perish all together in the flames; but we were betrayed by one of our own countrywomen, who slept with some of the head men of the ship, for it was common for the dirty filthy sailors to take African women and lie upon their bodies; but the men were chained and pent up in holes. It was the women and boys which were to burn the ship, with the approbation and groans of the rest; though that was prevented, the discovery was likewise a cruel bloody scene.

But it would be needless to give a description of all the horrible scenes which we saw, and the base treatment which we met with in this dreadful captive situation, as the similar cases of thousands, which suffer by this infernal traffic, are well known. Let it suffice to say, that I was thus lost to my dear indulgent parents and relations, and they to me. All my help was cries and tears, and these could not avail; nor suffered long, till one succeeding woe, and dread, swelled up another. Brought from a state of innocence and freedom, and, in a barbarous and cruel manner, conveyed to a state of horror and slavery: this abandoned situation may be easier conceived than described. From the time that I was kidnapped and conducted to a factory, and from thence in the brutish, base, but fashionable way of traffic, consigned to Granada, the grievous thoughts which I then felt, still pant in my heart; though my fears and tears have long since subsided. And yet it is still grievous to think that thousands more have suffered in similar and greater distress, under the hands of barbarous robbers, and merciless taskmasters; and that many even now are suffering in all the extreme bitterness of grief and woe, that no language can describe. The cries of some, and the sight of their misery, may be seen and heard afar; but the deep sounding groans of thousands, and the great sadness of their misery and woe, under the heavy load of oppressions and calamities inflicted upon them, are such as can only be distinctly known to the ears of Jehovah Sabaoth.

Document 10   Description of the Slave Ship, *Brookes*, 1789.[10]

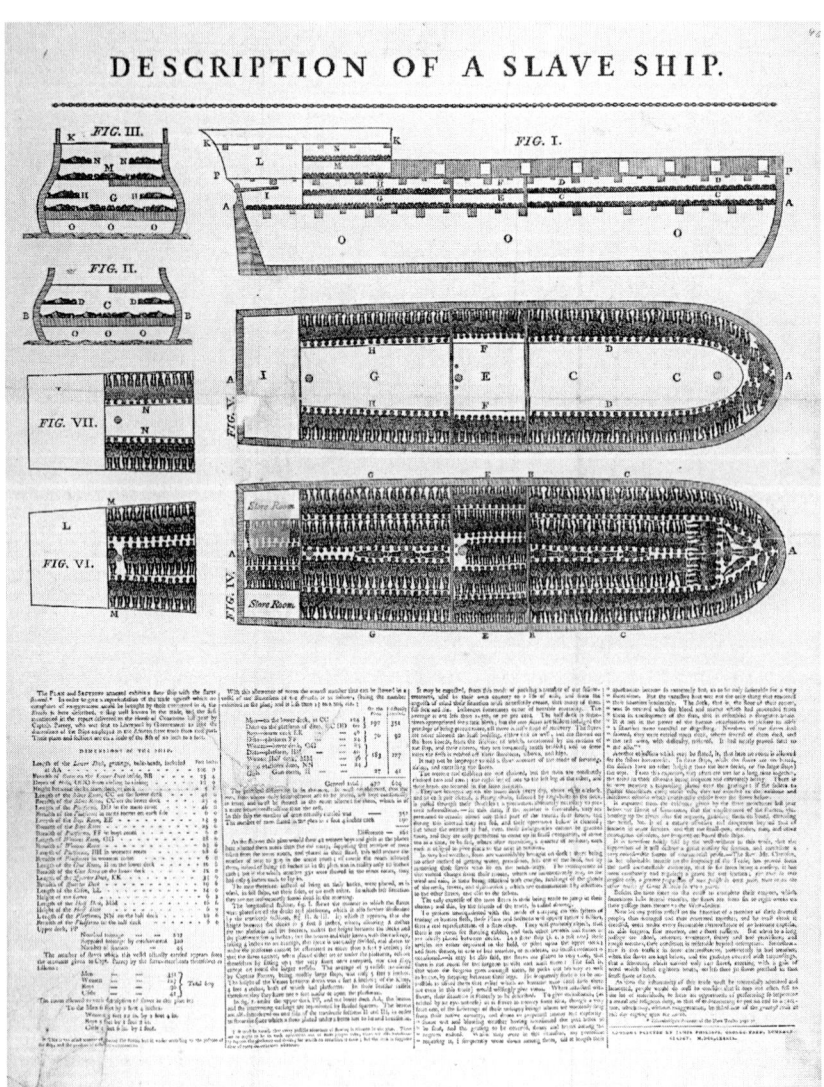

---

10   Description of the Slave Ship, Brookes, 1789. The British Library. http://www.bl.uk/learning/timeline/large106661.html

Document 11   Alexander Falconbridge, *An Account of the Slave Trade on the Coast of Africa*, 1788[11]

The Manner in which the Slaves are procured

After permission has been obtained for *breaking trade,* as it is termed, the captains go ashore, from time to time, to examine the negroes that are exposed to sale, and to make their purchases. The unhappy wretches thus disposed of, are brought by the black traders at fairs, which are held for that purpose, at the distance of upwards of two hundred miles from the sea coast; and these fairs are said to be supplied from an interior part of the country. Many negroes, upon being questioned relative to the places of their nativity have asserted, that they have travelled during the revolution of several moons, (their usual method of calculating time) before they have reached the places where they were purchased by the black traders. At these fairs, which are held at uncertain periods, but generally every six weeks, several thousands are frequently exposed to sale, who had been collected from all parts of the country for a very considerable distance round. While I was upon the coast, during one of the voyages I made, the black traders brought down, in different canoes, from twelve to fifteen hundred negroes, which had been purchased at one fair. They consisted chiefly of men and boys, the women seldom exceeding a third of the whole number. From forty to two hundred negroes are generally purchased at a time by the black traders, according to the opulence of the buyer; and consist of those of all ages, from a month, to sixty years and upward. Scarce any age or situation is deemed an exception, the price being proportionable. Women sometimes form a part of them, who happen to be so far advanced in their pregnancy, as to be delivered during their journey from the fairs to the coast; and I have frequently seen instances of deliveries on board ship. The slaves purchased at these fairs are only for the supply of the markets at Bonny, and Old and New Calabar.

There is great reason to believe, that most of the negroes shipped off from the coast of Africa are kidnapped. But the extreme care taken by black traders to prevent the Europeans from gaining any intelligence of their modes of proceeding; the great distance inland from whence the negroes are brought; and our ignorance of their language, (with which, very frequently, the black traders themselves are equally unacquainted) prevent our obtaining such information on this head as we could wish. I have, however, by means of occasional inquiries, made through interpreters, procured some intelligence relative to the point, and such, as I think, puts the matter beyond a doubt.

From these I shall select the following striking instances:--While I was in employ on board one of the slave ships, a negroe informed me, that being one evening invited to drink with some of the black traders, upon his going away, they attempted to seize him. As he was very active, he evaded their design, and got out of their hands. He was however prevented from effecting his escape by a large dog, which laid hold of him, and compelled him to submit. These creatures are kept by many of the traders for that purpose; and being trained to the inhuman sport, they appear to be much pleased with it.

I was likewise told by a negroe woman, that as she was on her return home, one evening, from some neighbours, to whom she had been making a visit by invitation, she was kidnapped; and,

---
11   Alexander Falconbridge, *Account of the Slave Trade on the Coast of Africa,* (London: J. Phillips, 1788).

notwithstanding she was big with child, sold for a slave. This transaction happened a considerable way up the country, and she had passed thorugh the hands of several purchasers before she reached the ship. A man and his son, according to their information, were seized by professed kidnappers, while they were planting yams, and sold for slaves. This likewise happened in the interior parts of the country, and after passing through several hands, they were purchased for the ship to which I belonged. It frequently happens, that those who kidnap others, are themselves, in their turns, seized and sold. A negroe in the West-Indies informed me, that after having been employed in kidnapping others, he had experienced this reverse. And he assured me, that it was a common incident among his countrymen. [....]

When the negroes, whom the black traders have to dispose of, are shewn to the European purchasers, they first examine them relative to their age. They then minutely inspect their persons and inquire into the state of their health; if they are afflicted with an infirmity, or are deformed, or have bad eyes or teeth; if they are lame, or weak in the joints, or distorted in the back, or of a slender make, or are narrow in the chest; in short, if they have been or are afflicted in any manner, so as to render them incapable of much labour; if any of the foregoing defects are discovered in them, they are rejected. But if approved of, they are generally taken on board the ship the same evening. The purchaser has liberty to retun on the following morning, but not afterwards, such as upon re-examing are found exceptionable.

The traders frequently beat those negroes which are objected to by the captains, and use them with great severity. It matters not whether they are refused on account of age, illness, deformity, or for any other reason. At New Calabar, in particular, the traders have frequently been known to put them to death. Instances have happened at that place, that the traders, when any of their negroes have been objected to, have dropped their canoes under the stern of the vessel, and instantly beheaded them, in sight of the captain.[....]

Nor do these unhappy beings, afer they become the property of the Europeans (from whom, as a more civilized people, more humanity might naturally be expected) find their situation in the least amended. Their treatment is no less rigorous. The men negroes, on being brought aboard the ship, are immediately fastened together, two and two, by handcuffs on their wrists, and by irons riveted on their legs. They are then sent down between the decks, and placed in an apartment partitioned off for that purpose. The women likewise are placed in a separate apartment between decks, but without being ironed. And, an adjoining room, on the same deck, is besides appointed for the boys. Thus are they all placed in different apartments.

But at the same time, they are frequently stowed so close, as to admit of no other posture than lying on their sides. Neither will the height between decks, unless directly under the grating, permit them the indulgence of an erect posture; especially where there are platforms, which is generally the case. These platforms are a kind of shelf, about eight or nine feet in breadth, extending from the side of the ship towards the centre. They are placed nearly midway between the decks, at the distance of two or three feet from each deck. Upon thse the negroes are stowed in the same manner as they are on the deck underneath.

In each of the apartments are placed three or four large buckets, of a conical form, being near two feet in diameter at the bottom, and only one foot at the top, and in depth about twenty-eight inches; to which, when necessary, the negroes have recourse. It often happens that those who are placed at a distance from the buckets, in endeavouring to get to them, tumble over their comapanions, in consequence of their being shackled. These accidents, although unavoidable, are productive of continual quarrels, in which some of them are always bruised. In this distressed situation, unable to proceed, and prevented from getting to the tubs, they desist from the attempt; and, as the necessities of nature are not to be repelled, ease themselves as they lie. This becomes a fresh source of broils and disturbances, and tends to render the condition of the poor captive wretches still more uncomfortable.[…]

About eight o'clock in the morning the negroes are generally brought upon deck. Their irons being examined, a long chain, which is locked to a ring-bolt, fixed in the deck, is run through the rings of the shacles of the men, and then locked to another ring-bold, fixed also in the deck. By this means fifty or sixty, and sometimes more, are fastened to one chain, in order to prevent them from rising, or endeavouring to escape. If the weather proves favourable, they are permitted to remain in that situation till four or five in the afternoon, when they are disengaged from the chain, and sent down.

The diet of the negroes, while on board, consists chiefly of horse-beans, boiled to the consistence of a pulp; of boiled yams and rice, and sometimes of a small quantity of beef or pork. The latter are frequently taken from the provisions laid in for the sailors. They sometimes make use of a sauce, composed of palm-oil, mixed with flour, water, and pepper, which sailors call *slabber-sauce*. Yams are the favourite food of the Eboe, or Bight negroes, and rice or corn, of those from the Gold and Windward Coasts; each preferring the produce of their native soil.

In their own country, the negroes in general live on animal food and fish, with roots, yams, and Indian corn. The horse-beans and rice, with which they are fed aboard ship, are chiefly taken from Europe. The latter, indeed, is sometimes purchased on the coast, being far superior to any other.[…]

Upon the negroes refusing to take sustenance, I have seen coals of fire, glowing hot, put on a shovel, and placed so near their lips, as to scorch and burn them. And this has been accompanied with threats, of forcing them to swallow the coals, if they any longer persist in refusing to eat. These means have generally had the desired effect. I have also been credibly informed, that a certain captain in the slave trade, poured melted lead on such of the negroes as obstinately refused their food.[…]

Exercise being deemed necessary for the preservation of their health, they are sometimes obliged to dance, when the weather will permit their coming on deck. If they go about it reluctantly, or do not move with agility, they are flogged; a person standing by them all the time with a cat-o'-nine-tails in his hand for that perpose. Their musick, upon these occasions, consists of a drum, sometimes with only one head; and when that is worn out, they do not scruple to make use of of the bottom of one of the tubs before described. The poor wretches are frequently compelled to sing also; but when they do so, their songs are generally, as may naturally be expected, melancholy lamentations of their exile from their native country.[…]

On board some ships, the common sailors are allowed to have intercourse with such of the black women whose consent they can procure. And some of them have been known to take the inconstancy of their paramours so much to heart, as to leap overboard and drown themselves. The officers are permited to indulge their passions among them at pleasure, and sometimes are guilty of such brutal excesses, as disgrace human nature.[…]

During the voyages I made, I was frequently a witness to the fatal effects of [the]exclusion of fresh air. [Falconbridge then reports a story told about a ship from the British port of Liverpool.]

This ship, ... took on board at Bonny, at least six hundred negroes; but according to the information of the black traders, from whom I received the intelligence immediately after the ship sailed, they amounted to near *seven hundred*. By purchasing so great a number, the slaves were so crowded, that they were even obliged to lie one upon another. This occasioned such a mortality among them, that, without meeting with unusual bad weather, or having a longer voyage than common, nearly one half of them died before the ship arrived in the West Indies.[…]

As very few of the negroes can so far brook the loss of their liberty, and the hardships they endure, as to bear them with any degree of patience, they are ever upon the watch to take advantage of the least negligence in their oppressors. Insurrections are frequently the consequence; which are seldom suppressed without much bloodshed. Sometimes these are successful, and the whole ship's company is cut off. They are likewise always ready to seize every opportunity for commiting some act of desperation to free themselves from their miserable state; and notwithstanding the restraints under which they are laid, they often succeed.

While a ship, to which I belonged, lay in Bonny River, one evening, a short time before our departure, a lot of negroes, consisting of about ten, was brought on board; when one of them, in a favourable moment, forced his way through the net-work on the larboard side of the vessel, jumped overboard, and was supposed to have been devoured by the sharks.[…]

It frequently happens that the negroes, on being purchased by the Europeans, become raving mad; and many of them die in that state; particularly the women. While I was one day ashore at Bonny, I saw a middle aged stout woman, who had been brought down from a fair the preceding day, chained to the post of a black trader's door, in a state of furious insanity. On board a ship in Bonny River, I saw a young negroe woman chained to the deck, who had lost her senses, soon after she was purchased and taken on board. […]

… I think it may be clearly deduced, that the unhappy Africans are not bereft of the finer feelings, but have a strong attachment to their native country, together with a just sense of the value of liberty.

Sale of the Slaves

When the ships arrive in the West-Indies, (the chief mart for this inhuman merchandise), the slaves are disposed of, as I have before observed, by different methods. Sometimes the mode of disposal, is that of selling them by what is termed a *scramble*; and a day is soon fixed for that purpose. But previous thereto, the sick, or refuse slaves, of which there are frequently many, are usually conveyed on shore, and sold at a tavern by vendue, or public auction. These, in general, are purchased by the Jews and surgeons, but chiefly the former, upon speculation, at so low a price as five or six dollars a head. I was informed by a mulatto woman, that she purchased a sick slave at Grenada, upon speculation, for the small sum of one dollar, as the poor wretch was apparently dying of the flux. It seldom happens that any, who are carried ashore in the emaciated state to which they are generally reduced by that disorder, long survive their landing. I once saw sixteen conveyed on shore, and sold in the foregoing manner, the whole of whom died before I left the island, which was within a short time after. Sometimes the captains march the slaves through the town at which they intend to dispose of them; and then place them in rows where they are examined and purchased.

The mode of selling them by scramble having fallen under my observation the oftenest, I shall be more particular in describing it. Being some years ago, at one of the islands in the West-Indies, I was witness to a sale by scramble, where about 250 negroes were sold. Upon this occasion all the negroes scrambled for bear an equal price; which is agreed uon between the captains and the purchasers before the sale begins.

One a day appointed, the negroes were landed and placed together in a large yard, belonging to the merchants to whom the ship was consigned. As soon as the hour agreed on arrived, the doors of the yard were suddenly thrown open, and in rushed a considerable number of purchasers, with all the ferocity of brutes. Some instantly seized such of the negroes as they could conveniently lay hold of with their hands. Others, being prepared with several handkerchiefs tied together, encircled with these as many as they were able. While others, by means of a rope, effected the same purpose. It is scarcely possible to describe the confusion of which this mode of selling is productive… The poor astonished negroes were so much terrified by these proceedings, that several of them, through fear, climbed over the walls of the court yard, and ran wild about the town; but were soon hunted down and taken […]

Various are the deceptions made use of in the disposal of the sick slaves; and many of these, such as must excite in every humane mine, the liveliest sensations of horror. I have been well informed, that a Liverpool captain boasted of his having cheated some Jews by the following stratagem: A lot of slaves, afflicted with the flux, being about to be landed for sale, he directed the surgeon to stop the anus of each of them with oakum. Thus prepared, they were landed, and taken to the accustomed place of sale; where being unable to stand but for a very short time, they are usually permitted to sit. The Jews, when they examine them, oblige them to stand up, in order to see if there be any discharge; and when they do not perceive this appearance, they consider it a symptom of recovery.

Document 12 James Ramsay, *On the Treatment and Conversion of African Slaves in the British Sugar Colonies*, 1784[12]

The discipline of a sugar plantation is as exact as that of a regiment: at four o'clock in the morning the plantation bell rings to call the slaves into the field. Their work is to manure, dig, and hoe, plow the ground, to plant, weed, and cut the cane, to bring it to the mill, to have the juice expressed, and boiled into sugar. About nine o'clock, they have an hour for breakfast, which they take in the field. Again they fall to work, and according to the custom of the plantation, continue until eleven o'clock, or noon; the bell then rings, and the slaves are dispersed in the neighborhood, to pick up about the fences, in the mountains, and sallow or waste grounds, natural grass and weeds for the horses and cattle. The time allotted for this branch of work, and preparation of dinner, varies from an hour and an half, to near three hours. […] At one, or in some plantations, at two o'clock, the bell summons them to deliver in the tale of their grass, and assemble to their field work. If the overseer thinks their bundles too small, or if they come too late with them, they are punished with a number of stripes from four to ten. Some masters, under a fit of carefulness for their cattle, have gone as far as fifty stripes, which effectually disable the culprit for weeks. If a slave has no grass to deliver in, he keeps away out of fear, skulks about in the mountains, and is absent from

---

12   James Ramsay, On the *Treatment and Conversion of African Slaves in the British Sugar Colonies* (London: James Philips, 1784) p. 69-72. Internet Archive https://archive.org/details/essayontreatment1784rams.

his work often for months; an aggravation of his crime, which when he is caught, he is made to remember. [...]

In crop-time, which may be when reckoned altogether on a plantation, from five to six months; the cane tops, by supplying the cattle with food, gives the slaves some little relaxation in picking grass. But some pretendedly industrious planters, men of much bustle, and no method, will especially in moon-light, keep their people till ten o'clock at night, carrying *wowra*, the decayed leaves of the cane, to boil off the cane juice. A considerable number of slaves is kept to attend in turn the mill and boiling house all night. They sleep over their work; the sugar is ill tempered, burnt in the boiler, and improperly struck; while the mill every now-and-then grinds off an hand, or an arm, of those drowsy worn down creatures that feed it. Still the process of making sugar is carried on in many plantations, for months, without any other interruption, than during some part of day light on Sundays. In some plantations it is the custom, during crop-time, to keep the whole gang employed as above, from morning to night, and alternately one half throughout the night, to supply the mill with canes, and the boiling house with *wowra*.

This labour is more or less moderated, in proportion to the method and good sense of the manager. In some plantations the young children and worn out slaves are set apart to pick grass, and bring cane tops from the field for the cattle, and do no other work. ... In most well ordered plantations, they leave off grinding and boiling before midnight, and begin not again till about dawn: it having been found, that the quantity of sugar made in the night, is not in proportion to the time; that it not only suffers in quality, but also lies open to pilferage;....

Every plantation contains little skirts, and portions of broken land, unfit for the cultivation of sugar. These are usually divided among the slaves for the growth of provisions; ... There is such a ready market for all the little articles which these spots produce, that the industrious slaves of a few, though but a few, plantations situated near the mountains, where the weather is seasonable and favours the growth of vegetables, maintain themselves in clothes and food, tolerably well, by the sale of their various fruits, with little other immediate aid from their master, besides a weekly allowance of herrings. But, in far the greater number of plantations, the quantity of provisions, or market vegetables, is uncertain and trifling; and necessity and hunger will not permit the wretches, to leave them in the ground to ripen sufficiently. Hence many diseases and ruined constitutions, from this scanty, rude, ill-prepared food, used among them. ...

Some masters, now-and-then, give their slaves Saturday afternoon, out of crop-time, to till their spots of ground; sometimes will turn in the whole gang among them to weed and put them in order, under the direction of the overseer. But, in general, the *culture of their private patches, and the picking of grass for their cattle, are their employments on Sunday.* ...

Added to the produce of their own provision lands, and the casualty of a fallow field, the slaves have a weekly allowance of grain, varying in different plantations, from one to three pounds, under the nominal measure of from two to eight pints. A few plantations go near to five pounds; one or two as far as six. They have also from three to eight herrings a week. In general, they are far from being well or plentifully fed.

They have an yearly allowance of two or three yards of coarse woolen cloth, called bamboo, to which sometimes is added for the men a woolen cap, for the women a handkerchief, and perhaps a few yards of Osnaburghs. At Christmas three holidays are pretended to be given them; but generally Sunday is foisted in for one, and now-and-then half of Christmas-day must be employed by them in digging yams for their allowance, and in receiving it afterwards, with a pound or two of salt-fish, or a scrap of coarse Irish beef. In Jamaica they have also two holidays at Easter, and two at Whitsuntide.

Their huts are framed of island timber, cut by each man for himself in the mountains, and carried down by him and his wife on Sundays. Sometimes the owner will supply a board or two to make a door or window shutter, but in general, such materials are stolen; nails and hinges are either stolen or bought from those who have stolen them.

Document 13   William Dickson, *Letters on Slavery*, 1788 [13]

LETTER III

Of the treatment of pregnant women, and of their babes on estates, while the former are lying in, I know almost nothing, but, before they are delivered, and while the latter are at the breast, their treatment is generally, I do not say universally, as Mr. Ramsay describes. When I first went to Barbadoes, I was particularly astonished to see some women far gone in their pregnancy, toiling in the field; and others, whose naked infants lay exposed to the weather, sprawling on a goat-skin, or in a wooden tray. I have heard, with indignation, drivers curse both them and their squalling brats, when they were suckling them.

… After the children on estates are weaned, and are able to run about, they are often put under the management of a careful old woman, and are employed picking vines, insects, etc. for the small and feathered stock. Hence they are called the *hog-meat-gang*, or the *pot-gang*, from their being fed with dressed victuals. Although an old woman, who has many to attend to, cannot be expected to supply the place of the mother; yet I have seen numerous gangs of such urchins, all in the best possible health and spirits. From the hog meat-gang, they are translated into what is called the *little gang*, which is employed in weeding, collecting grass, and other light work, till the individuals who compose it are able to take their station in the *great gang*, a transition which compleats the hardship and misery of a field negro. Till now he had been employed, as young people might be, and indeed sometimes, are employed, without injury, in this and other countries. Now he must till the ground, carry out the dung, and in short, must go through all the drudgery of husbandry, which cattle perform in every civilized country under heaven, except the West-Indian islands.

The weekly allowance of a field negro, in Barbadoes varies, like every other circumstance in his treatment. But I am of opinion, it may in general, be safely reckoned from six to to nine pints of Guinea corn, an excellent species of grain, or from nine to twelve pints of Indian corn, which is less nutritive; with three or four herrings, or from one pound and a half to two pounds of salted cod-fish, often of a bad quality…. Flour, and that worst of all species of food, horse-beans, form but a small part of the diet of the slaves, in Barbadoes; but they frequently have eddoes and sweet potatoes, and sometimes yams and plantanes, all of them excellent vegetables; the allowance of which, as well as of the small quantities of salted beef and pork, which are served

---

13   William Dickson, Letters on Slavery, (London: J. Phillips, 1789). Internet Archive. https://archive.org/stream/lettersonslavery00dick#page/30/mode/2up.

out to them (on holidays especially) I do not recollect. When they hole land, they each have about a gill of rum and molasses at noon. ... I forgot to mention, as part of their food, *pigeon peas*, so called for having been formerly given to pigeons, and other feathered stock; but which are now discovered to be very good food for men; and by many white people, are preferred to any kind of European peas. ... Okras and several other excellent vegetables enter more or less into their diet—It must be owned, that, when in health, the field negroes never do taste, at least they are not allowed, butchers meat, milk, butter, or any kind of fresh animal substance. ... The quality of their diet... is perhaps, not nearly so objectionable as its quantity, which, in general, is far from being proportioned to the toil they undergo. The grinding and sifting of their corn, after the labour of the day is over, may be regarded as a hardship, thought not as a great hardship. Most plantations are furnished with hand-mills for this purpose; but a few have wind-mills with mill-stones. Many negroes grind their corn, in their houses, between two stones. Artificers, when working at their trades, have a *bit,* or near 6d. sterling per day, a very sufficient allowance. Some domestics are wholly, and others partly, fed from the family-table....

In St. Kitt's, according to Mr. Ramsay, they punish with a *cart-whip*. The instrument of correction most commonly used in Barbadoes, is scalled a *cow-skin*, without which a negro driver would no more think of going into the field, than a coachman in England would think of setting out on a journey without his whip. It is composed of leathern thongs, platted in the common way, and tapers from the end of the handle (within which is a short bit of wood) to the point, which is furnished with a lash of silk-grass, hard platted and knotted, like that of a horse-whip, but thicker. Its form give it some degree of elasticity towards the handle; and when used with *severity*... it tears the flesh and brings blood at every stroke. The law has limited the number of lashes to forty, or rather, forty save one, which, if inflicted by an unfeeling hand, is very sever punishment; more severe, perhaps, though less tedious, than two hundred from the cat-o-nine tails used in the army. Nine and thirty lanshes are very seldom, I may say never, ordered by magistrates, unless for crimes which really do deserve such rigour, and which in this country would often be punished with the gallows; or for flagrant insults to white men, which seldom escape publick punishment, or private revenge. Owners very seldom go so far, in a regular way. But, Sir, punishment is not always regular. *Fits of passion*, to which even good owners are subject, disdain the restraints of law, of humanity, and of interest. *Intoxication, ill-nature*, and *revenge*, declare open war against humanity. In such cases, no trouble is taken to count the stripes; but they are laid on, furiously and indiscriminately, over all the body, the face, and the naked breasts of the women sometimes not excepted. Then it is that tyranny rages, without control....

Suppuration is always, and, in wet weather especially, convulsions are sometimes the consequence of a severe flogging; and the cicatrices of the wounds form large wheales, which the wretches carry to their graves. The backs and posteriors of many of the slaves, of both sexes, which are often covered with such wheales, are melancholy proofs of the severity of their owners and managers. I have seen both men and women, at their field labour, lacerated with the recent or suppurating wounds of the cow-skin. Some few work with a chain fastened around both ankles, which, from its length, they are obliged to tuck up, to enable them to walk; others have a chain locked, or an iron collar, with projecting prongs, riveted around the neck; others a *boot*, or ring of broad iron hammered around one ankle.

...Severe as the treatment of the field-negroes in Barbadoes may appear, I have reason to think that it is much milder than in most of the other, especially *new* islands; having repeatedly heard persons, from those islands, *ridicule* the lenity of the Barbadian discipline...

LETTER IV

By way of supplement or postscript to my last long, and I fear, tedious, letter, I now beg leave very briefly to describe the mode of cultivating a cane-field, or of *holing* land, and *turning* or carrying out dung, which I have always considered as the most laborious tasks of the negroes.

... I have seen land lined off into square spaces, four feet eacy way, which I believe, is the general rule in Barbadoes. The *holes*, therefore, may be about three feet square, and seven or eight inches deep, with a space of distance between each, and another space or bank at right angles to the distance, to receive the mould. The holes are dug, with hoes, by the slaves, in a row, with one driver at one end, to preserve the line. They begin and finish a row of these holes as nearly, at the same instants as possible; so that this equal task must be performed, in the same time, by a number of people who, it is next to impossible, should all be equally storng and desterous especially as few or no field negroes, who can wield a hoe, are exempted from it. Thus the weak must be oppressed. The driver is often obliged to set such negroes, as cannot keep up with the rest, to work, in a separate corner, by themselves; but, I am sorry to say, he too often first tries the effect of flogging, which is also sometimes the punishment for not digging the holes deep enough.

In turning dung, a task equally laborious, and, perhaps, more harassing than holing, each negro carries, on his head, a basketful of it. The gang must walk over a surface, now rendered very uneven by the holes, the driver bringing up the rear, and often smacking his whip, and I wish I could say, I never saw him apply it to the backs of the slaves, to increase their speed. But, I am sorry to add, I have more than once seen this.... Here, Sir, is another *equal* task, to be performed in an *equal* time, by people of *unequal* strength. In turning dung, therefore, as in holing, the weak, under strict drivers, at lest, are unavoidably oppressed. Both of them are very laborious tasks, considering the climate and scanty fare of the negroes, and the number of hours they work; especially, as those tasks are often performed rather in a hurry, as when advantage is to be taken of a heavy rain; or when the plantation-work, from various causes happens to be backward, or has not kept pace with the season.

...In this work, the negroes have *no help at all* from cattle or implements of husbandry, the *hoe* and the *basket*, only excepted. ... and, So long as the West Indians can import [slaves] from Africa, there is reason to fear that no other instruments than the *arms of those slaves* will ever be found to succeed, or indeed, be earnestly preservered in, in working the mines of the one or the plantations of the other.

ANALYZING THE EVIDENCE

1. How did Spaniards in their early encounters with Amerindian populations begin the process of relying on slave labor as they began to exploit the territories they had newly "discovered?"
2. Based on the evidence in Documents 3 and 4 what is the relationship between sugar consumption in England and Wales and population growth in the English colonies in America between 1650 and 1770?
3. Examine Pierre Pomet's engraving entitled "The Sugar Works" (Document 5) What tasks do you identify on the sugar plantation? What social hierarchies are evident on the sugar plantation? Why might economic historians have begun to characterize sugar plantations as among the first factories in European history? Why did Pomet include this engraving in his history of drugs?

4. Comparing Pomet's engraving (Document 5) and Richard Ligon's discussion of what was necessary to establish a plantation (Document 6). What elements in the latter did not feature in the former? Based on Ligon's description, what sorts of expenses, and profits, might one expect as a sugar planter in Barbadoes in the seventeenth century?

5. Why might slave ships have acquired the crops listed in Document 7? What does this listing of African-grown crops tell historians about the Columbian Exchange?

6. What does the image in Document 8 suggest about the relationship between African slave traders and African leaders?

7. Read Documents, 9-11. What do these documents tell us about the experiences of slaves as they were captured in Africa, transported across the Atlantic, and sold in the Americas?

8. Read Documents 12 and 13 and recall the Documents 5 and 6. What were the living and working conditions experienced by slaves on the sugar plantations?

Document Based Question:

Using the evidence provided, analyze the relationship between the development of the Atlantic slave trade and the growth of sugar production in the Caribbean between 1500 and 1800.

Regional Variations in the American South: Virginia and the Carolinas

CHAPTER 2

The British colonization of the Americas resulted in the establishment of three different slave-holding regions: the British West Indies with its enormously profitable sugar islands, the colonies of the American South (Virginia, Maryland, the Carolinas, and Georgia) where plantation economies depended to varying degrees on large numbers of African slaves, and finally the northeastern colonies (Connecticut, Delaware, Pennsylvania, Massachusetts, New Hampshire, New Jersey and New York). In each region, the role of coerced African labor played different roles in the establishment of the colonies and the development of their respective economies. Each region would differ in the degree to which it depended upon slave labor and the factors that contributed to the determination to turn to enslaved persons as a labor force. Additionally, the experiences of slaves in each of these regions differed significantly. But, in every region of the Americas where the British established their empire, it is fair to suggest that from the outset, enslaved Africans were vital to the regions' settlement and economic successes.

Plantation slavery developed first in the American South in the Chesapeake region (Virginia and Maryland) and was followed by its adoption in the Carolinas (North Carolina separated from the South Carolina in 1729). In the latter, plantation slavery and attendant importation of large numbers of Africans occurred almost from the outset of Carolina's establishment in 1663. In Virginia, however, slavery developed gradually before 1676 and then became the predominant feature of tobacco cultivation in the region thereafter. As a result the demographic and cultural contours of these two regions differed in important ways. The documents included in this chapter, however, will spotlight comparisons between the development of these two slave-based societies. Among the distinctions that should be observed in the documents in this chapter are differences in the dependency on indentured laborers in the two regions of the South. Another distinction may be seen in the ways in which Virginia's legal apparatus supporting slavery evolved gradually to differentiate white, Christian servants from black, African slaves. The gradual development of Virginia's dependency on African labor also provides an interesting case study with which to examine the evolving legal apparatus supporting slavery and with it the emergence of a racially divided society. South Carolina, because of its more immediate reliance on plantation slavery and because of its connections to the already established system of slavery in Barbadoes, set in place much more rapidly the legal apparatus for a racially-based slave system. Because the Carolinas turned more rapidly to imports of Africans, and because African slaves soon outnumbered their masters, the cultural and demographic makeup of the Carolina colony would differ significantly from the society developing in the Chesapeake.

TOBACCO PLANTATIONS ON THE CHESAPEAKE

The first permanent English settlement in North America, Jamestown, was founded in 1607. It was not properly speaking a colony, but instead was a "business enterprise," the property of the Virginia Company of London. The primary purpose of the enterprise was to turn a profit for the shareholders of the company. The first wave of Englishmen reached Virginia, explored the headwaters of the Chesapeake and established their position in Jamestown. These settlers were abysmal failures in almost every way. By the spring of 1610, after three years of violent struggle with the Powhatan Indian confederation, failure to farm or hunt sufficient food supplies, and inability to find any sustainable source of profit, only 60 settlers were left alive, huddled in the wooden stockade in Jamestown. To turn the fortunes of this company of adventurers around, the Virginia Company in 1611 tried to attract new laborers, first offering 50 acres of land as a "headright" to settlers who agreed to work for seven years in Virginia, then doubling the headright for workers who simply migrated to the region. To alleviate a severe shortage of women, and in the hopes of creating natural demographic growth and improving morale, the Virginia Company in 1619 even resorted to transporting a boatload of unmarried women to the colony. These reorganization and recruitment efforts helped the colony survive. But, tobacco in the end, as sugar transformed the Caribbean, provided the profitable cash crop that changed Virginia from a struggling and barely viable enterprise into a booming, if still unstable society.

Tobacco had been introduced into England in the 1580s as an expensive diversion for the upper classes. Virginia's first crop shipped to England in 1617. Within a decade, over 500,000 lbs. of the cured leaf was exported. By 1638 over 3 million lbs. of tobacco were grown in Virginia. By 1700, England was importing some 20 million lbs. of tobacco, most of it from the Chesapeake region. Virginians could still not grow enough corn to feed their growing population. They didn't need to. They "grew tobacco as though their lives depended on it" because their lives and livelihoods did depend on what King James I had called "that noxious weed." Though the profits in tobacco never approached those possible for sugar planters, a single laborer in the 1620s could tend one thousand tobacco plants, producing annually about 500 lbs. of leaf tobacco worth between £50 and £75. To cultivate their tobacco crop, planters sought laborers in England, offering them contracts or indentures to come to the Chesapeake region.

Indentured servants agreed to work for a period of between four and seven years to pay off the price of passage across the Atlantic, which was typically £6 per person. Following their time in service, these immigrants were entitled to the headrights granted to new arrivals. Indentured servants could also sell their headright, transferring the rights to speculators who often paid as much as £50. Life for these servants was nightmarish. Malarial fevers killed many new arrivals; overwork and insufficient rations killed many more. Abuse was commonplace, as masters had little incentive to treat their workers well. Indentured servants did not receive regular wages. The wages to which an indentured servant was entitled had been paid in advance as a price of transport. A meager severance package, a headright, and the possibility to turn that headright into a profitable tobacco farm were the primary incentives that motivated Englishmen to migrate to Virginia.

Virginia's reliance on white, indentured labor served the region well initially. However, it disguised a fundamental political and social instability, namely that every year a portion of poor, predominantly male Englishmen were released from their contracts and found themselves indebted to their former masters, pushed to marginal lands on the western fringes of the colony, faced with hostile Indians, and unable to earn sustainable livings. The discontentment and resentment that built against the tidewater elites eventually erupted in what became known as Bacon's Rebellion (1676). Nathaniel Bacon, a wealthy and arrogant recent arrival to Virginia resented the planter elite's refusal to afford him the respect he sought. His answer to this slight was to turn the frustrations of poor Virginians against the "grandees" and then to attempt to seize power. At the front of an undisciplined band of armed men, Bacon pressured the governor of Virginia into granting he and his men authorization to renew war against neighboring Indian villages. Tobacco cultivation, like most mono-cultures, wore out the soil, creating a near-constant hunger for more land. The annual discharge of indentured laborers meant that new tobacco-growing lands had to be found. After successfully waging war against the Indians, Bacon then led his men back to Jamestown, taking the city and forcing the governor and his allies to flee Jamestown. Bacon's men proceeded to loot the abandoned city, fired it and then abandoned it in a retreat into the surrounding swampland, where Bacon died of dysentery and the rebellion fizzled out in insignificance. But, the inherent tensions of the indentured servant system had been exposed, and Virginia's planter class determined to find an alternative labor force.

Virginia's elite had only to look to the Caribbean for a working model. Africans had been imported in small numbers to the Chesapeake since as early as 1619. As late as 1670, however, in Virginia only six percent of its population of around 35,000 were slaves. Barbados, by contrast had a slave population of over 20,000, vastly outnumbering white residents. Only 30 years later, Virginia would have over 16,000 slaves living in the colony, 28 percent of its population. Between 1700 and 1750 Virginia would become even more dependent on slave labor, importing over 75,000 enslaved persons into the colony during the first half of the eighteenth century.

The determination to shift from a labor force composed of indentured servants to a plantation economy dependent on enslaved Africans will be one of the features which the primary sources in this chapter will engage. A related concern of the documents included among this chapter's primary sources will be the development in Virginia of a code of laws that determinedly separated black Virginians from white Virginians, ensuring that Virginia's poor whites, whose grievances had led to Bacon's Rebellion, would never make common cause with the growing numbers of Africans enslaved in the colony. One feature of Virginia's two-stage development of slavery in the Chesapeake, before and after Bacon's Rebellion, would be the encouragement of a racial divide between African slaves and white servants and poor farmers, populations with a great deal in common economically. Before 1675 most slaves in Virginia lived in close contact with indentured servants and with the white residents of the colony in general. After 1675, Virginia's slave population experienced a heightened degree of "Africanization" as newly arrived Africans, predominantly male, were brought in to develop new upland plantations. As consequentially, however, would be the construction of separate legal identities. The result was that while Africans increased in number in the Chesapeake after 1675, they also found themselves differentiated from poor whites, and poor whites were granted a status that elevated them above that afforded African slaves.

THE CAROLINAS

In the Carolinas there was no similar process of gradual adoption of slavery, or significant reliance on indentured labor. Though initially Carolina's proprietors had conceived of the settlement of the colony by indentured labor and small farmers, almost from the outset, the Carolina's proprietors and founders had relied on shipments of enslaved men and women to develop their colony. The colony, centered at Charles Town in what is now South Carolina, was established in 1663 by eight courtiers of Charles II, who named the colony Carolina in his honor; *Carolus* is the Latin for Charles. The proprietors had close ties to British sugar planters in Barbados and saw the colony's role in Britain's Atlantic economy as provisioning the sugar islands with meat and grain. The profitability of sugar production in islands like Barbados, Grenada, or Jamaica meant that all available land and labor was devoted to growing cane and refining the sweet juices extracted from the cane. For slaves on Barbados to devote their time, or the planter's acerage to their own subsistence seemed a waste. The Carolinian founders thus initially hoped to attract settlers from Virginia and Maryland who would produce the necessary provisions for sale to the sugar islands, and perhaps tobacco for sale to European markets.

Rapidly, however, the Carolina colony became dependent upon slaves, first to clear the land and establish the plantations, and then to produce the food that would find ready markets in the sugar islands. The primary agricultural products exported from the Carolinas initially included beef, as its founders had imagined. But livestock management in the Carolinas proved quite different than the practices to which English settlers were accustomed. Cattle in large herds, as well as hogs, were allowed to graze the open ranges of the Carolina tidal regions, rather than being penned and fed forage as was the practice in much European husbandry. The labor force best equipped to manage these herds, it was soon understood, were Africans from the Senegambia region and elsewhere in Africa who were quite familiar with open-range cattle herding. As earlier noted, the first "cowboys" were not white men on horseback, or even *vaqueros*, but African men pejoratively called cowboys, in the same way that men who worked in the kitchens of their white owners were often called "houseboys." Africans also brought their skills as agriculturalists to the Carolinas to the profit of their English owners. In the 1680s varieties of rice from Madagascar were introduced into the Carolina lowlands, but few Englishmen had the requisite experience with rice cultivation. Africans familiar with rice growing were then imported and rice became a profitable export and an important staple for the many slaves forced to live in the Carolinas. A final crop, the purple dye plant, indigo, was introduced to the region. Again African know-how and labor made this a profitable export from the region.

Within the first forty years of the Carolina's establishment, the colony gained the reputation of a region with a "black majority." Many of the plantation owners followed the pattern established in the West Indies and preferred to spend their time away from the lowland rice-growing region, which had a reputation for malarial fevers and other mosquito-borne diseases, or preferred to stay in Charleston's more cosmopolitan and secure environs. With the clearing of new upland plantations as well the large number of slaves required as pioneers and agricultural laborers resulted in a system very different from the system that had earlier emerged in Virginia. In the Carolinas slaves lived in larger units, under brutal working conditions, while increasingly prosperous planters left supervision of field labor to overseers and black drivers. A Swiss newcomer noted, "Carolina looks more like a negro country than like a country settled by white people." This division between urban African-Americans, creolized and native born, and the African culture of the large plantations persisted. On the large plantations, slaves lived in relative isolation from white culture. They had truck gardens to supply their own food needs, labored in gangs. Here Gullah became the primary tongue. The ways in which Africans in the Carolinas and the Chesapeake maintained their African-ness, and contributed to the development of both African-American and an Afro-European culture will be the subject of Chapter Four.

REGIONAL VARIATIONS IN THE AMERICAN SOUTH: VIRGINIA AND THE CAROLINAS

As readers analyze the primary documents included in this chapter however, pay close attention to the following questions: In what ways did the system of indentured labor employed in the Chesapeake contribute to social and political instability? How did the importation of slaves address that instability? In what ways did slavery necessitate a new legal apparatus that worked to separate whites and blacks? With those questions in mind, compare the development of slavery in the Carolinas and Virginia noting, as was done in connecting the development of Barbados to sugar consumption in England, the role of commodity production and demand for labor in both regions. And, in both the Carolinas and Virginia, compare the legal apparatuses of slavery as they developed in both regions, considering how both sought to divide Africans from Europeans, creating a racial animus and legal divide that has persisted to the present.

PRIMARY SOURCE MATERIALS

Document 1 **William Marshall, woodcut for Richard Braithwait, *The Smoking Age*, 1617.**[1]

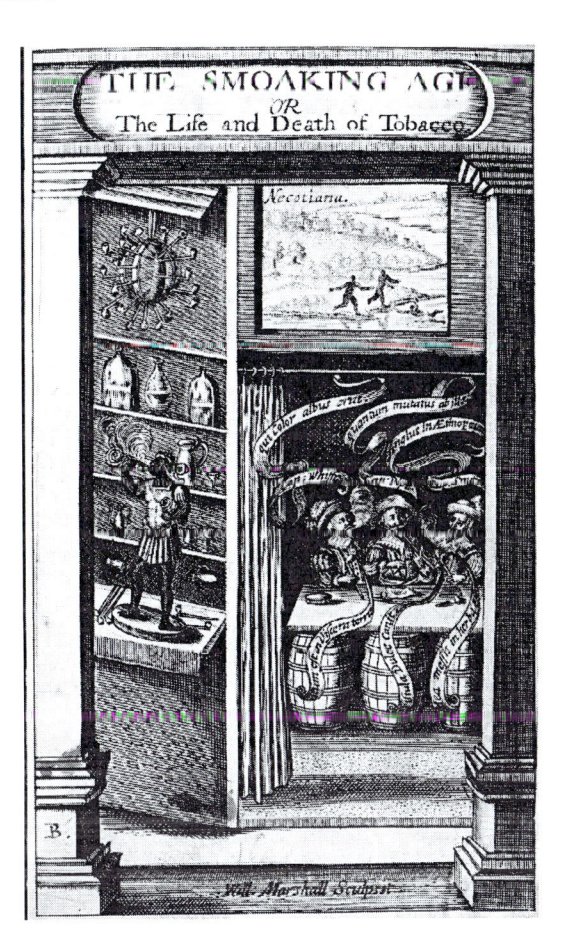

---

1 William Marshall, woodcut frontispiece, Richard Braithwait, The Smoking Age, or the Life and Death of Tobacco, (London: 1617). Out of copyright. Available through Bridgeman Images, the Bridgeman Art Library

Document 2   John Farrar, *A Perfect Description of Virginia*, 1649.[2]

These things that follow in this ensuing Relation are certified by divers Letters from Virginia, by men of worth and credit there, written to a Friend in England, that for his owne, and others satisfaction, was desirous to know these particulars, and the present estate of that Countrey. And let no man doubt the tenth of it, there be many in England, Land and Seamen that can beare witness of it. And if this Plantation be not worth Encouragement, let every *true* Englisman judge.

1. That there are in Virginia about fifteene thousand *English*, and of *Negroes* brought thither, three hundred good servants.
2. That of *Kine, Oxen, Bulls, Calves,* twenty thousand, large and good, and they make plenty of Butter and very good Cheese.
3. That there are of an excellent raise, about two hundred *Horses* and *Mares*.
4. That of *Asses* for burthen and use, there is fifty but daily increase.
5. That for *Sheepe* they have about three thousand, good wooll.
6. That for *Goates* there number is five thousand, thrive well.
7. That for *Swine* both tame and wilde (in the Woods) innumerable; the flesh pure and good, and Bacon none better.
9. That they yearly plow and sow many hundred Acres of *Wheat*, as good, and faire, as any in the world, and great increase.
10. That they have plenty of *Barley*, make excellent Mault.
11. That they have *Six publike Brewhouses,* and most brew their owne Beere, strong and good.
12. That their *Hopps* are faire and large, thrive well.
13. That they sell their Beefe at two pence half penny a pound, Pork at three pence a pound, plentifully.
14. That their Cattell are about the prices in *England,* and most of the Ships that come yearly hither, are there Victuall'd.
23. That their *Maize* or *Virgninia* Corne, it yeelds them five hundred for one, increase, ('its set as we doe garden Pease) it makes good Bread and Furmitie, will keep seven years, and maults well for Beere, and ripe in five Moneths, set in *April* or *May.*
26. *Indico* begins to be planted, and thrives wonderfully well, growes up to a little tree, and rich *Indico* made of the leaves of it, all men begins to get some of the seeds, and know it will be of ten-times the gaine to them as Tobacco. (and gaine now carries the Bell;) their hopes are great to gaine the Trade of it from the Mogulls Country, and to supply Christendome, and this will be many Thousands of pounds in the yeare.
27. Their Tobacco is much vented and esteemed in all places, yet the quantities so great that's made, that the price there is but three pence a pound. A man can plant two Thousand weight a yeare of it, and also sufficint Corne and Rootes, and other provisions for himselfe.

---

[2]   John Farrar, A Perfect Description of Virginia,... (Washington: P. Force, 1837).

31. There comes yearly to trade with them above 30 saile of ships, and in these not so little as seven or eight hundred Mariners employed, (some say above a thousand, this is a considerable thing) and they return laden home in *March*, (this is a good seminary for Mariners.)

32. The Commodity these ships bring, is Linnen Cloth of all sorts, and so of Woolen Cloth, Stockins, Shooes, and the like things.

33. Most of the Masters of ships and chief Mariners have also there Plantations, and houses, and servants, &c. in *Virginia*; and so are every way great gainers by Fraight, by Merchandize, and by Plantation and Pipe-staves, Clap-board, choice Walnut tree-wood, Ceader-tree timber, and the like, is transported by them if Tobacco is not their full lading.

34. They make Pitch and Tarre, (and there is materials in the Woods for abundance.) Also for Pot and Sop-ashes, Woods most proper and store: hands want.

37. … And in Tobacco they can make £20 a man, at 3 ½ a pound *per annum;* and this they find and know and the present gain is that, that puts out all endeavours from the attempting of others more Staple, and Sollid, and rich Commodities, out of the heads and hands of the Common people: So as I say, the wealthier sort of men must begin and give the example, and make the gain of other Commodities as apparent to them, by the affecting them to perfection, or it will not (as it hath not hither unto) go forward.

38. That they have health very well, and fewer die in a year there, according to the proportion, then in any place of *England*; since that men are provided with all necessaries, have plenty of victual, bread, and good beer, and housing, all which the Englishman loves full dearly.

39. That the Passengers also come safe and well: the seamen of late years having found a way, that now in 5, 6, and 7 weeks they saile to *Virginia* free from all Rocks, Sands, and Pirates; and that they return home again in 20 days sometimes, and 30 at most; the Winds commonly serving more constantly, being Westerly homeward, the Easterly outward bound.

Document 3 Virginia Legislation on Indentured Servants, 1660.[3]

Whereas the barbarous usage of some servants by cruel masters bring so much scandal and infamy to the country in general, that people who would willingly adventure themselves hither, are through fear thereof diverted, and by that means the supplies of particuler men and the well seating of his majesty' country very much obstructed, Be it therefore enacted that every master shall provide for his servants competent diet, clothing and lodging, and that he shall not exceed the bounds of moderation in correcting them beyond the meritt of their offences; and that it shalbe lawfull for any servant giving notice to their masters (having just cause of complaint against them) for harsh and bad usage, or else of want of diet or convenient necessaries to repair to the next commissioner to make his or their complaint, and if the said commisioner shall find by just proofs that the said servants' cause of complaint is just the said commissioner is hereby required to give order for the warning of such master to the next county court where the matter in difference shalbe determined, and the servant have remedy for his grievances.

---

3   A Complete Collection of all the Laws of Virginia Now in Force, (London: 1684), p. 76.

Document 4 "A Reward of Freedom and 5000 lbs. of tobacco to Berkenhead, who discovered the plot ot the 13th of September," *Laws of Virginia*, 16 September 1663.[4]

The house resolved into a grand committee while some propositions are treated of.

Since rewards for the encouragement of the good are as necessary as punishments for the terror of the cruel.

Whether it be not fit to bestow upon Berkenhead the discoverer of the horrid plot some considerable reward for encouragement of the good affections of others to the publick.

Resolved That Berkenhead have his freedom and five thousand pounds of tobacco given him in Gloster county and that his master be satisfaid in the said county for his time.

Resolved that the 13th of September be annually kept holy, being the day those villains intended to put the plot in execution.

Document 5 The Vain Prodigal Life AND Tragical Penitent DEATH of Thomas Hellier, born at Whitchurch near Lyme in DORSET-SHIRE: Who for Murdering his Master, Mistress, and a Maid, was Executed according to Law at *Westover* in *Charles City*, in the Country of Virginia, neer the Plantation called *Hard Labour*, where he perpetrated the said Murders. He Suffer'd on Monday the 5th of *August*, 1678. And was after Hanged up in Chains at *Windmill-Point* on *James River*.[5]

Thus had I trifled away and mis-spent my ten pounds and the price of my horse. Next, to supply necessity, I sold my Cloaths for want of money: so walking up *Tower*-ditch, I going in at the Eagle and Childe, enquired if there were any Ship-Captain quartered there? one replied, There was no Ship-Captain quartered in that house, but that he himself was concern'd about Sea-faring matters. I enquired to what parts he was concerned? He answered, To *Virginia*: So asked withal, if I were minded for that Country; if I were, I should have Meat, Drink, and Apparel, with other Necessaries provided for me. I replied, I had heard so bad a character of that Country, that I dreaded going thither, in regard I abhorred the Ax and the Haw. He told me, he would promise I should be onely employ'd in Merchants Accompts, and such Employments to which I had been bred, if they were here used.

On *August* the 10th, 1677, I being over-perswaded, went on board the *Young Prince*, Captain Robert Morris Commander; on the 5th of *September* ditto, the *Young Prince* weighed Anchor from the *Downs*; and on the 25th of *October* following, she arrived within the Capes of *Virginia*, and dropt Anchor at *Newpersnews*.

---

4   William Waller Hening, ed., *The Statutes at Large, Being a Collection of All the Laws of Virginia from the First Session of the Legislature, in the Year 1619,* Volume II, (Richmond,VA: R.W.& G. Bartow, 1823), 204.

5   T.H. Breen, James H. Lewis, and Keith Schlesinger, "Motive for Murder: A Servant's Life in Virginia, 1678, William and Mary Quarterly, 40:1 (1983), pp. 106-120.

I was delivered into the custody and dispose of one *Lewis Conner* of *Barmeodoe* hundred *Virginia*, who sold me off to one *Cutbeard Williamson*, living at a Plantation call'd *Hard Labour*, belonging to *Westover*-Parish, in *Charles* City, County *Virginia*: which said *Williamson* promised me I should be employed in Teaching his Children, and not be set to any laborious work, unless necessity did compel now and then, merely for a short spurt. But nevertheless, though I wanted not for Cloaths nor Victuals, yet I found their dealings contrary to their fair promises; which much disheartened me. And though my labour at the Howe was very irksome, and I was hoever resolved to do my utmost endeavor at it; yet that which embittered my life, and made every thing I gook in hand burdensome to me, was the unworthy ill-usage which I received daily and hourly from my ill-tongued Mistriss; who would not only rail, swear and curse at me within doors, whenever I came into the house, casting on my continually biting Taunts and bitter Flouts; but like a live Ghost would impertinently haunt me, when I was quiet in the Ground at work. And although I silently wrought as fast as she rail'd, plying my labour, without so much as muttering at her, or answering anything good or bad; yet all the silence and observance that I could use, would not charm her vile tongue. These things burning and broiling in my Breast, tempted me to take the trip, and give my Master the bag to hold; thereupon I vamped off, and got on board Captain *Larimore's* ship, where I remained eleven days, or thereabout, the Ship then riding at *Warwicks-Creek Bay*.

I was absent from my Master's business almost three Weeks, but at length my Master hunting about, and searching to and fro, had discover'd where I was, and so sending a Messenger, fetched me back home again. As I was upon my return homeward, I had a designe to have knocked the Messenger on the head; for which purpose I took up a great stone and carried it along in my hand a good way, unknown to the man: but my heart failing me, I let drop the designe. At length home I came, begg'd pardon of my Master for my fault, and all seemed pretty well again. But my usage proving still worse than before, my Mistress ever taunting me with her odious and inveterate Tongue, do all I would, and strive all the ways whatever I could, she, I found, was no whit pacified toward me. Whereupon I began to cast about and bethink my self, which way to rid me of that Hell upon Earth, yet still seeking if possible to weather it, but all in vain.

At last, Satan taking advantage of my secret inward regret, suggested to my vicious corrupt minde, that by ridding my Master and Mistress out of the way, I might with ease gain my Freedom, after which time I sought all opportunities to effectuate and bring to pass my said horrid contrivance: Concluding, when they were dead, I should be a Freeman. Which said execrable Project I attempted and put in execution *May* the 24, 1678. Thus.

Betimes in the Morning before day, I put on my best Cloaths, then got my Ax, and attempted two or three times to enter my Master's Lodging-room, still my heart failing me, I stept back again; but however at length in I rushed: A Servant-maid, who lay every night in the same Room, passed along by me the same time with her Bed on her shoulder, or under her arm, to whom I offer'd no violence, but let her pass untouched; nor had I meddled with her, had she kept out of my way. From her I passed on to my Masters Bed, and struck him with the Ax, and gave him several blows, as near as I could guess, upon the Head: I do believe, I had so unhappy an aim with my hand, that I mortally wounded him the first blow. My Mistress in the interim got out of Bed, and got hold of a Chair, thinking to defend her self; and when I came toward her, struggled, but I proved to hard for her; She begg'd me to save her Life, and I might take what I would, and go my way. But all in vain, nothing would satisfie but her Life, whom I looked on as my greatest Enemy; so down she went without Mercy. The Wench to whom I intended no hurt, returned, as I suppose to rescue her Mistress; whereupon she suffer'd the same cruel Fate with the other two.

After this Tragedy I broke open a Closet, and took Provision for my Journey, and rummaging my Mistriss Chest, I took what I thought fit, as much as loaded a good lusty Horse; So taking my Master's Gun in my hand, away I hastned: But while the Horse stood without door, a Neighbour came to the house, with an excuse to borrow the said Horse. To whom, I frowning, answered very roughly, and threatning him, bid him be gone, he could not have the Horse; who departed, and betrayed to the other Neighbours some jealousie he had conceived, concerning some Mischief I had been doing. A Childe also belonging to the Family was run forth to betray the business. But before any body came, I was gone upon my intended progress with my Master's Horse loaded, and his Gun in my hand.

Document 6   *A True Narrative of the Rise, Progresse, and Cessation of the Late Rebellion in Virginia, Most Humbly and Impartially Reported by His Majestys Commissioners Appointed to Enquire into the Affaires of the Said Colony, 1676.*[6]

…It soe happen'd that one Nathaniel Bacon Junior, a person whose lost and desparate fortunes, had thrown him into that remote part of the world about 14 months before, and fram'd him fit for such a purpose, as by the Sequel will appeare, which may make a short character of him no impertinent Digression.

Hee was a person whose erratique fortune had carryed and shewne him many Forraigne Parts, and of no obscure Family. Upon his first coming into Virginia hee was made one of the Councill, the reason of that advancement (all on a suddain) being best known to the Governour, which honor made him the more considerable in the eye of the Vulgar, and gave some advantage to his pernicious designes. Hee was said to be about four or five and thirty yeares of age, indifferent tall but slender, blackhair'd and of an ominous, pensive, melancholly Aspect, of a pestilent & prevalent Logical discourse tending to atheisme in most companies, not given to much talke, or to make suddain replyes, of a most imperious and dangerous hidden Pride of heart, despising the wisest of his neighbours for their Ignorance, and very ambitious and arrogant. But all these things lay hidd in him till after hee was a councilor, and until he became powerfull & popular.

…This fforwardnesse of Bacons greatly cheer'd and animated the People, who looked upon him as the onely Patron of the Country and preserver of their Lives and Fortunes.

For he p'tended and bostes what great Service hee would doe for the country, in destroying the Common Enemy, securing their Lives and Estates, Libertyes, and such like fair frauds hee subtily and Secretly insinuated by his owne Instruments over all the county, which he seduced the Vulgar and most ignorant People to believe (two thirds of each county being of that Sort) Soe that theire whole hearts and hopes were set now upon Bacon. Next he charges the Governour as negligent and wicked, treacherous and incapable, the Lawes and Taxes as unjust and oppressive and cryes up absolute necessity of redress.

…Bacon having got about 300 men together in armes prepared to goe out against the Indians, the Governour and his Friends endeavor to divert his designes, but cannot.

---

6   "Narrative of Bacon's Rebellion," The Virginia Magazine of History and Biography 4:2 (October 1896): 117-154.

Hee Proclames Bacon and his Followers Rebells and Mutineers for going forth against the Indians without a Commission, and (getting a company of Gentlemen together) the Governor marcheth up to the Falls of James River to pursue and take Bacon, or to seize him at his Returne; but all in vaine, ffor Bacon had got over the River with his Forces and hastning away into the woods, went directly and fell upon the Indians and killed some of them who were our best ffriends of Indians....

... The common cry and vogue of the Vulgar was away with these Forts, away with these distinctions, wee will have war with all Indians which come not in with their armes, and give Hostages for their Fidelity and to ayd against all others; we will spare none, and wee must bee hang'd for Rebells for killing those that will destroy us, let them hang us, wee will venture that rather than lye at the mercy of a Barbarous Enemy, and be murdered as we are, &c. Thus went the ruder sort raging and exclaiming agt. the Indians, expressing the calamity that befell New England by them. ...While the Governour was in the Upper Parts to wait Bacon's returne the people began to draw into armes, and to declare against the Forts. Hee to appease the commotions of the People leaves off that designe and comes immediately back to his own house, and caused at his returne the Surry and other Forts to be forthwith dismantled, and dissolving the assembly that enacted them, gave the country a free new election...

At this new election (such was the Prevalency of Bacon's Party) that they chose instead of Freeholders, Free men that had but lately crept out of the conditions of Servants, (which were never before Eligible) for their Burgesses and such as were eminent abettors to Bacon....

... At the Same time Bacon being come back from his Indian march with a thousand bragging lyes to ye credulous Silly People of what feats he had perform'd, was by the Inhabitants of the county of Henrico chosen a Burgess, as was also Crews for the Same county.

Document 7 Excerpts from Colonial Virginian Slave Laws—*Acts of Assembly, Passed in the Colony of Virginia: From 1662 to 1715.*[7]

1660 Runaways

... And in case any *English* Servant shall run away in Company of any Negroes, who are incapable of making Satisfaction by Addition of Time; It is Enacted, That the English, so running away in the Company with them, shall, at any Time of Service to their own Masters expired, serve the Masters of the said Negroes for their Absence, so long as they should have done by this Act, if they had not been Slaves, every Christian in Company serving his Proportion, and if the Negroes be lost or die in such Time of their being run away, the Christian Servants in Company with them shall, by Proportion among them, either pay Four thousand five hundred Pounds of Tobacco, and Cask, or Four Years Service, for every Negro so lost or dead.

1662 Status of Children born of Slave Women

Whereas some doubts have arisen whether children got by any Englishman upon a Negro woman should be slave or free, *be it therefore enacted and declared by this present Grand Assembly,* that all

---

7   Excerpts from Colonial Virginian Slave Laws—Acts of Assembly, Passed in the Colony of Virginia: From 1662 to 1715. Volume I. (London: John Baskett, 1727)

children born in this country shall be held bond or free only according to the condition of the mother; and that if any Christian shall commit fornication with a Negro man or woman, he or she so offending shall pay double the fines imposed by the former act.

1667 An Act declaring that Baptism of Slaves doth not exempt them from Bondage

Whereas some Doubts have arisen, whether Children, that are Slaves by Birth, and by the Charity and Piety of their Owners, made Partakers of the Blessed Sacrament of Baptism, should by Virtue of their Baptism, be made free: It is Enacted and Declared by this present Grand Assembly, and the Authority therof, That the conferring of Baptism doth not alter the Condition of the Person, as to his Bondage or Freedom, that diverse Masters, freed from this Doubt, may more carefully endeavor the Propagation of Christianity, by permitting Children, though Slaves, or those of greater Growth, if capable, to be admitted to that Sacrament.

1669 An Act About the Casual Killing of Slaves

Whereas the only Law in Force for Punishment of refractory Servants resisting their Masters, Mistresses, or Overseer, cannot be inflicted on Negroes, nor the Obstinacy of many of them, by other than violent Means suppressed: Be it Enacted and Declared by this Grand Assembly, and the Authority thereof, That if any Slave resist his Master, or others by his Master's Order, correcting him, and by the Extremety of the Correction should chance to die, such Death shall not be accounted Felony, but the Master, or that other Person by his Master appointed to punish him, be acquit from Molestation, since it cannot be presumed, that prepensed Malice, which alone makes Murder Felony, should induce any Man to destroy his own Estate.

1680 An Act for Preventing Negro Insurrections (p. 136)

Whereas the frequent Meetings of considerable Numbers of Negro Slaves, under Pretence of Feasts and Burials, is judged and deemed of dangerous Consequence; For the Prevention whereof for the future, Be it Enacted by the King's most Excellent Majesty, by and with the Consent of the General Assembly, and it is Enacted by the Authority aforesaid, That, from and after the Publication of this Law, it shall not be lawful for any Negro, or other Slave, to carry or arm himself with any Club, Staff, Gun, Sword, or any other Weapon of Defense of Offense, nor to go or depart from off his Master's Ground, without a Certificate from his Master, Mistress, or Overseer; and such Permission not to be granted, but upon particular and necessary Occasions; and every Negro or Slave so offending, not having Certificate, as aforesaid, shall be sent to the next Constable, who is hereby enjoyned and required to give the said Negro Twenty Lashes on the bare Back, well laid on, and so sent home to his said Master, Mistress, or Overseer.

And it is further Enacted by the Authority aforesaid, That if nay Negro, or other Slave, shall presume to lift up his Hand in Opposition against any Christian, shall for every such Offense, upon due Proof made thereof, by the Oath of the Party before a Magistrate, have and receive Thirty Lashes on his bare Back, well laid on.

And it is hereby further Enacted by the Authority aforesaid, That if any Negro, or other Slave, shall absent himself from his Master's Service and lie hid and lurking in obscure Places, committint Injuries to the Inhabitants, and shall resist any Person that shall, by any lawful Authority, be employed to apprehend and take the said Negro, that then in case of such Resistance, it shall be lawful for such Person or Persons to kill the said Negro or Slave, so lying out or resisting: And that this Law be once every Six Months published at the respective County Courts and Parish Churches within this Colony.

1691 An Act for Suppressing Out-lying Slaves

Whereas many times negroes, mulattoes, and other slaves unlawfully absent themselves from their masters and mistresses service, and lie hid and lurk in obscure places killing hogs and committing other injuries to the inhabitants of this dominion, for remedy whereof for the future, *Be it enacted by their majesties lieutenant governour, councell and burgesses of this present general assembly, and all authoritie thereof, and it is hereby enacted,* that in all such cases upon intelligence of any such negroes, mulattoes, or other slaves lying out, two of their majesties justices of the peace of that county, whereof one to be of the quorum, where such negroes, mulattoes or other slave shall be, shall be impowered and commanded, and are hereby impowered and commended to issue out their warrants directed to the sherrife of the same county to apprehend such negroes, mulattoes, and other slaves, which said sherriffe is hereby likewise required upon all such occasions to raise such and soe many forces from time to time as he shall think convenient and necessary for the effectual apprehending such negroes, mulattoes and other slaves, and in case any negroes, mulattoes or other slaves lying out as aforesaid shall resist, runaway, or refuse to deliver and surrender him or themselves to any person or persons that shall be by lawfull authority employed to apprehend and take such negroes, mulattoes, or other slaves that in such cases, it shall and may be lawfull for such person and persons to kill and destroy such negroes, mulattoes, and other slave or slaves by gunn or any other ways whatsoever.

Provided that where any negroe or mulattoe slave or slaves shall be killed in pursuance of this act, the owner or owners of such negro or mulatto slave shall be paid for such negro or mulatto slave four thousand pounds of tobacco by the publique.

And for prevention of that abominable mixture and spurious issue which hereafter may increase in this dominion, as well by negroes, mulattoes, and Indians intermarrying with English, or other white women, as by their unlawfull accompanying with one another, *Be it enacted by the authorities aforesaid, and it is hereby enacted,* that for the time to come, whatsoever English or other white man or woman being free shall intermarry with a negroe, mulatto, or Indian man or woman bond or free shall withint three months after such marriage be banished and removed from this dominion forever, and that the justices of each respective countie within this dominion make it their particular care, that this act be put in effectual execution. *And be it further enacted by the authorities aforesaid, and it is hereby enacted,* That if any English woman being free shall have a bastard child by any negro or mulatto, she pay the sume of fifteen pounds sterling within one month after such bastard child shall be born, to the Church wardens of the parish where she shall be delivered of such child, and in default of such payment she shall be taken into the possession of the said Church wardens and disposed of for five yeares, and the said fine of fifteen pounds, or whatever the woman shall be disposed of for, shall be paid, one third part to their majesties for and towards the support of the government and the contingent charges thereof, and one third part to the use the parish where the offence is committed, and the other third part to the informer, and that such bastard child be bound out as a servant by the said Church wardens until he or she shall attain the age of thirty years, and in case such English woman that shall have such bastard child be a servant, she shall be sold by the said church wardens, (after her time is expired that she ought by law to serve her master) for five yeares, and the money she shall be sold for divided as is before appointed, and the child to serve as aforesaid.

And forasmuch as great inconveniences may happen to this country by the setting of negroes and mulattoes free, by their either entertaining negro slaves from their masters' service, or receiving stolen goods, or being grown old bringing a charge upon the country; for prevention thereof, **Be it enacted by the authority aforesaid, and it is hereby enacted,** That no negro or mulatto be after the end of this present session of assembly set free by any person or persons whatsoever, unless such person or persons, their heirs, executors or administrators pay for the transportation of such negro or negroes out of the country within six months after such setting them free, upon penalty of paying of tenn pounds sterling to the Church wardens of the parish wehre such person shall dwell with, which money, or so much thereof as shall be necessary, the said Church wardens are to cause the said negro or mulatto to be transported out of the country, and the remainder of the said money to imploy to the use of the poor of the parish.

1705 An Act Concerning Servants and Slaves

Section I. *Be it enacted, by the governor, council, and burgesses, of this present general assembly, and it is hereby enacted, by the authority of the same,* That all servants brought into this country without indenture, if the said servants be Christians, and of Christian parentage, and above nineteen years of age, shall serve but five years; and if under nineteen years of age, 'till they shall become twenty-four years of age, and no longer.

Section IV. *And also be it enacted, by the authority aforesaid, and it is hereby enacted,* That all Servants imported and brought into this country, by sea or land, who were not Christians in their native country… shall be accounted and be slaves, and as such be here bought and sold notwithstanding a conversion to Christianity afterwards.

Section VII. *And also be it enacted by the authority aforesaid, and it is hereby enacted,* That all masters and owners of servants, shall find and provide for their servants, wholesome and competent diet, clothing, and lodging, by the discretion of the county court; and shall not, at any time, give immoderate correction; neigher shall, at any time, whip a Christian white servant naked, without an order from a justice of the peace: And if any, notwithstanding this act, shall presume to whip a Christian, white servant naked, without such order, the person so offending, shall forfeit and pay for the same, forty shillings sterling, to the party injured: To be recovered, with costs, upon petition, without the formal process of an action, as in and by this act is provided for servants complaints to be heard; provided complaint be made within six months after such whipping.

Section XI And for further Christian care and usage of all Christian servants, *Be it also enacted, by the authority aforesaid, and it is hereby enacted,* That no negros, mulattos, or Indians, although Christians, or Jews, Moors, Mahometans, or other infidels, shall at any time purchase any Christian servant, nor any other, except of their own complexion, or such as are declared slaves by this act: And if any negro, mulatto, or Indian, Jew, Moor, Mahometan, or other infidel, or such as are declared slaves by this act, shall, notwithstanding, purchase any Christian white servant, the said servant shall *ipso facto*, ecome free and acquit from any service then due, and shall be so held, deemed, and taken: And if any person, having such Christian servant, shall intermarry with any such negro, mulatto, or Indian, Jew, Moor, Mahometan, or other infidel, every Christian white servant of every such person so intermarrying, shall *ipso facto*, become free and acquit from any service then due to such master or mistress so intermarrying, as aforesaid.

Section XIII. And whereas there has been a good and laudable custom of allowing servants corn and clothes for their present support, upon their freedom; but nothing in that nature ever made certain, *Be it also enacted, by the authority aforesaid, and it is hereby enacted* That there shall be paid and allowed to every imported servant, not having yearly wages, at the time of service ended, by the master or owner of such servant, viz: To every male servant, ten bushels of Indian corn, thirty shillings in money, or the value thereof in goods, and one well fixed musket or fuzee, of the value of twenty shillings, at least: and to every woman servant, fifteen bushels of Indian corn, and forty shillings in money, or the value thereof, in goods: Which, upon refusal, shall be ordered, with costs, upon petition to the county court, in manner as is herein before directed, for servants complaints to be heard.

Document 8   Estimates of Virginia Population, 1650-1750[8]

Year	Black Population	White Population
1650	400	18,000
1680	3,000	40,000
1700	15,000	45,000
1710	19,000	55,000
1730	36,500	84,000
1750	107,000	130,000
1760	140,500	200,000
1770	187,500	260,000
1780	223,500	317,000
1790	305,000	432,000

---

[8]   Mechal Sobel, The World They Made Together: Black and White Values in Eighteenth-Century Virginia (Princeton: Princeton University Press, 1987), 243.

Document 9   Statistics of England's Tobacco Trade and Per Capita Consumption of Tobacco, 1686-1752.[9]

	Imports (lbs)	Re-Exports (lbs)	Retained Imports (lbs)
1686-1688	36,532,000	--	--
1689-1692	25,863,000	--	--
1693-1697	26,922,000	14,220,000	12,702,000
1698-1702	32,309,000	21,185,000	11,124,000
1703-1707	23,694,000	15,847,000	7,847,000
1708-1712	29,313,000	17,442,000	11,691,000
1713-1717	25,318,000	17,144,000	8,174,000
1718-1722	33,117,000	21,889,000	11,228,000
1723-1727	30,512,000	21,538,000	8,974,000
1728-1732	38,021,000	29,425,000	8,596,000
1733-1737	40,766,000	31,666,000	9,100,000
1738-1742	45,152,000	39,320,000	5,833,000
1743-1747	46,111,000	38,684,000	7,427,000
1748-1752	49,982,000	41,714,000	8,268,000

Document 10   Samuel Wilson, *An Account of the Province in Carolina*, 1682.[10]

The Province of Carolina, was in the Year 1663 Granted by Letters Pattents of his most Gracious Majesty, in Propriety unto the Right Honourable Edward Earl of Clarendon, George Duke of Albemarle, William Earl of Craven, John Lord Berkeley, Anthony Lord Ashby, now Earl of Shaftsbury, Sir George Careret, and Sir John Colleton, Knights and Barronets, Sir William Berkeley Knight, by which Letters Pattents the Laws of England are to be of force in Carolina: but the Lords Proprietors have power with the consent of the Inhabitants to make By-Laws for the better Government of the said Province.

... The Lords Proprietors do at present grant to all persons that come there to inhabit as follows, *viz.* To each Master or Mistriss of a Family fifty acres, and for every able son or man servant they shall carry or cause to be transported into Carolina fifty acres more, and the like for each Daughter or woman servant that is marriageable, and for each child, man or woman servant under sixteen years of age, forty acres, and fifty acres of Land to each servant when out of their time this Land to be injoy'd by them and their Heirs forever, they paying a Penny an Acre Quit-

---

9   Robert C. Nash, "The English and Scottish Tobacco Trades in the Seventeenth and Eighteenth Centuries: Legal and Illegal Trade," *The Economic History Review*, New Series, 35:3 (1982), p. 356.

10   Samuel Wilson, An Account of the Province of Carolina in America..., (London: Larckin, 1682). Accessed at https://blogs.ncl.ac.uk/speccoll/2016/10/07/samuel-wilsons-an-account-of-the-province-of-carolina-in-america%C2%B8-1682/

rent to the Lords' Proprietors, the Rent to commence in two years after taking up their Land. But forasmuch as divers persons who are already Inhabitants of Carolina and others that have Intentions to transport themselves into that Province, desire not to be combered with paying of a Rent, and also to secure to themselves good large convenient tracts of Land, without being forc'd to bring thither a great number of servants at one time; the Lords Proprietors have been prevail'd upon, and have agreed to sell to those who have a mind to buy Land, after the rate of fifty pounds for a Thousand Acres, reserving a Pepper Corn *per annum* Rent when demanded.

… The passage of a man or woman to Carolina is five Pound, Ships are going thither all times of the year. Some of the Lords Proprietors, or my self, will be every Tuesday at 11 of the clock at the Carolina Coffee house in Burching-Lane near the Royal Exchange to inform all people what Ships are going, or any other thing whatsoever.

Document 11 Preamble to, An Act to prevent Deceits by Double Mortgages and Conveyances of Lands, Negroes and Chattels, etc., 1689[11]

Whereas the want or neglect of registering and recording of sales, conveyances, and mortgages of lands and other goods and chattels, hath encouraged and given opportunity to several knavish and necessitous persons to make two or more sales, conveyances and mortgages of the same plantation, negroes, and other goods and chattels, the first sale, conveyance and mortgage being in force and not discharged, to several persons for considerable sums of money more than the same is worth, whereby buyers of plantations, and lenders of money upon second or after-mortgages, do often loose their money, and are put to great charges in suits of law and otherwise; for remedy whereof, *Be in Enacted*, That the sale, conveyance or mortgage of lands and tenements, except original grants, which shall be first registered in the register's office in Charles-Town, shall be taken, deemed, adjudged, allowed of and held to be the first sale, conveyance, and mortgage, and to be good, firm, substantial and lawful in all courts of judicature within South-Carolina, any former or other sale, conveyance or mortgage of the same land not before registered notwithstanding; and that that sale or mortgage of negroes, goods, or chattels which shall be first recorded in the secretary's office in Charles-Town, shall be taken, deemed, adjudged, allowed of and held to be the first mortgage, and good, firm, substantial and lawful in all courts of judicature within South Carolina, any former or other sale or mortgage for the same negroes, goods and chattels not recorded in the said office notwithstanding.

Document 12 An Act for the better ordering and governing of Negroes and Slaves, 17 June 1712.[12]

Since charity and the Christian religion which we profess, obliges us to wish well to the souls of all men, and that religion may not be made a pretence, to alter any man's property and right, and that no persons may neglect to baptize their negroes or slaves or suffer them to be baptized, for fear that thereby they should be manumitted and set fre: *Be it therefore enacted*, That it shall be, and

---

[11] Statutes relative to deeds made to defraud creditors, from in Touchstone of Common Assurance, containing the Laws of the Several States in the Union, by John Anthon, Volume III, (New York: I. Riley, 1810), p. 550.

[12] *The Statutes at Large of South Carolina*, Volume VII, David J. McCord, ed., (Columbia, SC: A.S. Johnston, 1840), pp. 352-365.

is hereby declared, lawful for any negro or Indian slave, or any other slave or slaves whatsoever, to receive and possess the Christian faith, and be thereunto baptized. But that notwithstanding such slave or slaves shall receive and profess the Christian religion, and be baptized, he or they shall not thereby manumitted or set free, or his or their owner, master or mistress loose his or their civil right, property and authority over such slave or slaves, but that the slave or slaves, with respect to his or their servitude, shall remain and continue in the same state and condition, that he or they was in before the making of this act.

Document 13 Excerpts of the Carolina Slave Code, 1712.[13]

Preamble

WHEREAS, the plantations and estates of this Province cannot be well and sufficiently managed and brought into use, without the labor and service of negroes and other slaves; and forasmuch as the said negroes and other slaves brought unto the people of this Province for that purpose, are of barbarous, wild, savage natures, and such as renders them wholly unqualified to be governed by the laws, customs, and practices of this Province; but that it is absolutely necessary, that such other constitutions, laws and orders, should in this Province be made and enacted, for the good regulating and ordering of them, as may restrain the disorders, rapines and inhumanity, to which they are naturally prone and inclined; and may also tend to the safety and security of the people of this Province and their estates; to which purpose,

Article II

And for the better ordering and governing of negroes and all other slaves in this Province, *Be it enacted* by the authority aforesaid, That no master, mistress, overseer, or other person whatsoever, that hath the care and charge of any negro or slave, shall give their negroes and other slaves leave, on Sundays, holidays, or any other time, to go out of their plantations, except such negro or other slave as usually wait upon them at home or abroad, or wearing a livery; and every other negro or slave that shall be taken hereafter out of his master's plantation, without a ticket, or leave in writing, from his master or mistress, or some other person by his or her appointment, or some white person in the company of such slave, to give an account of his business, shall be whipped; and every person who shall not (when in his power) apprehend every negro or other slave which he shall see out of his master's plantation, without leave as aforesaid, and after apprehended, shall neglect to punish him by moderate whipping, shall forfeit twenty shillings,…. And for the better security of all such persons that shall endeavor to take any runaway, or shall examine any slave for his ticket, passing to and from his master's plantation, it is hereby declared lawful for any white person to beat, maim or assault, and if such negro or slave cannot otherwise be taken, to kill him, who shall refuse to shew his ticket, or by running away or resistance, shall endeavor to avoid being apprehended or taken.

---

[13] *The Statutes at Large of South Carolina*, Volume VII, David J. McCord, ed., (Columbia, SC: A.S. Johnston, 1840), pp. 352-365.

Article III

And be it further enacted by the authority aforesaid, That every master, mistress or overseer of a family in this Province, shall cause all his negro houses to be searched diligently and effectually, once every fourteen days, for fugitive and runaway slaves, guns, swords, clubs, and any other mischievous weapons…; as also for clothes, goods, and any other things and commodities that are not given them by their master, mistress, commander or overseer, and honestly come by;

Article XVII

And be it further enacted by the authority aforesaid, That if any negro or slave whatsoever, shall offer any violence to any Christian or white person, by striking, or the like, such negro or other slave, for his or her first offence, by information given, upon oath, to the next justice, shall be severely whipped, or caused to be whipped, by the constable, who is hereby required to do the same, under the penalty of forty shillings, by order of any justice of the peace; for the second offence of that nature, … he shall be severely whpped, and his nose slit, or be burned in some part of his face with a hot iron, that the mark therof may remain; and for the third offence, be left to two justices and three freeholders, to inflict death, or any other punishment, according to their discretion. … And in case any negro or slave shall so assault and beat any white person, by which the said white person is maimed and disabled, in such case, the slave shall be punished as in the third offence… *Provided always*, that such striking, conflict, or maiming, be not by command of, or in the lawful defence of, their master, mistress, or owner of their families, or of their goods.

Document 14 *A Letter from South Carolina*; written by a Swiss Gentleman to his Friend at Bern. 1738.[14]

Description   Carolina is a Province of the English America, joining on the North-East to Virginia, between 36 and 29 degrees North Latitude. It is divided into two Governments, commonly call'd *North* and *South Carolina*. *North Carolina* joins to *Virginia*, and that Part thereof now inhabited by the *English*, lies between 35 and 36 Degrees N. Latitude. The Parts of *South Carolina*, now possess'd by the *English*, lie between 32 and 33 Degrees N. Latitude and about 60 Degrees Longitude, West from the Lands-End of England.

The Trade between *South Carolina* and *Great Britain*, does, one Year with another, employ 22 Sail of Ships, laden hither with all Sorts of Woolen Cloths, Stuffs and Druggets, Linens, Hollands, printed Linen and Callicoe, Silks, and Muslins, Nails of all sizes, Hoes, Hatchets, and all kinds of Iron-ware, Bed-ticks, strong Beer, bottled cider, Raisins, fine Earthen-ware, Pipes, Paper, Rugs, Blankets, Quilts, Hats from 2s. to 12s. Price, Stockings fro 1s. to 8 s. Price, Gloves, Pewter Dishes and Plates, Brass and Copper Ware, Guns, Powder, Bullets, Flints, Glass Beads, Cordage, Woolen and Cotton Cards, Steel Hand-Mills, Grind-stones, Looking and Drinking Glasses, Lace Thread coarse and fine, Mohair, and all Kinds of Trimming for Clothes, Pins, Needles etc. In return for which are remitted from hence about seventy Thousand Deer skins a Year, some Furs, Rosin, Pitch, Tar, Raw Silk, Rice, and formerly Indigo. But since all these don't balance the continual

---

14   *Letter from South Carolina; Giving an Account of the Soil, Air, Product, Trade, Government, Laws, Religion, People, Military Strength, etc. of that Province; Together with the Manner and necessary Charges of Setling a Plantation there, and the Annual Profit it will produce*, written by a Swiss Gentleman to his Friend at Bern. 2nd edition. (London: J. Clarke, 1732).

Demand of European Goods and Negro Slaves, sent us by the *English* Merchants, there is likewise sent to *England* some Cocoa-nuts, Sugar, Tortoise-shell, Money, and other Things, which we have from the *American* Islands, in return for our Provisions. Besides the 22 Sail above mentioned, there enter and clear annually at the Port of *Charlestown*, about 60 Sail of Ships, Sloops, and Brigantines, all from some Places of *Africa* or *America*.

From *Jamaica, St. Thomas's, Curaçao, Barbadoes,* and the *Leeward* Islands, we have Sugar, Rum, Molasses, Cotton, Chocolate made up, Cocoa-nuts, Negroes, and Money. In return whereof we send Beef, Pork, Butter, Candles, Soap, Tallow, Myrtle-wax Candles, Rice, some Pitch and Tar, Cedar and Pine-boards, Shingles, Hoop-staves, and Heads for Barrels.

From *New England, New York,* and *Pennsylvania*, we have Wheat-flower, Bisket, strong Beer, Cider, Salt Fish, Onions, Apples, Hops; and return them tan'd Hides, small Deer-skins, Gloves, Rice, Slaves taken by the *Indians* in War, some Tar and Pitch.

From *Madeira* and the Western Islands, we have Wine, and in return, supply them with Provisions, Staves, and Heads for Barrels, etc. Our Salt comes from the Bahama Islands.

From *Guinea,* and other Parts of the Coast of *Africa*, are imported Negro-slaves, but the Ships that bring them being sent, with the Effects to purchase them, from *England,* the Returns are sent thither. [...]

In order to live comfortably, after a Man's own and Family's Passage is paid, and Clothes bought for the first Year or two, he must have.[15*]

2 Negro Slaves, ... 40£ each	80 £
4 Cows and Calves, 1 £ 5 *shillings* each	5
4 Sows, 15 *shillings* each	6
A Steel Mill or a Pair of Querns (grindstones)	3
Axes, Hoes, Wedges, Handsaws, Hammers, And other tools	2
200 Acres of Land, 4£, Survey And other Charges, 2£	6
A small House for the first Year or two,	8
Corn, Peas, Beef, Pork etc. for the first year 14	
Expences and Contingencies	<u>26</u>
	150 £

This calculation is made in the Money of the Province, which is just 100£ Sterling. The Things mention'd here are of Necessity to one who would settle with any, tolerable Decency. And from this small Beginning, by moderate Industry, accompanied with the Blessing of Heaven, a Man may get a competent Estate, and live very handsomely. But there are many who settle without any Slaves at all, but Labour themselves.

---

15   *Note on English currency. £ designates the British pound. There are 20 shillings (s)in a pound and 12 pence (d) in a shilling. To compare these currency values with today's currency values you can use the following web site to get some idea of comparisons: http://www.historicalstatistics.org/Currencyconverter.html

Here follows an Account of what is necessary to settle an Estate of 300£ *per Annum*, with the Value of the Particulars, as they are most commonly sold there

30 Negroes, 15 Men and 15 Women,	40£	1200£
20 Cows and Calves, 1£ 5s each		25
2 Mares, 1 Stone-horse, 10£ each		
6 Sows and a Boar, 6£		36
1000 Acres of Land, 20£, Survey and other necessary charges, 7£		27
A large Periagoe, 20£, a small Canoe, 2£ A Steel Mill, 4£		26
10 Ewes and a Ram, 7£, 3 dozen Axes, 6£		13
Hoes, Hatchets, Broad Axes, Nails, Saws, Hammers, Wedges, Maul Rings, a Froe, And other necessary Tools.		23
Plows, Carts, with their Chains and Irons.		10
A small House for the first Year or two, Afterwards a Kitchen.		20
300 Bushels of *Indian* Corn and Peas, at 2 s 6 d per Bushel with some Beef, Pork for the first Years Provision		50
Expenses and Contingencies		70
	Total	1500 £

As for those who have no Substance to bring with them, they are either Labourers or Tradesmen, for whose Satisfaction I shall insert the usual Wages and Prices of Labour.

Per Diem Price of Labour	s.	d.
A Tailor	5	0
A Shoe-maker	2	6
A Smith	7	6
A Weaver	3	0
A Bricklayer	6	0
A Cowper	4	0

A Carpenter and Joiner have from 3 to 5 s. [per day]

A Day-labourer from 1 s. 3 d. to 2 s. with Lodging and Diet.

Those who oversee Plantations *per Annum* from 15 to 40 £.

Such as are employ'd to trade with the *Indians* from 20 to 100 £.

Document 15 English Imports of Indigo, 1736-1775[16]

Imports into England from (1,000s lbs. annual averages)

	Europe	Carolina	British West Indies	From all British colonies	Total English Imports
1736-1739	603	4	69	80	683
1740-1743	600	15	107	125	737
1744-1747	165	20	97	170	629
1748-1751	592	118	89	221	848
1752-1755	524	94	7	109	633
1756-1759	267	479	106	660	1323
1760-1763	130	397	83	531	1118
1764-1767	729	568	42	636	1365
1768-1771	588	533	106	663	1251
1772-1775	240	1076	143	1305	1545

Document 16 Rice Exports from South Carolina, 1695-1770[17]

Year	Lbs.	Year	Lbs.
1695	438	1735	21,259,800
1700	394,130	1740	43,326,000
1706	267,309	1745	29,813,375
1710	1,600,983	1750	27,372,500
1715	2,367,605	1755	59,057,775
1720	6,485,662	1760	35,327,250
1725	7,093,600	1765	65,710,575
1730	18,774,900	1770	83,708,625

ANALYZING THE EVIDENCE

1. Analyze the images in Documents 1. What was the English perception of tobacco as a product and source of wealth? What consumer items and practices were associated with the tobacco trade? How are racial hierarchies illustrated in this document?

---

16 Robert C. Nash, "South Carolina indigo, European textiles, and the British Atlantic Economy in the eighteenth century," *Economic History Review* 63:2 (2010), p. 366.

17 Adapted from Judith Carney, "Rice Milling, Gender, and Slave Labour in Colonial South Carolina," *Past & Present,* 153: (Nov. 1996), p. 109.

2. Analyze the description of Virginia in Document 2 and the descriptions of the Carolinas in Documents 11 and 15. What markets for raw materials and consumer items were maintained between Great Britain and these two colonies?

3. Analyze the conditions experienced by indentured servants in Documents 3, 4, 5, and 6 that may have contributed to Bacon's Rebellion.

4. Examine the evidence for increases in importation of African slaves in Document 2 and 9. How does that data support the view that unrest and instability among former indentured servants contributed to the determination to rely instead on an enslaved labor force.

5. Examine closely the various legal pronouncements in Document 7 and analyze the ways in which African slaves were increasingly differentiated from indentured servants.

6. Analyze the relationship between the English tobacco market and re-export market and slave imports in the seventeenth and eighteenth century using Documents 9 and 10.

7. Read carefully the excerpts from Carolina's slave laws in Documents 14 and 15. How does the evidence in these laws reflect the greater population denisity of enslaved persons in the Carolinas?

8. Compare the Carolina and Virginia slave laws. What similarities and differences do you notice?

DOCUMENT BASED QUESTION:

1. Using the documents in chapter two, analyze the similarities and differences in the way slavery developed in Virginia and the Carolinas.

Or

2. Using the documents in chapter two, compare the two systems of plantation agriculture that developed in Virginia and the Carolinas.

Slavery Above The Mason-Dixon Line

CHAPTER 3

Slavery in the northern colonies is often de-emphasized, particularly in courses that survey the first half of United States' history. Often these courses and the textbooks designed for them begin their story with an eye towards the Civil War. The conflict between the North and South is of such momentous impact and requires such explanation that often the end of the story is prefigured in the beginning. In other words the cultural and economic divide that ultimately erupts into the Civil War is rooted in the period of colonization. From 1607 with the establishment of Jamestown and 1620 with the landing of the Mayflower, it is as if the nation were on a collision course towards Fort Sumter. This approach leaves students with the false impression that New England and the Middle Colonies were largely disconnected from the currents of the slave trade and the implications of slavery. New England and the Middle Colonies, however, depended upon slaves, as sources of status, as the most important trade items in the "carrying trade" that profited northern shippers, and as sources of capital and labor.

It is perhaps, however, not entirely unfair to note the cultural, demographic, and economic differences between North and South that date to the colonial period of American history. The smaller numbers of slaves north of the Mason-Dixon line (the boundary between Pennsylvania and Maryland), for example, are indicative of the greater significance of slavery and plantation agriculture in the South. After all, in 1770, there were only 50,000 slaves north of Maryland, or about 4.5% of the total population. By contrast, in 1770, south of the Mason-Dixon line, there were over 400,000 slaves, or nearly 40% of the total southern population. The number of men and women of African descent in the northern colonies, many of them slaves, however, understates the importance of slavery to the economies of the North. In New England, blacks made up 2.5 percent of the population, and in the Middle Colonies, they represented 6.5 percent of the population before the American Revolution. The presence of slaves in the northern colonies, even in these small numbers, often comes as a surprise given the characteristics of northern agriculture, where grain crops and small farms were the norm. In the north, however, just as in the south, most of the enslaved population worked on farms as agricultural labor, though they were rarely grouped in large numbers on heavily capitalized farms. With the exception of a few areas in the north, for example, Naragansett county, Rhode Island, few slavers held more than one or two slaves.

Slavery also played a significant role in northern manufacturing and commerce. As a result, while the slave labor camps (or plantations if you will) that developed in the South were not as evident, slavery contributed in diverse ways to the flourishing of the northern economy. Slaves in Philadelphia, Boston, and New York City fulfilled a wide variety of functions. While many slaves represented status purchases and served as domestics in the household, or as coachmen and lackeys for the well-to-do, slaves also fulfilled more productive economic roles in in every northern urban center. At the top of northern cities' social hierarchies slaves served in these domestic roles and as symbols of the wealth and status of their owners. Northern professionals also owned slaves for similar reasons, or as investments. Some fifteen percent of the northern slaves that found themselves in bondage in northern cities were owned by clergymen, lawyers, judges, professors, and other professionals. Many slave owners ranked well below these northern elites. Artisans, craftsmen, ship captains, as well as tavern and innkeepers, figures who were not counted among the colonial elite, owned over fifty-five percent of slaves held in northern cities. Benjamin Franklin, for example, was a printer, an occupation not held in particularly high esteem. Nonetheless, over the course of his lifetime Franklin owned perhaps eight slaves, though not all at once. Many slaves also worked as dock workers and in construction. Northern merchants and shopkeepers also depended upon slave laborers. As many as thirty percent of all slaves held in northern cities were in the employ of merchants and traders.

The introduction and exploitation of slavery in the Middle Colonies and New England, however, just as was the case in the South, reflected both the particular labor demands of each colony and the relationship of each to the wider development of the Atlantic economy over the course of the seventeenth and eighteenth centuries. In the pages that follow and in the primary sources readers are asked to analyze in this chapter, observe specifically the diversity of both the ways in which slaves were employed, the many ways that slaves contributed to northern economies and culture, and the ways in which the slave system that developed in the North differed from the southern examples you have encountered in chapter two.

THE INTRODUCTION OF SLAVERY IN THE MIDDLE COLONIES

In the colonies of New York, Pennsylvania, New Jersey and Delaware slavery was first introduced by the Dutch, who settled the region beginning in the 1620s. The Dutch had established their colony of New Netherlands in the mid-1620s with the hope of encroaching on French fur-trading interests in North America. The hub of this enterprise was situated on Manhatten Island, re-christened New Amsterdam. The Hudson River valley, to the city's north, had lush farmland, which the Dutch West India Company hoped to exploit as well. The Dutch West India Company, however, had little interest in settling the Hudson River Valley with small farmers, instead hoping to attract larger land owners and the development of a plantation economy. They also were anxious to find an additional market for slaves as the Dutch West India Company already supplied its Caribbean sugar islands with African slaves. Beginning in 1626 the company began transporting slaves from their Caribbean island of Curaçao, at first using slaves to clear land along the Hudson and build roads and construct fortifications for New Amsterdam. The Dutch West India Company also employed slaves in New Jersey to clear lands and build forts. Possibly as early as 1623 slaves were used to build Fort Nassau. Across the Hudson from Manhattan, in what would later be the cities of Hoboken and Jersey City, between 1630 and 1655, slaves were used to clear and farm this land, supplying the residents of New Amsterdam with food.

When, in 1664, the English took New Netherlands from the Dutch, calling the colony New York, in honor of the newly restored King Charles II's brother, the Duke of York, the English proprietors remained open to both the possibilities of profits from the slave trade and from ownership of slaves. The first English legal codes promulgated for the colony recognized slavery's legality and endeavored to limit white indentured servitude. This served to heighten demand for slaves. By 1703 as many as 43 percent of New York City residents owned at least one slave.

Though the proportion of New Yorkers who owned slaves would decline over the course of the eighteenth century to one in fifteen, the number of slaves would continue to grow. Between 1700 and 1750 the number of slaves in the colony expanded from 2,000 to 10,000, mostly residing in New York city or its surrounding counties. A similar pattern developed in colonial New Jersey, which was granted to a separate group of proprietors after the British wrested control of it from the Dutch West India Company. The proprietors authorized slavery and encouraged its growth by offering 60 acres of free land for each slave brought into the colony. After New Jersey became a crown colony, its governor continued to encourage slave imports, thereby supporting the Royal Africa Company which had acquired a monopoly on British trade in slaves. And, when New York and Pennsylvania sought to profit by taxing slave imports, the port of Perth Amboy in New Jersey became an important smuggling route for secreting slaves into both colonies.

The Dutch also played a key role in the introduction of slavery into the area that would become Pennsylvania. As early as 1639 slaves had been imported into the Delaware River valley by Dutch vessels. When, in 1681, William Penn, an ally of Charles II, was rewarded for his support with the grant of a haven for his fellow Quaker co-religionists along the Delaware River, slaves would prove as important to the early establishment of Pennsylvania as they had New York and New Jersey. The Quakers have a deserved reputation of tolerance and support for abolition. In the eighteenth century, Quakers would be leaders in the movement to abolish the slave trade and then slavery itself. But Quakers only gradually developed a stand against slavery. As a result, the Quaker colony of Pennsylvania relied on enslaved Africans both during its initial founding and over the course of its colonial history.

William Penn, the founder and proprietor of the colony, was a slave owner who expressed a preference for slaves over servants, "for then, a man has them while they live." Penn intended the colony as a haven for Quakers, but not necessarily for Africans. Within three years of the colony's foundation over 150 Africans were brought to Philadelphia to do the work of clearing the forests, laying out the city's streets, and constructing homes. The numbers of African slaves continued to grow. By 1700 perhaps as many as one in every ten residents in the town owned a slave. Many of the slaves living in Philadelphia by that date were involved in ship building or worked in iron foundries. The surrounding countryside, producing wheat for consumption and export, relied on a mixture of indentured labor, yeoman farmers, and slaves. The high quality of the land exending westward from Philadelphia and the good farms attracted large numbers of Germans and Scots-Irish between 1727 and 1754, willing to work as indentured servants or able to establish their own farms. As a result slave labor in the countryside diminished in importance. But, Philadelphia continued to use slaves as domestics, lifters and loaders on the docks, and in manufacturing until the revolutionary period, despite the increasing unease over slavery expressed by the Quakers who governed the colony.

NEW ENGLAND:

The establishment and development of English settlements in New England also had their history of slavery. The founding of the different New England colonies have most often been associated with the desire to establish Biblically-based societies (in the case of Massachusetts, and to a lesser extent Connecticut and New Hampshire which were all outgrowths of the Puritan reform movements) or with a pursuit of a more religiously tolerant society (in the case of Rhode Island). The motive force for the settlement and expansion of New England colonies seems to have had little to do with either economic impulses or a connection to slavery. New England also had fewer slaves than either the Middle Colonies or the South, and consequently a smaller presence of Africans or men and women of African descent. Nonetheless, the importance to New England of the slave trade, and the "carrying trade" in provisions for plantations or in commodities produced by slave hands, cannot be ignored. And, despite the smaller number of slaves in New England, the New England colonies also relied on slave labor, though to a lesser degree than did the other regions of English colonization.

The Pilgrims, or Separatists, were English Protestants determined to separate from the Church of England. After earlier establishing their community in the Netherlands, the Pilgrims received approval to settle in the Americas. Though they had been authorized to go to the Jamestown colony, the Pilgrims ended up on the shores of New England, arriving at a place they called Plymouth Plantation in 1620. Not long after, the first slaves were imported to the region. In 1624, the first slave owner arrived in Massachusetts, bringing with him two slaves. The Pilgrims, however, had only established a beachhead on the rocky shores of the Atlantic. Beginning in 1629 the Plymouth settlers were followed by wave after wave of Puritans, who shared a similar theology and disenchantment with the Anglican church, but who were intent on purifying the church, rather than withdrawing from it. Their objective in New England was to establish a "Beacon on a Hill," a signal and model for the people of England, and a haven for others who believed as they did. Though the members of Plymouth Plantation and the Massachusetts Bay Company were motivated largely by religious impulses and a desire to escape persecution in England, neither had particular objections to slavery or slave ownership.

The Puritans regarded themselves as among "God's Elect" and saw Africans as people condemned to serve whites, predestined as it were to a life of servitude. This claim rested on both the view that "heathens" were rightly subject to Christian authorities, and upon interpretations of the Bible that characterized Africans as cursed by God and destined to lives in slavery. A Massachusetts law of 1641 specifically addressed the institution, and made clear that slavery was Biblical. The slave trade in New England would also result from the Puritans' difficult relationship with the Native Americans that surrounded their settlements. The Thanksgiving celebrations that form an important feature of American civic culture disguise what was in fact an often hostile interaction between Indians and the Englishmen that grew in number every year in the 1630s and demanded ever-increasing acreage for their farms and villages. In 1637 tensions between Puritans and the Pequot Indians erupted in violence. In retaliation for an attack on the town of Wetherfield, Puritan militias surrounded a Pequot village near Mystic, Connecticut, fired its stockade and huts, and slaughtered the Indian warriors who escaped the flames. The Indian women and children who survived were enslaved in the colony. The men and boys, however, posed too great a threat to keep in Massachusetts. They were transported to the West Indies and exchanged for "salt, cotton, tobacco, and Negroes." This pattern of capturing Indians and trading them for enslaved Africans in the Caribbean would be a commonplace during the seventeenth century. The practice, of course, fulfilled a number of functions: it served as a form of "ethnic cleansing" that opened up land for white settlement while also providing a commodity (Indian slaves) that could be exchanged for African slaves.

Despite the presence and cultural contributions of slaves to the New England colonies, Massachusetts, Connecticut, and Rhode Island had fewer slaves than did the other regions of the northern colonies. Moreover, most of the slaves who came to New England over the course of the colonial period arrived in the region as a consequence of the carrying trade to the Caribbean and to Africa. As early as 1644, Boston merchants began sailing to West Africa in search of slaves to sell in the Caribbean. In most years thereafter, from the ports of Boston, Portsmouth, Plymouth, Providence, Bristol, and Newport ships were outfitted with cargo destined for African shores. Many of New England's prominent figures would be involved in the trade, including such recognized revolutionary Americans as John Hancock and the Brown family of Rhode Island. Distilleries in New England produced rum from Caribbean molasses. The rum was traded in Europe or more often shipped to West Africa and exchanged there for African slaves, who then suffered the "Middle Passage" to the West Indies, where the slaves were exchanged for molasses destined for North America or Europe. The ships arriving in New England often carried a small number of slaves, frequently designated as "refuse slaves" that could not be sold in the West Indies. Often these slaves had been identified as troublemakers or difficult to manage. Because slaves in New England were more isolated from fellow Africans they could be more effectively controlled and posed less of a threat to New England masters than they might in the Caribbean, New England masters felt more comfortable taking in these "bad lots."

Though Boston merchants were active in the "carrying trade," Rhode Island played a particularly prominent role in the trade in African slaves. Rhode Island was established by Roger Williams in 1636. He had been banished from Massachusetts Bay Colony for his religious views. He settled on land at the tip of Narragansett Bay on a site renamed Providence. Other dissident Puritans, including Anne Hutchinson, soon joined him. As a result, Rhode Island is often remembered as the birthplace of American ideals of religious tolerance, and for positive relations with Native Americans.

Its place in the slave trade, however, is also noteworthy. The prominence of the slave trade and the proportionately high number of slaves in this little colony illustrate a rather different history. The first documented presence of slaves in Rhode Island dates to 1652. But in the eighteenth century, a higher proportion of slaves than indentured servants would be imported into the colony. By 1774, despite its small population, Rhode Island counted some 3,761 African slaves. Rather unlike the situation in nearby Massachusetts, where slaves were not prominent as agricultural laborers, in Rhode Island, particularly Narragansett County where large scale farming predominated, slaves were critical members of the agricultural labor force. Slaves made up one-third of the population in Narragansett County. The county consequently had slave laws that approached those in southern colonies for their draconian restrictions.

Rhode Island, though, is best known as a center of the North American slave trade. Between 1709 and 1807 Rhode Island merchants sponsored nearly 1000 slave voyages to Africa, and transported over 106,000 slaves to the New World. Every year in the middle of the 18th century Rhode Islanders sent 18 ships to Africa. This flotilla transported 1,800 hogsheads of rum to Africa, and earned annually over £40,000. One of the prominent families involved in this trade, the Brown family of Providence, Rhode Island, would feature in the debates leading to the American Revolution, and would turn some of the profits earned in the slave trade to good purpose by establishing Brown University.

In addition to considerations of the economic role of slavery in the northern colonies, it is worth while to reflect on the ways that residents of New England and the Middle Colonies were influenced culturally by the presence of African and West Indian slaves. One of the most fascinating ways in which African influence was felt played out in the well-known witch craze that swept the Massachusetts Bay Colony in the 1690s. One of the most important actors in this drama was Tituba, a West Indian slave. But African slaves would also be caught up in the investigations surrounding the "Salem Witch Trials." The Salem witch craze has often been seen as a belated example of the witch hunts that had erupted in the 1560s and lasted for around a century in western Europe. The role of Africans and slaves in the Salem Witch Trials, though illustrates the way in which African and European religious practices and beliefs often coincided and fueled mutual anxieties. Among the documents included in this selection of primary sources are documents from the Salem trials that feature enslaved Africans and West Indians. But Africans contributed in other ways do the development of society and culture in the northern colonies, as evident in this collection of documents by the interest in variolation or inoculation against small pox expressed by the Puritan Cotton Mather and his recognition of its long-standing practice among Africans.

CONCLUSION

North of the Mason-Dixon line, in the years after the American Revolution, slavery would be gradually phased out in some states and in other states ended outright with the stroke of a pen. Nonetheless, there were still slaves living in the northern states of the United States until well into the nineteenth century. Despite slavery's longevity in the North, the growing northern antipathy towards chattel slavery and the strength of the abolitionist movement in the North would eventually contribute to the coming of the American Civil War. One result of the North's rejection of the system of chattel slavery after 1776 would be the careful cultivation of a historical amnesia regarding slavery in the Middle Colonies and New England. This forgetfulness has allowed northerners to conclude that slavery was historically a "southern" problem and an institution "peculiar" to the South. This forgetfulness has allowed northern residents to congratulate themselves, perhaps without justification, as having been comparatively more progressive, while southerners held anachronistically to an outdated and inhumane labor system. In fact, each of the northern states has a history of slavery, which readers will observe in the primary sources included in this chapter.

In the documents below, however, readers will be able to see the many ways in which slaves and men and women of African descent were in fact present in the Middle Colonies and New England. The evidence in this chapter is perhaps most clearly indicative of the conditions of and role of slaves in New England, but this is only the accident of selection here. Slaves had similar roles and were somewhat more prevalent in the colonies of New York, Pennsylvania, and New Jersey than even in New England. In the documents that follow this introduction, however, it is evident that slaves were vital to the economy of the northern colonies, and that they played diverse roles in the cultural and economic life of the region.

PRIMARY SOURCES

Document 1   Extract from John Winthrop's *Journal*, 1638.[1]

26 February   Mr. Pierce, in the Salem ship, the *Desire*, returned from the West Indies after seven months. He had been at Providence, and brought some cotton, and tobacco, and negroes, etc., from thence, and salt from Tertugos. Dry fish and strong liquors are the only commodities

---

1   Documents Illustrative of the History of the Slave Trade to America. Elizabeth Donnan, ed. Vol. III. New England and the Middle Colonies. (New York: Octagon Books, Inc., 1965), 4.

for those parts. He met there two men-of-war, set forth by the lords, etc., of Providence with letters of mart, who had taken divers prizes from the Spaniard, and many negroes.

Document 2   The Massachusetts Body of Liberties, 1641.[2]

Source: *Documents Illustrative of the History of the Slave Trade to America*. Elizabeth Donnan, ed. Vol. III. *New England and the Middle Colonies*. (New York: Octagon Books, Inc., 1965), 4.

It is Ordered by this Court and the Authority thereof; That there shall never be any Bond-slavery, Villenage or Captivity amongst us, unless it be lawful Captives taken in just Wars, [and such strangers] as willingly sell themselves or are sold to us, and such shall have the Liberties and Christian usage which the Law of God established in Israel concerning such persons doth morally require; Provided this exempts none from servitude who shall be judged thereto by Authority.

Document 3   Report of the Board of Accounts on New Netherland. 1644.[3]

New Netherland, situated in America, between English Virginia and New England, …was first frequented by the inhabitants of this country in the year 1598, and especially by those of the Greenland Company, but without making any fixed settlements, only as a shelter in the winter. For which purpose they erected on the North and South Rivers there, two little forts against the incursions of the Indians. … In the years 1622 and 1623, the West India Company took possession, by virtue of their charter, of the said country, and conveyed thither, in their ship, the *New Netherland*, divers colonists under the direction of Cornelis Jacobus. [The report details the continued failings of the colony to succeed between its founding and 1644.]

To remedy this great decay, various suggestions were made by the Director and the Commonalty.

First, that to restore peace and quiet throughout the land, the Indians who had waged war against us, should be wholly destroyed and exterminated. …

Secondly, in order to prevent war in future, the Colonists ought to settle nearer each other, on suitable places, with a view of being thus formed into villages and towns, to be the better able to protect each other in time of need. …

Fifthly, it would be advisable, for the benefit of that country, first of all to facilitate emigration to New Netherland, as had been done a long time since; or at least to credit the passengers for a time, in order to allure Colonists thither, and afterward to introduce a goodly portion of farm servants and negroes into that country. By whose labor, agriculture would be so much promoted, that a great quantity of provisions could be exported thence to Brazil.

… And, for the advancement of the cultivation of the land there, it would not be unwise to allow, at the request of the Patroons, Colonists and other farmers, the introduction, from Brazil

---

2   Documents Illustrative of the History of the Slave Trade to America. Elizabeth Donnan, ed. Vol. III. New England and the Middle Colonies. (New York: Octagon Books, Inc., 1965), 4.

3   *Documents relative to the Colonial History of the State of New-York: Procured in Holland, England and France.* Volume I, Edited by E.B. O'Callaghan, (Albany: Weed, Parsons and Company, 1856), pp. 149-156.

there, of as many Negroes as they would be disposed to pay for at a fair price; which Negroes would accomplish more work for their masters, and at a less expense, than farm servants, who must be bribed to go thither by a great deal of money and promises.

Document 4 Act of the Director and Council of New Netherland, 25 February 1644.[4]

Having considered the petition of the Negroes named Paul d'Angola who have served the Company 18 to 19 years, to be liberated, especially as they have been many years in the service of the Honorable West India Company here and have been long since promised their Freedom; also that they are burdened with many children so that it is impossible for them to support their wives and children as they have been accustomed to do, if they must continue in the Company's service;

Therefore we, the Director and Council do release, for the term of their natural lives, the above named and their wives from Slavery, hereby setting them free and at liberty, on the same footing as other free people in New Netherland, where they shall be able to earn their livelihood by Agriculture, on the land shown and granted to them, on condition that they, the above named Negroes, shall be bound to pay for the freedom they receive, each man for himself annually, as long as he lives, to the West India Company or its Deputy here, thirty skepels of Maize, or Wheat, Pease or Beans, and one Fat Hog, valued at twenty guilders, which thirty skepels and the hog they, the Negroes, each for himself, promises to pay annually, beginning on the date hereof, on pain, if any one of them shall fail to pay the yearly tribute, he shall forfeit his freedom and return back into the said Company's slavery. With express condition, that their children at present born or yet to be born, shall be bound and obligated to serve the Honorable West India Company as Slaves. Likewise that the above mentioned men shall be obliged to serve the Honorable West India Company here, by water or on land, where their services are required, on receiving fair wages from the Company.

Document 5 Letter of Emanuel Downing to John Winthrop, 1645.[5]

To his evere-honored brother John Winthrop, Esq. at Boston.

Sir,

If upon a Just warre [with the Narragansetts] the Lord should deliver them into our hands, wee might easily have men women and children enough to exchange for Moores, which wilbe more gaynefull pilladge for us then wee conceive, for I doe not see how wee can thrive until wee get into a stock of slaves sufficient to doe all our business, for our children's children will hardly see this great Continent filled with people, soe that our servants will still desire freedome to plant for them-selves, and not stay but for verie great wages. And I suppose you know verie well how wee shall maintaine 20 Moores cheaper than one English servant.

---

[4] Ansel Judd Northrup, "Slavery in New York," *State Library Bulletin*, 4 (May 1900), pp. 250-251.

[5] Documents Illustrative of the History of the Slave Trade to America. Elizabeth Donnan, ed. Vol. III. New England and the Middle Colonies. (New York: Octagon Books, Inc., 1965), 8.

The ships that shall bring Moores may come home laden with salt which may beare most of the chardge, if not all of it…

Document 6   Records and Files of the Quarterly Courts of Essex County Massachusetts.[6]

17 September 1650   Katherine, a "negar" servant of Danyell Rumball, for having a bastard, fined 40 shillings, or to be whipped. Her master promised to pay the fine.

1 May 1653   James Thomas, for fornication with a "negar servant" of Danyell Rumball, fined and to pay 18 pence a week toward keeping the child.

29 September 1653   Kate, the blacmoore serv't to Daniell Rumboll presented for fornication, having a bastard Child." Fined 20 shillings or to be whipped.

25 September 1660   Jugg. Capt. White's negro, upon her presentment for fornication, was sentenced to be whipped.

23 October 1661   Jury of inquest appointed upon the death of one John, a negro of Mr. Henry Bartholomew, reported 23 October 1661, that they had "viewed the place

where the neargoe was found lying & a gun lying by him, & heard the relation of severall witnesses, that were called, before he was quite dead, & viewing his body & finding where the shot went into his body being about or Just beneath his short ribs one his leaft side, & came partly through about his shoulder blade behind, and being all agreed in our apprehentions, doe Judge according to our best apprehention, that he did willingly contrive & was the only actor in his owne death by shooting of ye said Gun into his own body. Sworn before William Hathorne.

26 August 1670   Mr. William Hollingworth v. Michael Powell, Jr. for several goods left with said Powell in Barbados and Virginia, and money in New England; dated 26/8/1670; signed by Hilliard Veren, for the court; and served by Edward Grove, constable of Salem, who attached a little negro boy "known by the name of Seaser, now in ye hands of Mr. William Hollingworth as ye "proper goods" of said Powell.

19 June 1673   Inventory of the estate of Henry Short of Newbury, who deceased May 5, 1673, by Richard Kent, Symon Tompson, and Anthonye Somerby, amounting to £1,842 8s; the new parlor, old parlor, new parlor chamber, kitchen chamber, buttery, kitchen and dairy house mentioned; he also owned a negro man. Debts owed, £68 2 s.

13 October 1674   John Clarke and James Kid were bound for the former's appearance to answer a complaint made by Robert Smart's negro called Bess, who charged him with being the father of her child

4 November 1674   Richard Dole's negro Grace, presented for fornication, was to be fined or whipped.

Juniper, John Hale's negro, presented for fornication, was to be fined or whipped.

---

6   Selections from Records and Files of the Quarterly Courts of Essex County, Massachusetts, Vol I-V (Salem, Mass.: Published by the Essex Institutie, 1916)

Document 7 John Josselyn, *Two Voyages in New England*, 1674.[7]

… the Second of *October*, about 9 of the clock in the morning, Mr. *Maverick's* Negro woman came to my chamber window, and in her own Countrey language and tune sang very loud and shrill, going out to her, she used a great deal of respect toward me, and willingly would have expressed her grief in *English*; but I apprehended it by her countenance and deportment, whereupon I repaired to my host, to learn of him the cause, and resolved to intreat him in her behalf, for that I understood before, that she had been a Queen in her own Countrey, and observed a very humble and dutiful garb used towards her by another Negro who was her maid. Mr. *Maverick* was desirous to have a breed of Negroes, and therefore seeing she would not yield by perswasions to company with a Negro young man he had in his house; he commanded him will'd she nill'd she to go to bed to her, which was no sooner done but she kickt him out again, this she took in high disdain beyond her slavery, and this was the cause of her grief.

Document 8 "Complaint v. Margaret Hawkes and Candy," July 1692.[8]

John Putnam, Jr. and Thomas Putnam of Salem complaines of Margret Hawkes late of Barbados, now of Salem and her negro Woman upon suspition they did afflict and torment by Witchcraft the bodeys of Mary Walcotte and Marry Warren, Ann Putnam, All of Salem Spinstrs and Pray that the said Margret Hawkes & her Negro Woman may be apprehended & Committed according to Law to answer the Complaint of the above said. Putnam.

"Examination of Candy," Salem Witchcraft Trials, 4 July 1692

The examination of Candy, a negro woman, before Bartholomew Gedney and John Hawthorne, Esqrs., Mr. Nicholas Noyes also present.

Q. Candy! Are you a witcth.

A. Candy no witch in her country. Candy's mother no witch. Candy no witch, Barbados. This country, mistress give Candy witch.

Q. Did your mistress make you a witch in this country?

A. Yes, in this country mistress give Candy witch.

Q. What did your mistress do to make you a witch?

A. Mistress bring book and pen and ink, make Candy write in it.

Q. What did you write in it?

--She took a pen and ink and upon a book or paper made a mark.

Q. How did you afflict or hurt these folks, where are the puppets you did it with?

--She asked to go out of the room and she would shew or tell; upon which she had liberty, one going with her, and she presently brought in two clouts [cloths], one with two knots tied it it, the other one; which being seen by Mary Warren, Deliverance Hobbs, and Abigail

---

[7] John Josselyn, An Account of Two Voyages to New England, in the Years 1638, 1663 (Boston: William Veazie, 1855) p. 26.

[8] Massachusetts Archives, Vol. 135 No. 31 A., in Salem Witch Trials Documentary Archive and Transcription Project, http://salem.lib.virginia.edu/home.html (accessed 12-1-2016).

Hobbs, they were greatly affrighted and fell into violent fits, and all of them said that the black man and Mrs. Hawkes and the negro stood by the puppets or rags and pinched them, and then they were afflicted, and when the knots were untied yet they continued as aforesaid. A bit of one of the rags being set on fire, the afflicted all said they were burned, and cried out dreadfully. The rags being put into water, two of the aforementioned persons were in dreadful fits almost choaked, and the other was violently running down to the river, but was stopped.

Attest. John Hawthorne, Just. Peace.

"Indictment v. Candy" December 1692

The Jurors for our Sovereign: Lord & Lady the King & Queen doe present That Candy, A Negro Woman Servant of Margarette Hawkes of Salem in and Upon the Second day of July last in the Year 1692 and divers other days & times as well before as after Certaine detestable Arts Called Witchcrafts & Sorceries Wickedly Mallitiously & feloniously hath Used practiced & exercised in the Towne of Salem afo [rbar] [sbar]'d Upon and Against One Mary Wallcot of Salem Single Woman by which Wicked Arts The Said Mary Wallcot the day & Year aforesaid & Divers other times as well before as after was & is Tortured Aflicted Consumed Wasted pined & Tormented Contrary to the peace of our Sovereign lord & lady the King & Queen their Crowne & dignity & The laws in that Case made & provided.

[On reverse of document] Candy Negro: for bewitching Mary Wallcott Billa Vera, *Robert Payne foreman. Ponet Se. The juery find the person here inditted not gilty of this indittement.

Document 9   Samuel Sewall, *The Selling of Joseph: A Memorial, 1700*.[9]

For as much as Liberty is in real value next unto Life: None ought to part with it themselves, or deprive others of it, but upon most mature Consideration.

The Numerousness of slaves at this day in the Province, and the Uneasiness of them under their Slavery, hath put many upon thinking whether the foundation of it be firmly and well laid; so as to sustain the Vast Weight that is built uon it. It is most certain that all Men, as they are Sons of Adam, are Coheirs; and have equal Right unto Liberty, and all other outward Comforts of Life. *God hath Given the Earth [with all its Commodities] unto the Sons of Adam,* Psalm 115:16. *And hath made of One Blood, all Nations of Men, for to dwell on all the face of the Earth, and hath determined the Times before appointed, and the bounds of their habitation: That they should seek the Lord. Forasmuch then as we are the Offspring of God &c.* Acts 17:26, 27, 29. Now although the Title given by the last ADAM, doth infinitely better Men's Estates, respecting GOD and themselves; and grants them a most beneficial and inviolable Lease under the Broad Seal of Heaven, who were before only Tenants at Will: Yet through the Indulgence of God to our First Parents after the Fall, the outward Estate of all and every of their Children, remains the same, as to one another. So that Originally, and Naturally there is no such thing as Slavery. *Joseph* was rightfully no more a Slave to his Brethren than they were to him; and they had no more Authority to *Sell* him, than they had to *Slay* him. And if they had nothing to do to Sell him; the *Ishmaelites* bargaining with them, and paying down Twenty pieces of Silver, could not make a

---

9   Samuel Sewall, *The Selling of Joseph: A Memorial* (Boston: Bartholomew Green and John Allen, 1700) Source: Massachusetts Historical Society. Collections Online. http://www.masshist.org/database/53.

Title. Neither could *Potiphar* have any better Interest in him than the *Ishmaelites* had. *Gen* 37:20, 27, 28. For he that shall in this case plead *Alteration of Poverty*, seems to have forfeited a great part of his claim to Humanity. There is no proportion between Twenty Pieces of Silver, and LIBERTY. The commodity it felt is the Claimer. If *Arabian* Gold be imported in any quantities, most are afraid to meddle with it, though they might have it at early rates; lest if it should have been wrongfully taken from the Owners, it should kindle a fire to the Consumption of their whole Estate. 'Tis pity there should be more Caution used in buying a Horse, or a little lifeless dust; than there is in purchasing Men and Women; Whenas they are the Offspring of GOD, and their liberty is *Auro pretiosior Omni!* [More precious than Gold.]

And seeing GOD hath said, *He that Stealeth a Man and Selleth him, or if he be found in his hand, he shall surely be put to Death.* Exodus 21:16. This Law being of Everlasting Equity, wherein Man Stealing is ranked among the most atrocious of Capital Crimes: What louder Cry can there be made of that Celebrated Warning: *CAVEAT EMPTOR!* [Let the buyer beware.]

And all things considered, it would conduce more to the Welfare of the Province, to hire White Servants for a Term of Years, than to have Slaves for Life. Few can endure to hear of a Negro's being made free; and indeed they can seldom use their freedom well; yet their continual aspiring after their forbidden Liberty, renders them Unwilling Servants. And there is such a disparity in their Conditions, Colour & Hair, that they can never embody with us, and grow up into orderly Families to the Peopling of the Land: but still remain in our Body Politick as a kind of extravasat Blood. As many Negro men as there are among us, so many empty places there are in our Train Bands, and the places taken up of Men that might make Husbands for our Daughters. And the Sons and Daughters of *New England* would become more like *Jacob* and Rachel, if this Slavery were thrust out of doors. Moreover it is too well known what Temptations Masters are under, to connive at the Fornication of their Slaves; lest they should be obliged to find them Wives, or pay their Fines. It seems to be practically pleaded that they might be Lawless; tis thought much of that the Law should have Satisfaction for their Thefts, and their immoralities; by which means, *Holiness to the Lord,* is more rarely engraven upon tis sort of Servitude. It is likewise most lamentable to think, how in taking Negros out of Africa, and Selling of them here, That which GOD has joyned together men do boldly rend asunder; Men from their Country, Husbands from their Wives, Parents from their Children. How horrible is the Uncleanness, Mortality, if not Murder, that the Ships are guilty of that bring great Crouds of these miserable Men, and Women. Methinks when we are bemoaning the barbarous Usage of our Friends and Kinsfolk in *Africa*: it might not be unseasonable to enquire whether we are not culpable in forcing the *Africans* to be Slaves amongst our selves. And it may be a question whether all the Benefit received by *Negro* slaves, will balance the Accompt of Cash laid out upon them.

Document 10   Black Population in New York, 1703 to 1771[10]

Census	Black Population	
	City	Colony
1703	630	2,383
1723	1,362	6,171
1731	1,577	7,231
1737	1,719	8,941
1746	2,444	9,107
1749	2,368	10,592
1756	2,278	13,548
1771	3,137	19,885

Document 11   An Act for Regulating of Slaves, New York, 27 November 1702.[11]

Further Enacted by the authority aforesaid, That hereafter it shall and may be lawful for any Master or Mistress of slaves to punish their slaves for their Crimes and offences at Discretion, not extending to life or Member. And for as much as the Number of slaves in the City of New York and Albany, and also in other Towns within this Province, doth daily increase, and that they have been found oftentimes guilty of Confederating together in running away, or other ill practices, Be it therefore Enacted by the authority aforesaid, That it shall not hereafter be lawful for above three Slaves to meet together at any one time, nor at any other place, than when it shall happen they meet in some servile Imployment for their Master's or Mistress's profit, and by their Master or Mistress consent, upon penalty of being whipt upon the naked back, at disretion of any Justice of the Peace, not exceeding forty lashes. And that it shall and may be lawful hereafter for any City or Town within this Province; to have and appoint a Common Whipper for their slaves. And for this salary it shall and may be lawful for any City or Town within this Province, at their Common Council or Town meeting, to agree upon which sum to be paid him by the Master or Mistress of slaves per head, as they shall think fit, not exceeding three shillins per head, for all such slaves as shall be whipt, as aforesaid.

And in case any slave presume to assault or strike any freeman or Woman professing Christianity, it shall be in the power of any two Justices of the Peace, who by this Act are thereunto authorized, to Committ such slave to Prison, not exceeding fourteen days for one fact, and to inflict such other Corporal punishment (not extending to life or limb) upon him, her, or them so offending, as to said Justices shall seem meet and reasonable.

And, be it further Enacted by the authority aforesaid, That no person or persons whatsoever do hereafter Imploy, harbor, Conceal, or entertain other men's slaves at their house, out-house or Plantation, w'thout the Consent of their Master or Mistress either signified to them verbally or by Certificate in writing, under the Said Master or Mistress hand, upon forfeiture of five pounds for

---

10   Adapted from James G. Lydon, "New York and the Slave Trade, 1700-1774," *The William and Mary Quarterly*, 35:2 (1978), p. 388.

11   Ansel Judd Northrup, "Slavery in New York," *State Library Bulletin*, pp. 260-261.

every night or day, to the Master or Mistress of such slaves, So that the penalty do not excuse the value of Said slave; and if any person or persons whatsoever shall be found guilty of harbouring, entertaining, or Concealing of any slave, or assisting to the Conveying of them away, if such slave shall thereupon be lost, dead, or otherwise destroyed, such person or persons So harbouring, entertaining, concealing, assisting or Conveying of them away, shall be also liable to pay the value of Such slave to the Master or Mistress, to be recovered by action of debt, in manner aforesaid. And whereas slaves are the property of Christians, and cannot without great loss or detriment to their Masters or Mistresses, be subjected in all cases Criminal, to the strict Rules of the Laws of England, Bee it Enacted by the Authority aforesaid, That hereafter if any slave by Theft or Trespass shall damnifie any person or persons to the value of five pounds or under, the Master or Mistress of such slave shall be liable to make satisfaction for such damage to the party injured, … and the slave shall receive Corporal Punishment, at Discretion of a Justice of the Peace, and immediately thereafter be permitted to attend his Master or Mistress service, without further punishment.

Document 12   Run-away Slave Notices in the *Boston News-Letter*[12]

Boston News-Letter Monday, 22 July 1706

Ran-away from his Master George Robinson Carver of Boston on Tuesday last the 16th, Currant, a Negro Man-Slave named Jo, of a middle Stature, well-set, Speaks good English, aged about 32 years, has on a sad coloured Jacket, white Shirt, and Leather Breeches. Whosoever shall apprehend and take up the said Runaway, so that he may be delivered unto his said Master, or give any true Intelligence of him, shall have a Sufficient reward.

Boston News-Letter Monday, 15 November 1708

Ran-away from his Master Col. *Nicholas Paige* of *Rumley*-Marsh, on Tuesday the 2d of this Instant *November*, a Negro Man-servant, aged about 45 years, call'd *Jack Bill,* of middle Stature, a comely Fellow, speaks good English: He has on a black Hat, black Coat, blew Jacket, a broad cloth pair of Breeches with Livery Lace, and a pair of white Stockings. Whoever shall apprehend the said Runaway, and him safely Convey to his said Master, or unto Mr. John Geeriss, Gunsmith, at the Upper-End of *Kings-Street* in *Boston;* or give any tru Intelligence of the said Negro Man-servant to either of them, so as that his Master may have him again, shall be sufficiently Rewarded, besides all necessary Charges paid.

Boston News-Letter, Monday, 6 April 1711

Ran-away from his Master Robert Rumsey at Fairfield in Connecticut Colony, on the 27th of March last, a Negro man call'd Jack, a tall thin fac'd Fellow, exceeding black, a considerable scar in his face, can play on a Violin, he hath carried his Fiddle with him, and a considerable bundle of Cloathes. Whoever shall apprehend the said Runaway Negro man, and him safely Convey to his said Master, or give any true Intelligence of him, so as his Master may have him again, shall be sufficiently Rewarded, besides all necessary Charges paid.

---

12   Selections from *The Boston News-Letter*, (Boston, Massachusetts).

Document 13   Probate Records: the Will of Samuel Arnold, 27 April 1739.[13]

I, Samuel Arnold of East Haddam, husbandman, do make this my last will and testament: I give unto my beloved wife Abigail 1/3 part of my moveable estate (excepting my negro slaves), to her, her heirs and assigns forever, and also the use of 1/3 part of my lands, house, barn, orchard or other commodity appertaining to my said land, to use and improve during her natural life. I give to my son Samuel Arnold one lot of land lying in the 3rd division of land in East Haddam, 43 ½ acres more or less, north on the land of Sergeant Samuel Andrews, and east and west on highways or commons, and south on a highway, to him, his heirs and assigns forever, as his or their own proper inheritance in fee simple, and also my negro man servant named Prince, yet 5th son of my eldest man servant named Prince and of Cate his wife, and also my will is that the aforesaid servant shall at my decease be in the hands of my executors and by them to be put in the hands of my son Samuel if they shall judge it best for him to have the said servant; but if my said executors shall judge it best to sell the said servant and my said to have ye money, then my will is that my executors shall sell my said servant in the following manner, viz: to such suitable master as will give most for my said servant, and to pay £10 a year annually until the payment be out: and also my will is that my said son shall have the money according to the foregoing proposal of payment, provided my said servant shall not be sold to any master living out of this town; and also £100 to be paid to him by my two sons, viz., Josiah and John, and in the following manner, viz., that Josiah Arnold shall pay unto his brother Samuel Arnold £3 a year annually for the space of 20 years next after my decease, and John Arnold shall pay unto his brother Samuel Arnold 40 shillings a year for the space of 20 years next after my decease. I give unto my son Joseph Arnold 1 lot of land in the fourth division of land in East Haddam joining land of Sergeant Samuel Ackley, containing about 60 acres be it more or less; and also 20 acres out of two lots of land in the 5th and 8th divisions, to him and his heirs forever; and also my negro man servant named Sampson. I give unto my son Enoch Arnold 120 acres of land laid out to me in the 5th and 8th divisions, to hm, his heirs and assigns in fee simple; and also my negro man servant named Ceaser. And further, my will is that my son Enoch shall have his 120 acres where it shall best suit him in the said two division lots. I give to my son Josiah Arnold my dwelling house and homelott, with all the fences, orcharding, buildings or other appurtenances thereto belonging; and also 1 small piece of land lying in the 6th division, containing about 4 ½ acres, lying west of the great highway; and also the west half of a small lot lying in the 2nd division; and also 4 negro servants, viz., my eldest man servant named Prince, and Cate his wife, and my man servant named Japhet and my woman servant named Rose. And further , my will is that my said son Josiah shall pay unto my son Samuel £3 a year for the space of 20 years after my decease, and also £5 a year for the space of 20 years after my decease, and also £5 a year for the space of 20 years annually after my decease to my daughter Mary Bates. I give to my son John Arnold 1 certain lott or tract of land lying partly on the hill called Bold Hill, being by estimation 40 acres be it more or less, and also the east half of a small lott lying in the 2nd division, to him and his heirs forever; and also my negro man servant named Peter. And further, my will is that my son John Arnold shall pay unto my son Samuel Arnold 40 shillings a year annually for the space of 20 years after my decease. I give to my daughter Mary Bates 6 ½ acres of land butting west on Connecticut River, south on the land of Jabez Chapman, east on a ledge of rocks, being half a certain tract of land laid out to me in the 6th division of land in East Haddam; and also £100 in money or bills of public credit,

---

13   *A Digest of the Early Connecticut Probate Records: Hartford District, 1729-1750*, edited by Charles William Manwaring, (Hartford, CT: R.S. Peck& Co., 1904), p. 219.

to be paid to her £5 a year annually, for the space of 20 years after my decease, by my son Josiah Arnold. I give unto my daughter Abigail Arnold 6 ½ acres of land butting west on the great rock, and north on the commons, being ½ of a certain tract of land laid out to me in the 6th division of land of East Haddam. I give to my said daughter Abigail my negro maid servant named Lois. I give my right in the undivided land, also the rest of my moveable estate, to be equally divided among my children. I appoint Ensign Daniel Cone and Sergeant Bezeleel Brainard, both of East Haddam, executors.

Witness: *Noadiah Brainard*   Samuel X Arnold, LS.

Henry Chapman, Thomas Smith

Document 14 *The Boston Gazette*, 7 July 1755.[14]

On Monday Evening last died suddenly at *Charlestown*, Captain *John Codman*, of that Place: Upon Suspicion of his being poyson'd, his Body was opened, and therein was found a Quantity of Poyson undissolv'd; since which, a Negroe Man (well known for his Roguery) who belong'd to the deceas'd was taken up and examin'd, who said, that two Negro Women belonging to the Family had commited this horrid Fact; but 'tis tho't they are innocent, as a Quantity of the same Stuff has been since found under his Possession: The Fellow is now in Gaol, and it is hoped he will soon meet with Justice adequate to this villainous Scene.

Document 15 *Boston Evening Post*, 22 September 1755.[15]

Thursday last, in the Afternoon, *Mark,* a Negro Man, and *Phillis*, a Negro Woman, both Servants to the late Capt. *John Codman*, of *Charlestown*, were executed at *Cambridge*, for poisoning their said Master, as mentioned in this paper some Weeks ago. The Fellow was hanged, and the Woman burned at a Stake about Ten Yards distant from the Gallows. They both confessed themselves guilty of the Crime for which they suffered, acknowledged the Justice of their Sentence, and died very penitent. After Execution, the Body of *Mark* was brought down to *Charlestown* Common, and hanged in Chains, on a Gibbet erected there for that Purpose.

Document 16 Nicholas Brown & Co. to Samuel Warner, Providence, 7 April 1761.[16]

Capt Samuel Warner

Sir

You being master of our Sloop *George* with our Cargo on board, Our Orders to You are that You Embrace all Oppotunities to gain Your Passage to Surinam and when Arrived there dispose of our

---

14 The *Boston Gazette*, (Boston, Massachusetts), 4 July 1755.
15 The *Boston Gazette*, (Boston, Massachusetts), 22 September 1755.
16 Nicholas Brown & Co, to Warner, Samuel, April 7, 1761, BFBR 549-3, item 1-4/7/61, Center for Digital Scholarship, Brown University, http://library.brown.edu/cds/catalog/catalog.php?verb=render&colid=17&id=116075543114406&view=showmods.

Cargo and lay out the Net Proceeds in good molasses and load the same on board your Vessel until she be full — Observing to make your Casks of such Bigness as will enable you to take on board the greatest Quantity she will Stow, or Carry. In the Hold, if you should be able to purchase more than your Vessel will Stow as aforesaid (of which we make no doubt In Case of a Tolerable Sale) then we advise to Take some upon Deck we suppose near Twenty hogsheads may be brought there with safety provided you are like to get home before winter all which must depend upon your prudence and Dispach. The over plus as aforesaid if any more than your Vessel will bring, Ship In good molasses if any oppotunity offers for this Colony. If Young male Slaves from 12 years & upwards can be got at about 220 Surinam Guilders or under that are likely fellows You are to Purchase Six or more provided you Come on the Coast in good Season. if good Duck can be got at 30 Surinam Guilder or under per Boult or any other Article that will Answer better than bills You may Lay out your over plus money there In, But In Case no Oppotunity Offers. Case You'l lay out the same In good Bills of Exchange. You'll make all possable Dispach while at Surinam and on Your Return Home. You are to make Tobago & Run between that & Trinedadad & make the Island of Tortugeses after that hall over for Porte Rico & so through between that & Hispaniola & so home at all times keeping a good lookout in order to shun the Enemie if You should be so unfortunate as to be Taken You have Liberty to Ransome upon the Best Terms You Can for Our Interest. Your Comissions for doing the Buisness of the Voyage is to be five percent for Sales & Two & a half percent for Returns and Ten hogsheads which will not hold more than One Hundred Ten Gallons each for priveledge Home. You are to take Special Care of your Vessel that She be graved in Season whiel there In Surinam & open your Lumber port as soon as may be after your arrival & Take all possable Care of your Vessel for her Preservation. You'l give us (Imbracing all Oppotunity) the timeliest & best Intelligence of Your proceedings during the Voyage by Letter; In Closing your Account of Sayles & Bill of Loading that we may be Able to prove our Property In Case of Loss. In case you should have Certain Intelligence before Sailing that Martineco should be Besieged by An English Fleet In that Case nevertheless for the aforesaid order upon Returning home Our Will & Orders are that You Come to windward of the Islands if possable.

Wishing a good Voyage we are &c.

Nicholas Brown

Document 17   Letter from Carter Braxton to Mr. Nicholas Brown & Co., 16 October 1763[17]

Sirs,

Yours dated the 5th Sept. came safe to hand, I was glad to hear my two Letters had been rec'd, for the distance is so great that It makes the conveyance uncertain. It affords me pleasure to hear of your Flourishing Prospect which I believe is more than you have had for some years past. I cannot think Ours so good as they wre last year or in general years and I am apt to believe Corn & Pork will be dear. Some Corn has been Bought at 10 s. per Barrill & I fancy it will rise. Pork will be high & I dare say will not be Bought under three pounds and upward per Barrill. Flour will be

---

17   "Braxton, Carter to Nicholas Brown & Co., October 16, 1763, BFBR 356-18-10/16/63, Center for Digital Scholarship, Brown University, http://library.brown.edu/cds/catalog/catalog.php?verb=render&colid=17&id=1160785113859089&view=showmods

from 15 *s.* to 16/8 per hundred. But what makes the Articles come considerably lower is the High Exchange which is not at 60#6*s*. If from what I have said you will still be encourag'd to send here and consign the cargo to me, you may rely I will do everything in my Power to make it Profit to your advantage, and shall be glad to have some Instructions of it before the Vessell arrives that I might procure the Load on the best terms & have it ready. I observe the Objection you make to the Commission I asked and readily own it is a great deal where the concern is large. But it is no more than they have in most parts of the World, especially the West Indies. In New York they have but £5 6s as you observe and I wonder at it. However I shall be glad to enter into a correspondence with you. I will do your business for £7 ½ 6 s. viz. £5 6s for selling. and £2 ½ 6 s for remittance which is what you offer. I shall be very glad to be concern'd in the African Trade and will be a fourth of the voyage if you choose it. Tobacco I can send any quantity at 20s per hund'd. I believe free of duty if your skipper will take it. I shou'd choose to be Insur'd and what ever expense came to my share more than the tobacco sent I wou'd remit by the Return of the Vessell that brought the slaves. The whole of the Voyage I should leave to you to conduct and you may begin to prepare if you please, But you will let me know the terms and everything relating to the Voyage before the Vessell sails. It ought to be forwarded so as to have the Vessell here in May, because the Negroes will sell better then, than later. The Gold Coast slaves are esteemed the most Valuable & sell best. The Prices of Negroes keep up amazingly. They have sold from £30 to £35 sterling a head clear of duty all this summer & I should not doubt of rendering such a sale if the Negroes were well and came early. I find two or three vessels have been here this summer from the Northwards and I suppose the Trade will be carried on with more negroes for the future. If you will undertake to befriend me in soliciting the consignment of some of them I will give you for your trouble 1/3 of my commissions which will be a pretty thing if the vessels consigns wholly to me. But if she is only half to me I will give you 1/3 of my commissions for all that you get and make my remittance in any manner they desire.

As Business cannot be carried on at such a distance without frequent writing, you will Please to answer this with that quickness you think the Subjects deserve.

I am … your most Obedient Servant,

Carter Braxton

Document 18   Receipt for 121 Ells of Ticklenberg 10 September 1764[18]

Providence

    Messrs. Nichs Brown & Co   10 Sept 1764

For the Brigg Sally   Bought of Thomas and John Greene

   *Ticklenberg** 121 Ells……………….. @ 17 ½ ….. £8 16s ½d

> [*Ticklenberg was a cheap cloth from Germany often sold in the West Indies to make clothing for slaves or traded in West Africa. An ell was a measure for cloth.]

---

18   Receipt for 121 Ells of Ticklenberg, BFBR 643-5, item 16 (JCB Manuscript ID), Center for Digital Scholarship, Brown University   http://library.brown.edu/cds/catalog/catalog.php?verb=render&colid=17&id=1157641645530916&view=showmods.

ANALYZING THE EVIDENCE

1. Based on the evidence in the Documents in Chapter Three, how were slaves acquired in New England and how was slavery justified legally (see Document 2)?

2. What factors contributed to the Dutch decision to import slaves into New Netherlands?

3. What does Document 4 tell us about the permanence of slave status in New Netherlands and how long slaves had been held in the colony?

4. How does Document 5 illustrate the relationship between "Indian Wars" and the slave trade in early New England

5. How do the court records in Document 6 and 7 provide evidence of close interaction between slave and free populations in colonial New England? What pressures on the enslaved populations are evident in these sources.

6. How do the court records in Document 8 provide evidence of connections between African and Puritan notions of spirituality and witchcraft?

7. While slavery was a fact of life in Puritan New England, there were those who felt it violated Biblical principles. How did Samuel Sewell use Biblical arguments to oppose ownership of slaves.

8. Compare the legal apparatus of slavery you have read about in Chapter Two with the laws on slavery outlined in Document 10. What differences or similarities do you notice?

9. Wills are often good sources for social and economic history. Samuel Arnold's will in Document 13 is a useful took for exploring social history of slavery in eighteenth-century Massachusetts. What does the will tell us about the importance of slavery to agriculture in colonial New England? To answer this question, consider the following intermediate questions:

    a. What was Arnold's listed occupation or status?

    b. How many acres of farmland are listed in Arnold's will?

    c. How many slaves are noted in Arnold's will?

    d. How is Arnold's wife cared for in the terms of the will?

    e. What were the bequests given to each of Arnold's children? What might help explain the differences in their bequests?

10. What does the story of Mark Codman (Documents 14 and 15) tell us about how slave resistance? What other acts of resistance are evidence in the documents in this chapter? What explains the response of Massachusetts authorities to this crime?

11. Analyze Documents 16, 17, and 18, all records of the Nicholas Brown & Company mercantile enterprise. What might historians be able to learn from these documents about the workings of the slave trade?

DOCUMENT BASED QUESTIONS:

1. Using your knowledge of the history of colonial New England and the evidence in the documents provided in this chapter, analyze the degree to which African slaves were integrated into the social, religious, and economic life of Colonial New England.

2. Using the evidence in the documents provided in this chapter, respond to someone who contended that slavery played an insignificant role in the history of the northern colonies.

Afro-European Culture in the Americas: Africans and Colonial Society

CHAPTER 4

The African slave trade, which began in the late 15th century and continued for the next 400 years is one of the most important phenomena in the history of the modern world. In simple numerical terms it represented the largest forced migration in human history. The African slave trade and the establishment of plantation economies throughout the Americas, coupled with the much smaller migration of Europeans to the Americas, which only really began to rival the African diaspora in numerical terms after the 1840s, resulted as well in significant processes of cultural diffusion. Cultural diffusion, or the spread of cultural practices, did not flow in one direction alone. Africans were of course "Europeanized" in this forced encounter. But Europeans were also profoundly "Africanized," often in ways they themselves didn't recognize or completely understand. This process would persist throughout the period of the slave trade creating what I have chosen here to describe as an Afro-European culture in the Americas. This chapter will focus attention first on ways in which Africans began to form African-American communities, beginning almost from their departure from their homelands. But, in this chapter we will also explore ways in which African folk-ways, manners, spirituality, and language began in the colonial period to shape the culture and values of the European settlers who also settled on the continent. Without question this process continues into the present in myriad ways; but, in this chapter we will concentrate on a number of key areas where African culture impacted the European settlers establishing themselves on the coast of the Atlantic and consider ways in which Africans adapted their own cultural traditions to the dictates of that same European society.

Frequently textbooks designed for college-level United States History courses contain a chapter that describes the ways in which the American colonies in British North America "matured" from the decidedly uncertain and often precarious communities that characterized the first century of English settlement in North America. Often the narrative of these studies stresses the ways in which the American settlements developed institutions of self-government, towns and small cities, and become more complex societies as the eighteenth century progressed. Additionally, during this period the textbooks emphasize the ways in which colonial economies grew both increasingly connected to the commercial currents of the Atlantic but also increasingly self-sufficient and economically stable. In some textbooks the impression given is that the American colonies, over the course of the eighteenth-century became more "English," and perhaps more like early modern Europe than had been the frontier settlements established by Puritans in New England or the merchant adventurers along the shores of the Chesapeake. In many ways this was the case. However, with the infusion of large numbers of Africans, a demographic current which was particularly noticeable in the eighteenth century, Africans inexorably and perhaps inevitably also made the American colonies more "African" as well.

Africans imported to the Americas had first, however, to try to maintain their own institutions, identities, and values and to attempt to establish communities despite their enslavement and brutal extraction from their native cultures and homelands. Among the most immediate challenges they had to face was the challenge of establishing linguistic communities. Enslaved Africans came from a wide variety of kingdoms, ethnic and linguistic groups, and regions across Africa. They came from varied religious and political traditions as well. They shared little save their status as slaves and the trauma of enslavement. Nonetheless, as we will see in this chapter, Africans from the outset sought to communicate with one another, to recreate fictional kinship groups in the absence of their own families, and to establish the foundations of community once they arrived in the colonies. They also managed over the course of the colonial period to fashion shared moral and religious values that helped sustain the enslaved and provide opportunities for leadership within the community. Among the populations of Africans captured in Africa and transported to the Americas, there were numerous religious traditions, including large numbers of Muslims from the region of the Sahel in West Africa, Christians from the Kongo region, as well as adherents to a wide variety of traditional animist religious traditions. Religion would prove to be an important unifying feature of developing African American culture. In this chapter, though the evidence is sometimes difficult to find, we will attempt to examine ways in which Africans shaped the emergence of an African-American culture over the course of the colonial period. Additionally, in this chapter the primary sources will illustrate the influence of that emerging African-American culture on the wider contours of colonial society.

While everywhere enslaved Africans and African Americans were present in the colonies they influenced the cultures of the Englishmen and women for whom they labored and with whom they interacted on a daily basis, not everywhere was the impact of the enslaved felt in the same way. Often this was the consequence of the kinds of labor fulfilled by enslaved persons. Slaves who worked as gang laborers on plantations in South Carolina or Virginia often spent much of their days in the company of other slaves with only the presence of a white overseer or driver to remind them that their labor was not their own. By contrast, slaves working alongside their owners on smaller farms, or on the docks of northeastern port cities, or in artisanal workshops of necessity had to assimilate themselves to white work and living spaces. But in either case, Africans were as surely shaping their environments and influencing their white overseers and owners. The timing and intensity of slave importations also contributed to the degree to which Africans and Europeans impacted one another culturally. Prior to 1700, for example, the small numbers of slaves imported into Virginia more rapidly assimilated to the society of their enslavers, adopting the English language, occasionally converting to Christianity, and adapting their dress and manners as best they could to the practices of white Virgnians. However, during the periods of the heaviest importation of slaves into Virginia between 1700 and 1750, Africans lived more often on frontier plantations in the colony's interior among populations of fellow Africans. As a result opportunities for trans-cultural sharing and diffusion of cultural practices diminished and "Africanisms" remained stronger in those areas.

One of the most easily traced areas where African culture influenced the emergence of American culture was in the realm of language. Slaves came from widely scattered parts of West and Central Africa and consequently had little in the way of a shared language. To communicate along the coast of West Africa where slavers plied their trade, on board ship, and then in the Americas, Africans communicated often with one another through what are called *pidgins*. These mixtures of African grammar, syntax, and vocabulary with European languages became the *lingua franca* of trade, and often became the most common way Africans in the Caribbean and in many parts of North America communicated with one another. Among the languages spoken in the colonial United States was *Gullah*, a kind of pidgin spoken most often in the Carolinas and in Georgia. There is debate over the degree to which *Gullah* is (the language still has some speakers) directly derived from African languages, or whether it reflects more strongly a derivation from the West Indies, particularly Barbados. In either case, *Gullah* would remain an important linguistic adaptation of African slaves to their enslavement in the Americas, and would also be one of the conduits through which African or Afro-Caribbean terms would enter American English.

It should not come as a surprise to hear that there are many terms in American English that derive from one of the many African tongues spoken by slaves transported to the Americas. For example, the word banana is an African word. Bananas were not a European fruit. The many varieties of this fruit, itself not native to Africa but to the Indonesian archipelago, had long been a staple across Africa before Europeans arrived along the continent's coast. In other cases, English-language words that were homonyms or near-homonyms (words that sound quite like the English language term) took on new meanings. For example, the word booty, or plunder, took on a more sexualized meaning, think "booty call," as it sounded much like the word *buedi*, a word used in multiple Bantu languages. Chick, with the connotation of an attractive young woman, derived from the Wolof term *jigen*, which meant woman. Occasionally these terms developed from the labor done by slaves. Cowboy and bronco are two words that would seem to have little likelihood of African origin. The Dallas Cowboys after all are America's team, and the Denver Broncos have their own Super Bowl history. But, the first "cowboys" were slaves employed to herd cattle in the Carolina Piedmont region. Just as slaves who served in planters' households were referred to as "houseboys," these cattlemen were referred to using this diminutive. Bronco was an Ibibio term for slaves that worked cattle. And, buckaroo, a reference to cattlemen on horseback, derived from *buckrah*, a pejorative term for white masters who often lorded it over their slaves from high on their own horses. These and the many examples which will follow in the Primary Sources section below will illustrate how thoroughly Americans interact in a language that is profoundly African.

Another area where Africans influenced Europeans living in North America was in the realm of religion and spirituality. Slaveowners were, as we have seen in the previous two chapters, deeply ambivalent about African conversions to Christianity and about the imperative that they concern themselves with the spiritual lives of people that were by law their property. Nonetheless, increasingly during the period, English colonists lived in a world where African spiritual practices and beliefs influenced their own. The continued impact of African spiritual practice can still be seen. It has often been noted by European observers of America that religion has a greater weight in American cultural life and politics than it does in contemporary Europe. Though certainly seventeenth and eighteenth century Europeans had strongly held religious values and deep convictions, Africans present in the towns and villages of New England and the Middle Colonies and in the plantations of the American South also shaped the development of that uniquely American religiosity.

Slaves brought with them a complex religious heritage which slavery never completely effaced. Religion was at the heart of African-American culture, and the development of slaves' Christianity in the 18th century reflected both their African heritage and their proximity to white masters. In the North, slaves more rapidly melded their own faiths with elements of Christianity. There it was more difficult to maintain African traditional practices. On Southern plantations, as slave masters were not eager to see their slaves instructed in Christianity, and as more Africans arrived, slaves could keep in touch with "Mother Africa" more easily. Enslavers then faced a dilemma. As African religion fostered a collective identity and fed the spirit of resistance, it was imperative to replace it with Christian belief. But, slave owners were not anxious to have their human property exposed to religion which would make them more difficult to handle. The dilemma of conversion extended to more practical concerns as well. The church buildings, their seating arrangements, and the sermons of the parson reinforced the importance of the gentry or planter class. Blacks and poor whites often felt unwelcome there. And, the gentry found the very presence of an African audience unsettling, even when they were relegated to the rear pews or balconies of the building. Yet, segregated facilities proved at once difficult to regulate. They also provided few opportunities to publicly display the planter elite's status. Nonetheless, during the eighteenth century missionary efforts were made to slaves in Virginia and the Carolinas. These efforts emphasized the Christian ideals of meekness, humility, obedience and not those of brotherhood of man or the story of the Hebrew flight from oppression. Separation of these features of Christianity, however proved difficult in practice. Slaves could find solace and justification for resistance in scripture where their masters hoped they would learn obedience and the certainty of heavenly reward rather than earthly satisfaction.

In addition, many African religious practices gradually became incorporated in both black and white services. For example, ritual dancing, speaking in tongues, and drumming were features of African religious practice which various sects of Christian believers, particularly in the South, gradually adopted. After 1750, spiritual revival became widespread in Virginia, a revival that had begun some decades earlier in New England. Beginning with the sermons of Jonathan Edwards, revival had spread through the colonies as George Whitefield and other itinerant evangelists spoke before large crowds of listeners, white and black alike. This religious revival has been called the Great Awakening. Historians have often noted the timing of this revival movement as coinciding closely with the period in early American history of the largest importation of African slaves. Whites and blacks across the colonies, thus encountered one another in larger numbers as religious and spiritual beings. Additionally, virtually all eighteenth-century Baptist and Methodist churches established as the revival spread were mixed churches, in which blacks sometimes, though rarely, preached to whites and where people of European descent witnessed together, shouted together, and shared ecstatic religious conversions with Africans and African Americans. The Great Awakening, and Evangelical Christianity itself, thus bears the imprint of African spirituality.

African medical knowledge and folk medicine also influenced European and American medical practices. For instance, Africans deserve credit for introducing "variolation" or the use of a serum from smallpox lesions to vaccinate against smallpox. In 1796 Edward Jenner, an English doctor introduced vaccination in England. But, among the Akan of Ghana, this practice had been commonplace for many generations. Colonial planters had a good deal of respect for Africans' skill and knowledge of herbs, medicines, and poisons. As a practical matter, reliance on African healing arts was a necessity on the plantation. African folk medicines and salves were often employed by slaves and owners alike to cure a wide variety of common ailments and life-threatening diseases. Whites, of course, feared the slaves' expertise in potions and poisons. Laws were passed against conjuring and poisoning, but whites also went to black doctors and magic workers as well.

The imperatives of the plantation also shaped the world of manners and comportment that surrounded slave owners and their children. Enslaved men and women raised planters' children and inculcated in them the most basic values, including expectations of respect for elders, proper addresses to their betters, and other rules of social interaction. Of course, they did not do so unilaterally or without supervision, but it is fair to say that over the course of the history of slavery, African parenting contributed significantly to shaping expressions of the family and social values of Southern whites. The influence of African parenting on white children in the American south persists to the present. As a young boy, I was struck when my friend from Alabama was told "Don't you sass me." Though my parents were not particularly permissive, this was not a phrase I had heard before. The word sass derives from the word, *sasi*, a Gullah term for a "proud one" or "boaster." This is but one of many illustrative examples of the influence on Englishmen and women of African parenting practices.

In countless other ways Africans influenced the development of colonial American culture. One area where early modern European and African values sometimes coincided and at other times clashed was over the meaning of time. A culture's sense of time has a profound influence on all other values. Historians have long been aware of the consequences of the introduction of industrial factory production on pre-modern notions of time. From concrete and functional understandings of time, the factory encouraged a change to more abstract conceptions of time, demarcated into uniformized and comparable units, easily measured in monetary terms. Early modern Europeans and colonial Americans lived in an earlier temporal world where time was tied to its function; there were times to pray, signaled by church bells; there were times to sow and times to reap. Rather than tracing the contours of ones life through easily recognizable age markers—the ages 16, 18, 21, and 65 all have easily identifiable significance—periods in the life cycle were more often associated with familial roles. The work week was not organized according to hours of required labor juxtaposed to weekend or evening leisure time. The work week changed according to the agricultural season in rural districts. Or, in towns and villages, the work week's routines were more varied and depended less on routines of factory life.

Traditional West African cultures shared many of the basic attitudes toward time common to early modern Europeans. But, for slaves, time took on different meanings. Nights, Sundays, and the the occasional holiday were the slaves' time and carefully husbanded. By contrast, daylight hours, work time, belonged to the master. Though masters often incentivized slaves use of work time, whether with the whip or greater rations, for most days there was less a job to do than a day to kill. Indeed, wasting time or making masters wait provided a form of subtle, yet unmistakable resistance. And, as we will see in a later chapter, masters in the nineteenth century cotton boom would, like the factory owners who routinized time and demanded uniformity in their factories, insist on a similarly regularized mastery of time. For masters, birth and aging signified profit and profitability, and were therefore noted carefully. For slaves, these dates that marked the anniversaries of their enslavement were less significant. As a result, slaves had often only a general sense of their birth dates and ages.

Africans also stamped their cultural values on Europeans' spatial sensibility and work lives. Whites worked alongside blacks in colonial America, whether as overseers or owners, or alongside slaves working on the docks or in workshops. The presence of African work rhythms and pace shaped the routines of the plantation and the workshop. Additionally, the disdain with which European elites considered manual labor was doubled when physical labor became associated with the degradation of the enslaved. This association would become particularly problematic in the nineteenth century. But it was already in evidence in the eighteenth century. If the world of work was shaped in part by African and African-American practice, so also were colonial environments. Historians have noticed the similarity between early plantation organization and African village complexes. The "Great House" with its separate out-buildings for toilets, cooking, washing, etc. reflected the African presence as Africans traditionally separated the various domestic functions, in order to keep houses "sweet" and free from unpleasant odors. Construction of homes reflected the influence of Africans in other ways. Roofing materials, and the size and shape of houses often revealed the impact of African building techniques.

In this chapter, readers will be asked to examine a variety of sources that illustrate the strategies of African slaves to reconstruct their own communities on a new footing, in a world that was largely hostile to and dismissive of their presence. In addition, the collection of primary sources that follow also reveal many of the ways that African values penetrated European society contributing to the construction of a new Afro-European society on the shores of the Atlantic Ocean. The "mature" British North America of 1776 was by the conclusion of the colonial period made up of thirteen colonies whose African roots, though unacknowledged, ran deep.

PRIMARY SOURCES

Document 1   Some Gullah terms with possible African Derivations[1]

Gullah Term	African origin, term, and meaning.
gulu (pig)	Kikongo, *gula*, pig or hog.
guba (peanut)	Kimbundu, *nguba*, peanut
gombo (okra)	Tshiluba, *tsingombo*, okra
jambi (a reddish sweet potato)	Vai, *djambi*, sweet potato
juk, juky (disorderly)	Wolof, *jug*, to lead a disorderly life
kush, fried corn bread cake	Hausa, *Kusha*, a thin cake made from peanuts
nana, mother, elderly woman, grandmother	Twi, *nana*, grandparent
tot, to carry	Kikongo, *tota*, to pick up
bukrah, white man	Ibibio, *mbakara*, white man

---

[1]   Adapted from Patricia A. Jones-Jackson, "Gullah: On the Question of Afro-American Language, *Anthropological Linguistics,* 20:9 (Dec. 1978), p. 425-426.

Document 2 Selected English Terms or Phrases with African Origins[2]

English Term or Phrase	African origin, term, and meaning.
to bad-mouth,	Mandingo, *da-jugu* and Hausa, *mugum-baki*, slander, abuse, literally to bad-mouth.
cut-eye or *bad eye*	Mandingo, *njeyugu*, hateful glance
bambi	Bantu, *mubambi*, one who lies down in order to hide.
banana	Wolof, *banana*
banjo	Kimbundu, *mbanza*, four-stringed musical instrument.
bogus, bogue	Hausa, *boko* or *boko-boko*, deceit, fraud
booboo	Bantu, *mbuku*, stupid, blundering act
booty	Bantu, *buedi*, act of emission, sex.
bozo	Bantu, *boza*, knock things over in passing
bronco	Ibibio, used to denote Spanish and African slaves who worked with cattle.
to bug	Mandigo, *baga*, to offend, annoy, harm.
chick	Wolof, *jigen*, woman, pretty young woman
cooter	Kongo, *nkuda*, a box turtle
dig	Wolof, *deg, dega*, understand, appreciate
do one's thing	Mandingo, *ka a fen ke* (literally to do one's thing)
jive	Wolof, *jev*, misleading talk.
ju ju	Bantu, *njiu*, danger, harm or charm against it
to kick the bucket	Krio, *kekerabu*, to die or wither, or Ga, *kekre* (dry, stiff)+*bo* (to become)
massa	Mandingo, *masa*, chief
okay	Mandingo, *o-ke*, Fula, *eeyi kay*, Wolof, *waw kay*, all mean "Yes," "That's it," etc.
poop	Wolof, *pup*, to defecate
zombie	Tshiluba, *Nzambi*, God, and *mujangi*, spirit of the dead.

---

2   Adapted from Joseph E. Holloway, "Africanisms in African American Names in the United States," in *Africanisms in American Culture,* Josehp E. Holloway, ed., (Bloomington, IN: Indiana University Press, 1984), pp. 82-110.

Document 3 Reverand Morgan Godwin, York County Virginia, 1665.[3]

The two last things objected, ... are the pretended barbarousness of their manners, both which for brevity, I shall dispatch together. Their Barbarousness, which I shall treat of first must be discernable either from their Demeanour and Conversation in the World, or else from their behavior and practice in their *Worship* and *Ceremonies* of *Religion*; or from both. Now for Religion; It cannot be denied but that nothing is more barbarous and contrary to Christianity, than their *Polygamy*, their *idolatrous Dances*, and *Revels*; in which they usually spend the Sunday after the necessity of labour for their Provisions (for the Planting of which, that Day alone is allotted to them) has been complied with. But as to these, the blame doth lie wholly upon such, who pretending themselves Christians, do suffer and even compel them to those Actions; part whereof are against their Wills, and where even a Check or Frown, would refrain them from the rest.

And here, that I may not be thought to rashly impute Idolotry to their Dances, my conjecture is raised upon this ground (besides their being *Gentiles*) for that they use their Dances as a means to procure Rain; Some of them having been known to beg this liberty upon the Week days in order thereunto. Now it is certain, that the *Gentiles* anciently did esteem and practice *Dancing*, as a part of *Divine Worship*: And no less also did the *Jews*; as may be proved from *Exod. 32.19* and from *David's Dancing before the Ark.* 2 Samuel 6. Add to this their placing confidence in certain Figures and ugly Representations, of none knows what besides themselves (which very decently for want of more *Magnificent Temples,* they usually enshrine in some stately *Earthen Potsherds*). The Fugitives and Runaways believing these *Deities* able to protect them in their Flight, and from Discovery (like as the *Egyptians* worshiping *Baal Zephon* was to detect them): Their companions and fellow Slaves also, that remain'd at Home, having been overheard upon the seizure of these *Puppets*, in a search after the other, instantly to give assurance that there was no possibility of their further concealment. And this doubtless is a manifest token of their *Impiety* in this kind, and no less of their *Barberity*. But as Christianity would soon (*if duly applied*) cure this evil; so I see not how it should prove them to be Brutes, more than the rest of the World, formerly, and even to this Day, more or less, addicted to the same vanity and deception of *false Worship*.

Document 4 William P. Bosman, "Describing the several Religions of the Negroes"[in West Africa], 1705.[4]

My last [letter] was very long; and if I treat the Subject largely, this will not be much shorter; For the Religion of the *Negroes,* of which I design to speak, will afford Matter enough for a Book alone, by reason of the numerous and different sorts of it: For there is no Village or Town, nay, I had almost said, no private Family which doth not differ from another on this Head; But not thinking it worth while to recount all the various Opinions, I shall therefore pass them over, and only speak of their publick Religion and Worship; in which they a'most all agree.

A'most all the Coast *Negroes* believe in one true God, to whom they attribute the Creation of the World and all things in it, though in a crude indigested Manner, they not being able to form

---

[3] Morgan Godwin, *The Negro's and Indian's Advocate, suing for their Admission into the Church, or A Persuasive to the Instructing and Baptizing the Negro's and Indians in our Plantations* (London: 1680), pp. 33-34.

[4] William P. Bosman, *A New and Accurate Description of the Coast of Guinea Divided into the Gold, the Slave, and the Ivory Coasts*, (London: Ballantyne and Co., 1707)

a just idea of a Deity. ... They tell us, that in the beginning God created black as well as White Men; thereby not only hinting but endeavouring to prove that their race was as soon in the World as ours; and to bestow a yet greater Honour on themselves, they tell us that god having created these two sorts of Men, offered two sorts of Gifts, *viz.* Gold, and Knowledge or Arts of Reading and Writing, giving the blacks the first Election, who chose Gold, and left the Knowledge of Letters to the White. God granted their Request, but being incensed at their Avarice, resolved that the Whites should for ever be their Masters and they obliged to wait on them as their Slaves. Others again affirm that Man at his first Creation was not shaped as at present; but that those parts which serve for the distinction of Sexes in Men and Women, were placed more in view for the convenience of Propagation.... I have found very few *Negroes* of this sentiment; but having asked those who are its Assertors, when the shape of Man was alter'd to its present State: they replied that God had done it out of respect to Modesty when the World became so well Peopled that the present Shape was sufficient to preserve the Race of Mankind. ...

I promised just now to explain the Word *fetiche*, which is used in various Senses. *Fetiche* or *Bossum* in the Negro language, derives its self from their False God.... Are they enclined to make Offerings to their Idols or desire to be informed of something by them? They cry out, "Let us make *Fetiche*; by which they express as much, as let us perform our Religious Worship, and see or hear what our God saith. In like manner, if they are injured by another they make *Fetiche* to destroy him in the following manner: they cause some Victuals and Drink to be Exorcised by their *Feticheer* or Priest, and scatter it in some place which their Enemy is accustomed to pass; firmly believing, that he who comes to touch this conjured Stuff shall certainly dye soon after. ... If they are robbed they make use of the same means for the discovery and condign Punishment of the Thief.... Is any obligation to be confirmed, their Phrase is, *let us as a farther Confirmation make Fetiche's*. When they drink the *Oath-Draught*, 'tis usually accompanied with an Imprecation, *that the Fetiche* may kill them if they do not perform the Contents of their Obligation.... Each Priest or *Feticheer* hath his peculiar Idol, prepared and adjusted in a particular and different manner....The second way of consulting their Idols, is by a sort of wild Nuts; which they pretend to take up by guess and let fall again: after which they tell them, and form their Predictions from the numbers falling even or odd.

If it was possible to convert the *Negroes* to the Christian Religion, the *Roman-Catholicks* would succeed beter than we should, because they already agree in several particulars, especially in their ridiculous Ceremonies; for do the *Romanists* abstain one or two Days weekly from Flesh; these have also their Days when they forbear Wine; which considering they are very great lovers of it, is somewhat severe. The *Romanists* have their allotted times for eating peculiar sorts of Food, or perhaps wholly abstaining from it, in which the *Negroes* out-do them....

How their Gods are represented to them, or what Idea they form of them, I never yet could learn, because indeed they do not know themselves: What we are able to observe is, that they have a great number of False Gods; that each Man, or at least each House-keeper, hath one; which they are perswaded narrowly inspects their Course of Life, and rewards Good, and Punished Wicked Men; but their Rewards consist in the Multiplicity of Wives and Slaves, and their Punishments in the want of them; though the most terrible Punishment they can imagine is Death; of which they are terribly afraid....

Their Notions of a Future State are different; most of them believe that immediately after Death of any Person he goes to another World, where he lives in the same Character as here, and makes use of all the Offerings of his Friends and Relations made here after his Death: But they have no Idea of future Rewards or Punishments for the good or ill Actions of their past Life; … Others are persuaded that after Death, they are transported to the Land of the Blanks or Whites and changed into white Men….

Since we are got on this Subject, I must not forget to inform you that the *Negroes* believe that there is a Devil, and that he frequently does them a great deal of Mischief: But what Authors write, that they pray and make Offerings to him, is utterly false….

They steadfastly believe the Apparition of Spirits and Ghosts, and that they frequently disturb and terrify some People: So that when any, but more especially any considerable Person, dies, they perplex one another with horrid Fears, proceeding from an Opinion that he appears for several Nights successively near his late Dwelling.

… Excepting what the *Negroes* have learn'd of the *Europeans,* they have no Notion of the divisions of the Year into Months and Weeks; but reckon their time by the shining of the Moon; whence they likewise collect when it is proper to sow; But that they have long been acquainted with the Division of Months into Weeks and Days seems very probable to me, by reason each Day of the Week has its proper Name in their Language. Their *Sabbath* falls on our *Tuesday,* but in *Ante,* like that of the *Mahometans,* on *Friday;* and differs from other Days no otherwise, than no Person is then permited to Fish: but all other works are allowed without the least interruption as freely as on other Days.

The Inland *Negroes* divide time in a very strange manner, into lucky and unlucky… The Inhabitants of one Country differ very much from those of another in this particular: This Nation accounting their happy Days at one time, and that fixing them at another…

Document 5   Somerset County, Maryland Judicial Decision, 1707[5]

Great complaints. . . [being] made. . . that diverse Negro slaves presume to ride horses on Sunday from their Masters' Plantations to those of others; the said horses sometimes belonging to themselves but generally to their Masters and others and that the said Negro slaves carry in their hands unlawful clubs, Bludgeons or Tom of Hawks and often gott Drunke on the Lord's Day beating their Negro Drums by which they call considerable numbers of Negros together in some certain places which if not timely Prevented may lead to a breach of the peace and be of evil consequence....

therefore it is hereby ordered that no Negros whatsoever within this Province presume hereafter without a lawful command therefore to ride on horseback from one plantation to another or to meeting of Negros in ye woods or beat upon any Drums whatsoever or otherwise bear or walk with any such unlawful Clubbs, Bludgeons or Tom of Hawks on pain of being whipt forty lashes for every such offense.......

---

[5]   Maryland Historical Archives (MdHr), 9169 Somerset County Judicials, 1707-1711, Second Tuesday of August, 1707, April 22 1/48/2/42 CR6396-1 (Unpublished manuscript in the Maryland State Historical Society, Annapolis, Maryland) cited in William H. Green, "'Tumultuous meetings' and the Fury of Freedom: Rethinking African American Religion," unpublished Ph.D. Dissertation, Syracuse University, 2004., p. 80-81.

Document 6   Excerpt, Letter of Cotton Mather, Puritan Minister, 12 July 1716.[6]

Therefore, I do assure you, that many months before I mett with any Intimations of treating ye *Small-Pox*, with ye Method of Inoculation, anywhere in *Europe*, I had from a Servant of my own, an Account of its being practiced in *Africa*. Enquiring of my Negro-man *Onesimus*, who is a pretty Intelligent Fellow, Whether he ever had ye *Small-Pox*; he answered, both, *Yes*, and, *No*; and then told me, that he had undergone an Operation, which had given him something of *ye Small-Pox*; & would forever preserve him from it; adding, That it was often used among ye *Goromantese*, & whoever had ye Courage to use it, was forever free from ye fear of the Contagion; He described ye Operation to me, and shew'd me in his Arm ye Scar, which it had left upon him, and his Description of it, made it the same, that afterwards I found related unto you by your *Timonius*.

Document 7   Excerpt, Letter of Cotton Mather, 20 November 1723.

There is at this Time a considerable Number of *Africans* in this Town, who can have no Conspiracy or Combination to cheat us. No body has instructed them to tell their Story. … For that these all agree in *one Story*. 'That abundance of poor Negro's die of the Small Pox, till they learn this Way; that People take the Juice of the *Small Pox*, and *Cut the Skin*, and put in a drop; then by'nd by a little *Sick*, then few *Small Pox*; and no body dye of it: no body have *Small Pox* any more.

Here we have clear Evidence that in *Africa*, where the Poor Creatures dye of the *Small Pox* in the common way like Rotten Sheep, a Merciful GOD has taught them a *wonderful Preservative*. It is a *Common Practice*, and is attended with *Success*. I have as full Evidence of this, as I have that there are *Lions* in *Africa*. And I don't know why 'tis more unlawful to learn of *Africans*, how to help against the *Poison* of the *Small Pox*, than it is to learn of our *Indians*, how to help against the *Poison* of a *Rattle-Snake*.

Document 8   George Whitefield, *Journal* entry, 11 May 1740.[7]

Sunday, May 11. Preached to about 15,000 people in the Morning, and observed a great Melting to follow the Word. Went twice to Church, and heard myself tasked by the Commissary, who preached from these Word: *I bear them Record, they have a Zeal of GOD, but not according to Knowledge.* I could have wished he considered the next Words: *For they being ignorant of GOD's Righteousness, and going about to establish their own Righteousness, have not submitted themselves unto the Righteousness of GOD.* Had he considered these Words, I might justly have said, Speaketh Mr. Commissary of this false Zeal in Reference to himself, or of some other Man? In the afternoon, the Tenth of the *Romans*, out of which his Text was taken, was appointed for the Lesson; and had he not been more perverse than *Balaam*, it must have restrained the Madness of this false Prophet. But he exclaimed loudly against me in the Pulpit, and, as I soon found, obliged many of his Hearers to do what they were before inclined to, *viz.* resolve to leave him entirely. I bear him Record, that Experience will soon convince him, that whatever mine be, his own Zeal is by no means according

---

[6] George L. Kittredge, "Some Lost Works of Cotton Mather," in the *Proceedings of the Massachusetts Historical Society*, 45 (January 1912), p. 422.

[7] *A Continuation of the Reverend Mr. Whitefield's Journal afer his Arrival at Georgia to a Few Days after his Second Return thither from Philadelphia*, (London: W. Strahan, 1741), pp. 38-40.

to Knowledge. After he had done, I preached my Farewell Sermon to I believe very nearly 20,000 Hearers.—As the Commissary's Sermon was chiefly full only of personal Reflections, I thought it not proper to render Railing for Railing…. One passage out of the second Lesson for the Morning, much affected me. *And the Lord had Compassion on the Multitude, because they were scattered, as Sheep having no Shepherd.* I then reminded them of our Lord's Command, *Pray ye therefore the LORD of the Harvest, that he may send out Labourers into his Harvest: For tho' the Harvest is so great, the Labourers are very few.* The poor People were much concerned at my bidding them Farewell. And after I had taken my Leave, oh how many came to my Lodgings, soring most of all that they were likely to see my Face no more for a long Season.—I believe 50 Negroes came to give me Thanks under God, for what had been done for their Souls. Oh how heartily did those poor Creatures throw in their Mites for my poor Orphans!—Some of them have been effectually wrought upon, and in an uncommon Manner. Many of them have now begun to learn to read.—And one that was free, said she would give me her two Children, whenever I settle my School.—I belive Masters and Mistresses will shortly see, that Christianity will not make their Negroes worse Slaves.—I intended, had Time permitted, to have settled a Society for Negroe Men and Negroe Women. But that must be deferred till it shall please GOD to bring me to *Philadelphia* again. I have been drawn out in Prayer for them, and have seen them exceedingly wrought upon under the Word preached.—I cannot well express how many others of all Sorts came to give me a last Farewell.

Document 9 Letter of Charles Brockwell to the Secretary of the Society for the Propagation of the Gospel, 18 February 1741.[8]

Reverend Sir,

It is impossible to relate the convulsions into which the whole Country is thrown by a set of Enthusiasts who stroll about haranguing the admiring Vulgar in *extempore* nonsense, nor is confined to these only, for Men, Women, Children, Servants, & Nigros are now becoming (as they phrase it) Exhorters. Their behavior is indeed shocking, as uncommon their groans, cries, screams, & agonies must affect the Spectators were they never so obdurate & draw tears even from the most resolute, whilst the ridiculous & frantic gestures of others cannot but excite both laughter & contempt, some leaping, some laughing, some singing, some clapping one another upon the back, &c. The tragic scene is performed by such as are entering into the pangs of the New Birth; the comic by those who are got through and those are so truly enthusiastic, ye they tell you they saw ye Joys of Heaven, can describe its situation, inhabitants, employments, & have seen their names entered into the Book of Life & can point out the writer, character & pen. And like the Papists support their fraud by recommending every dream as a Divine Vision & every idle untruth as a revelation to the admiring multitude. Their works may justly be called ye works of darkness as acted in the Night & often continued to the noon of ye next day & ye sleep of children depriv'd of their natural rest is called a trance, & their uncouth dreams (occasion'd from the awfulness of the place, the number of Lights, the variety of action among the People, some praying, some exhorting, some swooning, &c.) are deemed no less than heavenly discoveries. In Connecticut, the next Government, 'tis said many have laid their Bibles asicde; and some have

---

[8]   Charles Brockwell to the Secretary of the Society for the Propagation of the Gospel, Salem, Massachusetts, February 18, 1742. In William S. Perry, ed. *Historical Collections Relating to the American Colonial Church,* Volume III, (Hartford, Connecticut: 1873), pp. 453-454.

burnt them, as useless to those who are so plenteously fill'd with the Spirit, as to cry out Enough Lord! In short Sir, such confusion, disorder, & irregularity Eye never beheld. The illusion of the French Prophets Anno 1707, was nothing to this, & unless as to that, some unexpected accident put a period to this, I know not but this year for Enghusiasm may be as memorable as was 1692 for witchcraft for the converted cry out upon the unregenerated, as the afflicted did then upon the poor innocent wretches ye unjustly suffered. ….

Rev'd Sir,

Your most obliged Humble Servant,

Charles Brockwell.

Document 10 Charles Chauncy, *Seasonable Thoughts on the State of Religion in New England*, 1743.[9]

…Another Thing that very much tends, as I apprehend, to do Hurt to the Interest of Religion, is the Rise of so many *Exhorters*. A Stranger to this Land, and the present Appearance in it, may be at a Loss to know, who are meant by *these Exhorters*: And I'm really asham'd to say, that the Persons pointed out by them, are *Men of all Occupations*, who are vain enough to think themselves fit to be *Teachers* of others, Men who, though they have *no Learning*, and but *small Capacities*, yet imagine they are able, and without Study too, to speak to the *spiritual Profit* of such as are willing to hear them: Nay, there are among these Exhorters, *Babes* in *Age*, as well as Understanding. They are *chiefly* indeed *young Persons*, sometimes *Lads*, or rather *Boys*: Nay *Women* and *Girls*; yet, *Negroes*, have taken upon them to do the Business of *Preachers*. Nor has this been *accidental* only, or in a *single Place*, or at a *private House;* but there is scarce a Town in *all the Provinces*, where this Appearance has been, but there have been also *these Exhorters*, in smaller or greater Numbers: Neither have they contented themselves to speak in the *more private Meetings* of Christians, but have held forth in *the publick Congregations.*

Document 11 *Letters from the Reverend Samuel Davies, shewing the State of Religion in Virginia, particularly among the Negroes*, 1757.[10]

… As far as I can recollect, I gave you a pretty full account, in a former letter, of the numerous *African Slaves* in this colony; and now I only design to add a few particulars which are new; or which did not then occur to my mind.

When the books arrived, I gave public notice of it, after Sermon, at the next opportunity. I desired such *Negroes* as could read, and also such *white* People as would make a *good use* of them, and were so *poor*, that they could not buy such books, to come to me at my house, and I should distribute them among them. On this occasion, I also enlarged upon a new topic of conviction both to the *Slaves* themselves, and their *Masters*.

---

[9] Charles Chauncy, *Seasonable Thoughts on the State of Religion in New England*, (Boston: Rogers and Fowle, 1743), p.226.

[10] Samuel Davies, *Letters from the Reverend Samuel Davies shewing The State of Religion in Virginia, particularly among the Negroes.* (London: R. Pardon, 1757), pp. 16-17, 12.

"Since persons at so great a distance, who had no connexion with them, wer so generously concerned to Christianize the poor *Negroes*, and had been at so much pains and expence for that end; then, how much more concerned, how much more zealous and industrious should their *Masters* be, to whom the care of their souls, as well as their bodies, is committed, and who enjoy the advantage of their laborious service?—And how much more ought the *poor Negroes* to be concerned for themselves? And how much more aggravated would be their guilt and ruin, if they persisted in their obstinate infidelity and wickedness, after so much pains had been taken with them for their conversion?"

This as I found afterwards, proved a very popular topic of conviction, and made some impressions upon the minds of not a few.

For some time after this, the *poor Slaves*, whenever they could get an hour's leisure from their masters, would hurry away to my house; and received the Charity with all the genuine indications of passionate gratitude, which unpolished nature could give; and which affectation and grimace would mimic in vain. The books were all *very acceptable;* but none more so than the *Psalms* and *Hymns*, which enabled them to gratify their peculiar taste for *Psalmody*. Sundry of them have lodged all night in my kitchen; and, sometimes, when I have awaked about two or three-o'clock in the morning, a torrent of sacred harmony poured into my chamber, and carried my mind away to Heaven. In this seraphic exercise, some of them spend almost the whole night. I wish Sir, you and their other Benefactors could hear one of these sacred concerts: I am persuaded it would please and surprise you….

… That the Books themselves are valuable—that they are the system of Psalmody the Dissenters use in these parts—that the *Negroes* above all of the human species that ever I knew, have an ear for Music, and a kind of extatic delight in Psalmody; and there are no books they learn so soon, or take so much pleasure in, as those used in that heavenly part of divine Worship…

The good *effects* of this pious Charity are already apparent. It convinces the *Heathen* that however vicious, and careless about the Religion they profess, the generality of the white People are; yet, there are some who really look upon it as a matter of the utmost importance, and universal concern… It has excited some of their *Masters* to emulation; and they are ashamed that *Strangers*, on the other side of the *Atlantic*, should be at the pains to teach their domestics Christianity, and they should be quite negligent *themselves*.

Document 12 Letter, Jonathan Boucher to Reverend John Ames, 7 August 1759.[11]

Port Royal, Rappahanock River

Virginia, Aug't the 7th, 1759

…The Country here, to do it justice, is indeed most invitingly delightful. Plenty & Abundance are nowhere wanting; and this ye Inhabitants seem to know & therefore (differ't from some of you at Home) w'th Satisfaction & Pleasure Enjoy them. But then (w't a Pity!) their Manners &

---

11 "Letter from Jonathan Boucher to John Ames," *Maryland Historical Magazine,* 7:1 (March 1912), pp. 2-3.

Conversation are almost in every Thing ye very opposite to my Taste. Instead of manly instructive Discourse, subjects of Gaiety & Levity are always started and always attended to. … This may be said for them, w'e is no little Character, They are ye most hospitable generous People I ever saw: They are not Easy till you give them an Opportunity to shew you a kindness, And really they have ye Art of Enjoying Life, I think, in a Manner to be Envied. They live well and dress well, all without any Labour & almost with't any Concern of their own. So that it may truly enough be said of many of Them, *They toil not, neither do they spin, yet Solomon in all his Glory was not array'd like one of These.* I assure you Mrs. James, the common Planter's Daughters here go every Day in finer Cloaths than I have seen content you for a Summer's Sunday. You thought (homely Creatures as you are) my Sattin Wastecoat was a fine best, Lord help You, I'm noth'g amongst ye Lace & Lac'd fellows that are here….

… I must however be something particular about y't little Fellow, whom I cannot but think of. How does He thrive, can He walk or speak, when did He begin, Can you make Him understand who it is sends Compts to Him? Does Mary pett Him, or is She herself married & going to get One of Her Own? Dilattory as She is I must own I believe she'll now beat Me; for I expect to be obliged to stay till I come Home ag'n, as I cannot be reconcil'd to having my Bairns nursed by a Negro Wench. Seriously, that is a monstrous Fault I find with ye people here, & surely it is the source of many Disadvantages to their Children.

Document 13 "Sale of slaves," *Georgia Gazette*, 14 February 1765.[12]

George Baillie and Co. have just imported in the snow Leghorn Galley, from the West-Indies, a PARCEL of PRIME GRAIN COAST SLAVES. Barreled pork or rice will be taken in payment.

Document 14 "To be Sold in Savannah, Georgia," *Georgia Gazette*, May 23, 1770.[13]

TO BE SOLD

IN SAVANNAH

On Thursday the 31st Instant,

A C A R G O

Consisting of

Three Hundred and Forty Healthy

N E W N E G R O E S,

CHIEFLY MEN,

Just arrived in the Ship *Sally*, Capt. George Evans, after a short Passage

from the Rice Coast of Africa.

---

[12] "Advertisement," *Georgia Gazette*, (Savannah, GA), 14 February 1765, p. 3.
[13] "Advertisement, *Georgia Gazette*, (Savannah, GA), 23 May 1770, p. 2.

John Graham, Inglis, & Hall.

N.B. The sale will begin at 11 o'clock in the Forenoon, and no Slaves sold or bargained for 'till the Gun is fired.

Document 15 Yoruba Two Room House and Plan[14]

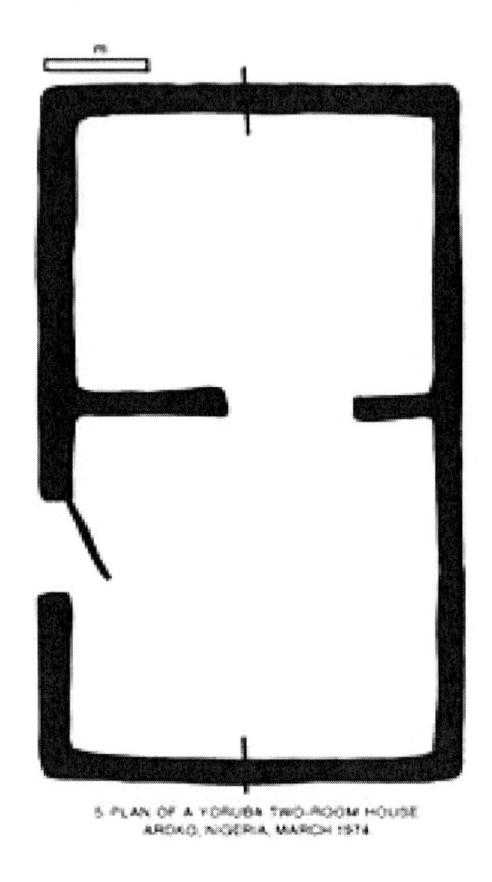

5. PLAN OF A YORUBA TWO-ROOM HOUSE
AROKO, NIGERIA, MARCH 1974

Document 16 Plan of a Shotgun House, Terrebone Parish, Louisiana.[15]

---

14   John Michael Vlach, "The Shotgun House: An African Architectural Legacy: Part II," *Pioneer America*, 8:2 (1976), p. 66.

15   John Michael Vlach, "The Shotgun House: An African Architectural Legacy: Part I," *Pioneer America*, 8:1 (1976), p. 48.

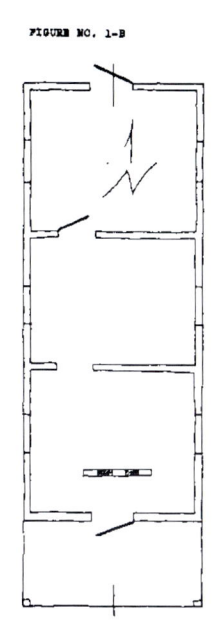

FIGURE 1. RURAL SHOTGUN HOUSES. A. Frame shotgun near Fairview, Chicot County, Arkansas. B. Plan of a shotgun south of Schriever, Terrebone Parish, Louisiana. C. Plan of a shotgun south of Theriot, Terrebonne Parish, Louisiana. D. Plan of a shotgun north of Theriot, Terrebonne Parish, Louisiana. (All of these illustrations are derived from personal fieldwork done in August 1973).

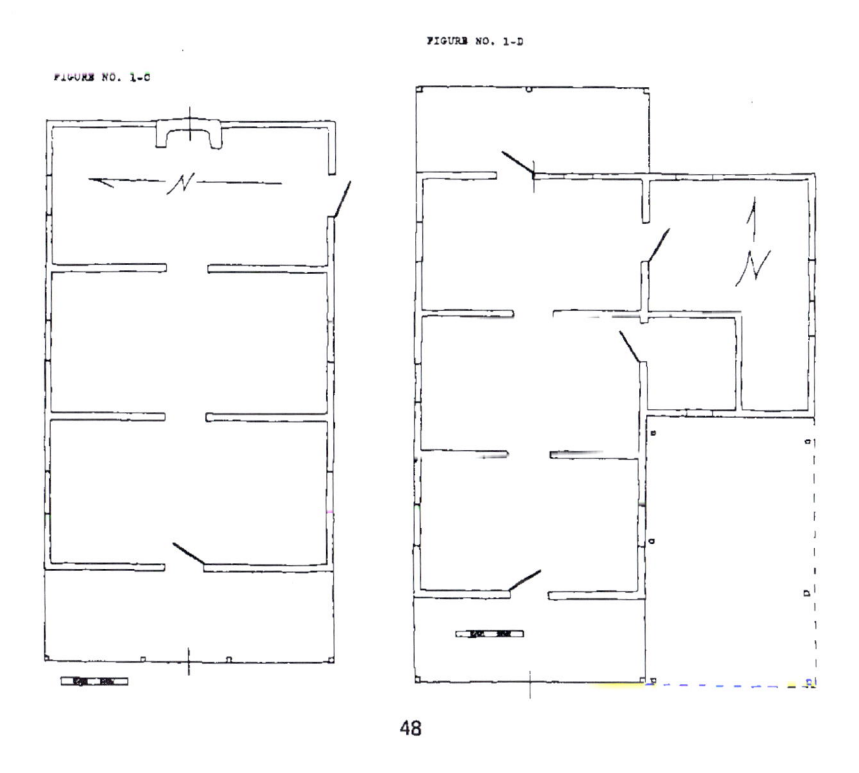

Document 17   Edward Long, *A History of Jamaica*, 1774[16]

They supply their ignorance of letters by a kind of technical memory. Few of them can ascertain their own age, or that of their children; but, when questioned about any event that has happened

---

16   Howard Long, *The History of Jamaica*, Volume II, (London: T. Lowndes, 1774), pp. 426-427.

in the course of their lives, they recur to a storm, a particularly dry or wet weason, and the like, and reckon by the number of Christmases they recollect since those periods. ... They have no computation for the fractional parts of a year; and consequently can never fix any fact or event nearer than about a twelvemonth before or after the time when it occurred. ... The language of the Creoles is bad English, larded with Guiney dialect, owing to their adopting the African words, in order to make themselves understood by the imported slaves; which they find much easier than teaching these strangers to learn English. ... In their conversation, they confound all the moods, tenses, cases, and conjugations, without mercy: for example, *I surprise* (for, I am surprised); *me glad for see you* (for I am glad to see you); *how you do* (for how do ye do?) ... This sort of gibberish likewise infects many of the white ... who learn it from their nurses in infancy, and meet with much difficulty, as they advance in years, to shake it entirely off, and express themselves with correctness.

Many of the plantation blacks call their children by the African name for the day of the week on which they are born: and these names are of two genders, male and female; as for instance:

Male.	Female.	Day.
Cudjoe,	Juba,	Monday.
Cubbenah,	Beneba,	Tuesday.
Quaco,	Cuba	Wednesday.
Cuffee,	Phibba,	Friday.
Quamin,	Mimba,	Saturday.
Quashee,	Quasheba,	Sunday.

Some good persons have expressed their wishes, that the plantation Negroes might be all converted to the Christian faith. The planters would be the last to oppose such a scheme, if it were thought practicable; well knowing, that their becoming true Christians would work no change of property, and might possibly amend their manners. But few, if any, of the African natives will listen to any proposition tending to deprive them of their favourite superstitions and sensual delights.

Document 18 J.F.D. Smyth, *A Tour in the United States of America*, 1784.

It is late at night before he returns to his second scanty meal, and even the time taken up at it, encroaches upon his hours of sleep, which, altogether do never exceed eight in number, for eating and repose.

But instead of retiring to rest, as might naturally be concluded he would be glad to do, he generally sets out from home, and walks six or seven miles in the night, be the weather ever so sultry, to a negroe dance, in which he performs with astonishing agility, and the most vigorous exertions, keeping time and cadence, most exactly, with the music of a banjo (a large hollow instrument with three strings), and a quaqua (somewhat resembling a drum) until he exhausts himself, and scarcely has time, or strength, to return home before the hour he is called forth to toil next morning.

When he sleeps, his comforts are equally miserable and limited; for he lies on a bench, or on the ground, with only an old scanty single blanket, and not always even that, to serve both for his bed and his covering. Nor his his cloathing less niggardly and wretched, being nothing but a shirt and trousers, made of coarse thin hard hempen stuff in the summer, with the addition of a sordid woolen jacket, breeches, and shoes, in the winter.

The female slaves fare, labour, and repose, just in the same manner; even when they breed, which is generally every two or three years, they seldom lose more than a week's work thereby, either in the delivery, or suckling the child.

In submission to injury and insults, they are likewise obliged to be entirely passive, nor dare any of them resist, or even defend himself against the whites, if they should attack him without the smallest provocation; for the law directs a negroe's arem to be struck off, who raises it against a white person, should it be only in his own defence, against the most wanton and wicked barbarity and outrage.

Document 19 "Pinkster," *The Spectator*, (New York, New York), 2 July 1803[17]

Pinkster

The convivial mirth which again enlivens every lane and alley of our city, as well as the verdant scenery which begins to display itself from our barren and dusty hills, notifies me of the return of the vernal holidays, and reminds me of my promise to give you some account of them.

The present anniversary is called, in the Dutch language, Pinkster, which corresponds to the Episcopal Whitsunday, and is in commemoration of the Day of Pentecost. The Monday after Pinkster, as are the other holidays, is religiously observed by the serious part of the Dutch congregation....

The public sports peculiar to the Pinkster holydays, commence on the Monday succeeding Pinkster Sabbath. The preceding week however is (if I may so call it) a time of preparations during which, the negroes patrol the streets in the evening more than usual, and begin to practice a little upon the Guinea drum.* This reminds the citizens of the approaching anniversary, wakes into anxious expectation juvenile curiosity, and kindles the latent spark of love for his native country and native dance in the bosom of the African. In the mean time, preparations are going forward on the hill, which the ensuing week, is to become the *theatre of action.*

The place of incampment is along the great western road,, on each side of which arbours of different sizes and figures are erected. These arbours for the most part are constructed with the shrub that grows upon the adjoining plain.... These arbours are divided into different apartments, filled with seats, and stored with fruit, cakes, cheeses, beer and liquors of various kinds. In the centre of this villa, and in front of the royal arbour, a sort of Ampitheatre is laid out, where the Guinea dance is to be performed.

All things being now in readiness, on Monday morning, the blacks and a certain class of whites, together with children of all countries and colours, begin to assemble on *Pinkster-Hill*, collected from every part of the city and from the adjacent country for many miles around, forming

---

17   "Pinkster," *The Spectator*, (New York, New York), 2 July 1803, p. 1.

on the whole a motley group of thousands, and presenting to the eye of the moral observer, a kind of chaos of sin and folly, of misery and fun.

An old Guinea Negro, who is called *King Charles,* is master of ceremonies, whose authority is absolute, and whose will is law during the whole of the Pinkster holidays.

On Monday, between the hours of ten and twelve o'clock, his majesty after having passed through the principal streets in the city, is conducted in great style to the *Hill* already swarming with a multifarious crowd of gaping spectators. ... At length he reaches his encampment, and after the ceremonies in his honor, he proceeds to collect his revenue. This consists in a levy of one shilling upon every black man's tent, and two upon *every* tent occupied by a white man. ...

The revenue being collected, sports of various kinds commence…

The most singular of these sports, and the only one which I shall particularly notice, is what the Negroes call *Toto,* or the Guinea dance. I have already observed, that in the centre of the villa there was a kind of Amphitheatre allotted for that purpose. On the one side of which is the royal tent, fronting the dancing ground, where the parties perform, and around which the spectators are assembled. Just at the entrance of this tent sits their chief musician… malling with both hands upon the hollow sounding Guinea drum….

In the mean time the dance in the approved African style, and free from the formalities and reserves with which the squeamish modesty of civilized life has invested the gyration of the ballroom, goes forward, in which two or more of the different sexes engage. As there is no regular air in the music, so neither are there any regular movements in this dance. Indeed the whole consists in placing the body in the most disgusting attitudes, and performing, without reserve, the most lewd and indecent gesticulations; at the crisis of which the parties meet and embrace in a kind of amorous Indian hug, terminating in a sort of masquerade capture, which must cover even a harlot with blushes to describe.

… When these days of fun are ended, King Charles, with his attendants, descend from the hill, patrol the principal streets, calling at one door after another, and demanding tribute; which demand he enforces by such a horrid noise, and frightful grimaces, that you are glad to bestow something to get rid of him, especially if you have a delicate wife, or timid children.

*The *Guinea Drum,* as it is called, is a log about four feet in length, and twelve or fourteen feet in diameter, burnt out at one end like a deep… mortar, and covered with a sheep-skin. On this one thumps with his fists a kind of barbarous ill composed, or uncomposed air, which is accompanied with a hoggish sort of grunting, a bawling, and mumbling which on any other occasion than Pinkster, would disgrace a savage.

Document 20 "Slave Chapels and Slave Worship," in Frederick Law Olmstead, *A Journey in the Seaboard Slave States*, 1856.[18]

On most of the large rice plantations which I have seen in this vicinity, there is a small chapel, which the negroes call their prayer-house. The owner of these told me that, having furnished the prayer-house with seats having a back-rail, his negroes petitioned him to remove it, because it

---

18 Frederick Law Olmsted, *A Journey in the Seaboard Slave States,* (New York: Dix & Edwards, 1856), p. 449-450.

did not leave them *room enough to pray*. It was explained to me that it is their custom, in social worship, to work themselves up to a great pitch of excitement, in which they yell and cry aloud, and finally, shriek and leap up, clapping their hands and dancing, as it is done at heathen festivals. The back-rail they found to seriously impede this exercise.

Mr. X. told me that he had endeavoured, with but little success, to prevent this shouting and jumping of the negroes at their meetings on his plantation, from a conviction that there was not the slightest element of religious sentiment in it. He considered to be engaged in more as an exciting amusement than from any really religious impulse. In the town churches, except, perhaps those managed and conducted almost exclusively by negroes, the slaves are said to commonly engage in religious exercises in a sober and decorous manner; yet, a member of a Presbyterian church in a Southern city told me, that he had seen the negroes, in his own house of worship, durin "a season of revival," leap from their seats, throw their arms wildly in the air, shout vehemently and unintelligibly, cry, groan, rend their clothes, and fall into cataleptic trances.

ANALYZING THE EVIDENCE

1. What features of the words borrowed from African languages do you observe from the lists of Gullah and English terms with African origins? (Documents 1 and 2) Do you have any theories that might explain why these words made the transition from Africa to the Americas?

2. What features of African and African American religious practice are evident in Documents 3, 4, and 5? How did Europeans perceive these practices?

3. What African medical knowledge does Cotton Mather identify in Documents 6 and 7?

4. Why did the revivalism of the Great Awakening appeal to enslaved Africans in the American colonies? What evidence in these documents suggests that African Americans helped shape the spirituality of the revivalists? How did critics of the Great Awakening characterize African Americans' roles in the movement? (Documents 8-12)

5. How did slave owners respond to efforts to convert their slaves to Christianity? Why? How did evangelical missionaries attempt to assuage their fears?

6. What was Jonathan Boucher's perception of Virginians and of their relationship with their slaves? (Document 12)

7. How do document 13 and 14 support the view that colonial slave traders marketed the skills of African populations to colonial buyers?

8. What might explain the similarities in floor plans in documents 15 and 16.

9. How did African Americans employ their leisure time according to these documents? (See Documents 5, 11, 18, and 19)

10. What does the "Pinkster" revelry suggest about the mixture of Dutch, English, and African cultures in New York? (Document 19)

11. How does Frederick Law Olmsted's description of a church service in the 1850s reveal a continuity in African-American religious practice from the 1700s to the mid-nineteenth century?

Document Based Question

1. Using the documents provided and your knowledge of American colonial history, analyze the extent to which African culture contributed to the shaping of colonial American society.

"Be not then, ye Negroes, tempted." Slavery and the American Revolution

CHAPTER 5

"We hold these truths self-evident," the Declaration of Independence opens with soaring certainty, "that all men are created equal, that they are endowed by their Creator with certain unalienable rights, that among these are Life, Liberty, and the Pursuit of Happiness." Thomas Jefferson, the author of these sentiments, it has often been noted, owned over 200 men and women at the time. John Hancock, who signed the document with a flourish, traded in slaves and smuggled rum produced by slaves in the Caribbean. Of the fifty-five signers of the Declaration, forty-one owned slaves at the time or had in the past. The irony of this fact was not ignored at the time. Samuel Johnson, the witty social critic wrote, "How is it that we hear the loudest yelps for liberty among the drivers of Negroes?" The historian Edmund Morgan, in his book, *Slavery and Freedom*, suggested that this paradox is central to the American experience. He argued that in fundamental ways, the ideology of American liberty was underwritten by the enslavement of hosts of Africans.

David Brion Davis has argued that the progress of the American Revolution itself had a paradoxical effect on the development of the institution of slavery and on the experience of African-Americans in the newly founded nation. While the American Revolution resulted in the gradual ending of slavery north of the Mason-Dixon line and substantial manumission of slaves in Virginia and Maryland, it was accompanied with significant discrimination against and marginalization of newly freed men and women, in short, an expansion of racism. At the same time, in the South, the commitment to slavery was only strengthened and new justifications were constructed to legitimize the possession of slaves in a republican nation. For, once revolutionary theory "made all persons free and equal with God-given inalienable rights" then slavery could only be justified by characterizing Africans and African-Americans through a different racial lens – a lens characterizing them as sub-human, morally degraded, and not subject to the same claims for rights guaranteed other human beings.

These paradoxes, however, are not the subject of this chapter. This chapter, instead, asks readers to reconsider the traditional narrative of the American Revolution as a rebellion against a tyrannical power bent on tightening control over its colonial possessions in North America and extracting greater revenues from provincial residents. This narrative, of course, regards the American rebellion against Great Britain through patriot eyes, accepting the logic of such revolutionary leaders as Thomas Jefferson, Samuel Adams, Patrick Henry, and John Dickinson that British infringements on American rights transformed the colonists inevitably into slaves. In fact, when actual African slaves marched through Charleston, South Carolina at the height of the Stamp Act Crisis in 1764 under banners proclaiming LIBERTY, they were not so well received.

Americans who have accepted Thomas Paine's statement that there is an absurdity in "supposing a continent to be perpetually governed by an island," and that the American Revolution originated fundamentally as a tax revolt, will likely receive with discomfort the possibility that among the primary causes of the American Revolution were efforts to protect slave holding and the racial hierarchies upon which this system of labor increasingly depended. This chapter therefore asks students to revisit the featured moments in the approach of the American Revolution and examine primary sources that reveal the role of slavery and the place of race in sparking the independence movement that ultimately separated the American colonies from the British empire. This chapter also requires students to reflect on the degree to which the promises of liberty, despite the assurances of the Declaration of Independence that they were the natural endowment of all men, rarely extended to men and women of African descent. In short, it asks readers to consider what happens when one examines the American Revolution with the issue of slavery at the forefront. And, it asks students to consider to what degree the American Revolution looks different through that lens.

BRITISH COLONIAL ADMINISTRATION AND THE MATTER OF SLAVERY

Following the French and Indian War (1754-1763) which cost the British greatly even as they expanded their empire substantially, the British needed to both tighten the administration of their colonies and to expand the revenues gained from their colonies. The American colonies cost the British government nearly £400,000 pounds per year while its tax revenues were substantially less. So, in the years after the end of the French and Indian War the British parliament enacted several new taxes to narrow this deficit. These taxes included the Sugar Act, taxes on molasses produced in the French, Spanish, and Dutch sugar islands, the Stamp Act, a direct tax on paper products, and after the uproar caused by each of these policies, the Townshend Acts, which largely fell on a variety of luxury items. In addition, the colonial administration tightened control over the unruly colonials, establishing better customs enforcement, insisting that taxes be paid in specie, or coin, rather than tobacco, or bills of exchange, a precursor to paper money.

The colonial response, which ranged from open and violent resistance, public protest, and efforts to coordinate the response of thirteen disparate colonies, often was stated in language that likened the colonists to slaves. John Dickinson, Philadelphia's largest slaveowner, and author of the Articles of Confederation, wrote in his *Letters from a Farmer*:

> These duties, which will inevitably be levied upon us—which are now levying upon us—are *expressly* laid *for the sole purpose of taking money*. This is the true definition of "*taxes*." … This money is to be taken from *us*. We are therefore *taxed*. Those who are taxed without their own consent, expressed by themselves or their representatives, are slaves. We are taxed without our own consent, expressed by ourselves or our representatives. We are therefore—SLAVES."

Pamphleteers repeatedly proclaimed, if the Stamp Act was not overturned, this would lead to "perpetual slavery" turning white Americans into bondsmen and bondswomen, into abject slaves. Joseph Montgomery, a minister, assured his listeners that Parliament's policies were designed "to reduce us from the glorious character of freemen to that of slaves." Another clergyman, Reverend

Oliver Noble, contended that the colonials' problem with Parliament resulted less from negotiable policy decisions, but from the determination of the colonists that "we WILL NOT BE SLAVES."

In 1774, George Washington observed that colonials could not afford to abandon their rights, because this would reduce them to the same status as black slaves. "The crisis is arrived," he wrote, "when we must assert our rights, or submit to every imposition, that can be heaped upon us, till custom and use shall make us tame and abject slaves, as the blacks we rule over with such arbitrary sway."

The colonists also feared that the extension of British authority threatened their slave property. The colonial charters that provided the legal authority under which each of the charters were established had granted the colonial governments legislative power, but had stipulated that "colonial laws should not be repugnant to the laws, statutes, and customs of England." These repugnancy clauses, had the effect of requiring colonial laws to remain in concordance with the laws in England. In addition, when in 1766, after the colonial uproar at the introduction of new and onerous taxes, Great Britain's Parliament had rescinded the Stamp Act and revised the terms of the Sugar Act, it had also proclaimed in the Declaratory Act 1766 that Parliament "had hath, and of right ought to have, full power and authority to make laws and statutes of sufficient force and validity to bind the colonies and people of America ... in all cases whatsoever." Predictably, the colonial leadership responded by imagining the colonies' enslavement: "In a word, we must be slaves, learn to grovel in the dust, and from thence look up to our imperious masters, in order to receive from their gripping hands, the scanty pittance which they might please to afford us." To the ears of colonial Britons, this assertion of the sovereignty of the British crown ruling through Parliament, echoed the language of racial repression that Americans understood all too well.

The rising influence of abolitionism in Great Britain, and its fainter echoes in the colonies, also concerned slave owners. Attacks in the press and courts on the slave trade alarmed merchants, most often from in northern port cities, who feared that disruptions of the "carrying trade" would adversely affect their commerce. Plantation owners feared that abolitionist tracts or worse, unfavorable legal decisions, might both disrupt the fragile control they had over slaves, or render their ownership of them illegal or impossible. In particular, the case *Somerset* v. *Stewart* (1772) and the decision in favor of the slave, James Somerset, suggested that British law and its courts might in the future find unfavorably on the legality of the institution or many of its practices. James Somerset was a slave sold in Virginia to a Scottish merchant named Charles Stewart. In 1769 Stewart took him to England, where Somerset escaped and was recaptured. Stewart decided to bind him over to traders who would transport him to Jamaica for sale. He was awaiting shipment to Jamaica, when Granville Sharp, the famed abolitionist along with several prominent British Quakers sought an injunction to free Somerset on the grounds that on English soil. Though there were some twelve to fifteen thousand slaves residing in England, and many thousands in the colonial territories, the status of slaves in England proper remained unsettled. English common law did not recognize the status of chattel slavery. And, in numerous cases in English courts, during the 18th century it was established that men could not be property in English law. The legal status of Africans brought to England was nonetheless unclear. After hearing the arguments, the judge, the Earl of Mansfield, determined that the only way that slavery in England could be maintained was by an act of parliament. This decision and the language that was used to describe slavery in Mansfield's ruling fueled anticipation among slaves and consternation among their owners that the practice of owning slaves would one day become repugnant to the laws and customs of Great Britain. Or, that Parliament might one day decide to abolish the slave trade or the right to own human beings as property. Other decisions by courts and royal administrators in the colonies further heightened these concerns.

RACE, SLAVERY AND REVOLUTION

Many of the featured moments of the American revolutionary period, when looked at carefully, highlight the role of race and slavery among the factors that contributed to the division between Great Britain and its North American colonies. The ways in which the Stamp Act Crisis and the rhetoric of liberty espoused by the "Liberty Boys" and others was appropriated by slaves who marched through Charleston, South Carolina is but one such example. The Boston Massacre, which resulted in the death of five Bostonians, including a black former slave named Crispus Attucks, when looked at with race and class conflict in mind hardly appears as the bloody outburst of violence unleashed by an oppressive British state against patriotic Americans. Instead, as you will read in the Documents that follow, the Boston Massacre occurred within a context of a long-standing rivalry on the docks between British regulars, the "Redcoats," many from the 29th Prince of Wales Infantry Regiment that included a contingent of Afro-Caribbean soldiers, and dock workers and sailors, among whom was the unlucky Crispus Attucks.

Neither did African slaves in the colonies during the revolutionary era from 1764 to 1783 sit idly by waiting for the wheels of justice to churn slowly toward their liberation. Slaves and freedmen actively sought their own liberty and political voice, in many instances encouraged by the rhetoric of liberty espoused by revolutionaries, or by the legal and administrative decisions of government officials. For many slaves, this meant simply running away from their masters, either hoping to find better circumstances in towns and cities, or perhaps on the frontier. Port cities also afforded the opportunity for some slaves to work on the docks, or on the many ships always in need of hands that traversed the Atlantic economy. For others it meant actively protesting under the banner of liberty widely proclaimed by their white counterparts as they challenged British authority. When active hostilities broke out between American patriots and the British authorities and their allies, slaves often faced a choice to join one side or the other. This proved another means of gaining their freedom. And, throughout the war slaves attempted to gain rights denied them through repeated petitions and remonstrances to colonial and later revolutionary governments.

For others, the promise of liberty required choosing sides in what was essentially a civil war. Crispus Attucks has been memorialized as an African-American patriot. However others more clearly made the choice to stand alongside the American revolutionaries. Alongside the "minutemen" who fought in the early battle of Bunker Hill were some 100 African-American militia men, the so-called "Bucks of America." Included in their number was Salem Poor, a former slave, who was signaled out for commendation for his role in that battle. James Armistead Lafayette served with his master's approval in the Continental Army during its final campaigns. The intelligence he gained as a spy in the British commander's headquarters proved instrumental to the eventual victory of the Continentals at the Battle of Yorktown. These men, the 1st Rhode Island Regiment, known as the "Black Regiment," and perhaps 5,000 other African Americans fought with the Continental Army for the patriot cause. Many more, however, concluded that the British promised greater hope of freedom, particularly after the issuance of Lord Dunmore's Emancipation Proclamation in November 1775. The estimates of the numbers of slaves who made the decision to flee to the British vary widely. At the time, observers concluded that perhaps as many as 55,000 slaves did so. More recently, however, historians have suggested that as many as 100,000 slaves escaped to the British, though many died trying, were struck down by epidemic disease, or eventually returned to their kin on plantations. Ten to twenty times the number of African Americans fought with the British than fought for the revolutionary cause.

Gerald Horne recently titled his history of the American Revolution, *The Counter-Revolution of 1776: Slave Resistance and the Origins of the United States of America*. He foregrounds the developments that threatened the American plantation and slave-based commercial system and the ways in which African Americans fought back against the peculiar institution in the pre-Revolutionary War period. Horne contends that the American Revolution was neither a tax revolt, nor a class uprising, nor finally an anti-colonial rebellion against a distant imperial power. Instead, Horne argues that it was the response of slave holding and slave trading Americans, intent on maintaining their rights to property in human beings which resulted ultimately in the independence of the thirteen colonies from Great Britain. Horne, however, shifts the lense through which the American Revolution is most often understood by contending that the truly revolutionary character of the American Revolution was most evident in the resistance of slaves to their enslavement, whether in commandeering slave ships, threatening and engaging in rebellion against their masters, pressing the case for freedom in the royal courts, petitioning legislative assemblies in North America, or fighting in both the patriot and British armies. The unmistakable conclusion, for Horne, is that the Patriot cause, by contrast, represented a "counter-revolution" that was ultimately enshrined in the Constitution of the United States, a compact that, while it did not mention slavery or slaves directly, nonetheless secured for the slave interest a stranglehold on political power and guarantees of the rights to own property in human beings. We will engage the debates that led to the fashioning of the United States Constitution in Chapter Six, but in this chapter, I encourage the reader to take seriously Horne's argument and test its validity by carefully analyzing the following primary documents.

PRIMARY SOURCES

Document 1   Runaway Notice, *Boston Gazette*, 2 October 1750[1]

Ran away from his master, William Brown, of Framingham, on the 30th of September last, a Mullato Fellow, about 27 years of age, named *Crispus*, 6 feet 2 inches high, short, curl'd hair, his knees nearer together than common; had on a light coloured Bearskin Coat, plain brown Fustain Jacket, or brown All Wool one, new Buck skin breeches, blue Yarn Stockings, and a checked woolen shirt. Whoever shall take up said Runaway and convey him to his abovesaid master, shall have *ten pounds* old Tenor Reward, and all necessary charges paid. And all Masters of Vessels and others, are hereby cautioned against concealing or carrying off said Servant on Penalty of the Law. Boston, October 2, 1750.

---

1   "Runaway Notice," *Boston Gazette*, (Boston, MA), October 2, 1750.

Document 2 Remonstrance of the Colony of Rhode Island to the Board of Trade [concerning the Sugar Act], 24 January 1764.[2]

… It is this quantity of molasses which serves as an engine in the hands of the merchant to effect the great purpose of paying for British manufactures; for part of it is exported to the Massachusetts Bay, to New York and Pennsylvania, to pay for British goods, for provisions and for many articles which compose our West India cargoes and part to the other colonies, southward of these last mentioned, for such commodities as serve for a remittance immediately to Europe; such as rice, naval stores, etc., or such as are necessary to enable us to carry on our commerce; the remainder (besides what is consumed by the inhabitants,) is distilled into rum, and exported to the coast of Africa; nor will this trade to Africa appear to be of little consequence, if the following account of it be considered.

Formerly, the negroes upon the coast were supplied with large quantities of French brandies; but in the year 1723, some merchants in this colony first introduced the use of rum there, which, from small beginnings soon increased to the consumption of several thousand hogsheads yearly; by which the French are deprived of the sale of an equal quantity of brandy; and as the demand for rum is annually increasing upon the coast, there is the greatest reason to think, that in a few years, if this trade be not discouraged, the sale of French brandies there will be entirely destroyed. This little colony, only, for more than thirty years past, have annually sent about eighteen sail of vessels to the coast, which have carried about eighteen hundred hogsheads of rum, together with a small quantity of provisions and some other articles, which have been sold for slaves, gold dust, elephants' teeth, camwood, etc. The slaves have been sold in the English islands, in Carolina, and Virginia, for bills of exchange, and the other articles have been sent to Europe; and by this trade alone, remittances have been made from this colony to Great Britain, to the value of £40,000 yearly; and this rum, carried to the coast, is so far from prejudicing the British trade thither, that it may be said rather to promote it; for as soon as our rum vessels arrive, they exchange away some of the rum with the traders from Britain, for a quantity of dry goods, with which each of them sort their cargoes to mutual advantage.

Besides this method of remittance by the African trade, we often get bills of exchange from the Dutch colonies of Surinam, Barbice, etc. and this happens when the sales of our cargoes amount to more than a sufficiency to load with molasses; so that, in this particular, a considerable benefit arises from the molasses trade, for these bills being paid in Holland, are the means of drawing from that republic so much cash yearly, into Great Britain, as these bills amount to….

The present price of molasses is about twelve pence, sterling, per gallon; at which rate, only, it can be distilled into rum for exportation; wherefore, if a duty should be laid on this article, the enhanced price may amount to a prohibition; and it may with truth be said, that there is not so large a sum of silver and gold circulating in the colony, as the duty imposed by the aforesaid act upon foreign molasses, would amount to in one year, which makes it absolutely impossible for the importers to pay it….

There are upwards of thirty distil houses… constantly employed in making rum from molasses. …These distil houses, for want of molasses, must be shut up, to the ruin of many

---

[2] *Documents Illustrative of the History of the Slave Trade to America.* Elizabeth Donnan, ed. Vol. III. New England and the Middle Colonies. (New York: Octagon Books, Inc., 1965).

families, and of our trade in general; particularly, of that to the coast of Africa, where the French will supply the natives with brandy, as they formerly did. Two-thirds of our vessels will become useless, and perish upon our hands; our mechanics and those who depend upon the merchant for employment, must seek for subsistence elsewhere; and what must very sensibly affect the present and future naval power and commerce of Great Britain… will be in a manner destroyed; and as an end will be put to our commerce, the merchants cannot import any more British manufactures, nor will the people be able to pay for those they have already received….

Document 3   Phyllis Wheatley, *On Being Brought From Africa*, 1768[3]

'Twas mercy brought me from my *Pagan* land,

Taught my benighted soul to understand

That there's a God, that there's a *Saviour* too:

Once I redemption neither sought nor knew.

Some view our sable rae with scornful eye,

"Their colour is a diabolic die."

Remember *Christians, Negros,* black as *Cain,*

May be refin'd, and join th'angelic train.

Document 4   Journal of Occurrences, [Reports from Boston published in Colonial Newspapers, many of them written by Samuel Adams] Boston, 1768[4]

October 6   In the Morning nine or ten soldiers of Colonel Carr's Regiment, for sundry Misdemeanors, were severely whipt on the Commons; ---to behold Britons scourg'd by Negro Drummers was a new and very disagreeable Spectacle.

October 31   In consequence of the late practices upon the Negroes of this Town, we are told that Orders have been given by the Selectmen to the Town Watch, to take up and secure all such Negro Servants as shall be absent from their Master's Houses at an unreasonable Time of Night.

The Subscribers Selectmen of the Town of Boston, complain of John Wilson, Esq; a Captain in his Majesty's 29th Regiment of Foot, a Detachment whereof is now quartered in the said Town of Boston, under his Command, that the said John, with others unknown, on the Evening of the 28th Day of October current, did, in the Sight and Hearing of divers Persons, utter many abusive and threatening Expressions, of, and against the Inhabitants of said Town, and in a dangerous and conspirative Manner, did entice and endeavor to spirit up, by a Promise of the Reward of Freedom, certain Negro Slaves in Boston aforesaid, the Property of several of the Town Inhabitants, to cut their Master's Throats, and to beat, insult, and otherwise ill treat

---

3   https://www.poetryfoundation.org/poems-and-poets/poems/detail/45465

4   "Boston: Journal of Occurrences," *The New York Gazette* (New York, New York) 24 October 1768, p. 2. "Boston: Journal of Occurences, 31 October 1768," *The New York Journal* (New York, New York) 17 November 1768, p. 2

their said Masters, asserting that now the Soldiers are come, the Negroes shall be free, and the Liberty Boys Slaves,--to the great Terror and Danger of the peacable Inhabitants of said Town, liege Subjects of his Majesty, our Lord the King, and the great Disturbance of the Peace and safety of said Town.

Wherefore your Complainants, solicitious for the Peace and Welfare of the said Town, as well as their own, as Individuals, humbly requests your Worship's Consideration of the Premises, and that Process may issue against the said John, that he me be dealt with herein according to Law.

Signed: Joshua Henshaw, John Hancock, Samuel Pemberton, Joseph Jackson, John Rowe, Henderson Inches

Document 5 Testimony before the Committee of Inquiry into the Boston "Massacre," 1770.

Margaret Swansborough, of lawful age, testivies and says, that a free woman, named Black Peg, who has kept much with the soldiers, on hearing the disturbance Monday evening, the 5th instant, said, "the soldiers were not to be trod upon by the inhabitants, but would know before morning, whether they or the inhabitants were to be masters." Since which time, the said Black Peg has sold off her household stuff and left the town, on her hearing what she had said before was given in to the committee of enquiry.

Her Margaret + Swansborough

mark

I John Hill, aged sixty-nine, testify, that in the forenoon of Friday the second of March current, I was at a house the corner of a passage way leading from Atkinson's street to Mr. John Gray's rope-walks, near Green's barracks so called, when I saw eight or ten soldiers pass the window with clubs. I immediately got up and went to the door, and found them returning from the rope-walks to the barracks; whence they again very speedily re-appeared, now increased to the number of thirty or forty, armed with clubs and other weapons. In this latter company was a tall negro drummer, to whom I called, you black rascal, what have you to do with white people's quarrels? He answered, I suppose I may look on, and went forward. I went out directly and commanded the peace, telling them I was in commission; but they not regarding me, knocked down a rope-maker in my presence, and two or three of them, beating him with clubs, I endeavored to relieve him; but on approaching the fellows who were mauling him, one of them with a great club struck at me with such violence, that had I not happily avoided it might have been fatal to me. The party last mentioned rushed in towards the rope-walks, and attacked the rope-makers nigh the tar-kettle, but were soon beat off, drove out of the passage-way by which they entered, and were followed by the rope-makers, whom I persuaded to go back, and they readily obeyed. And further I say not.   John Hill.

> Suffolk, ss. Boston March 19, 1770, John Hill Esq., above named, after due examination, made oath to the truth of the aforesaid affidavit, taken to perpetuate the remembrance of the thing.

"BE NOT THEN, YE NEGROES, TEMPTED." SLAVERY AND THE AMERICAN REVOLUTION

Document 6 "The Bloody Massacre perpetrated in King Street, Boston on March 5th 1770 by a party of the 29th Regiment." Engraving. Paul Revere, 1770.[5]

---

[5] Paul Revere, "The Bloody Massacre Perpretated in King-Street Boston on March 5th 1770 by a party of the 29th Regiment," Engraving, (Boston, MA: 1770) in the Gilder Lehrman Collection. Collection #GLC01868.

Document 7 Charge Delivered to the Grand Jury by Honorable Martin Howard, Esq., Superior Court Judge, North Carolina, 1771.[6]

A white man was indicted for the murder of a negro slave, and the grand jury returned the Bill IGNORAMUS. I cannot pretend to know their reasons for doing so; it might possibly be owing to want of sufficient evidence of the fact; but I am rather inclined to believe they found their opinion upon this principle; THAT IT IS NOT MURDER FOR A WHITE MAN TO KILL A NEGRO SLAVE.

Such a principle as this, I take to be of a most pernicious nature, tending to a gross corruption both of the understanding, and the heart, and at the same time repugnant to law.

It is not my intention to use arguments tending to annihilate the condition of slavery among us, and therefore I will not pretend to say, that slavery is inconsistent with Christianity....

Neither shall I take upon me to decide, that a state of slavery is inconsisten with the common law of England. How far ONE MAN can have the absolute property of ANOTHER MAN has been a point somewhat unsettled; though in the case of *Smith v Gould* (1706)... it was adjudged by the whole court, that a man could not have such a property....

But be that as it may, it must be confessed that in the plantations the lawfulness of slavery is generally admitted. Great part of the property here consists in negroes—and that sort of policy which avarice and luxury have made necessary, and which sacrifices justice and humanity to the acquisition of wealth, and the enlargement of commerce, has given sanction to slavery and incorporated it with our laws.

Nevertheless, I am not alone in my opinion that slavery is not only in itself a great evil, but roduces the worst effect upon our manners. Accustomed to an uncontrollable power over slaves, men become lazy, proud, and cruel; and we may reasonably conclude that these vices, so hurtful to ourselves and to society, would become still more enormous if we should adopt so barbarous a maxim as, that a white may man may murder a slave with impunity.

[In North Carolina law] We shall there find that when a negro slave runs away from his master, which hard usage some times compels him to do, advertisements are published and signed by two justices declaring, that if the slave does not surrender himself in a limited time, that then he may be hunted like a bast in the forest, and any person may kill or destroy him in what manner they please.

... Slavery is an adventitious, not a natural state. The souls and bodies of negroes are of the same quality with ours—they are our own fellow creatures, tho' in humbler circumstances, and are capable of the same happiness and misery with us.

Excepting the fruits of his labour, which belong to the master, a slave retains all the rights of subjects under civil government that are NATURALLY UNALIENABLE. Of this kind is self-defence, and personal safety from violence. No one has a right to take away his life without being punished for it. No civil law can confer such a right; it would confound every principle of nature.

---

6   Excerpted from Don Higginbotham and William S. Price, Jr. "Was it Murder for a White Man to Kill a Slave? Chief Justice Martin Howard Condemns the Peculiar Institution in North Carolina," The William and Mary Quarterly, 36:4 (1979): pp. 593-601.

But to show that the notion here opposed is contrary to law, as well as to reason, I shall conclude in giving you the definition of murder, as it is laid down in all the books.

"Murder is, when a man of sound mind and memory, and of the age of discretion, unlawfully killeth any REASONABLE CREATURE, being under the king's peace." So that if we can persuade ourselves, that a negro slave is a reasonable creature, it must be murder in any one that shall feloniously slay him.

Document 8   Lord Mansfield's Judgement, *Somerset v. Stuart*, 22 June 1772[7]

22nd June, 1772. JUDGEMENT—Lord Mansfield: On the part of Sommersett . . . the Court now proceeds to give its opinion. I shall recite the return to the writ of Habeas Corpus, as the ground of our determination; omitting only words of form. The captain of the ship on board of which the negro was taken, makes his return to the writ in terms signifying that there have been, and still are, slaves to a great number in Africa; and that the trade in them is authorized by the laws and opinions of Virginia and Jamaica; that they are goods and chattels; and, as such, saleable and sold. That James Sommersett is a negro of Africa, and long before the return of the king's writ was brought to be sold, and was sold to Charles Steuart, esq. then in Jamaica, and has not been manumitted1 since; that Mr. Steuart, having occasion to transact business, came over hither, with an intention to return; and brought Sommersett to attend and abide with him, and to carry him back as soon as the business should be transacted. That such intention has been, and still continues; and that the negro did remain till the time of his departure in the service of his master Mr. Steuart, and quitted it without his consent; and thereupon, before the return of the king's writ, the said Charles Steuart did commit the slave on board the Anne and Mary, to safe custody, to be kept till he should set sail, and then to be taken with him to Jamaica, and there sold as a slave . . . . We pay all due attention to the opinion of sir Philip Yorke, and lord chancellor Talbot, whereby they pledged themselves to the British planters, for all the legal consequences of slaves coming over to this kingdom or being baptized, recognized by lord Hardwicke, sitting as chancellor on the 19th of October, 1749, that trover 2 would lie: that a notion had prevailed, if a negro came over, or became a Christian, he was emancipated, but no ground in law: that he and lord Talbot, when attorney and solicitor-general, were of opinion, that no such claim for freedom was valid; that though the statute of tenures had abolished villeins3 regardant to a manor, yet he did not conceive but that a man might still become a villein in gross4 , by confessing himself such in open court . . . The only question before us is, whether the cause on the return is sufficient? If it is, the negro must be remanded; if it is not, he must be discharged. Accordingly, the return states, that the slave departed and refused to serve; whereupon he was kept, to be sold abroad. So high an act of dominion must be recognized by the law of the country where it is used. The power of a master over his slave has been extremely different, in different countries. The state of slavery is of such a nature, that it is incapable of being introduced on any reasons, moral or political, but only by positive law, which preserves its force long after the reasons, occasion, and time itself from whence it was created, is erased from memory. It is so odious, that nothing can be suffered to support it, but positive law. Whatever inconveniences, therefore, may follow from the decision, I cannot say this case is allowed or approved by the law of England, and therefore the black must be discharged.

---

7   "The Case of James Sommersett, A Negro," in Horace Nelson, Selected Cases, Statutes and Orders illustrative of the Principles of Private International Law as administered in England, (London: Stevens and Sons, Limited, 1889), pp. 64-65.

Document 9   "Slave Runaway Notice," *Virginia Gazette*, 30 June 1774.[8]

AUGUSTA, June 18, 1774. RUN away the 16th Instant, from the Subscriber, a Negro Man named BACCHUS, about 30 Years of Age, five Feet six or seven Inches high, strong and well made; had on, and took with him, two white Russia Drill Coats, one turned up with blue, the other quite plain and new, with white figured Metal Buttons, blue Plush Breeches, a fine Cloth Pompadour Waistcoat, two or three thin or Summer Jackets, sundry Pairs of white Thread Stockings, five or six white Shirts, two of them pretty fine, neat Shoes, Silver Buckles, a fine Hat cut and cocked in the Macaroni Figure, a double-milled Drab Great Coat, and sundry other Wearing Apparel. He formerly belonged to Doctor George Pitt, of Williamsburg, and I imagine is gone there under Pretence of my sending him upon Business, as I have frequently heretofore done; he is a cunning, artful, sensible Fellow, and very capable of forging a Tale to impose on the Unwary, is well acquainted with the lower Parts of the Country, having constantly rode with me for some Years past, and has been used to waiting from his Infancy. He was seen a few Days before he went off with a Purse of Dollars, and had just before changed a five Pound Bill; most, or all of which, I suppose he must have robbed me off [sic], which he might easily have done, I having trusted him much after what I thought had proved his Fidelity. He will probably endeavour to pass for a Freeman by the Name of John Christian, and attempt to get on Board some Vessel bound for Great Britain, from the Knowledge he has of the late Determination of Somerset's Case. Whoever takes up the said Slave shall have 5l. Reward, on his Delivery to GABRIEL JONES.

Document 10   Petition to Honor Salem Poor for Heroism at the Battle of Bunker Hill, 1775.[9]

To the Honorable General Court of the Massachusetts' Bay

The subscribers beg leave to report to your Honorable House, (which we do in justice to the character of so brave a man), that under our observation, we declare that a negro man named Salem Poor, of Col. Fry's regiment, Capt. Ame's company, in the late battle at Charleston, behaved like an experienced officer, as well as an excellent soldier. To set forth particulars of his conduct would be tedious. We only beg leave to say, in the person of this said negro, centers a brave and gallant soldier. The reward due to so great and distinguished a character, we submit to Congress.

Jonathan Brewer, Col.	Eliphalet Bodwell, Sg't.
Thomas Nixon, Lt. Col.	Josiah Foster, Lieut.
Wm. Prescott, Col.	Ebenezer Varnum, 2nd. Lieut.
Ephraim Corey, Lieut.	Wm. Hudson Ballard, Capt.
Joseph Baker, Lieut.	Wm. Smith, Cap.
Joshua Row, Lieut.	John Morton, Sergt.
Jonas Richardson, Capt.	Lieut. Richard Welsh

---

8   "Runaway slave notice," *Virginia Gazette*, (Williamsburg, VA), 30 June 1772.

9   "Notes" *The Journal of Negro History* 2: 1(1917), p. 203.

Cambridge, Dec. 5, 1775

    In Council Dec. 21, 1775.—Read, and sent down.

        Perez Morton, Dep'y Sec'y

Document 11 Lord Dunmore's *Emancipation Proclamation*, November 7, 1775.[10]

By His Excellency the Right Honorable JOHN Earl of DUNMORE, His MAJESTY'S Lieutenant and Governor General of the Colony and Dominion of VIRGINIA, and Vice Admiral of the fame.

A PROCLAMATION.

As I have ever entertained Hopes that an Accommodation might have taken Place between GREAT-BRITAIN and this colony, without being compelled by my Duty to this most disagreeable but now absolutely necessary Step, rendered so by a Body of armed Men unlawfully assembled, bring on His MAJESTY'S [Tenders], and the formation of an Army, and that Army now on their March to attack His MAJESTY'S troops and destroy the well disposed Subjects of this Colony. To defeat such unreasonable Purposes, and that all such Traitors, and their Abetters, may be brought to Justice, and that the Peace, and good Order of this Colony may be again restored, which the ordinary Course of the Civil Law is unable to effect, I have thought fit to issue this my Proclamation, hereby declaring, that until the aforesaid good Purposes can be obtained, I do in Virtue of the Power and Authority to ME given, by His MAJESTY, determine to execute Martial Law, and cause the fame to be executed throughout this Colony: and to the end that Peace and good Order may the sooner be [effected], I do require every Person capable of bearing Arms, to [resort] to His MAJESTY'S STANDARD, or be looked upon as Traitors to His MAJESTY'S Crown and Government, and thereby become liable to the Penalty the Law inflicts upon such Offences; such as forfeiture of Life, confiscation of Lands, &c. &c. And I do hereby further declare all indentured Servants, Negroes, or others, (appertaining to Rebels,) free that are able and willing to bear Arms, they joining His MAJESTY'S Troops as soon as may be, for the more speedily reducing this Colony to a proper Sense of their Duty, to His MAJESTY'S Leige Subjects, to retain their [Quitrents], or any other Taxes due or that may become due, in their own Custody, till such Time as Peace may be again restored to this at present most unhappy Country, or demanded of them for their former falutary Purposes, by Officers properly authorised to receive the fame.

GIVEN under my Hand on board the ship WILLIAM, off NORPOLE, the 7th Day of NOVEMBER, in the SIXTEENTH Year of His MAJESTY'S Reign.

DUNMORE.

(GOD save the KING.)

---

10   Document in public domain. Can be found at http://www.Blackpast.org/aah/lord-dunmore-s-proclamation-1775

Document 12   Patrick Henry, Response to Dunmore's Proclamation, reprinted in *The Pennsylvania Evening Post* from the *Virginia Gazette*, 5 December 1775.[11]

A COPY of the above proclamation having fallen into my hands, I thought it was necessary, for the welfare of two sorts of people, that its public appearance should be attended with comments of the following nature. Such as have mixed much in society, and have had opportunities of hearing the subject of the present unnatural contest discussed, will be little startled at the appellation of rebel, because they will know it is not merited; but others there may be whose circumstances may, in a great measure, have excluded them from the knowledge of public matters, who may be sincerely attached to the interests of their country, and who may yet be frightened to act against it from the dread of incurring a guilt which, by all good men, is justly abhorred. To these it may be proper to address a few remarks upon this proclamation, and as part of the proclamation respects the Negroes, and seems to offer something very flattering and desirable to them; it may be doing them, as well as the country, a service, to give them a just view of what they are to expect, would they be so weak and wicked as to comply with what Lord Dunmore requires. Those then, who are afraid of being styled rebels, I would beg to consider, that although Lord Dunmore, in this proclamation, insidiously mentions his having till now entertained hopes of an accommodation, yet the whole renown of his conduct, for many months past, has had the most direct and strongest tendency to widen the unhappy breach, and render a reconciliation more difficult. For what other purpose did he write his false and inflammatory letters to the Ministers of State? Why did he under cover of the night, take from us our powder, and render useless the arms of our public magazine? Why did he secretly and treacherously lay snares for the lives of our unwary brethren, snares that had likely to have proved but too effectual? Why did he, under idle pretenses, withdraw himself from the seat of government, where he alone could, had he been willing done essential service to our country? Why, by his authority, have continual depredations been since made upon such of our countrymen as were situated within the reach of ships of war and tenders? Why have our towns been attacked, and houses destroyed? Why have the persons of many of our most respectable brethren been seized upon, torn from all their connections, and confined on board of ships? Was all this to bring about a reconciliation? Judge for yourselves whether the injuring of our persons and properties be the readiest way to regain our affections. After insulting our persons, he now presumes to insult our understanding also. Do not believe his words, when his actions directly contradict them. If he wished for an accommodation, if he had a desire to restore peace and order, as he professes, it was to be upon terms which would have been disgraceful, and in the end destructive of everything dear and valuable.

Consider again the many attempts which have been made to enslave us. Nature gave us equal privileges with the people of Great Britain, we are equally with them, entitled to to the disposal of our own property, and we have never resigned to them these rights which we derive from nature. But they have endeavored, unjustly, to rob us of them. They have made acts of parliament, in which we in no manner concurred, which dispose of our property; acts which abridge us of liberties we once enjoyed, and which impose burdens and restraints upon us too heavy to be borne. Had we immediately taken up arms to assert our rights, and to prevent the

---

11   "Speech by Patrick Henry, reprinted from the Virginia Gazette," in *Pennsylvania Gazette* (Philadelphia, PA) 5 December 1775.

exercise of unlawful power, though our cause would have been just, yet our conduct would have been precipitate, and so far blamable. We might then, with some shadow of justice, have been charged with rebellion, or a disposition to rebel. But this was not the way we behaved. We petitioned once and again in the most dutiful manner; we hoped that the righteousness of our cause would appear, that our complaints would be heard and attended to; we wished to avoid the horrors of a civil war, and so long proceeded in this fruitless track that our not adopting a more vigorous opposition seemed rather to proceed from a spirit of meanness and fear than of peace and loyalty, and all that we gained was to be more grievously oppressed. At length we resolved to withhold our commerce from Britain, and by thus affecting her interest, oblige her to redress our grievances. But in this also we have been disappointed. Our associations have been deemed unlawful combinations, and opposition to government; we have been entirely deprived of our trade to foreign countries, and even amongst ourselves, and fleets and armies have been sent to reduce us to a compliance with the unjust and arbitrary demands of the British Minister and corrupt Parliament. Reduced to such circumstances, to what could we have recourse but to arms? Every other expedient having been tried, and found ineffectual, this alone was left; and this we have at last unwillingly adopted. If it be rebellion to take up arms in such a cause as this, rebellion then is not only justifiable but an honorable thing. But let us not be deceived with empty sounds. They who call us rebels cannot make us so. Rebellion is open, and avows opposition to lawful authority, but it is usurped and arbitrary power which we have determined to oppose. Societies are formed, and magistrates are appointed, that men may the better enjoy the blessings of life. Some of the rights which they have derived from nature they part with, that they may the more peaceably and safely possess the rest.

To preserve the rights they have reserved is the duty of every member of society, and to deprive a people of these is treason, is rebellion against the state. If this doctrine then be right, which no one, I believe, will venture to deny, we my countrymen, are dutiful members of society; and the persons who endeavor to rob us of our rights, they are rebels, rebels to their country, and to the rights of human nature. I repeat it again, let us not be deceived with empty sounds. We are acting the part of loyal subjects, of faithful members of the community, when we stand forth in opposition to the arbitrary and oppressive acts which Lord Dunmore has set up; and if any of you have been so far mistaken in your duty as to join him, fly from his camp, as an infected place, and speedily rejoin your virtuous countrymen, for be ye assured that the time will come when these invaders of the rights of human kind will suffer the punishment due to their crimes and when the insulted and oppressed Americans will, if they preserve their virtue, triumph over all their enemies.

The second class of people, for whose sake a few remarks upon this proclamation seem necessary, is the Negroes. They have been flattered with their freedom, if they be able to bear arms, and will speedily join Lord Dunmore's troops. To none then is freedom promised but to such as are able to do Lord Dunmore service. The aged, the infirm, the women and children, are still to remain the property of their masters who will be provoked to severity, should part of their slaves desert them. Lord Dunmore's declaration, therefore, is a cruel declaration to the Negroes. He does not even pretend to make it out of tenderness to them, but solely upon his own account; and should it meet with success, it leaves by far the greater number at the mercy of an enraged and injured people. But should there be any amongst the Negroes weak enough to believe that Lord Dunmore intends to do them a kindness, and wicked enough to provoke the fury of the Americans against their defenseless fathers and mothers, their wives, their women and children, let them only consider the difficulty of effecting their escape, and what they must expect to suffer if they fall into the hands of the Americans. Let them further consider what must be their fate, should the English prove conquerors in this dispute. If we can judge of the future from the past, it will not be much merited. Long have the Americans, moved by compassion, and actuated by sound policy, endeavored to stop the progress of slavery. Our Assemblies have repeatedly passed acts, laying heavy duties upon imported Negroes, by which they meant altogether to prevent horrid traffic; but their humane intentions have been as often frustrated by the cruelty and covetousness of a set of English merchants, who prevailed upon the King to repeal our kind and merciful acts, little indeed to the credit of his humanity. Can it then be supposed that the Negroes will be better used by the English, who have always encouraged and upheld this slavery, than by their present masters, who pity their condition, who wish in general to make it as easy and comfortable as possible, and who would willingly, were it in their power, or were they permitted, not only prevent any more Negroes from losing their freedom, but restore it to such as have already unhappily lost it? No, the ends of Lord Dunmore and his party being answered, they will either give up the offending Negroes to the rigors of the laws they have broken, or sell them in the West Indies, where every year they sell many thousands of their miserable brethren, to perish wither by the inclemency of weather, or the cruelty of barbarous masters. Be not then, ye Negroes, tempted by this proclamation to ruin yourselves. I have given you a faithful view of what you are to expect; and I declare before GOD, in doing it, I have considered your welfare as well as that of the country. Whether you will profit by my advice, I cannot tell; but this I know, that whether we suffer or not, if you desert us, you most certainly will.

Document 13 Slave Petition to the Governor, Council, and House of Representatives of the Province of Massachusetts, 25 May 1774.[12]

The Petition of a Grate Number of Blackes of this Province who by divine permission are held in a state of Slavery within the bowels of a free and Christian Country

Humbly Shewing

That your Petitioners apprehend we have in common with all other men a natural right to our freedoms without Being deprived of them by our fellow men as we are a freeborn Pepel and have never forfeited this Blessing by any compact or agreement whatever. But we were unjustly dragged by the cruel hand of power from our dearest friends and sum of us stolen from the bosoms of our tender Parents and from a Populous Pleasant and plentiful country and Brought hither to be made slaves for Life in a Christian land. Thus are we deprived of everything that hath a tendency to make life even tolerable, the endearing ties of husband and wife we are strangers to for we are no longer man and wife then our masters or mistresses thinks proper married or unmarried. Our children are also taken from us by force and sent many miles from us where we seldom or ever see them again there to be made slaves of for Life which somtimes is very short by Reason of Being dragged from their mothers Breast Thus our Lives are embittered to us on these accounts By our deplorable situation we are rendered incapable of shewing our obedience to Almighty God how can a slave perform the duties of a husband to a wife or parent to his child How can a husband leave master and work and cleave to his wife How can the wife submit themselves to their husbands in all things. How can the child obey their parents in all things.

---

12   "Petition of a Grate Number of Blackes," to Thomas Gage (May 25, 1774), in Herbert Aptheker, ed. *A Documentary History of the Negro People in the United States*, Vol. I, (New York: The Citadel Press, 1960), pp. 8-9.

There is a great number of us sincere . . . members of the Church of Christ how can the master and the slave be said to fulfill that command Live in love let Brotherly Love contuner and abound Bear yea one anothers' Burdens How can the master be said to Bear my Borden when he Bears me down with the Heavy chains of slavery and oppression against my will and how can we fulfill our part of duty to him whilst in this condition and as we cannot serve our God as we ought whilst in this situation Neither can we reap an equal benefit from the laws of the Land which doth not justify but condemns Slavery or if there had been any Law to hold us in Bondage we are Humbly of the Opinion there never was any to enslave our children for life when Born in a free Country. We therefor Beg your Excellency and Honors will give this its due weight and consideration and that you will accordingly cause an act of the legislative to be passed that we may obtain our Natural right our freedoms and our children be set at liberty at the year of Twenty one for whose sakes more petequeley your Petitioners is in Duty ever to Pray.

Document 15 Runaway Slave Advertisement, *South Carolina Gazette*, 7 November 1775.

Absented himself from the Subscriber, the 4th of this Instant, a NEGRO Man, named LIMUS; he is of a yellow Complexion, and has the Ends of three of his Fingers cut off his left Hand; he is well known in Charles-Town from his saucy and impudent Tongue, of which I have had many complaints; therefore, I hereby give free liberty, and will be also much obliged to any Person to flog him (so as not to take his Life) in such Manner as they shall thin proper, whenever he is found out of my Habitation without a Ticket; for though he is my Property, he has the audacity to tell me, he will be free, that he will serve no Man, and that he will be conquered or governed by no Man. I forewarn Masters of Vessels from carrying him off the Province, and all Persons from harbouring him in their Houses or Plantations.

Document 16 Lemuel Haynes, "Liberty Further Extended: Or Free Thoughts on the Illegality of Slave-keeping," 1776.[13]

We hold these truths to be self-Evident, that all men are created Equal, that they are Endowed By their Creator with Ceartain unalienable rights, that among these are Life, Liberty, and the pursuit of happyness. --Congress.

...Liberty, & freedom, is an innate principle, which is unmovebly placed in the human Species; and to see a man aspire after it, is not Enigmatical, seeing he acts no ways incompatible with his own Nature; consequently, he that would infring upon a mans Liberty may reasonably Expect to meet with oposision, seeing the Defendant cannot Comply to Nonresistance, unless he Counter-acts the very Laws of nature. Liberty is a Jewel which was handed Down to man from the cabinet of heaven, and is Coaeval with his Existance. And as it proceed from the Supreme Legislature of the univers, so it is he which hath a sole right to take away; therefore, he that would take away a mans Liberty assumes a prerogative that Belongs to another, and acts out of his own domain. One man may bost a superorety above another in point of Natural previledg; yet if he can produse no convincive arguments in vindication of this preheminence his hypothesis

---

[13] Lemuel Haynes, "Liberty Further Extended: Or Free Thoughts on the Illegality of Slave-Keeping," 1776. Text of address available at http://voiceslikeyours.com/pdfs/PSLemuelHaynesLibertyFurtherExtended.pdf

is to Be Suspected. To affirm, that an Englishman has a right to his Liberty, is a truth which has Been so clearly Evinced, Especially of Late, that to spend time in illustrating this, would be But Superfluous tautology. But I query, whether Liberty is so contracted a principle as to be Confin'd to any nation under Heaven; nay, I think it not hyperbolical to affirm, that Even an affrican, has Equally as good a right to his Liberty in common with Englishmen. I know that those that are concerned in the Slave-trade, Do pretend to Bring arguments in vindication of their practise; yet if we give them a candid Examination, we shall find them (Even those of the most cogent kind) to be Essencially Deficient. We live in a day wherein Liberty & freedom is the subject of many millions Concern; and the important Struggle hath alread caused great Effusion of Blood; men seem to manifest the most sanguine resolution not to Let their natural rights go without their Lives go with them; a resolution, one would think Every one that has the Least Love to his country, or futer posterity, would fully confide in, yet while we are so zelous to maintain, and foster our own invaded rights, it cannot be tho't impertinent for us Candidly to reflect on our own conduct, and I doubt not But that we shall find that subsisting in the midst of us, that may with propriety be stiled Opression, nay, much greater opression, than that which Englishmen seem so much to spurn at. I mean an oppression which they, themselves, impose upon others.... ... And the main proposition, which I intend for some Breif illustration is this, Namely, That an African, or, in other terms, that a Negro may Justly Chalenge, and has an Lemuel Haynes: Liberty Further Extended 2 undeniable right to his Liberty: Consequently, the practise of Slave-keeping, which so much abounds in this Land is illicit. Every privilege that mankind Enjoy have their Origen from god; and whatever acts are passed in any Earthly Court, which are Derogatory to those Edicts that are passed in the Court of Heaven, the act is void. If I have a perticular previledg granted to me by god, and the act is not revoked nor the power that granted the benefit vacated, (as it is imposable but that god should Ever remain immutable) then he that would infringe upon my Benifit, assumes an unreasonable, and tyrannic power. It hath pleased god to make of one Blood all nations of men, for to dwell upon the face of the Earth. Acts 1 7, 26. And as all are of one Species, so there are the same Laws, and aspiring principles placed in all nations; and the Effect that these Laws will produce, are Similar to Each other. Consequently we may suppose, that what is precious to one man, is precious to another, and what is irksom, or intolarable to one man, is so to another, consider'd in a Law of Nature. Therefore we may reasonably Conclude, that Liberty is Equally as pre[c]ious to a black man, as it is to a white one, and Bondage Equally as intollarable to the one as it is to the other: Seeing it Effects the Laws of nature Equally as much in the one as it Does in the other. But, as I observed Before, those privileges that are granted to us By the Divine Being, no one has the Least right to take them from us without our consen[t]; and there is Not the Least precept, or practise, in the Sacred Scriptures, that constitutes a black man a Slave, any more than a white one. Shall a mans Couler Be the Decisive Criterion whereby to Judg of his natural right? or Becaus a man is not of the same couler with his Neighbour, shall he Be Deprived of those things that Distuingsheth [Distinguisheth] him from the Beasts of the field?...

Document 17 Slaves' Petition the Massachusetts Legislature, 1777[14]

To The Honorable Counsel & House of Representatives for the State of Massachusetts Bay in General Court assembled, Jan. 13, 1777.

---

14   "Petition of a Great Number of Negroes," to the Massachusetts House of Representatives (January 13, 1777), in Herbert Aptheker, ed. *A Documentary History of the Negro People in the United States*, Vol. I, (New York: The Citadel Press, 1960), pp. 9-10..

The petition of A Great Number of Blackes detained in a State of slavery in the Bowels of a free & Christian Country Humbly shuwith that your Petitioners apprehend that thay have in Common with all other men a Natural and Unaliable Right to that freedom which the Grat Parent of the Unavers hath Bestowed equalley on all menkind and which they have Never forfuted by any Compact or agreement whatever—but thay wher Unjustly Dragged by the hand of cruel Power from their Derest friends and sum of them Even torn from the Embraces of their tender Parents—from A popolous Pleasant and plentiful contry and in violation of Laws of Nature and off Nations and in defiance of all the tender feelings of humanity Brough hear Either to Be sold Like Beast of Burthen & Like them Condemnd to Slavery for Life—Among A People Profesing the mild Religion of Jesus A people Not Insensible of the Secrets of Rational Being Nor without spirit to Resent the unjust endeavours of others to Reduce them to a state of Bondage and Subjection your honouer Need not to be informed that A Life of Slavery Like that of your petioners Deprived of Every social privilege of Every thing Requisit to Render Life Tolable is far worse then Nonexistence.

In Imitation of the Lawdable Example of the Good People of these States your petitiononers have Long and Patiently waited the Evnt of petition after petition By them presented to the Legislative Body of this state and cannot but with Grief Reflect that their Success hath ben but too similar they Cannot but express their Astonishment that It has Never Bin Consirdered that Every Principle form which Amarica has Acted in the Cours of their unhappy Dificultes with Great Briton Pleads Stronger than A thousand arguments in favowrs of your petioners they thertor humble Beseech your honours to give this petion [petition] its due weight & consideration & cause an act of the Legislatur to be past Wherby they may be Restored to the Enjoyments of that which is the Naturel Right of all men—and their Children who wher Born in this Land of Liberty may not be heald as Slaves after they arrive at the age of twenty one years so may the Inhabitance of this Stats No longer chargeable with the inconsistancey of acting themselves the part which they condem and oppose in others Be prospered in their present Glorious struggle for Liberty and have those Blessing to them, &c.

Document 18   The Constitution of Vermont—July 8, 1777[15]

Chapter I   A Declaration of the Rights of the Inhabitants of the State of Vermont

I. THAT all men are born equally free and independent, and have certain natural, inherent and unalienable rights, amongst which are the enjoying and defending life and liberty; acquiring, possessing and protecting property, and pursuing and obtaining happiness and safety. Therefore, no male person, born in this country, or brought from over sea, ought to be holden by law, to serve any person, as a slave, servant, or apprentice, after he arrives to the age of twenty one Years, nor female, in like manner, after she arrives to the age of eighteen years, unless they are bound by their own consent, after they arrive to such age, or bound by law, for the payment of debts, damages, fines, costs, or the like.

II. That private property ought to be subservient to public uses, when necessity requires it; nevertheless, whenever any particular man's property is taken for the use of the public, the owner ought to receive an equivalent in money.

---

15   Full text of the Vermont Constitution of 1777 is available at the Vermont State Archives, online at https://www.sec.state.vt.us/archives-records/state-archives/government-history/vermont-constitutions/1777-constitution.aspx

108 CHAPTER 5

Document 19 Bucks of America Flag, Paint on Silk, ca. 1785-1786.[16] [Flag of a Black Massachusetts militia unit]

---

16   Bucks of America Flag, paint on silk, ca. 1785-1786. Made in Boston. Massachusetts Historical Society, http://www.masshist.org/database/viewer.php?item_id=788&img_step=1&mode=large#page1

Document 20 Thomas Jefferson, "Births, Deaths etc. from 1779 to 1781 inclusive. Other Losses by the British in 1781," *The Farm Book*.[17]

Original manuscript from The Coolidge Collection of Thomas Jefferson Manuscripts at the Massachusetts Historical Society.

---

[17] Thomas Jefferson, *The Farm Book*, manuscript, 1774-1824, available on-line at the Massachusetts Historical Society, Boston, MA. https://www.masshist.org/thomasjeffersonpapers/farm/

Document 21 Richard Allen, "Eulogy of George Washington" printed in the *Philadelphia Gazette*, 31 December 1799[18]

At this time it may not be improper to speak a little on the late mournful event—an event in which we participate in common with the feelings of a grateful people—an event which causes 'the land to mourn' in a season of festivity. Our father and friend is taken from us—he whom the nations honoured is "seen of men no more."

We, my friends, have particular cause to bemoan our loss. To us he has been the sympathizing frind and tender father. He has watched over us and viewed our degraded and afflicted state with compassion and pity—his heart was not insensible to our sufferings. He whose wisdomthe nations revered thought we had a right to liberty. Unbiased by the popular opinion of the state in which is the memorable Mount Vernon—he dared to do his duty, and wipe off the only stain with which man could ever reproach him.

And it is now said by an authority on which I rely, that he who ventured his life in battles, whose "head was covered" in that day, and whose shield the "Lord of hosts" was, did not fight for that liberty which he desired to withhold from others—the bread of oppression was not sweet to his taste and he "let the oppressed go free"—he "undid every burden"—he provided lands and comfortable accomodations for them when he kept this "acceptable fast to the Lord"—that those who had been slaves might rejoice in the day of their deliverance.

If he who broke the yoke of British burdens "from off the neck of the people" of this land, and was hailed his country's deliverer, by what name shall we call him who secretly and almost unknown emancipated his "bondmen and bondwomen"—became to them a father, and gave them an inheritance.

Deeds like these are not common. He did not let "his right hand know what his left hand did"—but he who "sees in secret will openly reward" such acts of beneficence.

The name of Washington will live when the sculptured marble and statue of bronze shall be crumbled into dust—for it is the decree of eternal God that "the righteous shall be had in everlasting remembrance, but the memorial of the wicked shall rot."

ANALYZING THE EVIDENCE

1. How did the Sugar Act, according to the Rhode Island merchants (Document 2) threaten their trade and the African slave trade?
2. How did Phyllis Wheatley's poem (Document 3) challenge white Americans to a more Christian treatment of people of African descent?
3. After reading Documents pertaining to the Boston Massacre (Documents 1, 4, and 5) what role did class and racial tension in Boston play in the lead up to this event? How did the famous engraving by Paul Revere (Document 6) "white-wash" this event?
4. Read the two decisions by British judges pertaining to the status and treatment of slaves. How might the rulings by Justice Martin Howard in North Carolina (Document 7) and the

---

18 Richard Allen, "Eulogy of George Washington" *Philadelphia Gazette,* (Philadelphia, PA), 31 December 1799.

Somerset decision by Chief Justice Mansfield (Document 8) have threatened the institution of slavery in the British colonies in North America? How did slaves react to these rulings? (Document 9)

5. How did Lord Dunmore justify his decision to issue his "Emancipation Proclamation," (Document 11) and how did slaves respond to it? (Documents 15 and 20)

6. Analyze the different messages Patrick Henry (Document 12) gives to white and black residents of Virginia in response to the Dunmore Declaration. What specific grievances does Henry identify against the Dunmore and the British government? What is Henry's message to slaves residing in Virginia?

7. In what ways did African Americans who supported the Patriot cause contribute to the American Revolution?

8. How did African Americans living in Massachusetts (Document, 13, 16, 17, and 21) during revolutionary period couch their claims for political and social justice in the language of the American revolutionaries? How did they challenge the legitimacy of slavery?

Document Based Questions

1. Using the documents provided and your knowledge of the period, analyze the degree to which the American Revolutionary War was a "Counter-Revolution," the intent of which was to maintain ownership of property in slaves and the right to profit from them.

2. Using the documents provided and your knowledge of the period, analyze the ways in which those who objected to British rule and those who objected to slavery used the same arguments to justify their political demands.

"A Covenant with Death and An Agreement with Hell": Slavery at the Constitutional Convention

CHAPTER 6

The Declaration of Independence asserts that "all men are created equal," and the United States Constitution assures us that its purpose is to "secure the blessings of liberty." The degree to which the Constitution enshrined these values, however, has been in question almost from the outset of the republic. Woodrow Wilson, who said "The quick apotheosis of the American Constitution was a phenomenon without parallel in the western world," could not have been more wrong. The "cult of the Constitution" as one historian has termed this reverence for the republic's supreme law only gradually developed. And, for much of the history of the nation, perhaps even to the present, among the symbols of the American republic, the Constitution has ranked behind the flag, the Declaration of Independence (whose words are often wrongly assumed to be a part of the Constitution), coinage and paper money, and perhaps even the Pledge of Allegiance in the hearts and minds of the American public. Perhaps this is because the Constitution, despite its relative brevity and proclaimed clarity, has proven a more elusive guide framework for government and society than those who have touted its near-divine inspiration would suggest.

Among the early critics of the Constitution both immediately after its authorship and at the height of the sectional struggle over slavery were abolitionist voices. In the antebellum period, abolitionists were convinced that the Constitution had enshrined powerful protections for slavery and slave holders. William Lloyd Garrison, a leader of the abolitionist cause in the 1830s called the United States Constitution "a Covenant with Death" and an "agreement with Hell." Pro-slavery advocates, for their part, obliquely confirmed this conclusion by arguing vociferously that the Constitution confirmed slave ownership as a legitimate form of property and that it established a system of government that protected the slave-holding states from encroachments by the federal government that limited slave ownership.

This was despite the fact that the words, slave or slavery, or any overt mention of the enslaved persons composing over a quarter of the republic's populace in 1787 were absent from the document. Only with the Thirteenth Amendment, enacted into law in 1865, does the Constitution explicitly reference the institution of slavery. The Thirteenth Amendment, of course, abolished chattel slavery in the United States, at the end of a prolonged civil war that cost the nation over 600,000 lives. Nonetheless, it is clear from the debates at the constitutional convention and from the contentious arguments that followed during the ratification period that slavery was important to the concerns of those present at the convention, and prominent in the objections of those who opposed its ratification.

In this chapter, you will be asked to immerse yourselves in the debates that attended the Constitution, both at the convention and afterwards. You will be asked to set aside momentarily any reverence for the Constitution, and for the framers of the document, who after all were politicians not unlike contemporary political figures, with their own economic and political interests to defend. The primary sources you will have before you in this chapter are in three general categories. In the first instance, you will have the relevant portions of the United States Constitution at hand to review precisely where the Constitution directly or indirectly sustained the institution of slavery. A second category of documents will include the deliberations at the Constitutional Convention, in the form of excerpts from James Madison's notes on those discussions, which will be excerpted at length to make it possible for readers to immerse themselves in the deliberations of the convention. Finally, in the aftermath of the convention, a hotly contested ratification process took place where the debates at the convention were reprised. The last category of documents in this chapter will then be relevant pieces from Federalist and Anti-Federalist (supporters and opponents of the Constitution) propaganda, and speeches from a number of ratifying conventions. In the end, after a careful reading of the Constitution, the notes taken by Madison at the convention, and the ratifying debates, you will be asked to consider if Garrison, and of course, the pro-slavery apologists of the antebellum period, were not correct.

THE FIRST CONSTITUTION—THE ARTICLES OF CONFEDERATION

The United States Constitution that now stands as the supreme law of the land was not the first constitution to govern the new republic of the United States. The Philadelphia convention had been called to order in 1787 to amend the original constitution, *The Articles of Confederation and Perpetual Union,* which had been drafted to much less fanfare in 1777 and finally ratified in 1781. If ever there was a "weak state" in American history, it was this first constitution. The confederation was largely a wartime expedient established to coordinate the efforts of the states in their struggle for independence. It lacked as a consequence many of the powers typically associated with centralized government. The Congress, lacking an executive and judiciary, had the right to make war and to establish treaties, could requisition funds from the states, but lacked the authority to tax or to enforce laws in the several states that composed the confederation. The weaknesses of the Articles of Confederation were largely the result of the inability to reckon with the implications of slavery in a republic that proclaimed liberty its central ideal.

The deliberations that took place as the Articles were crafted frequently tiptoed around the issue of slavery to avoid offending slave holding members. Compromises made to insure the continued survival of the union so necessary to the ongoing success of the independence movement resulted in the "imbecility" of this weak state, as the framers often harshly judged it. Many of these compromises would be repeated in the fashioning of the United States Constitution. The matter of representation that dogged the Constitutional Convention, an issue that immediately resulted in debates about how to count the slaves, the Articles resolved by granting each state one vote. Under the Articles Congress depended upon requisitions from the states to fund its activities, and ultimately settled on an "impost" or import tax system administered by the states. This was the only tax system which required no discussion of taxing property, whether humans, lands, or capital, or of counting heads, which would again have led to the problem of counting slaves. And during the deliberations, when the matter of apportioning the tax burden arose, for the first time, the practice of counting slaves as three-fifths of a person was suggested. In the discussions that ensued during the writing of the Articles of Confederation, the same defense of slavery that had incited Virginians, Georgians, Carolinians, and Maryland's leaders to rise against Great Britain necessitated the establishment of a government that insured that the sovereignty of slave owners in their own states was not abridged.

This is not to suggest that the government under the Articles of Confederation had not had significant successes. Under the Articles of Confederation the thirteen states that had united to form a perpetual union had successfully defeated the Kingdom of Great Britain and negotiated their independence. But, problems of revenue harried the Congress from the outset, and this central inability to fund the government's operations or repay its debt efficiently provided one justification for calling a convention to amend the document.

This was not the only problem, or perhaps even the most pressing. Rebellions by farmers in the western portions of the original thirteen states, largely in response to high rates of foreclosure and in response to state governments' unfair tax policies illustrated a fundamental weakness of the government that was particularly worrisome to owners of slaves. As the Articles of Confederation remained a union of sovereign states, and as the Congress lacked the authority to intervene in the domestic affairs of the several states, insurrections could only be subdued using the repressive or police measures each of the states were capable of employing. This left all states vulnerable to the disaffection of their citizenry. But, none were so vulnerable as the slave-holding states. So, while Shays' Rebellion, an uprising expressing the discontent of western farmers in Massachusetts, is often cited as the immediate cause resulting in the calling of the Philadelphia convention, the spectre of slave rebellion was perhaps an even greater worry. As Shay's Rebellion was unfolding—it began in August 1786 and lasted until February of the following year--a meeting took place in Annapolis, Maryland to discuss reforms to the existing framework of government. At this assembly, a more extensive reform of the Articles of Confederation was called for, and Congress authorized the meeting of a convention to be held in Philadelphia the following year. This convention would then produce an entirely new system of government for the United States, the United States Constitution.

THE CONSTITUTIONAL CONVENTION

At the outset, slavery did not appear to be the principle dividing issue on which the reform of the Articles of Confederation would turn. Other concerns seemed more pressing. Most importantly, rivalries between more populous and more economically advantaged states and smaller states seemed to be the crucial divide. Under the Articles each state's vote had carried equal weight in the Confederation's deliberations, a fact deemed unjust by many in the larger states. Thus, the matter of how representation in a new government would be distributed was sure to be hotly debated. A related concern was whether the new government would have the power to tax, a recognized weakness of the Articles. The way taxes would be apportioned among the states also would prove a divisive issue. As importantly, particularly for the more commercially-oriented northern states, was the power of the national government to regulate trade both internally and internationally. Other matters were also on the table: paying off the debt accumulated by Congress during the war and afterwards, establishing a national judiciary and executive, and considering the differing powers of the state and national government. None of these issues, on the surface, necessitated consideration of slavery. However, as the debates ensued, the centrality of slavery to the United States, and the different ways in which each section of the country relied upon the sale, labor, and property of enslaved persons made it difficult to converse on any matter without touching on slavery. At every turn slavery, which nearly every member recognized as somehow at odds with the ideals of the recently-fought revolution, arose as a sticking point and obstacle which had to be accommodated or the enterprise of establishing a new Constitution would fail.

The Constitutional Convention opened May 25, 1787 and after a few days spent establishing the rules of order, selecting George Washington as presiding officer, and overturning the amendment process for the Articles of Confederation, on May 29 the work of the convention got underway in earnest. Almost immediately, so too did debates over the way slavery would be written into the national legal system. Edmund Randolph of Virginia submitted a series of resolutions that would later be known as the Virginia Plan to the body. Randolph's plan made population the basis for representation, overturning the Articles of Confederation's system of equal representation by state. Randolph's principled argument for representation based on population size was also a self-interested one. Virginia was the most populous state by a wide margin with its slaves, but only marginally so without. If slaves counted to congressional representation, Virginia, and the South would have greater voice in Congress than the northern states. Not surprisingly, neither less populous states nor northern states, where the numbers of enslaved persons were significantly fewer, were likely to support Randolph's plan. A number of alternative proposals were put forward, including one by William Patterson, often called the New Jersey plan, that called for a continuation of the Articles of Confederation's monocameral (or one chamber) legislature where each state had equal representation.

A compromise position was put forward jointly by Pennsylvania delegate James Wilson and the South Carolinian, Charles Pinckney to count slaves, but at a three-fifths ratio. The proposal was not a particular innovation. This ratio had been used under the Articles of Confederation as a way to calculate apportionment. As the Congress in 1783 struggled to pay off the war debt and fund minimal government functions, debate about how to apportion the payment of these expenses had split the Congress on grounds that by 1787 would have been familiar. A simple plan to implement required payment based on the size of the population of each state. Or, though it would have been nearly impossible to effectively calculate, the plan could have counted real property values (real estate, financial holdings, inventory, capital investments, and, of course, slaves). In both cases any measure of wealth required a negotiation about the numbers and status of slaves within the economy of the new republic. At the Constitutional Convention in Philadelphia in 1787 Pinkney and Wilson offered the three-fifths measure as a way to count slaves for the purposes of representation in the Congress.

As we will see in the debates included in this reader, while the three-fifths compromise gained ready acceptance by the convention, arguments over the principles involved would linger throughout the summer of 1787. They exposed the singular fault line over slavery that divided the delegates. Eldridge Gerry's often quoted remark revealed the heart of the problem: "blacks are property," Gerry observed, "and are used to the southward as horses and cattle to the northward; and why should their representation be increased to the southward on account of the number of slaves, than horses or oxen to the north?" Though Wilson, who had proposed the compromise, accepted the logic that if slaves were counted, "why is not other property admitted into the computation," he argued that this logic "must be overruled by the necessity of compromise." Counting slaves, even at a three-fifths ratio, gave the South greater political weight than it might otherwise have had. And, as William Peterson of New Jersey pointed out, the practice would only encourage the importation of slaves and the continuation of the slave trade. Southerners, for their part, argued that counting slaves, preferably on an equal footing, but if need be using the three-fifths ratio, was a required feature of any new constitution. Otherwise, as Charoles Cotesworth Pinckney of South Carolina contended, the South would be at the mercy of a northern-dominated Congress and southerners would be "nothing more than overseers for the Northern States." In the end, to insure that the Constitution would have any chance of acceptance in the South, slaves were counted according to the three-fifths ratio, and southern representation in Congress, and in the electoral college, would be accordingly increased, giving the South a political influence that belied the number of its recognized citizenry.

While determining the representational system most immediately involved the delegates in questions regarding slavery, other features of the new government's structure required delicate discussions of slavery's implications. One of the weaknesses of the Articles of Confederation was its lack of an executive authority. That such an executive was needed was readily acknowledged by the delegates. However, how to choose the executive was not at all clear. Many delegates believed in direct election by the people—state governors were elected by citizens—but others feared the prospect of a popular election. Southerners were particularly opposed to a popular election of what would only with Washington's inauguration be called "the President" of the United States. Some opponents of popular election objected to the competency of the people to choose so important a position. Others, James Madison among them, argued not that the people were not capable of making informed choices. Madison conceded that the people were "fittest" to make this decision, but nonetheless argued against direct popular election as the "right of suffrage was much more diffusive in the Northern than the Southern States; and the latter could have no influence in the election on the score of the Negroes." Virginians were not alone in recognizing that the large number of enslaved persons in their states reduced their influence in presidential elections. The electoral college, particurlarly with a composition that mirrored a congressional representation skewed by the three-fifths compromise, offered a system whereby southern slaveholders, without extending the franchise, could nonetheless dominate presidential electoral politics. Not surprisingly four of the first five presidents of the United States were Virginians, and slave holders. And eleven of the first sixteen presidents were also slave owners.

Another weakness of the Articles of Confederation that delegates to the Philadelphia convention were intent on addressing was Congress's inability to effectively regulate domestic or international commerce. For northern seaport merchants this weakness, or "imbecility," was fundamental. For both northern and southern delegates, however, debates about the commerce power involved once again discussions about the slave trade. The Philadelphia convention not infrequently divided the task of drafting the Constitution to subcommittees known as Committees of Detail. In early August one such committee returned to the entire convention a draft of what would eventually be the commerce clause. In this draft, Congress was forbidden to pass legislation that might end the African slave trade. Any "navigation acts" or regulations of international trade would also require a supermajority or favorable vote of two-thirds of the legislature. Finally, the report called for prohibitions against any taxes on exports in general and any taxes on imported slaves.

Deliberations about Congress's commerce and taxing powers again quickly turned to questions about slavery's significance to in the nation's political and economic fortunes. Did not the unending commitment to the African slave trade insure ever-increasing southern political influence? Gouverneur Morris of Pennsylvania immediately drew this conclusion, observing that by this means, South Carolina and Georgia, "shall have more votes in a Government instituted for protection of the rights of mankind," than would citizens in states where the slave trade was viewed with "a laudable horror." Northerners and southerners also disagreed over the practice of taxing exports. Southerners perceived export taxes as indirectly an attack on slavery. The power to tax, as Daniel Webster would note several decades later, is the power to destroy. Southerners feared that given the North's increasing antipathy to slavery and the slave trade inevitably a national government with the power to tax exports might use that power to limit or even end slavery. New England delegates, given the significance of the slave trade to their seaport economies, were also supportive of prohibitions on export taxes and protections of the slave trade. As a result, a coalition of New England delegates and southern delegates voted to prohibit any power to tax exports.

Debates about the African slave trade and Congressional powers to regulate trade resulted in a different alignment. The Virginia and Maryland delegations favored ending the African slave trade while the deep South (Georgia, South Carolina) and New England sought its continuation. Though their objections to the African slave trade were often couched in anti-slavery rhetoric, Virginia and Maryland planters had already concluded that they were burdened with a surplus of slaves. With the end of the slave trade, that surplus could be turned to their advantage. Their votes for an end to the external slave trade were effectively votes in favor of their financial interests in a flourishing internal slave trade, free from international competition that would lower the market price of their "surplus." New Englanders, who profited from the "carrying trade" in African slaves and in the produce of the plantations, and delegates from the deep South, thus aligned to extend the African slave trade for an additional twenty years. In a clear exchange, South Carolinians and Georgians agreed to support expanded Congressional power to regulate commerce. The South Carolinian, Charles Pinckney described this stance as a "pure concession on the part of the Southern states," because of the New England states' "liberal conduct towards the views of South Carolina," on the matter of the African slave trade. As a result, rather than the two-thirds vote initially required for Congressional commercial regulation, a simple majority vote became the standard.

With slaveowners' political influence firmly secured, other matters of concern to slavers were then incorporated into the document. The Fugitive Slave Clause guaranteed that slave owners' property rights were recognized and enforced even in states where slavery had been abolished. The responsibility of the federal government to guarantee against domestic violence, alongside the Congress's authorization to "call forth the militia… to suppress insurrection" meant that southern states that were formerly largely dependent on their own resources if faced with slave insurrections could now call on the military and financial resources of the federal government to put down slave rebellions.

On September 17, 1787, thirty-nine delegates to the Philadelphia convention signed the final draft, lending their endorsement to the work that had taken the previous four months to complete. In the end, a stronger national union had been established to replace the confederation under which the thirteen British colonies of North America had established their independence. A quick read of the document might lead one to conclude that slavery hardly troubled the authors of the Constitution. In fact, slavery had featured prominently in the debates in Philadelphia and had contributed significantly to shaping the document. During the ratification debates that followed, among the prominent objections to the new constitution was its expansion of the power of slaveholders and its enshrinement of slavery in a nation proud of its defense of liberty.

RATIFICATION

Perhaps the best evidence of the Constitution's support for slavery can be found in the ways northern and southern anti-Federalists, as opponents of the Constitution were known, respectively objected to the Constitution. Very few voices among southern anti-Federalists complained that the new constitution threatened either the power of slave holders or their rights to human property. Among those, Patrick Henry was the most adamant about the ability of the central government, in some not-so distant future, to undermine the enslavers' property rights. The same could not be said for northern critics who immediately perceived the protections of slavery in the Constitution and the inconsistency of the document with the precepts of the Declaration of Independence. Samuel Bryan perhaps best articulated this objection, concluding that the northern states had conceded too much to the South, whose loyalty had been "purchased too dearly." The Federalists, or supporters of the Constitution, emphasized the gradual ending of the slave trade, which they sold to the public as a "mortal wound" to the institution, which would ultimately prove slavery's death knell. They also contended for the propriety of the spirit of compromise that had prevailed at the convention, arguing that nothing short of the many compromises between the varied interests of the different states could have resulted in any form of union. The Federalists were able to carry the day and the Constitution was, of course, ratified by the thirteen original states becoming the law of the land. Many of the arguments which emerged over the course of the ratification process, mirroring those held at the convention, however, would form the basis of a lasting critique of the Constitution. Abolitionists would long criticize the document and its intent for its explicit, though unstated, defense of slavery. The purpose of this chapter is primarily then to understand those objections, and to momentarily set aside the reverence with which the Constitution is held to grapple with those criticisms.

PRIMARY SOURCES

Document 1   Document 3 *The Constitution of the United States of America*, 1787.

Art. I, sec. 2, par. 3. Representatives and direct Taxes shall be apportioned among the several States which may be included within this Union, according to their respective Numbers, which shall be determined by adding to the whole Number of free Persons, including those bound to Service for a Term of Years, and excluding Indians not taxed three fifths of all other Persons. The actual Enumeration shall be made withing three Years after the first Meeting of the Congress of the United States, and within every subsequent Term of ten Years, in such Manner as they shall by Law direct. The Number of Representatives shall not exceed one for every thirty Thousand, but each State shall have at Least one Representative; and until such enumeration shall be made, the State of New Hampshire shall be entitled to chuse three, Massachusetts eight, Rhode-Island and Providence Plantations one, Connecticut five, New York six, New Jersey four, Pennsylvania eight, Delaware one, Maryland six, Virginia ten, North Carolina five, South Carolina five, and Georgia three.

    Art. I, sec. 8, par. 15. The Congress shall have Power… To provide for calling forth the Militia to execute the Laws of the Union, suppress Insurrections and repel invasions;

Art. I, sec. 9, par. 1. The Migration or Importation of such Pesons as any of the States now existing shall think proper to admit, shall not be prohibited by the Congress prior to the Year one thousand eight hundred and eight, but a Tax or duty may be imposed on such Importation, not exceeding ten dollars for each Person.

Art. I, sec. 9, par. 4. No Capitation, or other direct, Tax shall be laid, unless in Proportion to the Census or enumeration herein before directed to be taken.

Art. I, sec. 10, par. 2. No State shall, without the Consent of the Congress, lay any Imposts or Duties on Imports or Exports, except what may be absolutely necessary for executing it's inspection Laws: and the net Produce of all Duties and Imposts, laid by any State on Imports or Exports, shall be for the Use of the Treasury of the United States; and all such Laws shall be subject to the Revision and Controul of the Congress.

Art. II, sec. 1, par. 2. Each State shall appoint, in such Manner as the Legislature thereof may direct, a Number of Electors, equal to the whole Number of Senators and Representatives to which the State may be entitled in the Congress: but no Senator or Representative, or Person holding an Office of Trust or Profit under the United States, shall be appointed an Elector.

Art. IV, sec. 2, par. 3. No Person held to Service or Labour in one State, under the Laws thereof, escaping into another, shall, in Consequence of any Law or Regulation therein, be discharged from such Service or Labour, but shall be delivered up on Claim of the Party to whom such Service or Labour may be due.

Art. IV, sec. 4. The United States shall guarantee to every State in this Union a Republican Form of Government, and shall protect each of them against Invasion; and on Application of the Legislature, or of the Executive (when the Legislature cannot be convened), against domestic Violence.

Art. V. The Congress, whenever two thirds of both Houses shall deem it necessary shall propose Amendments to this Constitution, or, on the Application of the Legislatures of two thirds of the several States, shall call a Convention for proposing Amendments, which, in either Case, shall be valid to all Intents and Purposes, as Part of this Constitution, when ratified by the Legislatures of three fourths of the several States, or by Conventions in three fourths thereof, as the one or the other Mode of Ratification may be proposed by the Congress; Provided that no Amendment which may be made prior to the Year One thousand eight hundred and eight shall in any Manner affect the first and fourth Clauses in the Ninth Section of the first Article; and that no State without its Consent, shall be deprived of its equal Suffrage in the Senate.

Document 2 Population of the United States, 1790 Census.[1]

State	Population	Slaves (percentage)	White Population
Virginia	747,610	292,697 (25.5%)	454,913
Pennsylvania	434,373	3,737 (>1)	430,636
North Carolina	393,751	100,572 (25.5)	293,179
Massachusetts	378,787	0	378,787
New York	340,120	21,234 (6.2)	318,886
Maryland	319,728	103,036 (32.2)	216,692
South Carolina	249,073	107,094 (43%)	141,979
Connecticut	237,946	2,764 (1.2)	235,182
New Jersey	184,139	11,423 (6.2)	172,716
New Hampshire	141,885	158 (.001)	141,727
Maine*	96,540	0	96,540
Vermont	85,530	16 (na)	85,514
Georgia	82,548	53,284 (35.5)	53,284
Kentucky*	73,677	12,430 (16.9)	61,247
Rhode Island	68,825	948 (1.4)	67,877
Delaware	56,096	8,887 (15)	50,209
Total (North)	**2,024,241**	**49,167 (2.7)**	**1,796,020**
Total (South)	**1,866,387**	**669,113 (35.3)**	**1,197,274**

*Maine and Kentucky were not states but included as territories of Massachusetts and Virginia respectively.

Document 3 James Madison, Notes on the Constitutional Convention, 1787.[2]

Mr. Randolph then opened the main business.[…]

1.He commented on the difficulty of the crisis, and the necessity of preventing the fulfilment of the prophecies of the American downfall.

He observed that in revising the federal system we ought to inquire 1. into the properties, which such a government ought to possess, 2. the defects of the confederation, 3. the danger of our situation & 4. the remedy.

1. The Character of such a government ought to secure 1. against foreign invasions: 2. against dissensions between members of the Union, or seditions in particular States: 3. to procure to

---

[1] Adapted from *Return of the Whole Number of Persons within the Several Districts of the United States according to "An Act Providing for the Enumeration of the Inhabitants of the United States..."*, (Philadelphia: J. Phillips, 1793), p. 2. http://www2.census.gov/prod2/decennial/documents/1790a.pdf

[2] James Madison, The Writings of James Madison, comprising his public papers and his private correspondence, including numerous letters and Documents now for the first time printed. Volume III, 1787 The Journal of the Constitutional Convention. Edited by Gaillard Hunt . (New York: G.P. Putnam's Sons, 1902) Accessed at the Online Library of Liberty http://oll.libertyfund.org/titles/madison-the-writings-of-james-madison-9-vols

the several States various blessings, of which an isolated situation was incapable: 4. to be able to defend itself against encroachment: & 5. to be paramount to the state constitutions.

2. In speaking of the defects of the confederation he professed a high respect for its authors, and considered them as having done all that patriots could do, in the then infancy of the science, of constitutions, & of confederacies,—when the inefficiency of requisitions was unknown—no commercial discord had arisen among any States—no rebellion had appeared as in Massts—foreign debts had not become urgent—the havoc of paper money had not been foreseen—treaties had not been violated—and perhaps nothing better could be obtained from the jealousy of the states with regard to their sovereignty.

2. He then proceeded to enumerate the defects.

1. that the confederation produced no security against foreign invasion; congress not being permitted to prevent a war nor to support it by their own authority—Of this he cited many examples; most of which tended to shew, that they could not cause infractions of treaties or of the law of nations to be punished: that particular states might by their conduct provoke war without controul; and that neither militia nor draughts being fit for defence on such occasions, enlistments only could be successful, and these could not be executed without money.

2, that the federal government could not check the quarrels between states, nor a rebellion in any, not having constitutional power nor means to interpose accordingly to the exigency.

3, that there were many advantages, which the U. S. might acquire, which were not attainable under the confederation—such as a productive impost—counteraction of the commercial regulations of other nations—pushing of commerce ad libitum,—&c &c.

4, that the fœderal government could not defend itself against encroachments from the states.

5, that it was not even paramount to the state constitutions, ratified as it was in many of the states.

3. He next reviewed the danger of our situation, appealed to the sense of the best friends of the U. S. the prospect of anarchy from the laxity of government every where; and to other considerations.

4. He then proceeded to the remedy; the basis of which he said must be the republican principle

He proposed as conformable to his ideas the following resolutions, which he explained one by one.

In Committee of the whole on Mr. Randolph's propositions.

The 3d. Resolution "that the national Legislature ought to consist of two branches" was agreed to without debate or dissent, except that of Pennsylvania, given probably from complaisance to Docr. Franklin who was understood to be partial to a single House of Legislation.

[On Direct Popular Vote for the Legislature]

Resol: 4. first clause, "that the members of the first branch of the National Legislature ought to be elected by the people of the several States," being taken up,

Mr. Sherman opposed the election by the people, insisting that it ought to be by the State Legislatures. The people he said, immediately should have as little to do as may be about the Government. They want information and are constantly liable to be misled.

Mr. Gerry. The evils we experience flow from the excess of democracy. The people do not want virtue, but are the dupes of pretended patriots. In Massts. it had been fully confirmed by experience that they are daily misled into the most baneful measures and opinions by the false reports circulated by designing men, and which no one on the spot can refute. One principal evil arises from the want of due provision for those employed in the administration of Governmt. It would seem to be a maxim of democracy to starve the public servants. He mentioned the popular clamour in Massts. for the reduction of salaries and the attack made on that of the Govr. though secured by the spirit of the Constitution itself. He had he said been too republican heretofore: he was still however republican, but had been taught by experience the danger of the levelling spirit.

Mr. Wilson contended strenuously for drawing the most numerous branch of the Legislature immediately from the people. He was for raising the federal pyramid to a considerable altitude, and for that reason wished to give it as broad a basis as possible. No government could long subsist without the confidence of the people. In a republican Government this confidence was peculiarly essential. He also thought it wrong to increase the weight of the State Legislatures by making them the electors of the national Legislature. All interference between the general and local Governmts. should be obviated as much as possible. On examination it would be found that the opposition of States to federal measures had proceeded much more from the officers of the States, than from the people at large.

Mr Madison considered the popular election of one branch of the national Legislature as essential to every plan of free Government. He observed that in some of the States one branch of the Legislature was composed of men already removed from the people by an intervening body of electors. That if the first branch of the general legislature should be elected by the State Legislatures, the second branch elected by the first — the Executive by the second together with the first; and other appointments again made for subordinate purposes by the Executive, the people would be lost sight of altogether; and the necessary sympathy between them and their rulers and officers, too little felt. He was an advocate for the policy of refining the popular appointments by successive filtrations, but thought it might be pushed too far. He wished the expedient to be resorted to only in the appointment of the second branch of the Legislature, and in the Executive & judiciary branches of the Government. He thought too that the great fabric to be raised would be more stable and durable, if it should rest on the solid foundation of the people themselves, than if it should stand merely on the pillars of the Legislatures.

Mr. Gerry did not like the election by the people. The maxims taken from the British Constitution were often fallacious when applied to our situation which was extremely different. Experience he said had shewn that the State legislatures drawn immediately from the people did not always possess their confidence. He had no objection however to an election by the people if it were so qualified that men of honor & character might not be unwilling to be joined in the appointments. He seemed to think the people might nominate a certain number out of which the State legislatures should be bound to choose.

Mr Butler thought an election by the people an impracticable mode.

On the question for an election of the first branch of the national Legislature, by the people,

Massts. ay. Connect. divd. N. York ay. N. Jersey no. Pena. ay. Delawr. divd. Va. ay. N. C. ay. S. C. no. Georga. ay.

[On the Principle of Legislative Representation]

Mr. Patterson considered the proposition for a proportional representation as striking at the existence of the lesser States. He wd. premise however to an investigation of this question some remarks on the nature structure and powers of the Convention. The Convention he said was formed in pursuance of an Act of Congs. that this act was recited in several of the Commissions, particularly that of Massts. which he required to be read: that the amendment of the Confederacy was the object of all the laws and Commissions on the subject: that the articles of the Confederation were therefore the proper basis of all the proceedings of the Convention. We ought to keep within its limits, or we should be charged by our Constituents with usurpation, that the people of America were sharpsighted and not to be deceived. But the Commissions under which we acted were not only the measure of our power, they denoted also the sentiments of the States on the subject of our deliberation. The idea of a National Govt. as contradistinguished from a federal one, never entered into the mind of any of them, and to the public mind we must accommodate ourselves. We have no power to go beyond the federal Scheme, and if we had the people are not ripe for any other. We must follow the people; the people will not follow us.—The *proposition* could not be maintained whether considered in reference to us as a nation, or as a confederacy. A confederacy supposes sovereignty in the members composing it & sovereignty supposes equality. If we are to be considered as a nation, all State distinctions must be abolished, the whole must be thrown into hotchpot, and when an equal division is made, then there may be fairly an equality of representation. He held up Virga. Massts & Pa. as the three large States, and the other ten as small ones; repeating the calculations of Mr Brearly, as to the disparity of votes which wd take place, and affirming that the small States would never agree to it. He said there was no more reason that a great individual State contributing much, should have more votes than a small one contributing little, than that a rich individual citizen should have more votes than an indigent one. If the rateable property of A was to that of B as 40 to 1, ought A for that reason to have 40 times as many votes as B. Such a principle would never be admitted, and if it were admitted would put B entirely at the mercy of A. As A. has more to be protected than B so he ought to contribute more for the common protection. The same may be said of a large State wch. has more to be protected than a small one. Give the large States an influence in proportion to their magnitude, and what will be the consequence? Their ambition will be proportionally increased, and the small States will have every thing to fear. It was once proposed by Galloway & some others that America should be represented in the British Parlt. and then be bound by its laws. America could not have been entitled to more than ⅓ of the no. of Representatives which would fall to the share of G. B. Would American rights & interests have been safe under an authority thus constituted? It has been said that if a Natl. Govt. is to be formed so as to operate on the people, and not on the States, the representatives ought to be drawn from the people. But why so? May not a Legislature filled by the State Legislatures operate on the people who chuse the State Legislatures? or may not a practicable coercion be found. He admitted that there was none such in the existing System.—He was attached strongly to the plan of the existing Confederacy, in which the people chuse their Legislative representatives; and the Legislatures their federal representatives. No other amendments were wanting than to mark the orbits of the States with due precision, and provide for the use of coercion, which was the great point. He alluded to the hint thrown out heretofore by Mr. Wilson of the necessity to which the large States might be reduced of confederating among themselves, by a refusal of the others to concur. Let them unite if they please, but let them remember that they have no authority to compel the others to unite. N. Jersey will never confederate on the plan before the Committee. She would be swallowed up. He had rather submit to a monarch, to a despot, than to such a fate. He would not only oppose the plan here but on his return home do every thing in his power to defeat it there. […]

Mr. King & Mr Wilson, in order to bring the question to a point moved "that the right of suffrage in the first branch of the national Legislature ought not to be according [to] the rule established in the articles of Confederation, but according to some equitable ratio of representation." The clause so far as it related to suffrage in the first branch was postponed in order to consider this motion.

Mr. Wilson read to the Committee in the words following—Mr. Chairman.

It has given me great pleasure to observe that till this point, the proportion of representation, came before us, our debates were carried on with great coolness & temper. If any thing of a contrary kind, has on this occasion appeared. I hope it will not be repeated; for we are sent here to *consult*, not to *contend*, with each other; and declarations of a fixed opinion, and of determined resolution, never to change it, neither enlighten nor convince us. Positiveness and warmth on one side, naturally beget their like on the other; and tend to create and augment discord & division in a great concern, wherein harmony & Union are extremely necessary to give weight to our Councils, and render them effectual in promoting & securing the common good. I must own that I was originally of opinion it would be better if every member of Congress, or our national Council, were to consider himself rather as a representative of the whole, than as an Agent for the interests of a particular State; in which case the proportion of members for each State would be of less consequence, & it would not be very material whether they voted by States or individually. But as I find this is not to be expected, I now think the number of Representatives should bear some proportion to the number of the Represented; and that the decisions shd. be by the majority of members, not by the majority of the States. This is objected to from an apprehension that the greater States would then swallow up the smaller. I do not at present clearly see what advantage the greater States could propose to themselves by swallowing up the smaller, and therefore do not apprehend they would attempt it....

It was then moved by Mr Rutlidge, 2ded. by Mr. Butler to add to the words "equitable ratio of representation" at the end of the motion just agreed to, the words "according to the quotas of contribution." On motion of Mr. Wilson [Pennsylvani] seconded by Mr. Pinkney [South Carolina], this was postponed; in order to add, after the words "equitable ratio of representation" the words following: "in proportion to the whole number of white & other free Citizens & inhabitants of every age sex & condition including those bound to servitude for a term of years and three fifths of all other persons not comprehended in the foregoing description, except Indians not paying taxes, in each State," this being the rule in the Act of Congress agreed to by eleven States, for apportioning quotas of revenue on the States, and requiring a Census only every 5, 7, or 10 years.

Mr. Gerry thought property not the rule of representation. Why then should the blacks, who were property in the South, be in the rule of representation more than the Cattle & horses of the North.....

Mr. Patterson considered the proposed estimate for the future according to the combined rules of numbers and wealth, as too vague. For this reason N. Jersey was agst. it. He could regard negroes slaves in no light but as property. They are no free agents, have no personal liberty, no faculty of acquiring property, but on the contrary are themselves property, & like other property entirely at the will of the Master. Has a man in Virga. a number of votes in proportion to the number of his slaves? And if negroes are not represented in the States to which they belong, why should they be represented in the Genl. Govt. What is the true principle of Representation? It is an expedient by which an assembly of certain individls chosen by the people is substituted in place of the inconvenient meeting of the people themselves. If such a meeting of the people was actually to take place, would the slaves vote? They would not. Why then shd. they be represented. He was also agst. such an indirect encouragemt. of the slave trade; observing that Congs. in their act relating to the change of the 8 art: of Confedn. had been ashamed to use the term "slaves" & had substituted a description.

Mr. Madison reminded Mr. Patterson that his doctrine of Representation which was in its principle the genuine one, must forever silence the pretensions of the small States to an equality of votes with the large ones. They ought to vote in the same proportion in which their Citizens would do, if the people of all the States were collectively met. He suggested as a proper ground of compromise, that in the first branch the States should be represented according to their number of free inhabitants; And in the 2d. which had for one of its primary objects the guardianship of property, according to the whole number, including slaves.....

Mr. Wilson did not well see on what principle the admission of blacks in the proportion of three fifths could be explained. Are they admitted as Citizens? then why are they not admitted on an equality with White Citizens? are they admitted as property? then why is not other property admitted into the computation? These were difficulties however which he thought must be overruled by the necessity of compromise. He had some apprehensions also from the tendency of the blending of the blacks with the whites, to give disgust to the people of Pena., as had been intimated by his Colleague (Mr. Govr. Morris). But he differed from him in thinking numbers of inhabts. so incorrect a measure of wealth. He had seen the Western settlemts. of Pa. and on a comparison of them with the City of Philada. could discover little other difference, than that property was more unequally divided among individuals here than there. Taking the same number in the aggregate in the two situations he believed there would be little difference in their wealth and ability to contribute to the public wants.

Mr. Govr. Morris was compelled to declare himself reduced to the dilemma of doing injustice to the Southern States or to human nature, and he must therefore do it to the former. For he could never agree to give such encouragement to the Slave Trade as would be given by allowing them a representation for their negroes, and he did not believe those States would ever confederate on terms that would deprive them of that trade.

Mr. Butler & Genl. Pinkney insisted that blacks be included in the rule of Representation *equally* with the whites; and for that purpose moved that the words "three-fifths" be struck out.

Mr. Gerry thought that ⅗ of them was to say the least the full proportion that could be admitted.

Mr. Ghorum. This ratio was fixed by Congs. as a rule of taxation. Then it was urged by the Delegates representing the States having slaves that the blacks were still more inferior to freemen. At present when the ratio of representation is to be established, we are assured that they are equal to freemen. The arguments on ye. former occasion convinced him that ⅗ was pretty near the just proportion and he should vote according to the same opinion now.

Mr. Butler insisted that the labour of a slave in S. Carola. was as productive & valuable as that of a freeman in Massts., that as wealth was the great means of defence and utility to the Nation they were equally valuable to it with freemen; and that consequently an equal representation ought to be allowed for them in a Government which was instituted principally for the protection of property, and was itself to be supported by property.

Mr. Mason could not agree to the motion, notwithstanding it was favorable to Virginia. because he thought it unjust. It was certain that the slaves were valuable, as they raised the value of land, increased the exports & imports, and of course the revenue, would supply the means of feeding & supporting an army, and might in cases of emergency become themselves soldiers. As in these important respects they were useful to the Community at large, they ought not to be excluded from the estimate of Representation. He could not however regard them as equal to freemen and could not vote for them as such. He added as worthy of remark, that the Southern States have this peculiar species of property over & above the other species of property common to all the States.

Mr. Williamson reminded Mr. Ghorum that if the Southn. States contended for the inferiority of blacks to whites when taxation was in view, the Eastern States on the same occasion contended for their equality. He did not however either then or now concur in either extreme, but approved of the ratio of ⅗.

On Mr. Butler's motion for considering blacks as equal to Whites in the apportionmt. of Representation. Massts. no. Cont. no. (N. Y. not on floor). N. J. no. Pa. no. Del. ay. Md. no. Va. no. N. C. no. S. C. ay. Geo. ay.

On Question for agreeing to include ⅗ of the blacks Massts. no. Cont. ay. N. J. no. Pa no. Del. no. Mard. no. Va ay. N. C. ay. S. C. no. Geo. ay.

[On the Slave Trade and Export Taxes]

August 8

Mr. King. The admission of slaves was a most grating circumstance to his mind, & he believed would be so to a great part of the people of America. He had not made a strenuous opposition to it heretofore… [but] In two great points the hands of the Legislature were absolutely tied. The importation of slaves could not be prohibited—exports could not be taxed. Is this reasonable? What are the great objects of the General System? 1. Defense against foreign invasion. 2. Against internal sedition. Shall all the States then be bound to defend each; & shall each be at liberty to introduce a weakness which will render defence more difficult? Shall one part of the U.S. be bound to defend another part, and that other part be at liberty not only to increase its own danger, but to withhold the compensation for the burden? If slaves are to be imported shall not the exports produced by their labor, supply a revenue the better to enable the General Government to defend their Masters? There was so much inequality & unreasonableness in all this, that the people of the Northern States could never be reconciled to it. No candid man could undertake to justify it to them. … At all events, either slaves should not be represented, or exports should be taxable.

August 22

Mr. L. Martin, proposed to vary Article VII Sect. 4 so as to allow a prohibition or tax on the importation of slaves. 1. As five slaves are to be counted as 3 free men in the apportionment of Representatives; such a clause would leave an encouragement to this traffic. 2. Slaves weakened one part of the Union which the other parts were bound to protect; the privilege of importing them was therefore unreasonable. 3. It was inconsistent with the principles of the revolution and dishonorable to the American character to have such a feature in the Constitution.

Mr. Rutlidge did not see how the importation of slaves could be encouraged by this section. He was not apprehensive of insurrections and would readily exempt the other States from the obligation to protect the Southern againt them. Religion and humanity had nothing to do with this question. Interest alone is the governing principle with nations. The true question at present is whether the Southern States shall or shall not be parties to the Union. If the Northern States consult their interest, they will not oppose the increase of slaves which will increase the commodities of which they will become the carriers.

Mr. Elseworth was for leaving the clause as it stands, let every State import what it pleases. The morality or wisdom of slavery are considerations belonging to the States themselves. What enriches a part enriches the whole, and the States are the best judges of their particular interest. The old confederation had not meddled with this point, and he did not see any greater necessity for bringing it within the policy of the new one:

Mr. Pinkney. South Carolina can never receive the plan if it prohibits the slave trade. In every proposed extension of the powers of Congress, that State has expressly & watchfully excepted that of meddling with the importation of negroes. If the States be all left liberty on this subject, S. Carolina may perhaps by degrees do of herself what is wished, as Virginia & Maryland already have done.

August 22

Article VII sect. 4 resumed. Mr Sherman was for leaving the clause as it stands. He disapproved of the slave trade; yet as the States were now possessed of the right to import slaves, as the public good did not require it to be taken from them, & as it was expedient to have as few objections as possible to the proposed scheme of Government, he thought it best to leave the matter as we find it. He observed that the abolition of Slavery seemed to be going on in the U.S. & that the good sense of the several States would probably by degreees complete it. He urged on the Convention the necessity of despatiching its business.

Colonel Mason. This infernal traffic originated in the avarice of British Merchants. The British Government constantly checked the attempts of Virginia to put a stop to it. The present question concerns not the importing States alone but the whole Union. ... Maryland and Virginia he said had already prohibited the importation of slaves expressly. N. Carolina had done the same in substance. All this would be in vain if S. Carolina & Georgia be at liberty to import. The Western people are already calling out for slaves for their new lands, and will fill that Country with slaves if they can be got thro' S. Carolina & Georgia. Slavery discourages arts & manufactures. The poor despise labor when performed by slaves. They prevent the immigration of Whites, who really enrich & strengthen a Country. They produce the most pernicious effect on manners. Every master of slaves is born a petty tyrant. ... As to the States bing in possession of the Right to import, this was the case with many other rights, now to be properly given up. He held it essential in every point of view that the General Government should have power to prevent the increase of slavery.

Mr. Elseworth. As he had never owned a slave could not judge of the effects of slavery on character. He said however that if it was to be considered in a moral light we ought to go farther and free those already in the Country.—As slaves also multiply so fast in Virginia & Maryland that it is cheaper to raise than to import them...

Mr. Pinkney. If slavery be wrong, it is justified by the example of all the world. He cited the case of Greece, Rome & other ancient States; the sanction given by France, England, Holland,

& other modern states. ... An attempt to take away the right as proposed will produce serious objections to the Constitution which he wished to see adopted.

General Pinkney declared it to be his firm opinion that if himself & all his colleagues were to sign the Constitution & use their personal influence, it would be of no avail towards obtaining the assent of their Constituents. S. Carolina & Georgia cannot do without slaves. As to Virginia she will gain by stopping the importations. Her slaves will rise in value, & she has more than she wants. It would be unequal to require S.C. & Georgia to confederate on such unequal terms.... He contended that the importation of slaves would be for the interest of the whole Union. The more slaves, the more produce to employ the carrying trade; The more consumption also, and the more of this, the more revenue for the common treasury....

Mr. Gerry thought we had nothing to do with the conduct of the States as to Slaves, but ought to be careful not to give any sanction to it.

Mr. Dickenson considered it as inadmissible on every principle of honor & safety that the importation of slaves should be authorized to the States by the Constitution. The true question was whether the national happiness would be promoted or impeded by the importation, and this question ought to be left to the National Government not to the States particularly interested.

... Mr. Sherman said it was better to let the Southern States import slaves than to part with them, if they made that a *sine qua non*. He was opposed to a tax on slaves imported as making the matter worse, because it implied they were *property*.

[On Fugitive Slaves]

August 28

... Mr. Butler and Mr. Pinkney moved "to require fugitive slaves and servants to be delivered up like criminals.

Mr. Wilson. This would oblige the Executive of the State to do it at the public expence.

Mr. Sherman saw no more propriety in the public seizing and surrendering a slave or servant, than a horse.

Mr. Butler withdrew his proposition in order that some particular provision might be made apart from this article.

Document 4 Alexander Hamilton or James Madison, *Federalist No. 54.*[3]

To the People of the State of New York:

THE next view which I shall take of the House of Representatives relates to the appointment of its members to the several States which is to be determined by the same rule with that of direct taxes.

It is not contended that the number of people in each State ought not to be the standard for regulating the proportion of those who are to represent the people of each State. The establishment

---

[3] Source: James Madison or Alexander Hamilton, Federalist No. 54, *The Avalon Project,* Yale Law School, Lillian Goldman Law Library. http://avalon.law.yale.edu/18th_century/fed54.asp

of the same rule for the appointment of taxes, will probably be as little contested; though the rule itself in this case, is by no means founded on the same principle. In the former case, the rule is understood to refer to the personal rights of the people, with which it has a natural and universal connection. In the latter, it has reference to the proportion of wealth, of which it is in no case a precise measure, and in ordinary cases a very unfit one. But notwithstanding the imperfection of the rule as applied to the relative wealth and contributions of the States, it is evidently the least objectionable among the practicable rules, and had too recently obtained the general sanction of America, not to have found a ready preference with the convention.

All this is admitted, it will perhaps be said; but does it follow, from an admission of numbers for the measure of representation, or of slaves combined with free citizens as a ratio of taxation, that slaves ought to be included in the numerical rule of representation? Slaves are considered as property, not as persons. They ought therefore to be comprehended in estimates of taxation which are founded on property, and to be excluded from representation which is regulated by a census of persons. This is the objection, as I understand it, stated in its full force. I shall be equally candid in stating the reasoning which may be offered on the opposite side. "We subscribe to the doctrine," might one of our Southern brethren observe, "that representation relates more immediately to persons, and taxation more immediately to property, and we join in the application of this distinction to the case of our slaves. But we must deny the fact, that slaves are considered merely as property, and in no respect whatever as persons. The true state of the case is, that they partake of both these qualities: being considered by our laws, in some respects, as persons, and in other respects as property.

In being compelled to labor, not for himself, but for a master; in being vendible by one master to another master; and in being subject at all times to be restrained in his liberty and chastised in his body, by the capricious will of another, the slave may appear to be degraded from the human rank, and classed with those irrational animals which fall under the legal denomination of property. In being protected, on the other hand, in his life and in his limbs, against the violence of all others, even the master of his labor and his liberty; and in being punishable himself for all violence committed against others, the slave is no less evidently regarded by the law as a member of the society, not as a part of the irrational creation; as a moral person, not as a mere article of property.

The federal Constitution, therefore, decides with great propriety on the case of our slaves, when it views them in the mixed character of persons and of property. This is in fact their true character. It is the character bestowed on them by the laws under which they live; and it will not be denied, that these are the proper criterion; because it is only under the pretext that the laws have transformed the negroes into subjects of property, that a place is disputed them in the computation of numbers; and it is admitted, that if the laws were to restore the rights which have been taken away, the negroes could no longer be refused an equal share of representation with the other inhabitants. "This question may be placed in another light. It is agreed on all sides, that numbers are the best scale of wealth and taxation, as they are the only proper scale of representation. Would the convention have been impartial or consistent, if they had rejected the slaves from the list of inhabitants, when the shares of representation were to be calculated, and inserted them on the lists when the tariff of contributions was to be adjusted? Could it be reasonably expected, that the Southern States would concur in a system, which considered their slaves in some degree as men, when burdens were to be imposed, but refused to consider them in the same light, when advantages were to be conferred? Might not some surprise also be expressed, that those who reproach the Southern States with the barbarous policy of considering as property a part of their human brethren, should themselves contend, that the government to which all the States are to be parties, ought to consider this unfortunate race more completely in the unnatural light of property, than the very laws of which they complain? "It may be replied, perhaps, that slaves are not included in the estimate of representatives in any of the States possessing them. They neither vote themselves nor increase the votes of their masters. Upon what principle, then, ought they to be taken into the federal estimate of representation?

In rejecting them altogether, the Constitution would, in this respect, have followed the very laws which have been appealed to as the proper guide. "This objection is repelled by a single abservation. It is a fundamental principle of the proposed Constitution, that as the aggregate number of representatives allotted to the several States is to be determined by a federal rule, founded on the aggregate number of inhabitants, so the right of choosing this allotted number in each State is to be exercised by such part of the inhabitants as the State itself may designate. The qualifications on which the right of suffrage depend are not, perhaps, the same in any two States. In some of the States the difference is very material.

In every State, a certain proportion of inhabitants are deprived of this right by the constitution of the State, who will be included in the census by which the federal Constitution apportions the representatives. In this point of view the Southern States might retort the complaint, by insisting that the principle laid down by the convention required that no regard should be had to the policy of particular States towards their own inhabitants; and consequently, that the slaves, as inhabitants, should have been admitted into the census according to their full number, in like manner with other inhabitants, who, by the policy of other States, are not admitted to all the rights of citizens. A rigorous adherence, however, to this principle, is waived by those who would be gainers by it. All that they ask is that equal moderation be shown on the other side. Let the case of the slaves be considered, as it is in truth, a peculiar one. Let the compromising expedient of the Constitution be mutually adopted, which regards them as inhabitants, but as debased by servitude below the equal level of free inhabitants, which regards the SLAVE as divested of two fifths of the MAN. "After all, may not another ground be taken on which this article of the Constitution will admit of a still more ready defense? We have hitherto proceeded on the idea that representation related to persons only, and not at all to property. But is it a just idea? Government is instituted no less for protection of the property, than of the persons, of individuals. The one as well as the other, therefore, may be considered as represented by those who are charged with the government.

Upon this principle it is, that in several of the States, and particularly in the State of New York, one branch of the government is intended more especially to be the guardian of property, and is accordingly elected by that part of the society which is most interested in this object of government. In the federal Constitution, this policy does not prevail. The rights of property are committed into the same hands with the personal rights. Some attention ought, therefore, to be paid to property in the choice of those hands. "For another reason, the votes allowed in the federal legislature to the people of each State, ought to bear some proportion to the comparative wealth of the States. States have not, like individuals, an influence over each other, arising from superior advantages of fortune. If the law allows an opulent citizen but a single vote in the choice of his representative, the respect and consequence which he derives from his fortunate situation very frequently guide the votes of others to the objects of his choice; and through this imperceptible channel the rights of property are conveyed into the public representation. A State possesses no such influence over other States. It is not probable that the richest State in the Confederacy will ever influence the choice of a single representative in any other State. Nor will the representatives of the larger and richer States possess any other advantage in the federal legislature, over the representatives of other States, than what may result from their superior number alone. As far, therefore, as their superior wealth and weight may justly entitle them to any advantage, it ought to be secured to them by a superior share of representation.

The new Constitution is, in this respect, materially different from the existing Confederation, as well as from that of the United Netherlands, and other similar confederacies. In each of the latter, the efficacy of the federal resolutions depends on the subsequent and voluntary resolutions of the states composing the union. Hence the states, though possessing an equal vote in the public councils, have an unequal influence, corresponding with the unequal importance of these subsequent and voluntary resolutions. Under the proposed Constitution, the federal acts will take effect without the necessary intervention of the individual States. They will depend merely on the majority of votes in the federal legislature, and consequently each vote, whether proceeding from a larger or smaller State, or a State more or less wealthy or powerful, will have an equal weight and efficacy: in the same manner as the votes individually given in a State legislature, by the representatives of unequal counties or other districts, have each a precise equality of value and effect; or if there be any difference in the case, it proceeds from the difference in the personal character of the individual representative, rather than from any regard to the extent of the district from which he comes. "Such is the reasoning which an advocate for the Southern interests might employ on this subject; and although it may appear to be a little strained in some points, yet, on the whole, I must confess that it fully reconciles me to the scale of representation which the convention have established. In one respect, the establishment of a common measure for representation and taxation will have a very salutary effect. As the accuracy of the census to be obtained by the Congress will necessarily depend, in a considerable degree on the disposition, if not on the co-operation, of the States, it is of great importance that the States should feel as little bias as possible, to swell or to reduce the amount of their numbers. Were their share of representation alone to be governed by this rule, they would have an interest in exaggerating their inhabitants. Were the rule to decide their share of taxation alone, a contrary temptation would prevail. By extending the rule to both objects, the States will have opposite interests, which will control and balance each other, and produce the requisite impartiality.

PUBLIUS.

Document 5 David Ramsay, *Address to the Freemen of South Carolina, on the subject of the* Federal Constitution, Proposed by the Convention, which met in Philadelphia, May, 1787. [4]

Friends, Countrymen, and Fellow Citizens:

You have, at this time a new federal constitution proposed for your consideration. The great importance of the subject demands your most serious attention. To assist you in forming a right judgment on this matter, it will be proper to consider,

---

[4] David Ramsay, "Address to the Freemen of South Carolina, on the subject of the Federal Constitution, Proposed by the Convention, which met in Philadelphia, May, 1787," in *The Federalist and other Contemporary Papers on the Constitution of the United States*, E.H. Scott, ed. (Chicago: Scott, Foresman and Company, 1894), pp. 918-924.

1st. It is the manifest interest of these states to be united. Internal wars among ourselves, would most probably be the consequence of disunion. Our local weakness particularly proves it to be for the advantage of South Carolina to strengthen the federal government; for we are inadequate to secure ourselves from more powerful neighbours

2d. If the thirteen states are to be united in reality, as well as in name, the obvious principle of the union will be, that the congress, or general government, should have power to regulate all general concerns. In a state of nature, each man is free, and may do what he pleases: but in society, every individual must sacrifice a part of his natural rights; the minority must yield to the majority, and the collective interest must controul particular interests. When thirteen persons constitute a family, each should forego everything that is injurious to the other twelve. When several families constitute a parish, or county, each may adopt what regulations it pleases with regard to its domestic affairs, but must be abridged of that liberty in other cases, where the good of the whole is concerned.

When several parishes, counties, or districts, form a state, the separate interests of each must yield to the collective interest of the whole. When several states combine in one government, the same principles must be observed. These relinquishments of natural rights, are not real sacrifices: each person, county, or state, gains more than it loses, for it only gives up a right of injuring others, and obtains in return aid and strength to secure itself in the peaceable enjoyment of all remaining rights. If then we are to be an united people, and the obvious ground of union must be, that all continental concerns should be managed by Congress—let us by those principles examine the new constitution. Look over the 8th section, which enumerates the powers of Congress, and point out one that is not essential on the before recited principles of union. The first is a power to lay and collect taxes, duties, imposts, and excises, to pay the debts, and provide for the common defence and general welfare of the United States.

When you authorised Congress to borrow money, and to contract debts, for carrying on the late war, you could not intend to abridge them of the means of paying their engagements, made on your account. You may observe that their future power is confined to provide *common defence* and *general welfare* of the United States. If they apply money to any other purposes, they exceed their powers. The people of the United States who pay, are to be judges how far their money is properly applied. It would be tedious to go over all the powers of Congress, but it would be easy to show that they all may be referred to this single principle, "that the general "concerns of the union ought to be managed by the general "government." The opposers of the constitution cannot show a single power delegated to Congress, that could be spared consistently with the welfare of the whole, nor a single one taken from the states, but such as can be more advantageously lodged in the general government, than in that of the separate states.

For instance, the states cannot emit money: This is not intended to prevent the emission of paper money, but only of state paper money. Is not this an advantage? To have thirteen paper currencies in thirteen states is embarrassing to commerce, and eminently so to travellers. It is *therefore*, obviously our interest, either to have no paper, or such as will circulate from Georgia to New Hampshire. Take another instance—the Congress are authorized to provide and maintain a navy.—Our sea-coast, in its whole extent needs the protection thereof; but if this was to be done by the states, they who build ships, would be more secure than they who do not. Again, if the local legislatures might build ships of war at pleasure, the Eastern would have a manifest superiority over the Southern states. Observe, how much better this business is referred to the regulations of Congress. A common navy, paid out of the common treasury, and to be disposed of by the united voice of a majority for the common defence of the weaker as well as of the stronger states, is promised, and will result from the federal constitution. Suffer not yourselves to be imposed on by declamation. Ask the man who objects to the powers of Congress two questions, is it not necessary that the supposed dangerous power should be lodged somewhere? And secondly, where can it be lodged, consistently with the general good, so well as in the general government? Decide for yourselves on these obvious principles of union.

It has been objected, that the eastern states have an advantage in their representation in Congress. Let us examine this objection—the four eastern states send seventeen members to the house of representatives, but Georgia, South-Carolina, North-Carolina and Virginia, send twenty-three. The six northern states send twenty-seven, the six southern thirty. In both cases, we have a superiority;—but, say the objectors, add Pennsylvania to the northern states, and there is a majority against us. It is obvious to reply, add Pennsylvania to the southern states, and they have a majority. The objection amounts to no more than that seven are more than six. It must be known to many of you, that the Southern states, from their vast extent of uncultivated country, are daily receiving new settlers; but in New England their country is so small, and their land so poor, that their inhabitants are constantly emigrating. As the rule of representation in Congress is to vary with the number of inhabitants, our influence in the general government will be constantly increasing. In fifty years, it is probable that the Southern states will have a great ascendency over the Eastern. It has been said that thirty-five men, not elected by yourselves, may make laws to bind you. This objection, if it has any force, tends to the destruction of your state government. By our constitution, sixty-nine make a quorum; of course, thirty-five members may make a law to bind all the people of South-Carolina.—Charleston, and any one of the neighboring parishes send collectively thirty-six members; it is therefore possible, in the absence of all others, that three of the lower parishes might legislate for the whole country. Would this be a valid objection against your own constitution? It certainly would not—neither is it against the proposed federal plan. Learn from it this useful lesson—insist on the constant attendance of your members, both in the state assembly, and Continental Congress; your representation in the latter, is as numerous in a relative proportion with the other states as it ought to be. You have a thirteenth part in both houses; and you are not, on principles of equality, entitled to more.

It has been objected, that the president, and two-thirds of the senate, though not of your election, may make treaties binding on the state. Ask these objectors—do you wish to have any treaties? They will say yes. Ask then who can be more properly trusted with the power of making them, than they to whom the convention have referred it? Can the state legislature? They would consult their local interests.—Can the Continental House of Representatives? When sixty-five men can keep a secret, they may.—Observe the cautious guards which are placed round your interests. Neither the senate nor president can make treaties by their separate authority.—They must both concur.—This is more in your favour than the footing on which you now stand. The delegates in Congress of nine states, without your consent, can now bind you; by the new constitution there must be two-thirds af the members present, and also the president, in whose election you have a vote. Two-thirds are to the whole, nearly as nine to thirteen. If you are not wanting to yourselves by neglecting to keep up the state's compliment of senators, your situation with regard to preventing the controul of your local interests by the Northern states, will be better under the proposed constitution than it is now under the existing confederation.

It has been said, we will have a navigation act, and be restricted to American bottoms, and that high freight will be the consequence. We certainly ought to have a navigation act, and we assuredly ought to give a preference, though not a monopoly, to our own shipping.

If this state is invaded by a maritime force, to whom can we apply for immediate aid?—To Virginia and North-Carolina? Before they can march by land to our assistance, the country may be overrun. The Eastern states, abounding in men and in ships, can sooner relieve us, than our next door neighbours. It is therefore not only our duty, but our interest to encourage their shipping. They have sufficient resources on a few months notice, to furnish tonnage enough to carry off all your exports; and they can afford, and doubtless will undertake to be your carriers on as easy terms as you now pay for freight in foreign bottoms.

On this subject, let us consider what we have gained, also what they have lost, by the revolution. We have gained a free trade with all the world, and consequently a higher price for our commodities; it may be said, and so have they. But they who reply in this manner, ought to know, that there is an amazing difference in our favour; their country affords no valuable exports, and of course the privilege of a free trade is to them of little value, while our staple commodity commands a higher price than was usual before the war. We have also gained an exemption from quit-rents, to which the eastern states were not subjected. Connecticut and Rhode Island were nearly as free before the revolution as since. They had no royal governor or councils to control them, or to legislate for them. Massachusetts and New Hampshire were much nearer independence in their late constitution than we were. The eastern states, by the revolution, have been deprived of a market for their fish, of their carrying trade, their ship-building, and almost of every thing but their liberties.

As the war has turned out so much in our favour, and so much against them, ought we to grudge them the carrying of our produce, especially when it is considered, that by encouraging their shipping, we increase the means of our own defence? Let us examine also the federal constitution, by the principles of reciprocal concession. We have laid a foundation for a navigation act. This will be a general good; but particularly so to our northern brethren. On the other hand, they have agreed to change the federal rule of paying the continental debt, according to the value of land, as laid down in the confederation, for a new principle of apportionment, to be founded on the numbers of inhabitants in the several states respectively. This is an immense concession in our favour. Their land is poor; our's rich; their numbers great; our's small; labour with them is done by white men, for whom they pay an equal share; while five of our negroes only count as equal to three of their whites. This will make a difference of many thousands of pounds in settling our continental accounts. It is farther objected, that they have stipulated for a right to prohibit the importation of negroes after 21 years. On this subject observe, as they are bound to protect us from domestic violence, they think we ought not to increase our exposure to that evil, by an unlimited importation of slaves. Though Congress may forbid the importation of negroes after 21 years, it does not follow that they will. On the other hand, it is probable that they will not. The more rice we make, the more business will be for their shipping; their interest will therefore coincide with our's. Besides, we have other sources of supply—the importation of the ensuing 20 years, added to the natural increase of those we already have, and the influx from our northern neighbours, who are desirous of getting rid of their slaves, will afford a sufficient number for cultivating all the lands in this state.

Let us suppose the union to be dissolved by the rejection of the new constitution, what would be our case? The united states owe several millions of dollars to France, Spain, and Holland. If an efficient government is not adopted, which will provide for the payment of our debt, especially of that which is due to foreigners—who will be the losers? Most certainly the southern states. Our exports, as being the most valuable, would be the first objects of capture on the high seas, or descents would be made on our defenceless coasts, till the creditors of the United States had paid themselves at the expense of this weaker part of the union. Let us also compare the present confederation with the proposed constitution. The former can neither protect us at home, nor gain us respect abroad; it cannot secure the payment of our debts, nor command the resources of our country, in case of danger. Without money, without a navy, or the means of even supporting an army of our own citizens in the field, we lie at the mercy of every invader; our sea-port towns may be laid under contribution, and our country ravaged.

By the new constitution, you will be protected with the force of the union, against domestic violence and foreign invasion. You will have a navy to defend your coast.—The respectable figure you will make among the nations, will so far command the attention of foreign powers, that it is probable you will soon obtain such commercial treaties, as will open to your vessels the West-India islands, and give life to your expiring commerce.

In a country like our's, abounding with free men all of one rank, where property is equally diffused, where estates are held in fee simple, the press free, and the means of information common, tyranny cannot reasonably find admission under any form of government; but its admission is next to impossible under one where the people are the source of all power, and elect either mediately by their representatives, or immediately by themselves the whole of their rulers.

Examine the new constitution with candor and liberality. Indulge no narrow prejudices to the disadvantage of your brethren of the other states; consider the people of all the thirteen states, as a band of brethren, speaking the same language, professing the same religion, inhabiting one undivided country, and designed by heaven to be one people. Content that what regards all the states should be managed by that body which represents all of them; be on your guard against the misrepresentations of men who are involved in debt; such may wish to see the constitution rejected, because of the following clause, "no state shall emit bills of credit, make any thing but gold and silver coin, a tender in payment of debts, pass any *expost facto* law, or law impairing the obligation of contracts." This will doubtless bear hard on debtors who wish to defraud their creditors, but it will be real service to the honest part of the community. Examine well the characters and circumstances of men who are averse to the new constitution. Perhaps you will find that the above recited clause is the real ground of the opposition of some of them, though they may artfully cover it with a splendid profession of zeal for state privileges and general liberty.

On the whole, if the proposed constitution be not calculated to better your country, and to secure to you the blessings for which you have so successfully contended, reject it: but if it be an improvement on the present confederation, and contains within itself the principles of farther improvement suited to future circumstances, join the mighty current of federalism, and give it your hearty support. You were among the first states that formed an independent constitution; be not among the last in accepting and ratifying the proposed plan of federal government; it is your sheet anchor; and without it independence may prove a curse.

CIVIS.

Document 6 Patrick Henry, Speech during the Debates of the Virginia Ratification Convention, 1788.[5]

It is exceedingly painful to me to be ojecting, but I must make a few observations. I shall not again review the catalogue of dangers which the honorable gentleman entertained us with. They appear to me absolutely imaginary. They have, in my conception, been proved to be such. But sure I am, that the dangers of this system are real, when those who have no similar interests with the people of this country are to legislate for us—when our dearest interests are left in the power of those whose advantage it may be to infringe them. How will the quotas of troops be furnished? Hated as requisitions are, your Federal officers cannot collect troops like dollars, and carry them in their pockets. You must make these abominable requisitions for them, and the scale will be in proportion to the number of your blacks as well as your whites, unless they violate the constitutional rule of apportionment. This is not calculated to rouse the fears of the people. It is founded in truth. How oppressive and dangerous must this be to the Southern States, who alone have slaves! This will render their proportion infinitely greater than that of the Northern States. It has been openly avowed that this shall be the rule. I will appeal to the judgments of the committee, whether there be danger.

... Suppose an insurrection in Virginia, and suppose there be danger apprehended of an insurrection in another State, from the exercise of the Government; or suppose a national war, and there be discontent among the people of this State, that produces or threatens an insurrection; suppose Congress, in either case, demands a number of militia, will they not be obliged to go? Where are your reserved rights, when your militia go to a neighboring State? Which call is to be obeyed, the Congressional call, or the call of the State Legislature? The call of Congress must be obeyed. I need not remind this committee, that the sweeping clause will cause their demands to be submitted to. This clause enables them "to make all laws which are necessary and proper to carry into execution all the powers vested in this Constitution in the Government of the United States, or in any department or officer thereof." Mr. Chairman, I will turn to another clause, which relates to the same subject, and tends to show the fallacy of their argument. The tenth section of the first article, to which reference was made by the worthy member, militates against himself. It says, that "no State shall engage in war, unless actually invaded." If you give this clause a fair construction, what is the true meaning of it? What does this relate to? Not domestic insurrections, but war. If the country be invaded, a State may go to war, but cannot suppress insurrections. If there should happen an insurrection of slaves, the country cannot be said to be invaded. They cannot therefore suppress it, without the interposition of Congress. The fourth section of the fourth article expressly directs, that in case of domestic violence, Congress shall protect the State, on application of the Legislature or Executive; and the eighth section of the first article gives Congress power to call forth the militia, to quell insurrections. There cannot, therefore, be a concurrent poer. The State Legislatures ought to have power to call forth the efforts of militia, when necessary. Occasions for calling them out may be urgent, pressing and instantaneous. The States cannot now call them, let an insurrection be ever so perilous, without an application to Congress. So long a delay may be fatal.

Among ten thousand implied powers which they may assume, they may, if we be engaged in war, liberate every one of your slaves, if they please; and this must and will be done by men,

---

[5] Daniel R. Goodloe, *The Southern Platform: or, Manual of Southern Sentiment on the Subject of Slavery*, (Boston: John P. Jewett & Co., 1858), pp. 20-26.

a majority of whom have not a common interest with you. They will, therefore, have no feeling of your interests. It has been repeatedly said here that the great object of a National Government was national defense. That power, which is said to be intended for security and safety, may be rendered detestable and oppressive. If they give power to the General Government to provide for the general defense, the means must be given to the Government which is intrusted with the public defense. In this State, there are 236,000 blacks; and there are many in several other States: but there are few or none in the Northern States; and yet, if the Northern States shall be of opinion that our slaves are numberless, they may call forth every national resource. May Congress not say *that every black man must fight?* Did we not see a little of this last war? We were not so hard pushed as to make emancipation general; but acts of Assembly passed, that every slave who would go to the army should be free. Another thing will contribute to bring this event about: Slavery is detested; we feel its fatal effects; we deplore it with all the pity of humanity. Let all these considerations, at some future period, press with full force on the minds of Congress—let that urbanity, which I trust will distinguish America, and the necessity of national defense—let all these things operate on their minds: they will search that paper, and see if they have the power of manumission. And have they not, Sir? Have they not power to provide for the general defense and welfare? May they not think that these call for abolition of Slavery? May they not pronounce all slaves free? And will they not be warranted by that power? There is no ambiguous implication or logical deduction. The paper speaks to the point. They have the power, in clear, unequivocal terms, and will clearly and certainly exercise it. As much as I deplore Slavery, I see that prudence forbids its abolition. I deny that the General Government ought to set them free, because a decided majority of the States have not the ties of sympathy and fellow-feeling for those whose interest would be affected by their emancipation. The majority of Congress is to the North, and the slaves are to the South. In this situation, I see a great deal of the property of the people of Virginia in jeopardy, and their peace and tranquility gone. I repeat it again, that it would rejoice my very soul, that every one of my fellow-beings was emancipated. As we ought, with gratitude, to admire that decree of Heaven which has numbered us among the free, we ought to lament and deplore the necessity of holding our fellow-men in bondage. But is it practicable by any human means, to liberate them, without producing the most dreadful and ruinous consequences? We ought to possess them in the manner we have inherited them from our ancestors, as their manumission is incompatible with the felicity of the country; but we ought to soften, as much as possible, the rigor of their unhappy fate. I know that in a variety of particular instances, the Legislature, listening to complaints have admitted their emancipation. Let me not dwell on this subject. I will only add, that this, as well as every other property of the people of Virginia, is in jeopardy, and put in the hands of those who have no similarity of situation with us. This is a local matter, and I can see no propriety in subjecting it to Congress.

EXAMINING THE EVIDENCE

1. What terms were used by the authors of the United States Constitution (Document 1) to refer to enslaved persons? Why might the framers of the Constitution have avoided using the terms "slaves" or "bondsmen"?

2. Examine the evidence from the United States Census of 1790 (Document 2). How would counting enslaved persons on an equal basis with free populations affect legislative representation and electoral college influence?

3. What did Edmund Randolph identify as the strengths and weaknesses of the Articles of Confederation? (Document 3)
4. What arguments were made in favor of direct popular election for the legislative branch at the Constitutional convention? What were the arguments against direct election? (Document 3)
5. What arguments were given in favor of "proportional representation" in the legislature? Against? (Document 3)
6. How did delegates at the Constitutional Convention argue for and against counting enslaved persons for the purposes of representation? (Document 3)
7. According to Madison's notes, what were the key reasons given for the Electoral College? (Document 3)
8. How did the delegates at the Constitutional Convention argue in favor and in opposition to the continuation of the African slave trade? (Document 3)
9. How did Federalist No. 54 (Document 4) support the contention that the Constitution would provide a more humane approach to slavery than that in existing law? How did it justify the legitimacy of counting slaves as property as well as persons?
10. What evidence did David Ramsay (Document 5) provide to the citizens of South Carolina that the new Federal Government would prove beneficial to the citizens of the state and to the South generally?
11. How did Patrick Henry (Document 6) fear the creation of the new Federal Government would threaten southern slave holding states?

Document Based Questions

1. Using the evidence in the documents provided and **your knowledge of** United States history, evaluate William Lloyd Garrison's contention that the United States Constitution represented a "Covenant with Death and an Agreement with Hell?"

Black Founders, American Democracy and White Supremacy

CHAPTER 7

The years following the tumult of the revolutionary period and the establishment of the United States Constitution are often seen as a period when the republic negotiated the transition to nationhood, setting in place many of the institutional practices that would remain in place until the present. Historical discussion of the early republic, from 1787 to the 1830s has emphasized the development of the political institutions and culture from the skeletal forms that had been laid out in the Constitution. In addition, historians have focused on the partisan and personal rivalries that soon became a common feature of politics in the new republic. The place of slavery as a lightening rod for political rivalry and symbol of sectional difference would not emerge in full until the 1840s, though there was a harbinger of this division in the Missouri controversy of 1819-1820. Instead, other concerns dominated the political debates of the early republic.

For example, the Constitution made no mention of political parties as the founders believed that political factionalism would be the death knell of the republic. Nonetheless, even before the end of George Washington's presidency political divisions within his administration had begun to form the outlines of the two-party political system that still characterizes American electoral politics. When George Washington determined to serve only two terms, these rivalries exploded into full view, with the Federalists, led by John Adams and Alexander Hamilton confronting the Jeffersonian Republicans, who would later be known as the Democratic Republicans, and finally the Democratic Party. In neither party was there a strong commitment to or defense of slavery. Jefferson recognized the threat posed to the republic by a reliance on slave labor, saw slavery as sapping the vitality of the white citizenry, and imagined the successful republic as one built on a foundation of yeoman farmers and a thriving merchant class. Slavery, while a present necessity, Jefferson imagined would sooner or later disappear naturally. Jefferson could conceive of no place within the American polity for freed men; African Americans were best returned to Africa. The Hamiltonian vision, likewise, saw little place for African slavery. But, rather than a republic constructed from a citizenry of independent farmers, Hamilton envisioned a thriving manufacturing sector, fostered by an activist government and a secure financial sector. For Hamilton, slavery seemed to be an anachronism. The fact that Jefferson and many of the party's other leaders were slave owners, and its base was in the South, meant that the Jeffersonian Republicans' interpretations of the role and limits of the federal government often coincided with slaveholders' interests. Nonetheless, both northerners and southerners could imagine the day when slavery was no longer a feature of the nation's economy.

Slavery, therefore, did not feature prominently in the political debates that energized partisans in the early republic. Instead, national political struggles turned on such issues as the constitutionality of the National Bank, the purchase of the Louisiana Territory, and foreign policy differences between the two national political parties. The Federalists and Jeffersonian Republicans bitterly contested power, and under John Adams' administration went so far as to jail political opponents under the terms of the Alien and Sedition Acts. Though both Federalists and Jeffersonians endeavored to keep the country free of entanglements in European conflicts, ultimately the nation was drawn into the waning conflict known as the Napoleonic Wars, our War of 1812. The Federalists, who had opposed entry into the war and who saw the British as a natural political and economic ally, were marginalized when the Democratic-Republican dominated Congress, led by President James Madison, entered the nation in a war with Great Britain. The Federalists emerged from this war the domestic losers and Jefferson's party, ascendant in the legislature and the executive branch, appeared poised to set in place the republic imagined by its founder, an expansive republic built on a yeoman farmer class focused on production for the market, allied with a planter and mercantile elite exporting cash crops to the Atlantic economy.

This would not be the case, however, and over the ensuing decades, a republic more akin to that envisioned by Alexander Hamilton developed. What began to emerge in the 1820s was a national economy that integrated three distinct regional economies: an urban, manufacturing sector centered in the Northeast, reliant on immigrant labor and sustained by the agricultural riches and natural resources of the Old Northwest (Michigan, Ohio, Wisconsin, Illinois, and Indiana) and the plantation economy spreading across the South, with cotton its most important product. The latter, of course, relied most directly upon slave labor, and the dispossession of the Native Americans living in Georgia, Tennessee, Alabama, and Mississippi. The removal of these Indian populations freed up over 25 million acres for cotton production. And with the booming of the cotton economy after 1815, the prominence of slavery in the national economy and the power of the slaveholders in the national polity did not diminish as many of the founding generation of white leaders had imagined.

BLACK FOUNDERS

The period of the American Revolution and its aftermath had seen thousands of slaves acquire their freedom, and the number of free blacks grow, both in the North and the South. As we have seen, during the Revolution slaves had gained their liberty by joining both the Patriot and Loyalist cause.Voluntary manumissions had increased as some slave owners recognized the incongruity between the rhetoric of liberty and equality and their ownership of other human beings. Pennsylvania had been the first state to abolish slavery in 1780 with the passage of a gradual emancipation bill. Other northern states followed suit. By 1804 each northern state had set in motion the gradual liberation of their enslaved populace. A corresponding increase in the numbers of free blacks took place. The Census of 1790 listed 59,557 free blacks across the republic. By 1830, that population had grown to 319,599 (over 181,000 residing in the South). Many of the free blacks in the early decades of the republic congregated in urban settings, rapidly outnumbering the slaves still present in northern cities. In New York, by 1810, for example, the free black population was three times greater than the slave population.

The growth in the number of free blacks during the period, however, corresponded with a waning in the fervor of abolitionism and with an increase in racial antipathy directed at African Americans. During the first decades of the early republic, most states had expanded the right to vote to include most adult property-holding, tax-paying males. In the northern states, Pennsylvania and New York included, the right to vote was also partially extended to free black men as well. Voter qualifications in the constitutions of Pennsylvania and New York made it possible for some freed African Americans to vote. As we will see, however, these gains would not last and during ground swell of "Jacksonian" democracy, new restrictions or outright bans on black voter participation were often imposed.

Free blacks in northern cities also faced particular difficulties transitioning from slavery. They were frequently confined to makeshift housing, ghettoized in alley housing or in other substandard conditions. They faced harsh employment discrimination and often lacked skills required in urban manufacturing or trade. In response to these hardships, free blacks across the country agitated for racial equality and argued strenuously for the end of slavery and the slave trade. Recent scholarship has begun to speak of this generation of black leaders as the "Black Founders," counterparts to the founders of the American republic. Just as Washington, Franklin, Adams, Jefferson, and Hamilton fashioned the institutions of the republic, putting flesh on the bones of the Constitution, this generation of "Black Founders," though restricted in their participation in the political sphere, were instrumental in the construction of key black institutions, and in the establishment of a tradition of protest that extends to the present. Lemuel Haynes, Richard Allen, Absalom Jones, Peter Williams and others deserve recognition as the precursors to African American civil rights leaders that will include W.E.B. Dubois, Marcus Garvey, Martin Luther King, Jr. Andrew Young, and Jesse Jackson. As has been the case from that generation to the era of the Civil Rights movement, black leaders frequently called upon the nation to reflect on and live up to its highest ideals. Despite these calls for greater equality and racial justice, for the most part, the national consciousness remained less focused on the conditions of free or enslaved African Americans, or on expansions of the franchise and civil rights.

JACKSONIAN DEMOCRACY AND WHITE SUPREMACY

During the period from 1820 to 1840 economic changes variously called the "Market Revolution" or "Industrial Revolution" or, sometimes, the "Communication Revolution" coincided with the emergence of a new political culture. As this new political culture came to fruition with the election in 1828 of Andrew Jackson, who claimed the presidency as a mandate of the people, the period is also known as the "Age of Jackson" or the era of "Jacksonian Democracy." Jackson's inauguration is most often cited as the symbol of this momentous change. Jackson had defeated John Quincy Adams in a most hostile political campaign. The election was so acrimonious that Adams refused to attend the swearing-in ceremony. When the crowd of Jackson supporters and members of the Washington establishment showed up to the White House for the inaugural reception, the White House wasn't prepared for the crush of people seeking political favors and appoints from Jackson. It is highly likely that the day's events have been exaggerated, but one of the most often quoted accounts numbered the crowd at 20,000 and described it as follows: "What a scene we did witness! The Majesty of the People had disappeared, and a rabble, a mob, boys, negros, women, children, scrambling, fighting, romping. What a pity. What a pity!" Jackson's inauguration has since been a symbol for the rise of popular sovereignty, or majority rule.

In fact, Jackson was the beneficiary of political changes that had begun in the first two decades of the nineteenth-century. In both the original thirteen states of the Union and in later additions, the suffrage was greatly extended during the period from 1815 to 1828. In part this resulted from both the fragmentation and weakness of the Federalists and the monopoly of national politics by the inheritors of Jefferson's party. In both cases there were incentives to encourage greater voter participation. Additionally, in the western states there were incentives to reduce restrictions on voting tied to property ownership. As a result, during the early nineteenth century the number of white male voters increased. Closely associated with this democratic sensibility was the ideal of white male equality. Andrew Jackson benefited from this sentiment and forged a coalition between southerners, western frontiersmen anxious to acquire Indian territory, and northern urban immigrants.

A corollary of Jacksonian democracy, however, was a corresponding growth of white racism and support for slavery, and animus towards free blacks. In a pattern that has been repeated at other times in American history when politicians have used populist rhetoric to justify their electoral claims, white supremacy and populism have been joined. Poor whites, whether in the South or West, or in the northern cities, gained immeasurably from Jackson's brand of populism. During the American Revolution the poor and propertyless had been distrusted, feared as "the rabble" or "the mob." In classical republican theory, poor and propertyless residents were considered unlikely participants in civic society because they were by definition dependent. The rise of "Jacksonian" democracy, however, afforded to all white males a promise of equality and the possibility of a political voice. It made "whiteness" and race the key distinguishing mark dividing society and provided a mechanism to surmount class and regional interests. Jackson's appeal to the "majority"and his development of the Democratic Party, which would dominate American electoral politics from 1828 to 1860, resulted in the establishment of perhaps the most truly democratic republic of its day. The Democratic Party however united three popular constituencies, which had little in common economically or socially. What united the coalition was "white supremacy."

The appeal to white supremacy was most effective in gaining the votes of "poor whites" in the southern highlands and immigrants in the northeast. Since the 1840s, Irish immigrants and afterwards Irish-Americans, have been the most consistently Democratic voters of any constituency. Between 1820 and 1860 nearly 2 million Irish immigrants came to the United States. These immigrants initially faced overt prejudice and discrimination. The historian Noel Ignatiev has argued that the Irish were initially seen through a racial lens that characterized them as "black." They were a "subject race" to the English. They "became white" according to Ignatiev, as a result of the Democratic Party's effort to establish a national political coalition that reached beyond the old Jeffersonian party's southern base. The Democratic party eased Irish assimilation and accorded them "whiteness" in the face of a history of English and Anglo-American denigration of their racial identity.[1] The social and political elevation of the Irish in northern cities, came at the expense of free blacks. As a result, poor Irish laborers, and other white workers, were able to control the work place and the ballot box, excluding African Americans from both. Before the 1830s, black men could expect to acquire a range of occupations, even if they were often poorly paid. Free blacks, after the 1830s, were increasingly marginalized in northern cities, closed off from occupational opportunities and housing. Additionally, the Democratic Party, unlike its Whig opponents, rarely voiced "nativist" or anti-immigration positions, and instead promised a "classless" egalitarianism and unity along white, racial lines.

If in northeastern cities "whiteness" became a currency with which to attract immigrant votes at the expense of increasingly disenfranchised free blacks, in the Southeast and West, the appeal of

---

[1] Noel Ignatiev, *How the Irish Became White*, (New York: Routledge, 1995).

democracy often came at the expense of Native Americans as well as enslaved African Americans. White settlers sweeping westward found desirable land already occupied by Indian populations. This was particularly so in the rich soil of the South where the "Five Civilized Tribes" (the Cherokees, Creeks, Choctaws, Seminoles, and Chickasaw) had adopted European agricultural methods, technology, and literacy. These Indian peoples, however, asserted longstanding claims to their land and to political sovereignty. Andrew Jackson, alongside many other western politicians, had long sought the removal of southeastern Indians from Georgia, Tennessee, and Alabama. Dispossession of the Native Americans in the South promised opportunity to poor whites and wealthy slaveowners alike. Perhaps as importantly, Indian claims of sovereignty confronted the principle that only white men were fully entitled to assert claims to power within the United States.

During the first decades of the American republic, the nation was a largely coastal nation, its attention concentrated on the Atlantic economy and its political institutions dominated by an elite composed of the South's landed gentry and the mercantile and professional classes of northeastern seaports. In the aftermath of the American Revolution the promise of liberty and equality, and gradual emancipation of the enslaved population seemed to promise the possibility of a racially just society. In the decades after the conclusion of the War of 1812, however, the insatiable demand for land and labor as the cotton economy blossomed was accompanied by the growth of a northeastern manufacturing sector equally dependent on the products of enslaved laborers. This economic change coincided with the emergence of a democratic political ideology founded upon what Frederick Douglass would later call "whitemanism." As a result, the Black Founders' appeals for racial justice and true equality failed to win over an industrializing nation, dependent upon slave labor and upon the populist currency of white supremacy.

PRIMARY SOURCES

Document 1 The Constitution of New York, 1777.[2]

Article VII That every male inhabitant of full age, who shall have personally resided within one of the counties of this State for six months immediately preceding the day of election, shall, at such election, be entitled to vote for representatives of the said county in assembly; if, during the time aforesaid, he shall have been a freeholder, possessing a freehold of the value of twenty pounds, within the said county, or have rented a tenement therein of the yearly value of forty shillings, and been rated and actually paid taxes to this State: *Provided always*, That every person who now is a freeman of the city of Albany, or who was made a freeman of the city of New York on or before the fourteenth day of October, in the year of our Lord one thousand seven hundred and seventy-five, and shall be actually and usually resident in the said cities, respectively, shall be entitled to vote for representatives in assembly within his said place of residence.

---

2   Constitution of New York, 1777. Accessible at The Avalon Project, Documents in Law, History and Diplomacy, Yale Law School, http://avalon.law.yale.edu/18th_century/ny01.asp

Document 2   Thomas Jefferson, *Notes on the State of Virginia*, 1781.[3]

Querry XIX   The present state of manufactures, commerce, interior and exterior trade?

We never had an interior trade of any importance. Our exterior commerce has suffered very much from the beginning of the present contest. During this time we have manufactured within our families the most necessary articles of clothing. Those of cotton will bear some comparison with the same kinds of manufacture in Europe; but those of wool, flax, and hemp are very coarse, unsightly, and unpleasant: and such is our attachment to agriculture, and such our preference for foreign manufactures, that be it wise or unwise, our people will certainly return as soon as they can, to the raising of raw materials, and exchanging them for finer manufactures than they are able to execute themselves.

The political economists of Europe have established it as a principle that every state should endeavor to manufacture for itself: and this principle, like many others, we transfer to America, without calculating the difference of circumstances which should often produce difference of result. In Europe the lands are either cultivated, or locked up against the cultivator. Manufacture must therefore be resorted to of necessity not of choice, to support the surplus of their people. But we have an immensity of land courting the industry of the husbandsman. Is it best then that all our citizens should be employed in its improvement, or that one half should be called off from that to exercise manufactures and handicrafts for the other? Those who labour in the earth are the chosen people of God, if ever he had a chosen people, whose breasts he has made his peculiar deposit for substantial and genuine virtue. It is the focus in which he keeps alive that sacred fire, which otherwise might escape from the face of the earth. Corruption of morals in the mass of cultivators is a phenomenon of which no age nor nation has furnished an example. It is the mark set on those, who not looking up to heaven, to their own soil and industry, as does the husbandman, for their subsistence, depend for it on casualties and caprice of customers. Dependence begets subservience and venality, suffocates the germ of virtue, and prepares fit tools for the designs of ambition. … While we have land to labour then, let us never wish to see our citizens occupied at a work-bench, or twirling a distaff…. The loss by the transportation of commodities across the Atlantic will be made up in happiness and permanence of government. The mobs of great cities add just so much to the support of pure government, as sores do to the strength of the human body.

Document 3   Pennsylvania Constitution of 1790[4]

Article III. Of Elections

Section I.   In elections by the citizens, every freeman of the age of twenty-one years, having resided in the state two years next before the election, and within that time paid a state or county tax, which shall have been assessed at least six months before the election, shall enjoy the rights of an elector: Provided that the sons of persons qualified as aforesaid, between the ages of twenty-one and twenty-two years, shall be entitled to vote, although they shall not have paid taxes.

---

[3] Thomas Jefferson, *Notes on the State of Virginia*, (Boston: Lilly and Wait, 1832), pp. 171-173.

[4] Pennsylvania Constitution of 1790, *Pennsylvania Archives, Third Series,* Volume 10, edited by William Henry Egle, (Harrisburg, PA: Clarence M. Busch, State Printer, 1896), pp. 739-754.

Document 4   Absalom Jones and Richard Allen, *A Narrative of the Proceedings of the Black People during the Late Awful Calamity in Philadelphia in the Year 1793 and a Refutation of the Censures thrown upon them in some late Publications.*[5]

Early in September, a solicitation appeared in the public papers, to the people of colour to come forward and assist the distressed, perishing, and neglected sick; with a kind of assurance, that people of colour were not liable to take the infection. Upon which we and a few others met and consulted how to act on so truly alarming and melancholy an occasion. After some conversation, we found a freedom to go forth, confiding in him who can preserve in the midst of a burning fiery furnace, sensible that it was our duty to do all the good we could to our suffering fellow mortals. We set out to see where we could be useful. … We administered what relief we could… We visited upwards of twenty families that day—they were scenes of woe indeed! The Lord was pleased to strengthen us, and disposed our hearts to be as useful as possible.

… We wish not to offend, but when an unprovoked attempt is made, to make us blacker than we are, it becomes less necessary to be over cautious on that account; therefore we shall take the liberty to tell of the conduct of some of the whites.

… We know six pounds was demanded by, and paid, to a white woman, for putting a corpse into a coffin; and forty dollars was demanded, and paid, to four white men, for bringing it down the stairs….

… A poor afflicted dying man, stood at his chamber window, praying and beseeching every one that passed by, to help him to a drink of water; a number of white people passed, and instead of being moved by the poor man's distress, they hurried as fast as they could out of the sound of his cries—until at length a gentlemen, who seemed to be a foreigner came up, he could not pass by, but had not resolution enough to go into the house, he held eight dollars in his hand, and offered it to several as a reward for giving the poor man a drink of water, but was refused by every one, until a poor black man came up, the gentleman offered the eight dollars to him, if he would relieve the poor man with a little water, "Master" replied the good natured fellow, "I will supply the gentleman with water, but surely I will not take your money for it" nor could he be prevailed upon to accept his bounty: he went in, supplied the poor object with water and rendered him every service he could.

An Address to those who keep Slaves, and approve the practice.

That God who knows the hearts of all men, and the propensity of a slave to hate his oppressor, hath strictly forbidden it to his chosen people, "thou shalt not abhor an Egyptian because thou wast a stranger in his land. Deut. 23:7." The meek and humble Jesus, the great pattern of humanity, and every other virtue that can adorn and dignify men, hath commanded to love our enemies, to do good to them that hate and despitefully use us. We feel the obligations, we wish to impress them on the minds of our black brethren, and that we may all forgive you, as we wish to be forgiven;

---

5   Absalom Jones and Richard Allen, *A Narrative of the Proceedings of the Black People during the Late Awful Calamity in Philadelphia in the Year 1793 and a Refutation of the Censures thrown upon them in some late Publications*, (Philadelphia: William W. Woodward, at Franklin's Head, 1794).

we think it a great mercy to have all anger and bitterness removed from our minds; we appeal to your own feelings, if it is not very disquieting to feel yourselves under the dominion of a wrathful disposition.

If you love your children, if you love your country, if you love the God of love, clear your hands from slaves, burden not your children or country with them. Our hearts have been sorrowful for the late bloodshed of the oppressors, as well as the oppressed, both appear guilty of each others blood, in the sight of him who said, he that sheddeth man's blood, by man shall his blood be shed.

Will you, because you have reduced us to the unhappy condition our colour is in, plead our incapacity for freedom, and our contented condition under oppression, as a sufficient cause for keeping us under the grievous yoke?....

To The People of Colour.

Feeling an engagement of mind for your welfare, we address you with an affectionate sympathy, having been ourselves slaves, and as desirous of freedom, as any of you; yet the bands of bondage were so strong, that no way appeared for our release, yet at times a hope arose in our hearts that a way would open for it, and when our minds were mercifully visited with the feeling of the love of God, then these hopes increased, and a confidence arose that he would make way for our enlargement, and as a patient waiting was necessary, we were sometimes favoured with it, at other times we were very impatient, then the prospect of liberty almost vanished away, and we were in darkness and perplexity.

We mention our experience to you, that your hearts may not sink at the discouraging prospects you may have, and that you may put your trust in God, who sees your condition, and as a merciful father pitieth his children, so doth God pity them that love him; and as your hearts are inclined to serve God, you will feel an affectionate regard towards your masters and mistresses, and the whole family where you live, this will be seen by them, and tend to promote your liberty, especially with such as feeling masters, and if they are otherwise you will have the favour and love of God dwelling in your hearts, which you will value more than any thing else, which will be a consolation in the worst condition you can be in, and no master can deprive you of it; and as life is short and uncertain, and the chief end of our having a being in this world, is to be prepared for a better, we wish you to think of this more than anything else; then will you have a view of that freedom which the sons of God enjoy: and if the troubles of your condition end with your lives, you will be admitted to the freedom which God hath prepared for those of all colours that love him; here the power of the most cruel master ends, and all sorrow and tears are wiped away.

To you who are favored with freedom, let your conduct manifest your gratitude toward the compassionate masters who have set you free, and let no rancor or ill-will lodge in your breasts for any bad treatment you may have received from any: if you do, you transgress against God, who will not hold you guiltless, he would not suffer it even in his beloved people Israel, and can you think he will allow it unto you?

There is much gratitude due from our colour towards the white people, very many of them are instruments in the hand of God for our good, even such as have held us in captivity, are now pleading our cause with earnestness and zeal; and we are sorry to say, that too many think more of the evil, than of the good they have received, and instead of taking the advice of their friends, turn from it with indifference; much depends upon us for the help of our colour more than many are aware; if we are lazy and idle, the enemies of freedom plead it as a cause why we ought not ot be free, and say we are better in a state of servitude, and that giving us our liberty would be an injury to us, and by such conduct we strengthen the hands of oppression, and keep many in bondage who are more worthy than ourselves; we intreat you to consider the obligations we lay under, to help forward the cause of freedom, we who know how bitter the cup is of which the slave hath to drink, O how ought we to feel for those who yet remain in bondage? Will even our friends excuse, will God pardon us, for the part we act in making strong the hands of the enemies of our colour.

Document 5   "An Act for the Gradual Abolition of Slavery," New York, 29 March 1799.[6]

Be it enacted by the People of the State of New York represented in Senate and Assembly, That any child born of a slave within this State after the fourth day of July next, shall be deemed and adjudged born free: *Provided nevertheless* that such child shall be the servant of the legal proprietor of his or her mother, until such servant if male shall arrive at the age of twenty eight years, and if a female at the age of twenty five years.

And be it further enacted, That such proprietor his, her, or their heirs or assigns shall be entitled to the service of such child until he or she arrive to the age aforesaid in the same manner as if such child had been bound to service by the overseers of the poor. …

And be it further enacted, That the person entitled to such service may nevertheless within one year after the birth of such child elect to abandon his or her right to such service by a notification of the same from under his or her hand and lodged with the clerk of the town or city where the owner of the mother of any such child may reside; in which case every child abandoned as aforesaid shall be considered as paupers of the respective town or city where the proprietor or owner of the mother of such child may reside at the time of its birth and liable to be bound out by the overseers of the poor on the same terms and conditions that the children of paupers were subject to before the passing of this act….

---

6   *Laws of the State of New York, passed at the Sessions of the Legislature Held in the Years, 1797-1800.* Vol. IV, (Albany: Weed, Parsons, and Co., 1887), pp. 368-369.

Document 6   Slave Population, Pennsylvania, 1780-1810.[7]

Philadelphia and Pennsylvania Counties	1780-1782	1790 (% of total population)	1810
Philadelphia	539	301 (0.7)	2
Philadelphia and Montgomery	400	196 (0.6)	9
Bucks	520	261 (1.0)	11
Chester & Delaware	493	65 (0.2)	4
Lancaster & Dauphin	838	586 (1.1)	70
York & Adams	793	499 (1.3)	93
Cumberland, Franklin & Perry	1,149	553 (1.6)	394
Westmoreland, Washington, Allegheny, & Fayette	1,140	834 (1.3)	159
Remainder	est. 693	271 (0.4)	46
Total Slaves	**6,855**	**3,760**	**795**

Document 7   James Thompson Callender, "The President Again," *The Richmond Recorder*, 1 September 1802.[8]

It is well known that the man, *whom it delighteth the people to honor*, keeps and for many years has kept, as his concubine, one of his slaves. Her name is SALLY. The name of her eldest is Tom. His features are said to bear a striking though sable resemblance to those of the president himself. The boy is ten or twelve years of age. His mother went to France in the same vessel with Mr. Jefferson and his two daughters. The delicacy of this arrangement must strike every person of common sensibility. What a sublime pattern for an American ambassador to place before the eyes of two young ladies!

As the reader does not feel himself *disposed to pause* we beg leave to proceed. Some years ago, this story had once or twice been hinted at in *Richmond's Federalist*. At that time, we believed the surmise to be an absolute calumny. One reason for thinking so was this. A vast body of people wished to debar Mr. Jefferson from the presidency. *The establishment of this* SINGLE FACT would have rendered his election impossible. We reasoned thus; that if the allegation had been true, it was sure to have been ascertained and advertised by his enemies, in every corner of the continent. The suppression of so decisive an enquiry serves to shew that the common sense of the federal party was overruled by divine providence. It was the predestination of the

---

[7] Adapted from Gary B. Nash and Jean R. Soderlund, *Freedom by Degrees: Emancipation in Pennsylvania and its Aftermath*, (New York: Oxford University Press, 1991), p. 5.

[8] "From the Recorder, The President Again," *The Republican*, (Baltimore, MD), September 6, 1802, p. 2.

supreme being that they should be turned out; that they should be expelled from office by the *popularity* of a character, which, at that instant was lying fettered and gagged, consumed and extinguished at their feet!

... By the wench Sally, our president has had several children. There is not an individual in the neighbourhood of Charlottsville who does not believe the story; and not a few who know it. If Duane sees this account, he will not prate any more about the treaty between Mr. Adams and Toussaint. Behold the favorite, the first born of republicanism! The pinnacle of all that is good and great! In the open consummation of an act which tends to subvert the policy, the happiness, and even the existence of this country!

'Tis supposed that, at the time when Mr. Jefferson wrote so smartly concerning negroes, when he endeavoured so much to belittle the African race, he had no expectation that the chief magistrate of the United States was to be the ringleader in shewing that his opinion was erroneous; or, that he should chuse an African stock whereupon he was to engraft his own descendants.

... The allegation is of a nature too black to be suffered to remain in suspence. We should be glad to hear of its refutation. We gave it to the world under the firmest belief that such a refutation *never can be made*. The African Venus is said to officiate, as house keeper at Monticello.—When Mr. Jefferson has read this article, he will find leisure to estimate how much has been lost or ganed by so many unprovoked attacks upon

J.T. Callender

Document 8 Congressional Authorization for Louisiana Purchase, 31 October 1803[9]

Be it enacted by the Senate and House of Representatives of the United States, in Congress assembled, That the President of the United States be, and he is hereby, authorized to take possession of and occupy the territories ceded by France to the United States by the Treaty concluded at Paris, on the 10th day of April last, between the two nations; and that he may for that purpose, and in order to maintain in the said territories the authority of the United States,...

And be it further enacted, That until the expiration of the present session of Congress, unless provision for temporary government of the said territories be sooner made by Congress, all the military, civil and judicial powers exercised by the officers of the existing government of the same, shall be vested in such person and persons, and shall be exercised in such manner, as the President of the United States shall direct for maintaining and protecting the inhabitants of Louisiana the free enjoyment of their liberty, property and religion.

---

9 *Debates and Proceedings in the Congress of the United States...*8th Congress, 1st session, 1803-1805, (Washington, 1852), p. 18.

Document 9 Secret Communication, President Thomas Jefferson to Senator John Breckinridge, 24 and 25 November 1803.[10]

Washington, Nov. 24, 1803.

Dear Sir,

--I thought I perceived in you the other day a dread of the job of preparing a constitution for the new acquisition. With more boldness than wisdom I therefore determined to prepare a canvass, give it a few daubs of outline, and send it to you to fill up. I yesterday morning took up the subject and scribbled off the inclosed. In communicating it to you I must do it in confidence that you will never let any person know that I have put pen to paper on the subject and that if you think the inclosed can be of any aid to you you will take the trouble to copy it & return me the original. I am this particular, because you know with what bloody teeth & fangs the Federalists will attack any sentiment or principle known to come from me, & what blackguardisms & personalities they make the occasion of vomiting forth. My time does not permit me to go into explanation of the inclosed letter. ...

Accept my friendly saluations.

Washington, Nov. 25, 1803

Th: J to mr. Breckenridge

Insert in some part of the paper of yesterday 'Slaves shall be admitted into the territory of Orleans from such of the United States or of their territories as prohibit their importation from abroad, but from no other state, territory or country.'

Salutations.

Document 10 By-Laws, Society of Free People of Color for promoting the instruction and school education of Children of African Descent, Philadelphia, 7 August 1804.

Whereas several Free People of Color, in the city of Philadelphia, have associated together for the purpose of uniting their efforts to promote the improvement, in School education, of the children of the African Race (without distinction of sects) and thereby enabling them to become useful members of society.

In order to secure the attainment of this object, they have resolved to form themselves into a Society, and have adopted the following constitution, viz.

ARTICLE I The name of the association shall be "The Society of Free People of Color for promoting the instruction and school education of Children of African descent."

---

10 In James E. Scanlon and Albert Gallatin, "A Sudden Conceit: Jefferson and the Louisiana Government Bill of 1804," *The Journal of the Louisiana Historical Association*, 9:2 (1968), pp. 152-153.

II. Every orderly person of colour, who desires to become a member of this Society, shall pay into the hands of the Treasurer, for the use thereof, on his admission, one dollar—shall subscribe a fair copy of this constitution, and shall also subscribe to pay one dollar annually, before he is entitled to membership. [...]

VII. The Society at its first meeting, after having chosen the officers before mentioned, shall proceed to elect by ballot, or otherwise, nine Trustees, a majority of whom shall constitute a quorum to transact business; they shall appoint a Chairman and Secretary, and keep regular minutes of their proceedings—being subject to such rules and regulations as the Society shall deem proper. Immediately after their first appointment, they shall divide themselves into three equal classes, and determine their time of service by lot: The first class shall be released at the end of six months—the second at the end of twelve months—and the third at the expiration of eighteen months from the time of their appointment; the vacancies being supplied by new members, or re-appointments, to serve eighteen months—and this rotation shall be regularly observed in order that there may always be a number of experienced members in the board, (some of whom shall visit the School or Schools, twice in every month)—The minutes of the Board of Trustees shall be read in society at every stated meeting. All applications for admission into the School or Schools which may be established under the superintendence of the Society shall be made to them—and two thirds of the whole number agreeing, shall have power to employ and dismiss Teachers, and direct what books may be used, but they are especially enjoined to give preference to those of a moral and religious tendancy, particularly the Holy Scriptures. It shall also be their duty in proportion to the state of the Treasury, to admit a certain number of pupils gratis.

N.B. The members present have agreed, that until the Society be duly organized, the following persons be appointed a Committee to solicit and receive subscriptions:--Richard Allen, William Brown, Joseph Alburt, Robert Green, James Champion, John Brown, Reuben Moore, Charles boston, and James Green.

August 7, 1804

Document 11 Runaway Slave Notice, *Tennessee Gazette*, 1804.[11]

FIFTY DOLLARS REWARD

Eloped from the subscriber, living near Nashville, on the 25th of June last, a Mulatto Man Slave, about thirty years old, six feet and an inch high, stout made and active, talks sensible, stoops in his walk, and has a remarkable large foot, broad across the root of the toes — will pass for a free man, as I am informed he has obtained by some means, certificates as such—took with him a drab greatcoat, dark mixed body coat, a ruffled shirt, cotton home-spun shirts and overalls. He will make for Detroit, through the states of Kentucky and Ohio, or the upper part of Louisiana. The above reward will be given any person that will take him. If taken out of the state, the above

---

[11] Runaway notice reproduced in Robert P. Hay, "'And Ten Dollars Extra, for Every Hundred Lashes Any Person Will Give Him, to the Amount of Three Hundred': A Note on Andrew Jackson's Runaway Slave Ad of 1804 and on the Historian's Use of Evidence," *Tennessee Historical Quarterly*, 36:4 (1977), p. 468.

reward, and all reasonable expenses paid—and ten dollars extra, for every hundred lashes any person will give him, to the amount of three hundred.

ANDREW JACKSON

Near Nashville, State of Tennessee

Document 12 Absolom Jones, "A Thanksgiving Sermon," preached January 1, 1808 in the African Episcopal Church, Philadelphia, On the Abolition of the Slave Trade.[12]

Oh thou God of all the nations upon the earth! We thank thee, that thou art *no respecter of persons,* and that thou *hast made of one blood all nations of men. We* thank thee, that thou hast appeared, in the fulness of time, in behalf of the nation from which most of the worshipping people, now before thee, are descended. We thank thee, that the sun of righteousness has at last shed his morning beams upon them. *Rend thy heavens,* O Lord, and *come down* upon the earth; and grant that *the mountains,* which now obstruct the perfect day of thy goodness and mercy towards them, may *flow down at thy presence.* Send thy gospel, we beseech thee, among them. May the nations, which now *sit in darkness,* behold and rejoice in its *light.* May *Ethiopia soon stretch out her hands unto thee,* and lay hold of the gracious promise of thy everlasting covenant. Destroy, we beseech thee, all the false religions which now prevail among them; and grant, that they may soon *cast* their *idols, to the moles and the bats* of the wilderness. O, hasten that glorious time, when the knowledge of the gospel of Jesus Christ, shall cover the *earth, as the waters cover the sea;* when *the wolf shall dwell with the lamb, and the leopard shall lie down with the kid, and the calf and the young lion and the fatling together, and a little child shall lead them;* and, *when, instead of the thorn, shall come up the fir tree, and, instead of the brier, shall come up the myrtle tree: and it shall be to the Lord for a name and for an everlasting sign that shall not be cut off.* We pray, O God, for all our friends and benefactors, in Great Britain, as well as in the United States: reward them, we beseech thee, with blessings upon earth, and prepare them to enjoy the fruits of their kindness to us, in thy everlasting kingdom in heaven: and dispose us, who are assembled in thy presence, to be always thankful for thy mercies, and to act as becomes a people who owe so much to thy goodness. We implore thy blessing, O God, upon the President, and all who are in authority in the United States. Direct them by thy wisdom, in all their deliberations, and O save thy people from the calamities of war. Give peace in our day, we beseech thee, O thou *God of peace! and* grant, that this highly favoured country may continue to afford a safe and peaceful retreat from the calamities of war and slavery, for ages yet to come. We implore all these blessings and mercies, only in the name of thy beloved Son, Jesus Christ, our Lord. And now, O Lord, we desire, with angels and arch-angels, and all the company of heaven, ever more to praise thee, saying, *Holy, holy, holy, Lord God Almighty: the whole earth is full of thy glory.* Amen.

---

12 Absalom Jones, *A Thanksgiving Sermon, preached January 1, 1808, in St. Thomas's, or the African Episcopal Church, Philadelphia on account of the Abolition of the African Slave Trade, on that day,* (Philadelphia: Fry and Kammerer, 1808).

Document 13 The Constitution of the State of New York, 1821.[13]

Article II.

Section 1. Every male citizen of the age of twenty-one years, who shall have been an inhabitant of this state one year preceding any election, and for the last six months a resident of the town or county where he may offer his vote; and shall have, within the next year preceding the election, paid a tax to the state or county, assessed upon his real or personal property; or shall by law be exempted from taxation; or being armed and equipped according to law, shall have performed within that year, military duty in the militia of this state; or who shall be exempted from performing militia duty in consequence of being a fireman in any city, town, or village in this state; and also, every male citizen of the age of twenty-one years, who shall have been, for three years next preceding such election an inhabitant of this state; and, for the last year, a resident in the town or county where he may offer his vote; and shall have been, within the last year, assessed to labor upon the public highways, and shall have performed the labor, or paid an equivalent therefor, according to law, shall be entitled to vote in the town or ward where he actually resides, and not elsewhere, for all officers that now are, or hereafter may be, elective by the people; but no man of colour, unless he shall have been for three years a citizen of this state, and for one year next preceding any election, shall be seized and possessed of a freehold estate of the value of two hundred and fifty dollars, over and above all debts and incumbrances charged thereon; and shall have been actually rated, and paid a tax thereon, shall be entitled to vote in any such election. And no person of colour shall be subject to direct taxation unless he shall be seized and possessed of such real estate as aforesaid.

Document 14 Constitution of the Cherokee Nation, 1827.[14]

WE THE REPRESENTATIVES of the people of the CHEROKEE NATION in Convention assembled, in order to establish justice, ensure tranquility, promote our common welfare, and secure to ourselves and our posterity the blessings of liberty, acknowledging with humility and gratitutde the goodness of the sovereign Ruler of the Universe, in offering as an opportunity so favorable to the design, and imploring his aid and direction in its accomplishment, do ordain and establish thie Constitution for the Government of the Cherokee Nation.

ARTICLE I

Sec. 1. THE BOUNDARIES of this nation, embracing the lands solemnly guaranteed and reserved forever to the Cherokee Nation by the Treaties concluded with the United States, are as follows; and shall forever hereafter remain unalterably the same, to wit. Beginning on the North Bank of Tennessee River at the upper part of the Chickasaw old fields; thence along the main channel of said river, including all the islands therein, to the mouth of the Hiawassee River, thence up the main channel of said river, including islands, to the first hill which closes in on said river, about two miles above Hiawassee Old Town; thence along the ridge which

---

13 Constitution of New York, 1821, accessible at https://www.nycourts.gov/history/legal-history-new-york/documents/Publications_1821-NY-Constitution.pdf

14 *Constitution of the Cherokee Nation,* accessible at https://arts-sciences.und.edu/native-media-center/_files/docs/1803-1860/1827cherokeeconstitution.pdf

divides the waters of the Hiawassee and Little Tellico, to the Tennessee River at Tallasasei, thence along the main channel, including islands, to the junction of the Cowee and Nanteyalee; thence along the ridge in the fork of said river, to the top of the Blue Ridge; thence along the Blue Ridge to the Unicoy Turnpike road; thence by a straight line to the main source of the Chestatee; thence along its main channel, including islands, to the Chattachoochy; and thence down the same to the Creek boundary at Buzzard Roost; thence along the boundary line which separates this and the Creek Nation, to a point on the Coosa River opposite the mouth of Will's Creek; thence down along the south bank of the same to a point opposite to Fort Strother; thence up the river to the mouth of Will's Creek; thence up along the east bank of said creek to the west branch thereof, and up the same to its source; and thence along the ridge which separates the Tombechee and Tennessee waters, to a point on the top of said ridge; thence due north to Camp Coffee on Tennessee River, which is opposite the Chickasaw Island; thence to the place of beginning.

Sec. 2. The Sovereignty and Jurisdiction of this Government shall extend over the country within the boundaries above described, and the lands therein are, and shall remain the common property of the Nation…

Document 15   James F. Smith, Cherokee Land Lottery, April 19, 1838.[15]

---

15 James F. Smith, *The Cherokee Land Lottery, containing a numerical list of the names of the fortunate drawers in said lottery, with an engraved map of each district*, (New York: Harper & Brothers, 1838).

The undersigned offers to the public in the following pages a work which he trusts will not only be acceptable, but highly valuable to many of his fellow-citizens. ... It contains the names and residence of all the fortunate drawers in the *Land Lottery* of the Cherokee country, arranged by districts in numerical order, and a map of each district, all carefully copied from the originals in the Executive Department and the Office of the Surveyor General, designating also the lots which have been granted....By reference to the numerical list, the drawer's name and residence can be readily ascertained, while the maps will give a pretty correct idea of the watercourses and local situation of any particular lot, as well as whether it has been granted or not.

Sixth District, First Section, Cherokee.

1. Arthur Turner, Summerlin's, Bulloch
2. Miles Shepherd, Hitchock's Muscogee
3. Absalom Ogletree, Ball's Monroe.
4. Aaron Palmer, Chastain's, Habersham.
5. Thomas Duren, sol., Newman's Thomas.
6. William A. Stewart, 559th, Walton.
7. George W. Bowen, Wolfskin's, Oglethorpe.
8. Edmund Bradley, Curry's Merriwether.

...

322. John Hembey, Phillip's, Talbot.
323. Jacob Freeman, Chastain's, Habersham.
324. John Williamson, Camp's, Baker.

Document 16 Peter Williams, "This is Our Country," 4 July 1830.[16]

ON THIS DAY the fathers of this nation declared, "We hold these truths to be self-evident, that all men are created equal, that they are endowed by their Creator with certain unalienable rights, among which are life, liberty, and the pursuit of happiness."....

From various causes ... the work of emancipation has within a few years been rapidly advancing in a number of States. The State we live in, since the 4th of July, 1827, has been able to boast that she has no slaves, and other States where there still are slaves appear disposed to follow her example.

But alas! the freedom to which we have attained is defective. Freedom and equality have been "put asunder." The rights of men are decided by the colour of their skin; and there is as much difference made between the rights of a free white man and a free coloured man as there is between a free coloured man and a slave.

Though delivered from the fetters of slavery, we are oppressed by an unreasonable, unrighteous, and cruel prejudice, which aims at nothing less than the forcing away of all the

---
16 Peter Williams, *Discourse delivered in St. Philip's Church for the Benefit of the Coloured Communit of Wilberforce, in Upper Canada*, (New York: G.F. Bunce, 1830).

free coloured people of the United States to the distant shores of Africa. Far be it from me to impeach the motives of every member of the African Colonization Society. The civilizing and Christianizing of that vast continent, and the extirpation of the abominable traffic in slaves (which notwithstanding all the laws passed for its suppression is still carried on in all its horrors), are no doubt the principal motives which induce many to give it their support....

We are natives of this country, we ask only to be treated as well as foreigners. Not a few of our fathers suffered and bled to purchase its independence; we ask only to be treated as well as those who fought against it. We have toiled to cultivate it, and to raise it to its present prosperous condition; we ask only to share equal privileges with those who come from distant lands, to enjoy the fruits of our labour. Let these moderate requests be granted, and we need not go to Africa nor anywhere else to be improved and happy. We cannot but doubt the purity of the motives of those persons who deny us these requests, and would send us to Africa to gain what they might give us at home.

The African Colonization Society is a numerous and influential body. Would they lay aside their own prejudices, much of the burden would be at once removed; and their example (especially if they were as anxious to have justice done us here as to send us to Africa) would have such an influence upon the community at large as would soon cause prejudice to hide its deformed head....

But, alas! the course which they have pursued has an opposite tendency. By the scandalous misrepresentations which they are continually giving of our character and conduct we have sustained much injury, and have reason to apprehend much more....

Without any charge of crime we have been denied all access to places to which we formerly had the most free intercourse; the coloured citizens of other places, on leaving their homes, have been denied the privilege of returning; and others have been absolutely driven out....

It is very certain that very few free people of colour wish to go to that land. The Colonization Society know this, and yet they do certainly calculate that in time they will have us all removed there.

How can this be effected but by making our situation worse here, and closing every other door against us?

Document 17 Appeal of Forty Thousand Citizens Threatened with Disfranchisement to the People of Pennsylvania, 1838.[17]

Philadelphia, March 14, 1838

A very numerous and respectable meeting of the colored citizens of Pennsylvania, was held in the Presbyterian Church, Seventh Street, below Shippen, on the evening of the 14th inst.

FELLOW CITIZENS:--We appeal to you from the decision of the "Reform Convention," which has stripped us of a right peaceably enjoyed during forty-seven years under the Constitution of

---

17 Appeal of Forty Thousand Citizens, threatened with Disfranchisement, to the People of Pennsylvania, (Philadelphia: Merrihew and Gunn, 1838).

this commonwealth. We honor Pennsylvania and her noble institutions too much to part with our birthright, as her free citizens, without a struggle. To all her citizens the right of suffrage is valuable in proportion as she is free; but surely there are none who can so ill afford to spare it as ourselves. ...

Was it made the business of the Convention to deny "that all men are born equally free," by making political rights depend upon the skin in which a man is born? Or to divide what our fathers bled to unite, to wit, TAXATION and REPRESENTATION? ... This is a question, fellow citizens, in which we plead *your* cause as well as our own. It is the safeguard of the strongest that he lives under a government which is obliged to respect the voice of the weakest. When you have taken from an individual his right to vote, you have made the government, in regard to him, a mere despotism; and you have taken a step towards making a despotism to all. ...

To us our right under the Constitution has been more precious, and our deprivation of it will be the more grievous, because our expatriation has come to be a darling project with many of our fellow citizens. Our abhorrence of a scheme which comes to us in the guise of Christian benevolence, and asks us to suffer ourselves to be transplanted to a distant and barbarous land, *because we are a "nuisance" in this*, is not more deep and thorough than it is reasonable. We love our native country, much as it has wronged us; and in the peaceable exercise of our inalienable rights, we will cling to it.... We are PENNSYLVANIANS, and we hope to see the day when Pennsylvania will have reason to be proud of us, as we believe she has now none to be ashamed. Will you starve our patriotism?....

... [The Pennsylvania Constitution] guarantees the right of suffrage to us as fully as to any of our fellow citizens whatsoever, for

1. Such was the intention of the framers. In the original draft, reported by a committee of nine, the word "WHITE" stood before "FREEMAN." On motion of ALBERT GALLATIN it was stricken out, for the express purpose of including colored citizens within the pale of the elective franchise.

2. We are CITIZENS. This, we believe, would never have been denied, had it not been for the scheme of expatriation to which we have already referred. But as our citizenship has been doubted by some who are not altogether unfriendly to us, we beg leave to submit some proofs, which we think you will not hastily set aside.

... What have we done to forfeit the inestimable benefits of this charter? Why should tax-paying colored men, any more than other tax-payers be deprived of the right of voting for their representatives? It was said in the Convention, that this government belongs to the *Whites*. We have already shown this to be false, as to the past. Those who established our present government designed it equally for all. It is for you to decide whether it shall be confined to the European complexion in the future. Why should you exclude us from a fair participation in the benefits of the republic? Have we oppressed the whites? Have we used our right to the injury of any class? ... As to the charge of idleness, we fling it back indignantly. Whose brows have sweat for our livelihood but our own? As to vice, if it disqualifies us for civil liberty, why not apply the same rule to the whites, so far as they are vicious? Will you punish the innocent for the crimes of the guilty? The execution of the laws is in the hands of the whites. If we are bad citizens let them apply the proper remedies. ... As to inferiority to the whites, if indeed we are guilty of it, either by nature or education, we trust our enjoyment of the rights of freemen will on that account be considered the less dangerous.

... By careful inquiry of a committee appointed by the "Pennsylvania Society for Promoting the Abolition of Slavery," it has been ascertained that the colored population of Philadelphia and its suburbs, numbering 18,768 souls, possess at the present time, of real and personal estate, not less than $1,350,000. They have paid for taxes during the last year $3,252.82; for house, water, and ground rent $166,963.50. This committee estimate the income to the holders of real estate occupied by the colored people, to be 7 ½ per cent. on a capital of about $2,000,000. Here is an addition to the wealth of their white brethren. But the rents and taxes are not all; to pay them, the colored people must be employed in labor, and here is another profit for the whites, for no man employs another unless he can make his labor profitable to himself. For a similar reason, a profit is made by all the whites who sell to colored people the necessaries or luxuries of life....

... Nor is the profit derived from us counterbalanced by the sums which we in any way draw from the public treasures. From a statement published by order of the Guardians of the Poor of Philadelphia, in 1830, it appears that out of 549 out-door poor relieved during the year, only 22 were persons of color, being about four per cent of the whole number, while the ratio of our population to that of the city and suburbs exceeds 8 ¼ per cent. ... Thus it has been ascertained that they pay more than they receive in the support of their own poor.

... That we are not neglectful of our religious interests, nor of the education of our children, is shown by the fact that there are among us in Philadelphia, Pittsburg, York, West Chester, and Columbia, 22 churches, 48 clergymen, 26 day schools, 20 Sabbath schools, 125 Sabbath school teachers, 4 literary societies, 2 public libraries, consisting of about 800 volumes, besides 8,333 volumes in private libraries, 2 tract societies, 2 Bible societies, and 7 temperance societies.

...Our fathers shared with yours the trials and perils of the wilderness. Among the facts which illustrate this, it is well known that the founder of your capital, from whom it bears the name of Harrisburg, was rescued by a *colored man*, from a party of Indians, who had captured, and bound him to the stake for execution.... When our common country has been invaded by a foreign foe, colored men have hazarded their lives in its defence. Our fathers fought by the side of yours in the struggle which made us an independent republic.

.. Are we to be disfranchised, that the purity of the *white* blood should be sullied by an intermixture with ours? It seems to us that our white brethren might well enough reserve their fear, till we seek such alliance with them. We ask no social favors. We would not willingly darken the doors of those to whom the complexion and features, which our Maker has given us, are disagreeable. The territories of the commonwealth are sufficiently ample to afford us a home without doing violence to the delicate nerves of our white brethren, for centuries to come. Besides, we are not intruders here, nor were our ancestors. Surely you ought to bear as unrepiningly the evil consequences of your fathers' guilt, as we those of our fathers' misfortune.

... We would not misrepresent the motives of the Convention, but we are constrained to believe that they have laid our rights a sacrifice on the altar of slavery. We do not believe our disfranchisement would have been proposed, but for the desire which is felt by political aspirants to gain the favor of the slave-holding States. This is not the first time that northern statesmen have "bowed the knee to the dark spirit of slavery," but it is the first time that they have bowed so low! Is Pennsylvania, which abolished slavery in 1780, and enfranchised her tax-paying colored citizens in 1790, now, in 1838 to gratify those who disgrace the very name of American Liberty, by holding our brethren as goods and chattels? ... Doubtless it will be well pleasing to the slaveholders of the South to see us degraded. They regard our freedom from chains as a dangerous example, much more our political freedom. They see in every thing which fortifies our rights, an obstacle to the recovery of their fugitive property. Will Pennsylvania go backwards towards slavery, for the better safety of southern slave property? … Fellow citizens, will you take the first step towards reimposing the chains which have now rusted for more than fifty years? Need we inform you that every colored man in Pennsylvania is exposed to be arrested as a fugitive from slavery? And that it depends not upon the verdict of a jury of his peers, but upon the decision of a judge on summary process, whether or not he shall be dragged into southern bondage?

… Fellow citizens, if there is one of us who has abused the right of suffrage, let him be tried and punished according to law. But in the name of humanity, in the name of justice, in the name of the God you profess to worship, who has no respect of persons, do not … [ratify] a Constitution which tears from us a privilege dearly earned and inestimably prized.

Document 18 Opinion of the Court of Quarter Sessions of Bucks County, delivered by Judge Fox, 28th December 1837.[18]

If the word *citizen* gives the negro the right to vote, then also *it gives him the right to be voted for*, and exercise the office of governor, senator, or any other office, because to be a *citizen*, (with residence,) is all the qualification required by the constitution. This clause of itself, makes this result sufficiently plain. But besides, all those parts of the constitution, which mention the election of the officers of government, provide that they shall be *citizens* and chosen *by the citizens.*

Who are citizens within the meaning of the constitution? The people, and their successors of the same caste, who established it. The people, in whom according to the declaration of rights, 2nd article, "*all* power is inherent," and by whose authority, "all free governments are founded," and for whose peace, safety, and happiness they are instituted." The *sovereign* people, in whom, collectively, is vested all political power, and who individually are component parts of the sovereign authority, and are equal to each other in all rights, powers, immunities and privileges. "WE THE PEOPLE," commences the constitution of the commonwealth of Pennsylvania, "ordain and establish this constitution for its government."

Is it possible that an inferior and degraded race were called in to take part in these high functions? That they composed a part of the *sovereign authority*, and suddenly were elevated from their abject condition, to be individually the equal in power and privileges, of the white man, who immediately before was immeasurably his superior in all these respects?...

But, further, *of the term citizen*. The framers of the constitution of Pennsylvania in making that instrument, manifestly, had in view the constitution of the United States. They adhered to it as inconsistent with the condition of the free negro in such state, and severe laws have always existed to prevent it. Therefore, when it is provided that the *People* shall bear arms, &c., it follows, that free negroes are not included in that term.

The determination of the people of the U.S. to exclude negroes from citizenship may also be strongly inferred from the fact, that the first naturalization law which passed on the 26th March, 1790, only one year after the adoption of the constitution, confineds, as do all the other

---
18 Opinion of The Honorable John Fox, against the Exercise of Negro Suffrage in Pennsylvania, (Harrisburg: Packer, Barrett and Parke, 1838).

naturalization laws, the right to become a citizen to FREE WHITE PERSONS.

... I have thus come to the conclusion, that the people of Pennsylvania, who framed the present constitution, were a political community of white men exclusively, and that colored persons of the African blood, were not contemplated by that constitution.

For the reasons given, the Court are of opinion that a negro in Pennsylvania, HAS NOT THE RIGHT OF SUFFRAGE,...

Document 19 The Constitution of the Commonwealth of Pennsylvania, 1838.

Article III.

Election franchise.

Section I. In elections by the citizens, every white freeman of the age of twenty-one years, having resided in the Sttate one year, and in the election district where he offers to vote, ten days immediately preceding such election, and within two years paid a State or county tax which shall have been assessed at least ten days before the election, shall enjoy the rights of an elector. But a citizen of the United States who had previously been qualified voter of this State, and removed therefrom and returned, and who shall have resided in the election district, and paid taxes, as aforesaid, shall be entitled to vote after residing in the State six months....

ANALYZING THE EVIDENCE

1. How might the wording of Article VII in the New York Constitution of 1777 (Document 1) and in Article III of the Pennsylvania Constitution of 1790 (Document 3) open up the possibility for African American suffrage? How might the wording also make it possible for African Americans to be excluded from the vote?

2. In what way did Jefferson's *Notes on the State of Virginia* (Document 2) describe a pre-industrial economy? What vision of republican citizenship is evident in Jefferson's *Notes*?

3. How did Absalom Jones and Richard Allen (Document 4) justify African American humanitarianism and compare it to white indifference to fellow Philadelphians during the epidemic in 1793? How did Jones and Allen employ Biblical arguments to support their arguments in favor of abolition? What admonitions and support did they give to enslaved persons? How do Jones and Allen call the society to a realization of a more just American republic?

4. What limitations on emancipation are evident in the New York law on gradual emancipation? (Document 5) Pennsylvania had a similar law. How does the enslaved population (Document 6) in Pennsylvania illustrate the slow process of emancipation?

5. How does J.T. Callendar's editorial (Document 7) reflect the bitterness of the political competition between Federalists and Jeffersonians? What racist attitudes are evident in Callendar's accusation against Jefferson?

6. How did Jefferson's acquisition of Louisiana (Documents 8 and 9) promise an economic windfall to Virginia and Maryland in the form of the domestic slave trade? Why did Jefferson not wish to have this made public?

7. In what ways were freed African Americans endeavoring to improve their educational opportunities in the early nineteenth century? (Document 10)

8. What does this runaway notice (Document 11) suggest about the "subscriber's" reputation as a humane master?

9. How does Absalom Jones in his Thanksgiving Sermon (Document 12) articulate a vision for a more just United States based on Christian principles.

10. Compare the 1821 New York Constitution (Document 13) and the 1838 Pennsylvania Constitution (Document 19) with the earlier New York and Pennsylvania constitutions (Documents 1 and 3). How were free men of color restricted from the suffrage in these later documents?

11. How does the preamble to the Cherokee constitution (Document 14) compare with the U.S. Constitution? Why does Article I so carefully outline the boundaries of the Cherokee nation?

12. What does the Land Lottery (Document 15) suggest links the Indian Removal and Trail of Tears to the spread of slavery in the early nineteenth century?

13. What evidence did Peter Williams (Document 16) provide for a new kind of racism that threatened African Americans in the first half of the nineteenth century? How did Williams defend African Americans' claims to citizenship and oppose "Colonization?"

14. In what ways did the "Appeal of 40,000 Citizens" (Document 17) support the claim that free blacks had originally been enfranchised by Pennsylvania? In what ways does the "Appeal" argue for African-Americans' rights to vote? Why do the authors of this appeal feel the effort is being made to disenfranchise African Americans in 1838? How do they support the view that "Democracy" was a coalition between whites in the South and North?

15. In what ways did Fox's decision (Document 18) support a white supremacist view of democracy and reject the possibility of African American citizenship? How does the decision challenge the arguments made in Documents 16 and 17?

DOCUMENT BASED QUESTION

1. Using the documents provided analyze the ways in which African American leaders fought for a republic that lived up to the ideals of the Declaration of Independence?

2. Using the documents provided and your knowledge of United States history, analyze the relationship between the development of anti-black racism and American democracy?

Cotton, Capital, and Industry—Slaves and the Making of the American Economy

CHAPTER 8

The relationship of slavery to capitalism is a critical question for students of American and world history. It is a question with two dimensions that need to be spelled out explicitly at the outset of this chapter. The first question, is to what degree did the slave-based, plantation economy reflect the technological and organizational developments associated with emerging capitalism in the nineteenth century? In other words, how capitalistic was the South's plantation economy? The second, related question, is to what degree did profits and labor from plantation slavery underwrite the emergence of modern industrial capitalism? In seeking answers to these two questions in the primary sources that follow, students will inevitably be drawn into questions about both the nature of slavery and its connection to American economic development and into a searching examination of the nature of liberal, free-market capitalism and its debt to the illiberal and coercive institution of slavery. These questions are not new. During the antebellum period, slave owners, abolitionists, industrialists, and critics of nineteenth-century capitalism had already begun the debate. The anwers they gave helped shape the way historians later would approach these same questions.

At the height of the anti-slavery movement, pro-slavery apologists and southern planters defended their system from claims that slavery was inhumane by contending that the plantation did not operate on the ruthless principles of industry seen in northern cities and factories. Instead, planters argued that plantations, like households, were organized and motivated by the benevolent and humane ideals of paternal obligation. As evidence, they pointed to the presence on plantations of elderly slaves who were no longer able to fulfill their duties in the fields, yet who continued to receive a maintenance. Sentiment rather than the unflinching logic of the marketplace directed the plantation. Industrialists and critics of capitalism alike often accepted this juxtaposition; they described a confrontation between a pre-modern, non-capitalist, technologically stunted, slave-based society and the progressive, liberal, efficiency-driven, wage economy of emerging industrial cities. More recently, however, historians of slavery have argued that the South's plantations were not immune to the "spirit of improvement" and the market-driven pursuit of efficiencies that seemed to govern northern factory and market developments.

During the antebellum period, if southerners were keen to demonstrate the humanity of the slave system and distinguish it from northern "wage-slavery," they were just as intent on emphasizing the North's, indeed the world's, dependence on the South. The famous boast by the South Carolina Senator and planter James Henry Hammond makes this connection directly:

> Without firing a gun, without drawing a sword, should they make war on us, we could bring the whole world to our feet... What would happen if no cotton was furnished for

three years?... Europe would topple headlong and carry the whole civilized world with her save the South. No, you dare not to make war on cotton. No power on the earth dares to make war upon it. Cotton is king.

Hammond was not alone, however, in identifying the flourishing industry of northern and English cities and the global ecomy with southern cotton. Karl Marx made the point as well, while also noting that the system of southern slavery was itself being transformed by market influences. The cotton textile industryin Great Britain and the North, Marx argued, "gave in the United States a stimulus... to the transformation of the earlier, more or less patriarchal slavery, into a system of commercial exploitation;" Marx continued, drawing a direct connection between the factory and the cotton field, "The veiled slavery of the wage-earners in Europe needed, for its pedestal, slavery pure and simple in the New World." In this chapter, then we will examine both the degree to which plantation slavery exhibited features of capitalism's "spirit of improvement" and its relationship to America's industrialization process.

The American "Industrial Revolution" and the emergence of American industrial capitalism, have often been explained as resulting from changes in the transportation sector, with a nod to the role of the National Bank and protectionist legislation, and with special attention to the can-do spirit of Yankee entrepreneurs and innovation. By the 1830s and 1840s, the United States was in the midst of a full-blown market and industrial transformation, with canals, roads, steamships, and then railroads connecting growing cities and towns with flourishing financial, retail, manufacturing and commercial centers. Agriculture expanded as well, with farmers across the country entering into the market economy to purchase consumer items with the sale of their agricultural commodities. Additionally, with the growth of internal markets, the United States' economy became less dependent on international trade; exports declined in their significance within the American economy, and the old colonial relationship with Europe, which had persisted long after the Revolution, ceased to define economic relations with the outside world. At least, this is the story that has most often been told in textbooks and is emphasized in state standards.

The significance of cotton to this developing American system, however, cannot be overemphasized. Slave-produced cotton was not only the dominant export, making up two-thirds of American exports, it provided the vital raw material for both Massachusett's textile mills and for Great Britain's even greater industrial expansion. Just as in the eighteenth century rum and molasses had been the lubricant of New England's trade, its manufacturing growth in the nineteenth century was also directly dependent on slavery and the internal slave trade as its mills could not continue without the raw material from the South. This fact southerners often noted with satisfaction, particularly as Massachusetts became a hotbed of abolitionist sentiment. New York also owed its commercial role to slave labor. The city's place as the financial center of the United States was cemented in the nineteenth century as its bankers financed investment in land and slaves, and insured the planters' property, often taking as collateral for their loans the souls of the slaves who at once were the most important capital in the American economy and the most productive labor force. As cotton farming spread from the Virginia and the Carolinas southward and westward into Georgia, Kentucky, Tennessee, Alabama, Mississippi, Arkansas and Florida, and finally into Texas, the South became interlinked in a vast cotton empire with a seemingly inexhaustible thirst for new land and enslaved laborers to make that investment profitable. It is no exaggeration to suggest that Manifest Destiny and American expansionism in the antebellum period was cotton imperialism. And, while after the Civil War cotton would be grown through a share-cropping system rather than by slave labor, cotton was the leading American export from

1803 to 1937. Well after Henry Ford introduced the Model-T and the "Age of the Automobile" had been declared, cotton was the United States' number one export.

In 1700 this would have hardly seemed a likely eventuality. India produced the lion's share of the world's cotton cloth and American and European traders purchased it primarily for trade with Africa, although cotton fabrics also were in hot demand in Europe as well. British and French weavers struggled to compete with these new fabrics. As a result European protectionist measures instituted in the early eighteenth century excluded Indian textiles, allowing textile producers, primarily in England, to develop the industrial technologies that made it possible for English weavers to compete with Indian producers, particularly at the low end of the market, making cheap cotton cloths. By the 1790s, English textile producers faced shortages of raw cotton.

The temperate climate and rich soils of the American South made the region ideally suited for growing short-staple cotton, a plant native to the highlands of central America. The fluffy cotton fibers of the plant were encased in a *boll* which had to be separated from the fibers before they could be cleaned, carded, spun and woven into fabric. Before the invention of the cotton 'gin, a single laborer might take an entire day to clean a single pound by hand. The high cost of labor, whether that of slaves or hired hands, made the expansion of cotton production a difficult prospect. In 1793 Eli Whitney acquired a patent for his engine, or 'gin. This machine could clean over 50 lbs. of cotton in a single day. While Whitney has received the lion's share of the credit for this innovation, recent scholars have argued that there is good evidence to suggest that one of Whitney's slaves should perhaps be recognized as the true inventor of the machine. Be that as it may, with the introduction of the cotton 'gin the slave-based, plantation economy in the United States gained a new lease on life.

The economic instability of the early republican period, and the War of 1812, slowed initial opportunities to profit from the demand for raw cotton, but after 1815, white southerners and their slaves began to move westward in increasing numbers. As they did, they encroached on the lands of Creek, Cherokee, Choctaw, and other native American communities. The Indian removal that reached its apogee in the American southeast with Jackson's removal of the Cherokee along the infamous "Trail of Tears," was in large part driven by this hunger for land on which to grow cotton. To exploit these vacated lands, slavers between 1815 and 1860 then marched over one million enslaved African Americans, chained in coffles just as Africans had been driven from the interior of Africa, or aboard ships in a repeat of the Middle Passage, from areas with surplus laborers like Virginia and Maryland to Alabama, Mississippi, Louisiana and later Texas, everywhere that "cotton fever" spread.

And, immediately following the conclusion of the war with Great Britain, financiers, factors, and merchants from Britain, eager to acquire this vital staple began to cultivate financial and market relations with southern planters. Before 1793, the United States exported to Great Britain only 11 million pounds of cotton. By 1800 that number had nearly doubled. Twenty years later American planters were exporting 128 million pounds. By 1860, the South grew three-fourths of the world's supply of cotton. The 1.8 billion pounds of cotton annually exported valued $200 million, fully two-thirds of all American exports. Elisée Reclus, in 1862, estimated that perhaps 20 million people worldwide were involved in producing raw cotton and cotton textiles, with three to four million of them enslaved persons in the American South. Indeed, as southerners trumpeted "King Cotton," it could also be said that the prosperity of the world's industrial economy, as John Marshman said, "has been based on the gigantic crime of holding three or four millions of human beings in a state of slavery."

Additionally, it is important to realize that key to the growth of cotton production were brutal measures applied to the slaver laborers to increase their efficiency and to expand their output. Much as the factory demanded uniformity, routinized labor, and long hours before the machine, African Americans who cultivated and picked cotton in countless slave labor camps across the South were likewise subjected to ruthless efficiency measures. As Sven Beckert and Seth Rockman have noted, "The whip made cotton. And whip-made increases in the efficiency of picking had global significance. They pushed down the real price of cotton, which by 1860 had fallen to one quarter of its 1800 price, even as demand had increased many times over."[1] The savings afforded by these brutal efficiencies were then absorbed into new technology in the mills, higher wages for mill workers, and cheaper, ready-made cotton clothing for European and American consumers.

The enslaved, however, should not be confused simply with a source of labor. Enslaved persons were property. Slaves were thus a form of capital, representing in a given year of the early nineteenth century, according to Michel Picketty, 150% of the United States national income. The value of enslaved persons was roughly equal to the total value of the nation's farmland during this period. According to Picketty, the value of slaves in 1860 was roughly three times greater than the total amount of money invested in the nation's banks. Comparisons to other sectors of national property further illustrate the significance of enslaved persons in the American economy. Slaves represented seven times the total value of all currency in circulation in 1860. They were three times the value of the entire livestock population and twelve times the value of the entire United States cotton crop. Finally, the value of the slaves in the South represented 48 times the total expenditure of the federal government in 1860.[2]

Prices paid for slaves, of course, fluctuated over the course of the nineteenth century, though they followed an upward secular trend. Additionally, prices paid for individual slaves reflected a number of factors; the age of the individual, their sex, physical appearance, strength, and even skin color played a role in the prices paid for each enslaved individual. Average prices reflected market conditions, often indicative of changes in the demand and price of cotton, or changes in general economic conditions. For example, during and after the War of 1812 there was a 40% increase in all prices, with the price of raw cotton more than doubling during the same period. Prices for slaves increased accordingly. In the 1830s, the price of slaves increased in response to discussions in Congress about returning the federal budget surplus to the states. Likewise, spending on "internal improvements" or infrastructure led to a boom in land prices and, once again, cotton prices. Slave prices rose in accord. After the "Panic of 1837," one of many cyclical downturns that have periodically plagued the global economy, prices for slaves fell precipitously. As the economy recovered from this depression, the price of slaves tripled after 1843. Several factors help explain this trend: worldwide demand for cotton increased; southern agricultural improvements and access to East Texas land increased demand for slaves and again prices rose in the very active market for slaves preceding the Civil War. By 1860, the average price paid for the purchase of a slave stood at around $800. But this average price was quite misleading. Young adult male field hands brought a much higher price, perhaps as much as $1800 to $2000. As the price of enslaved persons rose and fell, obviously, so did the fortunes of over one-third of

---

1 Sven Beckert and Seth Rockman, *Slavery's Capitalism: A New History of American Economic Development*, 52
2 Thomas Picketty, *Capital in the Twenty-first Century*, Translated by Arthur Goldhammer, (Cambridge, MA: The Belknap Press of Harvard University Press, 2014): 114-116.

white southerners and of many northern financial institutions that had invested in the immensely profitable cotton and internal slave markets.

While growth of cotton farming spread across the newly vacated Indian lands of the southeastern half of the United States, many northern families also made fortunes from the slave trade and from cotton textile production. The linkage between the eighteenth century slave trade and nineteenth century textile production is most clearly evident in the story of the establishment of Samuel Slater's textile mill in Pawtucket, Rhode Island. Slater's development of this textile mill, using technologies recently developed in England, was underwritten with financial backing from Moses Brown, and the firm, Almy and Brown. The Brown family had made its fortune in the "carrying trade" transporting slaves from Africa, rum from the Caribbean, and finished goods from England and British North America. Another prominent example of the interlinkages between the slave trade and urban industry in the North can be seen in the family of Francis Cabot Lowell. Lowell's father, John, was a member of the Continental Congress. His mother was the daughter of Francis Cabot. The Boston Cabots had made their wealth in the 18th century in the China trade (opium, tea, and Chinese luxuries) and in the Atlantic economy's carrying trade (rum and slaves). Francis Cabot Lowell had begun his business career in the same line importing silk and tea from China as well as textiles from India. He formed a partnership with other Bostonian merchants in1802 that became prominent in the opium trade in China and India. In 1804, Lowell purchased a rum distillery that processed slave-grown sugar from Jamaica. During a two-year visit to England and Scotland, Lowell reconnoitered British textile mills. The family had earlier invested heavily in the Beverly Cotton Manufactory in Beverly, Massachusetts. The enterprise had been the first textile mill in the United States, but had only been able to stay in business for little over a decade. With his knowledge of the operations in England, and by pooling family money and raising capital through the novel method of selling shares of stock in the business, Lowell established the Boston Manufacturing Company and constructed a mill in Waltham, Massachusetts. This successful operation was the first self-contained textile factory in the United States, combining all operations from processing raw cotton to weaving finished cloth under one roof. The mill would pioneer the practice of employing single women, "the Lowell Mill Girls," who earned lower wages than commanded by male workers, and were housed in a dormitory and kept under careful supervision. This factory model would transform American manufacturing.

Though the northern states had gradually eliminated slavery in the years after the Revolutionary War, and were often critical of the South's reliance on slave labor, as the example above illustrates, the northern economy was also deeply implicated in the internal slave trade and in the national dependency on enslaved labor. Abolitionists and southerners were alike fond of pointing out the inconsistency of northern citizens who expressed horror at the institution of slavery yet who profited in myriad ways from capital accumulated from the slave trade or commerce with the slave states. The abolitionist, William Lloyd Garrison, for example, characterized the North as a "partner in iniquity." Alexander McCaine, a southern apologist, observed, "Many of the abolitionists of the present day affect to have such tender consciences, and to feel such abhorrence of slavery, that they declare they will not wear the cotton of the South, because it has been cultivated by slaves. Yet, these extremely sensitive, and pre-eminently holy characters, feel no qualms of conscience, to sell Southern planters their boots and shoes, their negro cloth, and all the *et cetera* that make up a cargo of Yankee *notions*, and put the money, arising from the labour of slaves, in their pockets." In this chapter, you will be asked to examine the many ways in which the development of American capitalism in the nineteenth century owed its particular character to enslaved Americans, both in the cotton and cotton textile trades, but also in other industries associated with industrialization in the United States: railroads, coal and iron, finance, and commerce.

Northerners during the antebellum period often asked, "What have the people of the North to do with slavery?" Abolitionists answered "they have much to do with it." Today more than a century and a half after the Emancipation Proclamation, Americans from many walks of life ask a similar question, "What have we to do with slavery?" Is that not a distant memory? Was not the post-racial millennium entered into in 2008? Without reference to any of the events that have heightened racial tension in the intervening years since the election of President Barack Obama, it is possible to demonstrate that the American economy is still the beneficiary of the traffic in human beings that occurred before 1865, and from the labor of human chattel during the era of American slavery. So, in addition to asking readers to examine the impact of slavery on the development of American industrialization before 1865, in this chapter readers will also be asked to reflect on the may ways in which the American economy of the 21st century still benefits from that labor and from the capital generated by slaves. Within the past twenty years a number of corporations have opened their archives and uncovered the evidence of outright ownership of slaves, insurance contracts on the lives of slaves, loans granted with slaves as collateral, rental contracts for slave labor, and many other ways in which contemporary industries profited from the institution of slavery. A number of American universities have also acknowledged the importance of slave ownership to their early origins. So, when we ask at the beginning of the 21st century, "What have we to do with slavery?" It turns out, a great deal. As you analyse the documents that follow, all that can be asked is that each reader opens their heart and eyes to recognize the debt owed by every American to African Americans who labored in bondage before 1865.

PRIMARY SOURCES

Document 1   Letter from Samuel Slater to Moses Brown, 1789.

New York, December 2nd, 1789

Sir, -- A few days ago I was informed that you wanted a manager of *cotton spinning, &c.* in which business I flatter myself that I can give the greatest satisfaction, in making machinery, making good yarn, either for *stockings* or *twist,* as any that is made in England; as I have had opportunity, and an oversight, of Sir Richard Arkwright's works, and in Mr. Strutt's mill upward of eight years. If you are not provided for, should be glad to serve you; though I am in the New York manufactory, and have been for three weeks since I arrived from England. But we have but one *card,* two *mechanics,* two spinning jennies, which I think are not worth using. My encouragement is pretty good, but should much rather have the care of the perpetual carding and spinning. *My intention* is to erect a *perpetual card and spinning.* If you please to drop a line respecting the amount of encouragement you wish to give, by favour of Captain Brown, you will much oblige sir, your most obedient humble servant.

Samuel Slater

Document 2   Letter from Moses Brown to Samuel Slater, 1789.

Providence, 10th Twelfth Month, 1789

Friend,--I received thine of 2d instant and observe its contents. I, or rather Almy & Brown, who has the business in the cotton line, which I began, one being my son-in-law, and the other a kinsman, want the assistance of a person skilled in the frame or water spinning. An experiment has been made, which has failed, no person being acquainted with the business, and the frames imperfect. We are destitute of a person acquainted with water frame spinning; thy being already engaged in a factory with many able proprietors, we can hardly suppose we can give the encouragement adequate to leaving they present employ. As the frame we have is the first attempt of the kind that has been made in America, it is too imperfect to afford much encouragement; we hardly know what to say to thee, but if thou thought thou couldst perfect and conduct them to profit, if thou wilt come and do it, thou shalt have all the profits made of them over and above the interest of the money they cost, and the wear and tear of them. We will find stock and be repaid in yarn as we may agree for six months. And this we do for the information thou can give, if fully acquainted with the business. After this, if we find the business profitable, we can enlarge it, or before, if sufficient proof of it be had on trial, and can make any further agreement that may appear best or agreeable on all sides. We have secured only a temporary water convenience, but if we find the business profitable, can perpetuate one that is convenient. If thy prospects should be better, and thou should know of any other person unengaged, should be obliged to thee to mention us to him. In the mean time, shall be glad to be informed whether thou come or not. If thy present situation does not come up to what thou wishest, and from thy knowledge business, can be ascertained of the advantages of the mills, so as to induce thee to come and work ours, and have the *credit* as well as advantage of perfecting the first water mill in America, we should be glad to engage thy care so long as they can be made profitable to both, and we can agree. I am, for myself and Almy & Brown, thy frined,

Moses Brown

Document 3 "The First Cotton Gin," *Harper's Magazine,* 1869.

COTTON, CAPITAL, AND INDUSTRY—SLAVES AND THE MAKING OF THE AMERICAN ECONOMY

Document 4 Cotton Book of G.W. Lovelace, October 1817.[3] (Pounds of cotton picked daily)

	Monday	Tuesday	Wednesday	Thursday	Friday	Saturday	Totals
Sally	57	49	58	51	52	58	325
Bill	66	55	56	59	58	57	351
Charles	46	45	48	54	55	62	310
Elsy	31	37	26	28	31	39	192
Nancy	42	49	54	53	42	52	293
Dave	19	20	18	22	27	23	129
Harry	68	68	44	69	78	78	405
Joe	34	41	50	51	49	52	277
Lewis	23	38	34	33	44	43	215

DOCUMENT 5 Average Price of Slaves (1804-1861) In current dollars.

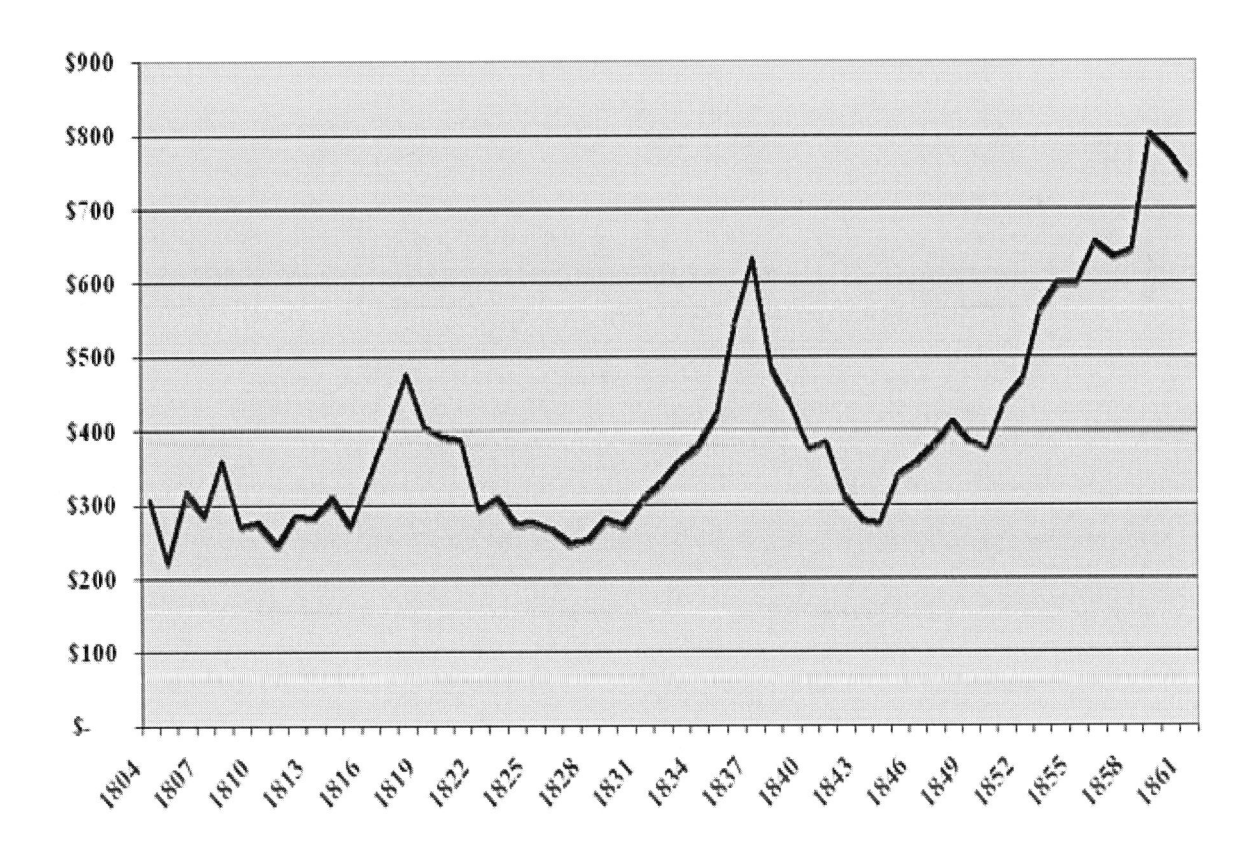

---

[3] Dr. Kilpatrick, "Historical and Stastical Collections of Louisiana: The Parish of Catahoula," Part 2, *De Bow's Review* 12 (1852), pp. 632-633.

DOCUMENT 6 Average Price of Slaves in 2015 dollars (1804-1861).

The prices below reflect simple calculation of the money price (based on the Consumer Price Index) of slaves in 2015 dollars.

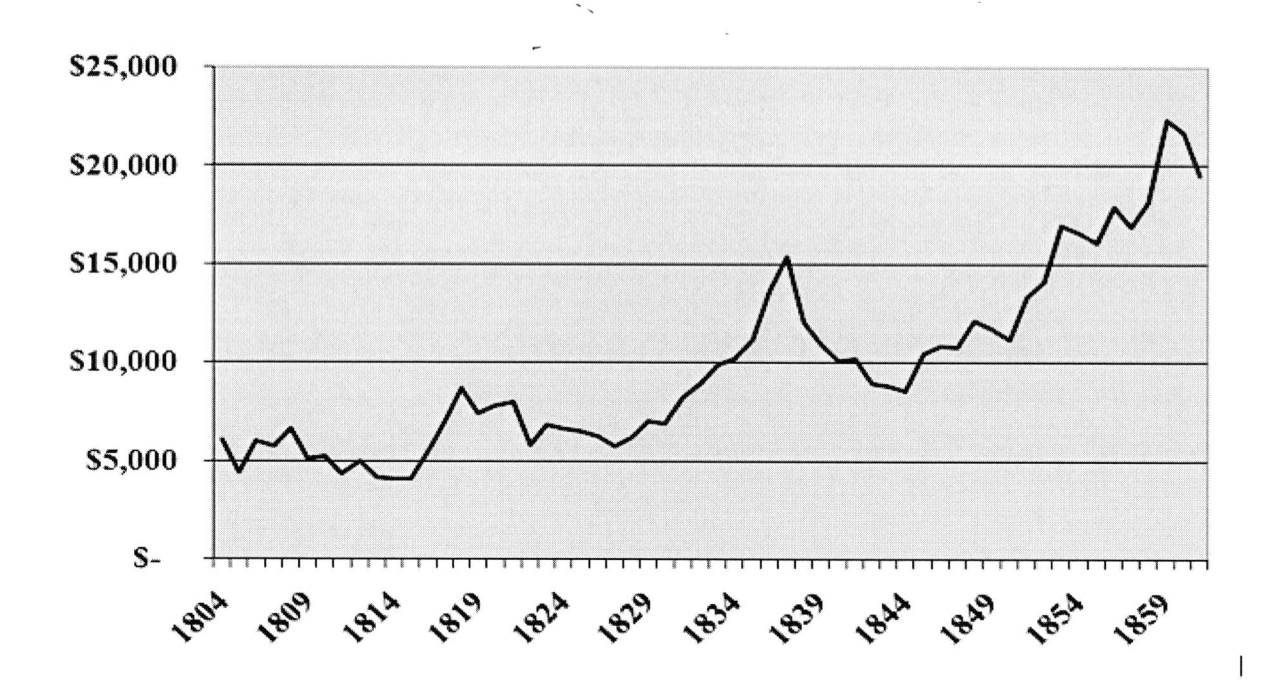

Document 7   Appraisal, 1815, of taxable property of William Pollard, of "Williamsville," Hanover County, Va.[4]

On the 31st May 1815 the Deputy Assessor called on me when he listed & valued

    1697 acres of land.... @ $16...........$16,455 ½

    Dwelling house........@ 4,000

    Out houses.............@ 610

    Furniture...............@.................... 700

    54 slaves................................ <u>8,720</u>

                                                $30,445 ½

    One Silver Watch

---

[4] Mss1 P7637 b 282, Unknown No Longer, Virginia Historical Society, http://unknownnolonger.vahistorical.org/record/9437/572, Accessed 11/20/2016.

The Slaves valued are mentioned below

Name	Age	Value		Name	Age	Value	
Jamey	Supposed to be 70 years of age	0		Milley	65	$20	$20
Ned	51	$50		Fanny	44	150	
Robin	55	30		Mary	16	300	
Frank	59	30	$110	Jenny	44	100	
Charles	45	350		Oncy	12	200	
Jacob	45	250		Muriah	45	20	
Moses	35	200		Mariah	16	300	
Balu	28	400		Sukey	26	100	
Solomon	35	350		Grace	30	200	
George	33	400		Salley	12	200	
Joshua	20	400		Sue	14	250	
Davey	21	350		Judy	29	300	
John	13	250		Nanny	17	300	
Dick	13	250		Sary	19	250	$2670
Edmond	14	250		Betty	9	130	
Wilson	15	300	$3750	Hannah	9	130	
Jamey	11	200		Abby	3	60	
Tawney	6	100		Janet	1	40	
Dago	5	50		Delphia	8	120	
Bartlet	6	100		Jane	4	60	
Thomas	10 (idiot)	0		Nelly	3	60	
Bob	9	150		Aggy	2	50	
William	5	100		Polly	7	100	
Armistead	8	150		Polly	7	100	
Billey	7	120		Kitty	7	100	
Joe	4	70		Sally (M)	5	90	
Henry	1	50	$1090	Judy-Ann	1	40	$1080
			$4950				

Document 8   Mortgage of land and 59 slaves by Eliphalet and Abigail Cutter Slack, 1836.[5]

State of Louisiana

Parish of Herville

Before me John Dutton, Parish judge ex-officio Notary public in and for and residing in the Parish of Herville in the State of Louisiana, and in presence of the witnesses hereafter named and subscribed.

Personally came and appeared M. Eliphalet Slack and his wife, Mistress Abigail Cutter Slack by him duly authorized domiciliated and residing in the Parish of Herville.

Which appearance did declare that this said Eliphalet Slack having subscribed for four hundred and twenty-six shares of stock of one hundred dollars each, forming altogether the sum of forty-two thousand six hundred dollars of capital stock of the Citizens Bank of Louisiana, created and incorporated by an act of the Legislature of the State of Louisiana approved the first day of April in the year eighteen hundred and thirty three, they the Said appearers acknowledge themselves to be indebted jointly and severally to the said Bank in the said sum of forty two thousand six hundred dollars, being the amount of their said capital stock in said Bank.

And now to secure the said capital stock agreeably to the provisions of the Charter of said Bank as well as to secure and assure the payment of capital and interests of the loan which had been or is to be taken to form the Capital of said Bank by the emission and issuing of obligations or Bonds to be signed by the President and countersigned by the cashier of said Bank or by any other persons authorized or who shall hereafter be authorized by law to sign and countersign such Bonds or obligations, the said Eliphalet Slack and Abigail Cutter Slack jointly and severally *in solido affectis* mortgage and hypothecate the following:

1. One tract of land situated in said Parish of Herville on the south side of Bayou Grosse Tête on said Bayou with a depth of forty arpents or more established and cultivated as a sugar and cotton plantation bounded above by land of said Eliphalet Slack and below by land owned by Ursin Daigle formerly by Madame Bosse together with all the buildings and improvements thereon consisting in dwelling houses, sugar works, cotton gin, cotton and corn houses, negro cabins, and other improvements—and all the cattle, horses, and implements of husbandry on or belonging to said plantation.

2. Another tract of land situated in said parish of Herville on the North side of the said Bayou Grosse Tête opposite to the plantation first, above described, and measuring twenty five arpents front, on said Bayou by a depth of forty arpents, cultivated in cotton and corn and used as pasture ground and woodland bounded above by land of said Eliphalet Slack and below by land of Arsin D'Aigle the said tract of land with all its improvements and establishments.

3. Fifty nine slaves whose names and ages follow:

---

[5]   Mortgage of land and 49 slaves by Eliphalet and Abigail Cutter Slack 3-2-1836, John Minor Wisdom Collection, 1790-1960, Manuscripts Collection 230, Box 10, Louisiana Research Collection, Tulane University Digital Library.

COTTON, CAPITAL, AND INDUSTRY—SLAVES AND THE MAKING OF THE AMERICAN ECONOMY 177

names	ages	names	ages	names	ages
Morris	35 yrs	Peggy	28 yrs	Lovey	24 yrs
Dinah	37 yrs	David	50 yrs	Fielding	26 yrs
Bird	34 "	Suzan	30 "	Rose	24 "
John	41 "	Dina	3 "	Hezekiah	36 "
Fanny	28 "	Jim Corbin	35 "	Michal	34 "
Minty	14 "	Martha	26 "	Rachael	32 "
Anne	12 "	Willis	30 "	Emeline	30 "
Harriet	4 "	Hannah	23 "	Beverly	20 "
Robin	52 "	Eliza	9 "	Becky	26 "
Levin	22 "	Dick	6 "	Izabella	18 "
Isaac	3 "	Abby	18 "	Phill	47 "
Thavous	14 "	Patsy	14 "	Kitty	30 "
Matilda	14 "	Henry	13 "	Winney	10 "
Hellen	12 "	Nelly	8 "	Peter	4 "
Little Phil.	6 "	Maria	30 "	Jonathan	4 "
Jane	14 "	Jacob	62 "	Ruth	10 "
Sally	62 "	Levi	3 "	Kitt	24 "
C.... Maria	3 "	Little Maria	20 "	Frederic	52 "
Celia	30 "	Lucy	16 "	Barnet	22 "
Jim Maria	26 "	Washington	14 "	----------------	

Which property land and slaves are to remain thus mortgaged and hypothecated until the full and final payment and extinction of the obligations and bonds aforesaid capital and interest, or until the said Eliphalet Slack and Abigail Cutter Slack shall have paid the amount of their capital stock and that they shall have reimbursed and paid in full capital and interest, any loan which they have obtained and to which they may be entitled to take as stock holders in said Bank in virtue of any of the provisions of the Charter of said Bank, unless previously to having obtained such loan they shall have transferred their stock and shall have been entirely and fully discharged by said Bank, the said Eliphalet and Abigail Cutter Slack agree that this hypothecary obligation by them given as security for their said stock and for any loan which they shall have obtained from said Bank, shall bear interest at the rate of ten per cent per annum, in case such loan shall not be punctually paid from the time it becomes due title fully paid and reimbursed and that the above mortgaged property shall also remain hypothecated to assure the payment of all such interest.

The said Mrs. Abigail Cutter Slack renounces in favour of said Bank all her rights and privileges dotal, paraphernal, or other or every nature and kind whatsoever which might affect in any manner the property mortgaged in the premises, ceding, transferring, pledging and affecting the said rights and privileges to the said Bank and consenting that the said Bank be fully subrogated in and to the said rights fully and without any kind of reserve, let or hindrance whatsoever; and the appearers further consent and agree, that if hereafter there should be by said Bank discovered any defect, vue, or deficiency in their title to the property or any other property mortgaged in the premises or that the said property be affected ...

... reserve the right to cause the said stock to be sold and to recover immediately any sum loaned to said appearers by the said Bank, unless the said appearers shall furnish other property the title of which shall be incontestable in lieu of that which the title shall be found to be defective or affected by tacit mortgage or privilege.

By the inspection of the records of mortgages of the said parish of Herville of which the said parish judge am the keeper, it appears that on the day of the date of this act the property mortgaged in the promises to the Citizens Bank of Louisiana is subject to and affected by the following Mortgages again and in the name of the said appearers and no others. [...]

And the said Eliphalet and Abigail Cutter Slack declare that any stock loan they may obtain shall be first applied to the extinguishment of the said judicial mortgage and consenting that the said Bank should retain a sufficient amount out of any monies they may be entitled to borrow, by reason of their being stock holders in said Bank to pay the said debt and interest due to the said William Eager or to his transferers.

So soon as this mortgage and hypothecary obligatons shall have been accepted by the President of the said Bank by authentic act and that the said acceptance, as well as this mortgage, shall have been inscribed in the paper office and upon this production of a certificate of the judge of said Parish of Herville that there shall have been accorded no new mortgage or privilege against said property and no act of alienation of any part or of the whole of said property the said Eliphalet and Abigail Slack shall be such is their will and intentions, de jure et de facto stock holders for four hundred and twenty six shares of stock in the capital of the said Citizens Bank of Louisiana.

This done and passed in my office the second day of March in the year of our Lord one thousand eight hundred and thirty six, in presence of William B. Savory and David G. Stacy, competent witnesses who have signed with the said Eliphalet Slack, the said Abigail Cutter Slack, the said Robert Fuller Slack and me the said judge. Signed.

Eliphalet Slack, Abigail Slack, Robert F. Slack for himself and as attorney for Charles Merriam, D.L. Stacy, and Wm. B. Savory. Signed. John Dutton, P. Judge

Document 9 Equity Mortgages in Virginia and Louisiana, Colonial and National Period[6]

		Sample size (percent of total)	Amount raised in 1791 dollars (percent of total)	Amount raised in 2015 dollars
Virginia (Fauquier, Culpepper, Albermarle, Goochland, Halifax, and Lunenburg counties)	Mortgages before 1776 not backed by slaves	257 (32%)	$406,832 (32%)	$20,564,554
	Slave-backed mortgages before 1776	192 (57%)	871,326 (68%)	42,722,963
	1812-1860 mortgages not backed by slaves	2,445 (72%)	2,114,234 (67%)	103,665,272
	1812-1860 mortgages backed by slaves	968 (28%)	1,050,723 (33%)	51,519,147
Louisiana (Opelousas and Baton Rouge Parish)	Mortgages before 1776 not backed by slaves	44 (49%)	26,637 (33%)	1,306,093
	Slave backed mortgages before 1776	46 (51%)	54,843 (67%)	2,689,072
	1812-1860 Mortgages not backed by slaves	545 (47%)	344,615 (12%)	16,897,207
	1812-1860 mortgages backed by slaves	493 (53%)	2,484,181 (88%)	121,805,555

Document 10 Charles Ball, *Slavery in the United States: A Narrative of the Life and Adventures of Charles Ball*, 1837.[7]

A Work Day in the Fields

The next morning I was waked, at the break of day, by the sound of a horn, which was blown very loudly. Perceiving that it was growing light, I came down, and went out immediately in front of the house of the overseer, who was standing near his own gate, blowing the horn. In a few minutes the whole of the working people, from all the cabins were assembled; and as it was now light enough for me distinctly to see such objects as were about me, I at once perceived the nature of the servitude to which I was, in future, to be subject.

---

[6] Table and data adapted from Bonnie Martin, "Slavery's Invisible Engine: Mortgaging Human Property," *The Journal of Southern History*, 76:4 (2010), pp. 837-838.

[7] Charles Ball, *Slavey in the United States: A Narrative of the Life and Adventures of Charles Ball, a Blackman who lived forty years in Maryland, South Carolina and Georgia, as a Slave, under Various Masters, and was one year in the Navy with Commodore Barney, during the Late War. Containing an Account of the manners and usages of the Planters and Slaveholders of the South—a description of the condition and treatment of the slaves, with observations upon the state of morals amongst the cotton planters, and the perils and sufferings of a fugitive slave, who twice escaped from cotton country*, (New York: John S.Taylor, 1837).

As I have before stated, there were altogether on this plantation, two hundred and sixty slaves; but he number was seldome stationary for a single week. Births were numerous and frequent, and deaths were not uncommon. When I joined them I believe we counted in all two hundred and sixty-three; but of these only one hundred and seventy went to the field to work. The others were children, too small to be of any service as labourers; old and blind persons, or incurably diseased. Ten or twelve were kept about the mansion-house and garden, chosen from the most handsome and sprightly of the gang.

…The overseer then led off to the field, with his horn in one hand and his whip in the other; we following—men, women, and children…--and a wretched looking troop we were.

…We walked nearly a mile through one vast cotton field, before we arrived at the place of our intended day's labour. At last the overseer stopped at the side of the field, and calling to several of the men by name, ordered them to call their companies and to turn into their rows. The work we had to do was to hoe and weed cotton, for the last time; and the men whose names had been called,… were designated as captains, each of whom had under his command a certain number of the other hands. The captain was the foreman of his company, and those under his command had to keep up with him. Each of the men and women had to take one row; and two, and in some cases where they were very small, three of the children had one. The first captain, whose name was Simon, took the first row,--and the other captains were compelled to keep up with him. By this means the overseer had nothing to do but to keep Simon hard at work, and he was certain that all the others must work equally hard.

..About seven o'clock in the morning the overseer sounded his horn [for breakfast]. The overseer had bread, butter, cold ham, and coffee for his breakfast. Ours was composed of a corn cake, weighing about three quarters of a pound, to each person, with as much water as was desired. … here, as everywhere in this country, each person received a peck of corn at the crib door, every Sunday evening, and that in ordinary times, every one had to grind this corn and bake it, for him or herself,… but that for some time past, the overseer, for the purpose of saving the time which had been lost in baking the bread, had made it the duty of an old woman, who was not capable of doing much work in the field, to stay at the quarter, and bake the bread of the whole gang. When baked, it was brought to the field in a cart, as I saw, and dealt out in loaves.

They still had to grind their own corn, after night, and as there were only three hand-mills on the plantation, he said they experienced much difficulty in converting their corn into meal. We worked in this field all day; and at the end of every hour, or hour and a quarter, we had pemission to… get water.

Our dinner was the same, in all respects, as our breakfast, except that, in addition to the bread, we had a little salt, and a radish for each person.

When we could no longer see to work, the horn was again sounded, and we returned home. I had now lived through one of the days—a succession of which make up the life of a slave—on a cotton plantation.

As we went out in the morning, I observed several women, who carried their young children in their arms to the field. These mothers laid their children at the side of the fence, or under the shade of the cotton plants, whilst they were at work; and when the rest of us went to get water, they would go to give suck to their children, requesting some one to bring them water in gourds, which they were careful to carry to the field with them. One young woman did not, like the others leave her child at the end of the row, but had contrived a sort of rude knapsack, made of a piece of coarse linen cloth, in which she fastened her child, which was very young, upon her back; and in this way carried it all day, and performed her task at the hoe with the other people.

I pitied this woman; and as we were going home at night, I came near her, and spoke to her…. I asked her why she did not do as the other women did, and leave her child at the end of the row in the shade. "Indeed," said she, "I cannot leave my child in the weeds amongst the snakes. What would be my feelings if I should leave it there, and a scorpion were to bite it? Besides, my child cries so piteously, when I leave it alone in the field, that I cannot bear to hear it. Poor thing, I wish were both in the grave, where all sorrow is forgotten."…

… I was deeply affected by the narrative of this woman, and as we had loitered on our way, it was already dark, whilst we were at a distance from the quarter; but the sound of the overseer's horn, here interrupted our conversation—at hearing which, she exclaimed, "We are too late, let us run, or we shall be whipped;" … At the time I joined the company, the overseer was calling over the names of the whole, from a little book…. Just as we had entered, Lydia came up out of breath, with the child in her arms; … and dropped on her knees before the overseer, and begged him to forgive her. "Where have you been?" said he. Poor Lydia now burst into tears, and said, "I only stopped to talk awhile to this man," pointing to me; "but, indeed, master overseer, I will never do so again." "Lie down," was his reply. Lydia immediately fell prostrate upon the ground; and in this position he compelled her to remove her old tow linen shift, the only garment she wore, so as to expose her hips, when he gave her ten lashes, with his long whip, every touch of which brought blood, and a shriek from the sufferer…. Then three other culprits were then put upon their trial. The first was a middle aged woman, who had, as her overseer said, left several hills of cotton in the course of the day, without cleaning and hilling them in a proper manner. She received twelve lashes. The other two were charged in general terms, with having been lazy, and of having neglected their work that day. Each of these received twelve lashes.

The Whip

…The whip used by the overseers on the cotton plantations, is different from all other whips, that I have ever seen. The staff is about twenty or twenty-two inches in length, with a large and heavy head, which is often loaded with a quarter or half pound of lead, wrapped in cat-gut, and securely fastened on, so that nothing but the greatest violence can separate it from the staff. The lash is ten feet long, made of small strips of buckskin, tanned so as to be dry and hard, and plaited carefully and closely together, of the thicknes, in the largest part, of a man's little finger, but quite small at each extremity. At the farthest end of this thong is attached a cracker, nine inches in length, made of strong sewing silk, twisted and knotted, until it feels as firm as the hardest twine.

…the best qualification of the overseer of a cotton plantation is the ability of using this whip with adroitness; and when wielded by an experienced arm, it is one of the keenest instruments of torture ever invented by the ingenuity of man. The cat-o'-nine tails, used in the British military service, is but a clumsy instrument beside this whip; which has superseded the cow-hide, the hickory, and every other species of lash, on the cotton plantations. The cow-hide and hickory, bruise and mangle the flesh of the sufferer; but this whip cuts, when expertly applied, almost as keen as a knife, and never bruises the flesh, nor injures the bones.

Picking Cotton

This business of picking cotton, constitutes about half the labour of the year, on a large plantation. … The manner of doing the work is this. The cotton being planted in hills, in straight rows, from four to five feet apart, each hand or picker, provided with a bag, made of cotton bagging, holding a bushel or more, hung around the neck, with cords, proceeds from one side of the field to the other, between two of these rows, picking all the cotton, from the open burs, on the right and left, as he goes. …The cotton is gathered into the bag, and when it becomes burdensome by its weight, it is deposited in some convenient place, until night, when it is taken home, either in a large bag or basket, and weighed under the inspection of the overseer. A day's work is not estimated by the number of hills, or rows, that are picked in the day, but by the number of pounds of cotton in the seed, that the picker brings into the cotton house, at night.

In a good field of cotton, fully ripe, a day's work is sixty pounds…. On all estates, the standard of a day's work is fixed by the overseer, according to the quality of the cotton; and if a hand gathers more than this standard, he is paid for it; but if, on the other hand, when his or her cotton is weighted at the cotton house, in the evening, it is found that the standard quantity has not been picked, the delinquient picker is sure to receive a whipping.

On some estates, settlements are made every evening, and the whipping follows immediately; on others, the whipping does not occur until the next morning, whilst on a few plantations, the accounts are closed twice, or three times a week. I have stated heretofore, that our overseer whipped twice a week, for the purpose of saving time….

It is estimated by the planters, or rather by the overseers, that a good hand can cultivate and pick five acres of cotton, and raise as much corn as will make his bread, and feed a mule or a horse. I know this to be a very hard task for a single hand, if the land is good, and the crops at all luxuriant…. Five acres of good cotton will yield ten thousand pounds of rough, or seed cotton. If he can pick sixty pounds a day, and works twenty-five days in a month, the picking of ten thousand pounds will occupy him more than six months.

… Picking of cotton may almost be reckoned among the arts. A man who has arrived at the age of twenty-five, before he sees a cotton field, will never in the language of the oversee, become a *crack picker*. By great industry and vigilance, I was able, at the end of a month, to return every evening a few pounds over the daily rate… but the business of picking cotton was an irksome, and fatiguing labour to me, and one to which I could never become thoroughly reconciled;….

Document 11 Articles of agreement between Thomas F. Mulledy, of Georgetown College, District of Columbia, of one part, and Jesse Beatty and Henry Johnson, of the State of Louisiana, of the other part. 19th June 1838.[8]

Thomas F. Mulledy sells to Jesse Beatty and Henry Johnson two hundred and seventy two negroes, to wit: - Isaac, a man sixty five years of age, Charles, his eldest son, forty years of age,

---

8   Maryland Province Archives, Special Collections, Lavinger Library, Georgetown University, Georgetown Slavery Archive, http://slaveryarchive.georgetown.edu/

COTTON, CAPITAL, AND INDUSTRY—SLAVES AND THE MAKING OF THE AMERICAN ECONOMY 183

Nelly his daughter, thirty eight years of age, Henny, a girl thirteen years of age, Julia, a girl eight years of age, Ruthy, a girl six years of age, Patrick a man thirty five years of age, Netty, his wife, thirty years of age, Cornelius, thirteen years of age, Francis, a boy twelve years of age, Susan, a girl ten, Gabriel, a boy eight, Peter a boy five, Jackson a boy three, Elizabeth, a child one, James a man twenty eight, Delia a woman twenty two, Susan a girl three, George a boy one, Isaac a man twenty six, Kitty his wife, twenty eight, Austin a boy six, Isaac a boy four, Elias a boy about one and a half, Sally a woman sixty five, Ned a man forty five, Rachel a woman forty three, Simon their son twenty, Anderson a boy eighteen, Louisa a girl fourteen, Ned a boy ten, Billy a man forty, Nelly a woman thirty eight, John a boy five, John a man thirty Nancy a woman twenty four, Patrick a boy three, Charles a man forty five, Sally a woman forty four, Nancy a woman seventeen, Margaret a girl fifteen, David a boy fourteen, Eliza a girl twelve, Martha a girl five, Thomas a boy five, Sarah Anne a child one, Nelly a woman sixty, Joseph a man forty, Nell a girl sixteen, Kitty a woman twenty two, Mary a girl six, Sam a boy four, Elizabeth a child one, Polly a woman sixty, Sally a woman fifty, William a man twenty one, Mary Anne a woman eighteen, Robert an idiot twelve, Henry eight, Harriett forty three Elizabeth twenty three, Louis a man twenty one, Mary Ellen seventeen, Nancy fifteen, Martha ten, Jenny one, Betsy a woman thirty two, Austin her son thirteen, Adolph ten, Henrietta seven, Harriett Anne four, Richard thirty six, Nancy Marly a woman thirty four, Margery sixty, Len sickly a man thirty eight Minty a woman thirty six, Nancy five Mary eighteen months, Charles sixty, Janus fifty, Tom forty five, Eliza twenty six, Reverdy seven, Noble five Edward three, William one Bill an idiot forty two Nana twenty six, Mary her daughter five, William six months, Charles [illegible] five, Benedict sixty five, Len Queen fifty, Sam [illegible] John Butler thirty five, John Gayle twenty one, [illegible] sixty five, Len [Enston?] fifty Daniel eighty, Nace fifty five Bernard thirty five, William eighteen, Tom sixteen, Jim twelve, Henry ten, Francis eight, Stephen lame sixty, Anne Ned Queen's wife, two sons and a daughter, Betsy [wife?] of Sam, and her two daughters, Matilda and her three daughters, Kitty wife of George, her son + daughter Margaret + her daughter, Ginny wife of Charles, and her daughter, Crissy, her two sons + two daughters, Celestia, Henry (not married) Louisa, Teresa, Mary, - all the women except Ginny, Kitty and the last three of last mentioned are under fifty, and over twenty years of age, the children attended to are from one to seven years of age, Harry sixty five, Livia his wife sixty, Joe fifty seven, Esther his wife fifty four, Bill twenty nine, Peter fifty seven, Stephen forty-nine, Sarah his wife forty eight, Bibiana forty nine, Mary fifty nine, Betty forty six, Bennet forty five, Clair his wife fortytwo, John thirty one, Abraham twenty seven, Susan twenty six, Priscilla seven, Perry twenty six, Jarred twenty four, Rose Anne his wife, twenty four, Charlotte twenty three, Mary twenty three, Julianne twenty two, Dick twenty seven, Greenfield twenty five, James twenty one, Ferdinand nineteen, Sylvester nineteen, Christianna eighteen, Harriette seventeen, Emmeline sixteen, Elenora fifteen, Mary twelve, Susanna fourteen, Ritta thirteen, Remus a man seventeen, Milly thirteen, Lucy eleven, Sall ten, Dina eight, Esther eight, Alexis thirteen, two children of one and two years of age, Nace fifty, Nace twenty, Biby forty five, Lucy twenty one, Bridget seventeen, Caroline fourteen, Basil thirteen, Martha eleven, Anne ten, Gabe eight, Biby seven, Henry six, Thomas five, Mary three, a child eighteen months old, Henry twenty eight, Emeline ten, Amanda eight, Elizabeth seven, Billy six, Biby five, Harriett five, Robert forty three, Mary thirty eight, Abraham sixteen, Robert fourteen, James twelve, Bridget eleven, Mary Jane ten, Susan eight, Sally Anne seven, Nelly six, Charles five, a child two, Bill Cush twenty eight, Phil fifty five, Nelly his wife, fifty three, Louis ten, Gusty eight, George thirty, Joseph twenty two, Harry seventy five, Anne seventy, Harry forty, Nelly thirty eight, Gabe twenty three, Daniel twenty five, Louise twenty three, Arnold twenty thirty eight, Anna his wife, twenty seven,

Arnold seven, Louisa five, Betsy thirty eight, Barney twelve, Lucinda ten, Greenfield five, Daniel four, Watt forty five, Teresa forty two, Frank twenty, Sam fourteen, Rachel eleven, Alexander ten, Charlotte seven, Emmeline thirty six, Watt three, a child one, Dick forty, Adeline thirty two, Matt ten, Jenny seven, Katherine four, a child six months, Nelly forty five, Eliza twenty two, Regis twenty eight, Kitty fifty three, Peter thirty seven, James sixty nine, Charl thirty three, Ned thirty, Sally fifty six, Alexis thirty six, Henney twenty two, Frederick twenty, Jenny nine, her child two, Zeke thirty two, Nathan sixty four, Henny his wife, sixty, James sixty years of age, it being understood, that if there be any children on either of the places where the said slaves now reside, belonging to any of the women herein named, that they are to be included in this sale.

It is understood that the said negroes are to be delivered at Alexandria in the District of Columbia, as follows. Fifty one contained in the list annexed, as soon as practicable, and all the others at such time as may be designated by the purchasers, between the 15th October & the 15th November next, with their beds:

Jesse Beatty & Henry Johnson agree on their part to pay to Thomas F. Muledy for the said negroes, the sum of one hundred & fifteen thousand dollars, to wit: - Twenty five thousand dollars on the delivery of the fifty one negroes if they shall be considered worth, agreeably to the average price of the whole, that sum, but if they should not be worth that amount agreeably to the said average, their estimated value is to be paid on their delivery, but the balance required to make up the amount of twenty five thousand dollars, shall be paid on the delivery of the other slaves in the fall. For the remaining sum of ninety thousand dollars, which J. Beatty & H. Johnson agree to pay, they are to have a credit of ten years, paying interest at the rate of six percent annually thereon; it being agreed and understood, that at the end of five years from the delivery of the said slaves at Alexandria, in the fall, as stipulated, the payments are to be made in five equal annual installments of eighteen thousand dollars each, from that time; that is, the first payment is to be made in the month of March next after the said time thus designated, and the other installments annually thereafter. It is distinctly understood, however, that the interest is to be paid from the time of the delivery of the slaves, as aforesaid, and that the first payment of interest will commence from the time of said delivery, and be calculated up to the period of payment, and that the interest thereafter is to be annually paid to T. F. Mulledy, at George Town College, District Columbia. –

It is further agreed, that on the delivery of the slaves in the fall, they are to be divided between Jesse Beatty and Henry Johnson, each agreeing to place his portion on a tract or tracts of land in the State of Louisiana, of the value of one thousand dollars, and to mortgage the said tract lands, together with the said negroes, (except those first to be delivered) to secure the payment of the said sum stipulated to be paid by him for his portion of the said slaves. And it also understood, that besides the said mortgages, the said J. Beatty and H. Johnson are to give their joint and several notes, or notes drawn in favor of one and endorsed by the other, for the amount stipulated to be paid for the negroes, and to cause each to be signed by some responsible person as security. –

It is further stipulated, that if the said negroes herein named shall be of different ages from that affixed to their names, and their value thereby impaired, or shall be unhealthy, or in any manner unsound, a fair deduction shall be made for such difference in age, or for such defects as shall lessen their value; and if the parties shall not agree as to the amount to be deducted, the question shall be submitted submitted for decision to two arbitrators to be chosen by the parties. It is further understood, that the fifty one negroes herein before alluded to, contained in the annexed list, are considered to be of the value of twenty five thousand dollars, and that the part of the contract relating to those to be immediately delivered, will be fulfilled when they are received, and the amount paid. City of Washington, June 19th 1838.

Thomas F. Mulledy

J. Batey

H. Johnson

Document 12 "Slavery and the Internal Slave Trade in the United States," *Tait's Edinburgh Review*, June 1841.[9]

The slave-trade flourishes in the capital, Washington, under the very eyes of the Congress; and we have this specimen of the advertisements which, openly and regularly, appear in the journals of that city:--

Cash for five hundred Negroes, including both sexes, from ten to twenty-five years of age. Persons having likely servants to dispose of, will find it their interest to give us a call, as we will give higher prices in cash than any other purchaser who is now or may hereafter come into the MARKET.

Franklin & Armfield, Alexandria.

Cash for three hundred Negroes.—The highest cash price will be given by the subscriber, for *negroes* of both sexes, from the ages of twelve to twenty-eight.

William H. Williams, Washington.

Cash for four hundred Negroes, including both sexes, from twelve to twenty-five years of age.

James H. Birch, Washington City.

Cash for Negroes.—We will at all times give the highest price in cash for likely young negroes of both sexes, from ten to thirty years of age.

J.W. Neil & Co., Washington

Here we find three traders in the district, advertising in one day for *twelve hundred* negroes, and a fourth offering to buy an indefinite number. In a later number of the *Intelligencer*, we find the following:-

Cash for Negroes.—I will give the highest price for likely negroes from ten to twenty-five years of age.

George Kephart

Cash for Negroes.—The subscriber wishes to purchase a number of negroes for the *Louisiana and Mississippi* market. Himself or an agent at all times can be found at his *jail* on Seventh Street.

William H. Williams.

---

9   "Slavery and the Internal Slave-Trade in the United States," *Tait's Edinburgh Review*, Vol. 8. (June 1841), pp. 373-378.

The unhappy beings purchased by these traders in human flesh, men and women, and children of eight years old, are sent to the south, either overland in coffles, or by sea, in crowded slavers. Fosered by Congress, these traders lose all sense of shame; and we have in the *National Intelligencer*, the following announcement of the regular departure of *three slavers*, belonging to a single factory:--

Alexandria and New Orleans Packets.—Brig *Tribune*, Samuel C. Bush, master, will sail as above on the 1st January; Brig *Isaac Franklin*, William Smith, master, on the 15th January; Brig *Uncas*, Nathan Boush, master, on the 1st of February. They will continue to leave this port on the 1st and 15th of each month, throughout the shipping season. *Servants that are intended to be shipped, will, at any time, be received for safe-keeping at twenty-five cents a-day.*

John Armfield, Alexandria

… This buying, imprisoning, and exporting of boys and girls eight years old; this tearing asunder of husbands and wives, parents and children, is all legalized *in virtue of authority delegated by Congress!!* The 249th page of the laws of the city of Washington, is polluted by the following enactment, bearing date 28th July, 1838:--

"For a LICENSE to trade or traffic in slaves for profit, four hundred dollars."

The following is from the "Anti-Slavery Manual," p. 114:--

… Franklin and Armfield alone shipped to New Orleans, during the year 1835, according to their own statement, not less than one thousand slaves. They own brigs of about 160 to 200 tons burthen, running regularly every thirty days, during the trading season, to New Orleans, each carrying about one slave to the ton.

Document 13 Assessed Property for Taxation, Texas, 1846-1855.[10]

Year	LAND No. Acres assessed	LAND Total assessed value	ENSLAVED PERSONS No. assessed	ENSLAVED PERSONS Total assessed value	ENSLAVED PERSONS Value of each	LIVESTOCK Total assessed value	OTHER PROPERTY Bank savings, store inventories, etc.
1846	31,967,480	$17,776,101	31,099	$10,142,198	$324	$2,929,378	$3,543,501
1847	30,440,210	17,326,994	39,251	12,174,593	310	3,392,784	4,668,134
1848	32,160,184	20,777,412	40,610	13,398,490	323	4,174,475	5,461,666
1849	32,890,887	20,874.641	43,534	14,658,837	337	4,419,015	5,847,516
1850	32,640,400	21,807,670	49,197	17,776,500	361	5,222,270	6,675,175
1851	37,731.774	31.415.604	59,959	26,246,668	404	6,638,115	8,639,797
1852	37,838,792	33,116,772	68,795	28,628,990	416	7,977,999	11,030,423
1853	39,175,858	39,256,612	78,713	35,946,473	456	10,217,499	13,734,530
1854	44,580,946	49,961,177	90,612	46,501,840	513	13,465,805	17,052,795
1855	45,893,869	58,671,126	105,603	53,373,924	505	16,936,423	20,539,978

---

10 Table adapted from Frederick Law Olmsted, *A Journey Through Texas or, A Saddle-Trip on the Southwestern Frontier: with a Statistical Appendix,* (New York: Dix, Edwards, & Co. 1857), p. 478.

Document 14 "Manufacture of Cotton by its producers" *De Bow's Commercial Review of the South and West,* 1;6 (1849), pp. 484-90

Cotton is the leading and controlling staple of the South, embracing nine States of the thirty, of the United States, and therefore worthy of consideration and study, by all who feel an interest in the prosperity of this end of the Union.

... An average crop now of United States is about 2,300,000 bales, which, at six cents, is $55,000,000. The estimated cost of spinning and weaving a pound of cotton is three cents, making two yards to the pound, equal to eighteen cents per pound, at nine cents per yard for Osnaburgs. The crop then, when spun and wove, is worth eighteen cents per pound, making $180,000,000, allowing ten per cent for waste, instead of $55,000,000 the yeld now, when sold as raw cotton.

The inequality between the labor and capital for growing, and that for spinning, is startling. A pound of cotton, plowed, hoed, picked, ginned, baled, spun, and wove is worth eighteen cents. The spinning and weaving, it is said, can be afforded for three cents cost, which would leave fifteen cents per pound for the labor of the planter, supposing the cotton mill in the cotton field, and the mill to get cost only. But as three cents may be too low an estimate, make it six—and then twelve cents is left for the planter. But now what does he get? Four, five, and six. The question may now be asked, who gets the balance—allowing six cents to the grower and six cents to the spinner, there will be six cents yet unaccounted for? It goes to pay warehouse charges, freight, insurance, drayages, storages, weighages, pickages, presage, commissions, postage, bills of lading, exchange, freight to Liverpool, dock dues, freight on railroad to Manchester, and then it is at the mill, and the same process brings it back, and this will fully account for the six cents per pound. Who pay these charges? The grower.

The growth and production of cotton are accomplished by the muscles of men and mules, laboring incessantly eleven months in every twelve; exposed to heat, to cold, to winds and rain, and to the malaria of swamps.

The spinning and weaving are done by the iron muscles of the spindle and loom, driven by the never-tiring engine, waited upon by boys and girls; and this labor is under roof, certain as to *quantity,* free from overflow, from frost, from caterpillar and bol worm. This simple statement is evidence clear and strong, that it is the grower's labor which is now sacrificed and greatly sacrificed. A firm and determined resolution among the planters, for they are the men who are suffering, and they must act for themselves, can arrest this policy in a few years.

Document 15 "Inventory of Negroes, 1850" Cappell Family Papers[11]

		Males				Females	
Name	Age	Value at commencement of year	Value at end of year	Name	Age	Value at commencement of year	Value at end of year
John	70	$50.00	$75.00	Hannah	60	$100.00	$125.00
Tom	49	1000.00	1200.00	Mary	34	800.00	900.00
Sandy	38	600.00	800.00	Fanny	23	800.00	900.00
Edmund	45	1000.00	1300.00	Rachel	32	675.00	750.00
Terry	40	700.00	950.00	Martha	27	675.00	700.00
Solomon	38	700.00	950.00	Celia	25	675.00	750.00
Peter		700.00	950.00	Rachel Ann	24	675.00	750.00
Isaac	50	700.00	950.00	Diana	31	600.00	700.00
Anthony	25	800.00	950.00	Chassy	32	600.00	675.00
Scott	25	800.00	950.00	Lucy	28	600.00	750.00
George	20	750.00	1000.00	Let	38	550.00	650.00
Tim	27	800.00	950.00	Azalia	13	600.00	700.00
Dotson	20	700.00	900.00	Amanda	13	400.00	600.00
Bill	18	700.00	900.00	Sarah	4	350.00	450.00
William	24	1000.00	1100.00	Harriet	8	300.00	400.00
Charles	10	500.00	650.00	Bet	7	350.00	400.00
Henry	19	375.00	400.00	Hannah	7	350.00	450.00
Henderson	8	300.00	350.00	Maryan	7	275.00	300.00
Johnson	6	250.00	275.00	Ellen	6	200.00	250.00
Stephen	4	200.00	225.00	Louisa	5	175.00	200.00
Tom	2	250.00	275.00	Susan	4	200.00	250.00
Monroe	4	200.00	225.00	Melissa	3	100.00	125.00
Daniel	2	150.00	175.00	Matilda	5	200.00	225.00
Tim	2	150.00	175.00	Jinny	3	100.00	150.00
Aaron	3	175.00	200.00	Caroline	3	150.00	150.00
Terry	1	75.00	100.00	Francis	2	100.00	125.00
		$9,625.00	$16,975.00	Laura	1	100.00	125.00
				Amarintha	1	75.00	100.00
				Sara An	6 mo	75.00	100.00
				Rose	6 mo	75.00	100.00
						$10,975.00	$12,850.00
				Ann			100
				Delia			100
							$13,050

---

11 Caitlin Rosenthal, "Slavery's Scientific Management: Masters and Managers," in *Slavery's Capitalism: A New History of American Economic Development*, Sven Beckert and Seth Rockman, eds., (Philadelphia: University of Pennsylvania Press, 2016): p. 80.

Document 16 Insurance Policy on Judy, a Slave, Richmond Fire Association, 15 August 1853[12]

No. 1853   Richmond Fire Association, Richmond, Virginia

This policy of Insurance witnesseth:

That THE RICHMOND FIRE ASSOCIATION, in consideration of the sum of *Six*---Dollars and *forty-eight*—cents, to them in hand paid by *Henry Curtis*—of *Hanover Co.*, Virginia.

Do Assure the life of *Judy*—a Slave in the *County of Hanover*, State of Virginia, in the amount of *Four hundred*—Dollars, for the term of One year, to wit: From the *fifteenth* day of *August*—One thousand eight hundred and fifty *three* (at noon) unto the *fifteenth* day of *August*—One thousand eight hundred and fifty *four* (at noon).

And the said Association do hereby promise and agree to and with the said assured *his* executors, administrators, or assigns, well and truly to pay or cause to be paid, the said sum insured, to the said assured, *his* executors, administrators, or assigns, within sixty days after due notice and satisfactory proof of ownership and of the death of the said slave.

Provided always and it is hereby declared to be the true intent and meaning of this Policy, and the same is accepted by the aforesaid upon these express conditions, that the said slave is the fee simple property of the party insuring, (or if otherwise, as stated in this declaration) and in case the said slave

Shall, without the consent of this Association, previously obtained and endorsed upon this policy, pass beyond the limits of the State of Virginia, or in case the assured shall have already any other insurance on the slave hereby insured and not notified to this Association, and mentioned in, or endorsed upon, this Policy, or shall hereafter affect any other insurance upon the said Slave without the consent of the Association first obtained and endorsed upon this Policy, or in case the said slave shall commit suicide, or shall die by means of an invasion, insurrection, riot, or civil commotion, or of any military or usurped power, or by the hands of justice, this policy shall be void, null and of no effect.

And it is also understood and agreed to be the true intent and meaning of this policy, that if the declaration made by the said *Henry Curtis* bearing same date of this policy and upon the faith of which this agreement is made, shall be found in any respect untrue, then in such case this Policy shall be null and void.

The interest of the assured in this Policy is not assignable, unless by consent of the Richmond Fire Association, manifested in writing.

This insurance may be continued for such farther term as shall be agreed upon, the premium therefore being paid and endorsed on the Policy, or a receipt given for the same.

In Witness whereof, *The Richmond Fire Association* have caused these present to be sealed with their seal, and signed by their President and Secretary, this *fifteenth* day of *August* in the Year of our Lord, *one thousand eight hundred and fifty-three*.

---

[12] Mss2 C9435 b 16. Unknown No Longer, Virginia Historical Society Richmond, VA http://unknownnolonger.vahistorical.org/record/1180/197# Accessed 11/20/2016.

Attested   James Bosher, President

J.G. Bosher, Assoc. Secretary

Document 17   Dr. Fred Ross, "Speech before the Presybterian General Assembly at Buffalo, 1853.

Friday May 27, 1853

Speech delivered at Buffalo, before the General Assembly of the Presbyterian Church. The order of the day was reached at a quarter before eleven, and the report read again,--viz.: ... 2. That with an express disavowal of any intention to be impertinently inquisitorial, and for the sole purpose of arriving at the truth, so as to correct misapprehensions and allay all causeless irritation, a committee be appointed of one from each of the synods of Kentucky, Tennessee, Missouri, and Virginia, who shall be requested to report to the next General Assembly on the following points:--1. The number of slaveholders in connection with the churches, and the number of slaves held by them. 2. The etent to which slaves are held from an unavoidable necessity imposed by the laws of the States, the obligations of guardianship, and the demands of humanity. 3. Whether the Southern churches regard the sacredness of the marriage relation as it exists among the slaves; whether baptism is duly administered to the children of the slaves professing Christianity, and in general, to what extent and in what manner provision is made for the religious well-being of the slave," &c. &c.

Dr. Ross moved to amend the report by substituting the following, with an express disavowal of being impertinently inquisitorial:--that a committee of *one* from each of the Northern synods be appointed, who shall be requested to report to the next General Assembly,-- 1. The number of Northern church-members concerned, directly or indirectly, in building and fitting out ships for the African slave-trade, and the slave-trade between the States. 2. The number of Northern church-members who traffic with slave-holders, and are seeking to make money by selling them negro-clothing, handcuffs, and cowhides. 3. The number of Northern church-members who have sent orders to New Orleans, and other Southern cities, to have slaves sold, to pay debts owing them from the South. [See Uncle Tom's Cabin.] 4. The number of Northern church-members who buy the cotton, sugar, rice, tobacco, oranges, pine-apples, figs, ginger, cocoa, melons, and a thousand other things, raised by slave-labor. 5. The number of Northern church-members who have intermarried with slave-holders, and have thus become slave-owners themselves, or enjoy the wealth made by the blood of the slave,--especially if there be any Northern ministers of the gospel in such a predicament. 6. The number of Northern church-members who are the descendants of the men who kidnapped negroes in Africa and brought them to Virginia and New England in former years. 7. The aggregate and individual wealth of members thus descended, and what action is best to compel them to disgorge this blood-stained gold, or to compel them to give dollar for dollar in equalizing the loss of the South by emancipation. 8. The number of Northern church-members, ministers especially, who have advocated *murder* in resistance to the laws of the land. 9. The number of Northern church members who own stock in underground railroads, running off fugitive slaves, and in Sabbath-breaking railroads and canals. ... 11. The number of Northern church-members who attend meetings of Spiritual Rappers, or Bloomers, or Women's-Rights Conventions. 12. The number of Northern church-members who are cruel husbands. 13. The number of Northern church-members who are hen-pecked husbands.

Document 18 *Calloway v. Jones*, Sumpter Superior Court, Georgia, before Judge Perkins, 1855.[13]

No. 53.—WILLIAM CALLAWAY, administrator of W.P. Gammage, plaintiff in error, vs. JONES & QUATTLEBUM, defendants in error.

1. Where the answer to a charge in a bill is mere matter of opinion, denial, founded upon belief only, does not swear off the equity, so as to entitle the defendant to a dissolution of the injunction.
2. A general warranty of soundness may cover even patent defects.
3. Where the Court gets jurisdiction of the person or property of a non-resident, it will retain it to administer justice to its own citizens, and will not send them to a foreign jurisdiction to seek relief.

In Equity, in Sumpter Superior Court. Decision by Judges PERKINS, August Term, 1855.

This bill was filed by William P. Gammage, in his lifetime, alleging that Jones & Quattlebum, in December, 1850, sold to complainant two negroes—Tenah and Rachel, for the sum of $1100, and gave a written warranty of soundness; that complainant gave them a mortgage upon the negroes for the purchase money, and has paid them a portioin of the same; that they had foreclosed the mortgage for the balance, $675, besides interest, and were proceeding with the *fi.fa.;* that both of the negroes were unsound, Tenah having a disease of the womb, and Rachel having a defect in one of her eyes; and that the amount already paid was the full value of the negroes; that defendants resided in the State of South Carolina. The prayer was for an injunction.

The defendants' answer denied that Tenah had any disease of the womb, or was unsound—admitted the defect in Rachel's eye, but insisted it was a patent defect, and not covered by the warranty.

The Court, on motion, dissolved the injunction, and this decision is assigned as error.

BROWN & BROWN, for plaintiff in error.

MILLER & HALL, for defendants in error.

By the Court.—Lumpkin, J. delivering the opinion.

The judgment of this Court is, that the injunction in this case should not have been dissolved, the answer not having sworn off the equity of the bill.

1. As to the womb disease alleged to have existed in one of the women at the time of the sale, the denial is, and of necessity must be, a matter of opinion—no disease is more subtle; none effects the whole system so completely; and consequently, none is more difficult to detect. And as to the defect in the eye, of the other woman, while the fact is admitted, it is insisted, that the blemish was obvious, and was not, therefore, covered by the general warranty of soundness.
2. That there are numerous elementary *dicta*, as well as reported cases, in favor of this proposition, we do not dispute. We believe, however, that principle and the weight of authority, are the

---

[13] *Calloway v. Jones*, in *Reports of Cases in Law and Equity, Argued and Determined in the Supreme Court of the State of Georgia* Volume XIX, (Athens, GA: Reynolds & Bro., 1856), pp. 277-278.

other way. (*Parson's on Contracts*, 459, *note*.) A purchaser chooses to rely upon the warranty of the vendor, rather than his own judgment; and if so, he should have the benefit of the protection which it gives him.

3. But it is argued, that the vendee has ample remedy at Law, by following the vendor to South Carolina. But the doctrine is, that when the Courts get jurisdiction of the person or property of non-residents, they will retain it, to administer justice to its own citizens, and not sent them to a foreign jurisdiction to seek redress; and this not considered a violation of the comity of States. And if this be true generally, how much strongly does it apply in the present case? Who would venture to assail one of the clan of the Quattlebums of historical notoriety in our chivalric sister State, with the significant device on her eschutcheon, *animus opibus que parati*.

Document 19 Daily Record of Cotton Picked during the week commencing on the 15th day of October, 1860. Eustatia Plantation Account Book[14]

Name	Monday	Tuesday	Wednesday	Thursday	Friday	Saturday	Week's Picking
Leah	45	40	30	50	35	40	240
Old Maria	60	65	75	55	70	65	340
Maria Anderson	45	sick	sick	sick	sick	sick	45
Big Amanda	175	215	220	215	235	235	1295
Celeste	75	100	50	sick	sick	sick	225
Big Sarah	135	150	160	160	160	180	945
Little Amanda	180	190	195	200	185	185	1135
Eliza Amy	140	160	155	155	160	155	925
Patsy Ann	135	155	165	150	sick	sick	605
Betty Cushman	100	child born					100
Elenaline	120	150	150	140	140	145	845
Sarah	105	115	145	135	140	155	795
Susan	35	45	80	70	85	85	400
Little Clarissa	155	170	175	165	190	180	1035
Little Patsy	135	145	155	150	170	170	925
Little Sarah	145	145	135	140	155	155	875

---

14 Caitlin Rosenthal, "Slavery's Scientific Management: Masters and Managers," in *Slavery's Capitalism: A New History of American Economic Development*, Sven Beckert and Seth Rockman, eds., (Philadelphia: University of Pennsylvania Press, 2016), p. 71.

Document 20 Wealth Estimates of the U.S. in 1860 by Economic Category from Joseph C.G. Kennedy, *Preliminary Report on the Eighth Census* (1860).[15]

Category	Estimated Value (1860)
Slaves	$3,000,000,000
Farms	6,638,414,221
Manufacturing investment	1,050,000,000
Investment in Railroads	1,166,422,729
Bank Capital	227,469,077
Home Productions	27,484,144
Livestock	1,098,862,355
Total	$13,452,000,000

Document 21 "One Dollar Bill," State of Florida, 1863.

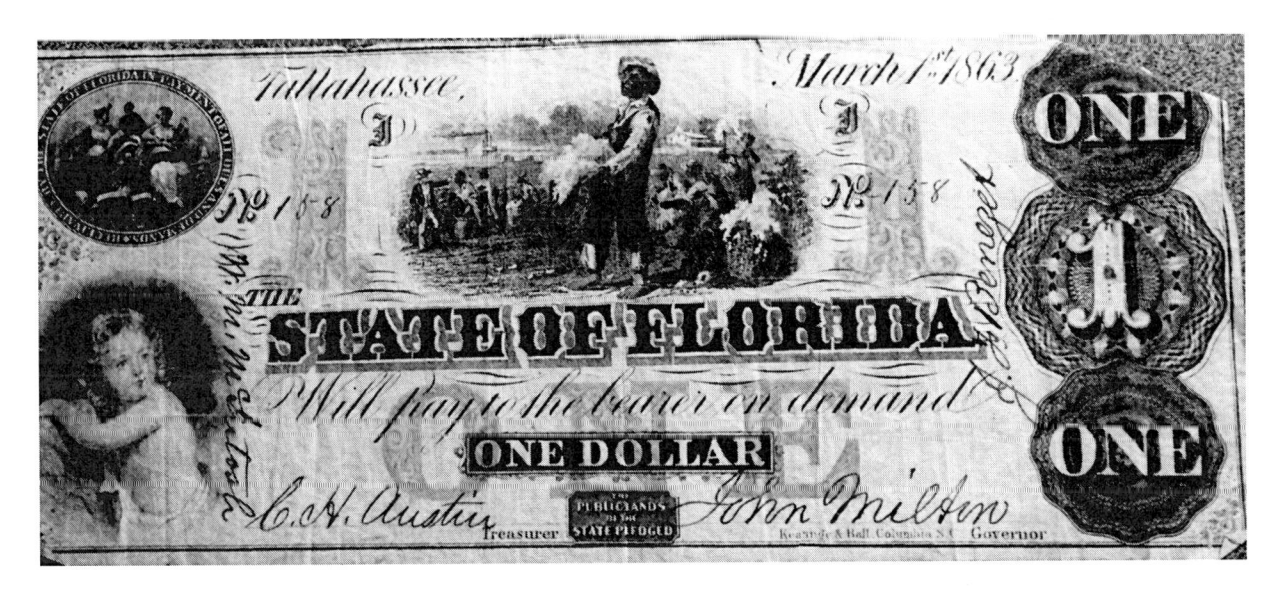

---

[15] James L. Huston, "Property Rights in Slavery and the Coming of the Civil War," Journal of Southern History, 65:2 (1999), p. 254. Data from Joseph C.G. Kennedy, Premliminary Report on the Eighth Census(Washington, D.C., 1862): 190, 192, 193, 195, 196, 209, 230-31.

EXAMINING THE EVIDENCE

1. Examine the letters between Moses Brown (of the Brown family in Providence, Rhode Island that made its fortune in the slave and carrying trade) and Samuel Slater (Documents 1 and 2). How do these letters illustrate the relationship between the slave trade and early industrialization in the United States?

2. How did the development of the cotton 'gin (Document 3) contribute to the growth of the cotton economy and the textile mills in New England (Documents 1 and 2)?

3. Analyze the average prices of slaves expressed in current and real dollar values (Documents 5 and 6). What factors might explain the different spikes in prices: 1816-1819, 1834-1837, and 1850-1861? What factors might help explain the precipitous declines in prices for slaves in 1819 and 1837?

4. The price of slaves expressed in 2015 dollars (Document 6) was derived from comparisons of a basket of comparable consumer items in the nineteenth century with similar items in 2015? How might this measure of the real value of slaves actually understate their value?

5. How did slaves figure in the net worth of the Pollard farm in 1815 (Document 7)? Compare the prices of slaves in Document 6 with the averages given in Document 5. How did the assessed value of the slaves on the Pollard plantation compare with the average prices of slaves across the United States?

6. How did the assessed value of the slaves on the Pollard plantation (Document 7) vary by age and gender?

7. Why did the Slacks (Document 8) mortgage their slaves in 1836?

8. How do Documents 8 and 9 illustrate the way in which slaves were used to underwrite investment in land and capital in the antebellum period?

COTTON, CAPITAL, AND INDUSTRY—SLAVES AND THE MAKING OF THE AMERICAN ECONOMY   195

9. Based on Charles Bell's narrative (Document 10) what was the daily routine on a cotton plantation? How did overseers and plantation owners increase productivity on their plantation?

10. What does the sale of slaves by Georgetown University in Washington, D.C. (Document 11) suggest about the development of non-agricultural institutions in the United States before 1865?

11. What does the sale of slaves by Georgetown University (Document 11), the exposé of the American slave trade (Document 12) and the evidence of growing slave numbers in Texas (Document 13) reveal about the workings of the internal slave trade? What explains the flow of slaves within the internal slave markets in the United States before the Civil War?

12. How does Document 14 support the view that industrialization was built on the labor of slaves?

13. Compare the average price of slaves in Document 5 with those listed in the Coppel's "Inventory of Negroes" (Document 15). How do these prices compare? Why might the Coppell plantation owner be interested in calculating the value (these are not sale prices) of his slaves? How might this relate to the practice of mortgaging slaves (Document 8) or insuring them (Document 16)?

14. What does the insurance policy on Sally (Document 16) suggest about slave owners' perceptions of their slaves? How does this document challenge the perception held by pro-slavery apologists that the plantation was a paternalistic household economic system?

15. Examine the daily record of cotton picking in Document 4 and Document 19. What do you notice about comparative productivity levels? How would you explain those differences? What other conclusions might you draw from these documents?

16. What does the court case, *Calloway v. Jones* (Document 19) tell historians about purchases of slaves in the antebellum period?

17. How do Document 7 and Document 17 and 20 support the view that slaves were critical to both individual planters in the South and to the national economy?

18. Examine the $1 bill issued by the State of Florida in 1862 (Document 21) Why does the bill read "The State of Florida will pay to the bearer on demand, One Dollar?" What is the significance of the image on the bill?

DOCUMENT BASED QUESTIONS

1. Using the documents provided analyze the degree to which southern cotton plantations reflected the values of capitalist industry in the period 1800 to 1860.

2. Using the documents provided analyze the relationship between the development of American capitalism and the institution of slavery in the period before the Civil War.

Gender and Family On and Off the Plantation

CHAPTER 9

In 1840, Alexis de Tocqueville published a two-volume work entitled *Democracy in America*. In this treatise, de Tocqueville had more than a little to say about the ways in which democracy was shaping gender relations in America and the ways in which American understandings of proper gender roles in turn influenced political and social institutions in the United States. Some of his remarks have been included among the primary sources in this chapter. De Tocqueville contended that one feature of American democracy that differed from the aristocratic societies of Europe, or even from revolutionary France, was the vitality of American womanhood, the high regard in which women were held in America, and the degree to which American women adhered without resistance to their place within the domestic sphere. De Tocqueville was identifying what has since been described as the "separate spheres" doctrine, an ideal that dominated American perceptions of gender and family relations through much of the nineteenth century, yet which only occasionally explained the lived realities of women across the social spectrum. This middle-class ideology of domesticity articulated a clear separation of public and private spheres, with men inhabiting the former and women the latter. This division, however, coincided with a certain empowerment of middle-class women, evident in increasingly positive images of women, greater educational attainment for middle-class women, and an acknowledgment of their unique suitability to shape household, church, and school. Over the course of the antebellum period, and often in concert with women's participation in social reform movements, northern women argued for expanded social and political rights precisely because of their nature, which promised a softening effect on the competitive and often harsh masculine public sphere.

This gender ideology shared a great deal with similar developments in western Europe. Both in the United States and across Europe, revolutionary and Enlightenment ideas combined with industrial capitalism's economic formation to shape gender roles and identities. A wide range of new consumer items and new forms of consumerism in the nineteenth-century also contributed to making the "Cult of Domesticity" possible, both in Europe and America. As de Tocqueville noted, however, in the United States, gender roles and expectations were different. He attributed these differences to the influence of democracy. However, it is worth remembering that unlike nineteenth-century Europe, where slavery and the presence of enslaved persons had never taken root, in the United States the institution of slavery was integrated into the political, economic, and social fabric of the nation. The significance of chattel slavery to the United States and the vehement defense of the institution during the first half of the nineteenth century, provided an important backdrop and context which helps explain unique American approaches to gender in the early nineteenth century. Moreover, even though slavery in the early nineteenth century had diminished to insignificance in the northern economy, racial categories that had resonance far beyond the slaveholding South helped shape the ways in which bourgeois ideals of gender roles and family relations would be understood in both North and South.

WOMEN'S WORK AND WHITENESS

Historians of immigrant women, female factory workers, and black women, whether slave or free, have made clear that the domestic ideal of separate spheres identified by de Tocqueville hardly corresponded with the lived experience of most American women. This was particularly the case when one looks closely at the economic activity of most American women. The mill girls who labored in textile mills or the immigrant women who took in boarders, or laundry, or in other ways helped cobble together household incomes shared little in common with middle-class housewives. Rural women who worked in "cottage industry" or on the farm, likewise lived very different lives than those held up as models for American women. What these women did share, however, were benefits of "whiteness" and opportunities made possible by the presence and labor of slaves, both men and women.

Mill girls in the textile industry, most obviously, processed raw cotton, grown by slaves, into fabric. This fabric was then sewn into ready-made, inexpensive cotton clothes in the garment districts of northern cities and sold across the country. Other manufactures depended on slaves either for their raw materials or as markets. In the 1830s, in Massachusetts alone, 33,000 women were employed in varied capacities in their homes making palm-leaf hats. The palms were cut by slaves in Georgia and the Carolinas, and the hats often sold in the South. Northern mills also produced "negro shoes," cheap mass-produced shoes sold to supply plantations. These women, at work in the market economy did not, of course, fulfill the ideals of middle-class domesticity. As you will see in the primary sources included in this chapter, the "factory girls" were stigmatized for their failure to live up to women's prescribed roles. Interestingly, their critics, including southern pro-slavery apologists, often likened the factory to the plantation as an institution of white, wage-slavery. The "factory girls," for their part, responded by differentiating themselves from slaves.

Of course, enslaved women at work in the fields also fell short of the domestic ideal. They were denied the opportunity to share fully in the consumer society their labor underwrote. Hard physical labor, as well, was only one of the areas where they did not measure up to the ideals of the "Cult of Domesticity." It was only with difficulty that black women could assert their domestic authority given the presence in the household of white plantation mistresses whose needs and the needs of their families took priority over those of their slaves, men or women. Slave women also faced the prospect, all too real in many cases, that their home and family could be broken up at the whim of their masters and mistresses. They also faced sexual exploitation and racist presumptions about African-American women's sexuality that again undermined their claims to moral authority of the sort that enabled middle-class, white women to lay claim to political and social influence in the antebellum period. In fact, much as the democratization of the male body politic had depended upon the expulsion of Native Americans and white supremacist assertions of middle-class and working-class males, white middle-class women's authority in the domestic sphere, in part derived from the benefits that accrued from "whiteness."

At the same time, reform movements, beginning with efforts to curtail Sunday labor, limit alcohol consumption, reform marriage laws, and advocate for the end of slavery, served to provide middle-class, white women with platforms to enter the public sphere and to argue for the positive contribution of women in the political realm. The reaction of male abolitionists to women's voices raised in the cause and women's exclusion from full participation in the abolition movement contributed to energizing many women (though not most) to argue from a moral authority derived from their stature in the home for such things as equal marriage and suffrage. In addition, the abolition movement provided a training ground for women's public activism. When women abolitionists objected to slavery, they often did so using the rhetoric of separate spheres doctrine. Indeed, the anti-slavery cause often depended upon the rhetoric of the Cult of Domesticity as justification for why slavery need be abolished.

MARRIAGE AND SEXUALITY

The subjects of slave marriage and African American sexuality provided another area in which to contest gender roles. For antebellum abolitionists, and for social scientists in the twentieth century, the sustainability of slave marriages and the stresses of plantation life on marriage proved a preoccupation. Among the primary sources included in this chapter are a number that examine the institution of slave marriages. A frequently-leveled criticism of slavery was that it destroyed the matrimonial bond between husband and wife, as slave owners denied legally-sanctioned marriages, arbitrarily separated husband and wife, subjected slave women to sexual pressure, and in myriad ways undermined black men's authority over their wives and daughters. Despite this fact, studies of slave marriages in the Freedmen's Bureau records collected during and after the Civil War, it is clear that slaves struggled successfully to maintain their marriages. According to Herbert Gutmann's study of a sampling of North Carolina marriages, over half of all marriage permits granted to former slaves recognized marriages that had lasted over a decade. But Gutman's study also revealed the enormous difficulties slave marriages faced. Of marriages registered in Mississippi's Freedmen's Bureau office where one of the partners was at least forty years of age over a third had experienced the termination of an earlier marriage by force. Gutman's survey of slave marriages, therefore, demonstrated the strength of slave marriages, despite the many impediments that slavery placed in the way of enslaved men and women.

Stereotypes of African American sexual behavior served important rhetorical purposes in the emerging ideology of domesticity. One of the stereotypes emphasized supposed sexual promiscuity among Africans and African Americans. For slave owners, presumptions of slave promiscuity served multiple purposes; the "natural lewdness" of African Americans justified social domination and sustained animosity towards black men. Presumptions of slave women's promiscuity served to legitimize slaveholders' own sexual exploitation of African American women. Northerners and abolitionists accepted the contention that slaves were sexually promiscuous, but argued that this was the result of enslavement, rather than the natural proclivity of people of African descent. In either case, the sexuality of African Americans, free or enslaved, served to establish the boundaries of sexual propriety. It was then only with difficulty that African American men and women could assert their own claims to moral and sexual virtue.

HOUSEHOLD MANAGEMENT AND TRUE MOTHERHOOD

The presence of enslaved African-Americans in the plantations of the South also had important consequences for developing ideals of domesticity in the South. The ideal of southern femininity, not unlike that in the North, emphasized the sanctity of virginity, the imperative of marriage, and the glorification of motherhood. Additionally, much as did middle-class northern women, plantation mistresses played critical roles in the management of the household, with the notable difference that where northern servants were free, "domestics" in the South were often enslaved African Americans. Plantation mistresses, like their northern counterparts, spent their lives caring for family members, supervising the daily tasks of cooking, cleaning, sewing, etc. Southern plantation mistresses, however, lacked the same domestic authority, because within the paternalistic model of the plantation, male authorities had not vacated the domestic space for the office or the factory. And, husbands' authority remained unchallengable, whether from wives or children, because such challenges threatened the structure of patriarchal power. Plantation women were also, to a much greater degree than was the case in northern cities, isolated on plantations, surrounded by their slaves. An important component of southern hospitality, and the ideal of gentility itself, was the encouragement of social ties across that distance.

A key feature of the domestic ideal of separate spheres as it emerged in the early nineteenth century was a glorification of women's maternal roles. This emphasis had emerged in the revolutionary era, as mothers were seen as central to the inculcation of the values of republicanism in the youth of the new nation. During the nineteenth century, declining family size, new forms of consumerism, and the emphasis on women's importance as nurturers of moral and religious values gave child-rearing and motherhood an increased significance. A new sentimentalism directed toward mother and child characterized the period. Attainment of the standards of "True Motherhood," however, would prove difficult for women outside the middle class. For slave women this was even more the case. Practices inherent in the institution of slavery ran entirely counter to the ideal.

The economic characteristics of the slave family contradicted the very sentimentality with which white families across the country endowed their own households. Families in the new domesticity stood outside the market, distanced from the cash nexus that defined relationships in the capitalist economy. But, slaves were labor, bought for a price; slaves were property that reproduced itself, akin to interest earned on savings. The birth of a child was an economic fact, with obvious import to the master, but also for its mother. Abolitionists claimed that this economic reality distorted the sentiments of true motherhood. A commonplace contention by slavery's apologists was that African Americans lacked the attachments to one another that white families maintained. Abolitionists countered that this was not the case and cited the memoirs of runaway slaves as evidence. In either case, however, the white, middle-class family, characterized by diminishing family size, spatially and emotionally differentiated from the presence of domestic servants, and built around the sentimental, nuclear family unit represented a model against which both white planters' families and slave families were unfavorably juxtaposed.

MASCULINITY

The new domestic ideal, of course, also shaped masculinity. Republican thought had emphasized the male property-holder, seeing dependency in any form as inimical to political participation. The "hireling"—or wage earner—was viewed as unable to fully participate as voter or officeholder. Wage earners, like servants, slaves, wives and daughters, all suffered from the impairment of being dependent. The development of an economy which relied much more on both wage-earners and salaried labor posed a significant challenge to models of masculinity in the early republic. The democratic impulses identified by de Tocqueville as contributing to the emergence of gendered separate spheres also depended upon a redefined masculinity capable of accommodating the wage earner and entrepreneur, as well as the yeoman farmer, planter, and merchant. The redefinition of masculinity during the "democratic" Age of Jackson was also shaped against the axis of race and slavery. Middle-class men found themselves, as salaried employees of manufacturing or financial firms, dependent on their employers, or if they had their own firms, faced with the uncertainties of volatile markets. Their claims to manhood then depended upon both success in business and the ability to afford the many markers of affluence that measured their success as providers. For working-class white men, as David R. Roediger has noted, "farm and household workers ... were becoming *white workers* who identified their freedom and their dignity in work [that was] suited to those who were 'not slaves' or 'not negurs'."[1] Consequently, working-class whites objected to being called servants, and to calling their employers masters, as was the custom before the American revolution. Ironically, they preferred to refer to their employers as "boss" which was simply the Dutch, *baas,* meaning master. To address a superior as master, in this democratic age, was to diminish oneself to the status of slave. Additionally, working-class white males, in both the North and South, asserted their right to participation in the public sphere, at the same time excluding men of color from the vote, ensuring that American democracy, as it emerged in the early nineteenth century was governed by what in Germany in the 1930s was designated the *herrenvolk,* or master race.

In the South, the planter elite, while not always office-holders, served to promote a culture that profoundly influenced smaller planters and poor whites. A feature of masculinity in the South was an emphasis on honor, virility, bravery, and racial identity. These ideals appealed to the planter elite as well as to poor whites, often with Scottish or Scots-Irish heritages. Family life in this context emphasized tradition and hierarchy in ways that northern families did not. It also stressed family honor, which could only be accumulated by male achievement and most often diminished by female impropriety. And, just as northern males feared loss of status associated with failures in business or loss of work, southern males' sensitivity to challenges to their honor reflected the recognition that they were surrounded by enslaved men who were dishonored and denied their manhood on a daily basis. A feature of white male culture in the South that has often been associated with this emphasis on individual and family honor was the common practice of dueling in the South, a practice largely outlawed in the North soon after the American Revolution. Additionally, respect for authority and recognition of the risks associated with a familial loss of honor became central features of the childrearing practices in southern families, with important implications for the development of educational institutions in the South.

KEY QUESTIONS

How did the institution of slavery and the prominence of slavery in the United States help shape the contours of gender and family life in the period before the Civil War? The documents included in this chapter will not enable readers to draw conclusive judgments. The complexity and scope of the question makes it impossible in one short chapter to fully incorporate the evidence needed to completely answer this question. But, hopefully the documents will permit readers to reflect on the relationship between the history of slavery and the history of gender and family in America? Additionally, my hope is that the evidence included in the pages that follow will encourage further questioning of the relationships between race, gender, and family in American history.

---

1   David R. Roediger, *The Wages of Whiteness: Race and the Making of the Working Class,* (London: Verso, 1991), p. 49.

Document 1   Alexis de Tocqueville, *Democracy in America*, 1840.[2]

Although the travelers who have visited North America differ on a great number of points, they all agree in remarking that morals are far more strict there than elsewhere....

The reason appears to me to be the principle of equality and the institutions derived from it. Equality of conditions does not itself engender regularity of morals, but it unquestionably facilitates and increases it.

Among aristocratic nations birth and fortune frequently make two such different beings of man and woman, that they can never be united to each other. Their passions draw them together, but the condition of society, and the notions suggested by it, prevent them from contracting a permanent and ostensible tie. The necessary consequence is a great number of transient and clandestine connections. Nature secretly avenges herself for the constraint imposed upon her by the laws of man.

This is not so much the case when the equality of conditions has swept away all the imaginary, or the real, barriers which separated man from woman. No girl then believes that she cannot become the wife of the man who loves her; and this renders all breaches of morality before marriage very uncommon: for, whatever be the credulity of the passions, a woman will hardly be able to persuade herself that she is beloved, when her lover is perfectly free to marry her and does not.

The same cause operates, though more indirectly, on married life. Nothing better serves to justify an illicit passion, either to the minds of those who have conceived it or to the world which looks on, than compulsory or accidental marriages.

In a country in which a woman is always free to exercise her power of choosing, and in which education has prepared her to choose rightly, public opinion is inexorable to her faults. The rigor of the Americans arises in part from this cause. They consider marriage as a covenant which is often onerous, but every condition of which the parties are strictly bound to fulfil, because they knew all those conditions beforehand, and were perfectly free not to have contracted them.

...Almost all men in democracies are engaged in public or professional life; and on the other hand the limited extent of common incomes obliges a wife to confine herself to the house, in order to watch in person and very closely over the details of domestic economy.

...The Americans have applied to the sexes the great principle of political economy which governs the manufactures of our age, by carefully dividing the duties of man from those of woman, in order that the great work of society may be better carried on.

In no country has such constant care been taken as in America to trace two clearly distinct lines of action for the two sexes, and to make them pace one with the other, but in two pathways which are always different. American women never manage the outward concerns of the family, or conduct a businesss, or take part in political life; nor are they, on the other hand, ever compelled to perform the rough labor of the fields, or to make any of those laborious exertions which demand the exertion of physical strength. No families are so poor as to form an exception to this rule. If on the one hand an American woman cannot escape from the quiet circle of domestic employments, on the other hand she is never forced to go beyond it. Hence it is that the women of America, who often exhibit

---

[2]   Alexis de Tocqueville, *Democracy in America*, Volume II, *The Social Influence of Democracy*, trans. Henry Reeve, esq. with an original preface by John C. Spencer, (New York: J&H.G. Langley, 1840), pp. 217-224, 225-227.

a masculine strength of understanding and a manly energy, generally preserve great delicacy of personal appearance and always retain the manners of women, although they sometimes show that they have the hearts and minds of men.

Nor have the Americans ever supposed that one consequence of democratic principles is the subversion of marital power, or the confusion of the natural authorities in families. They hold that every association must have a head in order to accomplish its object, and that the natural head of the conjugal association is man.

…This opinion is not peculiar to one sex, and contested by the other: I never observed that the women of America consider conjugal authority as a fortunate usurpation of their rights, nor that they thought themselves degraded by submitting to it. It appeared to me, on the contrary, that they attach a sort of pride to the voluntary surrender of their own will, and make it their boast to bend themselves to the yoke, not to shake it off.

…It is true that the Americans rarely lavish upon women those eager attentions which are commonly paid them in Europe; but their conduct to women always implies that they suppose them to be virtuous and refined; and such is the respect entertained for the moral freedom of the sex, that in the presence of a woman the most guarded language is used, lest her ear should be offended by an expression.

The legislators of the United States, who have mitigated almost all the penalties of criminal law, still make rape a capital offence, and no crime, is visited with more inexorable severity by public opinion. This may be accounted for; as the Americans can conceive nothing more precious than a woman's honour, …

Thus the Americans do not think that man and woman have either the duty or the right to perform the same offices, but they show an equal regard for both their respective parts; and though their lot is different, they consider both of them as beings of equal value. … Thus, then, while they have allowed the social inferiority of woman to subsist, they have done all they could to raise her morally and intellectually to the level of man; and in this respect they appear to me to have excellently understood the true principle of democratic improvement.

As for myself, I do not hesitate to avow, that, although the women of the United States are confined within the narrow circle of domestic life, and their situation is in some respects one of extreme dependence, I have nowhere seen women occupying a loftier position; and if I were asked, now that I am drawing to the close of this work, in which I have spoken of so many important things done by the Americans, to what the singular prosperity and growing strength of that people ought mainly to be attributed, I should reply—to the superiority of their women.

Document 2 An Act to Restrain the Horrid Practice of Duelling, Pennsylvania, 31 March 1806[3]

If any person within this commonwealth shall challenge by word or writing the person of another to fight at sword, rapier, pistol or other deadly weapon, or if any person so challenged shall

---

3 "An Act to Restrain the Horrid Practice of Duelling," *The General Laws of Pennsylvania, from the year 1700, to, 1853.* (Philadelphia: T.& J.W. Johnson, 1853), p. 228.

accept the said challenge, in either case, such person so giving, or sending, or receiving any such challenge, shall for such offense, being thereof lawfully convicted… by the testimony of one or more witnesses, or by confession, forfeit the sum of five hundred dollars, and shall suffer one year's imprisonment at hard labour, … and moreover shall forfeit and be deprived of all rights of citizenship within this commonwealth for the terms of seven years.

Document 3   Distribution of First Births by the Ages of Slave Mothers[4]

Age of Mothers	Distribution of First Births
Under 15	3%
15-19	37%
20-24	30%
25-29	15%
30-34	8%
Over 35	7%

Document 4   William Harper, *Memoir on Slavery* read before the Society for the Advancement of Learning of South Carolina, 1837.[5]

It has often been said by the denouncers of Slavery, that marriage does not exist among slaves. It is difficult to understand this, unless willful falsehood were intended. We know that marriages are contracted; may be, and often are, solemnized with the forms usual among other classes of society, and often faithfully adhered to during life. The law has not provided for making those marriages indissoluble, nor could it do so. If a man abandons his wife, being without property, and being both property themselves, he cannot be required to maintain her. If he abandons his wife, and lives in a state of concubinage with another, the law cannot punish him for bigamy. It may perhaps be meant that the chastity of wives is not protected by law from the outrages of violence. I answer, as with respect to their lives, that they are protected by manners, and their position. Who ever heard of such outrages being offered? At least as seldom, I will venture to say, as in other communities of different forms of polity. Our reason doubtless may be, that often there is no disposition to resist. Another reason also may be, that there is little temptation to such violence, as there is so large a proportion of this class of females who set little value on chastity, and afford easy gratification to the hot passions of men. It might be supposed, from the representations of some writers, that a slave-holding country were one wide stew for the indulgences of unbridled lust. Particular instances of intemperate and shameless debauchery are related, which may perhaps be true, and it is left to be inferred that this is the universal state of manners. Brutes and shameless debauchees there are in every country; we know that if such things are related as general or characteristic, the representation is false. Who would argue from

---

[4] Herbert G. Gutman, *Slavery and the Numbers Game: A Critique of Time on the Cross,* (Urbana: University of Illinois Press, 1975), p. 143.

[5] William Harper, "Memoir on Slavery" read before the Society for the Advancement of Learning of South Carolina at its Annual Meeting at Columbia, 1837. (Charleston, S.C.: James S. Burges, 1838), pp. 26-28.

the existence of a Col. Chartres in England, or of some individuals who might, perhaps be named in other portions of this country, of the horrid dissoluteness of manners occasioned by the want of the institution of Slavery. Yet the argument might be urged quite as fairly, and really it seems to me with a little more justice—for there such depravity is attended with much more pernicious consequences. Yet let us not deny or extenuate the truth. It is true that in this respect the morals of this class are very loose, (by no means as universally so as is often supposed,) and that the passions of men of the superior caste, tempt and find gratification in the easy chastity of the females. This is evil, and to be remedied, if we can do so, without the introduction of greater evil. But evil is incident to every condition of society, and as I have said, we have only to consider in which institution it most predominates.

Compare these prostitutes of our country, (if it is not injustice to call them so,) and their condition with those of other countries—the seventy thousand prostitutes of London, or of Paris, or the ten thousand of New-York, or our other Northern cities. Take the picture given of the first from the author whom I have before quoted. "The laws and customs of England, conspire to sink this class of English women into a state of vice and misery, below that which necessarily belongs to their condition. Hence, their extreme degradation, their troopers' oaths, their love of gin, their desperate recklessness, and the shortness of their miserable lives."

"English women of this class, or rather girls, for few of them live to be women, die like sheep with the rot; so fast that soon there would be none left; if a fresh supply were not obtained equal to the number of deaths. But a fresh supply is always obtained equal to the number of deaths. But a fresh supply is always obtained without the least trouble: seduction easily keeps pace with prostitution or mortality. Those that die are, like factory children that die, instantly succeeded by new competitors for misery and death." There is no hour of a summer's or a winter's night, in which there may not be found in the streets a ghastly wretch, expiring under the double tortures of disease and famine. Though less aggravated in its features, the picture of prostitution in New York or Philadelphia would be of like character.

In such communities, the unmarried woman who becomes a mother, is an outcast from society—and though sentimentalists lament the hardship of the case, it is justly and necessarily so. She is cut off from the hope of useful and profitable employment, and driven by necessity to further vice. Her misery, and the hopelessness of retrieving, render her desperate, until she sinks into every depth of depravity, and is prepared for every crime that can contaminate and infest society. She has given birth to a human being, who, if it be so unfortunate as to survive its miserable infancy, is commonly educated to a like course of vice, depravity and crime.

Compare with this the female slave under similar circumstances. She is not a less useful member of society than before. If shame be attached to her conduct, it is such shame as would be elsewhere felt for a venial impropriety. She has not impaired her means of support, nor materially impaired her character, or lowered her station in society; she has done no great injury to herself, or any other human being. Her offspring is not a burden, but an acquisition to her owner; his support is provided for, and he is brought up to usefulness; if the fruit of intercourse with a freeman, his condition is, perhaps, raised somewhat above that of his mother. Under these circumstances, with imperfect knowledge, tempted by the strongest of human passions—unrestrained by the motives which operate to restrain, but are so often found insufficient to restrain the conduct of females elsewhere, can it be matter of surprise that she should so often yield to the temptation? Is not the evil less in itself, and in reference to society—much less in the sight of God and man. As was said of theft—the want of chastity, which among females of other countries is sometimes vice, sometimes crime—among the free of our own, much more aggravated; among slaves, hardly deserves a harsher turn than that of weakness. I have heard of complaint made by a free prostitute, of the greater countenance and indulgence shewn by socity towards colored persons of her profession, (always regarded as of an inferior and servile class, though individually free,) than to those of her own complexion. The former readily obtain employment; are even admitted into families, and treated with some degree of kindness and familiarity, while any approach to intercourse with the latter is shunned as a contamination. The distinction is habitually made, and it is founded on the unerring instinct of nature. The colored prostitute is, in fact, a far less contaminated and depraved being. Still many, in spite of temptation, do preserve a perfectly virtuous conduct, and I imagine it hardly ever entered into the mind of one of these, that she was likely to be forced from it by authority or violence.

It may be asked, if we have no prostitutes from the free class of society among ourselves, I answer in no assignable proportion. With general truth, it might be said, that there are none. When such a case occurs, it is among the rare evils of society. And apart from other and better reasons, which we believe to exist, it is plain that it must be so, from the comparative absence of temptation. Our brothels, comparatively very few—and these should not be permitted to exist at all—are filled, for the most part, by importation from the cities of our confederate States, where Slavery does not exist. In return for the benefits which they receive from our Slavery, along with tariffs, libels, opinions, moral, religious, or political—they furnish us also with a supply of thieves and prostitutes. Never, but in a single instance, have I heard of an imputation on the general purity of manners, among the free females of the slave-holding States. Such an imputation, however, and made in coarse terms, we have never heard here—*here* where divorce was never known—where no Court was ever polluted by an action for criminal conversation with a wife—where it is related rather as matter of tradition, not unmingled with wonder, that a Carolinian women of education and family, proved false to her conjugal faith—an imputation deserving only of such reply as self-respect would forbid us to give, if respect for the author of it did not. And can it be doubted, that this purity is caused by, and is a compensation for the evils resulting from the existence of an enslaved class of more relaxed morals.

Document 5   Orestes Brownson, *The Laboring Classes: An Article from the Boston Quarterly Review*, 1840.[6]

We pass through our manufacturing villages; most of them appear neat and flourishing. The operatives are well dressed, and we are told, well paid. They are said to be healthy, contented, and happy. This is the fair side of the picture; the side exhibited to distinguished visitors. There is a dark side, moral as well as physical. Of the common operatives, few, if any, by their wages, acquire a competence. A few of what Carlyle terms not inaptly the *body-servants* are well paid, and now and then an agent or an overseer rides in his coach. But the great mass wear out their health, spirits, and morals, without becoming one whit better off than when they commenced labor. The bills of mortality in these factory villages are not striking, we admit, for the poor girls when they can toil no longer go home to die. The average life, working life we mean, of the girls that come to Lowell, for instance, from Maine, New Hampshire, and Vermont, we have been assured, is only about three years. What becomes of them then? Few of them ever marry; fewer still ever return to

---

[6] Orestes A. Brownson, *The Laboring Classes, an Article from the Boston Quarterly Review*, (Boston: Benjamin H. Greene, 1840), pp. 11-12.

their native places with reputations unimpaired. "She has worked in a Factory," is almost enough to damn to infamy the most worthy and virtuous girl. We know no sadder sight on earth than one of our factory villages presents, when the bell at break of day, or at the hour of breakfast, or dinner, calls out its hundreds or thousands of operatives. We stand and look at these hard working men and women hurrying in all directions, and ask ourselves, where go the proceeds of their labors? The man who employs them, and for whom they are toiling as so many slaves, is one of our city nabobs, reveling in luxury; or he is a member of our legislature, enacting laws to put money in his own pocket; or he is a member of Congress, contending for a high Tariff to tax the poor for the benefit of the rich; or in these times he is shedding crocodile tears over the deplorable conditions of the poor laborer, while he docks his wages twenty-five per cent; building miniature log cabins, shouting Harrison and "Hard cider." And this man too would fain pass for a Christian and a republican. He shouts for liberty, stickles for equality, and is horrified at a Southern planter who keeps slaves.

Document 6   "A Factory Girl," *The Lowel Offering*, December 1840.[7]

"SHE HAS WORKED IN A FACTORY, is sufficient to damn to infamy the most worthy and virtuous girl."

So says Mr. Orestes A. Brownson; and either this horrible assertion is true, or Mr. Brownson is a slanderer. I assert that it is *not* true, and Mr. B. may consider himself called upon to prove his words, if he can....

And, who has Mr. Brownson slandered? A class of girls who in this city alone are numbered by thousands, and who collect in many of our smaller towns by hundreds; girls who generally come from quiet country homes, where their minds and manners have been formed under the eyes of the worthy sons of the Pilgrims, and their virtuous partners, and who return again to become the wives of the free intelligent yeomanry of New England, and the mothers of quite a proportion of our future republicans.

... We are under restraints, but they are voluntarily assumed; and we are at liberty to withdraw from them, whenever they become galling or irksome. Neither have I discovered that any restraints were imposed upon us but those which were necessary for the peace and comfort of the whole, and for the promotion of the design for which we are collected, namely to get money, as much of it and as fast as we can; and it is because our toil is so unremitting, that the wages of factory girls are higher than those of females engaged in most other occupations. It is these wages which, in spite of toil, restraint, discomfort, and prejudice, have drawn so many worthy, virtuous, intelligent, and well-educated girls to Lowell, and other factories; and it is the wages which are in a great degree to decide the characters of the factory girls as a class. ... The avails of factory labor are now greater than those of many domestics, seamstresses, and school-teachers; and strange it would be, if in money-loving New England, one of the most lucrative female employments should be rejected because it is toilsome, or because some people are prejudiced against it. Yankee girls have too much *independence* for *that*.

... There are many who come here for but a short time, and who are willing for a while to forego every usual privilege, that they may carry back to their homes the greatest possible sum they can

---

7   "Factory Girls," *The Lowell Offering*, December 1840, p. 17.

save. There are widows earning money for the maintenance of their children; there are daughters providing for their aged and destitute parents; and there are widows, single women, and girls, endeavoring to furnish some other home than a factory boarding-house.

Document 7 Lewis Clark, "Leaves from a Slave's Journal of Life," *The Anti-Slavery Standard,* 20 and 27 October 1842.[8]

So I will, as well as I can. I want to tell you, not so much about the slave's being whipped, or about his not having enough to eat; though I could tell you enough of that, too, if I had a chance. But what I want to make you understand is, that A SLAVE CAN'T BE A MAN! Slavery makes a brute of man; I don't mean that he *is* a brute, neither. But a horse *can't* speak; and he *dar n't*. He dare n't tell what's in him; it wouldn't do. The worse he's treated, the more he must smile; the more he's kicked, the lower he must crawl. For you see the master *knows* when he's treated his slave too bad for human nature; and he *suspects* the slave will resent; and he watches him the closer, and so the slave has to be more deceitful.

... as I was telling ye, they hire these patter-rollers, and they have to take the meanest fellows above ground; and because they are so mortal sure the slaves don't want their freedom, they have to put all power into their hands, to do with the n___ just as they like. If a slave don't open his door to them, at any time of night, they break it down. They steal his money, if they can find it, and act just as they please with his wives and daughters. If a husband dares to say a word, or even look as if he wasn't quite satisfied, they tie him up and give him thirty-nine lashes. If there's any likely young girls in a slave's hut, they're mighty apt to have business there....

... Now who among you would like to have your wives and daughters, and sisters, in such a situation. This is what every slave in all these States is exposed to.— ... I told you in the beginning, that it wouldn't do to let the slave think he is a man. That would spoil slavery, clear entirely.—No; this is the cruelty of the thing—A SLAVE CAN'T BE A MAN. He *must* be made a brute;....

Document 8 A. J. Graves, *Woman in America: Being an Examination into the Moral and Intellectual Condition of American Female Society,* 1843.[9]

...When we ... hear an American mother, with her infant in her arms, giving utterance to such complaints as these: "We cannot go to Congress; we cannot stand in the pulpit; *we cannot be known*; we must toil at home;" and when we know that this individual represents an increasing class, it is time for us to tremble for our homes. ... Toil at home! Yes, thanks to Him who made us, this is at once our duty and our privilege; and may He, of his goodness, make every woman feel that it is also her highest happiness and her truest dignity. ... The sanctuary of domestic life is to her the place of safety as well as the "post of honour." From this quiet and secure point of observation she can look abroad with intelligent interest and calm reflection on the conflicting elements around her, dispassionately weigh opposing opinions, and study how she may best

---

8   Lewis Clark, "Leaves from a Slave's Journal of Life," *The Anti-Slavery Standard*, 20 and 27 October 1842, pp. 78-9, 83.

9   A.J. Graves, *Woman in America; Being an Examination into the Moral and Intellectual Condition of American Female Society*, (New York: Harper and Brothers, 1843).

fulfil her part in promoting the spiritual and intellectual advancement of society. She will then conclude, that, as the helpmate of man, she can best serve the great interests of humanity, not by rushing into the public arena to add feverishness to his excitements, but by shedding upon him, in his hours of home repose, the calm, clear light of truth, of peace, and of virtue....

... To woman it belongs, also, to elevate the intellectual character of her household, to kindle the fires of mental activity in childhood, and to keep them steadily burning with advancing years....There can be no doubt that "intellectual life" should have an existence in the souls of American women. The men of our country, as things are constituted among us, find but little time for the cultivation of science and general literature.... And this is the case even with those who have acquired a fondness for intellectual pursuits in early life. The absorbing passion for gain, and the pressing demands of business, engross their whole attention. Thus the merchant becomes a merchant, and nothing more; and the mind of the lawyer is little less than a library of cases and precedents, of legal records and commentaries. The physician loses sight of the scientific studies to which his profession so naturally directs him, contents himself with the same beaten track, and becomes a mere practitioner or operator. And the mechanic and agriculturalist too often settle down into mere manual labourers, by suffering practical details wholly to occupy their minds as well as their bodies. The only relief to this absorbing devotion to "material interests" is found in the excitement of party politics. These two engross the whole moral, intellectual, and physical man; and to be convinced of this, we need not follow the American to his place of business or to political meetings we have only to listen to his fireside conversation.... What is the perpetual theme of his conversation? Business and politics, six per cent., bank discounts, stock-jobbing, insolvencies, assets, liabilities—cases at court, legal opinions and decisions—neuralgia, gastric irritation, fevers, &c.—Clay, Webster, the Bank bill, and other political topics of the day: these are the subjects incessantly talked about by the male members of the family when at home, and which the females, of course, are neither expected to take any special interest in nor to understand.

Document 9   Josiah Priest, *Slavery as it relates to the Negro, or African Race examined in the Light of Circumstances, History, and the Holy Scriptures,* 1849.[10]

As justification of the severity of God against the race of Ham, we shall now give some account of their character,.... The baleful fire of unchaste amour rages through the negro's blood more fiercely than in the blood of any other people, inflaming their imaginations with corresponding images and ideas, on which account they are a people who are suspected of being but little acquainted with the virtue of chastity, and of regarding very little the marriage oath. In all the southern regions it is thus; promiscuous intercourse of the sexes every where prevails among the blacks all this is told and published to the world by abolitionists, with the view of having it understood that this awful and ruinous propensity of the negroes, as well as the practice, is wholly owing to the institutions of slavery. THIS, however, is not true; for they have always been thus. From the very days of Ham, their father, down through their whole history, whether in a civilized or savage state, whether enslaved or free, it was always so with them. That *one* passion conquers all, and will conquer every *mortal* endeavor to elevate the race much above their present level.

---

10   Josiah Priest, *Slavery as it relates to the Negro, or African Race, examined in the light of Circumstances, History, and the Holy Scriptures; with an account of the Origin of the Black Man's Color,* (Louisville: W.S. Brown, 1840), pp. 174-203.

Document 10 *Narrative of Henry Watson, A Fugitive Slave*, 1850.[11]

Much has been said about the marriage rites of slaves; but there exists no legal form, every slaveholder having a form of his own. Permit me, then, to give my readers the manner in which my master performed the ceremony. Whenever a vacancy occurred in any of the cabins of either sex, of marriageable age, it was immediately filled up by my master purchasing another slave, either a man or woman, as the case might be, and presenting them to the remaining inmates of the cabin, with the following words: "Kitty, stand out in the floor; I have bought this boy to-day for your husband, and I shall expect you to take good care of him, by washing and mending his clothes. You know my orders to the overseer; if either of you go to the field on Monday morning without your clothes being washed, you are to be whipped. You will also take care of his provisions, which will be weighed out with yours. Have it cooked and ready in his bucket in time for him to go to the field every morning. You understand what I have said to you;" which the slave must answer with a low bow, and replying, "I do sir." Then he will give the man the following charge: "Tom, you will take care of this girl for your wife, by bringing her wood, making her fire, bringing water. Should your wife or self want any thing, you can get it by working on Sunday, for which I will allow you fifty cents a day, out of the store." He would then ask them both if they understood his orders. They would answer as before, with a low bow and courtesy, replying that they did. He would then pronounce them man and wife, ….

Document 11 Sojourner Truth, *Ain't I a Woman*? Speech—Women's Convention, Akron, Ohio, 1851.[12]

Original report of Sojourner Truth's speech, as reported by Marcus Robinson in the <u>Anti-Slavery Bugle,</u> 21, June 1851.

One of the most unique and interesting speeches of the convention was made by Sojourner Truth, an emancipated slave. It is impossible to transfer it to paper, or convey any adequate idea of the effect it produced upon the audience. Those only can appreciate it who saw her powerful form, her whole-souled, earnest gesture, and listened to her strong and truthful tones. She came forward to the platform and addressing the President said with great simplicity: "May I say a few words?" Receiving an affirmative answer, she proceeded:

I want to say a few words about this matter. I am a woman's rights. [sic] I have as much muscle as any man, and can do as much work as any man. I have plowed and reaped and husked and chopped and mowed, and can any man do more than that? I have heard much about the sexes being equal. I can carry as much as any man, and can eat as much too, if I can get it. I am as strong as any man that is now. As for intellect, all I can say is, if a woman have a pint, and a man a quart – why can't she have her little pint full? You need not be afraid to give us our rights for fear we will take too much, – for we can't take more than our pint'll hold. The poor men seems to be all in confusion, and don't know what to do. Why children, if you have woman's rights, give it to her and you will feel better. You will have your own rights, and they won't be so much trouble. I can't read, but I can hear. I have heard the bible and have

---

11 *Narrative of Henry Watson, A Fugitive Slave,* (Boston: Bela Marsh, 1850). pp. 18-19.

12 Sojourner Truth, *Ain't I a Woman,* Speech at the Women's Convention in Akron, Ohio, 1851. http://www.sojournertruth.org/Library/Speeches/ for Frances Dana Gage's version see http://www.sojournertruth.org/Library/Speeches/AintIAWoman.htm

learned that Eve caused man to sin. Well, if woman upset the world, do give her a chance to set it right side up again. The Lady has spoken about Jesus, how he never spurned woman from him, and she was right. When Lazarus died, Mary and Martha came to him with faith and love and besought him to raise their brother. And Jesus wept and Lazarus came forth. And how came Jesus into the world? Through God who created him and the woman who bore him. Man, where was your part? But the women are coming up blessed be God and a few of the men are coming up with them. But man is in a tight place, the poor slave is on him, woman is coming on him, he is surely between a hawk and a buzzard.

Edited Version of the Ain't a Woman speech as reported by Frances Dana Gage in the <u>Anti-Slavery Standard</u>, May 2, 1863.

Well, children, when there is so much racket there must be something out of kilter. I think that twixt the negroes of the South and the women at the North, all talking about rights, the white men will be in a fix pretty soon. But what's all this here talking about?

That man over there says that women need to be helped into carriages, and lifted over ditches, and to have the best place everywhere. Nobody ever helps me into carriages, or over mud-puddles, or gives me any best place! And ain't I a woman? Look at me! Look at my arm! I have ploughed and planted, and gathered into barns, and no man could head me! And ain't I a woman? I could work as much and eat as much as a man—when I could get it—and bear the lash as well! And ain't I a woman? I have borne thirteen children, and seen most all sold off to slavery, and when I cried out with my mother's grief, none but Jesus heard me! And ain't I a woman?

They they talk about this thing in the head; what's this they call it? [An audience member called out "intellect."] That's it, honey. What's that got to do with women's rights or negroes rights? If my cup won't hold but a pint, and yours holds a quart, wouldn't you be mean not to let me have my little half measure full?

Then that little man in black there, he says women can't have as much rights as men 'cause Christ wasn't a woman! Where did your Christ come from? Where did your Christ come from? From God and a woman! Man had nothing to do with Him.

If the first woman God ever made was strong enough to turn the world upside down all alone, these women together ought to be able to turn it back, and get right side up again! And now they is asking to do it, the men better let them.

Obliged to you for hearing me, and now old Sojourner ain't got nothing more to say.

Document 12 George Fitzhugh, *Sociology of the South: Or the Failure of a Free Society*, 1854.[13]

Nothing in the signs of the times exhibits in stronger relief the fact, that free society is in a state of "dissolution and thaw," of demoralization and transition, than the stir about women's rights.... Northern newspapers are filled with the sufferings of poor needlewomen, and the murders of wives by their husbands. Woman *there* is in a false position. Be she white, or be she black, she is treated with kindness, and humanity in the slave-holding South. ... If American women wish to participate in the hard labor of men, they are right to curtail the petticoat. Queens wear the

---

13 George Fitzhugh, *Sociology for the South, or the Failure of Free Society,* (Richmond, VA: A. Morris, 1854).

longest trains, because they have least occasion to labor. The broom girls of Bavaria have to work hard for a living, and find it necessary to amputate the nether impediments. In France, woman draws the plough and the canal boat. She will be condemned to like labors in America, so soon as her dress, her education, and coarse sentiments fit her for such labors. Let her exhibit strength and hardihood, and man, her master, will make her a beast of burden.

So long as she is nervous, fickle, capricious, delicate, diffident, and dependent, man will worship and adore her. Her weaknesss is her strength, and her true art is to cultivate and improve that weakness. Woman naturally shrinks from public gaze, and from the struggle and competition of life. Free society has thrown her into the arena of industrial war, robbed her of the softness of her own sex, without conferring on her the strength of ours. In truth, woman, like children, has but one right, and that is the right to protection. The right to protection involves the obligation to obey. A husband, a lord and master, whom she should love, honor and obey, nature designed for every woman,--for the number of males and females is the same. If she be obedient, she is in little danger of mal-treatment; if she stands upon her rights, is coarse and masculine, man loathes and despises her, and ends by abusing her. Law, however, well intended, can do little in her behalf. True womanly art will give her an empire and sway far greater than she deserves. The best women have been distasteful to men, and unpopular with their own sex, simply for betraying, or seeming to betray, something masculine in their characters. ... On the other hand, men have adored the worst women, merely for their feminine charms and arts. Delilah, Cleopatra, Mary Stuart,... Marie Antoinette, ... ruled men as they pleased, by the exercise of all the charms, and more than the wiles and weakness of their sex. ... Women would do well to disguise strength of mind or body, if they possess it, if they would retain their empire.

The people of our Northern States, who hold that domestic slavery is unjust and iniquitous, are consistent in their attempts to modify or abolish the marriage relation. Marriages, in many places there, are contracted with as little formality as jumping over a broom, and are dissolved with equal facility by courts and legislatures. It is proposed by many to grant divorces at all times, when the parties mutually consent.... The ladies are promoting these movements by women's rights conventions. The prospects of these agitators are quite hopeful, because they have no conservative South to oppose them....

The men of the South take care of the women of the South, the men of slaveholding Asia guard and protect their women too. The generous sentiments of slaveholders are sufficient guarantee of the rights of woman, all the world over. But there is something wrong in her condition in free society, and that condition is daily becoming worse.

... To the husbands of pedantic, masculine women, the lines of Byron may be well applied—

> "But oh! Ye Lords of ladies intellectual,
>
> Inform us truly, have they not hen-pecked you all."

Document 13 "Slave 'Marriages' and Funerals," Frederick Law Olmsted, *A Journey in the Seaboard Slave States*, 1856.[14]

While watching the negroes in the field, Mr. X. addressed a girl, who was vigorously plying a hoe near us.

---

14 Frederick Law Olmsted, *A Journey in the Seaboard Slave States,* (New York: Dix & Edwards, 1856),

"Is that Lucy?—Ah, Lucy, what's this I hear about you?"

The girl simpered; but did not answer nor discontinue her work.

"What is this I hear about you and Sam, eh?"

The girl grinned; and, still hoeing away with all her might, whispered "Yes, sir."

"Sam came to see me this morning."

"If master pleases."

"Very well; you may come up to the house Saturday night, and your mistress will have something for you."

Mr. X. does not absolutely refuse to allow his negroes to "marry off the place" as most large slave-owners do, but he discourages intercourse, as much as possible, between his negroes and those of other plantations; and they are usually satisfied to choose from among themselves.

When a man and woman wish to live with each other, they are required to *ask leave* of their master; and, unless there are some very obvious objections, this is always granted: a cabin is allotted to them, and presents are made of dresses and house-keeping articles. A marriage ceremony, in the same form as that used by free people, is conducted by the negro preacher, and they are encouraged to make the occasion memorable and gratifying to all, by general festivity. The master and mistress, when on the plantation, usually honor the wedding by their attendance; and if they are favorite servants, it is held in the house, and the ceremony performed by a white minister.

A beautiful, dense, evergreen grove is used as the burial ground of the negroes. The funerals are always at night, and are described as being very quaint and picturesque—all the negroes of the neighborhood marching in procession from the cabin of the deceased person to the grave, carrying light-wood torches, and singing hymns, in their sad, wailing, chanting manner. At the head of each recent grave stands a wooden post.

Document 14   Harriet Ann Jacobs, *Incidents in the Life of a Slave Girl*, 1861.[15]

II. The New Master and Mistress

Dr. Flint, a physician in the neighborhood, had married the sister of my mistress, and I was now the property of their little daughter. … My brother William was purchased by the same family. My father, by his nature, as well as by the habit of transacting business as a skillful mechanic, had more of the feelings of a freeman than is common among slaves… One day, when his father and his mistress both happened to call him at the same time, he hesitated between the two; being perplexed to know which had the strongest claim upon his obedience. He finally concluded to go to his mistress. When my father reproved him for it, he said, "You both called me, and I didn't know which I ought to go to first."

"You are *my* child," replied our father, "and when I call you, you should come immediately, if you have to pass through fire and water."

---

[15]   Harriet Ann Jacobs, *Incidents in the Life of a Slave Girl, written by herself,* edited by Lydia Maria Child, (Boston: published for the author, 1861), pp. 18-19, 58-63.

Poor Willie! He was now to learn his first lesson of obedience to a master. [...]

I had been there nearly a year [when] ...grandmother,... said, "Come with me, Linda;" and from her tone I knew that something sad had happened. She led me apart from the people, and then said, "My child, your father is dead." Dead! How could I believe it? He had died so suddenly I had not even heard that he was sick. I went home with my grandmother. My heart rebelled against God,.... The good grandmother tried to comfort me. "Who knows the ways of God?" said she. "Perhaps they have been kindly taken from the evil days to come." ... She promised to be a mother to her grandchildren, so far as she might be permitted to do so; and strengthened by her love, I returned to my master's. I thought I should be allowed to go to my father's house the next morning; but I was ordered to go for flowers, that my mistress's house might be decorated for an evening party. I spent the day gathering flowers and weaving them into festoons, while the dead body of my father was lying within a mile of me. What cared my owners for that? He was merely a piece of property. Moreover, they thought he had spoiled his children, by teaching them to feel that they were human beings. This was blasphemous doctrine for a slave to teach; presumptuous in him, and dangerous to the masters.

VII. The Lover.

Why does the slave ever love? Why allow the tendrils of the heart to twine around objects which may at any moment be wrenched away by the hand of violence? When separations come by the hand of death, the pious soul can bow in resignation, and say, "Not my will, but thine be done, O Lord!" But when the ruthless hand of man strikes the blow, regardless of the misery he causes, it is hard to be submissive. I did not reason thus when I was a young girl. Youth will be youth. I loved, and I indulged the hope that the dark clouds around me would turn out a bright lining. I forgot that in the land of my birth the shadows are too dense for light to penetrate. A land

> "Where laughter is not mirth; nor thought the mind;
>
> Nor words a language, nor e'en men mankind.
>
> Where cries reply to curses, shrieks to blows,
>
> And each is tortured in his separate hell."

There was in the neighborhood a young colored carpenter; a free born man. We had been well acquainted in childhood, and frequently met together afterwards. We became mutually attached, and he proposed to marry me. I loved him with all the ardor of a young girl's first love. But when I reflected that I was a slave, and that the laws gave no sanction to the marriage of such, my heart sank within me. My lover wanted to buy me; but I knew that Dr. Flint was too willful and arbitrary a man to consent to that arrangement. From him, I was sure of experiencing all sorts of opposition, and I had nothing to hope from my mistress. She would have been delighted to have got rid of me, but not in that way. It would have relieved her mind of a burden if she could have seen me sold to some distant state, but if I was married near home I should be just as much in her husband's power as I had previously been,--for the husband of a slave has no power to protect her. Moreover, my mistress, like many others, seemed to think that slaves had no right to any family ties of their own; that they were created merely to wait upon the family of the mistress. I once heard her abuse a young slave girl, who told her that a colored man wanted to make her his wife. "I will have you peeled and pickled, my lady," said she, "if I ever hear you mention that subject again. Do you suppose that I will have you tending *my* children with the children of that nigger?" The girl to whom she said this had a mulatto child, of course not acknowledged by its father. The poor black man who loved her would have been proud to acknowledge this helpless offspring.

Many and anxious were the thoughts I revolved in my mind. I was at a loss what to do. Above all things, I was desirous to spare my lover the insults that had cut so deeply into my own soul. I talked with my grandmother about it, and partly told her my fears. I did not dare to tell her the worst. She had long suspected all was not right, and if I confirmed her suspicions I knew a storm would rise that would prove the overthrow of all my hopes.

This love-dream had been my support through many trials; and I could not bear to run the risk of having it suddenly dissipated. There was a lady in the neighborhood, a particular friend of Dr. Flint's, who often visited the house. I had a great respect for her, and she had always manifested a friendly interest in me. Grandmother thought she would have great influence with the doctor. I went to this lady, and told her my story. I told her I was aware that my lover's being a free-born man would prove a great objection; but he wanted to buy me; and if Dr. Flint would consent to that arrangement, I felt sure he would be willing to pay any reasonable price. She knew that Mrs. Flint disliked me; therefore, I ventured to suggest that perhaps my mistress would approve of my being sold, as that would rid her of me. The lady listened with kindly sympathy, and promised to do her utmost to promote my wishes. She had an interview with the doctor, and I believe she pleaded my cause earnestly; but it was all to no purpose.

How I dreaded my master now! Every minute I expected to be summoned to his presence; but the day passed, and I heard nothing from him. The next morning, a message was brought to me: "Master wants you in his study." I found the door ajar, and I stood a moment gazing at the hateful man who claimed a right to rule me, body and soul. I entered, and tried to appear calm. I did not want him to know how my heart was bleeding. He looked fixedly at me, with an expression which seemed to say, "I have half a mind to kill you on the spot." At last he broke the silence, and that was a relief to both of us.

"So you want to be married, do you?" said he, "and to a free nigger."

"Yes, sir."

"Well, I'll soon convince you whether I am your master, or the nigger fellow you honor so highly. If you *must* have a husband, you may take up with one of my slaves."

What a situation I should be in, as the wife of one of *his* slaves, even if my heart had been interested! I replied, "Don't you suppose, sir, that a slave can have some preference about marrying? Do you suppose that all men are alike to her?"

"Do you love this nigger?" said he, abruptly.

"Yes sir."

"How dare you tell me so!" he exclaimed, in great wrath. After a slight pause, he added, "I supposed you thought more of yourself; that you felt above the insults of such puppies."

I replied, "If he is a puppy I am a puppy, for we are both of the negro race. It is right and honorable for us to love each other. The man you call a puppy never insulted me, sir; and he would not love me if he did not believe me to be a virtuous woman."

He sprang upon me like a tiger, and gave me a stunning blow. It was the first time he had ever struck me; and fear did not enable me to control my anger. When I had recovered a little from the effects, I exclaimed, "You have struck me for answering you honestly. How I despise you!"

There was silence for some minutes. Perhaps he was deciding what should be my punishment; or, perhaps, he wanted to give me time to reflect on what I had said, and to whom I had said it. Finally, he asked, "Do you know what you have said?"

"Yes, sir; but your treatment drove me to it."

"Do you know that I have a right to do as I like with you,--that I can kill you, if I please?"

"You have tried to kill me, and I wish you had; but you have no right to do as you like with me."

"Silence!" he exclaimed, in a thundering voice. "By heavens, girl, you forget yourself too far! Are you mad? If you are, I will soon bring you to your senses. Do you think any other master would bear what I have borne from you this morning? Many masters would have killed you on the spot. How would you like to be sent to jail for your insolence?"

"I know I have been disrespectful, sir," I replied; "but you drove me to it; I couldn't help it. As for the jail, there would be more peace for me there than there is here."

"You deserve to go there," said he, "and to be under such treatment that you would forget the meaning of the word *peace*. It would do you good. It would take some of your high notions out of you. But I am not ready to send you there yet, notwithstanding your ingratitude for all my kindness and forbearance. You have been the plague of my life. I have wanted to make you happy, and I have been repaid with the basest ingratitude; but though you have proved yourself incapable of appreciating my kindness, I will be lenient towards you.... I will give you one more chance to redeem your character. If you behave yourself and do as I require, I will forgive you and treat you as I always have done; but if you disobey me, I will punish you as I would the meanest slave on my plantation. Never let me hear that fellow's name mentioned again. If I ever know of your speaking to him, I will cowhide you both; and if I catch him lurking about my premises, I will shoot him as soon as I would a dog. Do you hear what I say? I'll teach you a lesson about marriage and free niggers! Now go, and let this be the last time I have occasion to speak to you on this subject."

Document 15   John Lyde Wilson, *The Code of Honor: or Rules for the Government of Principals and Seconds in Duelling*, 1855.[16]

… if the question be directly put to me, whether there are not cases where duels are right and proper, I would unhesitatingly answer, there are. If an oppressed nation has a right to appeal to arms in defence of its liberty and the happiness of its people, there can be no argument used in support of such appeal, which will not apply with equal force to individuals…. In cases where the laws of the country give no redress for injuries received, where public opinion not only authorizes, but enjoins resistance, it is needless and a waste of time to denounce the practice. It will be persistend in as long as a manly independence, and a lofty personal pride in all that dignifies and enables the human character, shall continue to exist. If a man be smote on one cheek in public, and he turns the other, which is also smitten, and he offers no resistance, but blesses him that so despitefully used him, I am aware he is in the exercise of great Christian forbearance, highly recommended and enjoined by many very good men, but utterly repugnant to those

---

16   John Lyde Wilson, *The Code of Honor; or Rules for the Government of Principals and Seconds in Duelling,* (Charleston, SC: James Phinney, 1858).

feelings which nature and education have implanted in the human character. If it was possible to enact laws so severe and impossible to be evaded, as to enforce such rule of behavior, all that is honorable in the community would quit the country and inhabit the wilderness with the Indians. ... Those, therefore, who condemn ... dueling in every case, should establish schools where a passive submission to force would be the exercise of a commendable virtue. ...But I much doubt, if a seminary of learning was established, where this Christian forbearance was inculcated and enforced, where there would be many scholars.

Rules: Chapter I. The Person Insulted, Before Challenge Sent.

1. Whenever you believe that you are insulted, if the insult be in public and by words or behavior, never resent it there, if you have self-command enough to avoid noticing it. If resented there, you ofer an indignity to the company, which you should not.

2. If the insult be by blows or any personal indignity, it may be resented at the moment, for the insult to the company did not originate with you....

3. When you believe yourself aggrieved, be silent on the subject, speak to no one about the matter, and see your friend, who is to act for you, as soon as possible.

Rules: Chapter II. The Party receiving a Note before Challenge.

1. When a note is presented to you by an equal, receive it, and read it....

3. You may refuse to receive a note, from a minor; ... one that has been posted; one that has been publicly disgraced without resenting it; one whose occupation is unlawful; a man in his dotage and a lunatic. There may be other cases, but the character of those enumerated will lead to a correct decision upon those omitted.

Rules: Chapter VII. Arms, and Manner of Loading and Presenting them.

1. The arms used should be smooth-bore pistols, not exceeding nine inches in length, with flint and steel. Percussion pistols may be mutually used if agreed on....

2. Each second informs the other when he is about to load, and invites his presence, ...

3. The second, in presenting the pistol to his friend, should never put it in his pistol hand, but should place it in the other, which is grasped midway the barrel, with muzzle pointing in the contrary way to that which he is to fire, informing him that his pistol is loaded and ready for use. Before the word is given, the principle grasps the butt firmly in his pistol hand, and brings it round with the muzzle downward to the fighting position.

4. The fighting position, is with the muzzle down and the barrel from you; for although it may be agreed that you may hold your pistol with the muzzle up, it may be objected to, as you can fire sooner from that position, and consequently have a decided advantage, which ought not to be claimed and should not be granted.

Chapter VIII. The Degrees of Insult, and How Compromised.

1. The prevailing rule is, that words used in retort, although more violent and disrespectful than those first used, will not satisfy.—words being no satisfaction for words.

2. When words are used, and a blow given in return, the insult is avenged; and if redress be sought, it must be from the person receiving the blow.

Additional rules.

--All imputations of cheating at play, races &c., are considered equivalent to a blow; but may be reconciled after one shot, on admitting their falsehood, and begging pardon publicly.

--Any insult to a lady under a gentleman's care or protection, to be considered, as by one degree, a greater offense than if given to the gentleman personally.

--Offenses originating or accruing from the support of a lady's reputation, to be considered as less unjustifiable than any other of the same class, and as admitting of lighter apologies by the aggressor; this to be determined by the circumstances of the case,....

Document 16 Freedmen's Bureau Rules for Recording Marriages, 11 August 1863.[17]

Headquarters, Assistant Commissioner,

Beureau Refugees, Freedmen and Abandoned Lands,

South Carolina, Georgia, and Florida

Beaufort, S.C. Aug. 11, 1863

General Orders, No. 8

Marriage Rules

To correct as far as possible one of the most cruel wrongs inflicted by slavery, and also to aid the freedmen in properly appreciating and religiously observing the sacred obligations of the marriage state, the following rules are published for the information and guidance of all connected with this Bureau throughout the States of South Carolina, Georgia, and Florida:

Section I

--*Parties Eligible to Marriage.* 1.—All male persons, having never been married, of the age of twenty-one, and all females, having never been married, of the age of eighteen, shall be deemed eligible to marriage.

2. – All married persons who shall furnish satisfactory evidence of either the marriage or divorce of all former companions, according to the usages of slavery, or of their decease, will be eligible to marriage again.

3.—All married persons, producing satisfactory evidence of having been separated from their companions by slavery for a period of three years, and that they have no evidence that they are alive; or, if alive, that they will ever, probably, be restored to them, may be allowed to marry again.

Section II

Parties authorized to grant Permits of Marriage. 1.—All religious societies or churches of the freedmen or of other persons, whose organizations are recognized by their respective denominations, are authorized to grant permits for marriage, provided:

---

17   Found at Freedmen's Bureau Marriage Records, https://www.archives.gov/publications/prologue/2005/spring/freedman-marriage-recs.html

GENDER AND FAMILY ON AND OFF THE PLANTATION

First. That the parties are of lawful age, and that neither have never been married.

Second. That if either or both have been married, that such party has complied with the conditions of Section I., Rules 2 and 3.

Document 17   Freedmen's Bureau Marriage Permit for Benjamin Manson and Sarah White, 1866.[18]

Bureau Refugees, Freedmen and Abandoned Lands.

By the authority of Circular No. 5, dated Assistant Commissioner's Office Ky. and Tenn., *Nashville, Feb. 26, 1866, I certify that I have this day united* _B. B. Manson_ *and* _Sarah Ann B. (White)_, *colored, in the bonds of matrimony, they having been living together as man and wife* ~~for about~~ _since Oct 28, 1845_ _____ *years past, and have had, as the result thereof, the following children, viz:*

John L. W. (White) Manson Aged about 21 years, _died in 14 U.S.C.I_
Nancy Jane (do) Manson 20
Martin Clark (do) Manson 18 _died in 14 U.S.C.I_
Robt Dyer (do) Manson 17
Elenor Clifton (do) Manson 16
Sallie (do) Manson 14
Paul do Manson 12
William Loss (do) Manson 10
Patsy Agnes do, Manson 6

In witness whereof, I have hereunto set my hand in duplicate at office in Lebanon, Wilson County, Tennessee, April 19, 1866.

S. B. F. C. BARR, Sup't
Wilson County.

---

18   Found at Freedmen's Bureau Marriage Records, https://www.archives.gov/publications/prologue/2005/spring/freedman-marriage-recs.html

Document 18 "Causes of Marriage Disruption" from Arkansas Freedmen's Bureau Records.[19]

Reason for Disruption	Number of Marriages Disrupted
Quit	1
Deserted	6
Infidelity	7
Disagreement	9
No reason given	22
Power	45
Sale	64
Death of spouse	82
TOTAL	**236**

ANALYZING THE EVIDENCE

1. What does de Tocqueville (Document 1) suggest were the consequences for marriage of democratic ideals of equality and freedom? How did this result in "separate spheres" for men and women?

2. How did laws against dueling (Document 2) in the North illustrate very different masculine ideals than those evident in southern discussions of dueling (document 15)?

3. What might explain the high rates of first birth for slave mothers between the age of 15 and 19? Why might this have been encouraged by planation owners? How might this have contributed to perceptions of slave "promiscuity?"

4. Why did William Harper (Document 4) argue that legal sanction for slave marriage was unnecessary? How did Harper characterize African-American women's sexuality? How did Harper's explanation of African-American sexuality differ from Josiah Priest's? (Document 8) Why does he suggest that slavery provided a healthier outlet for satisfying sexual desire than did northern prostitution?

5. How were "factory girls" or women textile mill workers diminished in status according to Orestes Brownson? (Document 5) How does Brownson liken this work to slavery? How did the mill girls defend their virtue, and how did they differentiate themselves from enslaved laborers?(Document 6)

6. According to the Lewis Clark (Document 7) what was the impact of slavery on African American masculinity? How is Clark's perception supported by the other primary sources in this chapter?

7. According to A.J. Graves (Document 8), what were women's proper roles? How did Mrs. Graves characterize men's preoccupations?

---

19 From Randy Finley, *From Slavery to Uncertain Freedom: The Freedmen's Bureau in Arkansas, 1865-1869*, (Fayetteville, Arkansas: The University of Arkansas Press, 1996), p. 42.

8. How might the stereotypes of African American sexuality evident in Josiah Priest's observations (Document 9) result in the way masters regulated marriage as evident in Henry Watson's recollections of slave marriages? (Document 10)

9. Compare the two different recollections of Sojourner Truth's "Ain't I a Woman?" speech (Document 11). Why might they have been different? How did Sojourner Truth argue for women's right to participate in the public sphere? What gave her the moral authority to argue as she did as a former slave?

10. How does George Fitzhugh's (Document 12) portrayal of women reflect the "separate spheres" ideology described by de Tocqueville? (Document 1) In what ways did Fitzhugh suggest southern women were better off than those in the North? How does Fitzhugh view demands for women's rights and women's suffrage?

11. How do Frederick Law Olmsted's (Document 13) and Harriet Ann Jacob's (Document 14) portrayal of the sentiments of masters and mistresses differ? Why might they have had such different perceptions? Why did Harriet Ann Jacob's master object so strongly to her desire to marry?

12. On what grounds was it acceptable to challenge another to a duel? What were the rules for such an "affair of honor?" Why did John Lyde Wilson (Document 15) feel that dueling was sometimes a necessary recourse to defend one's honor? How did Wilson's defense of dueling illustrate southern notions of masculinity? How do you think the institution of slavery might have resulted in the development of southern definitions of masculinity?

13. What factors were considered by Freedmen's Bureau officials when determining whether to recognize a slave marriage? (Document 16) How might a historian use the Freedman's Bureau marriage certificate (Document 17) to learn about the history of enslaved African-American families? What conclusions can be drawn about the pressures on slave marriages from document 18?

DOCUMENT BASED QUESTION

1. Using the documents provided and your understanding of the history of the antebellum United States, analyze the ways in which gender roles and expectations of men and women differed.

2. Using the documents provided analyze the ways in which the insitituion of slavery in the United States contributed to shaping the development of gender roles and expectations in the antebellum period.

"Was Not Christ Crucified": Rebellion, Redemption, and Repression

Before the historian Herbert Aptheker began studying slave rebellions in the 1930s, the consensus among historians was that slaves in the United States rarely rebelled against their masters. This supposed fact was often proposed by pro-slavery apologists as evidence for both the benevolence of the South's slave system and for the passivity of African Americans. John Fiske, for example, observed that "It is one of the remarkable facts in American history that there have been so few insurrections of negroes." He explained why this was the case by referencing Robert Beverley, who wrote in 1705 that the labor of slaves "is no other than what the overseers, the freemen, and the planters themselves do....And I can assure you with a great deal of truth that generally their slaves are not worked near so hard, nor so many hours in a day, as the husbandmen and day-labourers in England." The work regimen of the enslaved was hardly oppressive. The historian James Schouler, however, argued that "Nothing... made American slavery on the whole so tolerable a condition for both enslaver and enslaved as the innate patience, docility, and childlike simplicity of the negro as a race. The slave, rarely unsusceptible to kindness, exhibited an attachment almost canine towards a kind master and mistress...."

The stereotype that slaves maintained a placid acceptance of their enslavement, even in the face of violent repression, has been entrenched in the popular imagination. Since the 1970s cinematic and television representations of plantation slavery have corrected the impression suggested in such popular movies as *Gone with the Wind* that slaves were quite content and well-treated. More recent representations of the plantation, however, have fed audiences a near-pornographic fascination with the violence meted out by sadistic overseers or planters. Only recently have films like *Django Unchanged*, a revenge fantasy, and Nate Parker's *The Birth of a Nation*, based on Nat Turner's 1831 rebellion, featured African Americans violently rebelling against their enslavement. These films, whatever their historicity, are an important response to the criticism the rapper, Snoop Dogg, leveled recently. Reacting to the airing in 2016 of a remake of the TV series *Roots*, the rapper complained, "They going to just keep beating that shit into our heads about how they did us, huh?... I ain't watching that shit."

In a reader such as this, which puts the institution of slavery at the center of United States history, it is often difficult not to leave the impression that more of this same "shit" is being pounded into students' heads, and that the history of enslaved persons is one of unmitigated exploitation and violence, without response. The asymmetry of power between plantation owners and the economic, social, and political institutions that supported white's power vis-à-vis the enslaved is hard to ignore. In this chapter, however, the aim is to examine the ways in which slaves overtly rebelled, despite the risks and often horrifying consequences. In doing so,

I hope to offer an answer to a student who asked early in my career as a teacher, "Why didn't the slaves fight back?" The short response, of course, is that they did, in many and varied ways.

Perhaps the most clear evidence that slaves did resist and violently, was the almost visceral terror at the possibility of rebellion frequently expressed by plantation owners, state governments, and even Federal officials. A dull ache in times of peace, the fear of rebellion was sharpened in times of war. Fears of slave rebellions provoked by the French or their Indian allies alarmed southern planters during the French and Indian War. Dunmore's Emancipation Proclamation, as we have seen, inspired flight and rebellion on the part of tens of thousands of slaves across the colonies. The War of 1812 resulted in similar panic. The slave system, always weakest along the nation's frontiers with the Indians, the Spanish, and eventually Mexico seemed particularly vulnerable to enemy encouragement of slave uprisings. In no small part, the foreign policy of the nation and the United States' obsessive pursuit of "border security" was often influenced by slave owners' desire to secure borders, not from the crossings into the country of "illegal" immigrants, but from the escape from the country of slaves intent on seeking their freedom. Additionally, the anti-slavery policies of the Mexican government contributed materially to dissension between the U.S. and Texas and the Mexican government, as slaves in Texas and Louisiana were prone to both seek support for rebellion and to flee to Mexico when it was possible. Finally, during the American Civil War, it would become the declared policy of the Union to encourage slaves to vote with their feet, flee their masters and join the Union armies. Lincoln's Emancipation Proclamation thus had real parallels with Lord Dunmore's issued some four score and eight years earlier. It also demonstrated the truth in southern fears that their slaves might not be trusted to remain their faithful servants if offered an opportunity to resist or escape.

But, times of war weren't the only moments that gave slave owners reason to fear slave uprisings. As often rebellions were occasioned by local conditions and by the personalities of the slaves themselves. Herbert Aptheker's survey of the country's many slave rebellions provides a long catalogue of these uprisings and conspiracies. The first serious conspiracy discovered involved a plot that saw indentured servants and slaves uniting in 1663 in Virginia in a failed conspiracy to overthrow their masters and gain their freedom. The response to this nightmare scenario—slaves and poor whites in coalition—perhaps explains the development across the south of a political style that sought guarantees of white solidarity by elevating the status of poor whites above oppressed African Americans. Militia service or participation as patrolers, or "paterollers" as slaves called them, afforded poorer white males psychological satisfaction and real power that came from being a part of the American master race.

Unable to call on class solidarities, African Americans nonetheless did not face the reality of their enslavement without direct and violent resistance, even if they only reached the level of unfulfilled conspiracies. Conspiracies were uncovered in the Chesapeake regions in 1672, 1688, 1690, and 1691, illustrating how volatile were conditions in the region well after Bacon's Rebellion. Across the colonies small-scale rebellions took place in 1702, 1708, 1709, 1710, 1711, and 1712. The last of these involved some twenty-five to thirty slaves in New York City who armed themselves, fired a building, and waited for unsuspecting whites to come douse the fire. Some nine men were murdered in the attack before the militia was called out and the rebels subdued. The reprisals, as was often the case, were designed to send a vivid message to other slaves not to consider a similar plot. Nonetheless, again in the 1740s a rash of fires in New York City were attributed to slaves setting fire to buildings and threatening their masters. The most alarming rebellion in colonial America, however, took place in 1739 near Charlestown, South

Carolina along the Stono River. The slaves in this rising, many of them Angolans with military experience in Africa, were led by a man named Jemmy. Their aim, in addition to escaping to the Spanish city of St. Augustine, Florida was to raise a generalized rebellion as they made their way southward. Marching to drummers and flying banners, the rebels attracted other slaves to their cause, but also drew the attention of the Carolina militia with which the rebels fought a number of pitched battles before falling to defeat. The Stono Rebellion would reverberate across South Carolina's history encouraging planters to engage in a much higher level of repression and closer supervision than had been the practice before 1739.

During the remainder of the eighteenth century, slave rebellion and conspiracy remained a constant worry of plantation owners in the South, and of authorities in northern cities. As we have seen, the potential for slave risings contributed in no small part to South Carolina's and Virginia's commitment to the patriot cause during the American Revolution, and was a preoccupation of some of the members at the Constitutional Convention. One of the most important inspirations for African-American slaves after the American Revolution, however, would be the Haitian Revolution. In 1791, two years after the French Revolution had begun, slaves on the island of Hispaniola, the French colony of Saint Domingue, overthrew their white masters and in 1793 established a black republic under the leadership of Toussaint L'Ouverture. When in 1800 Napoleon sent an expeditionary force to retake the colony, after three years he was forced to accept defeat and give up France's claim to the slaves and the lucrative sugar plantations that had once covered the island. Napoleon's inability to retake Saint Domingue would be one factor convincing Napoleon to give up thoughts of restoring France's North American empire. Shortly after withdrawing from Haiti, Napoleon authorized the sale of the Louisiana Territory to the United States. The uprising would also have unsettling effects on the slaves and freedmen of the United States. Some 10,000 refugees from the island relocated to the United States, settling mostly in Philadelphia, Baltimore, Norfolk, and New Orleans. The reports from these refugees' slaves and wider news from the island would represent an important inspiration for American slaves, and a cautionary tale to plantation owners, from the onset of that revolution until the end of the American Civil War. It would have a direct impact on at least two prominent American slave rebellions: the Gabriel Conspiracy (also known as the Prosser Rebellion) of 1800 and a rebellion that threatened the city of New Orleans in 1811. Reports from both of these episodes of slave resistance will feature in the primary sources included in this chapter.

The Denmark Vesey conspiracy that was brutally repressed in 1822 may have also been an echo of the Haitian rebellion, or at least it was so perceived by Charleston, South Carolina authorities. Denmark Vesey, originally known as Telemaque, was born a slave on the Danish island colony of St. Thomas. At fourteen he was acquired by a slaver and sea captain from Bermuda named Thomas, who later sold him to a plantation on Saint Domingue. The sale fell through, however, as Telemaque began to experience seizures (whether feigned or not is a question) and was returned to Vesey who would ultimately leave the slave trade and settle in Charleston. In 1799 Telemaque took winnings from a $1500 lottery and purchased his freedom from Vesey for $600, retaining the last name and his Americanized first name, Denmark. Vesey remained in Charleston, and gained prominence in the African American community, serving as a lay preacher and remaining actively involved in the development of the African Methodist Episcopal and black Presbyterian churches in the city. According to accusations made against him after the Vesey conspiracy was exposed, Vesey plotted for four years, inspired by his reading of scripture, by the heated debates in Congress over Missouri's entry into the United States, and by abolitionist tracts to unleash a rebellion in Charleston. The conspiracy was exposed when two slaves warned Charleston officials that an insurrection was planned for July 14 (perhaps in honor of Bastille Day) 1822. An intense investigation ensued and repression predictably followed with 131 slaves and free blacks arrested. Thirty-five were hanged, including Vesey, with an additional thirty-one deported.

At the time, however, there were those in Charleston who doubted that any conspiracy existed and questioned the means that were employed to gain confessions and try the accused. The governor, Thomas Bennett, Jr. whose own slaves were among the named conspirators, and William Johnson, Bennett's brother-in-law and Associate Justice of the Supreme Court, were both not convinced of the imminent threat posed in the conspiracy. As you read the documents included in this chapter that are associated with the Vesey conspiracy, it is worthwhile to keep in mind that fears of conspiracy can often lead to "witch hunts" that either exaggerate the nature of a threat or prove to be self-fulfilling prophecies as the extraordinary means taken to identify threats and prosecute the guilty frequently lead to the discovery of "plots" where none existed.

The last antebellum rebellion examined in this chapter, Nat Turner's rebellion, was no imagined conspiracy. Nat Turner's uprising convulsed the Virginia border with North Carolina in 1832, leading to massive and bloody reprisals and a recommitment to repression as the only effective way to insure against insurrection. In this chapter then we will examine the local context and historical factors that contributed to groups of slaves taking the courageous but often suicidal decision to rebel against their owners and the power and potential violence arrayed against them as they sought their freedom. In fact, one of the key factors shaping the development of southern and indeed American culture in this period, and which, unfortunately reverberates to the present in high rates of African-American imprisonment and in police shootings of unarmed black men, was the fear of rebellion and repression engendered by that fear.

Fear of rebellion resulted in the development of elaborate mechanisms of control which depended on local, state, and national policing. For southern planters could never relax their guard against the possibility of slave risings. Robert Y. Hayne, the Governor of South Carolina explained the situation: "A state of military preparation must always be with us a state of perfect domestic security. A period of profound peace and consequent apathy may expose us to the danger of domestic insurrection." The architect, Frederick Law Olmsted wrote that in Southern communities, one sees "police machinery such as you never find in towns under free government: citadels, sentries, passports, grapeshotted cannon, and daily public whippings of the subjects for accidental infractions of police ceremonies….. There is … nearly everywhere [in the South] always prepared to act, if not always in service, an armed force, with a military organization, which is invested with more arbitrary and cruel power than any police in Europe."

In this chapter readers will be directed to accounts and testimony regarding slave rebellions that occurred in the nineteenth century. The sources, unfortunately, are largely written by white observers and authorities. Keep in mind that in reading these accounts they often reflect as significantly the fears and concerns of the white population rather than the legitimacy of the African-American uprisings. One feature of white characterizations of these rebellions was an insistence that they represented insurrections rather than rebellions or revolutions. They were also as often described as paroxysms of looting and rioting. Rebellion and revolution suggest responses to real grievances while insurrection, looting, and rioting lack similar legitimacy. Another feature of accounts written by white authors was an effort to emasculate the participants in the rebellions by characterizing their behavior as cowardly or irrationally directed. While the voices of African Americans in rebellion unfiltered through white media or even written for white audiences are difficult to find, it is possible to identify the grievances and objectives of these acts of rebellion. The courage of these acts of rebellion are also evident in the sources, often despite the efforts of white authors to reduce them to spasmatic and unthinking explosions of a misguided people.

In addition to accounts and testimony of slave rebellions, the documents in this chapter include descriptions of the repressive measures taken to forestall slave uprisings and evidence of the systematic and near universal efforts taken in the South to insure that black men and women, whether free or enslaved, understood both the futility of any form of resistance and recognized their own subordinate status. The necessity of pervasive police measures serve as evidence of the falure of the plantation economy to live up to its paternalistic. The success of the plantation society that dominated the South depended as much on African-Americans' internal submission as it did on overt and violent oppression, as real as that oppression remained. As readers engage these tales of slave uprisings also pay close attention to the ways in which laws, policing authority, patrols, and racial oppression combined to respond to the threat, real and imagined, of enslaved peoples' pursuit of their liberty.

PRIMARY SOURCES

Document 1 Excerpts from Investigations into Gabriel's Conspiracy, Richmond, Virginia, 1800.[1]

Letter from Mosby Sheppard to the Governor of Virginia [James Monroe]

Aug. 30, Richmond   I have just been informed that the negroes were to rise (as they term it) in the neighborhood of Mr. Thomas H. Prosser's and to kill the neighbors, viz: Major William Mosby, Thomas H. Prosser, and Mr. Johnson; from thence they were to proceed to town, where they would be joined by the negroes of this place (Richmond), after which they were to take possession of the arms and ammunition, and then take possession of the town.

Here they stopped, appearing much agitated.

I then asked them two questions, viz:

When was it to take place?

Answer—Tonight.

Who is the principal man?

Answer—Prosser's Gabriel.

I have given you the substance of what I have heard, and there is not a doubt in my mind but what my information is true, and I have given you this information in order that the intended massacre may be prevented if possible.

I am, with due respect &c.

---

[1] *Calendar of Virginia State Papers and Other Manuscripts from January 1, 1799 to December 31, 1807*, Volume IX, Arranged and edited by H.W. Flournoy, (Richmond: James E. Goode, 1890), pp. 135-176.

N.B.—I will here recite to you the manner in which I got this information. I was sitting in the counting-room with the door shut, and no one near except myself; they knocked at the door, and I let them in; they shut the door themselves, and then began to tell what I have before recited.

M.S.

Sep. 8   Gervas Stoers and Joseph Selden to the Governor

This is to certify that we were examining magistrates in the case of the negroes charged with conspiracy and a design to rebel against the white people; and from every incident which appeared at the examination, we do not hesitate to say that Gabriel, property of Thomas H. Prosser, of Henrico county, was clearly proven to be the main spring and chief mover in the contemplated rebellion.

Sep 10   Manchester   Matthew Cheatham to the Governor

Had received the orders for calling out the militia of Chesterfield, and as soon as the men could be collected in Manchester and the requisite orders given, would send one hundred to Richmond.

Sep. 11 Henrico   Evidence Against the Negroes Tried September 11th

Solomon's Case.—Ben, the property of Thomas H. Prosser, deposed: That the Prisoner at the bar made a number of swords for the purpose of carrying into execution the plan of an insurrection which was planned by Gabriel, a negro man, the property of said Prosser, and that the said Solomon was to be the Treasurer. In the first place, Mr. Prosser and Mr. Johnson were to be killed and their arms seized upon; then they were to resort to and kill all the White Neighbours. This plan to be executed on the Saturday night on which there was such a great fall of rain. The place of meeting was near Prosser's blacksmith's shop in the woods. After Murdering the Inhabitants of the Neighbourhood, the assembly were to repair to Richmond and Seize upon the Arms and Ammunition—to-wit, the Magazine. Gabriel was to command at commencement of the business. The swords made by the prisoner were to be distributed by said Gabriel; swords have been making ever since last Harvest. 4,000 men was to be raised from Richmond, 600 from Ground Squirrel Bridge, and 400 from Goochland. Meetings were frequently held at William Young's under pretext of attending preachment, and at other times—viz., at Fish feast and Barbacues, to concert the plan of Insurrection, but whose names he did not hear.

Pharoah, the property of Philip Sheppard, deposed: That the prisoner at the bar on Saturday, the 30th August, enquired of this deponent whether the light horse of Richmond were out, he being then from Richmond, who informed him that he had seen some at Col. Goodall's tavern. The prisoner remarked that the business of the insurrection had so far advanced that they were compelled, even if discovered, to go forward with it; that he had four swords then to finish, which he must comlete by the time of his company meeting that evening, which would consist of 1,000 men, to wit: negroes.

Will's Case.—Ben, the property of T. H. Prosser, deposed: That the prisoner brought two scythe blades to Gabriel for the purpose of having them made into swords, and that four swords out of them by Solomon at request of Gabriel; that the said Will acknowledged in the presence of the deponent, in conversation with Gabriel, that he was concerned in the conspiracy and insurrection, and that he wanted the appointment of captain of the foot, but this being refused him, he was to act as a horseman; that the whites were to be murdered and killed indiscriminately, except [?] none of whom were to be touched.

Toby, the property of John Holman, deposed: That the prisoner proposed to join and fight the whites; that he had joined, and had to carry two scythe blades to Solomon to be made into swords; he was determined to kill his master; that he had his master's sorrel horse set apart for him to act upon as a horseman; but there was to be a grand meeting of the negroes near Prosser's, from whence they were to proceed and take the town; that 5,000 blacks were to meet the prisoner at the bar, and that all the blacks who did not join would be put to death; that he intended to kill his master on Saturday night, the 30th August last; that the prisoner had an appointment as captain, but was turned out, being under size.

John's Case.—Daniel, property of John Williamson, deposed: That the deponent being at plough at home, the prisoner, who at that time worked at the penitentiary and was passing by, invited him to come to a great barbecue which ws to be made by the negroes at Half Sink; and upon being informed that the purport of the barbecue was to concert measures for raising an insurrection and murdering and killing the whites and taking the country, of which he had no doubt, as Gabriel, and Solomon, and himself, being a captain, being at the head of the business; that the said John said he had a number of men at the Penitentiary, and was going up to Caroline, where he expected to raise several hundred; that they were to seize upon the arms at the penitentiary, and that all negroes who did not join in the insurrection would and should be put to death. That the whites were to be put to death indiscriminately.

Charles, property of William Winston, deposed: That about three weeks ago, the prisoner gave this deponent an invite to a barbecue to be at Mr. Moore's school-house, which was made on a particular occasion, but was not made known to him, the deponent, which invitation this deponent refused to accept.

Isaac's Case.—Ben, the property of T.H. Prosser, deposed, that the prisoner informed him the department, that he had joined Prosser's Gabriel, in order to take Richmond and that he the prisoner, was one of the foot soldiers; that he was if possible to supply himself with a sword which if he could not do, Gabriel was to furnish him, and he the prisoner was determined either to kill or be killed.

Daniel, the property of William Burton, deposed, that the prisoner informed the deponent, on Friday the 29th August last, that he the prisoner had been informed by Nanny, wife to Gabriel, that 1000 men were to meet said Gabriel near Prosser's Tavern the ensuing night, and that he also was to be one of them, for the purpose of murdering the White Citizens; that the Governor had in some measure, got an alarm of this business, and had caused the arms which had been kept in the Capitol to be removed to the Penitentiary—that they should not mind the guards which were placed over the arms as they were determined to rush through them and take both them and the magazine—that he communicated this information to the overseer that an army of negroes were raising against the whites, with an injunction to the said overseer to keep the communication secret, the blacks were determined to kill every black who should not aid in, and join them in the insurrection. The prisoner was much intoxicated at the time of the conversation above.

Michael's Case.—Ben, the property of T.H. Prosser, deposed: That about a fortnight before time appointed for the insurrection, the prisoner being on his way to Richmond, employed Gabriel to make him a sword, which was to be used by him in fighting the whites under the command of Gabriel, as a foot soldier; that he called on the Saturday evening appointed for carrying the plot into execution, the prisoner applied at the house of Gabriel and obtained his sword, and promised to meet Sunday night at the Tobacco house of Mr. Prosser, that being too rainy an evening for carrying their….

Pharoah, the property of Philip Sheppard, deposed: That in the week preceding the Saturday appointed for an insurrection, the prisoner informed him that Gabriel was to furnish him a sword, which he would call and get on Saturday evening ensuing; that he had joined the party.

Ned, the property of Judith Owen, deposed: That the prisoner informed him he had been requested by Gabriel to join him in an insurrection, which he had rejected, promising said Gabriel should he see the business progress well he would afterward join him.

William Gentry deposed: That he and Mr. Glenn being in pursuit of Gabriel and just on the return from said Gabriel's habitation, fell in with the prisoner, who they were about to take up when he fled into the woods; that being pursued by Mr. Glenn, was taken some time before the deponent arrived, and that Mr. Glenn informed him that a scythe blade made into the form of a sword was produced by the prisoner, with which he made battle against said Glenn, who had overcome the prisoner and had then the said sword in his possession.

Nat's Case:--Ben, the property of T.H. Prosser, deposed: That the prisoner had joined Gabriel to fight the White people, and for that purpose purchased a sword from one William, belonging to Ben Mosby; that upon falling in with Gabriel and this deponent, he informed Gabriel that he had his sword, and left it at the warehouse; that he had a stick in his hand, and flourishing it in his hand, observed that thus he would wield his sword. This was about three weeks previous to the time appointed for the commencement of thei insurrection. That the said Gabriel and the prisoner agreed that the prisoner should bear the rank of a captain, the said prisoner remarking that all the Warehouse boys had joined, and he would go on to get as many as he could until the appointed time.

Washington, belonging to Benj. Mosby, deposed: That he sold a sword to the prisoner, who informed him he wanted to stand Guard with it at the Warehouse, where he then lived and had the care of.

Sep 11 Henrico County Court, on September 11th, sentences John, a negro man slave, the property of Mary Jones, of Hanover, to death on charge of conspiracy and insurrection, and orders that he be hung at the usual place of execution on the 12th inst.

[Identical sentences were issued for: Solomon, "the property of Thomas H. Prosser," of Henrico; Nat, "the property of Anne Parsons," of Henrico; Isaac, "the property of William Burton, of Henrico; and Will, "the property of John Mosby, Senior," of Henrico.]

Sep 12 Further Trials of Insurgents

    Trial of Gregory's Billy.

Testimony of Ben against him: Billy was one. Gabriel asked Billy if he would be one. He said that he wanted to be a captain if Gabriel would find him arms, which Gabriel agreed to. Was to have Mr. Gregory's horse. This conversastion was on Wednesday night. He wanted to be a captain to fight the white people. He was to meet Gabriel the next night at Mr. Owns'. Guilty; excuted Monday. Valued £100

    Trial of Martin, Property of T.H. Prosser

Witnesses—John and Ben.

John—Gabriel carried some spirit to a spring where the prisoner was. When he was asked by Gabriel if he would join him to fight the white people he said he would.

Ben—Martin enlisted under Gabriel, but Gabriel said he was too old. Then Martin said he would run bullets and keep them in bullets. Guilty; executed on Monday. Valued £300.

Trial of Charles

Testimony of Patrick and Ben against him.

Patrick—Charles asked him at Gregory's Tavern if he was a man. He said he wanted him to meet him Saturday or Sunday; he wanted to talk with a man. He would pay him well.

Ben—Charles wanted to be a Cap't; Gabriel said he might be a sergeant—he was too trifling a fellow. Charles cursed mightily about. Charles was to meet Gabriel on a certain day at Mr. Gregory's, where there was 29 arms, where he was to be furnished with arms. He told Gabriel after he agreed to make him a Capt. That he would raise him 30 or 40 arms. Guildy; to be executed on Monday. Valued at £100.

Trial of Frank

Testimony of John and Ben against him.

John—Gabriel asked him to join him. He said he would. Those who were to join were to stand up; the prisoner stood up. They were to meet at Young's spring afterwards to confer on the same subject. The prisoner said he would enlist with Gabriel to fight the white people.

Ben—He agreed to join Gabriel to fight the white people for their liberty. George asked Frank why they did not start; Frank said the weather was too bad, but they were to meet—night. Guilty; to be executed on Monday. Valued £100.

Trial of Martin, Property of R. Gregory

Testimony of Billy and Ben against him.

Billy—Last Wednesday was a fortnight. He came to the witness and told him he could tell him news. He told him the boys on the Brook were going to fight the white people, and that he had joined them, and advised the prisoner to join also. The witness advised him not to join, and he said he believed he would not. The witness asked him what boys they were. He said he could not tell him, but that he would know in time.

Ben—Ben knew Martin, but did not know that he was concerned in the business

Moses, for the prisoner—The witness heard the prisoner, after the plot was discovered, curse the black people for intending to rise against the whites. Aquitted.

Sep 15 *Commonwealth against Isham, the property of William Burton The Evidence*

Ben deposed—On a Sunday on which the last Barbacue took place amongst the blacks, the prisoner [witness meant] went to the Bridge (Brook) about 12 o'clock, as he believed, where he found the prisoner at the Bar, and Sunday other negroes named by him, gaming with quaits pitching: The witness went below the bridge afishing and ws shortly after joined by Gabriel, the prisoner and a brother of his by name George, from hence the witness went to the Barbacue where the prisoner, Gabriel and some other negroes whom he saw at the Bridge were also present: That Gabriel, the prisoner, said George, the witness and some other negroes went home with Gabriel: Gabriel had asked the prisoner and his brother George to join him at the Barbecue; after being some time at Gabriel's house, he explained to the prisoner and George, for what purpose he asked them to join him: both agreed they would, and each shaking the other by the hand exclaimed, here are our hands and hearts, we will wade to our knees in blood sooner than fail in the attempt. The next Sunday was appointed as the day of Meeting, at Mrs. Owens, to settle the plan: About an hour by Sun, when they arrived at Gabriel's house, neither of them intoxicated, Mr. Burton's Frank was at the Bridge in company with the prisoner and others when he first arrived there.

Sep 17 Confessions of Ben alias Ben Woolfolk

The first time I ever heard of this conspiracy was from Mrs. Ann Smith's George; the second person that gave me information was Samuel alias Samuel Bird, the property of Mrs. Jane Clarke. They asked me last spring to come over to their houses on a Friday night. It was late before I could get there; the company had met and dispersed. I inquired where they were gone, and was informed to see their wives. I went after them and found George; he carried me and William (the property of William Young) to Sam Bird's, and after we got there he (Sam) enquired of George if he had any pen and ink; he said no—he had left it home. He brought out his list of men, and he had Elisha Price's Jim, James Price's Moses, Sally Price's Bob, Denny Wood's Emanuel. After this George invited me to come and see him the next night, but I did not go. The following Monday night William went over and returned with a ticket for me; likewise one for Gilbert. The Thursday night following, both George and Sam Bird came to see me. Bowler's Jack was with us. We conversed until late in the night upon the subject of the meditated war. George said he would try to be ready by the 24th of August, and the following Sunday he went to Hungry meeting-house to enlist men. When I saw him again he informed me he had enlisted 37 men there. The Sunday after he went to Manchester, where he said he had recruited 50-odd men. I never saw him again until the sermon at my house, which was about three weeks before the rising was to take place. On the day of the sermon, George called on Sam Bird to inform how many men he had; he said he had not his list with him, but he supposed about 500. George wished the business to be deferred some time longer. Mr. Prosser's Gabriel wished to bring on the business as soon as possible. Gilbert said the summer was almost over, and he wished them to enter upon the business before the weather got too cold. Gabriel proposed that the subject should be referred to his brother Martin to decide upon. Martin said there was this expression in the Bible, delays breed danger; at this time, he said, the country was at peace, the soldiers were discharge, and the arms all put away; there was no patrolling in the country, and that before he would any longer bear what he had borne, he would turn out and fight with his stick. Gilbert said he was ready with his pistol, but it was in need of repair; he gave it to Gabriel, who was put it in order for him. I then spoke to the company and informed them I wished to have something to say. I told them that I had heard in the days of old, when the Israelites were in the service of King Pharoah, they were taken from him by the power of God, and were carried away by Moses. God had blessed him with an angel to go with him, but that I could see nothing of that kind in these days. Martin said in reply: I read in my Bible where God says if we will worship Him we should have peace in all our land; five of you shall conquer an hundred, and a hundred a thousand of our enemies. After this they went on consultation upon the time they should execute the plan. Martin spoke and appointed for them to meet in three weeks, which was to be of a Saturday night. Gabriel said he had 500 bullets made. Smith's George said he was done the corn and would then go on to make as many cross-bows as he could. Bowler's Jack said he had got 50 spears or bayonets fixed at the end of sticks. The plan was to be as follows: We were all to meet at the briary spot on the Brook; 100 men were to stand at the Brook bridge; Gabriel was to take 100 more and go to Gregory's tavern and take the arms shich were there; 50 more were to be sent to Rocketts to set that on fire, in order to alarm the upper part of the town and induce the people to go down there; while they were employed in extinguishing the fire Gabriel and the other officers and soldiers were to take the Capitol and all the arms they could find and be ready to slaughter the people on their return from Rocketts. Sam Bird was to have a pass as a freeman and was to go to the nation of Indians called Catawbas to persuade them to join the negroes to fight the white people. As far as I understood all the whites were to be massacred, except the Quakers, the Methodists, and the Frenchmen, and they were to be spared on account as they conceived of their being friendly to liberty, and also they had understood that the French were at war with this country for the money that was due them, and that an army was landed at South Key, which they hoped would assist them. They intended also to spare all the poor white women who had no slaves.

The above communications are put down precisely as delivered to us by Ben, alias Ben Woolfolk. Given under our hands the 17th day of September 1800.

Gervas Storrs

Joseph Selden

Sep 18 Ben, alias Ben Woolfolk, sentenced to death for conspiracy and insurrection Sept. 16th, pardoned Sept. 18th.

Sep 23 Benjamin Oliver writes to the Governor asking that swords and pistols may be furnished the Hanover Cavalry, so that they may be able to do patrol duty. Thinks much danger is to be apprehended in the county from the great number of free negroes.

Sep 24 William prentis informs the Governor that he has caused the arrest of Reuben and Jesse Byrd of Petersburg, free men of color, who one of the convicted conspirators, stated were principally concerned in the late plot.

Sep 25, Richard E. Lee Gives Information to the Governor of Gabriel's Capture [captured aboard ship in Norfolk, VA. Refuses to confess to anyone but the Governor James Monroe]

The Trial of Gabriel

Oct 6 At a Court of Oyer and Terminer held for the county of Henrico on Monday, the sixth day of October, 1800, for the trial of Gabriel, a negro man slave, the property of Thomas Henry Prosser, of the said county, charged with conspiracy and insurrection, the said Gabriel was convicted and condemned to execution on Tuesday, the seventh day of October 1800.

Prosser's Ben—Gabriel was appointed Captain at first consultation respecting the Insurrection, and afterwards when he had enlisted a number of men was appointed General. That they were to kill Mr. Prosser, Mr. Mosby and all the neighbors, and then to proceed to Richmond, where they would kill everybody, take the treasury, and divide the money amongst the soldiers; after which he would fortify Richmond and proceed to discipline his men, as he apprehended force would be raised elsewhere to repel him. That if the white people agreed to their freedom they would then hoist a white flag, and he would dine and drink with the merchants of the city on the day when it should be agreed to.

Gabriel enlisted a number of negroes. The prisoner went with the witness to Mr. Young's to see Ben Woolfolk, who was going to Caroline to enlist men there. He gave three shillings for himself and three other negroes, to be expended in recruiting men.

The prisoner made the handles of the swords, which were made by Solomon. The prisoner shewed the witness a quantity of bullets, nearly a peck, which he and Martin had run, and some lead then on hand, and he said he had ten pounds of powder which he had purchased. Gabriel said he had nearly 10,000 men; he had 1,000 in Richmond, about 600 in Caroline, and nearly 500 at the Coal pits, besides others at different places, and that he expected the poor white people would also join him, and that two Frenchmen had actually joined, whom he said Jack Ditcher knew, but whose names he would not mention to the witness. That the prisoner had enlisted nearly all the negroes in town as he said, and amongst them had 400 Horsemen. That in consequence of the bad weather on Saturday night, an agreement was made to meet at the Tobacco House of Mr. Prosser the ensuing night. Gabriel said all the negroes from Petersburg were to join him after he had commenced the Insurrection.

Mr. Price's John—He saw the prisoner at a meeting, who gave a general invitation to the negro men to attend at the Spring to drink grog. That when there he mentioned the Insurrection, and proposed that all present should join them in the same, and meet in 3 weeks for the purpose of carrying the same into effect, and enjoined several of the negroes then present to use the best of their endeavors in enlisting men, and to meet according to the time appointed.

Ben Woolfolk—The prisoner was present at the meeting at Mr. Young's, who came to get persons to join him to carry on the war against the white people. That after meeting they adjourned to the Spring and held a consultation, when it was concluded that in 3 weeks the business should commence. Gabriel said he had 12 dozen swords made, and had worn out 2 pair of bullet moulds in running bullets, and pulling a third pair out of his pocket, observed that was nearly worn out. That Bob Cooley and Mr. Tinsley's Jim was to let them into the Capitol to get the arms out. That the lower part of the Town towards Rocketts was to be fired, which would draw forth the citizens (that part of the town being of little value); this would give an opportunity to the negroes to seize on the arms and ammunition, and then they would commence the attack upon them. After the assembling of the negroes near Prosser's, and previous to their coming to Richmond, a company was to be sent to Gregorie's Tavern to take possession of some arms there deposited. The prisoner said, at the time of meeting the witness at Mr. Young's, that he had the evening before received six Guns—one of which he had delivered to Col. Wilkinson's Sam. That he was present when Gabriel was appointed General and Geo. Smith second in command. That none were to be spared of the whites except Quakers, Methodists, and French people. The prisoner and Gilbert concluded to purchase a piece of silk for a flag, on which they would have written "death or Liberty," and they would kill all except as before excepted, unless they agreed to the freedom of the blacks, in which case they would at lest cut off one of their arms. That the prisoner told the witness that Bob Cooley had told him if he would call on him about a week before the time of the Insurrection he would untie the key of the room in which the arms and ammunition were kept at the Capitol and give it to him, or if he did not come, then on the night of the Insurrection being commenced, he would hand him arms out as fast as he could arm his men, and that he had on a Sunday previous to this, been shown by Cooley every room in the Capitol.

Document 2 "The Deslondes Uprising," *Louisiana Gazette,* 17 January 1811.[2]

January 11

The militia on the west side of the river crossed above the banditti of Negroes yesterday about ten o'clock and attacked them; killed several, took some prisoners, and dispersed the whole body; the fugitives retreated to the swamp several of whom soon after returned surrendered, amongst which is Charles, a yellow fellow, the property of Mr. Andry who was the leader of the miscreants.

From every account we have received the danger appears to be at and end. No nature plan had been arranged by blacks and the measures now adopted will ensure tranquility. General Hampton is on the coast with a respectable force—Major Milton, who was on his march to Baton Rouge, with about 150 regular troops, we are informed, was above where the ravages commenced and was coming down; so that there is little doubt but before third, the whole of the banditti are completely routed.

January 12

The accounts from the coast corroborate that of yesterday. The troops continue to kill and capture the fugitives, ten or twelve of who were brought to town this morning; and in a few days planters can with safety return to their farms. We expect soon (perhaps on Monday) to give a detailed account of damage done by the brigands.

January 17

It is very difficult to obtain anything like a correct statement of the damages done by the banditti on the coast. They commenced their depredations on the night of the 8th inst, at Mr. Andry's—killed young Mr. Andry and wounded the old gentleman. After seizing some public arms, liquor stores, and getting half drunk, they marched down the coast from plantation to plantation plundering and destroying property on their way; the inhabitants generally made their escape and the banditti continued on their march until 4 o'clock in the afternoon of Wednesday when they arrived at the plantation of Mr. Cadit Fortier. There they halted (having marched upwards of three leagues) and commenced killing poultry, cooking, eating, drinking and rioting.

When the alarm reached the city much confusion was manifested-no-regular corps of militia, no order nor discipline; yet with a strong disposition was shown by many to render every service in their power. The most active citizens armed themselves and in about an hour after three alarm (although the weather was extremely bad) commenced their march. Their force did not exceed thirty men, mounted on tolerable horses but were continually reinforced as they progressed up the coast. The road for two or three leagues was crowded with carriages and carts full of people making their escape from the ravages of banditti—negroes, half naked up to the knees in mud, with large packages on their heads driving along toward the city. The accounts we received were various. Fear and panic seized those that were making their escape. It was not possible to make any estimate of the force of the brigands. Some of them to be 500 strong, and that one half of them were armed with muskets and fusils and the others with [?] bres and cane knives. When we had arrived within a league of Mr. Fortier's where the banditti were feasting, our numbers had increased near one hundred, but badly armed and accountred. Major Darrington, of the United States Infantry, was named as our commandant—but indeed it was but a name for he

---

2   "The Deslondes Uprising," Louisiana Gazette, 17 January 1811.

was decidedly of the opinion that we ought not to attack the enemy with the small force we had until daylight. In this opinion he was supported by the informed characters in the detachment but without avail, for some of those were for attacking, had advanced—The major gave orders to prepare for action (this was about eight o'clock at night) and at the moment when every despositon was making for the attack, General Hampton arrived and decided against attacking them until the infantry could be brought up. This he was not able to effect although every exertion way made until 4 o'clock in the morning. Clouds had dispersed, the moon shine was clear and it was excessively cold; the arms of the United States troops glittered in the moonbeams and must have been the cause of the brigands discovering us; for soon after the foot filed off to take them in the rear, they rang an alarm bell and with a degree of extraordinary silence for such rabble, commenced and affected their retreat up the river.

When we took possession of the ground where the brigands had been committing their ravages all night, our troops and horses were so exhausted that we were unable to pursue the fugitives; however, by the activity of the militia and the promptness of Major Milton the regular force under his command that day and the next, the whole of the banditti were routed, killed, wounded and dispersed, and every thing is tranquil.

In this melancholy affair but two citizens have fell by the hands of the brigands, and three dwelling houses burned; not a single sugar house or sugar works were molested. The poor wretches who were concerned in the depredations have paid for their crime—upwards of one hundred, it is generally supposed, have been killed and hung; and more will be executed. This loss alone is expensive to the planters and the most [?] slaves were concerned or joined the poor deluded miscreants who first commenced the ravages.

This awful lesson should strike deep to the hearts of slave holders and those whose duty it is to keep our country in a state of defense; the time may not be distant when we shall be called... against a more formidable foe that the banditti lately quelled. The doctrine of passive obedience and non-resistance must and will be abandoned. Pleasant as sleep of peace with disgrace may be the sordid mind, it cannot be any longer. Let our rulers awaken from the lethargy and say by acts, not by deeds, that they are worthy of their station...

Document 3   An Official Report of the Trials of Sundry Negroes, charged with an attempt to raise an insurrection in the state of South-Carolina, 1822.[3]

At the head of this conspiracy stood Denmark Vesey, a free negro; with him the idea undoubtedly originated. For several years before he disclosed his intentions to any one, he appears to have been constantly and assiduously engaged in endeavoring to embitter the minds of the colored population against the white. He rendered himself perfectly familiar with all those parts of the Scriptures, which he thought he could pervert to his purpose; and would readily quote them, to prove that slavery was contrary to the laws of God; that slaves were bound to attempt their

---

[3]   *An Official Report of the Trials of Sundry Negroes, charged with an attempt to raise an Insurrection in the State of South-Carolina: preceded by an introduction and narrative: and, in an appendix, a report of the trials of four white pesons on indictments for attempting to excite the slaves to insurrection,* (Charleston: James R. Schenck, 1822), accessible at https://www.loc.gov/resource/

emancipation, however shocking and bloody might be the consequences, and that such efforts would not only be pleasing to the Almighty, but were absolutely enjoined, and their success predicted in the Scriptures. His favorite texts when he addressed his own color were, "Zecheriah, chapter 14th, verses 1,2, and 3*, and Joshua, chapter 4th, verse 21**; and in all his conversations he identified their situation with that of the Israelites. The number of inflammatory pamphlets on slavery brought into Charleston from some of our sister states, within the last four years, (and once from Siera Leone) and distributed amongst the colored population of the city, for which there was a great facility, in consequence of the unrestricted intercourse allowed to persons of color between the different States in the Union; and the speeches in Congress of those opposed to the admission of Missouri into the Union, perhaps garbled and misrepresented, furnished him with ample means for inflaming the minds of the colored population of the state; and by distorting certain parts of those speeches, or selecting from them particular passages, he persuaded but too many that Congress had actually declared them free, and that they were held in bondage contrary to the laws of the land. Even whilst walking through the streets in company with another, he was not idle; of if his companion bowed to a white person he would rebuke him, and observe that all men were born equal, and that he was surprised that any one would degrade himself by such conduct; that he would never cringe to the whites, nor ought any one who had the feelings of a man. When answered, "We are slaves," he would sarcastically and indignantly reply, "You deserve to remain slaves;" and if he were further asked, "What can we do?" he would reply, "Go and buy a spelling book and read the fable of Hercules and the Waggoner;" which he would then repeat, and apply it to their situation. He also sought every opportunity of entering into conversation with white persons when they could be overheard by negroes near by, especially in grog shops; during which conversation he would artfully introduce some bold remark on slavery; …He continued this course, until sometime after the commencement of the last winter; by which time he had not only obtained incredible influence amongst persons of color, but many feared him more than their owners, and one of them declared even more than his God.

At this period he sounded Rolla and Ned; two slaves of his Excellency Thomas Bennett, and finding them ready to acquiesce in his schemes, he made the same proposals to Jack, belong to Mrs. Purcell, and Peter, belonging to Mr. Poyas, who also consented with equal promptess. These men were his first four associates… Sometime after Christmas he was also joined by Gullah Jack, belonging to Mr. Pritchard and subsequently by Monday, belonging to Mr. Gell; who soon proved themselves to be as fit men for his purpose, and as active as Rolla, Ned, and Peter.—He also at his house held nocturnal meetings, for the purpose of interchanging opinions, maturing the plot, collecting and giving information &c.; at which meetings numbers of his insurgents, both from country and town attended; and where collecitons were made for the purpose of providing arms, ammunition, &c. and for defraying such expenses as might be indispensably necessary. … In order to induce the colored population to join them, every principle which could operate upon the mind of man was artfully employed: Religion, Hope, Fear, Deception, were resorted to as occasion required; All were told, and many believed, that God approved of their designs; those whose fears would have restrained them, were forced to yield to threats of death; those whose produce and foresight induced them to pause, were cheered with the assurance that assistance from St. Domingo and Africa were at hand; … And strange as it may appear; yet vast numbers of the Africans firmly believed that Gullah Jack was a sorcerer; that he could neither be killed nor taken; and whilst they retained the charms which he had distributed they would themselves be invulnerable. … This was about the time that the African congregation, (so called from its being composed wholly of persons of colour and almost entirely of blacks,) was formed, and their Church built in Hempstead; of which Vesey had been a member, and of which his principal associates, Gullah Jack, Monday, Ned and Peter, were also members; and the two last, were class leaders. ... The great impropriety of allowing meetings of any kind to be held solely by slaves, and at such times and places, must forcibly strike every reflecting mind.... Is it to be wondered at that, under all the foregoing circumstances, an attempt to create an insurrection should be contemplated!

*Behold the day of the Lord cometh, and thy spoil shall be divided in the midst of thee. For I will gather all nations against Jerusalem to battle; and the city shall be taken, and the women ravished; and half of the city shall go forth into captivity; and the residue of the people shall not be cut off from the city. Then shall the Lord go forth, and fight against those nations, as when he fought in the day of battle.

**And they utterly destroyed all that was in the city, both men and women, young and old, and ox, and sheep, and ass, with the edge of the sword.

Document 4   *Negro Plot: An Account of the late intended insurrection among a portion of the blacks of the city of Charleston, South Carolina, 1822.*[4]

On Thursday, the 30th of May last, about three o'clock in the afternoon, the intendant of Charleston was informed by a gentleman of great respectability,...that a favourite and confidential slave of his had communicated to him, on his arrival in town, a conversation which had taken place at the market on the Saturday preceding, between himself and a black man; which afforded strong reasons for believing that a revolt and insurrection were in contemplation among a proportion of our black population.... The gentleman who had conveyed the information ... having examined his slave, was induced to believe, that the negro fellow who had communicated the intelligence of the intended revolt to the slave in question, belonged to Messrs. J&D Paul, Broad street, and resided in their premises. Accordingly... without waiting for the interposition of the civil authority, he applied to the Messrs. Pauls, and had the whole of their male servants committed to the guardhouse, until the individual who had accosted the slave of this gentleman, on the occasion previously mentioned, could be identified from among them. On the assembly of the corporation at five, the slave of this gentleman was brought before them...:

"On Saturday afternoon last... I went to market; after finishing my business, I strolled down the wharf below the fish-market.... A black man (Mr. Paul's William) came up to me and... after some trifling conversation...he remarked with considerable earnestness to me, Do you know something serious is about to take place? To which I replied, No. Well said he, there is, and many of us are determined to right ourselves! I asked him to explain himself; when he remarked, why we are determined to shake off our bondage,.... many have joined and if you will go with me, I will show you the man, who has the list of names, who will take yours down... I left him instantly, lest, if this fellow afterwards got into trouble, and I had been seen conversing with him, in so publick a place, I might be suspected and thrown into difficulty.

---

4   *Negro Plot: An Account of the late intended insurrection among a portion of the blacks of the city of Charleston, South Carolina,* (Boston: J.W. Ingraham, 1822), accessible at https://www.loc.gov/resource/

On this witness being dismissed from the presence of the council, the prisoner (William) was examined. The mode resorted to in his examination was to afford him no intimation of the subject of the information which had been lodged against him, as it was extremely desirable in the first place, to have the testimony of the other witness corroborated as to time and place, that, from the confession of the prisoner himself, it might appear that he was at the fish-market at the period stated…. After a vast deal of equivocation, he admitted all these facts, but when the rest of the conversation was put home to him, he flatly denied it, but with so many obvious indications of guilt, that it was deemed unwise to discharge him. He was remanded, for the night, to the guardhouse, it having been decided to subject him to solitary confinement in the black-hole of the workhouse, where on the succeeding morning, he was to be conveyed.

On the morning of the 31st, he was again examined by the attending warden at the guardhouse on which occasion he admitted all the conversation which he had held at the fish-market, with the witness before mentioned, and stated that he had received his information from Mingo Harth, who was in possession of the muster-roll of the insurgents.

With the hope of still further disclosures, William was conveyed to the workhouse and placed in solitary confinement. The individuals (Mingo Harth and Peter Poyas) against whom he gave information, … were forthwith taken up by the wardens and their trunks examined. These fellows behaved with so much composure and coolness, and treated the charge, alleged against them, with so much levity… that the wardens were completely deceived, and these men discharged. One of these (Peter Poyas) proved afterwards,… to be one of the principal ringleaders in the conspiracy….

Council being still under the conviction that William Paul was in possession of more information than he had thought proper to disclose, a committee was appointed to examine him from time to time, with the hope of obtaining further intelligence. Although Peter and Mingo had been discharged, yet it was deemed advisable to have them watched, and consequently spies were employed of their own colour for this purpose, in such a manner as to give advices of all their movements.

Things remained in this state for six or seven days, until about the 8th of June, when William, who had been a week in solitary confinement, and beginning to fear that he would soon be led forth to the scaffold, for summary execution, in an interview with Mr. Napier, (one of the committee appointed to examine him.) confessed, that he had for sometime known of the plot, that it was very extensive, embracing an indiscriminate massacre of the whites, and that the blacks were to be headed by an individual, who carried about him a charm, which rendered him invulnerable. He stated, that the period fixed for the rising, was on the second Sunday in June. …

Measures were consequently promptly taken, to place the city guard in a state of utmost efficiency.

Three or four days now elapsed, and not withstanding all our efforts, we could obtain no confirmation of the disclosure of William, on the contrary, they seemed to have sustained some invalidation, from the circumstance of one of the individuals, (Ned Bennett), whom he named as a person who had information in relation to the insurrection, coming voluntarily to the intendant, and soliciting an examination, if he was an object of suspicion.

On the night, however, of Friday the 14th, the information of William was amply confirmed…. At 8 o'clock on this evening, the intendant received a visit from a gentleman who is advantageously known in this community for his worth and respectability. ...This gentleman... stated to the intendant, that having the most unbounded confidence in a faithful slave, ... he was induced to inform him, that rumours were abroad of an intended insurrection of the blacks, and that it was said, that this movement had been traced to some of the coloured members of Dr. Palmer's church, in which he was known to be a class leader.... This slave, it appears, was in no degree connected with the plot, but he had an intimate friend A--- (This witness gave the information under a pledge, that his name should not be divulged) who had been trusted by the conspirators with the secret, and had been solicited by them to join their association: ...

This gentleman, therefore, mentioned, that his servant had informed him, that A--- had stated, that about three months ago, Rolla, belonging to governor Bennett, had communicated to him the intelligence of the intended insurrection, and had asked him to join— "That he remarked, in the event of their rising, they would not be without help, as the people from San Domingo [Haiti] and Africa would assist them in obtaining their liberty, if they only made the motion first themselves. That if A---- wished to know more, he had better attend their meetings, where all would be disclosed." After this, at another interview, Rolla informed A----, that "the plan was matured, and that on Sunday night, the 16th June, a force would cross from James's Island and land on South Bay, march up and seize the arsenal and guardhouse, that another body at the same time would seize the arsenal on the neck, and a third would rendezvous in the vicinity of his master's mills. They would then sweep the town with fire and sword, not permitting a single white to escape."

...The following court was organized on the evening of the 17th.

Magistrates	Freeholders
Lionel H. Kennedy, Esq.	Colonel William Drayton
Tomas Parker, Esq.	Nathaniel Heyward, Esq.
	J.R. Pringle, Esq.
	James Legare, Esq.
	R.J. Turnbull, Esq.

On the night of the 17th, and during the ensuing twenty-four hours, the following slaves were committed: *Rolla, Batteau, Matthias,* and *Ned,* the property of the governour Bennett; *Mungo* and *Peter,* the property of James Poyas; *Amhurst,* the property of Mrs. Lining; *Stepehn,* the property of T.R. Smith; *Richard* and *John,* the property of Jonathan Lucas.

On the morning of the 19th of June, the court of magistrates and freeholders assembled at the courthouse, were sworn in, and proceeded to the arraignment of the above prisoners for trial; who were charged *"with attempting to raise an insurrection among the blacks against the whites."* ... Previous to their proceeding to the painful investigation with which they were charged, they laid down a variety of rules for their government, all of them subservient to justice as well as humanity.

In the first place, it was decided that the testimony should be regulated by those established rules of evidence which are elsewhere found so important in the exposition of truth; that no slave should be tried but in the presence of his master or his attorney; that the testimony of one witness, unsupported by circumstances, should lead to no conviction involving capital punishment; and that the statement of the party himself should be heard in explanation of such particulars as seemed most inculpatory.

THE COURT,

Being thus organized, they proceeded to the trial of ROLLA, the slave of governour Bennett. Jacob Axon, Esq. attending as attorney of his master.

It was proved, that *Rolla* had confessed to two persons, both of whom were examined by the court, that he belonged to the conspiracy, and with one of these witnesses (his friend) he used every effort to induce him to join in the insurrection, which Rolla stated was to take place on the night of the 16th of June. Finding that this friend (the witness in question) would not join the association, he urged him to go out of town on Sunday night, lest some harm should come to him. Rolla represented himself as the commander of the force which was to rendez-vous in the vicinity of his master's mills, & explained to the witness fully the order of attack; the division of the forces; and said,"that his troops, in their way into town, would fix his old buck (his master) and the intendant." On being asked whether it was intended to kill the women and children, he remarked when we have done with the men we know what to do with the women. On this testimony Rolla was found *guilty*, and sentenced to be executed on the 2d of July.

[Batteau, *guilty*, sentenced to be executed on the 2d of July; Stephen, belonging to Thomas R. Smith, Esq., *discharged*; Peter, the slave of Mr. James Poyas, *guilty*, sentenced for execution on the 2d of July; Amherst, belonging to Mrs. Lining, *not guilty*, discharged; Ned, property of Governour Bennett, *guilty*, sentenced for execution on the 2d of July; Jim, belonging to Mr. Ancrum, *not guilty*; Sandy, belonging to Mr. Holmes, *not guilty*, Friday, property of Mr. Rout, *not guilty*; Abraham, slave of Dr. Poyas, *not guilty*.}

[…]

… On Thursday, the 27th, DENMARK VESEY, a free black man, was brought before the court for trial, Assisted by his counsel, G.W. Cross, Esq.

It is perhaps somewhat remarkable, that at this stage of the investigation, although several witnesses had been examined, the *atrocious* guilt of *Denmark Vesey* had not been as yet fully unfolded From the testimony of most of the witnesses, however, the court found enough, and amply enough, to warrant the sentence of death, which, on the 28th, they passed on him. But every subsequent step in the progress of the trials of others, lent new confirmation to his overwhelming guilt, and placed him beyond a doubt, on the criminal eminence of having been the individual, in whose bosom the nefarious scheme was first engendered. There is ample reason for believing, that his project was not, with him, of recent origin, for it was said, he had spoken of it for upwards of four years.

These facts of his guilt the journals of the court will disclose—that no man can be proved to—that no man can be proved to have spoken of or urged the insurrection prior to himself. All the channels of communication and intelligence are traced back to him. His house was the place appointed for the secret meetings of the conspirators, at which he was invariably a leading and influential member; animating and encouraging the timid, by the hopes and prospects of success; removing the scruples of the religious, by the grossest prostitution and perversion of the sacred oracles, and inflaming and confirming the resolute, by all the savage fascinations of blood and booty.

The peculiar circumstances of guilt, which confer a distinction on his case, will be found narrated in the confession of Rolla, Monday Gell, Frank, and Jesse, in the appendix. He was sentenced for execution on the 2d July.

… Sentence of death was passed on these six men, on the 28th of June, and they were executed on the 2d of July. With the exception of Jesse and Rolla, they made no disclosures; all of them, with those exceptions, either explicitly or implicitly affirming their innocence. It is much to be lamented that the situation of the workhouse, at this period, precluded, after their sentence, their being separately confined; at least that Vesey could not have been subjected to the gloom and silence of a solitary cell. He might have been softened, and afforded the most precious confessions, as his knowledge and agency in the nefarious scheme very far exceeded the information of others, who, however guilty, seemed but the agents of his will. But these men mutually supported each other, and died obedient to the stern and emphatick injunction of their comrade, (Peter Poyas) *"Do not open your lips! Die silent, as you shall see me do!"*

CLASS No. 1 *Compromises those prisoners who were found guilty and executed*			
Prisoner's Names	Owners' Names	*Time of Commit*	*How disposed of.*
Peter	James Poyas	June 18	Hanged on Tuesday the 2nd of July 1822 on Blake's lands near Charleston
Ned	Governor Bennett	do.	do.
Rolla	do.	do.	do.
Batteau	do.	do.	do.
Denmark Vesey	A free black man	June 22	do.
Jessy	Thomas Blackwood	June 23	do.
John	Elias Horry	July 5	Hanged on the Lines near Charleston, Friday July 12, 1822
Gullah Jack	Paul Pritchard	do.	do.
Mingo	William Harth	June 21	Hanged on the Lines near Charleston, Friday July 26, 1822
Lot	Forrester	June 27	do.
Joe	P.L. Jore	July 6	do.
Julius	Thomas Forrest	July 8	do.
Tom	Mrs. Russell	July 10	do.
Smart	Robert Anderson	do.	do.
John	John Robertson	July 11	do.
Robert	do.	do.	do.
Adam	do.	do.	do.
Polydore	do.	do.	do.
Bacchus	Mrs. Faber	do.	do.
Dick	William Sims	July 13	do.
Pharaoh	Thompson	do.	do.
Jemmy	Mrs. Clement	July 18	do.

Mauidore	Mordecai Cohen	July 19	do.
Dean	---Mitchell	do.	do.
Jack	Mrs. Purcell	July 12	do.
Bellisle	Estate of Joseph Yates	July 18	do.
Naphur	do.	do.	do.
Adam	do.	do.	do.
Jacob	John S. Glen	July 16	do.
Charles	John Billings	July 18	do.
Jack	N. McNeill	July 22	Hanged Tuesday July 30, 1822
Caesar	Miss Smith	do.	do.
Jacob Stagg	Jacob Lankester	July 23	do.
Tom	William M. Scott	July 24	do.
William	Mrs. Garner	Aug 2	Hanged Fri. Aug. 9

Document 5 "Melancholy Effect of Popular Excitement," Charleston, June 21, 1822.[5]

Anonymous letter reprinted from the *Charleston Courier* but well known to be authored by William Johnson, Associate Justice and brother-in-law to South Carolina's governor.

The following anecdote may be relied on as a simple narrative of facts which actually occurred with the recollection of thousands.

In the year 1810 or 1811, Mr. Blount being Governor of N. Carolina, Mr. Milledge of Geo. and Mr. Drayton of S. Carolina, the two latter states were thrown into great alarm by a letter transmitted from Gov. Blount to Gov. Milledge, and by the latter despatched by express to Gov. Drayten. The militia of the two states in the counties adjacent to Augusta, were orderered to be held in readiness for action, *en masse*, and guards and patrols to scour the country.—The sufferings of the inhabitants, particularly the females, from apprehensions painfully excited, induced a gentleman of this city, then a resident near Augusta, to call on the Governor, then residing near that place, and request a sight of the letter. At the first glance of the eye he pronounced it a hoax: for it bore date on the 1st April, and had been picked up in one of the country towns in N. Carolina, where it had in fact been dropped by some thoughtless schoolboy. On the face of it also it bore such evidence of its origin, as must have struck any observer whose vision was not distorted by alarm. For it was dated Augusta, signed, "Your loving brother Captain Jack" and purported to be directed an associate in Lewisville, N.C. But it was in vain that these suggestions were made. The Governor of Georgia could not brook the mortifying discovery of his having been duped, and the whole country, on the designated night was kept in agitated motion.

Happy had it terminated in nothing more than the suffering and disturbance communicated to the people of both states, and the useless expenditure of some thousands of public money. But another hoax gave it a most tragical termination.

---

5 "Charleston, June 21," *Hallowell Gazette*, (Hallowell, Maine), 10 July 1822, p. 1.

The trumpeter of the Augusta Cavalry resided in the opposite district of Edgefield, and orders had been issued to him to attend the company that night. By some accident these orders did not reach him, in time to make Augusta that evening, and he halted at Moore's mills on Chever's Creek in South Carolina. Here he and a companion were shown into a garrett, where they were amusing themselves over their pint of whiskey, when the continual passing and repassing of the mounted militia drew their attention; and the half intoxicated bugleman resolved to try the effect of a blast of his music upon the fears of a party just gone by. The effect was electrical; it was deemed the expected signal; the detachments galloped off in all directions, in quest of the offender, and towards morning returned with a single poor half witted negro, who had been taken crossing a field on his way home without instrument of war or of music, But none else could be found, and he alone have given the significant blast, which so many had heard. It was in vain that he denied it: he was first whipped severely to extort a confession, and then, with his eyes bound commanded to prepare for instant death from a sabre, which a horseman was in the act of sharpening beside him.

He now recollected that a man named Billy belong to Capt. Key, had one of those long tubes which boatmen use on our rivers, and declared that he had sounded the horn, and done it at the command of Capt. Key's men: but still denied all sort of combination, and affirmed the innocence of the act.

An armed force was immediately detached to the house of Billy, and there found him quietly sleeping in the midst of a large family, in a degree of comfort very uncommon for a slave—for Billy was a blacksmith, a fellow of uncommon worth, and indulged in such privileges by his master as his fidelity justly merited.

But in one corner of the house, exposed to the view of every one, was found the terrific horn, and he was hurried away to be tried for his life. The Court of Magistrates and Freeholders was selected from men of the first respectability in the neighborhood; and yet it is a fact, although no evidence was given whatever as to a motive for sounding the horn, and the horn was actually found covered and even filled with cobwebs, they condemned that man to die the next day!—and, what will scarcely be believed, they actually received evidence of his having been once charged with stealing a pig, to substantiate the charge upon which he then stood on trial. Respectable bystanders have declared, that his guilt or innocence as to the pig soon took the lead of every other question on the trial. The owner, one of the worthiest men in all that country, thunderstruck at the sentence, entreated a more deliberate hearing; not being listened to, hastened away to his friends, and among them a judicial character in the neighborhood, to unite their entreaties with his. They promptly attended to his solicitations, procured a meeting of the court, and earnestly pressed the injustice and precipitation of the sentence, and their right to time to solicit a pardon, but in vain. The presiding magistrate actually conceived his dignity attacked, and threatened impeachment against the jude, who, as an individual, had interfered only to prevent a legal murder; and interfered upon the witness' retracting all he had testified to.

Billy was hung amidst crowds of execrating spectators; and such appeared to be the popular demand for a victim, that it is not certain that a pardon could have saved him.

Document 6 "Sentence of Gullah Jack," *Washington Reporter*, (Washington, PA), 16 September 1822.[6]

The court after deliberately considering all the circumstances of your case, are perfectly satisfied of your guilt. In the prosecution of your wicked designs, you were not satisfied with resorting to natural and ordinary means, but endeavored to enlist on your behalf, all the powers of darkness, and employed for that means the most disgusting mummery and superstition. You represented yourself as invulnerable; that you could neighter be taken nor destroyed; that all who fought under your banners would be invincible. While such wretched expedients are calculated to *inspire* the confidence, or to alarm the fears of the ignorant and credulous, they excite no other creation in the mind of the intelligent and enlightened, but contempt and disgust. Your boasted charms have not protected yourself, and of course could not protect others. "Your altars and your Gods have sunk altogether in the dust." The airy spectres, conjured by you, have been chased away by the special light of truth, and you stand exposed, the miserable and deluded victim of offended justice. Your days are literally numbered. You will shortly be consigned to the cold and silent grave, and all the powers of darkness cannot rescue you from your approaching fate! Let me then, conjure you to devote the remnant of your miserable existence, fleeing from the *"wrath to come."* This can only be done by a full disclosure of the truth. The court is willing to afford you all the aid in their power, and to permit any minister of the gospel, whom you may select, to have free access to you. To him you may unburthen your guilty conscience. Neglect not the opportunity, for there is "no device nor art beyond the tomb," to which you must shortly be consigned.

Document 7 Basil Hall, *Travels in North America in the Years 1827-1828*[7]

In walking round the Capitol at Richmond, in the course of the morning, my eyes were struck with the unusual sight of a sentinel marching in front of the building, with his musket on his shoulder. "Bless me!" I exclaimed, "has your legislature a guard of honour?—that is something new."

"Oh, no, no!" cried my companion, "that soldier is one of the guard stationed near the Capitol;--there are the barracks."

"I do not yet understand."

"It is necessary," he continued, "or at all events it is customary in these States to have a small guard always under arms;--there are only fifty men here. It is in consequence of the nature of our coloured population; but is done more as a preventive check than anything else—it keeps all thoughts of insurrection out of the heads of the slaves, and so gives confidence to those persons amongst us who may be timorous. But in reality, there is no cause for alarm, as it is sixteen years since such a thing was attempted here. And the blacks have become more and more sensible every day of their want of power."

On enquiring further into these matters, I learnt that there was in all these towns a vigorous and active police, whose rule is not to take for granted that any thing is secure which vigilance can watch. No negro, for example, is allowed to be out of doors after sunset, without a written

---

[6] "Sentence of Gullah Jack," *Washington Reporter*, (Washington, PA), 16 September 1822.
[7] Basil Hall, Travels in North America in the Years 1827-1828, Volume III (Edinburgh: Cadell and Co., 1829), p. 73-74.

pass from his master explaining the nature of his errand. If, during his absence from home, he be found wandering from the proper line of his message, he is speedily taken up and corrected accordingly.

Document 8   Frontispiece of Samuel Warner, *Authentic and impartial narrative of the tragical scene which was witnessed in Southampton County*, 1832.[8]

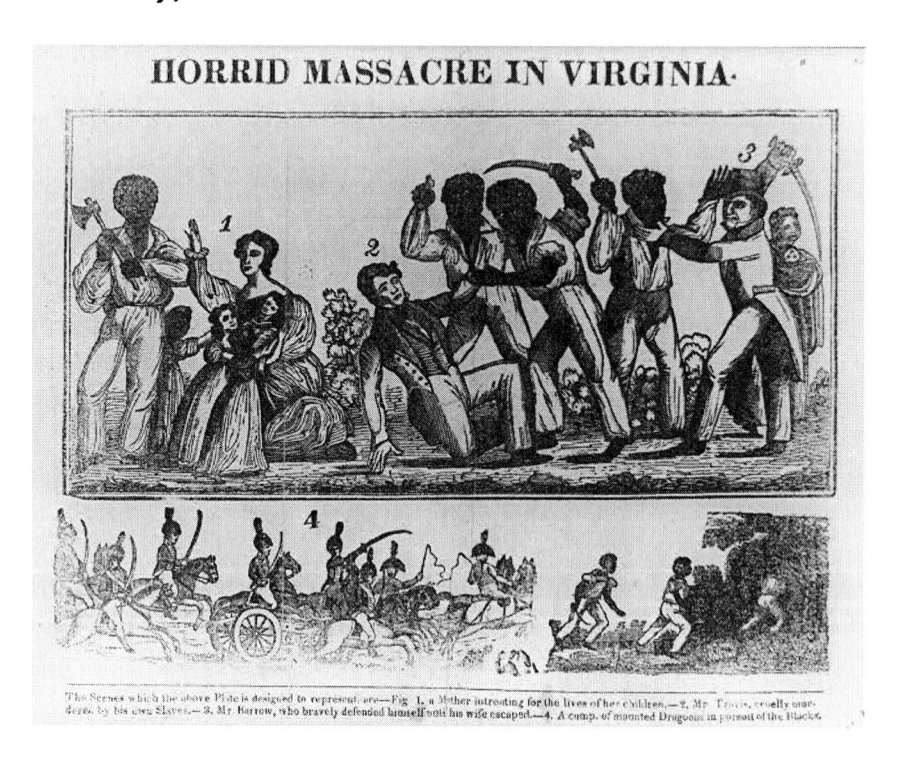

Document 9   *The Confessions of Nat Turner, the leader of the late insurrection in Southampton, VA. As fully and voluntarily made to Thomas R. Gray, in the prison where he was confined, and acknowledged by him to be such when read before the Court of Southampton; with the certificate, under seal of the Court, convened at Jerusalem, Nov. 5, 1831, for his trial.*[9]

Agreeable to his own appointment, on the evening he was committed to prison, with permission of the jailer, I visited NAT on Tuesday the 1st November, when, without being questioned at all, he commenced his narrative in the following words:--

---

8   Frontispiece of Samuel Warner, Authentic and impartial narrative of the tragical scene which was witnessed in Southampton County, 1832 http://digitalcollections.nypl.org/items/29666e80-51c2-0134-a964-00505686a51c

9   Source: Herbert Aptheker, Nat Turner's Slave Rebellion, Together with the Full Text of the So-Called "Confessions" of Nat Turner Made in Prison in 1831 (New York: Humanities Press, 1966).

SIR,--You have asked me to give a history of the motives which induced me to undertake the late insurrection, as you call it—To do so I must go back to the days of my infancy, and even before I was born. I was thirty-one years of age the 2nd of October last, and born the property of Benj. Turner, of this county. In my childhood a circumstance occurred which made an indelible impression on my mind, and laid the ground work of that enthusiasm, which hs terminated so fatally to many, both white and black, and for which I am about to atone at the gallows. It is here necessary to relate this circumstance—trifling as it may seem, it was the commencement of that belief which has grown with time, and even now, sir, in this dungeon, helpless and forsaken as I am, I cannot divest myelf of. Being at play with other children, when three or four years old, I was telling them something, which my mother overhearing, said it had happened before I was born—I stuck to my story, however, and related somethings which went, in her opinion, to confirm it—others being called on were greatly astonished, knowing that these things had happened, and caused them to say in my hearing, I surely would be a prophet, as the Lord had shewn me things that had happened before my birth. And my father and mother strengthened me in this my first impression, saying in my presence, I was intended for some great purpose, which they had always thought from certain marks on my head and breast—*a parcel of excrescences which I believe are not at all uncommon, particularly among negroes, as I have seen several with the same. In this case he has either cut them off or they have nearly disappeared*[10]—My grandmother, who was very religious, and to whom I was much attached—my master, who belonged to the church, and other religious persons who visited the house, and whom I often saw at prayers, noticing the singularity of my manners, I suppose, and my uncommon intelligence for a child, remarked I had too much sense to be raise, and if I was, I would never be of any service to any one as a slave—To a mind my like mine, restless, inquisitive, and observant of every thing that was passing, it is easy to suppose that religion was the subject to which it would be directed, and although this subject principally occupied my thoughts…. The manner in which I learned to read and write, not only had great influence on my own mind, as I acquired it with the most perfect ease, so much so, that I have no recollection whatever of learning the alphabet—but to the astonishment of the family, one day, when a book was shewn to me to keep me from crying, I began spelling the names of different objects—this was a source of wonder to all in the neighborhood, particularly the blacks….

Growing up among them, with this confidence in my superior judgment, and when this, in their opinions, was perfected by Divine inspiration, from the circumstances already alluded to in my infancy, and which belief was ever afterwards zealously inculcated by the austerity of my life and manners, which became the subject of remark by white and black.—By this time, having arrived to man's estate, and hearing the scriptures commented on at meetings, I was struck with that particular passage which says: "Seek ye the kingdom of Heaven and all things shall be added unto you." I reflected on this passage, and prayed daily for light on this subject—As I was praying one day at my plough, the spirit spoke to me, saying "Seek ye the kingdom of Heaven and all things shall be added unto you."

Question—what do you mean by the spirit? Answer: The Spirit that spoke to the prophets in former days—and I was greatly astonished, and for two years prayed continually, whenever my duty would permit—and then again I had the same revelation, which fully confirmed me in the impression that I was ordained for some great purpose in the hands of the Almighty. …

---

10   Italicized text are questions or commentary of the journalist, Thomas R. Gray. Text in brackets are this author's.

Now finding I had arrived to man's estate, and was a slave, and these revelations being known to me, I began to direct my attention to this great object, to fulfil the purpose for which, by this time, I felt assured I was intended. Knowing the influence I had obtained over the minds of my fellow servants,....I often communicated to them, and they believed and said my wisdom came from God. I now began to prepare them for my purpose, by telling them something was about to happen that would terminate in fulfilling the great promise that had been made to me— About this time I was placed under an overseer, from whom I ranaway—and after remaining in the woods thirty days, I returned, to the astonishment of the negroes on the plantation, who thought I had made my escape.... But the reason of my return was, that the Spirit appeared to me and said I had my wishes directed to the things of this world, and not to the kingdom of Heaven, and that I should return to the service of my earthly master—"For he who knoweth his Master's will, and doeth it not, shall be beaten with many stripes, and thus have I chastened you." And the negroes found fault, and murmured against me, saying that if they had my sense they would not serve any master in the world. And about this time I had a vision—and I saw white spirits and black spirits engaged in battle, and the sun was darkened—the thunder rolled in the Heavens, and blood flowed in streams. –And I heard a voice saying, "Such is your luck, such you are called to see, and let it come rough or smooth, you must surely bare it. I now withdrew myself as much as my situation would permit, from the intercourse of my fellow servants, for the avowed purpose of serving the Spirit more fully....

After this revelation in the year 1825, and the knowledge of the elements being made known to me, I sought more than ever to obtain true holiness before the great day of judgment should apper, and then I began to receive the true knowledge of faith. And from the first steps of righteousness until the last, was I made perfect; and the Holy Ghost was with me, and said, "Behold me as I stand in the Heavens"—and I looked and saw the forms of men in different attitudes and there were lights in the sky to which the children of darkness gave other names than what they really were—for they were the lights of the Savior's hands, stretched forth from east to west, even as they were extended on the cross on Calvary for the redemption of sinners. And I wondered greatly at these miracles, and prayed to be informed of a certainty of the meaning thereof—and shortly afterwards, while laboring in the field, I discovered drops of blood on the corn as though it were dew from heaven—and I communicated it to many, both white and black, in the neighborhood—and I then foundon the leaves in the woods hieroglyphic characters, and numbers, with the forms of men in different attitudes, portrayed in blood, and representing the figures I had seen before in the heavens. It was plain to me that the Savior was about to lay down the yoke he had borne for the sins of men, and the great day of judgment was at hand....

And on the 12th of May, 1828, I heard a loud noise in the heavens, and the Spirit instantly appeared to me and said the Serpant was loosened, and Christ had laid down the yoke he had borne for the sins of men, and that I should take it on and fight against the Serpent, for the time was fast approaching when the first should be last and the last should be first.

Question: Do you not find yourself mistaken now?

Answer: Was not Christ crucified?

And by signs in the heavens that it would make known to me when I should commence the great work—and until the first sign appeared, I should conceal it from the knowledge of men—And on the appearance of the first sign, (the eclipse of the sun last February) I should arise and prepare myself, and slay my enemies with their own weapons. And immediately on the sign appearing in the heavens, the seal was removed from my lips, and I communicated the great work laid out for me to do, to four in whom I had greatest confidence, (Henry, Hark, Nelson, and Sam)—It was intended by us to begun the work of death no the 4th July last—Many were the plans formed and rejected by us, and it affected my mind to such a degree, that I fell sick, and the time passed without our coming to any determination how to commence—Still forming new schemes, and rejecting them, when the sign appeared again, which determined me not to wait longer.

[At a late night meeting August 20, 1831 the slaves Nat Turner, Henry, Hark, Nelson, Sam, Will, and Jack decided to begin the attack at the home of Joseph Travis, Nat Turner's master beginning in 1830.]

It was quickly agreed we should commence at home on that night and until we had armed and equipped ourselves, and gathered sufficient force, neither age nor sex was to be spared. We remained at the feast, until about two hours in the night when we went to the house…. Hark went to the door with an axe, for the purpose of breaking it open, as we knew we were strong enough to murder the family, if they awaked by the noise; but reflecting that it might create an alarm in the neighborhood, we determined to enter the house secretly, and murder them whilst sleeping. Hark got a ladder and set it against the chimney, on which I ascended, and hoisting a window, entered and came down stairs, unbarred the door, and removed the guns from their places. It was then observed that I must spill the first blood. On which, armed with a hatchet, and accompanied by Will, I entered my master's chamber, it being dark, I could not give a death blow, the hatchet glanced from his head, he sprang from the bed and called his wife, it was his last word, Will laid him dead, with a blow of his axe, and Mrs. Travis shared the same fate, as she lay in bed. The murder of this family, five in number, was the work of a moment, not one of them awoke; there was a little infant sleeping in a cradle, that was forgotten, until we had left the house and gone some distance, when Henry and Will returned and killed it; we got here, four guns that would shoot, and several old muskets, with a pound or two of powder.

We remained some time at the barn, … I formed them in a line as soldiers, and after carrying them through all the manoeuvres I was master of, marched them off to Mr. Salathul Francis', about six hundred yards distant. Sam and Will went to the door and knocked. Mr. Francis asked who was there, Sam replied it was him, and he had a letter for him, on which he got up and came to the door; they immediately seized him, and dragging him out a little from the door, he was dispatched by repeated blows on the head; there was no other white person in the family. We started from there for Mrs. Reese's, maintaining the most perfect silence on our march, where finding the door unlocked, we entered, and murdered Mrs. Reese in her bed, while sleeping; her son awoke, but it was only to sleep the sleep of death, he had only time to say who is that, and he was no more. From Mrs. Reese's we went to Mrs. Turner's, a mile distant, which we reached about sunrise, on Monday morning. Henry, Austin, and Sam, went to the still, where, finding Mr. Peebles, Austin shot him, and the rest of us went to the house; as we approached the family discovered us, and shut the door. Vain hope! Will with one stroke of his axe, opened it, and we entered and found Mrs. Turner and Mrs. Newsome in the middle of a room, almost frightened to death. Will immediately killed Mrs. Turner, with one blow of his axe. I took Mrs. Newsome by the hand, and with the sword I had when I was apprehended, I struck her several blows over the head, but was not able to kill her, as the sword was dull. Will turning around and discovering it, despatched her also. A general destruction of property and search for money and ammunition, always succeeded the murders. By this time, my company amounted to fifteen, and nine men mounted, who started for Mrs. Whitehead's, (the other six were to go through a by way to Mr. Bryant's and rejoin us at Mrs. Whitehead's). …

[Mrs. Whitehead, her adult son, four daughters and a grandchild were killed as were Henry Bryant, his wife and mother-in-law, and their child. The group of rebels then divided, part going to Richard Porter's farm and then to Nathaniel Francis's plantation, and the others directed to Howell Harris's and Trajan Doyle's places. Turner went to Porter's place where he found that the family had escaped, and recognized that the alarm had been spread. Nathaniel Francis's overseer and two children were murdered, as was Trajan Doyle. Harris was not at home and thus spared. In the early hours of the uprising, Peter Edwards and John T. Barrows were also killed.]

… on their track to Capt. Newit Harris's, … I found the greater part mounted, and ready to start; the men now amounting to about forty, shouted and hurraed as I rode up, some were in the yards, loading their guns, others drinking. They said Captain Harris and his family had escaped, the property in the house they destroyed, robbing him of money and other valuables. I ordered them to mount and march instantly, this was about nine or ten o'clock, Monday morning. I proceeded to Mr. Levi Waller's, two or three miles distant. I took my station in the rear, and as it was my object to carry terror and devastation wherever we went, I placed fifteen or twenty of the best armed and most relied on, in front, who generally approached the houses as fast as their horses could run; this was for two purposes, to prevent escape and strike terror to the inhabitants—on this account I never got to the houses, after leaving Mrs. Whitehead's, until the murders were committed, except in one case. I sometimes got in sight in time to see the work of death completed, viewed the mangled bodies as they lay, in silent satisfaction, and immediately started in quest of other victims.….

… I determined on starting for Jerusalem—Our number amounted now to fifty or sixty, all mounted and armed with guns, axes, swords and clubs—On reaching Mr. James Parker's gate, immediately on the road leading to Jerusalem, and about three miles distant, it was proposed to me to call there, but I objected, as I knew he was gone to Jerusalem, and my object was to reach there as soon as possible; but some of the men having relations at Mr. Parker's it was agreed that they might call and get his people. I remained at the gate on the road, with seven or eight; the others going across the field to the house, about a half a mill off. After waiting some time for them, I became impatient, and started to the house for them, and on our return we were met by a party of white men, who had pursued our blood-stained track, and who had fired on those at the gate, and dispersed them. ….

… Immediately on discovering the whites, I ordered my men to halt and form, as they appeared to be alarmed—The white men, eighteen in number, approached us in about one hundred yards, when one of them fired [against their commander's orders]. –And I discovered half of them retreating, I then ordered my men to fire and rush them; the few remaining stood their ground until we approached within fifty yards, when they fired and retreated. We pursued and overtook some of them who we thought we left dead; (they were not killed) after pursuing them about two hundred yards, and rising a little hill, I discovered they were met by another party, and had halted, and were re-loading their guns… As I saw them reloading their guns, and more coming up than I saw at first, and several of my bravest men were wounded, the others became panick struck and squandered over the field; the white men pursued and fired on us several times. Hark had his horse shot under him, and I caught another for him as it was running by me; five or six of my men were wounded, but none left on the field; …. After trying in vain to collect a sufficient force to proceed to Jerusalem, I determined to return, as I was sure they would make back to their old neighborhood, where they would rejoin me, make new recruits, and come down again.... We stopped at Major Ridley's quarter for the night, and being joined by four of his men, with recruits made since my defeat, we mustered about forty strong. After placing out sentinels, I laid down to sleep, but was quickly roused ... one of the sentinels having given the alarm that we were about to be attacked. [In the confusion of the retreat, Turner's force was first reduced to twenty men most of whom deserted him soon after.]

... on Thursday night after having supplied myself with provisions from Mr. Travis's, I scratched a hole under a pile of fence rails in a field, where I concealed myself for six weeks, neve leaving my hiding place but for a few minutes in the dead of night to get water which was very near; thinking by this time I could venture out, I began to go about in the night and evesdrop the houses in the neighborhood; pursuing this course for about a fortnight and gathering little or no intelligence, afraid of speaking to any human being, and returning every morning to my cave before the dawn of day. I know not how long I might have led this life, if accident had not betrayed me....

Document 10   James Stirling, *Letters from the Slave States*[11]

New Orleans, 16 December 1856

We made many pleasant acquaintances on board the Cumberland and Mississippi steamers. When well-educated Southerners know that you mean no harm to them or theirs, although you may differ from them in opinion, they are most kind, one introducing you to another, and so passing you along a whole chain of kindly hospitalities. On the other hand, the lower set of people are morose and suspicious. They dog your steps, and watch your every word. I had to endure more espionage on the Mississippi than in Austrian Italy. There you have to do only with paid professional spies: here your fellow-traveller is your spy. Yet, after all, this suspicion is a necessity of the slave-owner's position. He must be watchful, for all around him there is danger.

The South seems to me in that mood of mind which foreruns destruction: there is a curse upon the land. Materially, its progress is naught; were it not for its cotton, it would be as wretched, poverty-stricken a country as Mexico. There is no enterprise, no capital. Then, in a social point of view, it is a sheer, downright despotism, without liberty of thought or speech. Fear and suspicion have taken possession of their souls, and no wonder. ... abortive attempts at insurrection, which will be put down by brute force; but the spirit of insurrection is a devil that will not be so easily laid, and sooner or later the fears of the South will be changed to a dread reality. Even at this moment the planter lays himself to bed with pistols under his pillow, never knowing when the wild whoop of insurrection may awaken him to a bloody fight. The whole South is like one of her own cotton-steamers—such as I have just left, filled from the hold to the topmost deck with the most inflammable matter; everything heated up to the burning point, a furious draft blowing from end to end, and a huge high pressure boiler in her belly, pressed to bursting. Is it pleasant to live in such a country? I have slept for nights over the boiler, and can tell you it is very far from pleasant.

---

11   James Stirling, Letters from the Slave States (London: John W. Parker and Son, 1857), p. 59.

Document 11 Testimony of Jane Sutton, 84 years old, Gulf Port, Mississippi, 1936[12]

"… I 'members de paterollers. Whenever de cullud folks would slip off an' have dey frolicks without gittin' a pass from Old Marster de paterollers would come. Lots-a time dey'd come while us was a-dancin' an' a-havin a big time. Dem paterollers would swarm in de room lak a lot o' bees. Fore anybody knowed it, dey'd begin grabbing at de mens. If dey didn' have dey pass wid 'em dey took 'em down in de woods an' whup 'em for runnin' off wid out asking dey white folks. Dey didn' bother de wimmins much. De wimmins mos' always got away while dey was catchin' de mens.

Onct I slipped off wid another gal an' went to a party dout asking Old Mis'. When dem Night Riders come dat night, de N___ was a-runnin' an' a-dodgin' an' a-jumpin' out-a winders lak dey was scairt to death. I runs too, me an' dat other gal.

Document 12 Frederick Law Olmsted, *A Journey in the Back Country*, 443.[13]

Will any traveler say that he has seen no signs of discontent, or insecurity, or apprehension, or precaution; that the South has appered quieter and less excited, even on the subject of slavery, than the North; that the negroes seem happy and contented, and the citizens more tranquilly engaged in the pursuit of their business and pleasure? Has the traveler been in Naples? Precisely the same remarks apply to the appearance of things there at this moment. The massacre of Haiti opened in a ball-room. Mr. Cobden judged there was not the smallest reason in the French king's surrounding himself with soldiers the day before the hidden forces of insubordination broke forth and cast him forth from his kingdom. It is true, however, that the tranquility of the South is the tranquility of Hungary and of Poland, rather than of France or the Two Sicilies; the tranquility of hopelessness on the part of the subject race. But in the most favored regions, this broken spirit of despair is as carefully preserved by the citizens, and with as confident and unhesitating an application of force, when necessary to teach humility, as it is by the army of the Czar, or the omnipresent police of the Kaiser. In Richmond, and Charleston, and New Orleans, the citizens are as careless and gay as in Boston or London, and their servants a thousand times as childlike and cordial, to all appearance, in their relations with them as our servants are with us. But to the bottom of this security and dependence, and you come to police machinery such as you never find in towns under free government: citidels, sentries, passports, grape-shotted cannon, and daily public whippings of the subjects for accidental infractions of police ceremonies. I happened myself to see more direct expression of tyranny in a single day and night at Charleston, than at Naples in a week; and I found that more than half the inhabitants of this town were subject to arrest, imprisonment, and barbarous punishment if found in the streets without a passport after the evening "gunfire."[curfew notice] Similar precautions and similar customs may be discovered in every large town in the South.

Nor is it so much better, as is generally imagined, in the rural districts. Ordinarily there is no show of government than at the North: the slaves go about with as much apparent freedom

---

12   Testimony of Jane Sutton, 84 years old, Gulf Port, Mississippi, *Slave Narratives from the Federal Writers' Project, 1936-1938. Mississippi,* (Bedford, MA: Applewood Books and Library of Congress, 1936).
13   Frederick Law Olmsted, *Travels through*

as convicts in a dock-yard. There is, however, nearly everywhere, always prepared to act, if not always in service, an armed force, with a military organization, which is invested with more arbitrary and cruel power than any police in Europe. Yet the security of the whites is in a much less degree contingent on the actions of the patrols than upon the constant, habitual, and instinctive surveillance and authority of all white people over all black. I have seen a gentleman, with no commission or special authority, oblige negroes to show their passports, simply because he did not recognize them as belonging to any of his neighbors. I have seen a girl, twelve years old, in a district where, in ten miles, the slave population was fifty to one of the free, stop an old man on the public road, demand to know where he was going, and by what authority, order him to face about and return to his plantation, and enforce her command with turbulent anger, when he hesitated, by threatenging that she would have him well whipped if he did not instantly obey. The man quailed like a spaniel, and she instantly resumed the manner of a lovely child with me, no more apprehending that she had acted unbecomingly, than that her character had influenced the slave's submission to her caprice of supremacy; no more conscious that she had increased the security of her life by strengthening the habit of the slave to the master race, ...

Document 13 *The Code of Alabama, 1852.*[14]

Chapter III Patrols

Section 983   All white male owners of slaves, below the age of sixty years, and all other free white persons, between the ages of eighteen and forty-five years, who are not disabled by sickness or bodily infirmity, except commissioned officers in the militia, and persons exempt by law from the performance of militia duty, are subject to perform patrol duty.

Section 991   Any member of a patrol detachment may send a substitute, who, if accepted by the leader, may patrol in his stead.

Section 992   The patrol has power to enter, in a peaceable manner, upon any plantation; to enter by force, if necessary, all negro cabins or quarters, kitchens and out houses, and to apprehend all slaves who may there be found, not belonging to the plantation or household, without a pass from their owner or overseer; or strolling from place to place, without authority.

Section 993   The patrol has power to punish slaves found under the circumstances recited in the preceding section, by stripes, not exceeding thirty-nine.

Chapter IV Slaves

Section 1005   No master, overseer, or other person having the charge of a slave, must permit such slave to hire himself to another person, or to hire his own time, or to go at large unless in a corporate town, by consent of the authorities thereof, evidenced by an ordinance of the corporation; and every such offence is a misdemeanor, punishable by fine not less than twenty nor more than one hundred dollars.

---

14   *Code of Alabama*, prepared by John J. Ormond, Arthur P. Bagby, George Goldthwaite, (Montgomery: Brittan and De Wolf, State Printers, 1852), pp. 234-237.

Section 1006   No master, overseer, or head of a family must permit any slave to be or remain at his house, out house, or kitchen, without leave of the owner or overseer, above four hours at any one time; and for every such offence he forfeits ten dollars, to be recovered before any justice of the peace, by any person who may sue for the same.

Section 1007   Any owner or overseer of a plantation, or householder, who knowingly permits more than five negroes, other than his own, to be and remain at his house, plantation, or quarter, at any one time, forfeits ten dollars for each and every over that number, to the use of any one who may sue for the same, before any justice of the peace; unless such assemblage is for the worship of almighty God, or for burial service, and with the consent of the owner or overseer of such slaves.

Section 1008   No slave must go beyond the limits of the plantation on which he resides without a pass, or some letter or token from his master or overseer, giving him authority to go and return from a certain place; and if found violating this law, may be apprehended and punished, not exceeding twenty stripes, at the disretion of any justice before whom he may be taken.

Section 1009   If any slave go upon the plantation or enter the house or out house of any person, without permission in writing from his master or overseer, or in the prosecution of his lawful business, the owner or overseer of such plantation or householder may give, or order such slave to be given ten lashes on his bare back.

Section 1012   No slave can keep or carry a gun, powder, shot, club, or other weapon, ecept the tools given him to work with, unless ordered by his master or overseer to carry such a weapon from one place to another. Any slave found offending against the provisions of this section, may be seized, with such weapon, by any one, and carried before any justice, who, upon proof of the offence, must condemn the weapon to the use of such person, and direct that the slave receive thirty-nine lashes on his bare back.

Section 1014   No slave can, under any pretence, keep a dog; and for every such offence must be punished by any justice of the peace with twenty stripes on his bare back.

Section 1016   Any person having knowledge of the commission of any offence by a slave against the law, may apprehend him, and take him before a justice of the peace for trial.

Section 1019   Any slave who writes for, or furnishes any other slave with any pass or free paper, on conviction before any justice of the peace, must receive one hundred lashes on his bare back.

Section 1020   Not more than five male slaves shall assemble together at any place off the plantation, or place to which they belong, with or without passes or permits to be there, unless attended by the master or overseer of such slaves, unless such slaves are attending the publish worship of God, held by white persons.

Section 1022   Any slave who preaches, exhorts, or harangues any assembly of slaves, or of slaves and free persons of color, without a license to preach or exhort from some religious society of the neighborhood, and in the presence of five slave-holders, must, for the first offence, be punished with tnirty-nine lashes, and for the second, with fifty lashes; which punishment may be inflicted by any officer of a patrol company, or by the order of any justice of the peace.

Chapter V   Free Negroes

Section 1033   Every free colored person who has come to this state since the first day of February, 1832, and has been admonished by any sheriff, justice of the peace, or other judicial officer, that he cannot, by law remain in this state; and does not, within thirty days, depart therefrom, must on conviction, be punished by imprisonment in the penitentiary for two years; and shall have thirty days after his discharge from the penitentiary to leave the state; and on failing to do so, must be imprisoned in the penitentiary for five years.

Section 1042   Any free person of color, found in company with any slave, in any kitchen, out house, or negro quarter, without a written permission from the owner, or overseer of such slave, must for every such offence, receive fifteen lashes; and for every subsequent offence, thirty-nine lashes; which may be inflicted by the owner or overseer of the slave, or by any officer or member of any patrol company.

ANALYZING THE EVIDENCE

1. Analyze carefully the court reports detailing investigations into Gabriel's conspiracy (Document 1). Answer the following questions as you read the document:
    a. How did Gabriel's conspiracy reveal evidence of careful planning on the part of the conspirators?
    b. What slaves were involved in the leadership of the conspiracy?
    c. How did the conspirators use social gatherings to plan and organize the rebellion?
    d. What were the different targets of the rebels? Why were these chosen?
    e. What motivated slaves to join the conspiracy?
    f. What hierarchies developed within the ranks of the conspirators? How did this mirror military hierarchies?
    g. What role did free blacks play in the conspiracy?
2. Analyze the Deslondes uprising in New Orleans in 1811. (Document 2)
    a. According to this account, what motivated the slaves in their uprising?
    b. What were the reactions of whites in Louisiana to the uprising?
    c. How were the rebels characterized in the media?
3. Analyze the Vesey Conspiracy in Charleston, South Carolina. (Document 3, 4, 5)
    a. According to the Official Account (Document 3)
        i. What factors led to the Vesey conspiracy?
        ii. How was Vesey characterized?
        iii. What motivated his leadership of this rebellion?
    b. In the "Negro Plot" (Document 4)
        i. What means were employed to discover the details of the plot? Why might William have disclosed the plot?

ii. What role did secret trials and anonymous witnesses have played in the discovery of the plot?

iii. What factors contributed to the large numbers of conspirators tried and executed (or exiled) as a result of their involvement in the Vesey conspiracy?

c. What did the "Melancholy Effect" (Document 5) letter suggest about the Vesey conspiracy? Why might the reports in Documents 3 and 4 have been written in response to the "Meloncholy Effect" letter?

d. Who was Gullah Jack (Document 6) and why was he such an important figure in the Vesey conspiracy?

e. Do you think the Vesey Conspiracy was actually being planned? Why or why not?

4. After having read the material on the Vesey conspiracy, what thoughts do you have on Gabriel Prosser's conspiracy?

5. How did the report of Basil Hall's travels reveal fears of insurrection in the South? (Document 7)

6. Analyze the sources relating to Nat Turner's Rebellion (Documents 8 and 9)

   a. Who was Nat Turner?

   b. What role did scripture reading play in motivating Turner in his rebellion?

   c. Compare the organization of the Turner, Vesey, and Gabriel conspiracies.

7. How did the fear of rebellion affect southerners? (Document 11-13)

8. What repressive police measures does Frederick Law Olmsted identify in the South? (Document 12)

9. How did Southern states use the patrol system to control African Americans and restrain the possibility of insurrection? (What parallels are there between the antebellum patrol system and the contemporary system of policing in the United States? What differences?)

DOCUMENT BASED QUESTIONS

1. Using the documents provided, analyze the methods and objectives of African American slave rebellions.

2. Using the documents provided, analyze the methods and objectives of southern efforts to restrain or repress slave rebellions in the antebellum period.

Antebellum Culture Wars

CHAPTER 11

Since the 1990s struggles for political power in the United States have often been cast as part of a "culture war" between those who consider themselves traditionalists or conservatives and those who favor liberal or progressive policies and values. The term itself is not new and recalls the German *Kulturkampf* or "culture struggle" of the late nineteenth century. And, while the term culture war was not used to describe the political and cultural confrontations of the antebellum period, Americans from the 1830s until the beginning of the Civil War engaged in what might rightly be called a culture war. The issue of slavery was at the heart of this cultural and political divide. And, just as in the contemporary "culture war" that has split the United States, opponents engaged along shifting fronts, facing off over a range of issues. Antebellum culture wars also saw a variety of political strategies made in a wide variety of media outlets as both sides sought to influence elections and control the national dialogue. This chapter asks readers to examine the arguments and changing strategies of the abolitionists and their allies and then engage the counter-arguments that pro-slavery advocates put forward in support of their positions.

The abolitionist movement, of course, was not a nineteenth-century development. It had its first flourishing in the second half of the eighteenth century, primarily in England, though there were important anti-slavery advocates in the Americas. Quakers like John Woolman and Benjamin Lay are often mentioned among the early and most effective opponents of slavery in the colonies. Lay had shocked Quakers in Philadelphia and elsewhere with his vehement opposition to slavery. He was known to smash tea sets, drawing the connection between tea, sugar, and slavery, or to splash sheeps' blood on worshipers, raging at the bloody slave trade. Woolman in 1754 published a tract entitled, *Some Considerations on the Keeping of Negroes*. Most of Woolman's outreach, however, took place in the context of the Quaker Meeting Houses that he visited and in his travels. In the former, he would express his "leading" to speak out against Quaker ownership of slaves. As Woolman traveled around the country, as a merchant and notary, he also made personal yet public sacrifices designed to highlight the injustices of slavery and his unwillingness to benefit from such an inhumane system of exploitation. He refused to draw up wills or other contracts involving transfers of slaves; he refused to drink or eat from utensils he believed had come from slave labor. Finally, he would insist on paying slaves who waited on him when he was visiting Quakers who owned slaves. Woolman's soft-spoken method and personal outreach had a positive effect on Quakers who gradually came to condemn the practice in their members. The Quakers were not alone among American religious groups advocating for an end to slavery. Methodists during the colonial period also took the lead among religious communities in calling for abolition. Religious reformers would also be prominent in the nineteenth century's abolitionist movement. Ministers also actively defended the institution as well.

Anti-slavery sentiment flourished in the Revolutionary era as well, despite the fact that British threats to the institution were prominent among the factors that led to the rebellion in the first place. Historians have frequently noted the vocal criticism directed at the institution of slavery by all the great American statesmen of the period from 1770 to 1810, even as many of these same figures continued to own slaves. John Adams, Samuel Adams, John Dickinson, Benjamin Franklin, Alexander Hamilton, Patrick Henry, John Jay, Thomas Jefferson, James Madison, George Mason, James Monroe, Thomas Paine, and George Washington are only the most prominent of the "Founding Fathers" who expressed reservations at the new republic's reliance on slavery. The inconsistency between the American creed outlined in the Declaration of Independence, "that all men are created equal, that they are endowed by their Creator with certain inalienable rights, that among these are life, liberty, and the pursuit of happiness," and the realities of slavery's persistence was not lost on the nation's leaders. But, fear of unsettling the delicate political status quo, fear of angering a populace that depended upon enslaved labor, and a commitment to the principle of property rights, even those in human beings, was coupled with a racist conviction that freed blacks could not be socially or politically integrated into the new republic and fear that the perpetuation of slavery could only lead to violent insurrection by the enslaved. In 1781 in his *Notes on the State of Virginia* Thomas Jefferson pessimistically considered the implications of the persistence of slavery:

> Deep rooted prejudices entertained by the whites; ten thousand recollections, by the blacks, of the injuries they have sustained; new provocations; the real distinctions which nature has made; and many other circumstances which will probably never end but in the extermination of the one or the other race.

In 1824, he more famously concluded, "…as it is, we have the wolf by the ear, and we can neither hold him, nor safely let him go. Justice is on one scale, and self-preservation in the other."

Jefferson, like most early 19th century white Americans, conceived the solution to the "problem" of slavery—a problem it should be noted for whites concerned largely with the effects of slavey on whites—as emancipation coupled with "colonization." According to these proposals, enslavers would be paid a fair reimbursement for the loss of their property, the enslaved would be granted their freedom, and they would be expatriated back to Africa. At its core, these colonization schemes were racist and poorly conceived on many fronts. Most importantly, African Americans had little interest in these proposals. Most African Americans were native to the country; few by this time were African born. Moreover, the prospects of freed slaves in Africa were uncertain at best. And, finally, slaves were both so numerous and so critical to the American economy that no colonization scheme had any hope of fulfilling the dubious and racist promises they held out.

Nonetheless, in 1816 the American Colonization Society was founded, with the express aim of establishing a colony on the coast of West Africa where freedmen and women might settle. In 1822, the Society began sending African Americans to what was called Liberia. By 1867 more than 13,000 African Americans had settled in the region. Though this number was not inconsequential and the role of these settlers in the establishment of the modern nation of Liberia was an important one, as a measure to end slavery and remove blacks from the South, it could only be considered a failure. Indeed, by 1830 the number of enslaved persons in the United States, despite the ending of the African slave trade in 1808, had grown to nearly 2 million from just under 700,000 in 1790.

During the first three decades of the republic, the most ardent opponents of slavery were African Americans themselves. These "Black Founders" were the true inheritors of the possibilities for social reform raised in the American Revolution. Lemuel Haynes, a theologian, and a soldier in the Continental Army, had intuitively grasped the abolitionist implications of republican ideals and united the revolutionary claims of human equality with earlier evangelical ideals of interracial harmony. The revival then that Haynes preached was a spiritual and political regeneration that resulted from a refashioning of race relations. As Peter Williams wrote July 4, 1830, "We are natives of this country, we ask only to be treated as well as FOREIGNERS.... We have toiled to cultivate it, and to raise it to its present prosperous condition; we ask only to share equal privileges with those who come from distant lands, to enjoy the fruits of our labor."

In the 1820s, however, there was a revival of abolitionist sentiment and activism both within and beyond the free black community. In part, the new abolitionism reflected the impact of the religious revival movement, often called the Second Great Awakening. This "awakening" was most prominent among Baptist, Methodist, and Wesleyan congregations. Revivalists in these denominations made a direct connection between individual conversion, the doctrine of "Holiness" which posited the possibility of personal spiritual perfectibility, and the need for social and political reform. The Calvinist strand of Protestantism had pessimistically emphasized the lasting effects of original sin and human depravity. This human condition was only overcome through the intervention of God's inscrutable grace, predestined to only a spiritual few, the elect. In the Calvinist tradition as well, human institutions, though necessarily flawed, were set in place to control human willfulness and sin. The revivalists of the Second Great Awakening, however, countered that individual sinners could through their own will and labor undergo conversion and achieve salvation. Following conversion, the "born again" might also experience a "sanctification" process that freed them from the effects of sin. For revivalists as well, human institutions could also be subjected to a similar process of Godly reform that brought social and political conditions into conformity with Godly design. These evangelicals then promoted a range of social reform platforms with the object of transforming American society and politics. These included a war against prostitution, the temperance movement, Sabbatarianism, and efforts to reform the penal system. The anti-slavery campaigns of the antebellum period derived from many of the same impulses for social and political reform of the United States. Slavery was in this context often cast as the quintessential American sin.

Though Quakerism did not precisely fit within the parameters of the evangelicalism of the early nineteenth century, Quakers once again were prominent in early calls for an end to slavery. Benjamin Lundy, a Quaker from New Jersey, was led at an early age to take a stand against slavery. A saddler by trade, he gave up the business to learn newspaper publishing. In 1819 he moved to St. Louis, Missouri, at the height of the controversy over Missouri statehood. He set up a printshop there to advocate for Missouri's entry as a non-slaveholding state. After Missouri's admission as a slave state, Lundy returned east, settling in Ohio where he began to print the abolitionist newspaper, the *Genius of Universal Emancipation*. Lundy also went on frequent and lengthy speaking tours promoting a gradualist agenda for ending slavery. Lundy also took his message into slave-holding states, and published his newspaper in cities like Baltimore, where he faced significant personal risk. In September 1829, Lundy hired William Lloyd Garrison to assist him in publishing the *Genius*. For the next three decades Garrison would represent one of the most visible figures in the movement to end slavery in the country.

Garrison had been associated with the American Colonization Society but came to favor immediate emancipation without repatriation. He also moved away from Lundy's more gradualist approach. In 1831 he began to publish his own newspaper, the *Liberator*. Garrison was considered a fanatic and extremist, even by many fellow abolitionists. For example, Garrison considered the United States Constitution unworkable as framework for government of a free society. Garrison was unusual among white abolitionists as well for his openness to the acceptance of free blacks into anti-slavery societies, and his willingness to call for black social and political equality. Like Lundy, Garrison faced physical threats; he was nearly tarred and feathered in Boston in 1835 and had a bounty of $5,000 offered by the Georgia legislature to anyone who would capture and bring him to trial in Georgia.

Garrison, and the new radicalism of the abolition movement in the 1830s was in many ways driven by African-American activism in the cause. Garrison's earliest audience and support came most clearly from free blacks in northern cities; nearly three-fourths of his early subscribers were African Americans. African-American churches, located theologically within the Baptist, Methodist, and Wesleyan evangelical traditions, not surprisingly were quick to identify the central sin of American society with slavery. Black church leaders then took on leading roles in the abolition movement, building on the abolitionism of the "Black Founders" who had employed the rhetoric of the American Revolution to challenge the institution.

Among the notable black leaders of the abolition cause, William Cooper Nell illustrates the commitment exhibited in opposition to slavery. Born a free man in Boston in 1816, Nell would recollect an early academic slight as one moment motivating him to struggle for equality and freedom. As a thirteen year-old his performance in a grammar-school writing competition had entitled him to receive a medal and recognition at a banquet dinner with the Boston mayor. He was not given the deserved medal, nor was he invited to the banquet. He recalled later that he vowed then, "I would do my best to hasten the day when color of the skin would be no barrier to equal school rights." He would ultimately become a minister, a practicing lawyer, and collaborator with William Lloyd Garrison on the *Liberator*. He fought adamantly against segregated anti-slavery organizations. His writing frequently criticized anti-black racism, both within the anti-slavery movement and in the wider society. He was among the founders of a "Freedom Association," an organization that, in violation of fugitive slave laws, assisted slaves in their passage to Canada. He was active in other ways in the Underground Railroad. He stood unsuccessfully for election to the Massachusetts legislature as a candidate from the Free Soil Party. He also published a history of African-American soldiers in the American Revolutionary War and the War of 1812. Nell was only one of many African Americans who actively pushed white America to live up to the ideals of liberty and equality.

Perhaps the most recognized African-American anti-slavery activists were Frederick Douglass and Sojourner Truth, both of whom had been born into slavery. The eloquence with which they described their experiences drew large audiences. Douglass would often open his lectures, even at a time when he was still legally the property of his owner, with the wry observation, "I appear before you this evening as a thief and a robber... I stole this head, these limbs, this body from my master, and ran off with them." Douglass was only legally freed on a visit to Great Britain in 1846 when money was raised there to pay for Douglass's freedom from his owner, Thomas Auld. By that time, he had long been active in the abolitionist cause, publishing his autobiography, *Narrative of the Life of Frederick Douglass, an American Slave*, in 1845. Douglass, unlike Nell, had disagreed with Garrison, primarily on the liberalism of the United States Constitution, and in 1847 began publishing his own abolitionist newspaper, *The North Star*.

Sojourner Truth, a name she took herself, was born Isabella Van Waganen, a slave in Ulster County, New York owned by a family of Dutch-speaking farmers. In fact, she spoke Dutch as her first language, a was the case often with rural New York slaves in the eighteenth century. She gained her freedom in 1827. Truth was influenced by the revivalist movement and the Holiness Doctrine preached by Methodists. As her owner, recalled decades later, she left behind her "fondness of liquor and tobacco." Truth also at this time struggled to regain her son, Peter, who had been sold illegally to an Alabama planter. As slavery was gradually ended in New York, many slave owners in the state had sought to profit by selling their slaves to southern owners. In a long legal process Truth was able to get Peter back, but the child bore the physical scars of the whippings and beatings his master had meted out to him over the year, as well as the psychological battering of losing his mother. In 1843, upon changing her name, Truth became an itinerant preacher and abolitionist, giving a speech that was entitled nearly twelve years later, *Ain't I a Woman?* The speech itself, not likely given in the stereotypical dialect which gave it its title, illustrated though the way in which abolitionism both relied on women's activism and was confronted by new gender categories of the early nineteenth century.

Women as we will see played a significant role in the abolitionist movement, much as they did in the other social reform movements of the period. Additionally, objections to slavery often emphasized the ways in which African American women were victimized sexually and economically, and denied their proper femininity. Pro-slavery advocates often made similar points, observing that women's place in the movement illustrated reversals in women's proper place. Pro-slavery voices also contended that women in the South, both black and white, were protected by the institution of slavery. Abolitionists also were ambivalent about the place women had in anti-slavery associations. The mast-head of Frederick Douglass's newspaper, *The North Star*, included the following words: "RIGHT IS OF NO SEX—TRUTH IS OF NO COLOR—GOD IS THE FATHER OF ALL, AND ALL WE ARE BRETHREN." But the vocal participation and leadership of women, black and white, in the abolition movement would both represent a dividing factor among abolitionists, a justification employed by pro-slavery advocates, and a goad to women to seek both the right to vote and more widespread political activism.

PRO-SLAVERY IDEOLOGY

It is difficult today to imagine a defense for slavery. The idea of owning another human being, as chattel, thankfully for most Americans, as for most of the world's citizens, seems an inconceivable prospect. This is not to deny that the practice of slavery does not persist today. But, in general where it does there is little public defense of the practice, and the sense shared by the greatest part of humanity is that it cannot be morally justified. It is nonetheless important to understand the development of the vigorous defense of slavery that developed in the early nineteenth century as slave owners sought to justify holding human beings in perpetual servitude.

Pro-slavery arguments and justifications of slavery have not received the same public attention or scholarly interest as has the history of the abolition movement. Garrison, Douglass, the Grimke sisters, Harriet Beecher Stowe, Sojourner Truth, and Harriet Tubman are well-known names. By comparison, Thomas Roderick Dew, James Henry Hammond, Josiah C. Nott, and other pro-slavery apologists are names only few will recognize. Perhaps this reflects the fact that in the aftermath of the South's defeat in the Civil War there seemed less need to explain the ideology that sustained the Confederacy. But there is another reason, I am convinced, for the convenient American amnesia on this point. It is because pro-slavery arguments were fundamentally American. Pro-slavery apologists, as we will see here, marshalled the Bible, the Constitution, science, laissez-faire economic dogma, paternalistic sentiment, claims to Christian charity, gender categories, and familiar critiques of industrial capitalism and consumerism to support the continuation of slavery. The same intellectual apparatus, employed differently perhaps, has been depended uponbe to call Americans to the great causes of the 20th century. It just simply would not do to recall how these same ideals were employed to justify chattel slavery.

Though the defense of slavery predated the American Revolution, it began in earnest in the early republic. Much of the early justification for slavery was not intended for northern audiences or for the nation as a whole. Instead, early arguments favoring slavery's continuation were largely directed to southerners who lacked slaves, and whose political demands threatened the landholding and slave-owning gentry of Virginia, Maryland, and the Carolinas. But, as the assault on slavery by northern abolitionists became more intense in the 1820s and thereafter, southern defensiveness on the subject increased. Additionally, as slavery became increasingly a marker of sectional identity and culture, the need to defend slavery to fellow southerners diminished and arguments in favor of slavery began to address the abolitionist movement point-by-point. In the process, short-comings and evils of slavery that had been acknowledged by slave owners across the South before 1820 were increasingly minimized as southerners closed ranks and developed a bulwark against abolitionist claims. In the process, pro-slavery arguments developed the features of a self-contained and self-perpetuating ideological character. And, in the process, the possibilities for dialogue between those who opposed and those who profited from slavery increasingly were cut off.

The first challenge to slave owners was the charge that slavery was a sin. This claim, leveled most stridently by revivalists was brushed aside on a number of grounds. Pro-slavery advocates emphasized slavery's Biblical roots in both the Old and New Testaments. Abraham, Isaac, Jacob, and other Old Testament patriarchs had owned slaves. The hierarchical and patriarchal principles evident in the Old Testament also supported a defense of slavery. While there were any number of sins identified in the Ten Commandments and Judaic Law, slavery was not among them. Though Methodists, Baptists, and Wesleyans were present in numbers in the South, the appeal of the Holiness doctrine did not reach as deeply into the South; most of the congregants drawn to the possibilities of perfectionism were centered in the Appalachian region, and represented precisely the non-slave holding populations of the South. It was not clear in any case that these possibilities were extended to African Americans. The "Curse of Canaan" (found in Genesis 12:15-16 and Genesis 13:2) was often offered as a Biblical explanation for why Africans and their descendents were slaves. "Cursed be Canaan; a servant of servants shall he be to his brethren," announced southern ministers from their pulpits. "Blessed be the Lord God of Shem; and Canaan shall be his servant." Europeans were identified as the historic inheritors of the lands of Shem, and Africans were identified as the descendents of Canaan, and rightfully, Biblically, enslaved.

African-American congregations emphasized the Exodus story, restorative justice of the "year of the Jubilee," and Jesus' "Sermon on the Mount" with its promise that "the first shall be last, and the last first." Pro-slavery theologians pointed instead to the legality of slavery in the Old Testament and argued that Jesus' had not come to "overturn" the law, but to fulfill it, thereby leaving slavery intact. They also frequently cited St. Paul's letter to the Christian, Roman slave-owner Philemon, where Philemon's ownership of his slave Onesimus, also a Christian, was reaffirmed. Slave owners emphasized Paul's admonition to Onesimus, "Servants be obedient to them who are your masters, according to the flesh, with fear and trembling, in singleness of your heart as unto Christ." Slavery then received a Biblical endorsement. And slaves converted to Christianity, even though remaining slaves, had the promise of a heavenly salvation denied Africans that remained on that continent.

The latter point, that slavery afforded the descendants of Africans opportunities denied them in their native land was an important feature of defenses of slavery that stressed the benevolence of the plantation and the sentimental attachment of slaves and masters to one another and to the soil. Harriet Beecher Stowe's and countless other northern representations of plantation life and the brutalities of slavery were adamantly rejected by pro-slavery apologists. Instead, the relationship between slaves and their masters was described as one of mutual affection, caring, and contentment on the part of the slaves. In part, slavery apologists argued that the contentment of slaves reflected their docility and child-like or, as often, near canine desire to please their masters. The plantation was described as an improved Eden. Slaves hadn't a care in the world, their needs provided for by others, their daily agricultural routines hardly more harsh than in that state of nature. Moreover, slave children and the aged, unable to contribute to planting, hoeing, or harvesting, nonetheless were cared for and maintained. As for the charge that slavery destroyed the black family, pro-slavery apologists denied this claim. They contended that sales of children or family members were rarely carried out, and that whenever possible families were maintained intact. Pro-slavery apologists also argued that the sentimental attachments of slaves to their family members were less severely felt than were the attachments of whites to their kin. When abolitionists objected that planters, overseers, or drivers took sexual advantage of slave women, they responded along two lines, first arguing that black women were naturally more licentious than were white women, and second that the presence of slave women as outlets for white men's sexuality resulted in less reliance upon prostitution than was the case in the North.

The culture and economy of the North came under a variety of attacks as well in this defense of slavery. Slavery was characterized as more humane than wage labor. Despite the evidence of the capitalist and efficiency-driven nature of the plantation described in chapter eight, planters maintained that slaves had been entrusted to their care, and that paternalistic sentiment rather than profit guided their treatment of their enslaved charges. By contrast, northern factory workers were "free but in name" and were instead wage slaves. The planters were no less strident in their critique of the Industrial Revolution's innovations than many followers of Karl Marx. The proletariat of wage earners, cast into the streets with every financial panic, or at every seasonal downturn, were worse off despite their vaunted independence than slaves who could count on their masters to insure that their basic needs were daily met. At the same time that the industrial economy came under attack for the abuse of its workforce, it also was criticized for destroying white womanhood. The prevalence of women in the factories and the reported incidence of prostitution in northern cities were both reported as evidence of the destructiveness of northern wage labor on families and femininity. At the same time that pro-slavery arguments were employed to critique the industrial, wage-earning economy of the North, pro-slavery arguments also emphasized the degree to which capital and the industrial world depended upon slave labor and the South for its own capital and mercantile success. Southerners extended this argument to emphasize the dependence of the industries of England and France on southern raw materials.

Perhaps the most convincing arguments for the connection between slavery and capitalism can be seen in the writings of pro-slavery apologists.

Finally, the authors that favored the continuation of slavery employed sometimes sophisticated scientific arguments in support of their beliefs. As frequently crude generalizations sustained by pseudo-scientific speculation were drawn upon. Scientific arguments that posited biological or racial differences (rather than religious or cultural distinctions) as justification for slavery dated to the eighteenth century. Enlightenment thinkers, like Thomas Jefferson and Benjamin Franklin, had speculated about the differeing rational faculties of Africans and African Americans. Eighteenth and nineteenth century Europeans often maintained that plantation crops, that flourished in tropical climates, required the labor of Africans who were genetically and physiologically able to work in the heat and humidity whereas Europeans could not, without risking disease and higher mortality. Geographic and demographic analyses provided pro-slavery scholars with the intellectual support for the view that Africans and African Americans were uniquely suited to the kind of labor the plantation required. Others drew on a science of racial difference to support the view that blacks lacked the intellectual capacity for solving the complex problems associated with management and ownership. Evidence from human skeletal remains and studies of cranial measurements were among the many scientific and pseudo-scientific methods used to justify the continued enslavement of people now characterized as racially and biologically inferior.

In the documents that follow, which are separated into abolitionist and pro-slavery groupings, pay particular attention to the ways in which the two kinds of claims about the injustice and inhumanity of slavery and the benevolence and necessity of the institution rely on many of the same textual and rhetorical devices. In other words, keep in mind that both the abolitionists and the southern pro-slavery writers are relying on very American arguments about the nature of abstract concepts like liberty, justice, equality, as well as the meaning of more concrete but still illusive terms such as gender, sexuality, race, class, and sectional identities. Also, observe the ways both sides of this "culture war" employ rhetorical tools from religion, law, and the social and physical sciences to support their positions. Finally, pay attention to the different media and communication methods that abolitionists and pro-slavery apologists employed to get their points across. For those who follow the development of our own "culture war" there is a lot that will be recognizable.

PRIMARY SOURCES

Document 1   Francis "Fanny" Wright, *A Plan for the Gradual Abolition of Slavery in the United States without danger or loss to the Citizens of the South*, 1825.[1]

It appears superfluous, in proposing a plan for the general abolition of slavery from the United States, to observe upon the immensity of the evil, and the gloomy prospect of dangers it presents

---

[1] *A Plan for the Gradual Abolition of Slavery in the United States, without Danger or Loss to the Citizens of the South.* (Baltimore: Printed by Benjamin Lundy, 1825). Accessible at http://antislavery.eserver.org/tracts/lundyplan

to the American people—disunion, bloodshed, servile wars of extermination, horrible in their nature and consequences, and disgraceful in the eyes of the civilized world.

It is conceived that any plan of emancipation, to be effectual, must consult at once the pecuniary interests and prevailing opinions of the southern planters, and bend itself to the existing laws of the southern states.—In consequence, it appears indispensable, that emancipation be connected with colonization, and that it demand no pecuniary sacrifice from existing slaveholders, and entail no loss of property on their children. The following plan is believed to embrace all these objects, and is presented to some southern and northern philanthropists, in the hope that, if meeting with their approbation, it will also meet with their support. It was originally suggested by the consideration of the German society, lately conducted by Mr. Rapp, at Harmony, Indiana and (since the purchase of that property, by Mr. Owen) .... It appears unnecessary to enlarge on the probable effect, which a mild but steady system of order and economy, together with the improved condition and future destinies of the children, and an induced personal and family interest in the thriving of the establishment, will produce on the dispositions and exertions of the parents. The better to insure those effects, the parents will be gradually brought to understand, in weekly evening meetings, the object of the establishment, and taught orally (in simple language) the necessity of industry, first for the procuring of liberty, and afterwards the value of industry when liberty shall be procured. Any deficiency of exertions, or other misconduct, may also be explained to them as charged to their account, and binding them to a further term of service. The duration of the term of service must be somewhat decided by experience. It must cover the first purchase money; the rearing of infancy, and loss of sickness or other accidents; and bring replacing labor into the community, according to the estimate subjoined. To prevent the separation of families, it would be proposed to value the labor, not by heads, but by families, retaining the parents for an additional number of years, rather than manumitting them and retaining the children to a certain age. It would be advisable also, to continue the labor for an additional year or years, the profits of which should defray the expences of removal, and supply implements of husbandry and other necessaries to the colonists. The term of five years has been chosen as an average term, in which a good laborer will return his first purchase money with interest. On sugar, rice, and some cotton lands, the term is now esteemed much shorter—from one to three—on other cotton lands, from four to five—in Kentucky, from six to ten—in Virginia, it is difficult to arrive at any estimate, so completely is the value of slave labor depressed. But as the proposed system admits of all kinds of industry—agriculture and manufactural—it may be expected to raise the value of labor in Virginia, Maryland, and Kentucky, to meet the term of five years; in which case, supposing an improvement in the labor of all the slave states, the average will not be taken too favorably. It should be observed, further, that so long as colonization shall be connected with emancipation, it may always relieve every establishment from the support of age; removing the parents annually, before the period of infirmity, in company with a vigorous youth, sufficient for their support. It is hoped that, after one successful experiment, a similar establishment will be placed in each state; and that when the advantages of the system shall be ascertained, many planters will lease out their property, to be worked in the same way, receiving an interest equal or superior to that returned at present, while the extra profits may be devoted to the forwarding of the general system. The experiment farm, which it is proposed to establish by subscription, will, as it is hoped, among other advantages, offer an asylum and school of industry for the slaves of benevolent masters, anxious to manumit their people, but apprehensive of throwing them unprepared into the world. It may not be superfluous to observe, that due care shall be taken to prevent all communication between the people on the proposed establishment, and laborers on the plantations. And to prevent this more effectually, it may be advisable, that the property shall be somewhat isolated.—Of course every possible facility to be afforded to planters and other strangers, for examination of the property and principles on which it shall be conducted. Should it be objected, that the price of laborers will rise in proportion to their scarcity: it may be answered, that, supposing the success of the emancipating system of labor to have reached the point at which the rise in the price of people would be anticipated, the supposition involves the competition of valuable with valueless or inferior labor; and that, consequently, the price of the old laborers could not rise. In general, however, these anticipations look too far ahead to admit of accuracy, either in objection or answer. It remains to meet a difficulty, frequently started at a first view of the plan. In removing the old laborers, how do you supply their place? It must, in general, be answered, that in all cases the supply is soon found to meet the demand. It is presumed, however, that a very large portion of the southern states is perfectly suited to white labor; and that this could, in a great measure, be furnished from the class of poor whites, throughout that section of the union, depressed by the slave system, and excluded from industry, to their loss and ruin. It must be remembered, also, that with the same facility that the door of colonization is opened, so also can it be closed. Whenever and wherever the improved system of black labor shall appear of value, it may be continued by retaining (on the footing perhaps of tenants, removable at will) as many, and no more, than the property can employ. The internal slave trade, which now paralizes the industry and disgraces the character of Virginia, Maryland, and Kentucky, may thus gradually decline, until the legislatures of those states, and other of other states, see proper to check it entirely. It is thought unnecessary, at present, to specify any place, or country, for the reception of the colonists.—Many ideas prevail on this subject; and all, perhaps may be consulted. Independent of Hayti, there is the Mexican territory of Texas, touching the line of the United States, free to all colors, with a climate suited to the complexion of the negro race, and a fine region beyond the rocky mountains, within the jurisdiction of the United States. This plan, proposed in a spirit of equal good will to master and slave, is intended to consult the interests of both. To prepare the later for liberty, before it is granted, and in no case to grant liberty, but in accordance with the laws of the state, by removal out of the state.—To remove, by gradual and gentle means, a system fraught with danger, as well as crime—To turn labor to account, which is, in many places, worse than profitless, and every where to heighten its value—To assimilate the industry of the south to that of the north, and enable it to multiply its productions, and improve all the rich advantages of southern soil and climate—To open also the field of industry to free white labor, now in a great measure closed throughout a large portion of this magnificent country.

Estimate of the first cost of the proposed Establishment.

100 Slaves, averaging $300…………….	$30,000
2 Sections of government land ………..	1,600
Provisions, clothing, medicines, $35 each ……	8,500
40 Axes ……	80
60 Hoes ……..	30
40 Grub Hoes ….	300
15 Ploughs ……	120
18 Horses x $40 each …..	1,720
Harness ……	150
Horse keeping for the first year ….	1,549
30 Cows x $15 …	450
20 Hogs …	100
Cotton, gin, and mill …	1,000
Overseer's wages ….	300
Incidental expenses….	<u>1,500</u>
	$42,168

Credits

Allowing 1,000 lbs. for cotton for each hand (200 lbs less than the statements supplied by southern planters) at 12 ½ cts.	$12,500
Deduct interest of money at 6 per cent.	<u>2,520</u>
Net profit	**$9,980**

Taking this low estimate, both as to price and quantity, it will be seen that hands, (between nine and fifty years of age,) will repay the purchase money, with interest in less than four years. But allowing deductions for sickness and deaths, the average term is stated at five years.

The above estimate is based upon the actual gains of southern slave labor, without any calculation as to expected advantages, to arise from an improved system of labor.

...

CALCULATION

Shewing at what period the labor of 100 people (doubling itself every five years) might redeem the whole slave population of the United States.

YEARS	SLAVE POPULATION AT PRESENT	PERSONS ON THE ESTABLISHMENT DOUBLING THEIR NUMBER EVERY YEARS FROM THEIR EARNINGS.	
	2,000,000	Begin with 100	Begin with 800
5		200	1,600
10		400	3,200
15		800	6,400
20		1,600	12,800
25	Natural increase 3,920,000	3,200	25,600
30		6,400	51,200
35		12,800	102,400
40		25,600	204,800
45		51,200	409,600
50		102,400	819,200
55		204,800	1,638,400
60		409,600	3,276,800
65	Natural increase 7,840,000	819,200	6,553,600
70		1,638,400	---
75		3,276,800	---
80		6,553,600	---
85		13,107,200	---

Document 2   "State of Maryland vs. Austin Woolfolk," *Niles Register*, 19 May 1827.[2]

As much has been said about the following case, we copy it from the Federal Gazette of the 11th instant.

State of Maryland vs. Austin Woolfolk, Baltimore City Court, February Term, 1827. Indictment for an assault and battery on Benjamin Lundy.

Submission to the court.

---

2   "State of Maryland vs. Austin Woolfolk," *Niles Register*, 19 May 1827.

It was proved on the part of the state, that the traverser, on the 9th of January, accosted Benjamin Lundy, in the street near the post-office, and enquired whether he had not published, in the *Genius of Universal Emancipation*, an account of the execution of William Hill, (alias Bowser), in New York; for the murder of the captain and mate of the schooner Decatur, with some remarks of his own; to which Lundy replied he had, and stated that he copied the article from a New York paper, the Christian Enquirer. Woolfolk then asked what the remarks were which he had made—Lundy then drew a paper from his pocket containing the remarks, offered it to Woolfolk, and told him he could read them for himself. Woolfolk refused to take the paper, but immediately seized Lundy, threw him to the ground, and beat and stamped upon his head and face in a most furious and violent manner, until pulled off by the byestanders—Lundy was confined to his bed for several days, in consequence of the beating he received from Woolfolk.

The counsel for the traverser admitted that he was guilty of a breach of the law, but in mitigation of the penalty they read several articles in the *Genius of Universal Emancipation*, which Lundy acknowledged he had written and published, in which the domestic slave trade from Maryland to the southern states was spoken of in the heaviest and bitterest terms of denunciation, as barbarous, inhuman and unchristian; and Woolfolk was called a "slave trader," "a soul seller," &c., and equally guilty in the sight of God with the man who was engaged in the African slave trade. The article about which Woolfolk interrogated Lundy, at the time of the assault and which appeared to have been the principle provocation, the traverser's counsel read to the court: ...

Chief Justice Brice, in pronouncing sentence, took occasion to observe, that he had never seen a case in which the provocation for a battery was greater than the present—that if abusive language could ever be a justification for a battery, this ws that case—that the traverser was engaged in a trade sanctioned by the laws of Maryland, and that Lundy had no right to reproach him in such abusive language for carrying on a lawful trade—that the trade itself was beneficial to the state, as it removed a great many rogues and vagabonds who were a nuisance to the state— that Lundy had received no more than a merited chastisement for his abuse of the traverser, and but for the strict letter of the law, the court would not fine Woolfolk anything. The court however was obliged to fine him something, and they therefore fined him *one dollar* and costs.

Document 3 Letter to Charles Fenton Mercer, from Robert Finley, 8 April 1832.[3]

Dear Sir,--

The tragical issue of the insurrection in Southampton, in which above sixty whites fell a sacrifice to the vengeance of their slaves, and subsequently to which, a great number of slaves suffered the penalties of the violated laws of the state, has awakened the slave states out of their slumbers, and excited considerable attention towards our colored population, and the awful conseqences that may ensue, sooner or later, from the admixture of two heterogenous castes in the country, without the least probability, at any future period, however remote, of an amalgamation between them, in consequence of the diversity of colour. [...]

---

3   *Letters on the Colonization Society with a view of its probable results*, addressed to the Hon. Charles F. Mercer, (Philadelphia: R.G. Dorsey, 1838), pp. 5-6.

In the discussion of the best means of averting, or at least of mitigating the evil to be dreaded, from the existence among us of a class of people, who, although free, and therefore entitled to the advantages and privileges of freemen, were, nevertheless, in a great degree, debarred from them by the inexorable force of public prejudice, and, in most of the states, werer subject to rules and regulations and proscriptions, of the most oppressive and galling kind, in this discussion, I say, public opinion unanimously settled down in favour of an extensive system of colonization.

On the subject of the location, there was not the same degree of unanimity. Some of our citizens were in favour of selecting a portion of the vacant territory of the United States, and setting it apart for the purpose. Others were, and some still are, for making an arrangement with the government of Mexico, and sending the class in question to Texas. Others, again, advocated a settlement on the western coast of Africa, being the *natale solum* [native soil] of their ancestors, the climate being better suited to the great majority of the coloured people of this country. The last plan was finally adopted.

The objects of the friends of colonization are—

I. To rescue the free coloured people from the disqualifications, the degradation, and the proscription to which they are exposed in the United States.

II. To place them in a country where they may enjoy the benefits of free government, with all the blessings which it brings in its train.

III. To avert the dangers of a dreadful collision at a future day of the two castes, which must inevitably be objects of mutual jealousy to each other.

IV. To spread civilization, sound morals, and true religion throughout the vast continent of Africa, at present sunk in the lowest and most hideous state of barbarism.

V. And, though last, not least, to afford slave owners who are conscientiously scrupulous about holding human beings in bondage, an asylum, to which they may send their manumitted slaves.

Document 4 Declaration of Sentiments of the American Anti-Slavery Convention, Philadelphia, 6 December 1833.[4]

…More than fifty-seven years have elapsed, since a band of patriots convened in this place, to devise measures for the deliverance of this country from a foreign yoke. The corner-stone upon which they founded the Temple of Freedom was broadly this—'that all men are created equal; that they are endowed by their Creator with certain inalienable rights; that among these are life, LIBERTY, and the pursuit of happiness.' At the sound of their trumpet-call, three millions of people rose up as from the sleep of death, and rushed to the strife of blood; deeming it more glorious to die instantly as freemen, than desirable to live one hour as slaves. They were few in number—poor in resources; but the honest conviction that Truth, Justice and Right were on their side, made them invincible.

---

[4] "Declaration of the American Anti-Slavery Convention," *From the Writings and Speeches of William Lloyd Garrison*, (Boston: F. Wallcut, 21 Cornhill, 1852), pp. 66-71.

We have met together for the achievement of an enterprise, without which that of our fathers is incomplete; and which, for its magnitude, solemnity, and probable results uon the destiny of the world, as far transcends their as moral truth does physical force. ...

Their principles led them to wage war against their oppressors, and to spill human blood like water, in order to be free. Ours forbid the doing of evil that good may come, and lead us to reject, and to entreat the oppressed to reject, the use of all carnal weapons for deliverance from bondage; relying solely upon those which are spiritual, and mighty through God to the pulling down of strong holds.

Their measures were physical resistance—the marshalling in arms—the hostile array—the mortal encounter Ours shall be such only as the opposition of moral purity to moral corruption—the destruction of error by the potency of truth—the overthrow of prejudice by the power of love—and the abolition of slavery by the spirit of repentance.

Their greivances, great as they were, were trifling in comparison with the wrongs and sufferings of those for whom we plead. Our fathers were never slaves—never bought and sold like cattle—never shut out from the light of knowledge and religion—never subjected to the lash of brutal taskmasters. ...

Hence we maintain—that in view of the civil and religious privileges of this nation, the guilt of its oppression is unequalled by any other on the face of the earth; and therefore, that it is bound to repent instantly, to undo the heavy burdens, AND TO LET THE OPPRESSED GO FREE.

We further maintain—that no man has the right to enslave or imbrute his brother—to hold or acknowledge him, for one moment, as a piece of merchandise—to keep back his hire by fraud—or to brutalize his mind, by denying him the means of intellectual, social, and moral improvement.

The right to enjoy liberty is inalienable. To invade it is to usurp the prerogative of Jehovah. Every man has a right to his own body—to the products of his own labor—to the protection of law—and to the common advantages of society. It is piracy to buy or steal a native African, and subject him to servitude. Surely, the sin is as great to enslave an American as an African.

Therefore we believe and affirm that there is no difference, in principle, between the African slave trade and American slavery:

That every American citizen, who detains a human being in involuntary bondage as his property, is according to Scripture, (Exoduce 21:16) a man stealer:

That the slaves ought instantly to be set free, and brought under the protection of law:

...That all those laws which are now in force, admitting the right of slavery, are therefore, before God, utterly null and void; being an audacious usurpation of the Divine prerogative, a daring infringement on the law of nature, a base overthrow of the very foundations of the social compact, a complete extinction of all the relations, endearments and obligations of mankind, and a presumptuous transgression of all the holy commandments; and therefore they ought instantly to be abrogated.

We further believe and affirm—that all persons of color, who possess the qualifications which are demanded of others, ought to be admitted forthwith to the enjoyment of the same privileges, and the exercise of the same prerogatives, as others; and the paths of preferment, of wealth, and of intelligence, should be opened as widely to them as to persons of a white complexion.

We maintain that no compensation should be given to the planters emancipating their slaves:

Because it would be a surrender of the great fundamental principle, that man cannot hold property in man:

Because slavery is a crime, and therefore is not an article to be sold:

Because the holders of slaves are not the just proprietors of what they claim; freeing the slave is not depriving them of property, but restoring it to its rightful owner; it is not wronging the master, but righting the slave—restoring him to himself:

Because immediate and general emancipation would only destroy nominal, not real property; it would not amputate a limb or break a bone of the slaves, but by infusing motives into their breasts, would make them doubly valuable to the masters as free labourers; and

Because if compensation is to be given at all, it should be given to the outraged and guiltless slaves, and not to those who have plundered and abused them.

We regard as delusive, cruel and dangerous, any scheme of expatriation which pretends to aid, either directly or indirectly, in the emancipation of the slaves, or to be a substitute for the immediate and total abolition of slavery.

We fully and unanimously recognize the sovereignty of each State, to legislate exclusively on the subject of slavery which is tolerated within its limits; we condede that Congress, under the present national compact, has no right to interfere with any of the slave States, in relation to this momentous subject:

But we maintain that Congress has a right, and is solemnly bound, to suppress the domestic slave trade between the several States, and to abolish slavery in those portions of our territory which the Constitution has placed under its exclusive jurisdiction.

We also maintain that there are, at the present time, the highest obligations resting upon the people of the free States to remove slavery by moral and political action, as prescribed in the Constitution of the United States. They are now living under a pledge of their tremendous physical force, to fasten the galling fetters of tyranny upon the limbs of millions in the Southern States; they are liable to be called at any moment to suppress a general insurrection of the slaves; they authorize the slave owner to vote for three-fifths of his slaves as property, and thus enable him to perpetuate his oppression; they support a standing army at the South for his protection; and they seize the slave, who has escaped into their territories, and send him back to be tortured by an enraged master or a brutal driver. This relation to slavery is criminal and full of danger: IT MUST BE BROKEN UP.

These are our views and principles—these our desires and measures. With entire confidence in the overruling justice of God, we plant ourselves upon the Declaration of Independence and the truths of Divine Revelation, as upon the Everlasting Rock.

Document 5 "Slavery" in *The Works of William E. Channing*, Unitarian Minister, 1835.[5]

---

5 "Slavery," in The Works of William E. Channing, D.D., (Boston: American Unitarian Association, 1891), pp. 692-697.

Chapter I. Property

The slave holder claims the slave as his Property. The very idea of a slave is, that he belongs to another, that he is bound to live and labor for another, to be another's instrument, and to make another's will his habitual law, however adverse to his own. […]

Now this claim of property in a human being is altogether false, groundless. No such right of man in man can exist. A human being cannot be justly owned. To hold and treat him as property is to inflict a great wrong, to incur the guilt of oppression.

This position there is a difficulty in maintaining on account of its exceeding obviousness. It is too plain for proof. To defend it is like trying to confirm a self-evident truth. To find arguments is not easy, because an argument is something clearer than the proposition to be sustained. The man who, on hearing the claim to property in man, does not see and feel disintinctly that it is a cruel usurpation, is hardly to be reached by reasoning, for it is hard to find any plainer principles than what he begins with denying. I will endeavor, however, to illustrate the truth which I have stated.

1. It is plain, that, if one man may be held as property, then every other man may be so held…. If the right of the free to liberty is founded, not on their essential attributes as rational and moral beings, but on certain adventitious, accidental circumstances,…then every human being, by a change of circumstances, may justly be held and treated by another as property…. Now let every reader ask himself this plain question: Could I, can I, be rightfully seized, and made an article of property; be made a passive instrument of another's will and pleasure; be subjected to another's irresponsible power, be subjected to stripes at another's will; be deined the control and use of my own limbs and faculties for my own good? …. Is there any moral truth more deeply rooted in us, that that such a degradation would be an infinite wrong….

2. A man cannot be seized and held as property, because he has Rights. What these rights are, whether few or many, or whether all men have the same, are questions for future discussion. … Now I say, a being having rights cannot justly be made property; for this claim over him virtually annuls all his rights.

3. Another argument against property is to be found in the Essential Equality of men. I know that this doctrine, so venerable in the eyes of our fathers, has lately been denied. Verbal logicians have told us that men are "born equal" only in the sense of being equally born. They have asked weter all are equally tall, strong, or beautiful; or whether nature, Procrustes-like, reduces all her children to one standard of intellect and virtue…. It is freely granted that there are innumerable diversities among men; but be it remembered, they are ordained to bind men together, and not to subdue one to the other; ordained to give means and occasions of mutual aid, … so that the good of all is equally intended in this distribution of various gifts…. …. Has nature conferred distinctions which tell us plainly who shall be owners and who be owned? Who of us can unblushingly lift his head and say that God has written "Master" there? Or who can show the word "Slave" engraven on his brother's brow?

4. That a human being cannot be justly held and used as property, is apparent from the very nature of property. Property is an exclusive right….. What then is the consequence of holding a human being as property? Plainly this. He can have no right to himself. His limbs are, in truth, not morally his own. He has not a right to his own strength. It belongs to another…. To deny the right of a human being to himself, to his own limbs and faculties,

to his energy of body and mind, is an absurdity too gross to be confuted by anything but a simple statement.

[…]

7. I come now to what is to my own mind the great argument against seizing and using a man as property. He cannot be property in the sight of God and justice, because he is a Rational, Moral, Immortal Being; because created in God's image, and therefore in the highest sense his child; because created to unfold godlike faculties, and to govern himself by a Divine Law written on his heart, and republished in God's Word. His whole nature forbids that he should be seized as property…. Did God make such a being to be owned as a tree or a brute? How plainly was he made to exercise, unfold, improve his highest powers, made for a moral and spiritual good! And how is he wronged, and his Creator opposed, when he is forced and broken into a tool to another's physical enjoyment!

Such a being was plainly made for an End in Himself. He is a Person, not a Thing. He is an End, not a mere Instrument or Means. He was made for his own virtue and happiness. […]

We have thus seen that a human being cannot rightfully be held and used as property. No legislation, not that of all countries or worlds, could make him so.

Document 6   Letter to E. Carpenter, from Lydia Maria Child, 4 September 1836.[6]

I have lately had a most interesting case brought under my observation. When in Boston I was entreated to exert myself concerning a little child, supposed to be a slave, brought from New Orleans, and kept shut up at No. 21 Pinkney Street. The object was to persuade the child's mistress to leave her at the colored asylum, and failing to effect this object, to ascertain beyond a doubt whether the child was a slave, whether there was intention to carry her back to New Orleans, and to obtain sight of her in order to be able to prove her identity…. I will not fill this sheet with particulars. Suffice it to say, the way was opened for us. We obtained all the evidence we wanted, carried it to a lawyer, who petitioned for a writ of habeas corpus; the judge granted the petition; and the man who held little Med in custody was brought up for trial. In consequence of the amount of evidence ready to be proved by three witnesses, the pro-slavery lawyers did not pretend to deny that the intent was to carry the child back into slavery; but they took the new and extraordinary ground that Southern masters had a legal right to hold human beings as slaves while they were visiting here in New England. Judge Wild expressed a wish to consult with the other judges; and our abolition friends, finding the case turn on such a very important point, resolved to retain the services of Webster, for want of a better man. He was willing to serve provided they would wait a few days. Rufus Choate, a man only second to himin abilities, and whose heart is strongly favorable to anti-slavery, was employed. The opposite counsel were full of sophistry and eloquence. One of them really wiped his own eyes at the thought that the poor little slave might be separated from its slave mother by mistaken benevolence. His pathos was a little marred by my friend E.G. Loring, who arose and stated that it was distinctly understood that litte Med was to be sold on her way back to New Orleans, to pay the expences of her mistress's journey to the North. The judges decided unanimously in favor of Med and liberty!

---

6   *Letters of Lydia Maria Child, with a biographical introduction by John G. Whittier and an appendix by Wendell Phillips*, (Boston: Houghton, Mifflin and Company, 1882), pp. 20-21.

The *Commercial Gazette* of the next day says: "This decision, though unquestionably according to law, is much to be regretted; for such cases cannot but injure the custom of our hotels, no so liberally patronized by gentlemen from the South." Verily, Sir Editor, thou art an honest devil; and I thank thee for not being at the pains to conceal thy cloven foot.

Document 7   Elizabeth Margaret Chandler, "Christmas," 1836[7]

Christmas

Mother, when Christmas comes once more,
    I do not wish that you
Should buy sweet things for me again,
    As you used to do:

The taste of cakes and sugar-plums
    Is pleasant to me yet,
And temptingly the gay shops look,
    With their fresh stores outset.

But I have learn'd, dear mother,
    That the poor and wretched slave
Must toil to win their sweetness,
    From the cradle to the grave.

And when he faints with weariness
    Beneath the torrid sun,
The keen lash urges on his toil,
    Until the day is done.

But when the holy angels' hymn,
    On Judea's plains afar,
Peal'd sweetly on the shepherds' ear,
    'Neath Bethlehem's wondrous star,

They sung of glory to our God,--
    "Peace and good will to men,"—
For Christ, the Saviour of the world,
    Was born amidst them then.

And is it for His glory, men
    Are made to toil,
With weary limbs and breaking hearts,
    Upon another's soil?

---

[7]   Elizabeth Margaret Chandler, "Christmas," in *Poetical Works of Elizabeth Margaret Chandler, with a Memoir of her Life and Character, by Benjamin Lundy,* (Philadelphia: Lemuel Howell, 1836), p. 124-125.

That they are taught not of his law,
> To know his holy will,
And that He hates the deed of sin,
> And loves the righteous still?

And is it peace and love to men,
> To bind them with the chain,
And sell them like the beasts that feed
> Upon the grassy plain?

To tear their flesh with scourgings rude,
> And from the aching heart,
The ties to which it fondliest clings,
> For evermore to part?

And 'tis because of all this sin, my mother,
> That I shun
To taste the tempting sweets for which
> Such wickedness is done.

If men to men will be unjust, if slavery must be,
Mother, the chain must not be worn; the scourge
> be plied for me.

Document 8 Speech by Angelina Grimke at Pennsylvania Hall, 17 May 1838

http://www.historyisaweapon.com/defcon1/grimke.html

Men, brethren and fathers—mothers, daughters and sisters, what came ye out for to see? A reed shaken with the wind? Is it curiosity merely, or a deep sympathy with the perishing slave, that has brought this large audience together?

[A yell from the mob outside the building interrupted her]

Those voices without ought to awaken and call out our warmest sympathies. Deluded beings! "they know not what they do." They know not that they are undermining their own rights and their own happiness, temporal and eternal. Do you ask, "what has the North to do with slavery?" Hear it—hear it. Those voices without tell us that the spirit of slavery is *here*, and has been roused to wrath by our abolition speeches and conventions: for surely liberty would not foam and tear herself with rage, because her friends are multiplied daily, and meetings are held in quick succession to set forth her virtues and extend her peaceful kingdom. This opposition shows that slavery has done its deadliest work in the hearts of our citizens. Do you ask, then, "what has the North to do?" I answer, cast out first the spirit of slavery from your own hearts, and then lend your aid to convert the South. Each one present has a work to do, be his or her situation what it may, however limited their means, or insignificant their supposed influence. The great men of this country will not do this work; the church will never do it. A desire to please the world, to keep the favor of all parties and of all conditions, makes them dumb on this and every other unpopular subject. They have become worldly-wise, and therefore God, in his wisdom, employs them not to carry on his plans of reformation and salvation. He hath chosen the foolish things of the world to confound the wise, and the weak to overcome the mighty.

As a Southerner I feel that it is my duty to stand up here to-night and bear testimony against slavery. I have seen it—I have seen it. I know it has horrors that can never be described. I was brought up under its wing: I witnessed for many years its demoralizing influences, and its destructiveness to human happiness. It is admitted by some that the slave is not happy under the *worst* forms of slavery. But I have *never* seen a happy slave. I have seen him dance in his chains, it is true; but he was not happy. There is a wide difference between happiness and mirth. Man cannot enjoy the former while his manhood is destroyed, and that part of the being which is necessary to the making, and to the enjoyment of happiness, is completely blotted out. The slaves, however, may be, and sometimes are, mirthful. When hope is extinguished, they say, "let us eat and drink, for tomorrow we die."

[Grimke was interrupted again, this time by the sound of stones thrown at the windows of the hall.]

What is a mob? What would the breaking of every window be? What would the levelling of this Hall be? Any evidence that we are wrong, or that slavery is a good and wholesome institution? What if the mob should now burst in upon us, break up our meeting and commit violence upon our persons—would this be any thing compared with what the slaves endure? No, no: and we do not remember them "as bound with them," if we shrink in the time of peril, or feel unwilling to sacrifice ourselves, if need be, for their sake. I thank the Lord that there is yet life left enough to feel the truth, even though it rages at it—that conscience is not so completely seared as to be unmoved by the truth of the living God.

...I have exiled myself from my native land because I could no longer endure to hear the wailing of the slave. I fled to the land of Penn; for here, thought I, sympathy for the slave will surely be found. But I found it not. The people were kind and hospitable, but the slave had no place in their thoughts. Whenever questions were put to me as to his condition, I felt that they were dictated by an idle curiosity, rather than by that deep feeling which would lead to effort for his rescue. I therefore shut up my grief in my own heart.... But how different do I feel now! Animated with hope, nay, with an assurance of the triumph of liberty and good will to man, I will lift up my voice like a trumpet, and show this people their transgression, their sins of omission towards the slave, and what they can do towards affecting Southern mind, and overthrowing Southern oppression.

[Shoutings, stones thrown against the windows, &c.]

....Women of Philadelphia! allow me as a Southern woman, with much attachment to the land of my birth, to entreat you to come up to this work. Especially let me urge you to petition. *Men* may settle this and other questions at the ballot-box, but you have no such right; it is only through petitions that you can reach the Legislature. It is therefore peculiarly *your* duty to petition. Do you say, "It does no good?" The South already turns pale at the number sent. They have read the reports of the proceedings of Congress, and there have seen that among other petitions were very many from the women of the North on the subject of slavery. This fact has called the attention of the South to the subject. How could we expect to have done more as yet? Men who hold the rod over slaves, rule in the councils of the nation: and they deny our right to petition and to remonstrate against abuses of our sex and of our kind. We have these rights, however, from our God. Only let us exercise them: and though often turned away unanswered, let us remember the influence of importunity upon the unjust judge, and act accordingly. The fact that the South look with jealousy upon our measures shows that they are effectual. There is, therefore, no cause for doubting or despair, but rather for rejoicing.

It was remarked in England that women did much to abolish Slavery in her colonies. Nor are they now idle. Numerous petitions from them have recently been presented to the Queen, to abolish the apprenticeship with its cruelties nearly equal to those of the system whose place it supplies. One petition two miles and a quarter long has been presented. And do you think these labors will be in vain? Let the history of the past answer. When the women of these States send up to Congress such a petition, our legislators will arise as did those of England, and say, "When all the maids and matrons of the land are knocking at our doors we must legislate." Let the zeal and love, the faith and works of our English sisters quicken ours—that while the slaves continue to suffer, and when they shout deliverance, we may feel the satisfaction of *having done what we could.*

Document 9 "Disgraceful Riot and Arson in Philadelphia," *The Emancipator* (New York, New York) 24 May 1838

The city of Philadelphia has been disgraced by one of the most wanton riots of modern times. The friends of liberty in that city, finding themselves shut out from all the most desirable places for holding public meetings, … built the PENNSYLVANIAN HALL for the express design of encouraging "free discussion on all subjects not on an immoral tendency—slavery and abolition being prominently in view. Last week was the time set for opening the Hall, and… numerous meetings were arranged to occupy the whole week…. On Wednesday evening the Women's Convention held a public meeting which was attended by an immense crowd, and addressed by WILLIAM LLOYD GARRISON, MRS. CHAPMAN, of Boston, ANGELINA GRIMKE WELD, LUCRETIA MOTT, and ABBY KELLY. During the evening, a large number of unruly persons gathered about the doors, and made what noise they could. They also broke some panes of glass by hurling stones,… The speakers, particularly Mrs. Weld, and the numerous women that made up a large part of the assembly maintained the most perfect composure. … As we retired, the colored members of the convention were protected by their white sisters, and oh! Shame to say, at both were thrown a shower of stones. … Soon several gentlemen rushed in and informed us that the hall was in flames and the fire rapidly spreading… … In a few moments the whole interior was enveloped in flames. The mob shouted, fire! fire!! which soon brought the fire department with their engines, but not a drop of water was permitted to be thrown upon the building, their whole attention was directed to the surrounding buildings…. The pretence for this atrocious deed, is that the whites and blacks were seated in the hall promiscuously, and that they walked together in the streets…."

Document 10 "Free Labor Dry Goods," *Pennsylvania Freeman* (Philadelphia, Pennsylvania), 26 April 1849, p. 4.[8]

Manufactured by the American Free Produce Association, and for sale at No. 51 North Fifth Street:-- Manchester Ginghams, Checks, Apron, and Furniture; Canton Flannel, unbleached; Muslin, bleached and unbleached, of various qualities and width; Bird Bye Towels, black and white Wadding; Cotton Laps; Lamp Wick; Bed Ticking, an excellent article; Calicoes, Stockings, Knitting Cotton, 4¢,

---

8 "Free Labor Dry Goods," *Pennsylvania Freeman*, (Philadelphia, Pennsylvania), 26 April 1849, p. 4.

Orders for goods, or letters desiring information may be addressed to J. Miller McKim, No. 31 N. Fifth Street.

>Daniel L. Miller, Jr., 139 N. Tenth St., or to
>James Mott, No. 35 Church Alley.
>A large and handsome assortment of Prints, now on hand.

Document 11 Thomas Roderick Dew, *An Essay on Slavery*, 1849.[9]

We take it for granted, that the right of the owner to his slave is to be respected, and consequently, that he is not required to emancipate him unless his full value is paid by the State. Let us, then, keeping this in view, proceed to the very simple calculation of the expense of emancipation and deportation in Virginia. The slaves, by the lates census (1830,) amounted within a small fraction to 470,000; the average value of each one of these is, $200; consequently, the whole aggregate value of the slave population of Virginia, in 1830, was $94,000,000; and allowing for the increase since, we cannot err far in putting the present value at $100,000,000. The assessed value of all the houses and lands in the State, amounts to $206,000,000, and these constitute the material items in the wealth of the State, the whole personal property besides bearing but a very small proportion to the value of slaves, lands, and houses. Now, do not these very simple statistics speak volumes upon this subject? It is gravely recommended to the State of Virginia to give up a species of property which constituted nearly one-third of the wealth of the whole State, and almost one half of that of Lower Virginia, and with the remaining two-thirds to encounter the additional enormous expense of transportation and colonization on the coast of Africa. But the loss of $100,000,000 of property is scarcely the half of what Virginia would lose, if the immutable laws of nature could suffer (as fortunately they cannot) this tremendous scheme of colonization to be carried into full effect. Is it not population which makes our lands and houses valuable? Why are lots in Paris and London worth more than the silver dollars which it might take to cover them? Why are lands of equal fertility in England and France, worth more than those of our northern States, and those again worth more than southern soils, and those in turn worth more than the soils of the distant west? It is the presence or absence of population which alone can explain the fact. It is in truth, the slave labor in Virginia which gives value to her soil and her habitations; take away this, and you pull down the atlas that upholds the whole system; eject from wthe State the whole slave population and we risk nothing in the prediction, that on the day in which it shall accomplished, the worn soils of Virginia will not bear the paltry price of the Government lands in the west, and the Old Dominion will be a "waste howling wilderness;" "the grass shall be seen growing in the streets and the foxes peeping from their holes.

Document 12 "The Farewell of a Virginia Slave Mother to her Daughters sold into Southern Bondage," by John Greenleaf Whittier, 1849.[10]

>Gone, gone, -- sold and gone,
>To the rice-swamp dank and lone.

---

9   Thomas R. Dew, *An Essay on Slavery*, (Richmond, VA: J.W. Randolph, 1849).

10 James Greenleaf Whittier, "Farewell of a Virginia Slave Mother to her Daughters sold into Southern Bondage," *Complete Poetical Works*, (Boston: James R. Osgood and Company,1876), p. 56

Where the slave-whip ceaseless swings,
Where the noisome insect stings,
Where the fever demon strews
Poison with the falling dews,
Where the sickly sunbeams glare
Through the hot and misty air,--
    Gone, gone, --sold and gone,
    To the rice-swamp dank and lone,
    From Virginia's hill and waters,--
    Woe is me, my stolen daughters!

    Gone, gone, --sold and gone,
    To the rice-swamp dank and lone.
There no mother's eye is near them,
There no mother's ear can hear them;
Never, when the torturing lash
Seams their back with many a gash,
Shall a mother's kindness bless them,
Or a mother's arms caress them.
    Gone, gone, --sold and gone,
    To the rice-swamp dank and lone,
    From Virginia's hill and waters,--
    Woe is me, my stolen daughters!

    Gone, gone, --sold and gone,
    To the rice-swamp dank and lone,
O, when weary, sad, and slow,
From the fields at night they go,
Faint with toil, and racked with pain,
To their cheerless homes again,
There no brother's voice shall greet
    Them,--
There no father's welcome meet them.
    Gone, gone, --sold and gone,
    To the rice-swamp dank and lone,
    From Virginia's hill and waters,--
    Woe is me, my stolen daughters!

    Gone, gone, --sold and gone,
    To the rice-swamp dank and lone,
From the tree whose shadow lay
On their childhood's place of play,--
From the cool spring where they drank,--
Rock, and hill, and rivulet bank,--
From the solemn house of prayer,
And the holy counsels there,--
    Gone, gone, --sold and gone,
    To the rice-swamp dank and lone,

From Virginia's hills and waters,--
Woe is me, my stolen daughters!

Gone, gone, --sold and gone,
To the rice-swamp dank and lone,

Toiling through the weary day,
And at night the spoiler's prey.
O that they had earlier died,
Sleeping calmly, side by side,
Where the tyrant's power is o'er,
And the fetter galls no more!
    Gone, gone, --sold and gone,
    To the rice-swamp dank and lone,
    From Virginia's hills and waters,--
    Woe is me, my stolen daughters!

    Gone, gone, --sold and gone,
    To the rice-swamp dank and lone,
By the holy love He beareth,--
By the bruised reed He spareth,--
O, may He to whom alone,
All their cruel wrongs are known,
Still their hope and refuge prove,
With a more than mother's love.
    Gone, gone, --sold and gone,
    To the rice-swamp dank and lone,
    From Virginia's hills and waters,--
    Woe is me, my stolen daughters!

Document 13 "Diseases and Peculiarities of the Negro Race," *De Bow's Review*, 1851[11]

This interesting subject has never before, we believe, been treated in an independent manner, by any of our physiological and medical writers, although it has a direct and practical bearing upon over three millions of people, and $2,000,000,000 of property! Dr. Cartwright of New Orleans deserves distinguished praise for the able investigations he has conducted in this recondite department, and we believe they will be received among the planters throughout the South as of inappreciable value. They are embodied in this paper, read by him before the late Medical Convention of Louisiana…:

    … Before going into the peculiarities of their diseases, it is necessary to glance at the anatomical and physiological differences between the negro and the white man; otherswise their diseases cannot be understood. It is commonly taken for granted, that the color of the skin constitutes the main and essential difference between the black and the white race; but there are other differences

---

11 "Diseases and Peculiarities of the Negro Race," De Bow's Review 11: (July 1851), pp. 64-69 continued pp. 330-336.

more deep, durable, and indelible, in their anatomy and physiology, than that of mere color. ... His bile is of a deeper color, and his blood is blacker than the white man's.... His bones are whiter and harder than those of the white race, owing to their containing more phosphate of live and less gelatin. His head is hung on the atlas differently from the white man; the face is thrown more upwards, and the neck is shorter and less oblique; the spine more inwards, and the pelvis more obliquely outwards; the thigh bones larger, and flattened from before backwards; the bones more bent; the legs curved outwards, or bowed; the feet, flat; the gastroenemii muscles so long, as to make the ankle appear as if planted in the middle of the foot; the gait, hopper-hipped, or what the French call *l'allure dahanchee,* not unlike that of a person carrying a burden. ... From the diffusion of the brain, as it were, into the various organs of the body, in the shape of nerves to minister to the senses, everything, from the necessity of such a conformation, partakes of sensuality, at the expense of intellectuality. Thus, music is a mere sensual pleasure with the negro. There is nothing in his music addressing the understanding; it has melody, but no harmony; his songs are mere sounds, without sense or meaning—pleasing to the ear, without conveying a single idea to the mind;.... It is this defective hematosis, or atmospherization of the blood, conjoined with a deficiency of cerebral matter in the cranium, and an excess of nervous matter, distributed to the organs of sensation and assimilation, that is the true cause of that debasement of mind, which has rendered the people of Africa unable to take care of themselves. It is the true cause of their indolence and apathy, and why they have chosen, through countless ages, idleness, misery and barbarism, to industry and frugality.... [Even] if let alone, they always prefer the same kind of government which we call slavery, but which is actually an improvement on the government of their forefathers, as it gives them more tranquility and sensual enjoyment, expands the mind and improves the morals, by arousing them from that natural indolence so fatal to mental and moral progress.

...Although their skin is very thick, it is as sensitive, when they are in perfect health, as that of children, and like them, they fear the rod. They resemble children in another very important particular: they are very easily governed by love combined with fear, and are ungovernable, vicious and rude under any form of government whatever not resting on love and fear as a basis. Like children it is not necessary that they kept under the fear of the lash;... Hence, from a law of his nature, the negro can no more help loving a kind master, than the child can help loving her who gives it suck.

Like children, they require government in every thing; food, clothing, exercise, sleep—all require to be prescribed by rule, or they will run into excesses. Like children, they are apt to over-eat themselves, or to confine their diet too much to one favorite article, unless restrained from doing so. They often gorge themselves with fat meat, as children do with sugar.

...I have thus hastily and imperfectly noticed some of the more striking anatomical and physiological peculiarities of the negro race. The question may be asked: does he belong to the same race as the white man? Is he a son of Adam? ... We learn from the Book of Genesis, that Noah had three sons, Shem, Ham, and Japtheth, and that Canaan, the son of Ham, was doomed to be servant of servants unto his brethren. From history, we learn, that the descendants of Canaan settled in Africa, and are the present Ethiopians, or black race of men; that Shem occupied Asia, and Japtheth, the north of Europe. In the 9th chapter and 27th verse of Genesis, one of the most authentic books of the Bible, is this remarkable prophecy: "God shall enlarge Japheth, and he shall dwell in the tents of Shem; and Canaan *shall be* his servant." Japtheth has been greatly enlarged by the discovery of a new world, the continent of America. He found in it the Indians, whom natural history declares to be of Asiatic origin, in other words, the descendants of Shem: he drove out Shem, and occupied his tents: and now the remaining part of the prophecy is in the process of fulfillment, from the facts everywhere before us, of Canaan becoming his servant. The question arises, is the Canaanite, or Ethiopian, qualified for the trying duties of servitude, and unfitted for the enjoyment of freedom? If he be, there is both wisdom, mercy and justice in the decree dooming him to be servant of servants, as the decree is in conformity to his nature. Anatomy and physiology have been interrogated, and the response is, that the Ethiopian, or Canaanite, is unfitted from his organization and the physiological laws predicated on that organization for the responsible duties of a free man, but like the child, is only fitted for a state of dependence and subordination.

...A radical reformation is greatly needed in our system of medical education, which is so defective as to lead to the fatal error in practice, that there is no physical or organic characters in the negro's organization different from that of the white man. ... It could easily be shown, by anatomy, physiology, and ethnographical investigations, that the debasement of mind supposed to arise from Southern slavery, arises from causes imprinted by the hand of nature on the sons of Ham, so far back as the time when the catacombs of Egypt were constructed. The vulgar error that there is no difference in the negro's organization, physiology, and psychology, and that all the apparent difference arises from Southern slaver is the cause of all those political agitations which are threatening to dissolve our Union.

Document 14 Speech of Senator A.P. Butler, during consideration of the Kansas-Nebraska Act, 24 February 1854.[12]

I am told, however,... by another Senator from Ohio, [Mr. Wade] who, it seems to me, has taken very contradictory positions, as have the other gentlemen who have sustained him, that the black man, under the sentimental idea contained in the Declaration of Independence, has a right to claim an equality with the white man; and I think that honorable Senator said, that "but for his degradation by the master, he would elevate himself to that equality...." ... The gentleman said however, notwithstanding all this, he guessed there would be no difference in the races in the sight of God.

Sir, I will not invade the province of God. I will not undertake to say in what point of view the white and the black man may be regarded at the bar of His tribunal. I should regard it as profanity in me to do so. Why, sir, if the purest moment of the purest being that ever lived on this earth were protracted into eternity, it might be a very inadequate conception of that happiness for which God may prepare the humblest and meanest being on earth. I do not, therefore, undertake to say what, before the Almighty eye, is the relative condition of the black man and the white man. Inequality pervades the creation of this universe. Yes, sir, with a chain of subordinate links and gradation, all existence upon this earth is connected together, from the lowest worm that crawls upon the earth, to the purest angel that burns before the altar of God. Inequality seems to characterize the administration of the Providence of God. I will not undertake to invade that sanctuary, but I will say, that the Abolitionists cannot make those equal whom God has made unequal, in human estimation. That He has made the blacks unequal to the whites, human

---

12   Congressional Globe, Senate, 33rd Congress, 1st Session, pp. 233-234.

history, as far as it can take cognizance of the matter, has pronounced its uniform judgment. The judgment of the earth, and the history of mankind, are alone the records which I presume to read. They lead to one judgment—revealing, perhaps, to us a melancholy truth.

… Is the black man equal with the white man, under human judgment? All history refutes it. Who ever heard of the African astronomer, statesman, general, poet? Who ever heard of the African soaring in those regions in which the Caucasian race have made their greatest developments? All history refutes the idea….

Is it not perfectly true, so far as regards the statutory provisions of the Federal and State legislation, that the black man has never been, and never can be equal with the white man? In your naturalization laws, it is provided that none but a white man shall be a citizen of the United States. Under your militia laws, it is provided that none but a white man can take a musket in the service of the country, or be enrolled among the militia. It is notorious that these very gentlemen who bestow so much tongue-expressed philanthropy upon the black man, do not themselves regard him as an equal, and they cannot so regard him.

Document 15   William Lloyd Garrison, "No Compromise with Slavery," 14 February 1854.[13]

Of necessity, as well as of choice, I am a "Garrisonian" Abolitionist—the most unpopular appellation that any man can have applied to him in the present state of public sentiment…. Representing, then, that phase of Abolitionism which is the most condemned,… let me define my positions, and at the same time Challenge anyone to show wherein they are untenable.

I. I am a believer in that portion of the Declaration of American Independence in which it is set forth, as among self-evident truths, "that all men are created equal; that they are endowed by their Creator with certain inalienable rights; that among these are life, liberty, and the pursuit of happiness." Hence, I am an Abolitionist. Hence, I cannot but regard oppression in every form—and most of all, that which turns a man into a thing—with indignation and abhorrence…. They who desire me to be dumb on the subject of Slavery, unless I will open my mouth in its defence, ask me to give the lie to my professions, to degrade my manhood, and to stain my soul. I will not be a liar, a poltroon, or a hypocrite, to accommodate any party, to gratify any sect, to escape any odium or peril, to save any interest, to preserve any institution, or to promote any object.

II. Notwithstanding the lessons taught us by Pilgrim Fathers and Revolutionary Sires, at Plymouth Rock, on Bunker Hill, at Lexington, Concord, and Yorktown; notwithstanding our Fourth of July celebrations, and ostentatious displays of patriotism, in what European nation is personal liberty held in such contempt as our own. Where are there such unbelievers in the natural equality and freedom of mankind…. As Nero fiddled while Rome was burning, so the slaveholding spirit of this nation rejoices, as one barrier of liberty after another is destroyed, and fresh victims are multiplied for the cotton-field and the auction-block…. The two great parties which absorb nearly the whole voting strength of the Republic are pledged to be deaf, dumb, and blind to whatever outrages the Slave Power may attempt

---

13   William Lloyd Garrison, "No Compromise with Slavery. An Address Delivered in the Broadway Tabernacle, New York, February 14, 1854," (New York: American Anti-Slavery Society, 1854).

to perpetrate. Cotton is in their ears—blinds are over their eyes—padlocks are upon their lips.... The reasons adduced among us in justification of slaveholding... are multitudinous. I will enumerate only a dozen of these: 1. "The victims are black." 2. "The slaves belong to an inferior race." 3. "Many of them have been fairly purchased." 4. "Others have been honestly inherited." 5. "Others have been honestly inherited." 6. "They are better off as slaves than they would be as freemen." 7. "They could not take care of themselves if set free." 8. "Their simultaneous liberation would be attended with great danger." 9. "Any interference in their behalf will excite the ill-will of the South, and thus seriously affect Northern trade and commerce." 10. "The Union can be preserved only by letting Slavery alone, and that is of paramount importance." 11. "Slavery is a lawful and constitutional system, and therefore not a crime." 12. "Slavery is sanctioned by the Bible; the Bible is the word of God; therefore God sanctions Slavery, and the Abolitionists are wise above what is written." ... But they are not valid. THEY ARE THE LOGIC OF BEDLAM, THE MORALITY OF THE PIRATE SHIP, THE DIABOLISM OF THE PIT. They insult the common sense and shook the moral nature of mankind.

III. The Abolitionism which I advocate is absolute as the law of God, and as unyielding as His throne. It admits of no compromise. Every slave is a stolen man; every slaveholder is a man-stealer.... The law that makes him chattel is to be trampled under foot; the compact that is formed at his expense, and cemented with his blood, is null and void; the church that consents to his enslavement is horribly atheistical; the religion that receives to its communion the enslaver is the embodiment of criminality. Such at least is the verdict of my soul.... And who am I but a man? What right have I to be free, that another man cannot prove himself to possess by nature Who or what are my wife and children, that they should not be herded with four-footed beasts, as well as others thus sacredly related? If I am white, and another is black, complexionally, what follows?... What if I am rich, and another is poor—strong, and he is weak—intelligent, and he is benighted—elevated, and he is depraved? "Have we not one Father? Hath God not created us?

... What then is to be done? Friends of the slave, the question is not whether by our efforts we can abolish Slavery, speedily or remotely—for duty is ours, the result is with God; but whether we will go with the multitude to do evil, sell our birthright for a mess of pottage, cease to cry aloud and spare not, and remain in Babylon when the command of God is, "Come out of her, my people, that ye be not partakers of her sins, and that ye receive not of her plagues." Let us stand in our lot, "and having done all, to stand." At least, a remnant shall be saved. Living or dying, defeated or victorious, be it ours to exclaim, "NO COMPROMISE WITH SLAVERY! LIBERTY FOR EACH, FOR ALL, FOREVER!..."

Document 16 John Forsyth, "The North and the South," *De Bow's Review*, 1854.[14]

It cannot be said that the excessive mortality among the males of the North, is owing to their unwholesome employments. For the females are employed in similar or more destructive avocations. In Massachusetts about fifty thousand women work in factories, and yet in that State there is an excess of 7,672 females, whereas, if the natural proportion of the sexes existed among

---

14 John Forsyth, "The North and the South," *De Bow's Review* 17 (October 1854): 307-312.

the native population, or such as is found in the South, Massachusetts ought to have an excess of twenty-two thousand males. So that at present she has about thirty thousand females beyond the due proportion. It is true that Massachusetts loses a portion of her male population by emigration to the West, although she is re-inforced again by the excess of males in the foreign emigrants that have settled there. But there still remains a large portion who must have perished by the sickness and vice of the towns and cities that contain so large a part of her people—Boston alone, with its suburb towns, having a population of 200,000 or nearly one third of all the State. So, then, the operation of the institution of this model State of the North, is to violate the laws of nature by a separation of the sexes; to send thousands of her sons away from their happy condition at home, to encounter the hardships of the West; to send multitudes of others to die by dissipation in her cities, and to place her lonely and deserted women not in convents, but in factories. I have said that there are about fifty thousand women employed in the factories of Massachusetts. Such is the testimony of the official census of the State in 1845. Those who are thus employed, it is well known, are generally young, unmarried women, as such a vocation would be rather incompatible with the domestic duties of wives. Now, according to the census of 1840, there were about 57,000 women in the State between the ages of 17 and 25. So that about seven-eighths of the marriageable women of Massachusetts, at a time of life that ought to be sacred to love and courtship, to pleasure and to hope, to home and to society, are sent forth from the parental roof, to labor for years, confined to over-heated rooms, containing a hundred persons each, confined to a space of five feet square, for thirteen hours a day, under a male overseer, and not permitted to receive a visit from a lover or a relative in the mill, except by the permission of the proprietor's agent, or at the boarding house except by permission of the proprietor's housekeeper.... This confinement to factories, postpones the marriage of the women of Massachusetts to an average of twenty-three or twenty-four years....

In determining the condition of civilized communities, it is generally considered essential to inquire into the state of their pauperism; not only because paupers themselves usually constitute a considerable class, but because their number affects vitally the condition of the entire laboring class.

In the State of New York, the progress of pauperism has been rapid. In 1830, the number supported or relieved was 15,506. In 1835 it was 38,362....In 1844, the number had increased to about 72,000 permanent, and the same number of occasional paupers, making the total of 144,000 as appears from the Journal of Commerce. These were for the whole State, and there was thus one pauper to every seventeen inhabitants. In 1847, there were received at the principal almshouses for the city of New York, 28,692 persons, and *out-door* relief was given, out of public funds, to 44, 572 persons, making a total of 73,624. So that about *one person out of every five* in the city of New York, was dependent more or less on public charity. The total cost, that year, of this pauperism was $319,298.88. For this present year of 1849, the estimate is $400,000, according to the mayor's message.

...Now, throughout the greater part of Virginia and Kentucky, pauperism is almost unknown. I passed some time ago, the poorhouse of Campbell county, Kentucky, on the opposite side of the river, and there was not a solitary inmate. And I have know a populous county in Virginia to have but one.

...When pauperism extends to the class that are able to labor, it is evident that the wages of labor are reduced to the cost of subsistence. And hence the whole class must be subjected to the melancholy and terrible necessity of working, rather to avoid the poorhouse, than of bettering their condition. And the pauper in an almshouse is a slave. He works under a master, and receives nothing but a subsistence. And there are already in New York and Massachusetts, about one hundred thousand persons in this condition....

...The number of convicts in the three penitentiaries of New York... is about two thousand. In the penitentiary of Virginia there are only 111 whites, 89 blacks. This indicates four times the amount of crime in proportion to the white population in New York as in Virginia. In Massachusetts there were, in 1847, 288 persons in the State prison, which incicates more than twice the crime in that State as in Virginia. Taking all the New England States together, their penitentiary convicts are twice as numerous in proportion to population, as in Virginia.... In Ohio there are 470 persons in the penitentiary—in Kentucky 130, Ohio being 25 percent, the most according to population....So much for the States of the North, agricultural, manufacturing, and commercial, old and new, as compared with the South, in crime. The results are uniformly and largely in favor of the South.

If we turn to the official reports of crime in the great cities of the North, we behold a state of society exhibited, at which the mind is appalled. In Boston the number of persons annually arraigned for crime exceeds four thousand, and of this number about one-third are females. So that one person out of every fourteen males, and one out of every 28 females, is arrested annually for criminal offenses....

In New York the proportion of crime is about the same, some eighteen thousand persons having been arrested there last year. Of these, it is said, six thousand for drunkenness, twelve thousand were committed to the tombs for examination, of whom ten thousand were committed for trial. Of these, there were sentenced to the State prison 119 men and 17 women—to the penitentiary 700 men and 170 women—to the city prison 162 men and 67 women—total 981 men, 254 women; showing an amount of crime in a single city, greater than in all the southern States together. In the Kentucky penitentiary, there is not a single woman—in the Virginia, I there believe there is none.

...There is a class of topics of a more intangible nature, but not the less important, and which are much insisted on in this controversy, that now remain to be briefly considered. It is urged that religion and education are more prevalent and flourishing in the North than in the South.... But it is in education that the North claims the great preeminence over the South. In Massachusetts, according to the census of 1840, there were but 4,448 white persons above the age of twenty who could not read and write—and in Virginia there were 58,787. In Ohio there were 35,364, in Kentucky 40,016....

But Virginia has a system of oral instruction which compensates for the want of schools, and that is her social intercourse. The social intercourse of the South is probably much greater than that of any people that ever existed. There is certainly nothing like the number of visits among the families of a city or even the same square in a city, as prevails in the country of the South. And these visits are not fashionable calls, but last for days and weeks—and they are the great resource of the South for instruction and amusement. It is true that persons are not taught at such places to read or write, but they are taught to think and converse. They are the occasions of interchanging opinions and diffusing intelligence; and to perform the duties, to enjoy the pleasures of such intercourse, to please, to shine, and to captivate, requires a degree of mental culture which no custom of the North so much demands. Accordingly the South exhibits the remarkable phenomenon of an agricultural people distinguished above all others of the present day by the elegance of their manners and the intellectual tone of their society.

The North excels in books.... But in individual character and individual action, the South excels. For a warm heart and open hand, for sympathy of feeling, fidelity of friendship, and high sense of honor; for knowledge of the sublime mechanism of man and reason and eloquence to delight, to instruct and to direct him, the South is superior; ....

Document 17 Reverend Fred Ross, "Speech delivered at the General Assembly of the Presbyterian Church," New York, 1856.[15]

The challenge to argue the question of slavery from the Bible was thrown down on the floor of the Assembly.

Dr. Wisner having said that he would argue the question on the Bible, ... Dr. Ross rose,... and, taking his position on the platform near the Moderator's chair, said,--

"I accept the challenge given by Dr. Wisner, to argue the question of slavery from the Scriptures."

Dr. Wisner.—Does the brother propose to go into it here?

Dr. Ross.—Yes, sir.

Dr. Wisner.—Well, I did not propose to go into it here.

Dr. Ross.—You gave the challenge, and I accept it.

Dr. Wisner.—I said I would argue it at a proper time; but it is no matter. Go ahead.

Sir, I come now to the Bible argument. I begin at the beginning of eternity! (Laughter.) WHAT IS RIGHT AND WRONG? *That's the question of questions.*

Two theories have obtained in the world. The one is, that right and wrong are eternal facts; that they exist *per se* in the nature of things; that they are ultimate truths above God; that he must study, and does study, to know them, as really as man. Ant that he comprehends them more clearly than man, only because he is a better student than man. Now, sir, *this theory is atheism.* For if right and wrong are like mathematical truths—fixed facts—then I may find them out, as I find out mathematical truths, without instruction from God. ... If, then, moral truths, if right and wrong, if rectitude and sin, are, in like manner, fixed, eternal facts,--if they are out from and above God, like mathematical entities,--then I may find them for myself.... The irrestible conclusion is, I may think I can live without God; that Jehovah is a myth, a name;...

The other theory, is that right and wrong are results brought into being, ... made to exist solely by the will of God, expressed through his word; or, when his will is not thus known, he shows it in the human reason by which he rules the natural heart. ... In his benevolent wisdom, he then *willed* LAW, to control *natural good and evil.* And he thereby made *conformity* to that law to be *right,* and *non-conformity* to be *wrong.*

---

15 Reverend Fred Ross, "Speech delivered at the General Assembly of the Presbyterian Church," New York, 1856, in *Slavery Ordained of God,* (Philadelphia: Lippincott & Co., 1857), pp. 32-65.

These two theories of Right and Wrong,--these two ideas of human liberty,--the right, in the nature of things, or the right as made by God,--the liberty of the individual man, of Atheism, of Red Republicanism, of the devil,--or the liberty of man, in the family, in the State, the liberty from God,--these two theories now make the conflict of the world. This anti-slavery battle is only part of the great struggle: God will be vicorious, and we, in his might.

I now come to the particular illustrations of the world-wide law that service shall be rendered by the inferior to the superior. The relations in which such service obtains are very many. Some of them are these:--husband and wife; parent and child; teacher and scholar; commander and soldier,--sailor; master and apprentice; master and hireling; master and slave. Now, sir, all these relations are ordained of God. They are all directly commanded, or they are the irresistible law of his providence.

... Do you say, The slave is held to *involuntary service?* So is the wife. Her relation to her husband, in the immense majority of cases, is made for her, and not by her.... O ye wives, I know how superior you are to your husbands in many respects,--not only in personal attraction,... in grace, in refined thought, in passive fortitude, in enduring love, and in a heart to be filled with the spirit of heaven. Oh, I know all this. Nay, I know you may surpass him in his own sphere of boasted prudence and worldly wisdom about dollars and cents. Nevertheless, he has authority, from God, to rule over you. You are under service to him. You are bound to obey him *in all things.* Your service is very, very, very often involuntary from the first.... But the husband may not so love you. He may rule you with the rod of iron. What can you do? Be divorced? God forbids it, save for crime. Will you say that you are free, that you will go where you please, do as you please? No; you cannot. ...

A word on the subject of divorce. One of your standing denunciations of the South is the terrible laxity of the marriage vow among the slaves. Well, sir, what does your Boston Dr. Nehemiah Adams say? ... He says, he is not sure but that the marriage relation is as enduring among the *slaves in the South* as it is among white people in New England. ... You seldom hear of a divorce in Virginia or South Carolina.

Do you say the slave is *sold and bought?* So is the wife world over. Everywhere, always, and now as the general fact, however done away or modified by Christianity. The savage buys her. The barbarian buys her. The Turk buys her. The Jew buys her. The Christian buys her,--Greek, Armenian, Nestorian, Roman Catholic, Protestant... the Frenchman, the Englishman, the New England man, the New Yorker,--*buy the wife*—in many, very many cases. She is seldom bought in the South, and never among the slaves themselves; for they always marry for love. (Continued laughter)

... Sir, God sanctioned slavery then, and sanctions it now. He made it right, they know, then and now.... Turn to the twenty-first chapter of Exodus, vs. 2-5. God, in these verses, gave the Israelites his command how they should buy and hold the Hebrew servant,--how, under certain conditions, he went free,--how, under other circumstances, he might be held to service forever, with his wife and her children. There it is.

But what have we here? Verses 7-11:--"And if a man sell his daughter to be a maid-servant, she shall not go out as the men-servants do. And if he hath betrothed her unto his son, he shall deal with her after the manner of daughters. If he take him another wife, her food, her raiment, and her duty of marriage shall he not diminish. And if he do not these three unto her, then shall she go out free without money." Now, sir, the wit of man can't dodge that passage, unless he runs away into the Hebrew. (Great laughter) For what does God say? Why, this: that an Israelite might sell his own daughter, not only into servitude, but into polygamy....

... In Leviticus 25:44-46, "Both thy bondmen and bondmaids, which thou-shalt have, shall be of the heathen that are round about you; of them shall ye buy bondmen and bondmaids." ... Sir, I do not see how God could tell us more plainly that he did command his people to buy slaves from the heathen round about them, ... The passage has no other meaning. Did God merely permit sin?—did he merely tolerate a dreadful evil? God does not say so anywhere. He gives his people law to buy and hold slaves of the heathen forever....

God in the New Testament made no law prohibiting the relation of master and slave.... The precepts in Colossians 4:18 and 23; I Timothy 6:1-6, and other places show, unanswerably, that God as really sanctioned the relation of master and slave as those of husband and wife, and parent and child; and that all the obligations of the moral law, and Christ's law of love, might and must be as truly fulfilled in the one relation as in the other.

.... Every Southern master. His Obligation is high, and great, and glorious. Yes, sir, *I know*, whether Southern masters fully know it or not, that *they hold from God*, individually and collectively, *the highest and the noblest responsibility ever given by Him to individual private men on all the face of the earth.* For God has entrusted them to train millions of the most degraded in form and intellect, but, at the same time, the most gentle, the most amiable, the most affectionate, the most imitative, the most susceptible of social and religious love, of all the races of mankind,--to train them, and to give them civilization, and the light and the life of the gospel of Jesus Christ.

Document 18 James Henry Hammond, "Letters on Slavery,"[16]

You will say that man cannot hold *property in man*. The anser is, that he can and *actually does* hold property in his fellow all the world over, in a variety of forms, and *has always done so.* I will show presently his authority for doing it.

... the first question we have to ask ourselves is, whether it is contrary to the will of God, as revealed to us in his Holy Scriptures—the only certain means given us to ascertain his will. If it is, then Slavery is a sin. ... Let us open these Holy Scriptures. In the twentieth chapter of Exodus, seventeenth verse, I find the following words: "Thou shalt not covet thy neighbor's house, thous shalt not covet thy neighbor's wife, nor his man-servant, nor his maid-servant, nor his ox, nor his ass, nor anything that is thy neighbor's"... Does it not emphatically and explicitly forbid you to disturb your neighbor in the enjoyment of his property; and more especially of that which is here specifically mentioned as being lawfully and by this commandment made sacredly his? Prominent in the catalogue stands his "man-servant and his maid-servant," who are thus distinctly *consecrated as his property,* and guaranteed to him for his exclusive benefit, in the most solemn manner.... It is well known that both the Hebrew and Greek words translated "servant" in the Scriptures, means also, and most usually, "slave."

---

[16] James Henry Hammond, "Letters on Slavery," in *The Pro-Slavery Argument; as maintained by the most Distinguished Writers of the Southern States,* (Charleston: Walker, Richards & Co., 1852), pp. 99-174.

... It is vain to look to Christ or any of his Apostles to justify such blasphemous perversions of the word of God.... On the contrary...[Christ and the Apostles] regarding Slavery as an *established*, as well as *inevitable condition of human society*, they never hinted at such as thing as its termination on earth....

It is impossible, therefore, to suppose that Slavery is contrary to the will of God. It is equally absurd to say that American Slavery differs in form or principle from that of the chosen people.... I think, then, I may safely conclude that American Slavery is not only not a sin, but especially commanded by God through Moses, and approved by Christ through his apostles. And here I might close its defence; for what God ordains, and Christ sanctifies, should surely command the respect and toleration of man.

.... Let us examine it in its influence on [the] political and social state.... I endorse without reserve the much abused sentiment of Goverher M'Duffie, that "Slavery is the corner-stone of our republican edifice;" while I repudiate, as ridiculously absurd, that much lauded but nowhere accredited dogma of Mr. Jefferson, that "all men are born equal." ...

.... In the slaveholding States, ... nearly one-half of the whole population, and those the poorest and most ignorant, have no political influence whatever, because they are slaves. Of the other half, a large proportion are both educated and independent in their circumstances, while those who unfortunately are not so, being still elevated far above the mass, are higher toned and more deeply interested in preserving a stable and well ordered government, than the same class in any other country....

With us every citizen is concerned in the maintenance of order, and in promoting honesty and industry among those of the lowest class who are our slaves; and our habitual vigilance renders standing armies, whether of soldiers or policemen, entirely unnecessary. Small guards in our cities, and occasional patrols in the country, ensure us a repose and security known no where else. You cannot be ignorant that, excepting the United States, there is no country in the world whose existing government would not be overturned in a month, but for its standing armies, maintained at an enormous and destructive cost.... Nor will it be long before the *"free States"* of this Union will be compelled to introduce the same expensive machinery, to preserve order among their "free and equal" citizens.

... It is a great mistake to suppose, as is generally done abroad, that in case of war slavery would be a source of weakness. It did not weaken Rome, nor Athens, nor Sparta.... I have no apprehension that our slaves would seize such an opportunity to revolt. The present generation of them, born among us, would never think of such a thing at any time, unless instigated to it by others....

Document 19 "The Dred Scott Decision," Speech delivered at the Anniversary of the American Abolition Society, Frederick Douglass, 1857.[17]

I base my sense of the certain overthrow of slavery, in part, upon the nature of the American Government, the Constitution, the tendencies of the age, and the character of the American people; and this, notwithstanding the important decision of Judge Taney. [the Dred Scott decision]

---

17 "Dred Scott Decision" in Two *Speeches by Frederick Douglass;*... (Rochester, NY: C.P. Dewey, 1857), pp. 35-37.

I know of no soil better adapted to the growth of reform than American soil. I know of no country where the conditions for affecting great changes in the settled order of things, for the development of right ideas of liberty and humanity, are more favorable than here in these United States.

The very groundwork of this government is a good repository of Christian civilization. The Constitution, as well as the Declaration of Independence, and the sentiments of the founders of the Republic, give us a platform broad enough, and strong enough, to support the most comprehensive plans for the freedom and elevation of all the people of this country, without regard to color, class, or clime.

There is nothing in the present aspect of the anti-slavery question which should drive us into the extravagance and nonsense of advocating a dissolution of the American Union as a means of overthrowing slavery, or freeing the North from the malign influence of slavery upon the morals of the Northern people. While the press is at liberty, and speech is free, and the ballot-box is open to the people of the sixteen free States; while the slaveholders are but four hundred thousand in number, and we are fourteen millions; while the mental and moral power of the nation is with us; while we are really the strong and they are the weak, it would look worse than cowardly to retreat from the Union.

If the people of the North have not the power to cope with these four hundred thousand slaveholders inside the Union, I see not how they could do so out of the Union. The strength necessary to move the Union must ever be less than is required to break it up. If we have got to conquer the slave power to get out of the Union, I for one would much rather conquer, and stay in the Union. The latter, it strikes me, is the far more rationale mode of action....

It is not in changing the dead form of the Union, that slavery is to be abolished in this country. We have to do not with the dead, but the living; not with the past, but the living present. Those who seek slavery in the Union, and who are everlastingly dealing blows upon the Union, in the belief that they are killing slavery, are most woefully mistaken. They are fighting a dead form instead of a living and powerful reality. It is clearly not because of the peculiar character of our Constitution that we have slavery, but the wicked pride, love of power, and selfish perverseness of the American people. Slavery lives in this country not because of any paper Constitution, but in the moral blindness of the American people, who persuade themselves that they are safe, though the rights of others may be struck down.

ANALYZING THE EVIDENCE

1. How did the proposals (Documents 1 and 3) to reimburse slaveowners and repatriate or "colonize" the slaves in either the American West or in Africa propose to end slavery without threatening the property rights of slavers? How did Francis Wright's proposal make this possible? Why did these two proposals contend that slaves had to be removed from the country on their emancipation?

2. What arguments were made in opposition to these "colonization" schemes? (See Document 4 and Document 11)

3. How did pro-slavery supporters frequently respond to anti-slavery activism? (Document 2 and 9) What support could abolitionists expect from authorities?

ANTEBELLUM CULTURE WARS

4. How did the Declaration of Sentiments (Document 4) connect the plight of slaves to the position of patriots in the American Revolution? What features of the institution of slavery does the declaration most object to?

5. How did William E. Channing use natural rights doctrine to justify his opposition to slavery?(Document 5)

6. What tactics used by the abolitionists are evident in Documents 3, and 6-10?

7. How did Angelina Grimke use her origins in the South to give her greater legitimacy in criticizing the practice of slavery? What criticisms did she level at northerners in her speech? (Document 8)

8. Why does Thomas Roderick Dew perceive to be the economic argument in favor of slavery an in rejection of colonization schemes? (Document 11)

9. How did Whittier's poem (Document 12) characterize the inhumanity of the domestic slave trade?

10. How did pro-slavery apologists support the argument that slavery was "natural" and "historical"? (Documents 13 and 14)

11. How does William Lloyd Garrison's tone and argument in this speech support the view that he was an anti-slavery "radical" in the 1850s? (Document 15) How did the pro-slavery arguments Garrison lists parallel those seen in the pro-slavery documents in this chapter?

12. What evidence did John Forsyth provide for the unhealthy nature of the northern "free" or "wage-labor" economy and of northern cities? (Document 16) How did such arguments support southern views of the morality of slavery?

13. How did Reverend Ross's defense of slavery use arguments from nature, family relations and scripture to support the view that slavery was God-ordained?(Document 17)

14. How did James Henry Hammond's argument make the case for "white supremacy" as the foundation of an orderly society? (Document 18)

15. How did Frederick Douglass's tone and objections to slavery (Document 19) compare with William Lloyd Garrison's? (Document 15)

Document Based Questions

1. Using the documents provided analyze the arguments made in favor of abolishing slavery in the nineteenth century.

2. Using the documents provided analyze the different strategies employed by abolitionists as they sought to do away with slavery in the United States.

3. Using the documents provided compare and contrast the arguments in opposition to and in favor of the institution of slavery by abolitionists and pro-slavery apologists.

"Oh, Liberty! What Crimes Have been Committed in Thy Name:" Manifest Destiny and the Politics of Slavery

CHAPTER 12

Between 1800 and 1860, the American republic grew from a nation precariously situated on the shores of the Atlantic with little real presence beyond the Appalachian mountain range, to a continental power extending to the Pacific. For an American born in 1800, his or her homeland had quadrupled during their lifetime. The most important acquisitions included the Louisiana Purchase in 1803, the annexation of Texas and the Oregon territory in 1845 and 1846 respectively, and the Mexican "Cession" in 1848 composing the contemporary states of California, Nevada, Colorado, New Mexico, and Arizona. The nation's expansion was neither inevitable nor are its present boundaries natural. The expansion of the United States came with significant costs to those in the way of that territorial enlargement, the native Americans who were removed from the eastern half of the country and the Mexican republic that lost nearly a quarter of its territory, and immeasurable economic resources at its defeat in the Mexican-American War.

The growth of the United States also exposed political and economic divisions within the young republic. Each territorial acquisition necessitated a revisiting of the fundamental question of what kind of nation the republic would become. Was the United States to be an "Empire of Liberty," an ideal first expressed by Thomas Jefferson? Or was it to be an "Empire of Slavery," as the opponents of slavery often contended. Jefferson's imagined future was itself a kind of oxymoron within republican intellectual traditions. Empires within republican thought were by definition conceived to be antithetical to liberty and to republican institutions. Jefferson had contended, however, that the new republic would only thrive if it expanded, spreading the ideals of liberty expressed in the Declaration of Independence and secured in the Constitution, and guaranteeing its citizenry opportunities for land ownership and freedom from dependency. Westward expansion, however, both reflected the imperatives of the plantation economy (cotton and tobacco rapidly reduced soil fertility and encouraged an extensive agriculture) and guaranteed the spread of chattel slavery. Each acquisition of new territory, nonetheless, threatened to destabilize the fragile balance of power that had been maintained since the drafting of the United States Constitution, a balance of power that confirmed the nation's commitment to recognize ownership of property in human beings and accepted the economics of an industrial capitalism built on a foundation of financial dependency on chattel slavery.

The challenge to those who hoped to maintain the Union fashioned in Philadelphia in 1787 was often manifested as an ideological divide (pitting abolitionists against defenders of slavery). It as often appeared to be an economic conflict between the commercial interests of an urban industrial society united with the market-oriented agriculture of the Old Northwest confronting a tradition-bound plantation economy. The economic differences between North and South, as we saw in an earlier chapter, may have been more rhetorical than real. It is quite possible that each of these ways of conceptualizing the differences between North and South had more to do with simple political calculations and struggles for electoral victories. Over the course of the antebellum period, the ways in which political leaders energized distinct groups of voters and mobilized different regional, cultural, and economic arguments to appeal for votes had a great deal to do with destabilizing the coalition of cultural and economic interests that had papered over their differences with the United States Constitution.

THE MISSOURI CRISIS

The first moment of political crisis stemming from territorial acquisition occurred in 1819-1820, in a period often characterized as the "Era of Good Feelings," when residents of Missouri applied to enter the Union. Missouri was the second region in the Louisiana Territory, after Louisiana, to meet the requirements for application to statehood. As the area had been settled by residents of Tennessee and Kentucky, many of whom were slaveholders, the Missouri constitution submitted to Congress defended residents' rights to own slaves and the rights of immigrants to bring into the state their human property. The constitution and Missouri's application for statehood had to be approved by the United States Congress, however, and in the debates over its entry, political and ideological opposition to slavery threatened to derail the process. The New Yorker, James Tallmadge, Jr. proposed an amendment to the resolution establishing Missouri's statehood, which required that Missouri agree to the gradual end of slavery as a condition for its entry into the Union. Abolitionists and religious reformers quickly celebrated Tallmadge's amendment and southerners decried what they characterized as an unconstitutional Congressional intrusion into the process for application to statehood. They also feared that, despite Tallmadge's protestations to the contrary, were this Congressional regulation of the property rights of slaveholders wishing to settle in Missouri permitted to stand, southerners emigrating elsewhere into the Louisiana Territory would face similar obstacles. Southerners also feared that the door would be opened to further meddling with the slave holding rights of states where slavery was established practice. Tallmadge and his abolitionist allies contended that slavery was an evil that should not be permitted to spread beyond the Mississippi, and that Congress had the Constitutional authority to limit its expansion. Moreover, Tallmadge's Congressional allies argued that Missouri's admission as a slave state violated the precedent laid out in the Northwest Ordinances of 1787 that established the Northwest Territories (north of the Ohio River) as free states. The debates surrounding Missouri's application, in short, gave voice to arguments on both sides that would become features of the debate over slavery in newly acquired lands. Underlying the ferocity of Congressional debates was the threat to the sectional balance in the legislative body. The number of slave states (eleven) equaled the number of free states. Addition of Missouri as a slave state would result in southern dominance in the Senate. Southerners countered that the North maintained a substantial lead (105-81) in the House of Representatives. Similar political considerations would feature in each of the ensuing episodes of rivalry over how to include new states into the Union.

The "Missouri Compromise" that resolved this dispute admitted Missouri to the Union but counterbalanced this inclusion with the addition of Maine as a free state. Additionally, Congress passed a law outlawing slavery north of the southern boundary of Missouri. The constitutional crisis was momentarily averted. But with Texas's war for independence and agitation to annex its vast territory, the issue was again renewed. Because Texas had been settled largely by slave holders from the South and because its prosperity depended upon cotton cultivation and the growth of global demand for cotton, it seemed apparent that Texas, were it to become a part of the United States, would seek admission as a slave state.

TEXAS SECESSION AND STATEHOOD

When Mexico achieved its independence from Spain in 1821, Mexico stretched from California and the present-day U.S. Southwest and encompassed all of Central America except Panama. The state of "Coahuila y Tejas," which included Texas, was on the northeastern boundary of the new United States of Mexico. With Mexico's independence the country legalized immigration from the United States. In particular, Mexico sought to encourage settlement in Texas to try to stabilize a region with few Spanish-speaking inhabitants. In 1821 Texas was largely the domain of the Comanche and other native Americans. The Comanche during this period had terrorized Mexican settlements, in part as they raided for horses and mules that could be sold to southern planters in Louisiana and Mississippi. The Mexican government hoped that the settlement of Anglo planters along the Gulf Coast would reverse the decline in the region's fortunes.

Moses Austin was the first American immigrant authorized to settle in the state. He died before he was able to move to Texas. His son, Stephen F. Austin took over the land grant, and in 1822 brought 300 immigrants from the United States. Austin's colony was composed mostly of immigrants from the American South, with their African slaves. Under Austin's plan, an immigrant was entitled to acquire an additional 50 acres of land for each slave brought to Texas. The plan was successful in attracting southern slave holders. By 1825 one out of every five settlers was an enslaved African American. Anglo settlers were not the only immigrants encouraged to come to Texas. Mexico offered land ownership and other privileges to free blacks, who were entitled to full citizenship rights as well. As we have seen in an earlier chapter, proposals for "colonization" frequently mentioned Texas as a potential destination for freed slaves.

This was only the most immediate indicator that Mexico shared a somewhat different perspective on race relations and slavery than that held by most American southerners. Additionally, successive Mexican governments and Mexican state governments often differed on the matter of slavery. After welcoming southern slave holders to Texas, the government of Mexico in 1823 forbade the sale or purchase of slaves, and required manumission of the children of slaves at the age of fourteen. In 1827, the legislature of Coahuila y Tejas, in Saltillo, outlawed further imports of slaves and granted freedom at birth to all children born to enslaved parents. Then in 1829, President Vicente Guerreroa, an Afro-Mestizan himself, ordered the abolition of slavery. Two and a half months later, after lengthy and heated negotiations, Texas was granted an exemption, but Anglo-Texan slave holders were increasingly ill-at-ease with the apparent growing hostility to their property rights in human beings. In 1830 a nationwide prohibition of slave imports was enacted. Texans exploited a loophole allowing them to bring in slaves as "indentured servants," under "contracts" for lifetime servitude in repayment of a debt (their purchase price) which could hardly be paid off given their hopelessly low wages. The debt was also inheritable, passing the debt on to the children of enslaved persons, effectively ensuring the continued enslavement of generations of black Texans.

Efforts to limit or eliminate slavery resulted in tensions between Mexican governments and Anglo slaveowners from the United States. Slaves also took advantage of opportunities to flee to tribal lands or across the Rio Grande in search of their freedom. These tensions came to a head what became known as the Anahuac Disturbances, in 1832 and again in 1835. These uprisings of Anglo settlers resulted in part from dissatisfaction at the imposition of taxes on imports and exports, which were perceived as a threat to slave owners, and from the Mexican military commander's protection of two escaped slaves from Louisiana. William B. Travis was the attorney hired to bring the slaves back; he was also arrested for forging a letter to the governor threatening that the Louisiana militia were going to intervene. These and other issues resulted in the Texans declaring their independence in 1835. It is fair to say, as one recent historian has done, that the "Texas Revolution," was a precursor to the American Civil War and had little of a revolutionary character about it. Texans seceded from the United States of Mexico, largely with the objective of maintaining the institution of slavery and securing ownership of human property.

Perhaps the best evidence of the counter-revolutionary nature of the "Texas Revolution" might be seen in the preoccupations of the Texas Constitution of 1836. Among the features of this framework for Texas government, persons who had been indentured for life were formally declared property; Congress could pass no law restricting immigrants from bringing their slaves into the Republic; Congress was forbidden to emancipate slaves; freedmen had to petition the Texas Congress for permission to remain in the country and were disqualified, even if free from being classified as persons having rights; and, finally slave owners were not free to manumit slaves, unless the freed slave left the republic, immediately. Unlike the American Revolution, which did destabilize the pre-revolutionary social and political hierarchy the Texas Revolution represented the victory of slavers challenged by Mexicans' revolutionary and abolitionist impulses.

For the United States, however, possibility of annexation of Texas by the United States—which Texans had overwhelmingly voted for shortly after their independence from Mexico was secure—once again exposed fault lines in the republic. Andrew Jackson, though he favored annexation, in his last year in office, and not wishing to either impair the election of his Vice President, Martin Van Buren, or involve the United States in a dispute with Mexico, refused to recognize the new republic until after Van Buren's presidency had been assured. Abolitionists had opposed annexation even before the Texas war for independence had concluded, seeing southern migration into Texas, defiance of Mexican law, and the revolution itself as part of a southern conspiracy to spread slavery. In March 1837, with Van Buren's election secure, Congress finally recognized the Republic of Texas. But under Van Buren, with the economic depression of 1837 pre-occupying his presidency, and with fears that annexation would fracture the union, talk of annexation waned. The majority of southerners favored adding Texas to the Union. In the North, both Whigs and Democrats were divided, and the national leadership of both the Whig and Democratic Parties feared that debates over Texas would fracture party unity. In 1840, William Henry Harrison, a Whig was elected as the nation reacted to the economic downturn that had characterized Van Buren's administration. But, Harrison died a month into his presidency and was replaced by John Tyler. Tyler had been added to the Harrison ticket, rather as an afterthought; a New York power-broker contended that "Tyler was finally taken because we could get nobody else to accept." Tyler believed that territorial expansion promised the best hope to strengthen and preserve the Union. As a Virginian he was also committed to both slave-holding and states' rights. Tyler, who had been a Democrat until 1836, was by 1843 also *persona non grata* in the Whig Party. Hoping to build his personal popularity, Tyler departed from previous administrations' position on annexation and opened secret negotiations with Texas president Sam Houston to secure Texas' annexation. Ratification of the treaty, however, would prove a most serious obstacle. The Whig-dominated Senate soundly defeated the treaty and Tyler was unable to win re-election. Instead, James K. Polk, who had run a pro-expansion campaign calling for the annexation of Texas and acquisition of Oregon Territory won the election of 1844. It would be Tyler then who signed the treaty accepting Texas into the Union.

THE MEXICAN "CESSION" AND THE "APPLE OF DISCORD"

The annexation of Texas, Mexican leaders had warned, would soon lead to war. They were not wrong. Mexico's northern provinces of New Mexico and California, in a pattern not unlike that which had led to the settlement in Texas by Anglo immigrants from the southeastern United States, were also becoming increasingly interlinked with the United States economy as U.S. merchants and settlers arrived and forged relations with local Indian and Mexican populations. These ties, coupled with tensions between Mexico's Far North and the centralizing government in Mexico City, provided a window of opportunity for American political leaders to further extend the project of Manifest Destiny. For many southern slaveholders this meant an opportunity to expand the reach of the plantation economy. Mercantile interests saw expansion to the Pacific largely as an opportunity to increase possibilities of Asian trade. Once again, mercantile interests and slaveholders' interests coincided.

After the acquisition of Texas, Polk's administration turned to California and New Mexico. A diplomatic mission to Mexico offered to purchase these two northern provinces for between $24 and $40 million. The Mexican President José Joaquín Herrera, refused to meet with the envoys, a snub that Polk took as justification for war. United States had also taken up the boundary dispute between the Republic of Texas and Mexico, claiming that the boundaries of Texas extended to the Rio Grand River, a vast extension of territory, while Mexico maintained the border was the Nueces River. Polk had earlier ordered an "army of observation" stationed in Corpus Christi, where they took up a position along the Nueces, but soon began to make excursions into the Nueces Strip between the Nueces and Rio Grande rivers. When on April 25, 1846 one of these excursionary units confronted a Mexican force at the "Battle of Buena Vista" Polk revised his already written war message to include the language that Mexican troops had "invaded our territory and shed blood on American soil." Congress then overwhelmingly approved the declaration of war.

Many Whigs, however, opposed the war and what they believed to be blatant expansionism. Daniel Webster expressed this objection most clearly, "We want no extension of territory; we want no accession of new states. The country is large enough already." Moreover, Northern Whigs characterized the war as a conflict engineered by a conspiracy of slave interests. Northern Whigs feared that expansion into Mexican territory would lead to a repeat of the divide opened by the Missouri application for statehood. But, as has often been the case in United States history, the fever of nationalist enthusiasm and fear of being politically cast as unwilling to support the sacrifices of the troops led most Whigs to acquiesce to the declaration of war and to increased military appropriations. The war was not a lengthy one, and by September 1847 Mexico City had fallen. The final surrender would be signed in February 1848 with the Treaty of Guadalupe-Hidalgo.

Even as the war was underway in the midst of the patriotic furor, David Wilmot, a Democrat from Pennsylvania offered up what southerners would call an "apple of discord," his proviso. A proviso is an addendum to a bill likely to pass, in this case, an appropriations bill to fund the war. The text of his proviso read forbade the expansion of slavery into the territories acquired from Mexico. Wilmot offered this rider in the hopes of currying favor with voters in Pennsylvania who voted for the Liberty Party or the Free-Soil Party, both single issue parties opposed to the spread of slavery. "Wilmot's Proviso" and the debate over whether slavery should be permitted to spread into the territories annexed from Mexico would once again divide the nation, with southern Whigs and southern Democrats making cause against it and northern politicians of both parties voting in favor. Not only did political parties divide over the issue of what to do with the new southwestern territories, churches and other social organizations increasingly divided along sectional lines over the issue of western expansion of slavery. The argument over what to do with the territories acquired from Mexico shaped national politics between 1846 and 1850, with a temporary resolution reached only with the Compromise of 1850. Under the terms of this compromise, California with its current boundaries was incorporated into the Union as a free state, Texas's borders were definitively settled, and the remainder of the Mexican territories were left without a determined status.

A feature of the Compromise of 1850 was the passage of the Fugitive Slave Act, which aimed to put teeth into the Fugitive Slave Clause and to stop the "nullification" of northerners unwilling to be party to enforcement of the constitutional requirement that escaped slaves be returned to their owners. The law authorized a fine of $1,000 as a penalty for law-enforcement officials who failed to arrest alleged runaways and a similar fine for private citizens who gave runaway slaves food and assistance. As a result of this "poison pill" the Compromise of 1850 did little to eliminate the sectional tensions that had arisen with Wilmot's "apple of discord." Moreover, the Fugitive Slave Act shifted the terms of the debate from a focus on the status of slavery in the West to the place of slavery in the existing states of the Union. As has already been explored in Chapter Ten, during the 1850s an increase in abolitionist sentiment across the North and Midwest, and the influence of key anti-slavery activists and publications increasingly made communication and political compromise across this cultural and economic divide difficult.

THE KANSAS-NEBRASKA ISSUE

Perhaps the matter that finally resulted in the opening of hostilities over the question of slavery's presence in the western territories was the question of what to do in the Indian territories north of the Missouri Compromise line. Stephen Douglass, an Illinois Senator with an ambition to become president, and the desire to bridge this divide, would in 1854 offer a compromise solution designed to keep the country together. Douglas proposed to open the Indian Terrritory, now Kansas and Nebraska, to statehood. Kansas, like Oklahoma, had been largely settled in the previous decade by Indian populations driven west in the 1830s. Kansas was offered as a potential slave state, even though its admission as such would violate the principles of the Missouri Compromise. Nebraska was seen by Douglas as a likely free-state. Douglas considered the area likely to attract small farmers rather than slaveholders. In order to attract southern votes in favor of this expansion of settlement, Douglas argued that the determination of whether Kansas and Nebraska should be "free" or "slave" states should be left to majority rule in the territory.

Kansas would be the first of the two likely states to test Douglas's proposed solution. For Kansas the consequence of placing the issue before the voters, in one of the most high-stakes contests for both the territory and for the nation, was massive voter fraud and electoral violence. The first referendum resulted in more than double the number of ballots cast as there were eligible voters. Missourians crossed the boarder to vote and to settle, hoping to swing the balance toward the pro-slavery camp. Free-soilers from New England came to northeastern Kansas establishing the town of Lawrence. The town was attacked by pro-slavery Kansans and Missourians. In retaliation, the pro-slavery town of Pottawatomie Creek nearby was attacked by freesoilers led by John Brown. The Kansas countryside deteriorated into violence and disorder.

Douglas would not ride the measure to the White House. Instead, the Kansas-Nebraska Act, would divide the parties along sectional lines, this time with the end result being the destruction of the 2nd Party system. When the Kansas-Nebraska Act came to a vote, southern Whigs voted with southern Democrats in its favor, while northern Whigs rejected it unanimously, completely fracturing the Whig Party. In 1856, the Whigs were so divided they could not agree on a presidential candidate. Meanwhile, northern Democrats were so tainted by the national Democratic Party's support for Douglas's proposal that they were punished in the elections of 1854 with losses that reduced their presence in Congress to less than a third of their former influence. Out of the wreckage arose a third party, the Republican Party. The Republicans drew their support from anti-slavery voters, Northern Whigs unable to forgive southern Whigs who had voted for the Kansas-Nebraska Act, and northern Democrats who saw southern slave holders as monopolizing and distorting the Democratic Party for their own ends.

As a result of the inability of the national political institutions to resolve the conflicts that inevitability arose with each new territory's inclusion or with each new state's application for statehood, the dreams of an "Empire of Liberty" as Jefferson had proclaimed, and the unifying possibilities of Manifest Destiny, no longer seemed realistic. In a political climate reminiscent of our own in the early decades of the twenty-first century, conversations across the cultural and political divide became ever more difficult. Southerners and pro-slavery advocates increasingly associated moderate free-soilers with abolitionists, and abolitionists with race mixers, free love advocates, suffragists, and socialists. Such fears seemed to be confirmed in 1859 when John Brown led a failed attempt to take the United States arsenal at Harpers Ferry, Virginia with the intent of raising a slave insurrection and arming the slaves with the stolen weaponry. Remembering how northerners had feted Brown after his return from Kansas, southerners felt they no longer lived in a republic that accepted their constitutional right to human property. The election of Abraham Lincoln in November of 1860 confirmed them in that conviction.

PRIMARY SOURCES

Document 1 "Admission of Missouri," Debate in the House of Representatives, 1819.[1]

Admission of Missouri

The House having again resolved itself into a Committee of the Whole, (Mr. Smith of Maryland in the chair) on the bill to authorize the people of the Missouri Territory to form a constitution and State government, and for the admission of the same into the Union—

The question being on the proposition of Mr. TALLMADGE to amend the bill by adding to it the following proviso:

"And provided, That the further introduction of slavery or involuntary servitude be prohibited,

except for the punishment of crimes, whereof the party shall have been fully convicted; and that

---

1 "Admission of Missouri," Debates in Annals of Congress, House of Representatives, 15th Congress, 2nd Session, pp. 1169-1185. http://memory.loc.gov

all children born within the said State, after admission thereof into the Union, shall be free at the age of twenty-five years:"

The debate commenced on Saturday was today resumed on this proposition; which was supported by Mr. Taylor, Mr. Mills, Mr. Livermore, and Mr. Fuller; and opposed by Mr. Barbour, Mr. Pindall, Mr. Clay, and Mr. Holmes.

Mr. John W. Taylor (New York): First, has Congress power to require of Missouri a Constitutional prohibition against the introduction of slavery, as a condition of admission into the Union?

Second: If the power exist, is it wise to exercise it? Congress has no power unless it be expressly granted by the Constitution, or necessary to the execution of some power clearly delegated. What then are the grants made to Congress in relation to the Territories? The third section of the fourth article declares, that "the Congress shall have power to dispose of and make all needful rules and regulations respecting the territory or other property belonging to the United States." It would be difficult to devise a more comprehensive grant of power. ...

...Having proved, as I apprehend, our right to legislate in the manner proposed, I proceed to illustrate the propriety of exercising it. And here I might rest satisfied with reminding my opponents of their own declarations on the subject of slavery. How often, and how eloquently, have they deplored its existence among them? What willingnesss, nay what solicitude have they not manifested to be relieved from this burden? How have they wept over the unfortunate policy that first introduced slaves into this country! How have they disclaimed the guilt and shame of that original sin, and thrown it back upon their ancestors! ... Gentlemen have now an opportunity of putting their principles into practice; if they have tried slavery and found it a curse; if they desire to dissipate the gloom with which it covers the land; I call upon them to exclude it from the Territory in question; plant not its seeds in this uncorrupt soil. ...

... History will record the decision of this day as exerting its influence for centuries to come .... If we reject the amendment and suffer this evil, now easily eradicated, to strike its roots so deep in the soil that it can never be removed, shall we not furnish some apology for doubting our sincerity....

Mr. Philip Pendleton Barbour, (Virginia) said that, as he was decidedly opposed to the amendment... he asked the indulgence of the House whilst he made some remarks ... for the purpose of showing the impropriety of its adoption. ... The first objection, said he, which meets us at the very threshold of the discussion, is this, that we have no Constitutional right to enact the proposed provision. ... "Congress has the power to make all needful rules and regulations respecting the territory of the United States;" and although, therefore, whilst the proposed State continued a part of our territory,... it would have been competent for us, .. to make needful rules and regulation—to have established the principle now proposed; yet the question assumes a totally different aspect when that principle is intended to apply to a State.... [and] Sir, this provision would be in violation of another principle of this Constitution... that "the citizens of each State shall be entitled to all privileges and immunities of citizens in the several States." Now, he would ask, whether a citizen of the State of Missouri, who (if this amendment prevail) cannot hold a slave, could, ... be said to enjoy the same privileges with a citizen of Virginia who now may hold a slave, or even with a citizen of Pennsylvania, who, though he cannot now hold one, yet may be permitted by the Legislature of his own State? ... if we pursue this reasoning still further... we shall be more forcibly struck with its impropriety. If we have a right to go one step in relation to a new State, beyond the footing upon which the original States stand; if we have a right to shear them of one beam more of sovereignty, we have the same right to take from them any other attribute of sovereign power. Thus, sir, we should equally possess the power to require ... that their Chief Executive Magistrate should or should not have [a veto] upon the acts of their Legislature; [or] that their Legislature should consist either of one or two chambers, as in our discretion we thought right. ... For, the question now before us, is not what regulations we shall prescribe for a territory which is to continue as such, but upon what forms and conditions we will admit a State into the Union. Our business is, then, to create a political community of a particular character, as prescribed by the Constitution; to itself it will belong to regulate its interior concerns, and amongst others, to decide whether it will or will not admit involuntary servitude.

...But, as it respected the justice of the measure, he would beg leave to submit some remarks to the House. Throughout all the Southern States, it was well known a very large portion of the population consisted of slaves, who, at the same time, stood towards the white population of the same States in the relation of property; although they were held as property, yet they were considered and treated as the most valuable, as the most favored property; their masters remembered that they were men, and although certainly degraded in the scale of society, by reason of their servitude, we felt for them those sympathies which bind one man to another, though that other may be our inferior. We were attached to them...; in short, such were the feelings of the Southern people towards their slaves, that nothing scarcely but the necessity of the master, or the crime of the slave, would induce him to sell his slave. If the master emigrated, he would carry his slave with him, not only for the various reasons ... already stated, but because, going into a wilderness, where much labor ws necessary to clear a country, they were, on that account, peculiarly necessary. Under these circumstances, a prohibition of the importation of slaves would in almost every instance, be tantamount to a prohibition of the emigration of the Southern people to the state of Missouri.

...Let it be remembered that we are not now called upon to decide, whether slavery shall be introduced into this country; it existed at the formation of the Constitution, and was recognized by that instrument, in reference both to representation and taxation. Nor, sir, are we called upon to decide whether there shall be an increase of the number of our slaves by importation from abroad. But the real question is, what disposition shall we make of those slaves who are already in the country/ Shall they be perpetually confined on this side of the Mississippi, or shall we spread them over a much larger surfact by permitting them to be carried beyond that river? ... By spreading them over a more extended surface, you secure these advantages. First by diminishing the proportion which the slaves bear in point of numbers to the whites, you diminish their motives to insurrection. Secondly, that if that even ever should occur, it would obviously be much more easily and certainly suppressed....

... Gentlemen mistake when they suppose that, if slaves be permitted to be carried to Missouri, the Northern people will not emigrate to that State; look at the fact in the Southern States; the Northern hive is continually pouring forth its swarms of emigrants, and many of them, especially of the mercantile class, light and settle amongst us, they soon become familiar with our habits and modes of life, prosper in an eminent degree. ... Gentlemen equally mistake, when they suppose that their countrymen of the North, who are obliged to labor, would be degraded to a level with the slaves....

...Another effect of this amendment would be, in an essential degree to affect the value of the countless millions of public lands beyond the Mississippi.

... Upon the whole, said Mr.Barbour, I believe that we have no power to enact the proposed amendment; and that, if we had, it would be highly impolitic and unjust. I am, therefore, decidedly opposed to its adoption.

Mr. James Tallmadge, (New York) rose.—Sir,... When I had the honor to submit to this House the amendment now under consideration, I accompanied it with a declaration, that it was intended to confine its operation to the newly acquired territory across the Mississippi; and I then expressly declared that I would in no manner intermeddle with the slaveholding States, nor attempt manumission in any of the original States in the Union. ... But, sir, such has been the character and the violence of this debate, and expressions of so much intemperance, and of an aspect so threatening have been used, that continued silence on my part would ill become me, who had submitted to this House the original proposition.

... Sir, the honorable gentleman from Missouri, (Mr. Scott) who has just resumed his seat, has told us of the *ides of March* and has cautioned us to "*beware of the fate of Caesar and of Rome.*" Another gentleman (Mr. Cobb) from Georgia, in addition to other expressions of great warmth, has said "that if we persist, the Union will be dissolved;" and, with a look fixed on me, has told us, "we have kindled a fire which all the waters of the ocean cannot put out, which seas of blood, can only extinguish."

Sir, language of this sort has no effect on me; my purpose is fixed, it is interwoven with my existence, its durability is limited with my life, it is a great and glorious cause, setting bounds to a slavery most cruel and debasing the world ever witnessed; it is the freedom of man; it is the cause of unredeemed and unregenerated human beings.

Sir, if a dissolution of the Union must take place, let it be so! If civil war, which gentlemen so much threaten, must come, I can only say, let it come! ... If blood is necessary to extinguish any fire which I have assisted to kindle, I can assure gentlemen, while I regret the necessity, I shall not forbear to contribute my mite.... I have the fortune and the honor to stand here as the representative of freemen... I know the will of my constituents, and regardless of consequences I will avow it; as their representative, I will proclaim their hatred to slavery in every shape;

Document 2   Henry L. Pinckney, Resolution on Petitions, 26 May 1836.[2]

That all petitions, memorials, resolutions, propositions, or papers, relating in any way or to any extent whatever to the subject of slavery, or the abolition of slavery, shall, without being either printed or referred, be laid upon the table, and that no further action whatever shall be had thereon.

Document 3   "Abolition Petitions," *Congressional Globe*, 9 January 1837.[3]

In the House of Representatives—Mr. ADAMS having presented a petition for the abolition of slavery within the District of Columbia, and the question being "Shall the memorial be received?:"

Mr. UNDERWOOD, of Kentucky, said that he had just voted against receiving a petition presented by the gentleman from Massachusetts (Mr. Adams) but he had been overruled by a large majority of the House. The petition was received and laid on the table, there to sleep the sleep of death. No sooner is this done, than the same gentleman offers another petition of the same character, praying for the abolition of slavery and the slave trade in the District of Columbia coming from a portion of the people of Massachusetts represented by him. ...

---

2   *Abridgement of the Debates of Congress, from 1789 to 1756,* Volume XIII, (New York: D. Appleton, & Co., 1860), p. 28.
3   Abolition Petitions, *Congressional Globe*, 9 January 1837.

Now, sir, I desire to know what *right* (for I shall consider the question as one of *right*) the people of Massachusetts have to petition us to repeal or modify the local regulations and laws which do not operate upon them, or within their territory, but which govern a different people, who do not complain, and who may be entirely satisfied, and wholly opposed to any change. We are told that we must receive and act upon this and all similar petitions, lest we subvert the *revered right of petition*. I deny that there is any *right* of petition, where the grievance complained of does not operate upon the petitioners. I admit that you may receive any petition through courtesy, without regard to its object, or the quarter from whence it comes; and in general it would be best to do so. But the attempt is made to force these abolition petitions upon the consideration of Congress as a matter of *right*; and it is against that attempt, upon such a pretext, I protest. Sir, these petitioners, as I conceive, are officiously intermeddling with the affairs of other people, when they had better mind their own business. …

Mr. REED of Massachusetts said he differed entirely in opinion with the gentleman who had last spoken, (Mr. Underwood) and as he had the charge of a number of memorials of similar character to the one now under consideration, he begged leave to say a few words upon the subject.

Let it be remembered that these memorials, so obnoxious to some members of this House, pray for the abolition of slavery and the slave trade in the *District of Columbia. They go no further.* The gentleman from Kentucky… denies the right secured by the Constitution, peaceably to assemble and petition Government for a redress of grievance, applied to the present case, because the evil complained of, if any evil exist, is only a national evil and is no personal grievance to the petitioners.

I cannot for a moment assent to the position of the gentleman. To my mind they are subversive of the right of petition, and of the rights of a free people. …In my opinion the *right* of the citizens of a free and representative Government to petition their representatives for a redress of grievances, is a perfect right. It exists independent of the Constitution. It must exist whre the people are free, and where it does not exist there is despotism. I am aware that, from abundant caution, this sacred right of petition is secured by the Constitution. The right so secured is not limited or enlarged by the security. It is a perfect right, which we must never permit to be impaired by ingenious arguments, to avoid the consideration of an unpleasant subject…. The right is the same, whether the evil complained of be national and remote, or direct and personal.

Document 4 Robert J. Walker, *Letter of Mr. Walker of Mississippi, Relative to the Annexation of Texas,* 1844.[4]

… If slavery be considered by the States of the North as an evil, why should they prefer that its location should be continued in States on their border, rather than in the more distant portions of the Union. It is clear that, as slavery advanced in Texas, it would recede from the States bordering on the free States of the North and West; and thus they would be released from actual contact with what they consider an evil, and also from all influx from those States of a large and constantly augmenting free black population.

… Here, then, if Texas is reannexed throughout the vast region and salubrious and delicious climate of Mexico, and of Central and Southern America, a large and rapidly increasing portion of the

---

[4] Robert J. Walker, *Letter of Mr. Walker, of Mississippi, relative to the Annexation of Texas*, (Washington: Printed at the Globe Office, 1844).

African race will disappear from the limits of the Union. The process will be gradual and progressive, without a shock, and without a convulsion; whereas, by the loss of Texas, and the imprisonment of the slave population of the Union within its present limits, slavery would increase in nearly all the slaveholding States, and a change in their condition would become impossible; ...

... The reannexation of Texas would strengthen and fortify the whole Union,... To the South and Southwest it would give peace and security; to agriculture and manufactures, to the products of the mines, the forest, and fisheries, new and important markets, that otherwise must soon be lost forever. To the commercial and navigating interests, it would give a new impulse; and not a canal or a railroad throughout the Union, that would not derive increased business, and augmented profits; whilst the great city of New York, the centre of most of the business of the Union, would take a mighty step in advance towards that destiny which must place her above London in wealth, in business and population. ... Shall, then, Texas be our own, with all its markets, commerce, and products, or shall we drive it into the arms of England, now outstretched to receive it, and striving to direct its destiny?

Document 5 Resolutions passed by the Massachusetts' Legislature on the Annexation of Texas, 1843-1847.[5]

16 March 1843.—"*Resolved,* That we, the Senate and House of Representatives, in General Court assembled, do, in the name of the people of Massachusetts, earnestly and solemnly protest against the incorporation of Texas into this Union, and declare than no act done, or compact made, for such purpose, by the Government of the United States, will be binding on the States or the People."

March 1845.—"*Resolved,* that the annexation of a large slaveholding territory, at the will of the Government of the United States, with the declared intention of giving strength to the institution of domestic slavery in these States, is an alarming encroachment upon the rights of the freemen of the Union, a perversion of the principles of republican government, a deliberate assault upon the compromises of the Constitution, and demands the strenuous, united and persevering opposition of all persons, without distinction, who claim to be the friends of human liberty."

February 1847.—"*Resolved, unanimously,* That the people of Massachusetts will strenuously resist the annexation of any new territory to this Union in which the institution of slavery is to be tolerated or established; and the Legislature, in behalf of the people of this Commonwealth, do hereby solemnly protest against the acquisition of any additional territory, withouth an express provision by Congress, that there shall be neigher slavery nor involuntary servitude in such territory, otherwise than for the punishment of crime.

---

5 "Note," *Mr. Daniel Webster's Speech in the U.S. Senate, March 23, 1848, upon the War with Mexico,* (Boston: Eastburn's Press, 1848), p. 24.

Document 6   E. W. Clay, "Young Texas in Repose," Lithograph, 1852.[6]

YOUNG TEXAS IN REPOSE.

An abolitionist view of the new republic featured a murderous cowboy and his victim.

---

6   E.W. Clay, "Young Texas in Repose," Lithograph, 1852. Yale Library Collection of Western Americana, Beinecke Rare Book and Manuscript Library. This particular image was accessed at https://www.csub.edu/~gsantos/img0041.html

Document 7   David Wilmot, "The Wilmot Proviso," August 8, 1846.[7]

Provided, That, as an express and fundamental condition to the acquisition of any territory from the Republic of Mexico by the United States, by virtue of any treaty which may be negotiated between them, and to the use by the Executive of the moneys herein appropriated, neither slavery nor involuntary servitude shall ever exist in any part of said territory, except for crime, whereof the party shall first be duly convicted.

Document 8   Mr. Daniel Webster's Speech in the U.S. Senate, upon the War with Mexico, 1848.[8]

Sir, we are in possession, by military power, of New Mexico and California, countries belonging hitherto to the United States of Mexico. We are informed by the President that it is his purpose to retain them, to consider them as territory fit to be attached, and to be attached to these United States of America. And our military operations and designs now before the Senate, are to enforce this claim of the Executive of the United States. We are to compel Mexico to agree, that the part of her dominion called New Mexico, and the other called California, shall be ceded to us; that we are in possession, as is said, and that she shall yield title to us.... Sir it is the identical object, in my judgment, for which the war was originally commenced, for which it has hitherto been prosecuted, and in furtherance of which this treaty is to be used, but as one means to bring about the general result, that general result depending, after all, on our own superior power, and on the necessity of submitting to any terms which we may prescribe to fallen, fallen, Mexico!

Sir, the members composing the other House... has passed a resolution affirming that "the war with Mexico was begun unconstitutionally and unnecessarily by the Executive government of the United States." I concur in that sentiment; ... and equally true, and equally capable of demonstration... this was was begun, has been continued, and is now prosecuted, for the great and leading purpose of the acquisition of new territory, out of which to bring in new States, with their Mexican population, into this our Union of the United States. ... However often it may be said that we did not go to war for conquest—"*Credut Judaeus Appella, Non ego.*" [Literally translated: Let the Jew *Appella* believe it, not I. We might say, "Tell that s--- to someone else."] Does not every body see, that the moment we *get possession* of territory we must retain it and make it our own?

But sir,

This war was waged for the object of creating new States, on the southern frontier of the United States, out of Mexican territory, and with such population as should be found resident thereupon.

I have opposed this object. I am against all accessions of territory to form new States. ... And, therefore I say, sir, that if I were asked today whether ... I will take a treaty for adding two new States to the Union on our southern border, I say *no*, distinctly, NO. ... I stated my reasons on the occasion now referred to [the annexation of Texas] in language which I have now before me and which I beg to present to the Senate:

---

7   David Wilmot, "The Wilmot Proviso," August 8, 1846, in Thomas Hart Benton, ed., *Abridgment of the Debates of Congress, from 1789 to 1856,* Vol. 15 (New York: D. Appleton & Co., 1861), p. 646.

8   *Mr. Daniel Webster's Speech in the U.S. Senate, March 23, 1848, upon the War with Mexico,* (Boston: Eastburn's Press, 1848), p. 23-23.

"I say then, gentlemen, in all frankness, that I see objections, I think insurmountable objections, to the annexation of Texas to the United States.... Gentlemen, we all see, that by whomsoever possessed, Texas is likely to be a slaveholding country, and I frankly avow my entire unwillingness to do anything which shall extend the slavery of the African race on this Continent, or add other slaveholding States to the Union. When I say that I regard slavery in itself as a great moral, social, and political evil, I only use language which has been adopted by distinguished men, themselves citizens of slaveholding States. I shall do nothing, therefore, to favor or encourage its further extension. We have slavery already amongst us. The Constitution found it among us; it recognized it, and gave it solemn guaranties. To the full extent of those guaranties we are all bound, in honor, in justice, and by the Constitution.... But when we come to speak of admitting new States, the subject assumes an entirely different aspect. Our rights and our duties are then both different.... In my opinion, the people of the United States will not consent to bring a new, vastly extensive and slaveholding country, large enough for half a dozen or dozen States, into the Union. In my opinion they ought not to consent to it. Indeed, I am altogether at a loss to conceive what possible benefit any part of this country can expect to derive from such annexation; all benefit to any part is at least doubtful and uncertain; the objections obvious, plain, and strong.

Document 9 Ichabod Spencer, Presbyterian Minister, Sermon: "Fugitive Slave Law. The Religious Duty of Obedience to Law," 24 November 1850.[9]

The 'New York Evangelical Congregational Association" recently passed the following Resolution in respect to the "Fugitive-Slave Law," a Law regularly enacted by the Congress of the United States:--

"Resolved, That we cannot recognize this Law, as of any binding force upon the citizens of our country."—(I am thankful that these modest men did not go on, like him of the triple crown [the pope], to absolve "the citizens of our country" from all allegiance to the government, and give our rulers over into the hands of a majesty fit to take care of them.)

A *religious* paper, edited by Congregational clergymen, holding respectable stations, Pastors of churches,--a paper professedly devoted to the cause of Christ,--holds the following language in an *Editorial* article, under the caption, "How to oppose the Fugitive-Slave Law":--

This *religious* paper says,--"To the fugitives themelves... this Law is no Law...and to resist it even unto death, is their right, and it may be their duty..... To each *individual* fugitive, to every man or woman, who having escaped from bondage and tasted liberty, is in hourly peril of being seized and dragged back to slavery, we say,--Be fully prepared for your own defense. If to you death seems better than slavery, then refuse not to die—whether on the way-side, at your own threshold, or even as a felon upon the gallows. Defend your liberty and the liberty of your wife and children, as you would defend your life and theirs against the assassin. If you die thus, you die nobly, and your blood shall be the redemption of your race. Should you destroy the life of your assailant, you will pass into the custody of the criminal Law.....under any indictment for murder; but the verdict of the community, and the verdict of almost any jury will be, justifiable homicide in self-defense..... Or should a different

---

9 Ichabod S. Spencer, "Fugitive Slave Law: The Religious Duty of Obedience to Law," Sermon Preached in the Second Presbyterian Church, in Brooklyn, Nov. 24, 1850, (New York: M.W. Dodd, 1850).

verdict be found, and you be condemned to die as a murderer, your ignominious death shall be luminous with the halo of a martyr, and your sacrifice shall be for the deliverance of your people."

Such are the *religious* principles, and such is the *religious* advice of these *religious* ministers!

I am sorry to see this. I *never read more wicked and abominable principles!* They deserve not only the reprehension of every Christian, but the entire indignation of *all civilized mankind!* They advise private arming with bloody weapons—they advise violent resistance and murder—the murder of officers of civil Law engaged in the discharge of the duty which they have sworn to perform! I have no words to express my abhorrence of these wicked and outrageous sentiments, so directly contrary to the whole nature of all civilized society, to the precepts of the Bible, and the whole spirit of Christianity!

... I am not justifying slavery. I am pleading obedience to the texts before me. Slavery may be wrong. Be it so; there is still a *righteous* method to get rid of it. But if slavery *is* wrong, that does not make violence and murder *right.*

I am not justifying the Fugitive-Slave Law. It may be wrong: it may be unwise and unconstitutional. I think that any wise and modest man would hesitate much to pronounce it unconstitutional, ... But, be it wrong—be it unwise and unconstitutional; there are civil courts to decide upon its constitutionality, and no man has *any right* to decide for *himself* that it is unconstitutional, and act upon that decision: if he had such a right, then every man would be his own Lawmaker....

I have nothing to do with politics or party. I am only insisting upon religious obedience to Law. I am preaching the texts before me. Such obedience is a religious duty. It is the will of God. I appeal to the texts. They proclaim the Law of God. Peaceful subjection to government *is* his law; and men are guilty of sophistry and falsehood, when, to excuse wicked evasion of Law or violent resistance, they pretend to appeal to what they call "the higher laws of God." *There are no such higher laws.*

Document 10 Speech of Senator R.M.T. Hunter of Virginia, 24 February 1854[10]

The Senate having under consideration the bill to organize the Territories of Nebraska and Kansas—

Mr. Hunter said:

Mr. President, Complaints have been made that this question of the repeal of the Missouri compromise has been unnecessarily thrust upon us....

The legislation which has been denominated as the Missouri compromise of 1820, if founded upon any principle, was founded upon that of a division of territory between the slaveholding and the nonslaveholding States of this Confederacy. It seemed to proceed upon the assumption that the States were jointly entitled to that territory, and that if social possession became either impossible or inconvenient, then justice required a partition of it amongst them, for purposes of use and occupation. Accordingly, when the slave territory of Texas was annexed, a proposition was made to run the line of $36°30°$ through it, and to prohibit slavery in all that portion of the territory north of that line. To that proposition the South cheerfully acceded. And when it became a question as to the

---

[10] Speech of Senator R.M.T. Hunter of Virginia, 24 February 1854.

organization of the Territory of Oregon and of that acquired from Mexico, then, too, the proposition was made to settle that question upon the same principle of division, the South being found to favor it almost unanimously, and the North generally voting against it. ... On the contrary, the North wished to introduce a new principle, and insisted upon permitting a few people on our western coast to come in as a State without the previous invitation or consent of Congress, and not only to include the territory which they themselves occupied, and which might be of a convenient size for the new State, but to assign to themselves what limits and boundaries they pleased.

Document 11 John Forsyth, "The North and the South," *De Bow's Review* 17 (October 1854): 313-314.[11]

When the North American colonies confederated for resistance to Great Britain, the territorial area of the southern portion of them was 648,202 square miles—that of the northern only 164,084, or about one-fourth as large. Virginia alone had, by royal charter, the whole northwestern territory in her limits, and, during the war, had confirmed her title by the patriotism and valor of her own citizens—who rescued even Illinois from British power. But before the present constitution was formed, Virginia, with a magnanimity almost infatuated, had ceded to the Confederacy, for the formation of free States, the whole north-western territory now constituting the States of Ohio, Indiana, Illinois, Michigan, and Wisconsin, containing 261,681 square miles, and making the territory of the free States rather more than that of the slaveholding. The object of this cession, and the ordinance of 1787, was to equalize the area of the two sections. The acquisition of Louisiana, in 1803, added 1,138,103 square miles to our territory, of which, by the Missouri compromise, the South obtained only 226,013 square miles, or about one-fifth—the other four-fifths, notwithstanding it came to use as a slaveholding province, were allotted to the North, which thus had acquired more than 700,000 square miles of territory over the South. Florida and Oregon were acquired by the treaty of 1819, by which the South got 59,268 square miles, and the North 341,463, making the North about 1,000,000 square miles the most. In 1845 Texas was annexed, which added only 325,520 square miles to the South, even if all Texas were included. In 1848, we obtained 526,078 square miles more in the territories of New Mexico and California. And now the North claims the whole of this also—and not only this but half of Texas besides, which would make the share of the North exceed that of the South nearly 1,500,000 square miles; a territory about equal in extent to the whole valley of the Mississippi, and leaving the South only about 810,812 square miles, while the North retains 2,097,124 or nearly three-fourths of the whole! And this, too, when the South contributed her full share of men and money by which the whole territory was obtained. In the Revolutionary war, the South furnished an average of 16,714 men in each year, and the North 25,875 which nearly corresponds with their respective number of citizens, and that, too, although the war was waged chiefly against the large cities of the North—cities being, in war, the most tempting and the most vulnerable points of attack. In the war with Mexico, the South supplied two-thirds of the volunteers which constituted three-fourths of the entire force employed. The revenue by which these wars have been supported, the public debt paid, and the price for the territory furnished, has been raised chiefly by duties which have notoriously operated designedly and incidentally to promote the industry and capital of the North, and to oppress those of the South.

---

11 John Forsyth, "The North and the South," De Bow's Review 17 (October 1854): 313-314.

If, after all this, the South should submit to be plundered of her share of the territory now in dispute, when as an agricultural people, she requires her full proportion, she would be recreant to her interests, her power, her right, her honor, and her fame—recreant to her history and her destiny.

Document 12   Charles Sumner, Senator from Massachusetts, "The Crime Against Kansas," 19 May 1856.[12]

… But the wickedness which I now begin to expose is immeasurably aggravated by the motive which prompted it. Not in any common lust for power did this uncommon tragedy have its origin. It is the rape of a virgin territory, compelling it to the hateful embrace of slavery; and it may be clearly traced to a depraved longing for a new slave State, the hideous offspring of such a crime, in the hope of adding to the power of slavery in the national government.

… But, before entering upon the argument, I must say something of a general character, particularly in response to what has fallen from Senators who have raised themselves to eminence on this floor in championship of human wrongs; I mean the Senator from South Carolina [Mr. Butler] and the Senator from Illinois, [Mr. Douglas] …. The Senator from South Carolina has read many books on chivalry, and believes himself a chivalrous knight, with sentiments of honor and courage. Of course he has chosen a mistress to whom he has made his vows, and who, though ugly to others, is always lovely to him; though polluted in the sight of the world, is chaste in his sight—I mean the harlot, Slavery. For her, his tongue is always profuse in words. Let her be impeached in character, or any proposition made to shut her out from the extension of her wantonness, and no extravagance of manner or hardihood of assertion is then too great for this Senator. The frenzy of Don Quixote, in behalf of his wench Dulcinea del Toboso, is all surpassed. The asserted rights of Slavery, which shock equality of all kinds, are cloaked by a fantastic claim of equality. If the slave States cannot enjoy what, in mockery of the great fathers of the Republic, he misnames equality under the Constitution—in other words, the full power in the National Territories to compel fellow-men to unpaid toil, to separate husband and wife, and to sell little children at the auction-block—then sir, the chivalric Senator will conduct the State of South Carolina out of the Union! Heroic knight! Exalted Senator! A second Moses come for a second exodus!

… As the Senator from South Carolina is the Don Quixote, the Senator from Illinois [Mr. Douglas] is the squire of Slavery, its very Sancho Panza, ready to do all its humiliating offices.

… It belongs to me now, in the first place, to expose the Crime against Kansas, in its origin and extent. … Now, the Nebraska Bill, on its very face, openly cleared the way for Slavery, and it is not wrong to presume that its originators intended the natural consequences of such an act, and sought in this way to extend slavery. Of course they did. And this is the first stage in the crime against Kansas. … Then was conceived the consummation of the Crime against Kansas. What could not be accomplished peaceably, was to be accomplished forcibly. The reptile monster, that could not be quietly and securely hatched there, was to be pushed full-grown into the Territory. All efforts were now given to the dismal work of forcing Slavery on Free Soil. In flagrant derogation of the very

---

12   Senator Charles Sumner, "The Crime Against Kansas," Speech on the Senate Floor, May 19, 1856. Accessed at https://archive.org/stream/crimeagainstkans00sumn#page/n1/mode/2up .

Popular Sovereignty, whose name helped to impose the Bill upon the country, the atrocious object was not distinctly avowed. And the avowal has been followed by the art.

... The violence, for some time threatened, broke forth on the 29th November, 1854, at the first election of a Delegate to Congress, when companies from Missouri, amounting to upwards of one thousand, crossed into Kansas, and, with force and arms, proceeded to vote for Mr. Whitfield, the candidate of Slavery. An eye-witness... thus describes the scene:

"The first ballot-box that was opened upon our virgin soil was closed to us by overpowering numbers and impending force. So bold and reckless were our invaders, that they dared not to conceal their attack.... They came directly from their homes, 'and in compact and organized bands, with arms in hand and provisions for the expedition, marched to our polls, and, when their work was done, returned whence they came."

This infliction was a significant prelude to the grand invasion of the 30th March 1855, at the election of the first Territorial Legislature... when an armed multitude from Missouri entered the Territory,... organized in companies, with officers, munitions, tents, and provisions, as though marching upon a foreign foe, and breathing loud-mouthed threats that they would carry their purose, if need be by the bowie knife and revolver.... With this force they were able, on the succeeding day, to intimidate the judges of elections; in others to substitute judges of their own appointment; in others, to wrest the ballot-boxes from their rightful possessors, and everywhere to exercise a complete control of the election, and thus... impose a Legislature upon the free people of Kansas.

Document 13 David Rice Atchinson, Speech to the "Border Ruffians" before their second assault on the town of Lawrence, Kansas, 1855.[13]

"Boys, this day I am a Kickapoo Ranger, by God! This day we have entered Lawrence with 'Southern Rights' inscribed upon our banner, and not one damned Abolitionist dared to fire a gun. Now, boys, this is the happiest day of my life. We have entered that damn town, and taught the damned Abolitionists a Southern lesson that they will remember until the day they die. And now, boys, we will go in again, with our highly honorable Jones, and test the strength of that damned Free-State Hotel, and teach the Emigrant Aid Company that Kansas shall be ours. Boys, ladies should, and I hope will, be respected by every gentleman. But when a woman takes upon herself the garb of a soldier carrying a Sharpe's rifle, then she is no longer worthy of respect. Trample her under your feet as you would a snake! Come on boys! Now do your duty to yourselves and your Southern friends. Your duty I know you will do. If one man or woman dare stand before you, blow them to hell with a chunk of cold lead."

---

13 Quoted in *The Life and Letters of John Brown, Liberator of Kansas and Martyr of Virginia*, F.B Sanborn, ed., (Concord, MA: F.B. Sanborn, 1910), pp. 234.

Document 14 John Steuart Curry, "Tragic Prelude," Mural, Kansas State House, Topeka, Kansas, 1937.

Document 15 *Dred Scott v Sandford,* Opinion rendered by Chief Justice Taney, 1857.[14]

There are two leading questions presented by the record:

1. Had the Circuit Court of the United States jurisdiction to hear and determine the case between these two parties? And
2. If it had jurisdiction, is the judgment it has given erroneous or not?

The plaintiff…was, with his wife and children, held as slaves by the defendant, in the state of Missouri; and he brought this action in the circuit court of the United States for that district, to assert the title of himself and his family to freedom. […]

The defendant pleaded….that the plaintiff was not a citizen of the State of Missouri, as alleged in his declaration, being a negro of African descent, whose ancestors were of pure African blood, and who were brought into this country and sold as slaves.

---

[14] *Dred Scott v John F.A. Sandford*, Supreme Court of the United States, December term, 1856. Chief Justice Taney Opinion, in Horace Gray, *A Legal Review of the Case of Dred Scott as decided by the Supreme Court of the United States*, Volume I (Boston: Crosby, Nichols, and Company, 1857).

The question is simply this: Can a negro whose ancestors were imported into the country, and sold as slaves, become a member of the political community formed and brought into existence by the Constitution of the United States and as such become entitled to all the rights and privileges and immunities guaranteed to the citizen? One of which rights is the privilege of suing in a court of the United States in the cases specified in the Constitution. [...]

The words "people of the United States" and "citizens" are synonymous terms, and mean the same thing.... The question before us is, whether the class of persons described in the plea... compose a portion of the people, and are constituent members of this sovereignty? We think they are not, and that they are not included, and were not intended to be included under the word "citizens" in the Constitution, and can therefore claim none of the rights and privileges which this instrument provides for and secures to citizens of the United States. [...]

It is not the province of the court to decide upon the justice or injustice, the policy or impolicy, of these laws. The decision of that question belonged to the political or law-making power; to those who formed the sovereignty and framed the Constitution. The duty of the court is, to interpret the instrument they have framed, with the best lights we can obtain on the subject, and to administer it as we find it, according to its true intent and meaning when it was adopted.

In discussing this question, we must not confound the rights of citizenship which a State may confer within its own limits, and the rights of citizenship as a member of the Union. It does not by any means follow, because he has all the rights and privileges of a citizen of a State, that he must be a citizen of the United States....

...Does the Constitution of the United States act upon him [any African American] whenever he shall be made free under the laws of a State, and raised there to the rank of a citizen, and immediately clothe him with all the privileges of a citizen in every other State, and in its own courts?

The court thinks the affirmative of these propositions cannot be maintained. And, if it cannot, the plaintiff ... could not be a citizen of the State of Missouri, within the meaning of the Constitution of the United States, and consequently, was not entitled to sue in its courts.[...]

We proceed therefore, to inquire whether the facts relied on by the plaintiff entitled him to his freedom.

The case, as he himself states it, on the record brought here...is this:

The plaintiff was a negro slave, belonging to Dr. Emerson, who was a surgeon in the army of the United States. In the year 1834, he took the plaintiff from the State of Missouri to the military post at Rock Island, in the State of Illinois, and held him there as a slave until the month of April or May, 1836. At the time last mentioned, said Dr. Emerson removed the plaintiff from said military post at Rock Island to the military post at Fort Snelling, situate on the west bank of the Mississipi river, ... north of the latitude of thirty-six degrees thirty minutes north, and north of the State of Missouri. Said Dr. Emerson held the plaintiff in slavery at said Fort Snelling, from said last mentioned date until the year 1838.

In the year 1833, Harriet, who is named in the second count of the plaintiff's declaration, was the negro slave of Major Taliaferro, who belonged to the army of the United States. In that year, 1835, said Major Taliaferro took said Harriet to said Fort Snelling... and kept here there as a slave until the year 1836, and then sold and delivered her as a slave... unto the said Dr. Emerson.... Said Dr. Emerson held said Harriet in slavery at said Fort Snelling until the year 1838.

In the year 1838, the plaintiff and Harriet intermarried... with the consent of Dr. Emerson, who then claimed to be their master and owner. Eliza and Lizzie, ... are the fruit of that marriage....

... Before the commencement of this suit, said Dr. Emerson sold and conveyed the plaintiff, and said Harriet, Eliza, and Lizzie, to the defendant, as slaves, and the defendant has ever since claimed to hold them, and each of them, as slaves.

In considering this part of the controversy, two questions arise: 1. Was he, together with his family, free in Missouri by reason of the stay in the territory of the United States hereinbefore mentioned? And, 2. If they were not, is Scott himself free by reason of his removal to Rock Island, in the State of Illinois, as stated in the above admissions?

We proceed to examine the first question. [...] it is the opinion of the court that the act of Congress which prohibited a citizen from holding and owning property of this kind in the territory of the United States north of the line therein mentioned, is not warranted by the Constitution, and is therefore void; and that neither Dred Scott himself, nor any of his family, were made free by being carried into this territory;...

And it is contended on the part of the plaintiff, tht he is made free by being taken to Rock Island, in the State of Illinois, independently of his residence in the territory of the United States; and being so made free, he was not again reduced to a state of slavery by being brought back to Missouri.

Our notice of this part of the case will be very brief; for the principle on which it depends was decided in this court... in the case of *Strader, et al v Graham*... In that case, the slaves had been taken from Kentucky to Ohio, with the consent of the owner, and afterwards brought back to Kentucky. And this court held that their *status* or condition, as free or slave, depended upon the laws of Kentucky, when they were brought back into that State, and not of Ohio; and that this court had no jurisdiction to revise the judgment of a State court upon its own laws....

So in this case. As Scott was a slave when taken into the State of Illinois by his owner, and was there held as such, and brought back in that character, his *status*, as free or slave, depended on the laws of Missouri, and not of Illinois.

Document 16   Abraham Lincoln, "The 'House Divided Against Itself' Speech, 16 June 1858.[15]

[The following speech delivered at Springfield, Illinois at the close of the Republican State Convention. Lincoln had just been nominated by the Republican party to run against Steven Douglas for Senator from Illinois]

MR. PRESIDENT AND GENTLEMEN OF THE CONVENTION:

If we could first know where we are, and whither we are tending, we could better judge what to do, and how to do it. We are now far into the fifth year since a policy was initiated with the avowed object and confident promise of putting an end to slavery agitation. Under the operation of that policy, that agitation has not only not ceased, but has constantly augmented. In my opinion, it

---

[15] *Political Speeches of Abraham Lincoln and Stephen A. Douglas,* ed. Alonzo T. Jones, (Battle Creek, MI: International Tract Society, 1895), pp. 52-60.

will not cease until a crisis shall have been reached and passed. "A house divided against itself cannot stand." I believe this Government cannot endure permanently half slave and half free. I do not expect the Union to be dissolved; I do not expect the house to fall; but I do not expect it will cease to be divided. It will become all one thing, or all the other. Either the opponents of slavery will arrest the further spread of it, and place it where the public mind shall rest in the belief that it is in the course of ultimate extinction, or its advocates will push it forward till it shall become alike lawful in all the States, old as well as new, North as well as South.

Have we no tendency to the latter condition?

Let any who doubts, carefully contemplate that now almost complete legal comination—piece of machinery, so to speak—compounded of the Nebraska doctrine and the Dred Scott decision.[...]

The new year of 1854 found slavery excluded from more than half the States by State Constitutions, and from most of the National territory by Congressional prohibition. Four days later, commenced the struggle which ended in repealing that Congressional prohibition. This opened all the National territory to slavery, and was the first point gained.

But, so far, Congress *only* had acted; and an indorsement by the people... was indispensable....

This necessity... had been provided for... in the notable argument of "squatter sovereignty," otherwise called "sacred right of self-government," which latter phrase, though expressive of the only rightful basis of any government, was so perverted in this attempted use of it as to amount to just this: That if any *one* man choose to enslave *another*, no *third* man shall be allowed to object. That argument was incorporated into the Nebraska bill itself, in the language which follows:

"It being the true intent and meaning of this Act not to legislate slavery into any Territory or State, nor to exclude it therefrom, but to leave the people thereof perfectly free to form and regulate their domestic institutions in their own way, subject only to the Constitution of the United States."

Then opened the roar of loose declamation in favor of "squatter sovereignty," and "sacred right of self government." [...]

While the Nebraska bill was passing through Congress, a *law case*, involving the question of a negro's freedom,... was passing through the United States Circuit Court.... The negro's name was "Dred Scott." [...] The several points of the Dred Scott decision, in connection with Senator Douglas's ... policy, constitute the piece of machinery, in its present state of advancement. ... The working points of that machinery are:--

First, That no negro slave, ... and no descendant of such a slave, can ever be a citizen of any State.... This point is made in order to deprive the negro, in every possible event, of the benefit of that provision of the United States Constitution which declares that "The citizens of each State shall be entitled to all the privileges and immunities of citizens in the several States."

Secondly, That "subject to the Constitution of the United States," neither Congress nor a Territorial Legislature can exclude slavery from any United States Territory. This point is made in order that individual men may fill up the Territories with slaves, without danger of losing them as property....

Thirdly, That whether the holding a negro in actual slavery in a free State, makes him free, as against the holder, the United States courts will not decide, but will leave to be decided by the courts of any Slave State the negro may be forced into by the master. ... [Thus] what Dred Scott's master might lawfully do with Dred Scott in the Free State of Illinois, every other master may lawfully do with any other one, or one thousand slaves, in Illinois, or any other Free State. [...]

It should not be overlooked that by the Nebraska bill the people of a *State* as well as Territory were to be left "perfectly free," "subject only to the Constitution." ... Put this and that together, and we have another nice little niche, which we may, ere long, see filled with another Supreme Court decision, declaring that the Constitution of the Unitd States does not permit a *State* to exclude slavery from its limits. ...

Such a decision is all that slavery now lacks of being alike lawful in all the States. Welcome or unwelcome, such decision is probably coming, and will soon be upon us, unless the power of the present political dynasty shall be met and overthrown. We shall lie down pleasantly dreaming that the people of Missouri are on the verge of making their State free, and we shall awake to the reality instead that the Supreme Court has made Illinois a Slave State. To meet and overthrow the power of that dynasty is the work now before all those who would prevent that consummation. That is what we have to do.

Document 17 Questioning of John Brown, at Harper's Ferry, 25 October 1859.[16]

In the afternoon of the day he was taken prisoner, Senator Mason [James Murray Mason, Senator from Virginia], Lieutenant Stuart [J.E.B. Stuart], Colonel Faulkner, M.C. and Clement L. Vallandigham [Representative from Ohio] had an interview with Brown at the Office of the Paymaster of the Armory, where he had been removed from the engine house. A verbatim report was made of this by one who was present, as follows:

Mr. Mason: Can you tell us, at least, who furnished money for your expedition?

Brown: I furnished most of it myself. I cannot implicate others. It is by my own folly that I have been taken. I could easily have saved myself from it had I exercised my own better judgment, rather than yielded to my feelings.

Mason: You mean if you had escaped immediately? ...

Brown: I should have gone away, but I had thirty odd prisoners, whose wives and daughters were in tears for their safety, and I felt for them. Besides, I wanted to allay the fears of those who believed we came here to burn and kill....

Mason: But you killed some people passing along the streets quietly.

Brown: Well, sir, if there was anything of that kind done, it was without my knowledge... I did not allow my men to fire, nor even to return fire, when there was danger of killing those we regarded as innocent persons, if I could help it....

Mason: If you would tell us who sent you here—who provided the means—that would be information of some value.

Brown: I will answer freely and faithfully about what concerns myself—I will answer anything I can honor, but not about others.

Vallandigham: Mr. Brown, who sent you here?

---

16   John Davison Lawson, ed., *American State Trials*, Volume VI, (St. Louis: F.H. Thomas Law Book Co., 1916), pp. 711-718.

Brown:	No man sent me here; it was my own prompting and that of my Maker, or that of the devil, which ever you please to ascribe it to. I acknowledge no man in human form.
Vallandigham:	Did you get up the expedition yourself?
Brown:	I did.
Vallandigham:	Did you get up this document that is called a constitution?
Brown:	I did. They are a constitution and ordinances of my own contriving and getting up.
Vallandigham:	How long have you been engaged in this business?
Brown:	From the breaking of the difficulties in Kansas. Four of my sons had gone there to settle, and they induced me to go. I did not go there to settle, but because of the difficulties. […]
Mason:	What was your object in coming?
Brown:	I came to free the slaves, and only that. […]
Mason:	How do you justify your acts?
Brown:	I think, my friend, you are guilty of a great wrong against God and humanity—I say it without wishing to be offensive—and it would be perfectly right in any one to interfere with you so far as to free those you willfully and wickedly hold in bondage. I do not say this insultingly. I think I did right, and that others will do right who interfere with you at any time and all times. I hold that the golden rule, "Do unto others as you would that others should do unto you," applies to all who would help others to gain their liberty.
Lieut. Stuart:	But you don't believe in the Bible.
Brown:	Certainly I do. […]
Vallandigham:	… Did you attend the Fugitive Slave Convention [in Cleveland?]
Brown:	No, I was there about the time of the sitting of the court to try the Oberlin rescuers. I spoke there publicly on that subject. I spoke on the Fugitive Slave law and my own rescue. Of course, so far as I had any influence at all, I was disposed to justify the Oberlin people for rescuing the slave, because I have myself forcibly taken slaves from bondage. I was concerned in taking eleven slaves from Missouri to Canada last winter. […]
A Bystander:	Do you consider this a religious movement?
Brown:	It is, in my opinion, the greatest service a man can render to God.
A Bystander:	Do you consider yourself an instrument in the hands of Providence?
Brown:	I do.
A Bystander:	Upon what principle do you justify your acts?
Brown:	Upon the golden rule. I pity the poor in bondage that have none to help them; that is why I am here; not to gratify any personal animosity, revenge, or vindictive spirit. It is my sympathy with the oppressed and the wronged, that are as good as you and as precious in the sight of God.
Vallandigham:	Who are advisers in this movement?

Brown:	I cannot answer that. I have numerous sympathizers throughout the entire North.
A Bystander:	The New York *Herald* of yesterday, in speaking of this affair, … predicts that the next movement made in the direction of negro emancipation would be an insurrection in the South.
Brown:	I have not seen the New York *Herald* for some days past; but I presume, from your remarks about the gist of the letter, that I should concur with it. I agree… that moral suasion is hopeless. I don't think the people of the slave states will ever consider the subject of slavery in its true light till some other argument is resorted to than moral suasion. […]
Herald reporter:	I do not wish to annoy you; but if you have anything further you would say I will report it.
Brown:	I have nothing to say, only that I claim to be here carrying out a measure I believe perfectly justifiable, and not to act the part of an incendiary or ruffian, but to aid those suffering great wrong. I wish to say, furthermore, that you had better—all you people at the South—prepare yourselves for a settlement of that question that must come up for settlement sooner than you are prepared for. The sooner you are prepared the better. You may dispose of me very easily; I am nearly disposed of now; but this question is still to be settled—the negro question I mean—the end of that is not yet. […]
A Bystander:	Brown, suppose you had every nigger in the United States, what would you do with them?
Brown:	Set them free.
A Bystander:	To set them free would sacrifice the life of every man in this community.
Brown:	I don't think so.
A Bystander:	I know it. I think you are fanatical.
Brown:	And I think you are fanatical. "Whom the gods would destroy they first make mad," and you are mad.
A Bystander:	Was it your only object to free the negroes?
Brown:	Absolutely our only object.
A Bystander:	But you demanded and took Col. Washington's silver and watch?
Brown:	Yes; we intended freely to appropriate the property of slaveholders to carry out our object. It was for that, and only that, and with no design to enrich ourselves with any plunder whatever.
… The COURT inquired if the prisoners had counsel.	
Brown:	I did not ask for any quarter at the time I was taken. I did not ask to have my life spared. The Governor of the State of Virginia tended me his assurance that I should have a fair trial; and under no circumstances whatever will I be able to have a fair trial. If you seek my blood, you can have it at any moment, without this mockery of a trial. … if we are to be forced with a mere form—a trial for execution—you might spare yourselves that trouble. I am ready for my fate.

Document 18 "What Should Georgia Do? *Daily Constitutionalist*, 11 November 1860[17]

The most inveterate and sanguine Unionist in Georgia, if he is an observant man, must read, in the signs of the times, the hopelessness of the Union cause, and the feebleness of the Union sentiment in this State. The differences between North and South have been growing more marked for years, and the mutual repulsion more radical, until not a single sympathy is left between the dominant influences in each section. Not even the banner of the stars and stripes excites the same thrill of patriotic emotion, alike in the heart of the northern Republican and the southern Secessionist. The former looks upon that flag as blurred by the stain of African slavery, for which he feels responsible as long as that flag waves over it, and that it is his duty to humanity and religion to obliterate its stigma. The latter looks upon it as the emblem of a gigantic power, soon to pass into the hands of that sworn enemy, and knows that African slavery, though panoplied by the Federal Constitution is doomed to a war of extermination.

... The election of Mr. Lincoln to the Presidency gives a tremendous onward impulse to anti-slavery sentiment. So far from the possibility of its being induced to recede, its steps are now nerved with new energy, and soon its arm will be clothed with the huge power of Executive patronage....

... The time was, when it was not patriotic to despair of the Republic. The time has come when the indulgence of hopes for its preservation is apt to delude the imagination and blind the judgment. The 'ties of Union,' if by the term is meant ties of fraternal sympathy, can never again be strengthened, for they no longer exist to bind the two sections together. They are broken—utterly sundered between portions of the South, and portions of the North. The antagonism amounts not simply to aversion, but to bitter disgust and hatred.

ANALYZING THE EVIDENCE

1. What constitutional arguments are put forward in favor of the Tallmadge amendment excluding slavery from the territory of Missouri? What constitutional arguments are made against the amendment? (Document 1) What other arguments are made in favor of and against the amendment?

2. How did Pinckney's resolution (Document 2) threaten 1st Amendment rights according to northern representatives to Congress? How did southerners justify the restriction? (Document 3)

3. Why did Robert J. Walker contend that annexation of Texas would strengthen the Union and reduce tensions caused by slavery?(Document 4) How did the Massachusetts' Resolutions (Document 5) and the image of "Young Texas in Repose" (Document 6) reflect the view that the annexation of Texas would only strengthen slavers' hold on African Americans and power over the United States.

4. How did the proposed annexation of Mexican territory following the Mexican War reopen the debate over slavery's presence in the West?(Documents 7 and 8) What arguments did Daniel Webster make against territorial acquisitions from Mexico?

---

17 "What Should Georgia Do?" *Daily Constitutionalist*, Augusta, Georgia, 11 November 1860, p. 2.

5. How did Ichabod Spencer (Document 9) defend the Fugitive Slave Law and object to New York religious leaders' call to "nullify" the law?

6. How did Senator R.M.T. Hunter argue that the Kansas-Nebraska Act did not violate the principles of the Missouri Compromise? (Document 10)

7. How did John Forsyth (Document 11) employ historical arguments to support the view that the North was unfairly restraining the economic and political interests of the slaveholding states and of slave owners by trying to limit their ability to take their slaves into western territories?

8. Why might Charles Sumner's speech (Document 12) have been so offensive to Preston Brooks, the second cousin of Senator Andrew Butler, that he would assault Sumner on the floor of the Senate and severely beat him? Why did Sumner liken Stephen Douglas of Nebraska to Don Quixote's henchman, Sancho Panza, or as the henchman of the southern Slave Power? What did Sumner see as the crime against Kansas?

9. Why might the presence of David Rice Atchinson (Document 13) and John Brown, the central figure in John Stueart Curry's mural (Document 14) in Kansas in the late 1850s have presaged the Civil War as portrayed in Curry's mural?

10. On what grounds did Chief Justice Taney conclude that Dred Scott had no right to sue for his and his family's freedom? (Document 15) What did this decision imply for the conditions of the Missouri Compromise or the Kansas-Nebraska act?

11. What did Abraham Lincoln in his "House Divided" speech (Document 16) suggest were the consequences of the Dred Scott decision? What did he conclude were the consequences of the principle of popular sovereignty as a way to resolve the matter of whether slavery would be permitted in the territories? How might Lincoln's speech be used as evidence that he favored a war to conclude the issue of slavery once and for all?

12. What did John Brown set out to do at Harper's Ferry (Document 17) and how did he justify this act? Why might John Brown be justifiably called both an "American Terrorist" and an "American Hero?"

13. Why did the editor of this Georgia newspaper (Document 18) conclude that secession from the Union was the only option left open for southern states?

DOCUMENT BASED QUESTION

1. Using the documents provided and your knowledge of United States history analyze the different arguments made in favor of and in opposition to the spread of slavery into western territories between 1820 and 1860.

2. Using the documents provided and your knowledge of United States history analyze the relationship between American expansionism and political division along sectional lines between 1815 and 1860.

"Cannot we Prove Ourselves Men!": Civil War and Emancipation

CHAPTER 13

In April 1861, with the fall of Fort Sumter, northerners and southerners rushed to enlist. Their enthusiasm for the fight bore no relationship to the horror the war would become. Northern volunteers were wildly cheered as they paraded off to trains that would take them to the war. The Second New Hampshire Regiment, in June 1861, for example, escorted by an honor guard, marched through the town of Portsmouth to a twenty-car transport train to martial airs supplied by the Manchester Cornet Band and an accompanying drum corps. As their train made its way to Boston, large crowds greeted them, "cheering, firing salutes, &c.; and scattered along the route for nearly the whole distance were swinging hats and waving handkerchiefs...." In Boston, they were received warmly, marching to a hall where a "sumptuous and inviting repast" of "strawberries and cream, rolls, cold meats, coffee, pastry, and other substantial viands" were provided. Colonel Gilman Marston, the 2nd New Hampshire's commander, thanked the organizers of the welcoming party with the following words:

> Whatever scenes of danger we may hereafter be called upon to encounter, I am sure that the recollection of the scenes which have transpired this day will fire our hearts and nerve our arms to dare and endure everything which men can dare and endure in honor of our native State, New Hampshire—God bless her! (Great applause) and the glory of our common country.

Marston continued, "Gentlemen, this 2nd Regiment of New Hampshire have no acquaintance with war. They are all civilians." And, uninterested in conquest.

> We have not left our homes, our friends, the peaceful pursuits in which we have always been engaged all our lives for the purpose of entering upon a war of conquest and aggression upon the rights of anybody. (Good, good.) We have taken up arms to preserve, defend and protect the freest and best government which ever existed upon earth, against the most causeless rebellion the sun in heaven ever shone upon, and by the help of God we will do it.

What was missing from Marston's remark was any expression of desire to put an end to slavery.

This was not the case for all the soldiers preparing themselves for battle against the Confederacy. John Worthington Ames, in a letter to his mother explaining his reasons for volunteering, said, "Slavery has brought death into our own households already in its wicked rebellion.... There is but one way [to win the war] and that is emancipation.... I want to sing 'John Brown' in the streets of Charleston, and ram red-hot abolitionism down their unwilling throats at the point of the bayonet."[1] Ames was not alone in identifying the reason for the war and the justification for his participation with abolitionist objects. However, despite Ames' fervor to end slavery, few volunteers signed up for such a crusade. Instead, like Colonel Marston, they fought to uphold the republic that had been established in the Revolutionary War eighty years earlier and for the liberty that the republic represented. "This is the first test of a modern free government in the act of sustaining itself against internal enemys" an Irish-born private in the 28th Massachusetts wrote to his wife, "...if it fail then the hopes of millions fall and the designs and wishes of all tyrants will succeed..."[2] The "Glorious Cause" for which they fought and died was, however, a patriotic cause, for "*union* and *liberty*" rather than for the promise of freedom extended to millions of slaves.

Southerners who joined the Confederate forces fought for the abstractions, *Constitutional liberty* and *self government*, often without mention of their interest in protecting rights to property in slaves. Southern volunteers, did however often stress that the consequences of their defeat would be their own subjugation and enslavement. In this regard, the rhetoric of southern independence resembled that often heard during the earlier American Revolution. The Confederate defense of the South was often described as "the holy cause of southern freedom," and southern authors often likened their succession to the rebellion against England, a fight motivated by "the same principles which fired the hearts of our ancestors in the revolutionary struggle." Confederate soldiers also considered their war to be one in defense of their "life, liberty, and property," concretely embodied in their hearths, homes, and womenfolk. However, just as the Union soldiers did not often make abolition of slavery their stated purpose, Confederate soldiers did not often overtly make their fight a defense of slavery.

Despite Abraham Lincoln's objections to slavery, his administration did not at the outset of the conflict make abolition the objective of Union military and political strategy. Instead, Lincoln's policy statements and prosecution of the war implied a limited strategy of restoration of the Union and the Constitution and suppression of the illegal succession of the southern states. Even as his more radical Republican critics demanded that the war become a crusade to "free the slaves," Lincoln considered such a strategy to be one that overstepped his constitutional authority. Moreover, it also promised to turn the war from one with a limited political objective to a total war with little possibility of a negotiated settlement and little hope for a restoration of the Union to the *status quo ante* before 1861. In short, to transform the war into an abolitionist crusade required a revolutionary transformation with significant legal, political, economic, and social repurcussions. Lincoln's more conservative approach and his attention to constitutional forms coincided with unavoidable political realities. Lincoln did not lead a united Union. His critics in the Democratic Party, backed by nearly half of northern voters many of whom were fearful of the consequences of a generalized emancipation, made Lincoln's desire to free the slaves a politically difficult position. In addition, the Union included four slave-holding states (Kentucky, Missouri, Maryland, and Delaware) that might also secede were Lincoln to make abolition the hallmark of the war effort.

It is therefore critical to our study of the Civil War to explain how the prosecution of the war itself transformed the conflict from a struggle in which slavery was the predominant

---

1 James M. McPherson, *For Cause and Comrades: Why Men Fought in the Civil War* (New York: Oxford University Press, 1997), p. 19.
2 Ibid., 32.

cause, but the abolition of slavery not a stated war aim of the Union, into a war that explicitly promised an end to slavery. The answer to that question requires a survey of the war itself and its transformation from a limited war of short duration with achievable political objectives, into a revolutionary struggle for the transformation of the nation that required its total mobilization. But perhaps more important than why Union or Confederate soldiers enlisted, or the stated aims of the President or Congress, were the actions of African Americans who effectively made the objectives of northern or southern leaders to defend or abolish slavery moot. For, from the opening moments of the conflict, slaves began to make themselves free in a myriad of ways. This then is the story of emancipation. It did not take place with blacks on bended knee before "Massa Lincum, de Sabiour ub de Negro" as portrayed so often in popular and official representations. It occurred as slaves and freedmen took matters in their own hands and forced the nation to reckon with a wrong that had persisted for too long.

MOBILIZING FOR TOTAL WAR

As the Union and Confederacy entered into conflict, it was apparent that neither North nor South were prepared for war. The United States Army before the war had scarcely 16,000 men, most of them stationed on the frontier. With southern secession one-third of its officer corps resigned to join the Confederacy. Southerners were proud of their martial heritage and disdained the northern fighting men, characterizing the Yankees as "blue-bellied shopkeepers." They were confident that a single rebel soldier could defeat three Union men. In either case, however, both sides were going to require manpower on an unprecedented scale in American history. By the end of the Civil War, at least two and a half million men had served in the Union Army, and over eight-hundred thousand men had fought for the Confederacy. The pressing need for soldiers would test to the breaking point both sides' objections to conscription and standing armies. And, as we will see, the demand for military manpower would also result in the service of significant numbers of African-American soldiers in the Union army and even recruitment of slaves into the Confederate forces.

Supplying such large armies completely outmatched the capacity of American finance. The resources needed to feed, clothe, and arm the soldiers arrayed against each other required the total mobilization of both sides' fiscal and logistical potential. The tax structure, however, non-existent in the South, and quite limited in the North, hardly seemed capable of sustaining a prolonged conflict. Both sides would be forced to raise taxes, borrow heavily, and print money to sustain the war effort. Though the United States had the world's most extensive rail system, the transportation system was unevenly distributed across the country, to the advantage of the Union. The Union states had significant advantages in industrial capacity, population, and raw material resources, but the Confederacy produced fully two thirds of the nation's exports, and the value of slave property was greater than the value of all housing stock, or agricultural land. The Confederacy hoped to leverage that wealth to cultivate a political alliance and economic partnership with Great Britain, or perhaps another European power capable of aiding the southern cause.

The military necessities of both sides dictated very different strategies as well. For the Union to succeed in its objective it had to invade successfully and occupy the entirety of the South. It had to destroy the will of southerners to resist. With no measurable technological advantage and with only a three to one advantage in troop strength, the North's success was hardly inevitable. Consider the United States military's failure to accomplish a similar objective in Vietnam a century later; with vastly superior firepower and with a much larger army and better supplied soldiers, the United States could not impose its will on the Vietnamese. The Confederacy, for its part, required only to fight a defensive war, on their own familiar ground, and convince Lincoln and the northern populace that the human and economic costs of reuniting the country were simply too great. The South, however, had an often overlooked Achilles heel, the presence of nearly four million slaves, roughly 13% of the South's population. While it would prove impossible to "win the hearts and minds" of southerners—Redeemers, the Ku Klux Klan, and 20th century segregationists remained committed to the "Lost Cause" long after Appomattox—African Americans would play the key role in their own liberation, and provide an important source of new troops for the Union armies. Moreover, elevating emancipation as a central war aim, both gave new legitimacy to the war effort and struck directly at the South's most important asset. But, determining on a course of abolition would only result from the difficulties and enormous costs of the war itself.

The development of improved weapons, particularly breech-loading and repeating rifles, that expanded the range and rapidity of firing meant that the number of casualties in Civil War battles vastly surpassed those in earlier American wars. Even the weaponry used in the the Mexican-American war, scarcely fifteen years earlier hardly compared. Ulysses S. Grant, who had served as an officer in that conflict, had remarked that "At a distance of a few hundred yards, a man could fire at you all day without your finding out." But, the tactics used in the Civil War had not adapted to the new firepower. Battle planning still relied on methods that involved amassing infantry opposite an enemy's vulnerabilities and attempting to overwhelm the enemy lines by marching units into the teeth of the opponent's firepower. The resulting casualties were horrific. At just three battles, Shiloh (April 6-7, 1862), Antietam (September 17, 1862) and Gettysburg (July 1-3, 1863) both sides had nearly 100,000 men killed, wounded or captured. At Gettysburg, in what has become known as "Pickett's Charge" of approximately 12,500 men who attacked Cemetary Ridge over a one mile front, at least 1,123 Confederate soldiers were killed in the field, over 4,000 wounded, and many more captured.

For southerners such losses could be justified as a necessary cost of protecting their homes, families, and property from the Yankee Vandals. Northerners had no such claim. As one Union officer observed, "They are fighting from different motives from us. We are fighting for the Union… a high and noble sentiment, but after all a sentiment." In the end, the cause of emancipation would provide both a legitimizing sentiment for northern soldiers, and as importantly, a way to attack the South at its most vulnerable point. Abraham Lincoln and the northern commanders would by fits and starts come to the same conclusion that John Murray, the Earl of Dunmore, had arrived at in November 1775: emancipation of the slaves was the surest way to attack the Confederacy at its core and either hasten its defeat or render its cause meaningless.

EMANCIPATION

Emancipation only gradually emerged as a vital war aim, and hardly derived initially from a conscious policy decision. Instead, it was largely a consequence of the determinations made by "men on the spot" who had to decide what to do with the slaves who fled to Union lines as the military advanced into the South. Congressional leaders would later conclude that confiscation of rebel property including slaves might prove to be a useful military tool. In August 1861, Congress passed a Confiscation Act allowing rebel property to be seized. Included in that property, of course, were southern slaves. Slaves, however, remained slaves under this act, as Congress remained committed to the principle of property rights and saw the slaves as a potential bargaining chip to bring to the table in the inevitable negotiations that would conclude hostilities. Additionlly, the slave states that had remained in the Union were made uneasy by a policy that seemed to promise full emancipation. As the war continued into its second year, and as success on the battlefield proved difficult, using the promise of emancipation as a military tactic gathered momentum. In July 1862 a second Confiscation Act reauthorized the earlier law, and offered the incentive to slaves from rebel territory to flee to Union lines, where their freedom would be guaranteed.

Abraham Lincoln, however, remained committed to a strategy of negotiated re-unification under the terms of the existing national constitution, which, as we have seen, permitted or perhaps enshrined slavery as the law of the land. Only gradually did his commitment to abolition override his commitment to the Constitution. In September of 1862, after the military victory at Antietam, Lincoln issued the Emancipation Proclamation, which would go into effect the first day of January of the following year. In it, Lincoln promised emancipation to all slaves in the states in rebellion, though not to those in the border states that had remained in the Union. The Emancipation Proclamation freed few slaves and could only be enforced as an outcome of a definitive victory over the South. But, it changed the war aims of the federal government, and committed the government to the abolition of slavery in the South. It made the war a war to free the slaves.

THE END OF SLAVE TIME

In the final analysis, it was not the Emancipation Proclamation that freed the slaves. Neither can it be said that the Thirteenth Amendment did so. The latter merely confirmed a fact that was already becoming apparent. In large part, the slaves freed themselves. Slaves crossed the front lines to freedom, voting with their feet, whenever and wherever the Union armies approached. The "contraband" camps that followed the military saw freedmen employed as cooks, teamsters, and laborers. Freedmen in the camps were also leased out to farmers and planters desparate to plant or harvest their corn, cotton, or tobacco, who agreed to swear allegiance to the Union in exchange for being able to hire for wages African Americans who had formerly been slaves. Even in areas where the Union armies did not provide this ready protection, slaves began to negotiate new working conditions and in some cases, even insisted on receiving wages for their labor. The slave system was already weakening before the end of the war.

African Americans also freed themselves by soldiering for the U.S. Army. By the end of the Civil War, roughly 186,000 black men composed 10% of the Union's troops. black soldiers served in artillery and infantry companies. They also served in noncombat roles as chaplains, cooks, guards, scouts, spies, and teamsters. Another 19,000 black men served in the Navy. Though most Black troops were led by white officers, nearly 80 black commissioned officers proved their leadership potential. Black women, as well, though they could not formally serve, nonetheless aided the war effort as nurses, spies, and scouts. Harriet Tubman, whose importance as an abolitionist and leader of the Underground Railroad has landed her on the ten dollar bill, scouted for the 2nd South Carolina Volunteers.

Black infantrymen fought gallantly in a number of key battles, and over 40,000 died during the course of the war. Perhaps the most famous combat role played by black troops occurred at the assault on Fort Wagner, South Carolina in which the 54th Regiment of Massachusetts Volunteers lost two-thirds of their officers and half of their troops. This unit and the battle of Fort Wagner was memorialized in the movie *Glory*, the first overtly pro-war Hollywood film produced after the Vietnam War. By war's end, sixteen black soldiers had been awarded the Medal of Honor for their valor. Black soldiers however, often faced violent retribution when they were captured by the Confederacy. Black captives were typically treated more harshly than white captives. In one particularly egregious case, Confederate soldiers shot to death already surrendered black Union soldiers captured at the battle of Fort Pillow in Tennessee.

CONCLUSION

Barbara Fields in the last episode of PBS's *The Civil War*, directed by Ken Burns, remarked, "I think what we need to remember, most of all, is that the Civil War is not over until we, today, have done our part in fighting it, as well as understanding what happened…." Richard Slotkin expressed a similar sentiment, noting that the Civil War was merely "the beginning of a contest over the fundamental questions of social justice which remains the central unfinished business of American history."[3] We opened this chapter by noting the relative absence of anti-slavery fervor in the motivations of those marching off to fight in 1861. We have also observed how slowly the emancipation of the slaves emerged as a main war aim of the North. This should not be taken as support for the view that slavery was a minor factor in the coming of the Civil War. Textbooks in the 1950s, before the Civil Rights movement, often repeated this claim, a "form of Southern apologetics," according to James W. Loewen.[4] Textbooks have been one field in the ongoing battle over the meaning of the Civil War that both Slotkin and Fields describe. The purpose of this chapter therefore is to understand what happened, and to recognize how this contest over the fundamental questions of social justice played out in the period of the American Civil War

PRIMARY SOURCES

DOCUMENT 1 Letters between Thomas T. Gantt and General William S. Harney, 1861[5]

Saint Louis Mo. May 14, 1861.

To: General William S. Harney, Commanding the Military Department of the West, St. Louis, Mo.

Sir: In common with thousands who have perused your admirable proclamation of this morning, I return you the thanks of a citizen of Missouri for its pratriotic tone and tranquilizing assurances.

---

[3] Richard Slotkin, "What Shall Men Remember?": Recent Work on the Civil War," *American Literary History*, Vol. 3, No. 1 (Spring 1991), p. 121.

[4] James W. Loewen, *Lies My Teacher Told Me: Everything Your American History Textbook Got Wrong*, (New York: Simon and Schuster, 1996), 141.

[5] " Reports Made by General William S. Harney During his Command of the United States Forces in the State of Missouri," in *Executive Documents and Reports of Committees*, printed by order of the House of Representatives during the First Session of the Thirty-Seventh Congress, (Washington: Government Printing Office, 1861), pp. 16-17.

There is nothing in this paper which in my opinion needs explanation; yet I wish to be able to answer, with the authority of your name, a question which I have already replied to on my own judgment. Last evening, a gentleman, of the highest respectability, and intelligence, from Greene county, Mo. asked me whether I supposed it was the intention of the United States Government to interfere with the institution of negro slavery in Missouri or any Slave State, or impair the security of that description of property. Of course, my answer was most unqualifiedly, and almost indignantly in the negative. I told him that I had no means of forming an opinion which were not open to every other private citizen; but that I felt certain that the force of the United States, would, if necessary, be exerted for the protection of this, as well as any other kind of property. Will you be good enough to spare from your engrossing military duties so much time as may be required to say whether I answered correctly?

I have the honor to be, with the highest respect, your most obedient Servant.

(Sgd) Thomas T. Gantt.

[*St. Louis, Mo.*] May 14, 1861.

To: Thomas T. Gantt

Sir: I have just received your note of this date, inquiring whether, in my opinion, you were correct in replying to a citizen of Southwestern Missouri as to the purpose of the United States Government respecting the protection of negro property.

I must premise by saying that I have no special instructions on this Head from the War Department. But I should as soon expect to hear that the orders of the Government were directed towards the overthrow of any other kind of property as of this in negro slaves.

I entertain no doubt whatever that you answered the question you mention correctly. I should certainly have answered it in the same manner, and I think with the very feelings you describe. I am not a little astonished that such a question could be seriously put. Already since the commencement of these unhappy disturbances, slaves have escaped from their owners, and have sought refuge in the camps of United States troops from Northern states and commanded by a Northern General. They were carefully sent back to their owners. An insurrection of slaves was reported to have taken place in Maryland. A Northern General offered to the Executive of that State the aid of Northern troops under his own command, to suppress it. Incendiaries have asked of the President permission to invade the Southern States, and have been warned that any attempt to do this will be punished as a crime. I repeat it, I have no special means of knowledge on this subject, but what I have cited, and my general acquaintance with the statesmanlike views of the President, makes me confident in expressing the opinion above given. Very respectfully, Your obedt. Servant:

William S. Harney, Brigadier General

Document 2   Excerpt of Letter from General Benjamin F. Butler to Lieutenant General Winfield Scott, 27 May 1861.[6]

Fortress Monroe, Virginia 27 May 1861

Sir,

Since I wrote my last dispatch the question in regard to slave property is becoming one of very serious magnitude. The inhabitants of Virginia are using their negroes in the batteries, and are preparing to send the women and children South. The escapes from them are very numerous, and a squad has come in this morning to my pickets bringing their women and children. Of course these cannot be dealt with upon the Theory on which I designed to treat the services of able bodied men and women who might come within my lines and of which I gave you a detailed account in my last dispatch. I am in the utmost doubt what to do with this species of property. Up to this time I have had come within my lines men and women with their children—entire families—each family belonging to the same owner. I have therefore determined to employ, as I can do very profitably, the able-bodied persons in the party, issuing proper food for the support of all, and charging against their services the expense of care and sustenance of the non-laborers, keeping a strict and accurate account as well of the services as of the expenditure having the worth of the services and the cost of the expenditure determined by a board of Survey hereafter to be detailed. I know of no other manner in which to dispose of this subject and the questions connected therewith. As a matter of property to the insurgents it will be of very great moment, the number that I now have amounting as I am informed to what in good times would be of the value of sixty thousand dollars. Twelve of these negroes I am informed have escaped from the erection of the batteries on Sewall's point which this morning fired upon my expedition as it passed by out of range. As a means of offence therefore in the enemy's hands these negroes when able bodied are of the last importance. Without them the batteries could not have been erected at least for many weeks. As a military question it would seem to be a measure of necessity to deprive their masters of their services. How can this be done? As a political question and a question of humanity can I receive the services of a Father and a Mother and not take the children? Of the humanitarian aspect I have no doubt. Of the political one I have no right to judge. I therefore submit all this to your better judgement, and as these questions have a political aspect, I have ventured—and I trust I am not wrong in so doing—to duplicate the parts of my dispatch relating to this subject and forward them to the Secretary of War.

Benjamin F. Butler

DOCUMENT 3 An Act to confiscate Property used for Insurrectionary Purposes. 6 August 1861.[7]

Be it enacted by the Senate and House of Representatives of the United States of America in Congress assembled, That if, during the present or any future insurrection against the Government of the United States, after the President of the United States shall have declared, by proclamation,

---

[6]   *The War of the Rebellion: A Compilation of the Official Records of the Union and Confederate Armies*, Series I, Volume II, (Washington: Government Printing Office, 1880), p. 52.

[7]   U.S., *Statutes at Large, Treaties, and Proclamations of the United States of America*, vol. 12 (Boston, 1863), p. 319.

that the laws of the United States are opposed, and the execution thereof obstructed, by combinations too powerful to be suppressed by the ordinary course of judicial proceedings, or by the power vested in the marshals by law, any person or persons, his, her, or their agent, attorney, or employé, shall purchase or acquire, sell or give, any property of whatsoever kind or description, with intent to use or employ the same, or suffer the same to be used or employed, in aiding, abetting, or promoting such insurrection or resistance to the laws, or any person or persons engaged therein; or if any person or persons, being the owner or owners of any such property, shall knowingly use or employ, or consent to the use or employment of the same as aforesaid, all such property is hereby declared to be lawful subject of prize and capture wherever found; and it shall be the duty of the President of the United States to cause the same to be seized, confiscated, and condemned.

SEC. 2. *And be it further enacted,* That such prizes and capture shall be condemned in the district or circuit court of the United States having jurisdiction of the amount, or in admiralty in any district in which the same may be seized, or into which they may be taken and proceedings first instituted.

SEC. 3. *And be it further enacted,* That the Attorney-General, or any district attorney of the United States in which said property may at the time be, may institute the proceedings of condemnation, and in such case they shall be wholly for the benefit of the United States; or any person may file an information with such attorney, in which case the proceedings shall be for the use of such informer and the United States in equal parts.

SEC. 4. *And be it further enacted,* That whenever hereafter, during the present insurrection against the Government of the United States, any person claimed to be held to labor or service under the law of any State, shall be required or permitted by the person to whom such labor or service is claimed to be due, or by the lawful agent of such person, to take up arms against the United States, or shall be required or permitted by the person to whom such labor or service is claimed to be due, or his lawful agent, to work or to be employed in or upon any fort, navy yard, dock, armory, ship, entrenchment, or in any military or naval service whatsoever, against the Government and lawful authority of the United States, then, and in every such case, the person to whom such labor or service is claimed to be due shall forfeit his claim to such labor, any law of the State or of the United States to the contrary notwithstanding. And whenever thereafter the person claiming such labor or service shall seek to enforce his claim, it shall be a full and sufficient answer to such claim that the person whose service or labor is claimed had been employed in hostile service against the Government of the United States, contrary to the provisions of this act.

DOCUMENT 4 *Anti-Slavery Advocate,* II (February 1, 1862), 498-499.[8]

There are now in Beaufort District alone, I am informed by official personages, nearly sixteen thousand slaves, whose masters have fled, and Beaufort District is but a small portion of the country at present in our hands. I have accompanied a number of the reconnaissances made in all directions from this post, both by sea and land; have witnessed the exploration of the country

---

[8] John W. Blassingame, ed., *Slave Testimony: Two Centuries of Letters, Speeches, Interviews, and Autobiographies* (Baton Rouge: Louisiana State Press, 1977): 358-363.

from Tybee Island on the south to North Edisto on the north, an extent of sixty miles, and have penetrated as far into the interior, on some of these excursions, as our troops have yet gone. Everywhere I find the same state of things existing; everywhere the blacks hurry in droves to our lines; they crowd in small boats around our ships; they swarm upon our decks; they hurry to our officers, from the cotton-houses of their masters, in an hour or two after our guns are fired. I am writing now not what I have heard, but what I have seen. I am not sending you opinions, or conclusions at which I have arrived, but facts that I have observed. I mean each statement to be taken literally; it is not garnished for rhetorical effect, but put into such a form as will most exactly convey to the mind of a reader the impression made on me. I have seen negroes who reported themselves as just escaped from their masters, who came breathless to our forces, and said they dared not go back, for their masters would kill them; who told that their masters were at that moment armed and threatening to shoot any slave who did not fly with them; who declared they had tricked their owners and came away in boats that they were bidden to take back to the whites. I have talked with drivers and field-hands with house-maids, and coachmen, and body-servants, who were apparently as eager to escape as any. I have heard the blacks point out how their masters might be caught, where they were hidden, what were their forces. I have seen them used as guides and pilots. I have been along while they pointed out in wht houses stores of arms and ammunition were kept, and where bodies of troops were stationed. I have known this information verified. I have asked them about the sentiment of the slave population, and been invariably answered that everywhere it is the same.

I have invariably been told by the negroes that they were not well fed. The first reason a black man, or woman, or child assigns for deserting his owner is the small quantity and poor quality of food given him; the next reason is the same story about clothing; then comes the complaint of hard usage, hard work, and occasionally of cruelty. The last is rare, in my experience....

The absurd attempts of Southern papers to pretend that the blacks are still loyal can only excite a compassionate smile. The poor wretches cling to this hope, the absence of which would present to them so appalling a future. The slaves not yet escaped of course pretend to be faithful, but some have told me how they said to their masters and mistresses on the day of the fight, "The Yankees will be whipped, Massa and Missus," but all the while they prayed and believed otherwise. So, casual allusions are made in Charleston papers to the fidelity of their "servants," as if it were a matter of course, but there is no labored discussion of a subject too terrible for discussion. As for my own judgement—it may not be worth much—but I came hither prepared to find all the negroes attached to their masters, and I have gradually observed a feeling of bitterness displayed by the blacks; at first there was only elation at their own escape; of late this has been mingled with indignation at the insane attempt of the masters to fire on them. I have known of several instances where slaves asked for arms to fire on their own masters (this was the case with colonel Whitmarsh Seabrook's live stock near Edisto); I have known where slaves assisted in the capture of their masters; I have sometimes asked myself whether the time might not come when arming the blacks and regularly drilling them as soldiers under white officers might not prove the only means of averting the odious horrors of a servile insurrection. That time appears to me not to have yet come even here; but it may be nearer than any of us suppose. The blacks fall to plundering as soon as their masters flee, and go by our lines confidently with their arms or their boats laden with plunder; and it is hardly the business of Federal troops to look after the property of rebels.

Document 5   An Act for the Release of Certain Persons Held to Service of Labor in the District of Columbia, signed into law by President Abraham Lincoln, 16 April 1862.[9]

Be it enacted by the Senate and House of Representatives of the United States of America in Congress assembled, that all persons held to service or labor within the District of Columbia by reason of African descent are hereby discharged and freed of and from all claim to such service of labor; and from and after the passage of this act neither slavery nor involuntary servitude except for crime whereof the party shall be duly convicted shall hereafter exist in said District.

Sec. 2. And be it further enacted, That all persons loyal to the United States holding claims to service or labor against persons discharged therefrom by this act may within ninety days from the passage thereof but not thereafter present to the Commissioners hereinmentioned their respective statements or petitions in writing verified by oath or affirmation setting forth the names, ages, and personal description of such persons the manner in which said petitioners acquired such claim and any facts touching the value thereof and declaring his allegiance to the government of the United States; and that he has not borne arms against the United States during the present rebellion nor in any way given aid or comfort thereto Provided that the oath of the party to the petition shall not be evidence of the facts therein stated.

Sec. 3. And be it further enacted, That the President of the United States with the advice and consent of the Senate, shall appoint three commissioners residents of the District of Columbia any two of which shall have power to act who shall receive the petitions above mentioned and who shall investigate and determine the validity and value of the claims therein present as aforesaid and appraise and apportion under the procedure hereto annexed the value in money of the several claims by them found to be valid. Provided however That the entire sum so appraised and apportioned shall not exceed in the aggregate an amount equal to three hundred dollars for each person shown to have been so heldby lawful claim.

Document 6   David Hunter, Major-General, Commander of Union Troops in South Carolina, 1862[10]

Headquarters, Department of the South

Hilton Head, S.C., June 1862

To the Hon. E.M. Stanton, Secretary of War, Washington, D.C.

Sir:--I have the honor to acknowledge the receipt of a communication from the Adjutant-General of the Army, dated June 13, 1862, requesting me to furnish you with the information necessary to answer certain Resolutions introduced in the House of Representatives June 9, 1862, on motion of the Hon. Mr. Wickliffe, of Kentucky; their substance being to enquire:

---

[9] "Act abolishing Slavery in the District of Columbia, April 16, 1862," *Select Statutes and Other Documents illustrative of the History of the United States, 1861-1898*, William MacDonald, ed., (New York: The Macmillan Company, 1909), p. 35.

[10] Joseph Thomas Wilson, *Black Phalanx: A History of the Negro Soldiers of the United States in the Wars of 1775-1812, 1861-'65*, (Hartford, Conn.: American Publishing Company, 1890), p. 152.

"1st—Whether I had organized, or was organizing, a regiment of 'fugitive slaves' in this department.

"2d—Whether any authority had been given to me from the War Department for such an organization; and

"3rd—Whether I had been furnished, by order of the War Department, with clothing, uniforms, arms, equipments, and so forth, for such a force?

"Only having received the letter at a late hour this evening, I urge forward my answer in time for the steamer sailing tomorrow morning.—this haste preventing me from entering, as minutely as I could wish, upon many points of detail, such as the paramount importance of the subject would seem to call for. But, in view of the near termination of the present session of Congress, and the wide-spread interest which must have been awakened by Mr. Wickliffe's resolutions, I prefer sending even this imperfect answer to waiting the period necessary for the collection of fuller and more comprehensive data.

"To the first question, therefore, I reply: That no regiment of 'fugitive slaves' has been, or is being, organized in this department. There is, however, a fine regiment of loyal persons whose late masters are fugitive rebels—men who everywhere fly before the appearance of the national flag, leaving their loyal and unhappy servants behind them, to shift, as best they can, for themselves. So far, indeed, are the loyal persons composing the regiment from seeking to evade the presence of their late owners, that they are now, one and all, endeavoring with commendable zeal to acquire the drill and discipline requisite to place them in a position to go in full and effective pursuit of their fugacious and traitorous proprietors.

"To the second question, I have the honor to answer that the instructions given to Brig.-Gen. W.T. Sherman by the Hon. Simon Cameron, late Secretary of War, and turned over to me, by succession, for my guidance, do distinctly authorize me to employ 'all loyal persons offering their service in defence of the Union, and for the suppression of this rebellion,' in any manner I may see fit, or that circumstances may call for. There is no restriction as to the character or color of the persons to be employed, or the nature of the employment—whether civil or military—in which their services may be used. I conclude, therefore, that I have been authorized to enlist 'fugitive slaves' as soldiers, could any such fugitives be found in this department. No such characters, however, have yet appeared within view of our most advanced pickets.— the loyal negroes everywhere remaining on their plantations to welcome us, aid us, and supply us with food, labor and information. It is the masters who have in every instance been the 'fugitives,' running away from loyal slaves as well as loyal soldiers; and these, as yet, we have only partially been able to see—chiefly their heads over ramparts, or dodging behind trees, rifles in hand, in the extreme distance. In the absence of any 'fugitive master law,' the deserted slaves would be wholly without remedy had not the crime of treason given them right to pursue, capture and bring those persons of whose benignant protection they have been thus suddenly and cruelly bereft.

To the third interrogatory, it is my painful duty to reply that I have never received any specific authority for issue of clothing, uniforms, arms, equipments, and so forth, to the troops in question.—my general instructions from Mr. Cameron, to employ them in any manner I might find necessary, and the military exigencies of the department and the country, being my only, but I trust, sufficient justification. Neither have I had any specific authority for supplying those persons with shovels, spades, and pick axes, when employing them as laborers; nor with boats and oars, when using them as lighter-men; but these are not points included in Mr. Wickliffe's resolution. To me it seemed that liberty to employ men in any particular capacity implied and carried with it liberty, also, to supply them with the necessary tools; and acting upon this faith, I have clothed, equipped and armed the only loyal regiment yet raised in South Carolina, Georgia, or Florida.

I must say, in vindication of my own conduct, that had it not been for the many other diversified and imperative claims on my time and attention, a much more satisfactory result might have been achieved; and that, in place of only one regiment, as at present, at least five or six well-drilled, and thoroughly acclimated regiments should, by this time, have been added to the loyal forces of the Union.

The experiment of arming the blacks, so far as I have made it, has been a complete and even marvelous success. They are sober, docile, attentive, and enthusiastic; displaying great natural capacities in acquiring the duties of the soldier. They are now eager beyond all things to take the field and be led into actions; and it is the unanimous opinion of the officers who have had charge of them that, in the peculiarities of this climate and country, they will prove invaluable auxiliaries, fully equal to the similar regiments so long and successfully used by the British authorities in the West India Islands.

In conclusion, I would say, it is my hope—there appearing no possibility of other reinforcements, owing to the exigencies of the compaign in the Peninsula—to have organized by the end of next fall, and be able to present to the government, from forty-eight to fifty thousand of these hardy and devoted soldiers.

Trusting that this letter may be made part of your answer to Mr. Wickliffe's resolutions, I have the honor to be,

Very respectfully your most obedient servant,

David Hunter, *Maj.-Gen. Commanding.*

APPROVED, August 6, 1861.

Document 7 Letter from William Tecumseh Sherman, Commander of the 5th Division of the Army of the Tennessee to Thomas Hunton, Tennessee Slaveholder. 24 August 1862.[11]

My dear Sir, I freely admit that when you recall the times when we were schoolfellows, when we were younger than now, you touch me on a tender point, and cause me to deeply regret that even you should style yourself a Rebel. I cannot believe that Tom Hunton, the Companion of Gaither, Rankin, and Irvin and many others long since dead, and of Halleck, Ord, Stevens and others still living can of his own free will admit the anarchical principle of secession or be vain enough to suppose the present Politicians Can frame a Government better than that of Washington, Hamilton & Jefferson. We cannot realize this but delude ourselves into the belief that by some strange but successful jugglery the managers of our Political Machine have raised up the single issue, North or South, which shall prevail in America? or that you like others have been blown up, and cast into the Mississippi of Secession doubtful if by hard fighting you can reach the shore in safety, or drift out to the Ocean of Death. I know it is no use for us now to discuss this war is on us. We are Enemies, still private friends. In the one Capacity I will do you all the harm I can, yet on the other if here, you may have as of old my last Cent, my last shirt and pants. You ask of me your negroes, and I will Immediately ascertain if they be under my Military Control and I will moreover see that they are one and all told what is true of all–Boys if you want to go to your master, Go– You are free to choose. You must now think for yourselves. Your Master has seceded from his Parent Government and you have seceded from him–both wrong by law–but both exercising an

---

[11] Maj. Genl. W. T. Sherman to Thomas Hunton, Esq., 24 Aug. 1862, vol. 3, pp. 51–53, Letters Sent, W. T. Sherman Papers, Generals' Papers & Books, series 159, Adjutant General's Office, Record Group 94, National Archives.

undoubted natural Right to rebel. If your boys want to go, I will enable them to go, but I won't advise, persuade or force them– I confess I have not yet seen the "Confiscation Act," but I enclose you my own orders defining my position. I also cut out of a paper Grant's Orders, and I assert that the Action of all our Leading Military Leaders, Halleck, McClellan, Buell, Grant & myself have been more conservative of slavery than the Acts of your own men. The Constitution of the United States is your only legal title to slavery. You have another title, that of posession & Force, but in Law & Logic your title to your Boys lay in the Constitution of the United States. You may say you are for the Constitution of the United States, as it was–You know it is unchanged, not a word, not a syllable and I can lay my hand on that Constitution and swear to it without one twang. But your party have made *another* and have another in force. How can you say that you would have the old, when you have a new? By the new if sucessful you inherit the Right of Slavery, but the new is not law till your Revolution is successful. Therefore we who contend for the old existing Law, Contend that you by your own act take away Your own title to all property save what is restricted by *our* constitution, your slaves included. You know I don't want your slaves; but to bring you to reason I think as a Military Man I have a Right and it is good policy to make *you all* feel that you are but men–that you have all the wants & dependencies of other men, and must eat, be clad &c. to which end you must have property & labor, and that by Rebelling you risk both. Even without the Confiscation Act, by the simple laws of War we ought to take your effective slaves. I don't say to free them, but to use their labor & deprive you of it; as Belligerents we ought to seek the hostile Army and fight it and not the people.–We went to Corinth but Beaureguard declined Battle, since which time many are dispersed as Guerillas. We are not bound to follow them, but rightfully make war by any means that will tend to bring about an end and restore Peace. Your people may say it only exasperates, widens the breach and all that, But the longer the war lasts the more you must be convinced that we are no better & no worse than People who have gone before us, and that we are simply reenacting History, and that one of the modes of bringing People to reason is to touch their Interests pecuniary or property.

We never harbor women or children–we give employment to men, under the enclosed order. I find no negroes Registered as belonging to Hunton, some in the name of McGhee of which the Engineer is now making a list–I see McClellan says that the negroes once taken shall never again be restored. I say nothing. My opinion is, we execute not make the Law, be it of Congress or War. But it is Manifest that if you won't go into a United States District Court and sue for the recovery of your slave property, You can never Get it, out of adverse hands. No U.S. Court would allow you to sue for the recovery of a slave under the Fugitive Slave Law, unless you acknowledge allegiance. Believing this honesty, so I must act. though personally I feel strong frindship as ever, for very many in the South. With Great Respect Your friend,

W. T. Sherman

Documnt 8 The "Second Confiscation Act," 17 July 1862.[12]

An Act to suppress Insurrection, to punish Treason and Rebellion, to seize and confiscate the Property of Rebels, and for other Purposes.

---

[12] "An Act to Suppress Insurrection, to Punish Treason and Rebellion, to seize and confiscate the Property of Rebels, and for other Purposes," *United States Statutes at Large, Treaties, and Proclamations of the United States of America*, Vol. 12, (Boston: Little, Brown and Company, 1863), p. 589-592.

Be it enacted by the Senate and House of Representatives of the United States of America in Congress assembled, That every person who shall hereafter commit the crime of treason against the United States, and shall be adjudged guilty thereof, shall suffer death, and all his slaves, if any, shall be declared and made free; or, at the discretion of the court, he shall be imprisoned for not less than five years and fined not less than ten thousand dollars, and all his slaves, if any, shall be declared and made free; said fine shall be levied and collected on any or all of the property, real and personal, excluding slaves, of which the said person so convicted was the owner at the time of committing the said crime, any sale or conveyance to the contrary notwithstanding.

SEC. 2. *And be it further enacted*, That if any person shall hereafter incite, set on foot, assist, or engage in any rebellion or insurrection against the authority of the United States, or the laws thereof, or shall give aid or comfort thereto, or shall engage in, or give aid and comfort to, any such existing rebellion or insurrection, and be convicted thereof, such person shall be punished by imprisonment for a period not exceeding ten years, or by a fine not exceeding ten thousand dollars, and by the liberation of all his slaves, if any he have; or by both of said punishments, at the discretion of the court.

SEC. 5. *And be it further enacted*, That, to insure the speedy termination of the present rebellion, it shall be the duty of the President of the United States to cause the seizure of all the estate and property, money, stocks, credits, and effects of the persons hereinafter named in this section, and to apply and use the same

SEC. 9. *And be it further enacted*, That all slaves of persons who shall hereafter be engaged in rebellion against the government of the United States, or who shall in any way give aid or comfort thereto, escaping from such persons and taking refuge within the lines of the army; and all slaves captured from such persons or deserted by them and coming under the control of the government of the United States; and all slaves of such person found on [*or*] being within any place occupied by rebel forces and afterwards occupied by the forces of the United States, shall be deemed captives of war, and shall be forever free of their servitude, and not again held as slaves.

SEC. 10. *And be it further enacted*, That no slave escaping into any State, Territory, or the District of Columbia, from any other State, shall be delivered up, or in any way impeded or hindered of his liberty, except for crime, or some offence against the laws, unless the person claiming said fugitive shall first make oath that the person to whom the labor or service of such fugitive is alleged to be due is his lawful owner, and has not borne arms against the United States in the present rebellion, nor in any way given aid and comfort thereto; and no person engaged in the military or naval service of the United States shall, under any pretence whatever, assume to decide on the validity of the claim of any person to the service or labor of any other person, or surrender up any such person to the claimant, on pain of being dismissed from the service.

SEC. 11. *And be it further enacted*, That the President of the United States is authorized to employ as many persons of African descent as he may deem necessary and proper for the suppression of this rebellion, and for this purpose he may organize and use them in such manner as he may judge best for the public welfare.

SEC. 13. *And be it further enacted*, That the President is hereby authorized, at any time hereafter, by proclamation, to extend to persons who may have participated in the existing rebellion in any State or part thereof, pardon and amnesty, with such exceptions and at such time and on such conditions as he may deem expedient for the public welfare.

SEC. 14. *And be it further enacted*, That the courts of the United States shall have full power to institute proceedings, make orders and decrees, issue process, and do all other things necessary to carry this act into effect.

APPROVED, July 17, 1862.

Document 9 President Abraham Lincoln, "Address on Colonization to a Deputation of Negroes," 14 August 1862.[13]

This afternoon the President of the United States gave audience to a Committee of colored men at the White House.... Having all been seated, the President, after a few preliminary observations, informed them that a sum of money had been appropriatd by Congress, and placed at his disposition for the purpose of aiding the colonization in some country of the people, or a portion of them, of African descent, thereby making it his duty, as it had for a long time been his inclination, to favor that cause; and why, he asked, should the people of your race be colonized, and where? Why should they leave this country? This is, perhaps, the first question for proper consideration. You and we are different races. We have between us a broader difference than exists between almost any other two races. Whether it is right or wrong I need not discuss, but this physical difference is a great disadvantage to us both, as I think your race suffer very greatly, many of them by living among us, while ours suffer from your presence. In a word, we suffer on each side. If this is admitted, it affords a reason at least why we should be separated. You here are freemen I suppose? ... Your race are suffering, in my judgment, the greatest wrong inflicted on any people. But even when you cease to be slaves, you are yet far removed from being placed on an equality with the white race. You are cut off from many of the advantages which the other race enjoy. The aspiration of men is to enjoy equality with the best when free, but on this broad continent, not a single man of your race is made the equal of a single man of ours. Go where you are treated the best, and the ban is still upon you.

I do not propose to discuss this, but to present it as a fact with which we have to deal. I cannot alter it if I would. It is a fact, about which we all think and feel alike, I and you. We look to our condition, owing to the existence of the two races on this continent. I need not recount to you the effects upon white men, growing out of the institution of Slavery. I believe in its general evil effects on the white race. See our present condition—the country engaged in war!--our white men cutting one another's throats, none knowing how far it will extend; and then consider what we know to be the truth. But for your race among us there could not be war, although many men engaged on either side do not care for you one way or the other. Nevertheless, I repeat, without the institution of Slavery and the colored race as a basis, the war could not have an existence.

It is better for us both, therefore, to be separated. I know that there are free men among you, who even if they could better their condition are not as much inclined to go out of the country as those, who being slaves could obtain their freedom on this condition. I suppose one of the principal difficulties in the way of colonization is that the free colored man cannot see that his comfort would be advanced by it. You may believe you can live in Washington or elsewhere in the United States the remainder of your life, as easily, or perhaps more so than you can in any foreign

---

[13] Abraham Lincoln, *Collected Works of Abraham Lincoln*, Volume 5, Roy P. Basler, ed., Marion Dolores Pratt and Lloyd A. Dunlap, asst. eds., (New Brunswick, N.J.: Rutgers University Press, 1953), pp. 370-375.

country, and hence you may come to the conclusion that you have nothing to do with the idea of going to a foreign country, and hence you may come to the conclusion that you have nothing to do with the idea of going to a foreign country. This is (I speak in no unkind sense) an extremely selfish view of the case.

But you ought to do something to help those who are not so fortunate as yourselves. There is an unwillingness on the part of our people, harsh as it may be, for you free colored people to remain with us. Now, if you could give a start to white people, you would open a wide door for many to be made free. If we deal with those who are not free at the beginning, and whose intellects are clouded by Slavery, we have very poor materials to start with. If intelligent colored men, such as are before me, would move in this matter, much might be accomplished. It is exceedingly important that we have men at the beginning capable of thinking as white men, and not those who have been systematically oppressed. ...

The colony of Liberia has been in existence a long time. In a certain sense it is a success.... The question is if the colored people are persuaded to go anywhere, why not there? One reason for an unwillingness to do so is that some of you would rather remain within reach of the country of your nativity. ... The place I am thinking about having for a colony is in Central America. It is nearer to us than Liberia. ... The country is a very excellent one for any people, and with great natural resources and advantages, and especially because of the similarity of climate with your native land—thus being suited to your physical condition. The particular place I have in view is to be a great highwat from the Atlantic or Caribbean Sea to the Pacific Ocean, and this particular place has all the advantages for a colony. ...

The practical thing I want to ascertain is whether I can get a number of able-bodied men, with their wives and children, who are willing to go, when I present evidence of encouragement and protection. ... I want you to let me know whether this can be done or not.

... The Chairman of the delegation briefly replied that "they would hold a consultation and in a short time give an answer." The President said: "Take your full time—no hurry at all."

The delegation then withdrew.

Document 10 Abraham Lincoln, Letter to Horace Greeley, 22 August 1862.[14]

Executive Mansion

Washington, August 22, 1862

Hon. Horace Greeley:

Dear Sir,

I have just read yours of the 19th, addressed to myself through the New-York Tribune. If there be in it any statements, or assumptions of fact, which I may know to be erroneous, I do not, now and here, controvert them. If there be in it any inferences which I may believe to be falsely

---

14 Abraham Lincoln, Letter to Horace Greeley, August 22, 1862, in *Collected Works of Abraham Lincoln,* Roy Prentice Basler, ed., (Springfield, Ill.: Rutgers University Press, 1860), accessible at https://www.abrahamlincolnonline.org/lincoln/speeches/greeley.htm

drawn, I do not now and here, argue against them. If there be perceptible in it an impatient and dictatorial tone, I waive it in deference to an old friend, whose heart I have always supposed to be right.

As to the policy I "seem to be pursuing" as you say, I have not meant to leave any one in doubt.

I would save the Union. I would save it the shortest way under the Constitution. The sooner the national authority can be restored; the nearer the Union will be "the Union as it was." If there be those who would not save the Union, unless they could at the same time *save* slavery, I do not agree with them. If there be those who would not save the Union unless they could at the same time *destroy* slavery, I do not agree with them. My paramount object in this struggle *is* to save the Union, and is *not* either to save or to destroy slavery. If I could save the Union without freeing *any* slave I would do it, and if I could save it by freeing *all* the slaves I would do it; and if I could save it by freeing some and leaving others alone I would also do that. What I do about slavery, and the colored race, I do because I believe it helps to save the Union; and what I forbear, I forbear because I do *not* believe it would help save the Union. I shall do *less* whenever I shall believe what I am doing hurts the cause, and I shall do *more* whenever I shall believe doing more will help the cause. I shall try to correct errors when shown to be errors; and I shall adopt new views so fast as they shall appear to be true views.

I have here stated my purpose according to my view of my *official* duty; and I intend no modification of my oft-expressed *personal* wish that all men everywhere could be free.

Yours,

A. Lincoln

Document 11   The Emancipation Proclamation, 1 January 1863.

A Proclamation.

Whereas, on the twenty-second day of September, in the year of our Lord one thousand eight hundred and sixty two, a proclamation was issued by the President of the United States, containing, among other things, the following, to wit:

"That on the first day of January, in the year of our Lord one thousand eight hundred and sixty-three, all persons held as slaves within any State or designated part of a State, the people whereof shall then be in rebellion against the United States, shall be then, thenceforward, and forever free; and the Executive Government of the United States, including the military and naval authority thereof, will recognize and maintain the freedom of such persons, and will do no act or acts to repress such persons, or any of them, in any efforts they may make for their actual freedom.

"That the Executive will, on the first day of January aforesaid, by proclamation, designate the States and parts of States, if any, in which the people thereof, respectively, shall then be in rebellion against the United States; and the fact that any State, or the people thereof, shall on that day be, in good faith, represented in the Congress of the United States by members chosen thereto at elections wherein a majority of the qualified voters of such State shall have participated, shall, in the absence of strong countervailing testimony, be deemed conclusive evidence that such State, and the people thereof, are not then in rebellion against the United States."

Now, therefore I, Abraham Lincoln, President of the United States, by virtue of the power in me vested as Commander-in-Chief, of the Army and Navy of the United States in time of actual armed rebellion against the authority and government of the United States, and as a fit and necessary war measure for suppressing said rebellion, do, on this first day of January, in the year of our Lord one thousand eight hundred and sixty three, and in accordance with my purpose so to do publicly proclaimed for the full period of one hundred days, from the day first above mentioned, order and designate as the States and parts of States wherein the people thereof respectively, are this day in rebellion against the United States, the following, to wit:

Arkansas, Texas, Louisiana, (except the Parishes of St. Bernard, Plaquemines, Jefferson, St. Johns, St. Charles, St. James Ascension, Assumption, Terrebonne, Lafourche, St. Mary, St. Martin, and Orleans, including the City of New Orleans) Mississippi, Alabama, Florida, Georgia, South-Carolina, North-Carolina, and Virginia, (except the fortyeight counties designated as West Virginia, and also the counties of Berkley, Accomac, Northampton, Elizabeth-City, York, Princess Ann, and Norfolk, including the cities of Norfolk and Portsmouth[)], and which excepted parts, are for the present, left precisely as if this proclamation were not issued.

And by virtue of the power, and for the purpose aforesaid, I do order and declare that all persons held as slaves within said designated States, and parts of States, are, and henceforward shall be free; and that the Executive government of the United States, including the military and naval authorities thereof, will recognize and maintain the freedom of said persons.

And I hereby enjoin upon the people so declared to be free to abstain from all violence, unless in necessary self-defence; and I recommend to them that, in all cases when allowed, they labor faithfully for reasonable wages.

And I further declare and make known, that such persons of suitable condition, will be received into the armed service of the United States to garrison forts, positions, stations, and other places, and to man vessels of all sorts in said service.

And upon this act, sincerely believed to be an act of justice, warranted by the Constitution, upon military necessity, I invoke the considerate judgment of mankind, and the gracious favor of Almighty God.

In witness whereof, I have hereunto set my hand and caused the seal of the United States to be affixed.

Done at the City of Washington, this first day of January, in the year of our Lord one thousand eight hundred and sixty three, and of the Independence of the United States of America the eighty-seventh.

By the President: ABRAHAM LINCOLN

WILLIAM H. SEWARD, Secretary of State.

Document 12   Law on Prisoners of War, Congress of the Confederate States of America, 12 January 1863[15]

Section 4   That every white person, being a commissioned officer, or acting as such, who, during the present war, shall command Negroes or mulattoes in arms against the Confederate States, or who shall arm, train, organize, or prepare Negroes or mulattoes for military service against the Confederate States, or who shall voluntarily aid Negroes or mulattoes in any military enterprise, attack, or conflict in such service, shall be deemed as inciting servile insurrection, and shall, if captured, be put to death, or be otherwise punished at the discretion of the Court.

Document 13   Frederick Douglass, *Men of Color, to Arms!* 2 March 1863.[16]

When first the Rebel cannon shattered the walls of Sumter, and drove away its starving garrison, I predicted that the war then and there inaugurated would not be fought out entirely by white men. Every month's experience during these two dreary years has confirmed that opinion. A war undertaken and brazenly carried on for the perpetual enslavement of colored men, calls logically and loudly upon colored men to help to suppress it. Only a moderate share of sagacity was needed to see that the arms of the slave was the best defense against the arms of the slaveholder. Hence with every reverse to the National arms, with every exulting shout of victory raised by the slaveholding Rebels, I have implored an imperiled nation to unshaken against her foes her powerful black hand. Slowly and reluctantly that appeal is beginning to be heeded. Stop not now to complain that it was not heeded sooner. It may or it may not have been best that it should not. This is not the time to discuss that question. Leave it to the future. When the war is over, the country saved, peace established, and the black man's rights secured, as they will be, history with an impartial hand, will dispose of that and sundry other questions. Action! Action! Not criticism is the plain duty of this hour. Words are now useful only as they stimulate to blows. The office of speech now is only to point out when, where, and how to strike to the best advantage. There is no time to delay. The tide is at its flood that leads on to fortune. From East to West, from North to South, the sky is written all over 'NOW OR NEVER.' Liberty won by white men would lose half its lustre. 'Who would be free, themselves must strike the blow.' 'Better even die free, than to live slaves.' This is the sentiment of every brave coloured man amongst us. There are weak and cowardly men in all nations. We have them amongst us. They tell you this is the 'white man's war;' that you will be no 'better off after than before the war;' that the getting of you into the army is to 'sacrifice you on the first opportunity.' Believe them not; cowards themselves, they do not wish to have their cowardice shamed by your brave example. Leave them to their timidity, or to whatever motive may hold them back. I have not thought lightly of the words I am now addressing you. The counsel I give comes of close observation of the great struggle now in progress, and of the deep conviction that this is your hour and mine. In good earnest then, and after the best deliberation, I now for the first time during this war, feel at liberty to call and counsel you to arms. By every consideration which

---

15   Text of resolution in Horace Greeley, *The American Conflict: A History of the Great Rebellion in the United States of America 1860-'65.* Vol II. (Hartford, Conn.: O.D. Case & Company, 1866), pp. 523-524.

16   Frederick Douglass, *The Life and Times of Frederick Douglass, written by himself,* (Hartford, Conn.: Parck Publishing, 1882), pp. 414-416.

binds you to your enslaved fellow-countrymen, and the peace and welfare of your country; by every aspiration which you cherish for the freedom and equality of yourselves and your children; by all the ties of blood and identity which makes us one with the brave black men now fighting our battles in Louisiana and South Carolina, I urge you to fly to arms and smite with death the power that would bury the Government and your liberty in the same hopeless grave. I wish I could tell you that the State of New York calls you to this high honor. For the moment her constituted authorities are silent on the subject. They will speak by and by, and doubtless on the right side; but we are not compelled to wait for her. We can get at the threat of treason and Slavery through the State of Massachusetts.

She was first in the war of Independence; first to break the chains of her slaves; first to make the black man equal before the law; first to admit colored children to her common schools, and she was first to answer with her blood the alarm cry of the nation—when its capital was menaced by rebels. You know her patriotic Governor, and you know Charles Sumner—I need add no more.

Massachusetts now welcomes you to arms as her soldiers. She has but a small colored population from which to recruit. She has full leave of the General Government to send one regiment to the war, and she has undertaken to do it. Go quickly and help fill up this first colored regiment from the North. I am authorized to assure you that you will receive the same wages, the same rations, the same equipments, the same protection, the same treatment and the same bounty secured to white soldiers. You will be led by able and skillful officers—men who will take especial pride in your efficiency and purpose. They will be quick to accord to you all the honor you shall merit by your valor—and see that your rights and feelings are respected by other soldiers. I have assured myself on these points—and can speak with authority. More than twenty years unswerving devotion to our common cause, may give me some humble claim to be trusted at this momentous crisis.

I will not argue. To do so implies hesitation and doubt, and you do not hesitate. You do not doubt. The day dawns—the morning star is bright upon the horizon! The iron gate of our prison stands half open. One gallant rush from the North will fling it wide open, while four millions of our brothers and sisters shall march out into Liberty! The chance is now given to you to end in a day the bondage of centuries, and to rise in one bound from social degradation to the place of common equality with all other varieties of men. Remember Denmark Vesey of Charleston. Remember Nathaniel Turner of South Hampton; remember Sheilds, Green, and Copeland, who followed noble John Brown, and fell as glorious martyrs for the causes of the slaves. Remember that in a contest with Oppression, the Almighty has no attribute which can take sides with oppressors. The case is before you. This is our golden opportunity—let us accept it—and forever wipe out the dark reproaches unsparingly hurled against us by our enemies. Win for ourselves the gratitude of our country—and the best blessings of our prosperity through all time. The nucleus of this first regiment is now in camp at Readville, a short distance from Boston. I will undertake to forward to Boston all persons adjudged fit to be mustered into this regiment, who shall apply to me at any time within the next two weeks.

Frederick Douglass

Rochester, March 2, 1863

Document 14 Letter from Black Officers formerly serving in a Louisiana Black Regiment to the Commander of the Department of the Gulf, 7 April 1863.[17]

New Orleans [La.] April 7th 1863

Sir,

We the undersigned in part resigned officers of the Third Regular Louisiana Volunteer Native Guards and others desiring to assist in putting down this wicked rebellion. And in restoring peace to our once peaceful country. And wishing to share with you the dangers of the battle field and serve our country under you as our forefathers did under [Andrew] Jackson in eighteen hundred and fourteen and fifteen — On part of the ex officers we hereby volunteer our services to recruit A regiment of infantry for the United States army. — The commanding General may think that we will have the same difficulties to surmount that we had before resigning. But sir give us a commander who will appreciate us as men and soldiers, And we will be willing to surmount all other difficulties. We hope also if we are permitted to go into the service again, we will be allowed to share the dangers of the battle field and not be Kept for men who will not fight. If the world doubts our fighting give us A chance and we will show then what we can do. — We transmit this for your perusal and await your just conclusion. And hope that you will grant our request. We remain respectfully your obedient servants.

Adolph J Gla	James E. Moore	Charles W. Gibbons
Samuel Laurence	William Hardin	Daniel W. Smith, Jr.
Joseph G. Parker	William Moore	
Joseph W. Howard	Charles A. Allen	

Document 15 Letter from Abraham Lincoln to A. G. Hodges, Esq. Executive Mansion, Frankfort, Ky. Washington, April 4, 1864.[18]

My dear Sir: You ask me to put in writing the substance of what I verbally said the other day, in your presence, to Governor Bramlette and Senator Dixon. It was about as follows:

I am naturally anti-slavery. If slavery is not wrong, nothing is wrong. I can not remember when I did not so think, and feel. And yet I have never understood that the Presidency conferred upon me an unrestricted right to act officially upon this judgment and feeling. It was in the oath I took that I would, to the best of my ability, preserve, protect, and defend the Constitution of the United States. I could not take the office without taking the oath. Nor was it my view that I might take an oath to get power, and break the oath in using the power. I understood, too, that in ordinary civil administration this oath even forbade me to practically indulge my primary abstract judgment on the moral question of slavery. I had publicly declared this many times, and

---

17 Letter from Black Officers formerly serving in a Louisiana Black Regiment to the Commander of the Department of the Gulf. 7 April 1863. Accessed at Freedman and Southern Society Project http://www.freedmen.umd.edu/Gla.html

18 Reproduced in "President Lincoln," *Macmillan's Magazine*, Volume XI (November 1864-April 1865), ed. David Masson, (London: Macmillan and Co., 1865), pp. 300-306.

in many ways. And I aver that, to this day, I have done no official act in mere deference to my abstract judgment and feeling on slavery. I did understand however, that my oath to preserve the constitution to the best of my ability, imposed upon me the duty of preserving, by every indispensable means, that government---that nation---of which that constitution was the organic law. Was it possible to lose the nation, and yet preserve the constitution? By general law life *and* limb must be protected; yet often a limb must be amputated to save a life; but a life is never wisely given to save a limb. I felt that measures, otherwise unconstitutional, might become lawful, by becoming indispensable to the preservation of the constitution, through the preservation of the nation. Right or wrong, I assumed this ground, and now avow it. I could not feel that, to the best of my ability, I had even tried to preserve the constitution, if, to save slavery, or any minor matter, I should permit the wreck of government, country, and Constitution all together. When, early in the war, Gen. Fremont attempted military emancipation, I forbade it, because I did not then think it an indispensable necessity. When a little later, Gen. Cameron, then Secretary of War, suggested the arming of the blacks, I objected, because I did not yet think it an indispensable necessity. When, still later, Gen. Hunter attempted military emancipation, I again forbade it, because I did not yet think the indispensable necessity had come. When, in March, and May, and July 1862 I made earnest, and successive appeals to the border states to favor compensated emancipation, I believed the indispensable necessity for military emancipation, and arming the blacks would come, unless averted by that measure. They declined the proposition; and I was, in my best judgment, driven to the alternative of either surrendering the Union, and with it, the Constitution, or of laying a strong hand upon the colored element. I chose the latter. In choosing it, I hoped for greater gain than loss; but of this, I was not entirely confident. More than a year of trial now shows no loss by it in our foreign relations, none in our home popular sentiment, none in our white military force,---no loss by it any how or anywhere. On the contrary, it shows a gain of quite a hundred and thirty thousand soldiers, seamen, and laborers. These are palpable facts, about which, as facts, there can be no cavilling. We have the men; and we could not have had them without the measure.

And now let any Union man who complains of the measure, test himself by writing down in one line that he is for subduing the rebellion by force of arms; and in the next, that he is for taking these hundred and thirty thousand men from the Union side, and placing them where they would be but for the measure he condemns. If he can not face his case so stated, it is only because he can not face the truth.

I add a word which was not in the verbal conversation. In telling this tale I attempt no compliment to my own sagacity. I claim not to have controlled events, but confess plainly that events have controlled me. Now, at the end of three years struggle the nation's condition is not what either party, or any man devised, or expected. God alone can claim it. Whither it is tending seems plain. If God now wills the removal of a great wrong, and wills also that we of the North as well as you of the South, shall pay fairly for our complicity in that wrong, impartial history will find therein new cause to attest and revere the justice and goodness of God. Yours truly

A. LINCOLN

Document 16 Testimony, Investigation into the Fort Pillow Massacre, 22 April 1864[19]

Elias Falls, (colored) private, company A, 6th United States heavy artillery, or 1st Alabama artillery, sworn and examined.

Question:	Were you at Fort Pillow when the battle took place there, and it was captured by the rebels?
Answer:	I was there; I was a cook, and was waiting on the captain and major.
Question:	What did you see done there? What did the rebels do after they came into the fort?
Answer:	They killed all the men after they surrendered, until orders were given to stop; they killed all they came to, white and black, after they had surrendered.
Question:	The one the same as the other?
Answer:	Yes, sir, till he gave orders to stop firing.
Question:	Till who gave orders?
Answer:	They told me his name was Forrest.
Question:	Did you see anybody killed or shot there?
Answer:	Yes, sir; I was shot after the surrender, as I was marched up the hill by the rebels.
Question:	Where were you wounded?
Answer:	In the knee.
Question:	Was that the day of the fight?
Answer:	The same day.
Question:	Did you see any men shot the next day?
Answer:	I did not.
Question:	What did you see done after the place was taken?
Answer:	After peace was made some of the secesh soldiers came around cursing the boys that were wounded. They shot one of them about the hand, aimed to shoot him in the head, as he lay on the ground, and hit him in the hand; and an officer told the secesh soldier if he did that again he would arrest him, and he went off then.
Question:	Did they burn any buildings!
Answer:	Yes, sir.
Question:	Was anybody burned in the buildings?
Answer:	I did not see anybody burned; I saw them burn the buildings; I was not able to walk about; I stayed in a building that night with some three or four white men.
Question:	Do you know anything about their going into the hospital and killing those who were there sick in bed?

---

19 Committee on the Conduct of the War, investigation into the "Fort Pillow Massacre," 38th Congress, 1st Session, House of Representatives, Report No. 65.

Answer:	We had some three or four of our men there, and some of our men came in and said they had killed two women and two children.

Nathan Hunter, (colored) private, company D, 6th United States heavy artillery, sworn and examined.

Question:	Were you at Fort Pillow when it was captured?
Answer:	Yes, sir.
Question:	What did you see done there?
Answer:	They went down the hill, and shot all of us they saw; they shot me for dead, and I lay there until the next morning when the gunboat came along. They thought I was dead and pulled my boots off. That is all I know.
Question:	Were you shot when they first took the fort?
Answer:	I was not shot until we were done fighting.
Question:	Had you any arms in your hands when you were shot?
Answer:	No, sir.
Question:	How long did you lie where you were shot?
Answer:	I lay there from three o'clock until after night, and then I went up in the guard-house and stayed there until the next morning when the gunboat came along.
Question:	Did you see any others shot?
Answer:	Yes, sir; they shot down a whole parcel along with me. Their bodies were lying along the river bank the next morning. They kicked some of them into the river afer they were shot dead.
Question:	Did you see that?
Answer:	Yes, sir; I thought they were going to throw me in too; I slipped away in the night.
Question:	Did you see any men burned?
Answer:	No sir; I was down under the hill next the river.
Question:	They thought you were dead when they pulled your boots off?
Answer:	Yes, sir; they pulled my boots off, and rolled me over, and said they had killed me..

Document 17 Photograph, Timothy H. O'Sullivan, "Bombproof quarters on the lines in front of Petersburg, Va. August 18, 1864."[20]

Document 18 General Orders, No. 14 Confederate Law Authorizing the Enlistment of Black Soldiers, as Promulgated in a Military Order, 1865.[21]

Richmond, Va., March 23, 1865.

GENERAL ORDERS, No. 14.

I. The following act of Congress and regulations are published for the information and direction of all concerned:

AN ACT to increase the military force of the Confederate States.

The Congress of the Confederate States of America do enact, That, in order to provide additional forces to repel invasion, maintain the rightful possession of the Confederate States, secure their

---

20 Timothy H. O'Sullivan, photographer, "Bombproof quarters on the lines in front of Petersburg, Va. Aug. 7, 1864, LC-DIG ppmsca-32443 (digital file from original item) LC-B8184-802A (b&w film copy neg.), LOT 4166-E, no. 43 [P&P], Library of Congress Prints and Photographs Division Washington, D.C. 20540 USA http://hdl.loc.gov/loc.pnp/pp.print

21 General Orders, No. 14 Confederate Law Authorizing the Enlistment of Black Soldiers, as Promulgated in a Military Order, 1865. Source: Freedman and Southern Society Project http://www.freedmen.umd.edu/csenlist.htm

independence, and preserve their institutions, the President be, and he is hereby, authorized to ask for and accept from the owners of slaves, the services of such number of able-bodied negro men as he may deem expedient, for and during the war, to perform military service in whatever capacity he may direct.

SEC 2. That the General-in-Chief be authorized to organize the said slaves into companies, battalions, regiments, and brigades, under such rules and regulations as the Secretary of War may prescribe, and to be commanded by such officers as the President may appoint.

SEC 3. That while employed in the service the said troops shall receive the same rations, clothing, and compensation as are allowed to other troops in the same branch of the service.

SEC 4. That if, under the previous sections of this act, the President shall not be able to raise a sufficient number of troops to prosecute the war successfully and maintain the sovereignty of the States and the independence of the Confederate States, then he is hereby authorized to call on each State, whenever he thinks it expedient, for her quota of 300,000 troops, in addition to those subject to military service under existing laws, or so many thereof as the President may deem necessary to be raised from such classes of the population, irrespective of color, in each State, as the proper authorities thereof may determine: *Provided*, That not more than twenty-five per cent. of the male slaves between the ages of eighteen and forty-five, in any State, shall be called for under the provisions of this act.

SEC 5. That nothing in this act shall be construed to authorize a change in the relation which the said slaves shall bear toward their owners, except by consent of the owners and of the States in which they may reside, and in pursuance of the laws thereof.

Approved March 13, 1865.

By order:

S. COOPER,

Adjutant and Inspector General.

Document 19 Major Alexandria S. Johnson, 116th Colored Infantry Regiment, 1865.[22]

As a participant in these events I will speak merely of what came under my own observation. The 116th Colored Infantry, in which I commanded a company, belonged to the Third Brigade, Second Division of the 25th Army Corps, and during the winter of 1864-65 held the lines on Chapin's farm, the left resting on Fort Burnham. The division was commanded by Major-General Birney. The winter was passed in endeavoring to get the troops in as high a state of discipline as possible by constant drill and watchful training. When the spring opened we had the satisfaction of feeling that they were the equal, as soldiers, of most of the white troops. They were a contented body, being well fed and clothed, and they took delight in their various duties. The news of the capture of Savannah by Sherman and the defeat of Hood at Nashville had a cheering effect upon the whole command, and we looked forward with confidence that the end was drawing near.

---

22 Recorded in Joseph Thomas Wilson, *The Black Phalanx; A History of the Negro Soldiers of the United States in the Wars of 1775-1812, 1861-'65*, (Hartford, Conn.: American Publishing Company, 1890), pp. 455-458.

... on the afternoon of April 1st, [the order was given] to advance on the lines in our front at dawn on the following day. That night the Union artillery opened along the whole line. Hissing and bursting shells from Appomattox river to Hatcher's Run filled in a scene never to be forgotten by those who witnessed it. It was as if demons incarnate were holding a jubilee. As far as the eye could reach there was one blaze of fiery shot. The world has seldom seen its like. Where our brigade was to operate was a dense wilderness of pines with matted underbrush, but in the morning it looked as though a sirocco had kissed it.

With the dawn of day the brigade was in line of battle. Not a breath of air was stirring. A misty vapor shed its gloom and hung like a pall among the tree-tops. The silk covers were taken from our flags, but their folds hung lazily along the staff when the command, 'Forward! Guide Centre! March! Was given. ... The dusky line broke through the abattis, however, as if the stakes had been so many reeds, and charged over the breastworks and into the Confederate camp. The rush must have been a surprise, as the enemy offered little resistance. .. Swinging by the right flank we kept our way along the Boydton road. A Confederate light battery in position alongside of a cottage, which stood in a hollow, shelled the column as it advanced, and so accurate had the gunners got the range that almost every shell did damage. ... One of our batteries was brought into position, and engaging the Confederate battery, the latter was silenced, when the column again resumed the march, arriving in front of Petersburg about noon.... We went into bivouac for the night, and at early dawn of the 3rd we entered the city, the Confederates having evacuated the forts during the night. The field music played "John Brown's Body," and a tiny Union flag in the hands of a girl of ten years waved us a welcome. Resting an hour in the city the division started in pursuit of the Confederates. For a mile or two outside of the city the road was strewn with plug tobacco. Blood could be seen also at intervals in patches along the road. We bivouacked some fifteen miles from the city. A few of our officers took supper in a house close to our camping ground. Our fare was "corn pone," scraps of bacon, sorghum molasses, and a solution of something called coffee, for which we gave our host, a middle-aged Virginian, one dollar. The colored troops encamped on his farm his indignation was stirred and he exclaimed, while the tears trickled down his cheeks, "Poor old Virginia! Poor old Virginia! That I should have lived to see this day!"

At dawn of the 4th the column resumed the pursuit. It is needless for me to tell in detail how our cavalry destroyed and burned over five hundred Confederate wagons on the 5th and 6th, and how Ewell's command was defeated and captured at Sailor's creek on the 6th.... Nothing of interest took place until the 8th, which was noted for the forced march made by the brigade, starting at day-break and going into bivouac at twelve midnight. The morning of the 9th broke calm and serene. It was a lovely morning, the sun had not yet gotten above the horizon when the brigade was on the march again, but it went only a short distance when it was halted. To the right of the road, in a clearing was a portion of the 24th Corps, with arms stacked and the men cooking breakfast. Sides of bacon at intervals hung from their bayonets. Although the woods were full of our cavalry, and three divisions of our infantry were in close proximity, all was as quiet as a Sabbath morning... Such was the situation at Appomattox at sunrise on the morning of the 9th.

Our brigade, after resting some thirty minutes, resumed the march. It soon filed to the right. In a few minutes the command was given—'Right shoulder, shift arms! Double quick, march!' Onward we went, the objective point being the Lynchburg pike. Dismounted cavalry retreating from the front broke through the column, saying as they passed us, 'Give it to them, boys! They are too many for us!' In a few minutes the head of the column reached the pike, when it halted and faced to the front. The command—'Unsling knapsacks!'—was given, and then we knew we were stripping for a fight. Skirmishers were deployed on our front, and as we advanced the Confederate skirmishers retired before us. After advancing some eight hundred yards the brigade was ordered to halt and form in line of battle. It formed into columns of companies. Some eight hundred yards away was the Army of Northern Virginia, with its three lines of battle awaiting us.

We had not been at a halt more than twenty minutes when the news of Lee's surrender reached us. Our brigade celebrated the event by firing volleys of musketry in the air. Officers hugged each other with joy. About four hundred yards to the rear was a portion of the 24th Corps, which had been marching to our support. The men in that long line threw their caps upwards until they looked like a flock of crows. From wood and dale came the sound of cheers from thousands of throats. Appomattox will never hear the like again.

Document 20   United States Constitution. *Amendment XIII.* Ratified 6 December 1865.

Section 1.

Neither slavery nor involuntary servitude, except as a punishment for crime whereof the party shall have been duly convicted, shall exist within the United States, or any place subject to their jurisdiction.

Section 2.

Congress shall have power to enforce this article by appropriate legislation.

ANALYZING THE EVIDENCE

1. What concerns about property rights in slaves are reflected in the two letters in Document 1? In what ways were slaves taking advantage of the war to achieve their freedom, regardless of official policy?

2. How did Benjamin Butler (Document 2) and David Hunter (Document 6) argue that the contribution of slaves to the Confederacy justified policies that enabled their escape or employment? How did both propose to employ slaves in the war effort?

3. What legal justifications were given for the First Confiscation Act? (Document 3) What slaves were the subject of this Act?

4. What were slaves doing to affect their liberation according to the *Anti-Slavery Advocate* (Document 4) and what specific grievances were given to justify their doing so? How did these slaves' actions contradict the claims made by Southern planters about the loyalty of their slaves?

5. How did the Emancipation Proclamation of the District of Columbia (Document 5) both grant freedom to slaves while simultaneously recognizing the importance of property rights?

6. What arguments did William Tecumseh Sherman (Document 7) offer to his childhood friend as wartime justifications for his "freeing" of southern slaves? What was his "constitutional" argument?

7. How did the Second Confiscation Act (Document 8) expand on the provisions of the First Confiscation Act?

8. How did Lincoln's presentation to leading northern free blacks (Document 9) and his letter to Horace Greeley (Document 10) illustrate Lincoln's continuing effort to find a compromise solution on the issue of slavery which would permit a political solution to the Civil War? What political and social factors might have contributed to Lincoln's "middle-of-the-road" approach here?

9. How did the Emancipation Proclamation (Document 11) continue Lincoln's policy of moderation? In what ways did the Emancipation Proclamation, nonetheless, change the war from a war to restore the Union to a war to free the slaves?

10. How did the Confederate order (Document 12) contribute to the events that took place at Fort Pillow? (Document 16)

11. Why did Frederick Douglass (Document 13) feel comfortable counseling African Americans to volunteer for service in the Union army? What arguments does Frederick Douglass offer for why African Americans should join the Union cause? How did his invocation of Denmark Vesey and Nat Turner illustrate a different war aim for African Americans than for northern whites?

12. In what ways did Frederick Douglass (Document 13) and the Louisiana volunteers (Document 14) illustrate the desires of African American men to be accorded respect as men?

13. How does Lincoln's letter to the Governor of Kentucky (Document 15) offer a clear rationale for the military necessity of the Emancipation Proclamation? How did Lincoln view the participation of African American soldiers in this letter?

14. How did the Confederacy's General Order No. 14 (Document 18) illustrate a) the military effectiveness of Lincoln's earlier Emancipation Proclamation, and b) the degree to which African Americans were already "freeing themselves?"

15. How do Documents 17 and 19 illustrate the importance of African American soldiers in the final stages of the war?

16. To what degree did the 13th Amendment represent a culmination or a departure from the initial objectives of Lincoln and the Federal Government?

DOCUMENT BASED QUESTIONS

1. Using the documents provided and your knowledge of United States history, analyze the ways in which African Americans contributed to liberating themselves and turning the war into a "Crusade" to "Free the Slaves."

2. Using the documents provided and your knowledge of United States history, analyze the ways in which Union policy towards slavery gradually changed over the course of the Civil War.

Epilogue

Reconstruction

A war that had begun with the express purpose of restoring the Union had been by 1863 transformed into a war to free the slaves. The shift in wartime objectives had been both the consequence of wartime exigency and the result of African Americans pursuing their own liberation. As Eric Foner has noted, the Emancipation Proclamation resulted in the "end of a labor system," and "the uncompensated liquidation of the nation's largest concentration of private property." The Thirteenth Amendment would solidify Lincoln's executive directive as law, though it was ultimately ratified after his assassination. The nation had come late to abolition, but pushed by slaves, freedmen, and white abolitionists, emancipation had been achieved. Abolition however, represented the birth of a new republic, with all the promise that had attended the establishment of the nation's first Constitution. Unfortunately, after the initial euphoria of possibility, in many ways the new republic was stillborn. Reverence for private property and for the structures of the Constitution coupled with the persistence of anti-black racism and an unwillingness to truly compensate slaves and the descendents of slaves, has meant that slavery's shadow has been longer than it might have been. Rather than build meaningful reconciliation upon an open and heartfelt repentence for the evils of slavery and upon a system of reparation for labor and lives lost, reconstruction meant primarily an effort to rebuild the republic along its former lines, absent the institution of slavery of course, but also without a true reckoning with it.

This failure to reckon with the history of slavery and its implications began with Lincoln's Proclamation for Amnesty and Reconstruction, which offered all white southerners willing to swear allegiance to the United States, with the exception of the Confederacy's most prominent military and civilian leaders, a full pardon and restoration of property other than slaves. Additionally, once ten percent of a state's electorate in 1860 had taken the oath of allegiance, the state could reconstitute its state government. Lincoln has been lauded for the generosity of this plan, at least as it represented outreach to white southerners. The more radical members of Lincoln's party rightly perceived this plan as not accomplishing the fundamental reformation of southern society that they believed necessary. To affect significant amelioration of the slaves' conditions, as part of Congressional efforts to take the lead in the reconstruction process even before Lincoln's assassination, the Freedmen's Bureau was established to address former slave's housing, clothing, provisioning, and land management. But these measures, as positive as they were, placed the freedmen at the mercy of Federal generosity and local administration, both of which would prove to be inadequate to meet the needs. More critically, they left the freedmen and women without the means of their own independence.

Perhaps the most egregious failure of the Reconstruction proposals, which perhaps more than anything ensured both the eventual return of white southerners to the Union and later exploitation of freedmen and women was the failure to address former slaves' demand for their own land, or independent livelihood. The varied arrangements proposed by military commanders, most notably William Tecumseh Sherman's offer to grant the slaves who flocked to his armies "forty acres and a mule." "Sherman's land," was mostly an expedient designed to disencumber Sherman's armies from these slaves, promised a modest redistribution that ultimately was not followed by either civilian or military authorities. Former slaves justifiably argued that they were entitled to either a share of the land of their former masters or reparations that would enable them to fashion economic independence. Instead, African Americans in the South were increasingly drawn into a variety of labor arrangements that varied in the level of coercion and exploitation. In some instances, this implied simple money wages; in others share wages or sharecropping. The sharecropping system, which was favored by ex-slaves, afforded the greatest degree of autonomy and freedom from white supervision, but also left former slaves vulnerable to market forces and debt peonage.Had some creative empowerment and propertied compensation been on offer, Reconstruction might well have represented a more complete transformation of the American republic.

With Lincoln's assassination and the accession of Andrew Johnson to the presidency, control of reconstruction shifted to a Congress dominated by a Republican majority. Among the features of Congressional reconstruction was the passage of a Civil Rights bill that overturned the Dred Scott decision, defining citizenship to include all persons born in the United States. The law also eliminated the legal supports of slavery, the Slave Laws found throughout the South. The final legislative pillar of Congressional reconstruction would be the Fourteenth Amendment that extended full citizenship rights and due process to all former slaves.

The response of the South was largely intransigence, terroristic violence against former slaves and their white allies, and efforts to re-establish political dominance over African Americans and to reassert control over their labor. "Black Codes" reminiscent of the slave laws were enacted. Limits on African American civil rights—exclusion from juries, voting, testifying in court, inter-racial marriage—became the norm. The planters also employed the courts to force former slaves into new forms of coerced labor. African Americans charged with misdemeanors or even found without employment were often jailed and leased to planters. African American political leadership and black office holders were gradually driven from office through assassination and intimidation. Black voters were similarly intimidated or silenced. African Americans who successfully transitioned to land ownership or independence then were subjected to terroristic assaults and violence. Only the presence of an occupying force could protect the rights of freedmen and women. In 1877 a war-weary northern populace unwilling to sacrifice further for African Americans withdrew Federal troops from the South and turned the region over to the largely unrepentant and unreformed planters and political class that had led the southern states to secede in 1861. Reconstruction had accomplished little in the way of reconciliation or recompense for over two centuries of enslavement.

This did not mean that for the over four million slaves in the South, freedom had not been achieved. One feature of the enslaved populations' new reality involved a new degree of mobility.

Interestingly former slaves migrated, not to northern cities, where they were no less subject to racist indignities and threat, but to counties in the deep South, following the sixty year pattern of the internal slave trade. Why this was the case is best explained by the desire to be reunited with family members that had been sold southwards, or by the desire to find strength in numbers. Emancipation, in its most tangible form, meant the opportunity to reconstitute families broken up over generations. For enslaved men, enlistment in the Union army, voting, holding office, and taking on public roles white men had long characterized as markers of their masculinity became hallmarks of emancipation. For women, formerly required to work in the fields in back-breaking labor while being denied the dignity accorded white mothers and wives, the opportunity to take on domestic and childrearing duties proved key to the meaning of freedom. Emancipation also implied freedom to worship together and to acquire the education that had been so long denied them. Churches and schools proliferated, many of the latter staffed by northern missionary societies and by free blacks from the North. Freedom had arrived, but independence had been constrained and the full harvest of liberty postponed.

That harvest is still only partially realized, even after the sacrifices of the Civil Rights movement. Even with the election of an African-American president, it is not possible to exult as Martin Luther King, Jr. dreamed, "Free at last. Free at Last." The day of jubilee still awaits. And not just for Americans of African descent. One purpose of this reader has been to illustrate the ways in which all Americans have been held in bondage by slavery and continue to be restrained by our failure to confront the legacy of slavery and make tangible recompense for that crime. Michelle Obama in her speech before the Democratic National Convention in July 2016 observed, "I wake up every morning in a house built by slaves." Her statement comes as a reminder that so do we all. The White House, like the nation itself, was built by slaves.